Inside Wills and Trusts

What Matters and Why

D1567915

Inside Wills and Trusts

What Matters and Why

William P. LaPiana

Rita and Joseph Solomon Professor of Wills, Trusts, and Estates
New York Law School

Wolters Kluwer
Law & Business

Copyright © 2012 CCH Incorporated.

Published by Wolters Kluwer Law & Business in New York.

Wolters Kluwer Law & Business serves customers worldwide with CCH, Aspen Publishers, and Kluwer Law International products. (www.wolterskluwerlb.com)

No part of this publication may be reproduced or transmitted in any form or by any means, electronic or mechanical, including photocopy, recording, or utilized by any information storage or retrieval system, without written permission from the publisher. For information about permissions or to request permissions online, visit us at www.wolterskluwerlb.com, or a written request may be faxed to our permissions department at 212-771-0803.

To contact Customer Service, e-mail customer.service@wolterskluwer.com, call 1-800-234-1660, fax 1-800-901-9075, or mail correspondence to:

Wolters Kluwer Law & Business
Attn: Order Department
PO Box 990
Frederick, MD 21705

Printed in the United States of America.

1 2 3 4 5 6 7 8 9 0

ISBN 978-0-7355-8426-6

Library of Congress Cataloging-in-Publication Data

LaPiana, William P.
Inside wills and trusts : what matters and why / William P. LaPiana.
    p. cm.
ISBN 978-0-7355-8426-6
1. Trusts and trustees — United States. 2. Wills — United States. I. Title.

KF730.L35 2012
346.7305'6 — dc23

                                                              2011052973

About Wolters Kluwer Law & Business

Wolters Kluwer Law & Business is a leading global provider of intelligent information and digital solutions for legal and business professionals in key specialty areas, and respected educational resources for professors and law students. Wolters Kluwer Law & Business connects legal and business professionals as well as those in the education market with timely, specialized authoritative content and information-enabled solutions to support success through productivity, accuracy and mobility.

Serving customers worldwide, Wolters Kluwer Law & Business products include those under the Aspen Publishers, CCH, Kluwer Law International, Loislaw, Best Case, ftwilliam.com and MediRegs family of products.

CCH products have been a trusted resource since 1913, and are highly regarded resources for legal, securities, antitrust and trade regulation, government contracting, banking, pension, payroll, employment and labor, and healthcare reimbursement and compliance professionals.

Aspen Publishers products provide essential information to attorneys, business professionals and law students. Written by preeminent authorities, the product line offers analytical and practical information in a range of specialty practice areas from securities law and intellectual property to mergers and acquisitions and pension/benefits. Aspen's trusted legal education resources provide professors and students with high-quality, up-to-date and effective resources for successful instruction and study in all areas of the law.

Kluwer Law International products provide the global business community with reliable international legal information in English. Legal practitioners, corporate counsel and business executives around the world rely on Kluwer Law journals, looseleafs, books, and electronic products for comprehensive information in many areas of international legal practice.

Loislaw is a comprehensive online legal research product providing legal content to law firm practitioners of various specializations. Loislaw provides attorneys with the ability to quickly and efficiently find the necessary legal information they need, when and where they need it, by facilitating access to primary law as well as state-specific law, records, forms and treatises.

Best Case Solutions is the leading bankruptcy software product to the bankruptcy industry. It provides software and workflow tools to flawlessly streamline petition preparation and the electronic filing process, while timely incorporating ever-changing court requirements.

ftwilliam.com offers employee benefits professionals the highest quality plan documents (retirement, welfare and non-qualified) and government forms (5500/PBGC, 1099 and IRS) software at highly competitive prices.

MediRegs products provide integrated health care compliance content and software solutions for professionals in healthcare, higher education and life sciences, including professionals in accounting, law and consulting.

Wolters Kluwer Law & Business, a division of Wolters Kluwer, is headquartered in New York. Wolters Kluwer is a market-leading global information services company focused on professionals.

To
Sebastian
My sole distributee

Summary of Contents

Contents

Chapter 8. Trusts: Creation, Modification, and Termination 161

Chapter 11. The Revocable Trust: The Ultimate Will Substitute 243

Chapter 12. Trust Duration: The Rule Against Perpetuities 259

Chapter 14. Dealing with Illness, Disability, and Last Things 319

Chapter 15. Charitable Trusts 333

Acknowledgments

Much of the work on this book was accomplished during a sabbatical from my regular teaching duties at New York Law School and over summers during which I received financial support from the school's faculty research funds.

Over decades of teaching I have learned more than I can ever properly acknowledge from fellow lawyers, both practitioners and teachers, and from my students. I owe a special debt to my late colleague Pamela R. Champine, whose skill as a practitioner, creativity as a scholar, and patience as a teacher was, is, and will continue to be a source of light and inspiration.

The anonymous readers of the manuscript made criticisms and suggestions that have greatly improved this book. I have also received much appreciated help from Prof. Linda S. Whitton of Valparaiso University School of Law; Prof. Bridget J. Crawford of Pace Law School; and especially Emily F. Johnson, Esq., of New York City, Adjunct Professor of Law at New York Law School. Much that is good here comes from their unselfish help; the errors of substance and barbarities of style that remain are very much my own.

There would be no book without the patience, skill, and good humor of my editors at Aspen, especially Carmen Corral-Reid, assistant editorial director, and copyeditor extraordinaire Lisa A. Wehrle, who labored mightily to civilize those barbarities of style; any absence of civilization that remains must be laid at my door.

WPLaP
January 2012

Preface

This book is a thorough introduction to the vast body of law that governs the making of gifts at death. It is a body of law that is inextricably involved with some of the deepest emotions we feel: fear of death, the responsibilities we have for those we love, the deep desire "to leave something behind," and the painful wisdom of knowing we must, at some time, "let go." And for almost as long as human beings have felt those desires and emotions, groups or communities of humans—society—have shaped their expression through law. With a history so long and rich and deeply intertwined with human experience, this is a body of law that's more Frankenstein's monster than Adonis. In other words, this is truly law that is as complex, contradictory, and messy as life itself.

I hope this book will be of use to law students who are studying this area of law whether in class or in preparation for the bar exam, lawyers who want a basic introduction, and anyone who wants to know something about how wills and trusts work. As a study aid, this book is different from many. Like other books in Aspen's *Inside* series, it incorporates several features designed to aid understanding:

- Figures and tables are designed to reinforce the text by presenting basic materials in ways that speak to those who find visual representations and graphical summaries helpful.
- Each chapter begins with an **Overview** that gives readers a broad picture of the chapter's topic and an idea of why it's important.
- Each chapter ends with a **Summary** of the basic information and **Connections** that link topics across chapters and help to situate individual topics in the broad sweep of wills and trusts law.
- **FAQs** and **Sidebars** provide answers to questions students often have, present additional information about how law works in the world, provide basic historical background, and sometimes are there simply for fun.
- **Key terms** are presented in boldface and defined in context. "Terms of art" are the heart of the language of the law, and learning their meanings is a critical step to understanding.
- The **Table of Contents** is particularly detailed and is designed to be the primary guide to finding information to answer particular questions.

In every sense, this book is the product of almost 30 years of teaching the law of wills and trusts. I have worked diligently to present a comprehensive picture and to explain the basics in terms that my experience has taught me students understand. Writing this book has been a labor love. I offer it to all who read it in the humble hope that it will help them understand this interesting, dynamic, and very human area of the law.

William P. LaPiana
January 2012

Introduction

1

This chapter introduces the concepts that under-lie the law governing how property is distributed after death. Few things are as personal as making sure our wishes regarding our property are carried out after we die. To understand the legal principles and rationales behind wills and trusts law, you must first grasp its most basic concepts: the distinction between property that is distributed through wills versus that distributed through intestacy statutes, non-will arrangements used to distribute property, the cast of characters involved, the procedural mechanisms that are involved in making gifts at death, and the general structure of the entire body of law. In other words, read this chapter carefully first!

D. PROCEDURES

1. Probate
2. Administering the Estate
3. The Cost

E. TAXES

Most of you, I'm betting, are law students currently enrolled in a course in wills and trusts, decedents' estates and trusts, or a course that has at least one of those words in its title. A few of you may be reviewing for the bar exam, and a few more might be general readers who simply want to explore the topic. Needless to say, you are all welcome. If you are a law student enrolled in your school's course in this topic, you should congratulate yourself because, unless you intend to follow a life of crime, you are taking the law school course that is most relevant to your life. Why? It's simple. We're all going to die, and we can't take anything with us: clothes, electronics, books, household items, cars, homes, and financial assets. All these things stay when we leave through the exit marked "death."

In a sense, however, we do not abandon our property when we die because we can leave instructions for what is to happen to it after we're gone. That's what this book is about—the law that provides the structures we use to make sure that our plans for what happens to our property after death are carried out. In other words, the law you will read about here governs how a person makes a gift at death. So let's get going!

A. Making a Gift at Death—Probate and Nonprobate Property

You probably remember the rules governing lifetime gifts from your course in property, rules that can be summed up in three words: intent, delivery, and acceptance. Let's discuss these in reverse order. Acceptance is something that the donee does, and the donee of a gift made at death, usually called a "beneficiary," has the choice whether to accept the gift or not. (There are statutes that govern a refusal of the gift, and we'll deal with those a bit later.) Delivery, of course, cannot be made by the donor who is, well, dead. (That's why the most general term referring to the person making a gift at death is **decedent**.) Some living person must be given the authority to carry out the donor's wishes. As for intent, a living donor can express intent in many different ways, but a decedent has to leave written instructions. For centuries, that writing has been the will. If a person does not give instructions by writing a will, the state provides a ready-made, one-size-fits-all set of instructions in its intestacy statute. You must understand the difference between property governed by a will or by the intestacy statute and property that is given away at death through other means, and so it is time to talk about probate property (sometimes called the probate estate) and nonprobate property.

When the owner of property dies, some of the property will be orphaned. That is, no living person will have the authority to transfer it. (Table 1.1 gives some concrete examples.) This property is literally stuck in place. Someone has to succeed to the decedent's authority over it, or, as we described earlier, someone has to acquire the authority to deliver the property in accordance with either the decedent's will or the provisions of the intestacy statute.

TABLE 1.1	Why It's Probate Property
Property	**What the Decedent Cannot Do**
Checking account	Sign a check
Savings account	Sign a withdrawal slip
Stock certificate	Sign a stock power giving a broker authority to transfer the stock
Brokerage account	Give instructions to a broker
Motor vehicle	Sign the certificate of transfer
Real property	Sign a deed

This property is called "probate property" or the "probate estate." Why? **Probate** is the term applied to the legal procedures necessary to confirm the authority of the personal representative who deals with the decedent's property. If the decedent was **testate**, that is, left behind a valid will, the will must be admitted to probate as the true will of the decedent before the personal representative can act. Probate is described at greater length below, but for now you need to understand only that when probate is complete, a legal institution (usually but not always a court) issues a document to the appropriate personal representative that gives him the authority to distribute the decedent's property. Therefore, **probate property** is the decedent's property that can be disposed of after death only though the probate process.

It is possible to make arrangements during life so that one's property is not probate property. In the modern world, **nonprobate property** is usually subject to a contract between the property owner and some entity, which includes an agreement that the entity will deliver the property to a beneficiary selected by the property owner. One example you are almost certainly familiar with is a life insurance contract. As part of the contract, the insurance company agrees to deliver the death benefit to the beneficiary selected by the insured. Other examples include various sorts of retirement savings vehicles like IRAs and Keogh plans, which are managed for the plan owner by, for example, a bank or brokerage house under a contract that allows the owner to name a beneficiary who will receive any remainder of the property not exhausted at the time of the owner's death. For all arrangements like this, when the owner dies, the named beneficiary need provide only proof of death to the other party to the contract, usually in the form of a death certificate, and the property is delivered to the beneficiary.

Nonprobate property is not a completely new idea. In studying property, you no doubt came across two ancient forms of nonprobate property: the joint tenancy with right of survivorship and the legal life estate and remainder in real property. (Both are discussed in more detail in Chapter 6.) Until relatively recently in the history of Anglo-American law, the only way I could keep complete control of my property and designate who would have the property after my death was to write a will. A non-will instrument such as a deed that purported to convey real property to my child at my death would be an invalid will substitute. The only way such an arrangement would be valid is if some interest passed to the beneficiary during my life. That was the case, at least, until what one eminent scholar has described as "the nonprobate revolution." In Chapter 6, we'll discuss this revolution in detail, but for now all you have to know is that through a combination of court decisions and statutes, all sorts of arrangements that were once invalid will substitutes now are valid methods of creating nonprobate property. In fact, every one of the types of property listed in Table 1.1 can be turned into nonprobate property, although not in every state.

There is another way to create nonprobate property, and it involves the use of **trusts**. The trust is one of the superstars of Anglo-American law, the legal systems descended from the English common law. It has a long, complex, and interesting history, the unraveling of which has presented challenges to generations of scholars. Today the trust is an important device for the management of property. Businesses, retirement schemes, mutual funds, and securitization vehicles can all be organized as trusts. Most people, however, think of trusts as things that are used to manage private wealth, and that is the sort of trust that is one of the subjects of this book. In other words, trusts are another way of making a gift, including a gift at death. There is much to learn about trusts in general, and revocable lifetime trusts in particular, and we will discuss them in great detail in Chapters 8, 9, and 11. For now, you should realize that a well-drafted trust can take the place of a will and is the ultimate device for avoiding the probate system.

Figure 1.1 sums up the basics of making gifts at death.

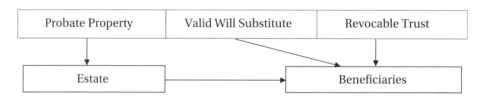

FIGURE 1.1   **ROUTES FROM THE DECEDENT TO THE BENEFICIARIES OF GIFTS AT DEATH**

B. Where Does the Law Come From?

Does this question's answer seem hopelessly obvious to you? After all, law comes from legislatures and courts, and is written in statute books and case opinions. That's an accurate answer, of course, but it does not come anywhere near doing justice to the complexity of the law of wills and trusts.

One complicating factor is the antiquity of the law. Human beings probably have been concerned about the disposition of their property after death for as long as the concept of "mine" has been part of human society, and that's a very long time. For our purposes, however, the story begins with the Norman conquest of England in 1066, when the Duke of Normandy, William the Bastard (yes, he was a nonmarital child; and yes, when you win, you get to write history and call yourself the

"Conqueror"), brought with him a new way to govern. **Feudalism** was founded on the idea that the king was the owner of all the land in the kingdom, which he parceled out to his major supporters in return for their promise to supply him with an army. Theoretically, the king controlled the disposition of the land on the death of its holder. Very quickly, however, land became heritable, passing from the decedent to his eldest son. It took a long time, but eventually statutes were passed allowing the making of wills of land. The story of personal property is somewhat different, but the important point is that the law of wills is statutory and that today in the United States, in theory at least, the legislatures of the various states are in complete control of the passing of property at death. In addition, many of the statutes are the descendants of much older statutes and decisional law so that there are a lot of fossils embedded in the modern law.

The law of trusts, on the other hand, was created by courts and, until the twentieth century in many states, was barely represented in the statute books. Indeed, some states had very little trust law of any kind. Many courts found themselves relying on decisional law from other jurisdictions, including England; and just as in the law of wills, there are lots of fossils embedded in the modern structure. At the beginning of the twenty-first century, however, the law of wills and trusts has entered a new era.

This new era began with the promulgation of the Uniform Probate Code (UPC) in 1969. Like the Uniform Commercial Code (UCC), the UPC was the work of the National Conference of Commissioners on Uniform State Laws (now known as the Uniform Law Commission (ULC)). Although the UPC has not been anywhere near as widely adopted as the UCC, it has been extremely influential, and parts of the code — sometimes individual sections, sometimes much larger portions — have been adopted in many states. The UPC from the beginning was inspired by the desire to simplify and modernize the substantive law of wills and probate procedure. Beginning in the 1990s, development of the UPC became closely linked to the creation of Restatement (Third) of Property: Wills and Other Donative Transfers. The spirit of Restatement (Third) is unabashedly reformist, and today the UPC proclaims in statutory form what the Restatement suggests should be the law applied by courts.

Sidebar

INHERITANCE AND THE CONSTITUTION

While it is absolutely true that the legislature is in control of passing of property at death and could theoretically abolish inheritance, it seems that public opinion is otherwise. In addition, there are two U.S. Supreme Court opinions that can be read as equating the abolition of the "right" to inherit and the "right" to make a gift at death with a taking, which is unconstitutional unless just compensation is provided. The cases, *Hodel v. Irving*, 481 U.S. 704 (1987), and *Babbitt v. Youpee*, 519 U.S. 234 (1997), invalidated federal statutes aimed at preventing further fractionalization of ownership interests in Native American lands by requiring that small interests pass to the tribe of which the decedent was a member rather than by intestacy or under the decedent's will.

Sidebar

FOSSILS

Among the fossils in the law of wills and trusts are lots and lots of vocabulary. Traditionally, a gift of land in a will is a "devise" to a "devisee," and a gift of personal property is a "bequest" to a "legatee." The corresponding verbs were used in wills: I devise Blackacre to my daughter, Jane. I bequeath my gold watch to my son, John. Today the noun "gift" and the verb "give" are perfectly acceptable, and everyone who takes under a will can be called a "beneficiary." It was also traditional to call a female testator a "testratrix," a female administrator an "administratrix," and a female executor an "executrix." Today these words are truly obsolete and we'll try to avoid them (although you will certainly see them even in relatively recent cases). Note too that the UPC calls every gift in a will a "devise."

The recent history of the law of trusts has had a similar development. The ULC promulgated the Uniform Trust Code (UTC) in 2000. Like the UPC, its development has been closely linked to a Restatement, in this case Restatement (Third) of Trusts. The UTC has been controversial to some degree, but on the whole it has been well received and more widely adopted than the UPC.

Both the UPC and the UTC are almost always extensively discussed in and sometimes are the very foundation of casebooks and teaching materials for courses in wills and trusts. Not only have both codes greatly influenced current statutes, but, taken together, they come closest to providing a national law of the subject. Nevertheless, state laws vary widely and often are at odds with many of the provisions of the UPC and UTC. In this book, I discuss the UPC and the UTC as well as other approaches to the legal questions the codes address.

The long history of the law that governs wills and trusts is responsible for another important characteristic of the law discussed in this book. There is a large body of case law dealing with most of the topics we will consider. Even when a statute is directly applicable to the question at hand, the statute may very well have been the subject of many decisions, and its meaning cannot be understood apart from those decisions. When you are seeking the answer to a question raised by a client's plan for disposition of her property at death or by possible litigation, remember that research must include both statutes and cases.

C. Persons

Understanding the cast of characters involved in the production and carrying out of plans to dispose of property at death, usually called **estate plans**, is an important first step in mastering the law.

(1) The Personal Representative

Personal representative is the most general term for the person who has the authority to deal with a decedent's probate property. If the decedent died intestate, the personal representative is designated by statute and called an **administrator**. A typical statute governing appointment of an administrator creates a hierarchy under which a surviving spouse has priority above all others. If the decedent had no spouse or the spouse cannot or does not wish to serve, an adult child is next in line. Under UPC § 2-302(a), any heir of the decedent may qualify if the surviving spouse does not; if 45 days pass after the decedent's death without anyone qualifying, a creditor of the decedent may seek to be appointed personal representative if the decedent died without a will (the UPC uses the term "personal representative" for both intestate and testate administration). In any event, the universe of persons who may be administrator is not unlimited. The significance of allowing a creditor of the decedent to be administrator will be clear in a bit.

If no one mentioned in the relevant statute becomes administrator, the state may provide someone either by appointing a lawyer or by providing a public official to undertake the task. In New York, for example, this official is accurately but unimaginatively called the "public administrator."

You no doubt have already concluded that one of the reasons to write a will is to make a gift at death different from what the intestacy statute provides. Even if the disposition of your probate property under the intestacy statute is exactly what you want, however, you may still want to write a will so that you can select the person you want to be personal representative. When named in a will, the personal representative is usually called an **executor**, although as noted above, the UPC uses the more general term "personal representative."

Although many (perhaps most) **testators** (persons who have a will) select an individual to be executor, under some circumstances the testator might name a bank. Most large commercial banks as well as many smaller (often local) banks have the legal authority to act as personal representatives or trustees. You might choose a bank to be executor if administration of the estate will be especially complicated because of the nature of the assets (think of closely held business interests or interests in complex investments vehicles) or because relationships among the beneficiaries are equally complex (think of descendants from multiple marriages). Of course, an individual executor can always hire appropriate expert help so that it is often not really necessary to make a bank executor to get the advantages of professional management of estate administration.

F   A   Q

Q: Can anyone act as executor?

A: The short answer is no. Every state sets a minimum age, and the drafters of the UPC suggest a minimum age of 21 (UPC § 3-204(f)(1)). In addition, the UPC in § 3-204(f)(2) also disqualifies "a person whom the Court finds unsuitable in formal proceedings." Other statutes may be more specific, disqualifying, for example, a convicted felon. Some states impose a residency requirement that prevents nonresident individuals from serving as personal representatives.

F   A   Q

Q: Can a partnership be a personal representative or trustee?

A: Because the duties of the fiduciary are enforced in equity and equity can enforce its decrees only by acting on the person (i.e., holding a person in contempt), only natural persons and specially qualified banks can be any sort of fiduciary. Therefore a law firm organized as a partnership, a professional corporation (PC), or a limited liability corporation (LLC) usually cannot be a personal representative or trustee (there are exceptions).

(2) The Trustee

Much of what the previous section has to say about personal representatives also applies to trustees of trusts created in wills or during life, including trustees of revocable lifetime trusts other than the settlor of the trust. Like personal representatives, trustees are **fiduciaries** (parties who are obligated to behave toward certain other persons in ways that further those other persons' interests rather than the fiduciaries') and can be either natural persons or banks with the appropriate legal authority. While many of the considerations in selecting a corporate executor apply to selecting a corporate trustee, there is an additional consideration applicable only to trustees. Because even under the traditional rule against perpetuities a trust may last longer than the lifetime of an individual named as trustee, it may be especially wise to nominate a bank as trustee of a long-term trust.

(3) Beneficiaries

Because Anglo-American law generally gives a testator wide latitude in deciding the terms of a gift made at death, there are few constraints on selecting the persons or organizations to benefit from those gifts. As we will see in Chapter 13, there is law requiring that some family members, especially a surviving spouse, are not left out entirely, but on the whole almost anything goes. There are also broad restraints related to public policy. For example, a bequest to finance the overthrow of the Constitution would certainly be barred by public policy. The parameters set by public policy change over time, and what is unthinkable at one time might be unexceptional decades later.

(4) The Lawyer

Because wills and trusts law is so complex, many people seek the assistance of a lawyer in making their estate plans. But not all do; the number of reported cases concerning "homemade" wills and trusts indicate that many people, wisely or not, engage in do-it-yourself estate planning, and with advice and forms just a click away, the number of homemade documents is likely to increase.

Estate planning attorneys, like all lawyers, are governed by professional responsibility rules. Some aspects of that law are especially applicable to estate planning because a lawyer often has as the client not an individual but a couple, married or not. Even when the two persons involved have perfectly compatible ideas about making gifts at death — creating, for example, reciprocal wills in which both partners leave everything to the surviving partner or, if that partner dies first, to their descendants — one or both may want to keep certain facts hidden from their partner (e.g., the existence of a child by someone other than the current partner). If so, a lawyer's duties of loyalty and client confidentiality may conflict.

The universal suggestion for coping with this sort of problem is to have the couple sign a representation agreement in which they agree to one of two ways of handling the loyalty and confidentiality problems. The first is the option of transparency. By signing such an agreement, the clients consent to have all information shared with the lawyer communicated to both clients. The other, apparently less frequently used, option is to promise to keep each client's secrets from the other. Of course, having been entrusted with a secret, the lawyer may have to withdraw from representing the couple.

Example 1.1: Husband and Wife hire a lawyer to create reciprocal wills. Husband tells their lawyer, however, that he wants to make a provision in the estate plan for a non-marital child that Wife doesn't know about. Based on their reciprocal wills, Wife is expecting the probate property of both clients to pass to their descendants. If she dies first, however, Husband may very well make a gift to the child, diminishing what passes to the descendants of both clients. Wife, then, is relying on a falsehood in making her will. If the lawyer has promised not to share secrets, then the lawyer's only option is to withdraw.

A related problem involves these same professional duties of loyalty and keeping confidences, but with regard to an entire family. It is common for one lawyer, perhaps with the help of the lawyer's partners and associates, to represent an entire family, handling tax matters, dealing with issues related to a family-owned business, and doing estate planning for the parents and adult children. The often close relationship between clients and their lawyer and the lawyer's position as trusted family counselor is much admired, but problems may arise if the lawyer does not make the limits of her representation clear at the outset.

Example 1.2: Husband and Wife have built up a business and have three children, who have varying degrees of interest in and aptitude for running the business after their parents' deaths. For years, one lawyer has handled all of the family's legal needs. When the time comes to plan what is going to happen after both parents die — called **succession planning** — the lawyer follows the parents' wishes, making all three children co-executors and equal beneficiaries of the will of the last parent to die, but also turning the parents' interest in the business into nonprobate property, perhaps by transferring it to a revocable lifetime trust. The favored child is successor trustee after the parents are dead, and the other children know nothing of the trust. The disfavored children all see the will and believe that the family business is to belong to all the children equally. When both parents are dead, the disfavored children are outraged to learn that, in effect, they have been disinherited.

Do the unhappy children have a claim against the lawyer? They may, if they can prove that they were clients of the lawyer as well and that he breached his duty of loyalty to them by not fully explaining the parents' estate plan. The attorney could have avoided this whole problem by initially informing the children that they are not his clients and that they should seek their own lawyers.

Another aspect of professional responsibility law that concerns estate planning lawyers is the extent of lawyers' potential liability for committing malpractice. When malpractice comes to light after the testator's death, beneficiaries traditionally have no cause of action against the lawyer because of lack of privity. They were not the lawyer's clients, and therefore the lawyer owes them no duty. The testator's estate might be able to recover the fees paid to the lawyer, but that will be cold comfort for the disappointed beneficiaries.

Beginning with a 1961 decision of the California Supreme Court, the privity barrier to recovery began to collapse,[1] and a good many state high courts followed California's lead by holding that disappointed beneficiaries could sue the lawyer who had prepared the will or created the estate plan for the decedent. Not every court jumped on the bandwagon, and beginning in the mid-1990s, several state supreme courts reaffirmed the privity barrier to suits by disappointed beneficiaries.[2] This rebuilding of the privity barrier may be an expression of disillusionment with malpractice litigation in general; but in any event, in the second decade of the twenty-first century, privity is not the dead issue many once assumed it would be.

A few states that have eliminated the privity barrier have nonetheless severely limited the effects of the change by requiring that the lawyer's error appear on the face of the will.

---

[1]Lucas v. Hamm, 364 P.2d 685 (Cal. 1961).
[2]For one of the first examples, see Barcelo v. Elliott, 923 S.W.2d 575 (Tex. 1996).

Example 1.3: Husband's will states that he gives his estate to Wife if she survives him by 30 days, but if he and Wife die "in a common disaster," his estate is to be divided equally between two of his nephews. Husband then dies unexpectedly, and Wife dies 15 days later after a long illness. The nephews sue the lawyer who drafted the will, alleging that their uncle wanted his estate to pass to his nephews if Wife did not survive him by 30 days, and not only if he and Wife died in a common disaster. A court with a constrained approach to the matter would hold that the will is not negligently drafted on its face. It simply provides that the estate pass in intestacy if Wife dies within 30 days of Husband but not as a result of a common disaster. That might seem to be a ridiculous conclusion, but in some instances, it is what courts have held.[3]

D. Procedures

(1) Probate

The word "probate" has already appeared many times in this first chapter. The time has come to say more about it and to learn more about how probate works. We'll begin at the beginning, which involves opening intestate administration if there is no will or having the will admitted to probate if the decedent died testate. The procedure followed in intestacy parallels testate procedure closely enough that we'll limit this discussion almost exclusively to probating wills.

The person seeking to have the will admitted to probate is almost always the executor named in the will, and that person must first bring the will to the right place. In most states, the right place is a court, although in some states the official who deals with at least some probate proceedings is an official known as the registrar of wills or similar title. Some states have specialized courts that deal with probate of wills and the administration of estates. The nature and powers of these courts vary. In some states, they handle only uncontested probates and are staffed by judges who need not be lawyers and who often are elected. In others, these courts may have a wider jurisdiction dealing not only with admitting wills to probate but with will contests, actions seeking interpretation of wills, actions by beneficiaries alleging misbehavior by executors and trustees, and formal procedures for closing administration of estates and winding up trusts. Almost always the court or official is located in the county where the decedent was domiciled at death.

Once the person who wants to have the will admitted to probate (the **proponent** of the will) gets to the right place, the next step is to begin procedures for admission of the will to probate. If the proponent is fortunate, the venue for probate will be in a jurisdiction where these procedures are quite simple. This type of probate, which the UPC calls informal probate, is an ex parte proceeding that requires only that the proponent prove the testator's signature, usually through the sworn statements of the witnesses or the named executor. The will is admitted to probate immediately, and the executor receives **letters testamentary**, which are the official evidence of the executor's authority to proceed with administration of the estate. (An administrator receives **letters of administration**.) If the will creates a trust, the trustee named in the will receives **letters of trusteeship**.

---

[3]This example is taken from Ogle v. Fuiten, 466 N.E.2d 224 (Ill. 1984), in which the court rejected the reasoning discussed and allowed the nephews to pursue their suit.

Notice of the will's admission is given through publication or perhaps by mailed notice to those interested in the will and those intestate heirs who are disinherited. Anyone challenging the will has a certain period of time, usually a year or less, to file a **caveat** or formal objection to probate. Once the caveat is filed, procedures for a will contest begin.

States that have simple ex parte probate usually also have procedures for formal or solemn form probate. (The UPC provides for both.) In some states, most notably New York, this more elaborate procedure is the *only* procedure. **Solemn form probate** is a noticed proceeding like any lawsuit and begins with formal notice to anyone who has an interest in opposing the admission of the will to probate. At the very least, these persons are the intestate heirs. The heirs may very well be the beneficiaries of the will, but that is not always the case. The notice tells those receiving it that they have the right to oppose the admission of the will. If they do, procedures for a will contest begin. If they do not or if they waive the notice and consent to admission of the will, the letters testamentary and letters of trusteeship issue to the appropriate persons and administration of the estate can begin.

(2) Administering the Estate

(a) Supervision of Administration

Once the executor receives letters testamentary, administration of the estate simply goes forward until it is complete. In some states, however, an executor is subject to supervision by the appropriate court. Under UPC § 3-501, supervised administration is an option that the testator can select or that the court can order "upon a finding that it is necessary for protection of persons interested in the estate" or if the court finds it "is necessary under the circumstances." Once supervised administration is in place, UPC § 3-504 prohibits the personal representative from making a distribution without prior approval of the court, and § 3-501 makes the personal representative "subject to direction concerning the estate made by the Court on its own motion or on the motion of any interested party."

(b) Collecting Assets and Paying Debts

Once the personal representative receives letters, the collection of the decedent's probate assets can begin. Sometimes the collection is literal: the personal representative may present the letters testamentary (letters of administration in an intestate administration), or more usually a certificate from the court evidencing the grant of letters, to a bank where the decedent had an account, withdraw the funds, and add them to an account opened in the name of the personal representative as personal representative. As we will see in Chapter 16, one of the duties of the personal representative as a fiduciary is to keep the estate's property separate from her own.

Sidebar

UNIVERSAL SUCCESSION

UPC §§ 3-312 to 3-322 authorize and provide detailed procedures for a system of succession without administration, which is modeled on the civil law concept of universal succession. The statute allows the decedent's heirs or the residuary beneficiaries of the decedent's will to take on the task of paying taxes, the decedent's debts and claims against the estate, and distributing assets to others entitled to property in the probate estate. By assuming this task, the "universal successors" assume personal liability for these various payments and distributions.

In some instances, the personal representative needs only change the title of probate property. For example, using the authority evidenced by the appropriate letters, the personal representative could direct a brokerage firm where the decedent had an account to change the title of the account from "John Doe" to "Jane Doe as executor of the will of John Doe." The personal representative then gives instructions to the broker necessary to carry out administration of the estate. The personal representative could instead close the account and open a new account to hold the securities in the probate estate.

Handling real property varies from state to state. Some jurisdictions adhere to the older common law view that on death the title to real property vests immediately in the heirs or in the beneficiaries of the will. The personal representative never deals with the property, and the heirs or beneficiaries establish their chain of title by filing a death certificate and a certified copy of the will or an "affidavit of heirship" establishing their claim. In some jurisdictions, including those with "automatic" passing of title, it is conventional for the personal representative to execute a deed passing title to the real property from the estate to the beneficiaries or heirs.

Once the personal representative has collected the probate estate, it's time to pay the decedent's debts. As a general rule, if the probate estate is not sufficient to pay the decedent's debts, the creditors are simply out of luck unless, of course, they have a security interest in particular property. In some instances, some forms of nonprobate property are also subject to paying the decedent's debts, and we'll examine those instances at much greater length in Chapter 6.

In many instances, of course, paying the decedent's debts is a pretty straightforward undertaking, and every jurisdiction has a statute of limitations called a **nonclaim statute** applicable to the decedent's creditors. The need for such a statute should be obvious; without it, the personal representative and the heirs or beneficiaries who succeed to the decedent's property could never be completely sure that they have no liability to some unknown creditor.

Sidebar

NONCLAIM STATUTES AND THE CONSTITUTION

In *Tulsa Professional Collection Services v. Pope,* 485 U.S. 478 (1988), the U.S. Supreme Court held that the Oklahoma nonclaim statute giving all creditors two months from publication of the notice of probate to present their claims violated the due process rights of creditors known to or who reasonably should be known to the personal representative. The Court held that the probate court was so connected to the working of the statute that the entire procedure involved "state action" and was therefore subject to the due process requirement of the Fourteenth Amendment. In response, some jurisdictions made explicit the personal representative's responsibility to give individual notice to creditors the personal representative knows or should know about. The decision is especially notable for its extension of the state action concept to probate proceedings.

There are situations, however, in which even though the decedent left behind probate property, probate might not be necessary. If the only probate property is tangible personal property and cash, the persons entitled to it, either in intestacy or under the decedent's will, can simply divide the property. Unless the tangible property is of exceptional value, there is no need to show any sort of written title to it if it is sold or even given away. Think of children disposing of a parent's clothes and other personal property. They may keep some items for their sentimental value and give others to charity, or sell them in a yard sale, through a consignment shop, or in an Internet auction. No charity accepting the property or purchaser is going to demand "prove to me that you own this." Of course, if the children are trying to sell a valuable painting or other work of art, any reputable dealer or purchaser will require proof of the work's **provenance**, that is, how the seller came to have title to it. A probate proceeding would provide the link in the chain of title to the work.

(c) Distribution and Closing the Estate

With debts and expenses paid, or at least sums set aside to pay them, the personal representative can distribute the probate estate to heirs in intestacy or the beneficiaries of the decedent's will. Once the property has been distributed, the personal representative must still close the estate. Administrators usually must make a formal report to the court that granted the letters of administration. This report, called an **accounting**, is a complete record of everything the administrator has done with the probate property. It shows the collection of every penny of probate property and the expenditure of every penny, whether to pay debts and expenses or in distribution to the heirs. Executors usually have a range of choices. If administration of the estate presented no unusual complications and if all the beneficiaries are competent adults and are agreeable, the executor may present an accounting to the beneficiaries and ask them to execute a formal approval of what the accounting contains. Otherwise, the executor can submit the accounting to the appropriate court, ask the court to send formal notice to all those interested in the estate, and request a decree approving the accounting and releasing the executor from any further responsibility. This **judicial accounting** provides the executor with the greatest protection but involves greater time and expense than an informal accounting presented only to the beneficiaries.

> **Sidebar**
>
> **SMALL ESTATE PROCEDURES**
>
> Every state has simplified procedures for "small" amounts of probate property (common limits are $30,000 or $50,000). States also have a procedure for collecting particular items of probate property below a certain value by affidavit of the person claiming to be entitled to it. A surviving spouse or child might be able to collect a bank account belonging to the decedent by making an affidavit giving the facts that entitle them to the account under the relevant statute. The statute also protects the bank from claims by others. Amounts that can be collected this way vary, but $5,000 seems to be a common limit. Motor vehicles can also be transferred by affidavit, again to a surviving spouse or child or other close relative.

(3) The Cost

For decades the probate system has been criticized, often vehemently, as archaic, time-consuming, and above all, too expensive. Reinforced by several books written for nonlawyers, this perception has helped fuel the nonprobate revolution, especially the use of revocable lifetime trusts as will substitutes. It is worth taking a moment, however, to consider in a general way the costs of probate.

First, there are filing fees associated with opening testate or intestate administration, and they are often on a sliding scale keyed to the estimated value of the probate estate. If the personal representative uses a judicial accounting to close the estate, there will be more filing fees. Remember too that if a testate probate estate is being distributed to adult family members, one of whom is executor, an informal accounting may be sufficient, although the services of an accountant may be necessary to properly prepare a complete account.

An executor might want to hire a lawyer to handle admitting the will to probate and the various tasks of administration. The trustee of a revocable trust, of course, doesn't have to worry about the probate process, but might still need professional legal help to deal with a judicial accounting. If the value of decedent's estate is large enough to incur federal or state estate or inheritance taxes, it is likely that a lawyer's help will be required to complete the proper tax returns. The amount of the legal fees is a matter of agreement between the executor or trustee and the lawyer, although in a few states legal fees for representing an executor are set by statute. It is also not uncommon for a court to have the last word on the amount of the legal fees paid by an executor, and if an executor or a trustee of a revocable trust seeks a formal discharge through a judicial accounting, the relevant court will pass on the fee as part of its approval of the executor's or trustee's expenditures.

Both executors and trustees are entitled to commissions, which are their pay for performing the tasks they are required to do. In some states, commissions for executors and trustees are set by statute; in others, it is a matter of what is "reasonable." In any event, the testator or the settlor of the revocable trust can set the compensation of the executor or trustee in the document. A bank acting as executor or trustee will almost certainly expect payment according to its own fee schedule.

Finally, there is the cost of the will or trust itself. As we will see, there is no requirement that a testator have a lawyer write the will or that someone who wants to have a revocable trust hire a lawyer to draft it. If someone does seek professional help, however, fees vary widely according to the complexity of the will or trust, the region, the lawyer's experience, and so on.

In short, it is very difficult to say anything generally true about the relative costs of using the probate system versus avoiding it through the use of nonprobate property devices and the revocable trust. And whatever the out-of-pocket costs may be, there are other considerations. The law governing nonprobate property devices is not as well developed as the law of wills and the workings of the probate system. One striking example is the treatment of creditors. The opening of a probate proceeding, testate or intestate, is often a prerequisite to quickly resolving claims against the estate and thus relieving beneficiaries from concerns about claims on the property they have received.

E. Taxes

As Benjamin Franklin pointed out several hundred years ago, "in this world nothing can be said to be certain, except death and taxes."[4] And he couldn't have been more right. Paying taxes is, in fact, an important part of the entire process of making a gift at death and of the probate process. First, the decedent will owe income taxes for the year of death. The personal representative will file whatever returns are due, and if no personal representative qualifies, whoever is in possession of the decedent's property is responsible for filing the final federal income tax return. For example, the successor trustee of the decedent's revocable trust will have the responsibility for filing the final return if no personal representative qualifies. States and localities that levy income taxes generally track the federal procedures.

In addition to income taxes, there are taxes that are levied on the making of a gift both during life and at death. These are the wealth transfer taxes: the estate tax, the gift tax, and the generation-skipping transfer tax. These taxes are explained in much

---

[4]Benjamin Franklin to Jean-Baptiste Leroy (Nov. 13, 1789), in *Bartlett's Familiar Quotations* 310 (Justin Kaplan ed., 16th ed. 1992).

greater detail in Chapter 17, but for now what you need to know is that very few Americans ever have to be concerned about these taxes. The numerous exemptions from the gift tax make it unlikely that most of us will ever have to give any thought to the gift tax when we give presents to mark holidays, birthdays, weddings, and other events. In 2012, the federal estate tax applies only to taxable estates of at least $5,120,000 which means that very few estates need worry about it (although some states levy estate taxes on smaller taxable estates). The generation-skipping transfer tax is also structured to exempt the vast majority of transfers that would otherwise be subject to it.

You must understand two things about taxes before we continue. First, most nonprobate property is part of the taxable estate on which the estate tax is computed. In other words, avoiding probate will not avoid estate taxes. Second, so important is taxation that the property law of making a gift at death has been strongly influenced by the tax laws. We will see many examples of this influence as we go along.

SUMMARY

- This book is about the law of wills and trusts, which is the law governing making a gift at death.

- Probate property is disposed of by will or passes in intestacy.

- There are numerous devices for creating nonprobate property; the most comprehensive is the revocable lifetime trust.

- The personal representative obtains authority to deal with the decedent's probate property through the probate process.

- Administering a probate estate involves qualification by a personal representative, collection of the probate property, payment of the decedent's debts and expenses, including taxes, distribution of the property, and, finally, closing the estate.

- While few estates are liable for federal estate tax, tax provisions have greatly influenced the law of making gifts at death.

CONNECTIONS

The Law Governing Wills and Trusts

Although the UPC and the UTC have been fairly widely enacted by the states and have influenced a good deal of legislation in others, they do not provide the kind of nationwide uniformity provided by their sibling, the UCC. There is no substitute for consulting the law of the state that applies to a particular problem (or on which your bar exam will be based).

Personal Representatives, Trustees, and Fiduciary Duties

Personal representatives and trustees are fiduciaries. Their actions are governed by the fiduciary duties owed to the beneficiaries of estates and trusts. Chapter 16 discusses these duties in detail.

Nonprobate Property and the Revocable Lifetime Trust

A full understanding of the workings of a revocable lifetime trust requires understanding the discussion of revocable trusts in Chapter 11, the law of trusts discussed in Chapters 8 and 9, and the law of future interests discussed in Chapter 7.

Wills and Gifts at Death

Chapters 3, 4, and 5 are all about wills: Chapter 3 discusses how to create a valid will and how to revoke one, Chapter 4 examines the law that governs challenges to wills, and Chapter 5 deals in detail with the large body of law that makes wills work.

Intestacy and Family

Chapter 2 discusses intestacy statutes in detail with a special emphasis on the UPC. But the chapter is as much about the persons to whom the intestacy statute distributes the decedent's probate estate as it is about how much they get. Because intestacy statutes are all based on the idea of family, understanding them requires some hard thought about who are a decedent's family. Questions raised by changing definitions of marriage and by medical advances that are changing the idea of parenthood are especially relevant to the discussions of class gifts in Chapters 5 and 7 and all of Chapter 13 on protection of the family.

Wealth Transfer Taxes and Gifts at Death

Chapter 17 is an introduction to the workings of the wealth transfer taxes discussed at the end of this chapter. The discussion there should help you understand how the tax law has influenced the law of making gifts at death.

Intestacy

2

Intestacy statutes distribute a decedent's probate property when no valid will exists. The recipients of such property are some — but not all — of the

O V E R V I E W

decedent's family members. Which family members receive how much is what intestacy statutes are all about. Intestacy law is vital to understand not only because large numbers of people die without leaving valid wills, but also because the terms and definitions used in intestacy statutes are often the same ones used in wills and trusts. In addition, because society's definition of what defines a "family" continues to evolve, so must the law's, making intestacy a legal barometer of sorts, registering changes that affect all of us.

A. HOW INTESTACY STATUTES WORK

B. THE MECHANICS OF DISTRIBUTION

    1. The Three Basic Schemes of Distribution
    2. Minors and Incapacitated Persons as Heirs

C. THE INTESTACY STATUTES AND THE FAMILY

    1. Who Is a Spouse?
    2. The Legal Relationship of Parent and Child
    3. How Far Do We Go, or Who's Your First Cousin Once Removed?
    4. Relatives of the Half Blood

D. **BARS TO TAKING IN INTESTACY (OR IN ANY OTHER WAY)**

   1. Advancements
   2. Slayers
   3. Disclaimers
   4. Bad Behavior

E. **WHAT INTESTACY RULES MEAN FOR WILLS AND TRUSTS**

A. How Intestacy Statutes Work

Probate property has to go somewhere, and if a decedent does not leave a valid will, the intestacy statute tells us where that "somewhere" is. Remember that because of the peculiarities of history (the answer is always "because the Normans conquered England"), the state controls the passing of property at death. In the United States, then, individual state legislatures write the intestacy statutes, which contain one important common denominator: probate property goes to decedents' families. To put it more formally, the heirs designated in a statute to take a decedent's probate property are those persons related to the decedent by blood or adoption (**consanguinity**), *not* by marriage (**affinity**), except in very limited circumstances.

An intestacy statute is a **default statute** because it governs the distribution of the decedent's probate property if she dies without a valid will. In other words, it takes effect if a person does nothing, just like the default setting in a computer application operates unless you change it. Default statutes are very common in the law of wills and trusts. Take a moment to think about why this might be.

Next consider how a legislature should proceed in writing a default statute. Should it try to decide what the average person would do in the situation and write that solution into law? Should it decide what the best solution is, irrespective of what a majority of people would want? Can the legislature even know who represents an average person, let alone what that average person wants? Can it know who is included in a majority of people (those who have some minimum amount of probate property? are married? are in unmarried relationships? have children, regardless of marital status?); if not, how can it know what that majority wants? And even if the legislature could agree on who belongs to the majority, could it agree on what a best solution is? You see the point, I hope. As we learn about what default statutes provide, give some thought to what you believe they *should* provide.

Sidebar

PARTIAL INTESTACY

Partial intestacy occurs when (1) a will does not dispose of all of the testator's probate property or (2) when a **negative will** excludes an heir from taking any property, but all inheriting heirs die before the disinherited heir does. Under the common law, negative words intended to disinherit someone do not override the intestacy statute if the will does not make an otherwise effective gift of the probate property. Today, however, the law of many states, often by adopting UPC § 2-101, gives effect to negative wills by treating a disinherited party as if he had died before the testator. Restatement (Third) of Property (Wills and Other Donative Transfers) § 2.7 also expressly authorizes negative wills and therefore reverses the common law rule.

Q: Which state's intestacy law governs the decedent's estate?

A: The law of the state of the decedent's domicile. We each have only one domicile, and that's the place of residence to which we always intend to return no matter how much time we spend elsewhere. The passing of real property in intestacy, however, is always governed by the law of the state in which the property is located.

B. The Mechanics of Distribution

Before we turn to the perhaps surprisingly complex questions involved in deciding who qualifies as a family member, and therefore an heir, we're going to examine the mechanics of distribution in intestacy. In almost every intestacy statute, heirs other than the surviving spouse, parents, or grandparents of the decedent are described as a class, such as the decedent's descendants or those of the decedent's parents or grandparents. These **multigenerational classes** include persons in more than one generation. Whenever an intestacy statute designates the members of a multigenerational class as a decedent's heirs, the statute also says that the class members take "by representation." What does that mean?

Q: Who are a person's descendants, issue, and heirs?

A: **Heirs** are the persons who take a decedent's probate estate under the intestacy statute. While a person is alive, who those persons are is unknown. We usually refer to those who would take under the intestacy statute were a person to die right now as **presumptive heirs**. **Descendants** (or **issue**) describe everyone descended from a person: children, grandchildren, great-grandchildren, and so on. Both descendants and issue are **multigenerational classes** because they can embrace persons belonging to more than one generation.

Taking **by representation** means that a person does not get a share of the property that is being distributed if she has a living ancestor among the group of descendants. Take a look at the following chart depicting Decedent's descendants; persons who survive Decedent appear in *underlined italics*.

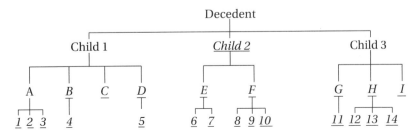

If Decedent dies intestate, the portion of the probate estate that is going to Decedent's descendants by representation will go to Child 2, B, C, D, G, H, 1, 2, and 3. The only great-grandchildren of Decedent who are heirs are 1, 2, and 3 because their parent, A, and their grandparent, Child 1, did not survive Decedent. All the other great-grandchildren are not heirs because their parent or grandparent survived Decedent.

If you want help in understanding this result, think first of all of Decedent's descendants looking up the family tree to their dead ancestor. If there is a living person between them and the dead ancestor whose property is being distributed, they are not going to get any; they are not heirs. Another way to visualize the result is from the point of view of the property that is going to be distributed. Once it is released from Decedent's dead hands, it starts to travel down the family tree. It is grabbed by and belongs to the first pairs of living hands it encounters. So Child 2 grabs 1/3 of the property. Another 1/3 slips through the dead hands of Child 1. B, C, and D each grab 1/4 of that 1/3, and the other 1/4 passes in equal shares to 1, 2, and 3. The final 1/3 slips through the dead hands of Child 3. G, H, and I each grab 1/3 of that 1/3.

Why the initial division into thirds? Because of Decedent's three children, one survived the Decedent and the other two have descendants of their own who survive Decedent. There are three branches to Decedent's family tree — at least in this example. There are three systems of representation currently in use in the United States. We're going to consider each one of them in turn, using the family tree we've just worked with.

(1) The Three Basic Schemes of Representation

The three basic schemes of representation are **English** (or **strict**) **per stirpes**, **modern** (or **modified**) **per stirpes**, and **per capita at each generation**.

(a) English (or Strict) Per Stirpes

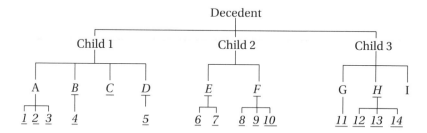

English per stirpes is the system of English common law, thus its name. It is "strict" in the sense that it identifies the branches of the family by their origin in the generation of Decedent's children. In this case, there are three branches of the family tree. (A "stirp" is a root or stock, so the idea is that there are three roots or stocks issuing out of Decedent and forming three families.) Under English per stirpes, the initial division of the property is made in the generation of the named person's children, *even if none of them are alive at the time the distribution is to be made.* Once this initial division is made, the property moves down the family lines dividing and subdividing until it is all distributed to living people.

The distribution of Decedent's property under English per stirpes is therefore as follows:

- The 1/3 set aside for Child 1 is divided into four parts, one part for each living child of Child 1 and one part of the deceased child (A) who has living descendants. Therefore, B, C, and D each take 1/12 of the property (1/4 × 1/3); and 1, 2, and 3 each get 1/36 (1/3 × 1/12). (Yes, this involves multiplying fractions. Fourth-grade arithmetic strikes again.)
- The 1/3 set aside for Child 2 is divided into two parts, and E and F each take 1/6 of the property (1/2 × 1/3).
- The 1/3 set aside for Child 3 is divided into two parts, and H takes 1/6 (1/2 × 1/3) and 11 takes 1/6.

Note first that Child 3's 1/3 is divided into two not three parts because grandchild I is dead without any living descendants. There are only two branches of the family issuing out of Child 3, so the 1/3 is divided into only two parts. Note also that 11 gets 1/6 because 11 is the only living child of G. Great-grandchildren 1, 2, and 3 each took only 1/36 because Child 1's 1/3 had to be divided first into four parts, one for each of branches of the family issuing out of Child 1, and then again so that each child of A takes an equal share. Thus in English per stirpes, persons receiving distributions who are in the same generation will not necessarily receive the same share. It all depends on how many living siblings and how many dead siblings with living descendants they have at the time of distribution.

(b) Modern (or Modified) Per Stirpes

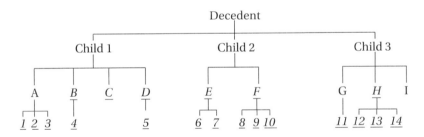

Under modern per stirpes, the initial division of Decedent's property *is at the eldest generation in which there are living persons.* Because the stirps begin in the eldest generation in which people survive, this family tree now has eight branches instead of three.

Now Decedent's property is divided into eight parts, one part of each living grandchild and one part of each dead grandchild who has living descendants. (Remember, there is no share set aside for I because I is dead without living descendants; there is no branch of the family tree there.) Each living grandchild— B, C, D, E, F, and H—takes 1/8. Great-grandchildren 1, 2, and 3 each take 1/24 (1/3 × 1/8), and great-grandchild 11 takes 1/8. The other great-grandchildren are not heirs because their parents are alive. Note once again that 11 takes three times what 1, 2, and 3 take because 11 is an only child and doesn't have to share with siblings.

(c) Per Capita at Each Generation

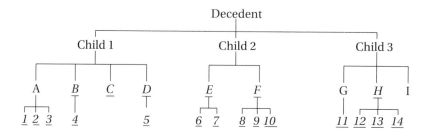

Under per capita in each generation, just as under modern per stirpes, the initial division of Decedent's property *is at the eldest generation in which there are living persons.* So once again, Decedent's property is divided into eight parts, and once again each living grandchild — B, C, D, E, F, and H — takes 1/8.

Now things get interesting. The one-eighths that were set aside for each A and G, the two grandchildren who did not survive Decedent but who have living descendants, *are combined and distributed in equal shares to the persons in the next generation who are entitled to take.* Great-grandchildren 1, 2, 3, and 11, therefore, each take 1/16 ($1/4 \times 2/8 = 2/32$, or 1/16). Per capita in each generation is exactly that: *each person entitled to share in the property being distributed receives the same share as every other person in that generation who is entitled to take.* Now the great-grandchildren who are entitled to take each receive exactly the same share.

Per capita in each generation is the meaning of "by representation" under the UPC § 2-107. For more illustrations of this system of representation, take a look at the comment following § 2-107. A handful of states have adopted statutes that define "by representation" as per capita in each generation.

Table 2.1 summarizes the three systems of representation as applied to the family tree we've been using.

TERMINOLOGY CONFUSION AND REPRESENTATION

The names we've given the three systems of representation are not necessarily those that appear in statutes. Most statutes define "representation" to mean whatever system is used in intestacy. The statutes may also define what "representation" and "per stirpes" mean when used in wills and trusts. While "representation" probably will be defined as the system used in intestacy, "per stirpes" might mean English or modern, if those are not the meaning of "representation."

As you can see, which system is used certainly makes a difference. Which one is the "best" is a difficult question. The drafters of the UPC selected per capita in each generation based on some empirical evidence showing a preference for distributing equal shares to all heirs in the same generation. The catch phrase has become "equally near, equally dear." Some practitioners maintain that many of their clients prefer English per stirpes when drafting wills that give property to their descendants "by representation." When it comes to the intestacy statute, however, the legislature has to make a choice. (Remember that intestacy is a default rule that can be overridden by drafting a valid will.)

TABLE 2.1	Summary: Systems of Representation		
Heirs (Persons Taking)	English Per Stirpes	Modern Per Stirpes	Per Capita in Each Generation
B	1/12	1/8	1/8
C	1/12	1/8	1/8
D	1/12	1/8	1/8
E	1/6	1/8	1/8
F	1/6	1/8	1/8
H	1/6	1/8	1/8
1	1/36	1/24	1/16
2	1/36	1/24	1/16
3	1/36	1/24	1/16
11	1/6	1/8	1/16

(2) Minors and Incapacitated Persons as Heirs

If any of a decedent's heirs are **minors**, that is, under the age of 18, or **incapacitated** (as a legal concept, a word with a variety of definitions), the distribution of the decedent's probate property involves some additional work. Because a minor or an incapacitated person cannot enter into a binding contract, he can do little more than hold title to the property. He cannot invest, sell, or lease it. Now what?

You will not be surprised to learn that the law provides rules to govern this situation; after all, minors and incapacitated persons have been inheriting property since property could be inherited. The problem is that the law does not handle the problem very well, at least in most states.

F   A   Q

Q: What's the difference between a guardian of the property and a guardian of the person?

A: Both types of court-appointed guardians act on behalf of a minor or incapacitated person, but they have different roles. The guardian of the property makes decisions concerning the inherited property. The guardian of the person is responsible for the personal care of the minor or incapacitated person. A parent can name a guardian of the person for minor children in a will, but if the parent dies intestate and the other parent is also dead, a court will select someone, usually from among the minor's relatives, making the selection "in the best interests of the child."

A court appoints a **guardian** (or, in some states and under the UPC, a **conservator**) to act on behalf of a minor or an incapacitated heir. In many states, the guardian has only limited authority over the property and may invest in only a limited range of assets, sometimes only insured bank deposits and federal governmental debt. In addition, guardians are sometimes limited to spending the income from the property. If they need to use some of the property itself to provide for the person, they must seek court approval. The guardian may also be required to **account** to the appointing court, presenting for approval a detailed explanation of every expenditure of guardianship property. Finally, the guardian is often required to post a bond, the cost of which is paid by the guardianship property. All in all, a guardianship can be an expensive proposition.

One alternative to guardianship for a minor in all states is a **custodial account** under the state's version of the Uniform Transfer to Minors Act (UTMA). The property in the account belongs to the minor but is managed by a **custodian** who has broad powers to expend the property for the minor's benefit. In some states, the administrator of an intestate estate can distribute the share of a minor heir to a custodian selected by the administrator; in others, a court might have that authority. In any event, the breadth of the custodian's authority and the fact that the custodianship will end when the minor reaches 18 (in some states, 21) make this device suitable for relatively small amounts, probably no more than several tens of thousands of dollars. Larger amounts are probably best dealt with in a trust, especially because an 18- or 21-year-old might not be capable of managing wealth.

C. The Intestacy Statutes and the Family

As we've seen, the decedent's heirs are defined in terms of consanguineous family relationships. The meaning of family is basically a traditional one. With the exception of the decedent's spouse, the decedent's heirs are persons related to the decedent by blood or adoption (a relatively late addition as these things go). The inclusion of adopted persons shows that the concept of family has evolved in the last fifty years, and the process is not ended. Today, medical advances have altered the once timeless truths of human reproduction so the idea of "blood" relationship simply isn't what it used to be. The idea of "spouse" is also changing. The struggle over the recognition of same-sex committed partnerships is an important public issue that is far from settled. The law of wills and trusts may be focused on death, but it is at the heart of social change.

(1) Who Is a Spouse?

Until relatively recently, determining who qualifies as surviving spouse involved little difficulty. Marriage involved one man and one woman, and in most states marriage requires a license from the state and some sort of ceremony presided over by a government official or a religious official to whom the state, in essence, delegates the authority to perform ceremonial marriages. A few states still recognize what is colloquially called **common law marriage**, more accurately described as **nonceremonial marriage**. In these jurisdictions, a man and a woman are legally married if they "hold themselves out" as husband and wife and are regarded by others as being married.

It is relatively easy to identify the surviving spouse of a ceremonial marriage because formal paperwork exists. The existence of a nonceremonial marriage is more difficult to prove and often is settled in litigation. Even if a state does not recognize nonceremonial marriages contracted within its borders, it will recognize such marriages validly created in another state so long as the marriage *does not violate the public policy of the state.*

And therein lies the rub when it comes to a related and pressing current issue, that of same-sex relationships. Although logic might suggest that states would treat out-of-state same-sex marriages like they do out-of-state nonceremonial marriages, this does not hold up in practice. Why? For the reason given in italics in the preceding paragraph.

The uproar over the possibility of same-sex couples marrying began with a decision of the Hawai'i Supreme Court in *Baehr v. Lewin* in 1993.[1] The court held that denial of a marriage license to a same-sex couple was discrimination based on sex and therefore could be upheld against a challenge based on equal protection analysis only if the state had a "compelling interest" in denying marriage to same-sex couples, and the court couldn't find one. In response, in 1996 Congress passed and the president signed into law the Defense of Marriage Act (DOMA).[2] DOMA limits federal recognition of marriage to opposite sex unions and sanctions a state's refusal to recognize same-sex marriages validly performed in another state. Several states have similar laws (so-called mini-DOMAs), and some have amended their constitutions to define marriage as limited to one man and one woman. In some instances, these constitutional amendments purport to prohibit same-sex **civil unions** (which give couples who cannot marry all of the rights and responsibilities of marriage) or other "marriage substitutes," although many of these provisions are less than clear.

States without mini-DOMAs or constitutional provisions have taken a variety of approaches to the question of legal recognition for same-sex couples. Connecticut, Iowa, Massachusetts, New Hampshire, New York, Vermont, and the District of Columbia do not limit marriage to opposite-sex couples. Delaware, Hawai'i, Illinois, New Jersey, and Rhode Island have civil union legislation. In California, legislation gives registered domestic partners all the statutorily based rights of married couples by the simple expedient of directing that wherever a statute uses the term "spouse," the phrase "registered domestic partner" is included. Colorado, Nevada, Oregon, Washington, and Wisconsin all have some form of domestic partnership legislation, even though some of these states have constitutional provisions banning same-sex marriage.

---

[1]852 P.3d 44 (Haw. 1993).
[2]1 U.S.C. § 7 (2004).

Although these marriage substitutes certainly are advantageous for the same-sex couples who live in the states where they are authorized, the question remains of what happens when same-sex couples who are married, partners in civil unions, or registered domestic partners move to a state where same-sex marriage, civil unions, or registered domestic partnerships are not available to the residents of the state. The law is developing rapidly, and in some instances same-sex marriages valid where the parties were married have been recognized at least for some purposes by states where same-sex marriage is not possible. There is a lot more law to be made.

One last word on the surviving spouse as heir. It is obvious that if the marriage is dissolved before the death of one of the parties, the survivor is not the decedent's surviving spouse. The UPC provides that result expressly in § 2-802. Many non-UPC states have similar statutory provisions, some of which go further than UPC provisions. For example, a legal separation may end inheritance rights between the spouses. Bad behavior on the part of the survivor may also be disqualifying. The grounds can include abandonment of the decedent, refusal to fulfill the obligation of spousal support, or physical or mental abuse.

Now, finally, after we've established *who* is a surviving spouse, the question remains *what* does the surviving spouse get? You're going to hate the answer: it depends. Bad law professor joking aside, it should be clear that what a surviving spouse inherits depends on the provision of the applicable intestacy statute. In most cases, it's safe to say that if a decedent is not survived by descendants but does have a surviving spouse, the spouse is the sole heir. In a few states, a surviving spouse may have to share the intestate estate with the decedent's surviving parents or parent if no descendants of the decedent survive. UPC § 2-102(1) gives the entire intestate probate estate to the decedent's surviving spouse if the decedent is not survived by descendants or parents. If at least one of the decedent's parents survives the decedent, under UPC § 2-102(2) the surviving spouse receives the first $300,000 of the intestate probate estate and three-fourths of the remainder; the other one-fourth goes to the decedent's surviving parent or parents.

F   A   Q

Q: Why are the dollar amounts in UPC § 2-102 in square brackets?

A: Square brackets indicate that the material they enclose is suggested by the Uniform Law Commission and that a state enacting the provision should make a choice. In this case the legislature should decide on the dollar amounts going to the surviving spouse "off the top." In some uniform acts, however, square brackets indicate alternative provisions among which the legislature should choose.

When the decedent does have descendants who survive her, most statutes give the surviving spouse an amount "off the top" and divide the rest of the probate estate between the spouse and the decedent's descendants. The off-the-top amount is designed to give all of smaller probate estates ("small" being defined by the legislature) to the surviving spouse.

The UPC provisions (§ 2-120) are more complex. The amount the surviving spouse is entitled to depends on whether all of the decedent's descendants are also descendants of the surviving spouse and whether the surviving spouse has descendants who are not also descendants of the decedent. (Go ahead, read that aloud.

Because "descendant" and "decedent" sound so much alike, the UPC intestacy provisions sometimes read like tongue twisters.) The idea is that how much the surviving spouse gets depends on the structure of the families of the spouses:

TABLE 2.2

Surviving descendants of decedent	Amount to surviving spouse	Fraction of balance to surviving spouse
Are all descendants of spouse, and spouse has no descendants not also descended from decedent	n/a	100%
Are all descendants of spouse who has other descendants not descended from decedent	$225,000	50%
Are not all descendants of surviving spouse	$150,000	50%

The drafters of the UPC had two thoughts in mind when they formulated § 2-102. First, as the comment to the section states, at the time of the 1990 revision there were empirical studies showing that wills of married persons with "smaller" probate estates "tend to devise their entire estate to their surviving spouses, even when the couple has children." The key here is "smaller" estates. The comment goes on to say that intestate estates "overwhelmingly tend to be" smaller estates. The relatively large amounts set aside to the surviving spouse off the top of the intestate estate are designed, therefore, to make sure that the intestacy statute does what the decedent would have done had the decedent written a will — give the entire probate estate to the surviving spouse. As already noted, many non-UPC-based intestacy statutes give some amount off the top to the surviving spouse, although the reason for the provision may not be as empirically based as that behind the UPC.

The second goal of the UPC intestacy provisions for the surviving spouse is quite different from the first. The UPC provisions try to strike a balance between providing for the surviving spouse and honoring the decedent's presumed intent to pass property through the surviving spouse to the decedent's children by giving differing shares of larger intestate estates to surviving spouses depending on the assumed inclination of the surviving spouse to provide for the decedent's children (and the descendants of children who die before the surviving spouse). That's why the surviving spouse gets the smallest amount off the top when the surviving spouse is not the ancestor of all of the decedent's descendants. The entire scheme reflects the fact that we live in a society marked by serial monogamy: one spouse at a time, but several different spouses (or unmarried relationships) over the course of a lifetime.

Non-UPC-based intestacy statutes generally do not attempt to take the fact of serial monogamy into account, remaining content with a provision dividing the intestate probate estate between the surviving spouse and the decedent's descendants that applies in all situations. Note also that all intestacy provisions for the surviving spouse do not take into account the length of the marriage. Being your deceased spouse's heir comes with being married until your spouse's death, no matter how long or short the time between wedding and death.

(2) The Legal Relationship of Parent and Child

The intestacy statutes do not mention children. They all refer to descendants (or sometimes to issue) of the decedent. Remember that one cannot have descendants without first having children. Then those children have to have children if the intestate decedent is going have descendants beyond the children's generation. So who is whose child is a critical question.

In all cases, the question is greatly simplified by the long-standing and all but irrebuttable presumption that a child born to a married woman is the child of her husband. Of course, that presumption does not apply to a child born to an unmarried woman, and questions of paternity have long been important. Medical and scientific advances such as DNA matching have made answering paternity questions easier and more certain.

What medical science contributes to certainty with one hand, however, it sometimes takes away with the other. In addition to the legal presumption about the fatherhood of a child born to a married woman, the laws of nature seemed to make it absolutely certain that a child born to a woman was that woman's genetic child. Today, certain medical and scientific advances have changed the rules and complicated the question of whose child is whose. We are still working out the answers, as we will see.

(a) Posthumous Children

One question about who is a child has been around for a very long time. It is possible for a man to die while a woman is pregnant with the man's child. If the child is eventually born alive, can this child born after the father's death, this **posthumous child**, be an heir of the father? Answering that question involves answering two other questions. First, can the child be considered to be alive at the father's death, which is when heirs are determined? Second, and really more important, is the child really the decedent's child?

The common law has long answered the first question with a yes. Under the common law, an unborn child is said to be *en ventre sa mere*, which is old law French for "in the mother's womb" or, more literally, "in the mother's belly." Once born alive, the child's legal existence relates back to the moment of conception. Therefore, if a man's child is born after his death, the child can be an heir if the child was conceived during the man's lifetime.

Of course, we still have to know whether the decedent really is the child's father. We'll deal with the status of children born outside of marriage in a bit, but that discussion does not usually apply to a child born to a woman recently widowed. There is a well-established rebuttable presumption of common law that a child born to a widow within 280 days (the average gestational period for humans) of her husband's death is the child of her late husband. In some states, that is still the law. The intestacy statute may require an heir to be in gestation before the father's death or to be conceived before the father's death, but whether that requirement is fulfilled is decided through the use of the traditional presumption if the parents were married. Remember that if the parents were not married, once paternity is proved, something we discuss below, proof of the child's conception before the father's death will have to be made without the benefit of the presumption.

(b) Adoption

There is a complication to determining "who is a child" that is unrelated to medical technology. Adoption is a familiar concept today, but it is not part of the Anglo-American legal heritage. The **civil law system**, the legal system descended from Roman law, recognized from very early times the possibility of making someone a family member by choice rather than birth. One famous instance is Julius Caesar's adoption of his great-nephew Octavian, who eventually became the emperor Augustus. Adoption became part of the Anglo-American legal landscape in the nineteenth century by legislative action, meaning that adoption is purely statutory. Strictly speaking, there is no common law of adoption. The role of the courts has been to answer questions that the statutes have not addressed.

At the beginning of the twenty-first century, two rules governed the status of adopted persons as heirs:

- An adopted person is completely integrated into the adopting family, acquiring new parents, siblings, ancestors, and collateral relatives, and can inherit in intestacy from any of them.
- An adopted person is completely separated from his or her genetic family and therefore cannot inherit from any of them.

A handful of states and the UPC (§ 2-119) have statutes that modify the second rule. One of the most common modifications (which could also be established by case law) is to allow a person adopted by a stepparent to continue to inherit as the child of the adoptive person's other parent, the stepparent's spouse. It makes sense to assume that you do not expect to cease to be your child's parent when your spouse adopts your child.

A less usual modification also involves adoption by a stepparent but allows the adopted person to continue to inherit as the child of the other parent, the parent not married to the stepparent. Here's a diagram of this scenario:

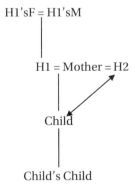

The lines represent genetic relationships; the double arrow represents the adoptive relationship. The equal sign indicates that the persons on either side of it are the genetic parents of the person to whom the line leads. Child, the genetic child of H1 and Mother, has been adopted by H2, who before the adoption was Child's stepfather. Some statutes, including the UPC, allow Child to inherit from H1, the genetic father, if H1 dies intestate just as if Child had never been adopted by H2. In addition, once Child can inherit from H1, Child can also inherit as a descendant of H1's parents (that is, Child can inherit "through" H1). Should a parent of H1 die intestate after H1's death, then Child will be an heir of that parent of H1. H1, however, cannot inherit *from* Child should Child die intestate. In that case, Child's parents are Mother and H2. In addition, if Child dies before H1 but Child's Child survives H1 (and it doesn't matter who Child Child's other parent is; the significant fact is the relationship with Child), then Child's Child, the descendant of the adoptee, inherits from H1 just as if Child had never been adopted.

A handful of state statutes and UPC § 2-119 go even further and allow an adopted person to inherit in his genetic relationships when the adoptive parent is related to a genetic parent. This diagram illustrates the situation such statutes address:

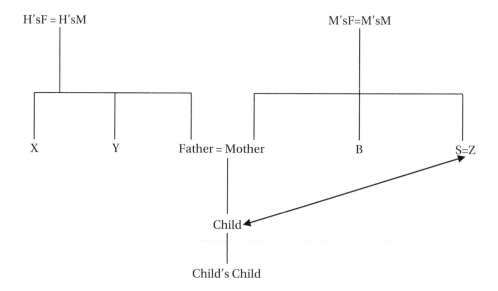

Under the general rule of complete separation from the genetic family, Child would no longer be the child of Mother and Father for inheritance purposes. Child could not inherit from Father or anyone in Father's family through Father; and for purposes of inheritance from members of Mother's family, Child would inherit as the child of S and not from or through Mother. Statutes that change this result preserve the parent-child relationship between the adopted person and his genetic parents for purposes of inheritance by the adopted person and the adopted person's descendants from or through the genetic parents whenever the adopted person, Child in our diagram, has been adopted by a relative of a genetic parent. Usually (and under UPC § 2-119), "relative" means a grandparent or descendant of a grandparent.

F A Q

Q: Does an adopted person whose adoption is subject to a statute like UPC § 2-119 *really* inherit from more than two sets of grandparents?

A: In a word, yes. The provisions of the UPC and similar statutes represent a policy choice to preserve the adopted person's inheritance rights from the genetic family under the circumstances covered by the statutes.

Applying such a statute to the situation in the diagram means Child and Child's descendants inherit as if Mother and Father were still Child's parents. Child will inherit from Father, from Father's family, and from Mother; and Child will be an heir of Mother's parents if they die intestate after Mother's death. For purposes of inheritance, Child's Child is still a grandniece or grandnephew of Mother and Father's siblings and a great-grandchild of Mother and Father's parents. Remember, too, that Child, Child's Child, and all of Child's other descendants also inherit from and through Z, the adoptive parent who is not related to a genetic parent. In effect, Child has three sets of grandparents for inheritance purposes: H's parents, the parents of W and S, and Z's parents.

There is another aspect to adoption that is completely a matter of court-made law. **Equitable adoption** is a doctrine used by courts to find a parent-child relationship where there has been no adoption. The cases that address it almost always arise when a person dies intestate and the only heirs are distant relatives or the state under the doctrine of escheat (which we discuss below). A person who lived as a child with the decedent then comes forward and claims that she should be recognized as the decedent's child and heir.

The facts of these cases are often emotionally moving, but the courts have generally been reluctant to recognize equitable claims to being a child. Many of the cases take a fairly rigid doctrinal approach. The reasoning starts with the proposition that equity will treat as done that which ought to have been done but was not. Here what ought to have been done was a formal adoption of the child. Some cases have required proof not only of intent to adopt but of a binding promise to adopt between the alleged parent and someone who had the authority to offer the child for adoption.[3] Even courts that have not required a formal, binding promise to adopt

Sidebar

SECOND PARENT ADOPTION

Consider the situation of a same-sex couple, one of whom is the genetic or adoptive parent of a child whom the other partner wishes to adopt so that the child will have two parents. The couple cannot marry in the state where they live, nor will that state recognize a valid marriage performed elsewhere. Even under the UPC and similarly expansive statutes, the adoption will sever the parent-child relationship between the existing parent and the child because the adoptive parent is not married to the existing parent. In other words, the statutes make no provision for **second parent adoption**. Such adoptions are recognized in a few states, however, usually by court decision; and in those states, the child will indeed have two parents after the adoption is final, even though the parents are not married.

---

[3]O'Neal v. Wilkes, 439 S.E.2d 490 (Ga. 1994).

have required that the intention to adopt or the decedent's representations to the child or to others that the child was indeed a genetic or formally adopted child be shown by clear and convincing evidence.[4] If an equitable adoption is found, the benefits almost always run only one way—the child is an heir of the decedent, but the decedent's relatives cannot inherit from the child through the decedent should the child later die intestate.

F   A   Q

Q: Are stepchildren ever the heirs of their stepparents and are in-laws ever the heirs of spouse's family?

A: Generally, no. Inheritance follows family lines as defined by genetic and adoptive relationships. Persons who are related through marriage of their genetic or adoptive relations are not related to one another for purposes of inheritance. However, under UPC § 2-103(b), stepchildren and descendants can inherit when the decedent has no other heirs. California also makes certain exceptions that allow stepchildren, foster children, and in-laws to inherit. See Cal. Prob. Code §§ 6402(f) (in-laws), 6454 (step- or foster children); see also Estate of Joseph, 949 P.2d 472 (Cal. 1998).

(c) Nonmarital Children

Under the common law, a child who was born to an unmarried woman was literally the child of no one. William Blackstone summed up the traditional common law in the first volume of his *Commentaries on the Laws of England*, first published in 1765: a nonmarital child "can *inherit* nothing, being looked upon as the son of nobody, and sometimes called *filius nullius.* . . ."[5] The situation was not quite that grim in practice, but it took some time before the nonmarital child was officially an heir of her mother and even longer before the law recognized the possibility of inheriting from the father.

By the third quarter of the twentieth century, it was common for statutes to allow the nonmarital child to inherit from the father only if the father had married the mother or had in some way acknowledged the child as his. The situation was completely changed in 1977 by the U.S. Supreme Court's decision in *Trimble v. Gordon.*[6] The Court held that limiting the right of a nonmarital child to inherit from his or her father to situations where the father had admitted paternity was a denial of equal protection.

Since *Trimble*, states have gradually liberalized their statutes to expand the ways in which a nonmarital child can prove paternity and thus inherit from his or her father. This development has gone hand in hand with scientific advances that have made DNA matching an all but infallible test of paternity. What was once always open to some doubt can today be established beyond doubt.

[4]Estate of Ford, 82 P.3d 747 (Cal. 2004).
[5]1 William Blackstone, *Commentaries* *447.
[6]430 U.S. 762 (1977).

The UPC does not contain rules for determining parentage of nonmarital children, although § 2-117 eliminates all distinctions between marital and nonmarital children. The Uniform Parentage Act does contain rules that put great weight on genetic testing. The effect of scientific advances, however, is not always to make it easier to answer questions about who is related to whom.

(d) Assisted Reproduction

Three advances in medical science concern what the UPC terms **assisted reproduction**, defined in UPC § 2-115(2) to mean "a method of causing pregnancy other than sexual intercourse." These advances remade the law of parentage and therefore the law of intestate succession. The first is the development of techniques for the cryopreservation of human gametes and embryos. Cryopreservation of sperm, the first technique to be perfected, allowed **artificial insemination** in which sperm enters a woman's body not through sexual intercourse but through mechanical means — the use of a syringe, for example. Sperm banks throughout the United States supply frozen sperm from screened, anonymous donors to women who wish to conceive by artificial insemination. Because there is no doubt that the woman is the genetic mother of a child born as a result of artificial insemination, she is the legal mother of the child.

Identifying the father of the child is another matter. Because artificial insemination with donated sperm has been practiced for some time, there are statutes that address the question. Generally, the anonymous sperm donor is not the legal father of the resulting child. He has neither obligations to the child nor any parental rights over the child. If the woman who conceives using the anonymously donated sperm is married and the artificial insemination is done with her husband's consent, the husband is the father of the child even though he is not the genetic father. The child inherits as a child of the couple. A child born to an unmarried woman who has been artificially inseminated with sperm from an anonymous donor does not have a legal father and therefore will inherit only from and through his mother.

F　A　Q

Q: What happens if the donor of sperm used in artificial insemination is not anonymous?

A: In some instances, the donor and the mother enter into an agreement that defines their rights and obligations with respect to the child. Such agreements do not always prevent disputes, which must be settled by a court. If there is no agreement, disputes often end up in court where the intent of the parties at the time of the conception of the child will be important, as will their subsequent behavior toward the child. Inheritance rights are governed by the rules applicable to any nonmarital child.

The second scientific advance is **in vitro fertilization**, where a human ovum is fertilized outside a woman's body (*in vitro* is Latin for "in glass"); the resulting embryo is then implanted in the womb of the genetic mother or another woman (who is termed the **gestational carrier** in UPC § 2-121). If an embryo resulting from in vitro fertilization is carried to term, who are the child's parents? The answer to this question depends both on the source of the sperm and ova and the identity of the woman who carries the child to term. Generally speaking, no matter what the source of the sperm and ova and no matter who bears the child, the law will recognize as the child's parents the persons who made the in vitro arrangement happen, although the use of such a rule is most likely where the woman who gave birth and the donors of the gametes are not asserting parental rights. When there are competing claims to parentage, courts have given differing weight to genetic and gestational relationships as opposed to intent to become a parent by making the arrangements.

Finally we come to the third and newest technology of assisted reproduction. **Posthumous conception** occurs after the death of the person from whose sperm or ova the child was conceived. Whose child is this? The cases that have been decided up to now have all involved children conceived by widows using their dead husbands' sperm. The facts have been similar. Husband is diagnosed with a serious illness, treatment for which, even if successful, will leave him sterile. He freezes several samples of his sperm. Unfortunately, treatment is not successful, and sometime after his death his widow uses the sperm to conceive, either in vitro using her ova or by artificial insemination. At least one child is born, and the mother then applies for Social Security benefits on their behalf as the children of her deceased husband.

At the time the first cases were brought, an important factor in deciding when a dependent of a decedent was entitled to Social Security benefits based on the decedent's earnings record was whether the person claiming benefits was an heir of the decedent. The Social Security Administration denied the claims, and the mother appealed on the children's behalf. Sometimes the litigation was in state court seeking a declaration that the children were the deceased father's heirs; sometimes it was in federal court, which decided the issue or certified the question of whether the children were heirs under state law to the highest court of the state where the litigation was taking place. The most influential decision came from such a certification to the Massachusetts Supreme Judicial Court. In *Woodward v. Commissioner,*[7] the court held that posthumously conceived children could be the legal children of their deceased parent and therefore heirs if the genetic relationship could be adequately proved, if conception and birth took place within a reasonable time after the parent's death, and if the deceased parent had "clearly and unequivocally consented" to the use of the stored gametes for posthumous reproduction and to the support of any resulting child. The second requirement is related to the state's interest in the prompt and efficient administration of estates, which must be balanced against the surviving spouse's need to carefully consider the important decision of whether to have children only after an appropriate period of mourning. The third is related to the need to prevent fraud, presumably the defrauding of the decedent's other heirs as well as of private and governmental entities that might provide benefits to the decedent's children.

Not every court that has considered the question has found that it is possible for posthumously conceived children to be the legal children or heirs of their deceased parents.[8] These cases have generally turned on the wording of the respective state intestacy statutes, which require an heir to be conceived during the decedent's lifetime or refer to the decedent's issue living at the decedent's death. Many of these opinions, whatever they decide, call on the legislature to settle the matter.

---

[7]760 N.E.2d 257 (Mass. 2002).
[8]See Finley v. Astrue, 270 S.W.3d 849 (Ark. 2008); Khabbaz v. Commr., 930 A.2d 1180 (N.H.2007).

Nevertheless, very few states have legislation dealing with posthumously conceived children. What statutes there are usually require that the consent to posthumous reproduction be made in writing. This is also the position of the Uniform Parentage Act (§ 707).

F   A   Q

Q: What's a record referred to in many uniform Acts?

A: A **record** is a defined term used in uniform acts that means "information that is inscribed on a tangible medium or that is stored in an electronic or other medium and is retrievable in perceivable form" (UPC § 1-201(41)). This definition gives a text file stored on a computer hard drive or a memory flash card the same status as words written on paper. UPC § 1-201(45) is a definition of "sign" that includes electronic signatures and that allows a record to be signed just as a writing can be signed.

Restatement (Third) of Property: Wills and Other Donative Transfers § 2.5 comment *l*, in contrast, states that

> to inherit from the decedent, a child produced from genetic material of the decedent by assisted reproductive technology must be born within a reasonable time after the decedent's death in circumstances indicating the decedent would have approved of the child's right to inherit.

The comment goes on to state that "a clear case" of approval would be the conception of the child by the decedent's widow using his frozen sperm. This is a much less rigorous standard than the requirement of a signed consent and is probably less demanding than even the Massachusetts court's requirement of clear and unequivocal consent. It is, however, much closer to the UPC provisions.

UPC § 2-120 deals with the parentage of children of assisted conception in all circumstances, not just posthumous reproduction. The child is always the child of the woman who gives birth to the child, the **birth mother**, unless that woman is a gestational carrier (the parentage of children born to gestation carriers is dealt with in UPC § 2-121). When it comes to deciding if the child has a second parent, the child is also presumptively the child of any other person named on the birth certificate. If the mother is not married, if the child is conceived after her husband's death, or if no other person is named on the birth certificate, UPC § 2-120 provides several ways in which a person other than the birth mother can become the other parent of the child:

- A writing ("record," in uniform act speak) signed before or after the child's birth that "considering all the facts and circumstances" evidences consent to be the child's parent
- In the absence of the required writing:
  - The person "functioned as a parent" within the first two years of the child's life
  - The person intended to function as a parent within the first two years of the child's life but was prevented from doing so "by death, incapacity, or other circumstances"

- The person intended to be treated as the parent of a posthumously conceived child if the intent can be established by clear and convincing evidence

All of these methods, as well as the birth certificate presumption, apply whether or not the birth mother and the other parent are married. In fact, there is nothing that prevents the birth mother's same-sex partner from fulfilling these tests and being the parent of the child born to the birth mother. Except for functioning as a parent during the first two years of the child's life, these methods of establishing parenthood also apply to a posthumously conceived child. In addition, UPC § 2-120 includes a special rule applicable when the birth mother is married or a surviving spouse. In both cases, her husband is presumed to satisfy one of the three different ways of giving consent to be a parent other than by signing a writing.

F   A   Q

Q: What does the UPC mean by "functioned as a parent"?

A: UPC § 2-115(4) defines the term to mean behaving toward the child in a way "consistent" with being the child's parent and performing the functions customarily performed by a parent, fulfilling parental responsibilities, holding the child out as one's own, participating in the child's upbringing, and residing with the child in the same household or "as a regular member of that household." The comment to § 2-115 further explains this statutory language, which is based on Reporter's Note no. 4 to § 14.5 of Restatement (Third) of Property, which in turn is based on another ALI project, the *Principles of the Law of Family Dissolution: Analysis and Recommendations* § 2.03 (2002).

Establishing parentage under UPC § 2-120, however, does not necessarily establish inheritance rights. A writing evidencing intent to be a parent must be signed within two years of the child's birth in order for the person signing it to be an heir of the child, unless that person also functions as a parent before the child reaches 18. In order to be an heir of the person whose gametes were used for posthumous conception, the child must *en ventre sa mere* no later than 36 months after the death of the gamete donor or be born no later than 47 months after that person's death. That provision means that the birth mother has three years after the decedent's death to decide whether to conceive.

(3) How Far Do We Go, or Who's Your First Cousin Once Removed?

As we've seen, inheritance within the immediate family follows the same pattern just about everywhere. If the intestate decedent is survived by a spouse, the surviving spouse is the primary and sometimes the only heir, especially if the decedent is not survived by any descendants. If there are descendants of the decedent alive when the decedent dies, they usually are heirs, and if there is no surviving spouse they are the only heirs.

What if the decedent is not survived by a spouse or by descendants? Again, the pattern is pretty much the same under every statute: the decedent's surviving parent or parents are the heirs. If neither of the decedent's parents survives the decedent, then once again all of the intestacy statutes agree and make the decedent's parents' descendants the decedent's heirs. In other words, the decedent's brother and sisters and their descendants are the decedent's heirs. The descendants of the decedent's parents take by representation, of course.

So far so good, but what if the decedent outlives her parents, has no surviving issue or spouse, and was her parents' only child? Here's where the intestacy statutes in the United States begin to differ. To understand the various statutory provisions, we need to know a little about family relationships beyond parents, brothers and sisters, and descendants of brothers and sisters (nieces, nephews, great-nieces and great-nephews, and so on).

Most intestacy statutes are based on the **parentelic system**. A **parentela** is a line of descent. The decedent's own descendant make up the first parentela, the decedent's parents and their descendants (other than the decedent, of course) are the second parentela, and the decedent's grandparents and their descendants (other than the decedent's parents and their descendants) are the third parentela. *Most American intestacy statutes do not make relatives beyond the third parentela heirs of the decedent.*

To make sense of that last sentence, take a look at Figure 2.1. In this figure, the parentelas are indicated by the shape containing the description of the persons involved.

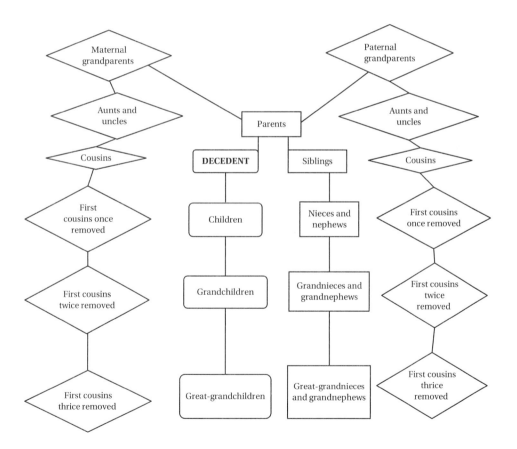

FIGURE 2.1   **PARENTELIC SYSTEM**

First, a couple of things to note about the figure. One, it has two parentelas of the third degree because we each have two sets of grandparents. (Of course, some of us might not have two sets of legal grandparents — think of the child of an unmarried woman who conceives through anonymous sperm donation.) Two, the children of your first cousins are your first cousins once removed. Why "removed"? Because they are one generation more distant from you. Thus your first cousin's great-grandchildren are your first cousins three times or thrice removed.

Now we can use the chart to understand what happens when our intestate decedent has no relatives in the first or second parentelas. Under most intestacy statutes, including UPC § 2-103, the probate property splits in half and moves up the family tree, one-half to the paternal side and one-half to the maternal side. Any living grandparent is an heir. Thus in Figure 2.1, if the maternal grandmother survived the decedent, she would take one-half of the probate estate as the decedent's heir. If both the paternal grandfather and the paternal grandmother survived the decedent, they would each take one-quarter of the probate estate as the decedent's heirs.

If no grandparents survive the decedent on one side of the family, the one-half of the intestate probate estate that would have gone to the grandparents moves down the family tree to the grandparents' descendants. If there are no living persons in one of the third parentelas, all of the intestate probate estate passes to the other third parentela.

If there are no living persons in either of the third-degree parentelas, under most statutes the probate estate **escheats**, that is, the state becomes the decedent's heir. Modern statutes seldom go beyond the third parentela in looking for heirs, so escheat is the result in probably only a small number of cases. Also, UPC § 2-103(b) makes the decedent's stepchildren her heirs if the only alternative is escheat. And of course, escheat can be prevented by writing a will giving the probate estate to whomever the testator wishes.

So much for the way almost all intestacy statutes deal with inheritance from descendants who have no living relatives in the first two parentelas. It is possible for an intestacy statute to look for heirs beyond the third parentela. Some statutes do not provide for escheat when the third parentela is empty but rather give the intestate probate estate to the decedent's **kindred** or **next of kin**. These two terms mean the same thing, and that thing is the determination of kinship by **degrees of relationship**. A degree of relationship is one generational link between the decedent and the person related to the decedent. In Figure 2.1, each line that connects a box is a degree of relationship. The decedent and a sibling are in the second degree of relationship — one link from the decedent to the parents and one link from the parents to the sibling. The decedent and a first cousin are in the fourth degree of relationship — two links from the decedent to the common grandparents, one link from the grandparents to the first cousin's parent, the decedent's aunt or uncle, and one link from the aunt or uncle to the first cousin. When heirship is determined by degrees of relationship, the statutes usually provide that everyone of the same degree of relationship to the decedent receives the same share of the probate estate. Some statutes provide that if relatives of the same degree of relationship are related to the decedent through different ancestors, the person related through the closest ancestor is the heir and the other person is not.

Illustrating the workings of the degree of relationship system gets a little messy, so Figure 2.2 shows a really simple chart focusing on one side of the decedent's family. It doesn't matter which, and we'll arbitrary select the paternal side.

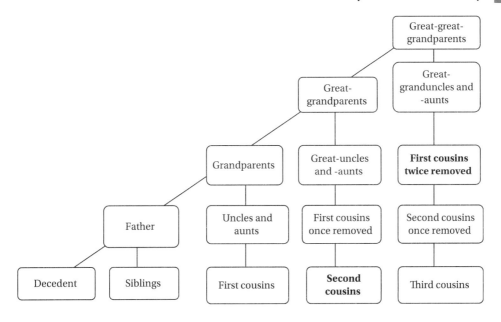

FIGURE 2.2   **DEGREES OF RELATIONSHIP**

Now we know that the decedent's parents and siblings are the second parentela, grandparents and their descendants the third parentela, great-grandparents and their descendants the fourth parentela, and great-great-grandparents and their descendants the fifth. Let's assume that none of the decedent's descendants and no one in the second or third parentelas survives the decedent. The only persons who do survive are in boldface in the chart: second cousins (the children of the decedent's father's cousins, who themselves are the decedent's first cousins once removed—not to be confused with the decedent's first cousins once removed in the third parentela, the child of the decedent's first cousins) and first cousins twice removed, the children of the decedent's great-granduncles and aunts. If you count the number of lines linking these groups of people to the decedent, you will see that both groups are in the sixth degree of relationship to the decedent. The second cousins, however, are related to the decedent through the decedent's great-grandparents, or in other words, the decedent and the second cousins share a common ancestor in their great-grandparents. The first cousins twice removed and the decedent are related through the decedent's great-great-grandparents. The second cousins are related to the decedent through the closer common ancestor, so in a degree of relationship system the second cousins would be the decedent's heirs and the first cousins twice removed would not be.

Figure 2.2's system can be pretty confusing; it's not encouraging to learn that the term "first cousin once removed" describes both the children of your first cousins and your parent's first cousins, the children of your great-aunts and -uncles. Given the growing tendency to restrict inheritance to relatives no more distant than the third parentela, the overlap in terminology becomes less and less important. (Think about your own family situation—are you personally acquainted with any of your relatives in the fourth parentela, let alone any persons even more distantly related to you?) Remember, too, that while a person is alive, she does not have heirs, only presumptive heirs.

(4) Relatives of the Half Blood

There's one more type of relationship we have to note before we can go on. Collateral relatives who share only one common ancestor are related by the **half blood**. The simplest example is illustrated by this family tree:

$$H1 = W = H2$$
$$\begin{array}{ccc} | & | & \\ A & B & C \end{array}$$

B and C are full siblings who are half-siblings to A. A on one hand and B and C on the other have only one ancestor, in this case a parent, in common. W is their mother, but H1, W's first husband, is A's father and H2, W's second husband, is the father of B and C. If A, B, and C have children, the children of B and C are full first cousins to one another, but they and the children of A are half first cousins because once again they have only one ancestor in common, their grandmother, W.

Almost all states have statutes that treat relatives of the half blood as if they were relatives of the whole blood. That is also the rule under UPC § 2-107. Under these statutes, if W and H2 are both dead and C then dies unmarried and without surviving descendants, but A and B both survive C, A and B are C's heirs. If C had died intestate, A and B would each take one-half of C's probate property.

D. Bars to Taking in Intestacy (or in Any Other Way)

Sometimes the intestacy statute, the words of a valid will, or even designations of persons to take nonprobate property do not result in the person entitled to take property actually coming into possession. In this section we examine first an all but obsolete way in which an heir can be barred from taking in intestacy. Then we deal with the two most important ways in which the law rewrites these designations, one of which is in control of the heir or beneficiary; the other, which we take up first, most decidedly is not. We'll also take a look at a third form of disqualification that is not yet as widely accepted as the others.

(1) Advancements

Under American statutes that traced their lineage to the English Statute of Distributions of 1670, a gift to someone who turned out to be an heir of the donor could be counted as a down payment or an anticipation of the donee's share of the intestate probate estate. This down payment is called an **advancement**. The law of advancements used to be a misery. The English statute did not define what made a gift an advancement; it only prescribed the way to take account of such a gift in determining the intestate share of the donee. In light of the statute's silence, the English courts treated almost all gifts made during life as advancements. American courts, however, usually went on a case-by-case basis in an attempt to determine if the donor intended the gift to be an advancement or an outright gift, which would have no effect on distribution of the probate estate in intestacy. The cases are many and often difficult to reconcile.

F   A   Q

Q: Does a presumptive heir have any sort of property interest?

A: No. The presumptive heir has an **expectancy**, which is not property. However, the presumptive heir can *release* the expectancy to the person whose heir he would be. A proper release cuts off the rights in intestacy of the person making the release and of all of his descendants. A presumptive heir can also assign the expectancy. If the presumptive heir actually becomes an heir by surviving the decedent and the assignment is valid, the assignor's intestate share passes to the assignee. If the assignor does not survive the decedent, the rights of the assignor's descendants are not cut off.

Contracts for release or assignment of expectances can be enforced only in equity and only if the person releasing or assigning receives fair consideration. In other words, the equity court will decide whether the deal was fair to the presumptive heir.

Enter true legal reform. Under modern statutes in effect in almost all of the states, a gift is not an advancement unless there is a writing by the donor or donee stating that the gift is to be counted against what the donee would otherwise receive as an heir of the donor. This is the position of Restatement (Third) of Property § 2.7. The UPC provision, § 2-109, requires a declaration by the decedent in a "contemporaneous writing" or "the heir's written acknowledgment" indicating that the gift "is to be taken into account in computing the division and distribution of the decedent's estate." No writing, no advancement.

(2) Slayers

You should not be surprised to learn that if you kill a person from whom you can inherit, you are not going to get the property. Makes sense, right? In the United States, the modern history of that principle begins with a decision of New York's highest court in 1889.[9] Grandfather's will made a significant gift to grandson. Fearing that his grandfather would change his will, and, as the court put it, "to obtain the speedy enjoyment and immediate possession of his property," the grandson "willfully murdered him by poisoning him." The court decided that the grandson could

Sidebar

ACCOUNTING FOR ADVANCEMENTS — THE HOTCHPOT

The method for taking an advancement into account in computing the intestate share of the heir who has received an advancement is a matter of common law. It's called the **hotchpot** and works like this. Say Parent dies intestate survived by three children, A, B, and C. Parent's probate estate is valued at $300,000. Parent also made lifetime gifts to A of $180,000 and to B of $30,000, both of which were described as advancements in a writing that meets the statutory requirements. To calculate the intestate shares of the three children, we add the value of the advancements at the time of the gifts to the probate estate. That gives us a total of $510,000; this is "hotchpot estate." The share of each child is $170,000. A, however, has received an advancement greater than the share to which she is entitled. A can keep the $180,000, but then is entitled to nothing more. The remaining $330,000 is divided between B and C. Each is entitled to $165,000. B has already received $30,000 and therefore is entitled to $135,000 from the probate estate, leaving $165,000 for C.

---

[9]Riggs v. Palmer, 22 N.E. 158 (N.Y. 1889).

not take under the will, and the probate property was distributed as if the grandson had died before the grandfather.

The common law principle of forfeiture by a slayer still exists in that form in some states. In those states, one has to carefully research the cases to answer questions that commonly arise. For example, is it sufficient that the slayer be convicted of any degree of homicide? Sometimes the line is drawn between voluntary and involuntary manslaughter. Does acquittal in a criminal proceeding prevent forfeiture, or can guilt be proved in a civil action by a preponderance of the evidence standard as in a wrongful death action? Usually the answer is yes. What happens to nonprobate property, especially property held by the slayer and victim as joint tenants with right of survivorship or as tenants by the entirety? This question has a variety of answers.

It is easier to find answers to these questions in states with **slayer statutes** that deal with the subject. Many of these statutes are modeled more or less closely on UPC § 2-803, which applies to someone who feloniously and intentionally kills. The slayer forfeits all benefits that would be received because of the victim's death, including in intestacy, under the victim's will, and as beneficiary of a wide range of nonprobate property arrangements. Any appointment of the slayer as personal representative or as trustee is also undone by the statute. Jointly held property (which under UPC § 1-201 is defined to include tenancy by the entirety property) is transformed into an equal tenancy in common so that the victim's share passes through the victim's probate estate. If the accused slayer is acquitted in a criminal proceeding, forfeiture will still occur if the appropriate court determines that the accused slayer would be found "criminally accountable" under a preponderance of the evidence standard. Property that has been forfeited passes as if the slayer had disclaimed the property. (We discuss disclaimers in the next section.) Finally, if the slayer somehow acquires property in a way that is not covered by § 2-803, the acquisition "must be treated in accordance with the principle that a killer cannot profit from his or her wrongdoing" (§ 2-803(f)).

Remember that the law of the state whose bar exam you plan to take or in which you live or might plan to practice may or may not be statutory, and, if statutory, may or may not be set out in a statute as comprehensive as UPC § 2-803. The result is that understanding the extent of forfeiture imposed on a slayer in any particular situation requires good old-fashioned legal research.

(3) Disclaimers

At the very beginning of this book we talked about making a gift at death and drew an analogy to making a gift during life. We noted then that there are statutes that govern a beneficiary's refusal to accept a gift made at death. Now is the time to talk about them.

Under the common law, an heir could not refuse property passing in intestacy, but the beneficiary of a will or trust could refuse to accept property passing to the beneficiary under a will or trust. That distinction has long since passed away, and **renunciations** of property passing in intestacy and **disclaimers** of property passing under wills, trusts, and other nonprobate devices have long been possible. In all states today, they are governed by statutes (almost all of which use the term "disclaimer" for all sorts of refusals). Many of these statutes, however, are not exclusive, and a refusal under the common law might still be possible.

Why in the world would anyone reject an intestate share or a gift under a will or some nonprobate device? The answer comes in two words: taxes and creditors. Let's start with the first. Take another look at the family tree we used to illustrate the three representational systems. Once again, the living are in _underlined italics_.

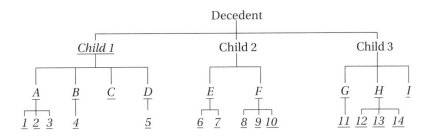

Let's assume that Decedent has died intestate (although, as we will see, the basic situation is the same if Decedent's will makes a gift to "my descendants by representation" or at the termination of a trust the trust property is being distributed to Decedent's descendants by representation). The heirs are Child 1 and grandchildren E, F, G, H, and I. Child 1 is quite prosperous and believes that she really doesn't need her share of Decedent's probate property. All she's likely to do is save or invest it, and when she dies it will be part of her estate that is likely to be large enough to incur federal estate tax and perhaps state estate tax as well. Her children, however, certainly could use the property for their own families. If Child 1 simply gives the property she inherits to A, B, C, and D, she may have adverse gift and estate tax consequences. (We'll see how that might happen in Chapter 17.) Of course, if Child 1 had not survived Decedent, then her children would indeed be Decedent's heirs. If Child 1 properly disclaims her interest in Decedent's estate, the probate property will be distributed as if Child 1 did not survive Decedent. The result of the disclaimer is that Child 1 is pretend dead.

This result comes from the statutory law governing disclaimers of the state whose law governs Decedent's estate. If Child 1 does not want this to be treated as a taxable gift, however, her disclaimer must conform to the requirements of Internal Revenue Code § 2518. The most important requirement if Child 1's disclaimer is to be a **tax-qualified disclaimer** is that it must be made within nine months of Decedent's death. There are additional requirements, but studying those is more appropriate for a course in estate and gift taxation or estate planning. There is another reason Child 1 might disclaim her share of Decedent's intestate estate. The result of being pretend dead is that the **disclaimant**, and here that's Child 1, has never had any interest in the property at all and the disclaimer is not a transfer of any sort. Under the law of most states, that means that a creditor of Child 1 cannot reach the disclaimed property. Even if there is an outstanding judgment against Child 1, in most states a properly done disclaimer will prevent the judgment holder from satisfying the judgment from the disclaimed property.

There is one more aspect of disclaimers we need to examine. Let's go back to the family tree we used to illustrate why Child 1 might disclaim her inheritance from Decedent. Realize that no matter what system of representation is used, Child 1's share of Decedent's intestate probate property is 1/3. Realize too that if Child 1 really had not survived Decedent, under both modern per stirpes and per capita in each generation all of the grandchildren would be Decedent's heirs and they would each take a 1/9 share of Decedent's intestate probate property. If Child 1 is now pretend dead because of a disclaimer, do the nine grandchildren now receive equal share of Decedent's estate? If the answer is yes, Child 1's branch of the family would receive 4/9 of the estate rather than the 3/9 (1/3) that Child 1 would have received. Wouldn't that be sufficient incentive for Child 1 to disclaim? It would be, except that all disclaimer statutes prevent that result. Although the language can be convoluted, all state disclaimer statutes contain language that prevents a disclaimer from altering the size of shares in the disclaimed property.

This short section is only the most basic of introduction to how disclaimers work. There are many other property law issues involved in being pretend dead. Tax-qualified disclaimers have many uses in estate planning, both planned and unplanned. For example, the key aspect of a tax-oriented estate plan might be contemplated disclaimer by a beneficiary. On the other hand, mistakes in tax planning can sometimes be cured by timely disclaimers. As with just about all of the subjects dealt with in this book, there is much, much more to learn.

(4) Bad Behavior

In discussing inheritance by surviving spouses, we noted that some states have statutes preventing a surviving spouse from inheriting from the decedent if the surviving spouse had abandoned, neglected, refused to support, or abused the decedent, even though the marriage existed until the decedent's death. In relatively recent times, these statutes have been joined by statutes that disqualify parents from taking as heirs of their children if they have neglected or failed to support the child, even if parental rights have not been terminated by a court. UPC § 2-114 bars a parent inheriting from a child who dies before reaching 18 years of age where "there is clear and convincing evidence" that the parental rights could have been terminated under the laws of the state "on the basis of non-support, abandonment, abuse or neglect, or other actions or inactions of the parent toward the child."

F   A   Q

Q: Since an 18-year-old is unlikely to have accumulated a lot of probate property, how much does a parent who is disqualified as an heir really lose?

A: It's likely that a disqualification statute like UPC § 2-114 will have its greatest impact on wrongful death recoveries. If a child's death is caused by criminal or negligent actions, it is likely that any recovery for pain and suffering and any damages will pass through the child's estate to the heirs. Disqualification prevents an unworthy parent from sharing in a recovery that, depending on the facts, could be a substantial sum.

California has gone one step beyond UPC § 2-114 and similar statutes by equating a person who mistreats "an elder or dependent adult" as if that person were a slayer—the person is deemed to have predeceased the victim. Under California Probate Code § 259, the mistreatment must involve physical abuse, neglect, or abuse of a fiduciary relationship with the victim. In addition, the bad actor must be found to have acted in bad faith and to have been "reckless, oppressive, fraudulent, or malicious." Under this statute, the bad actor would not take in intestacy, under a will, or as the beneficiary of a nonprobate property arrangement and, like a slayer, is deemed to predecease the victim.

Sidebar

UNWORTHY HEIRS

While California's disqualification of the unworthy heir or beneficiary of a will or non-probate property arrangement is unusual, there has been much academic discussion about disqualifying bad actors from taking in intestacy and even as beneficiaries. The discussion has been inspired to a great degree by discussions of the Chinese system, which penalizes bad actors and rewards those who have cared for the decedent, even if they are nonrelatives. One of the first influential discussions of the Chinese system and a good place to begin understanding the issue is Frances H. Foster, *Towards a Behavior-Based Model of Inheritance? The Chinese Experiment,* 32 U.C. Davis L. Rev. 77 (1998).

E. What Intestacy Rules Mean for Wills and Trusts

This has been a long chapter—and we haven't even begun to really talk about wills, let alone trusts. But the time you've invested in dealing with the material in this chapter certainly has not been wasted. Intestacy is of course an important subject in itself. Much of what we've discussed in this chapter, however, is basic to the entire subject of making a gift at death. Wills and trusts refer to spouses, children, descendants, and issue. When those terms are used without names of individuals attached, the law we've looked at in this chapter give those terms meaning. Systems of representation are used in wills and trusts, and disclaimers are important in many aspects of estate planning. And besides, now you know who your first cousin once removed is.

SUMMARY

■ The intestacy statute is a default statute that distributes probate property not disposed of by the decedent's will.

■ Heirs are the beneficiaries of the intestacy statute and, with very few exceptions, are members of the decedent's family.

■ The three schemes of representation—English (or strict) per stirpes, modern (or modified) per stirpes, and per capita at each generation—can each give different results when property is distributed to a multigenerational class.

■ Any probate property passing to a minor or to an incapacitated person must be managed on the person's behalf. The traditional guardianship of the property is an expensive and often wasteful way to do that.

■ Inheritance laws governing the rights of same-sex couples is evolving. Courts and legislatures continue to grapple with the legal status of these couples.

■ Adopted persons inherit just as if they were the genetic children of their parent or parents. In some situations defined by statute, an adopted person can inherit as a member of his or her birth family.

■ Persons born to an unmarried woman inherit as members of their mothers' families. They are the children of their fathers for purposes of inheritance if paternity has been established in conformity with the applicable state law.

■ Advances in medical technology allow the separation of conception from sexual intercourse. The legal status of children born through assisted reproduction is evolving.

■ A slayer is disqualified from inheriting from the victim and from taking as a beneficiary under the victim's will or under nonprobate property arrangements. In the absence of a comprehensive statute, the rules governing disqualification may not clear.

■ A disclaimer is a voluntary refusal to accept a gift a death. Disclaimers are often made to avoid gift taxes or to protect the property disclaimed from the disclaimant's creditors.

■ Bad behavior (short of homicide) on the part of the beneficiary of a gift at death can result in disqualification, although this rule is often applied only to surviving spouses. California has a far-reaching statute that may be a harbinger of change.

CONNECTIONS

Children, Descendants, and Issue and Beneficiaries of Wills and Trusts

The rules that decide who is a descendant of the decedent for purposes of intestacy often apply to gifts in wills and trusts to the children, descendants, or issue of the testator or settlor of the trust. Chapters 5 and 7 discuss these rules in the context of wills and trusts.

Children, Descendants, and Issue and Future Interests

Gifts to persons described as children, descendants, or issue often involve the creation of future interests. In Chapter 7 we'll see how the law of future interests defines the limits of such gifts.

Incapacitated Persons as Beneficiaries

A testator or the settlor of a will who knows or foresees that a minor or incapacitated person will or might be a beneficiary of a gift made at death can make arrangements for dealing with the property which are much more efficient than a guardianship of the property. A trust for the benefit of the minor or incapacitated person is often used, and Chapter 9 discusses some of the types of trusts used in these situations.

Spouses and Wills

While the surviving spouse is the primary heir of the deceased spouse, the intestacy statute is a default rule so that the decedent could use a will or a trust to give to property to someone other than the surviving spouse. There is, however, a strong public policy against the disinheritance of a surviving spouse which is discussed in Chapter 13.

Community Property and Spouses

The community property regime under which at the death of one spouse one-half of the community property belongs to the survivor with the other half forming part of the deceased spouse's probate property is discussed in Chapter 13.

Wealth Transfer Taxes and Disclaimers

Taxation of the transfer of wealth both at death and during life is discussed in Chapter 17. The usefulness of the disclaimer as a tax planning tool can be best understood in the context of the system of wealth transfer taxation.

Disclaimers and How Wills Work

As we've seen, it is possible to disclaim gifts in a will as well as property received as an heir. The result of the disclaimer is the same: the person disclaiming is pretend dead just before the testator. As we'll see in Chapter 5, the effect of the deemed death on who gets the property depends on the application of the common law of lapse and of statutes that modify it.

Wills: Execution and Revocation

3

Although you can't avoid death, you can avoid the intestacy statute. How? You can write a will — but not any which way you please. To be valid,

O V E R V I E W

the document must comply with your state's statutory requirements for executing a will. State execution statutes vary, but all require you to sign your will and to have that signature witnessed by at least two other persons. Some states have alternative rules too, which may include some rather untraditional provisions for executing a will. Revoking a valid will is also governed by statutes that require certain formalities. And all of these statutory schemes cannot be understood apart from the numerous cases and judicial opinions applying them.

A. EXECUTION, OR MAKING A WRITING INTO A WILL

1. Statutes
2. Attested Wills
3. Holographic Wills
4. Related Doctrines

B. REVOCATION

1. Revocation by Act of the Testator
2. Revocation by Operation of Law

A. Execution, or Making a Writing into a Will

The will is a creature of statute: "no statute, no will." Why? Because the Normans conquered England (you recall, no doubt, from Chapter 2). And while it might no longer be completely accurate in the twenty-first century to say that the state controls all mechanisms of making gifts at death, it is accurate to say that statutory requirements must be followed to make a will valid. Not surprisingly, those statutory requirements have changed over time. Today they are entering a new era defined by the provisions of Restatement (Third) of Property, which have been incorporated into the UPC.

Before we examine these statutory requirements, let's pause. Why have any requirements at all? The reasons most often given are to prevent fraud (e.g., by requiring witnesses) and to create a document that is recognized as a will (e.g., by requiring certain formalities, it is more certain that testators are expressing their testamentary intent rather than mere whims).

If you think carefully about that last sentence, it begs a very large question. Who cares, besides you, if you've thought carefully about what happens to your property after you die? The state controls the mechanisms of making gifts at death, but except for a prohibition on disinheriting a surviving spouse (in most states), you have **testamentary freedom**. You can dispose of your property at death as you like.

Public policy concerns create a few limitations, of course. You can't leave your property to an organization that advocates the violent overthrow of the government or direct that it be used to commit crimes. Nor can you direct that valuable property be destroyed, no matter what you can do with property while still alive to bear the economic cost of the destruction. After you're dead, you have no economic stake in your property, and your whims should not be allowed to deprive society of valuable assets (although a direction to destroy your personal papers, even if you are an important public figure, is almost certainly not contrary to public policy). So we're back where we started: why have statutory rules dictating how to make a valid will? That's not a question that can be answered easily and quickly. As we'll see in Chapter 4, the concept of **testamentary capacity**, the level of cognitive awareness a person must have in order to make a valid will, is tied to the prospective testator's knowledge of who his family members are. Society acting through law seems to take a dim view of using wills to disinherit members of the testator's family, even though the only legally binding restriction involves the testator's surviving spouse, as we'll see in Chapter 13.

Whatever conclusions you come to about the why, we're going to concern ourselves in the remainder of this chapter with the "how" as we explore the requirements for making a valid will.

Sidebar

STATUTE OF WILLS

Sometimes in judicial opinions you'll see references to the **Statute of Wills**, which rarely refers to a specific statute. Instead, it is a shorthand way of saying "the statutory requirements for a valid will as explained by all the cases in this particular jurisdiction."

(1) Statutes

Every one of the fifty states and the District of Columbia have will execution statutes. These statutes are similar in their broad outlines (with the exception of Louisiana's, which incorporates some aspects of the civil law system). Valid wills come in two flavors: **attested wills**, whose validity comes from their being signed by the testator and witnesses, and **holographic wills**, whose validity comes from their being signed by the testator and their provisions being at least in part in the testator's handwriting.

(2) Attested Wills

Restatement (Third) of Property § 3.1 explains attested wills this way:

> A will is validly executed if it is in writing and is signed by the testator and by a specified number of witnesses under procedure provided by applicable law.

(a) Writing

While the writing requirement seems pretty straight forward, it is likely that technology will soon make it possible to create an electronic will that is valid although never printed in hard copy. In addition, it has long been possible for a testator to make an oral, or **nuncupative,** will under very limited circumstances. The most common are wills of members of the armed forces in combat zones and mariners at sea. A few statutes also authorize oral wills if made during the testator's last illness when death is at hand and there is no time to do anything else. The statutes require that the will be uttered in front of witnesses who must within some prescribed period of time reduce what they were told to writing. (For more on oral wills, see Restatement (Third) of Property § 3.2 cmt. h & stat. note 3.)

(b) Signature

Let's start with the first requirement, signed by the testator. A professionally drafted will begins with an **exordium** ("I, [name of testator], residing at, [city, county, state], declare this to be my last will and testament and hereby revoke all wills and codicils previously made by me") and ends with the **testimonium**, which includes the testator's signature and the date of signing. It usually looks like this:

> IN WITNESS WHEREOF, I have signed my name, this _____ day of _____, 20_____
> _____ [Name of testator] _____ (L.S.)

The testator should sign the will the same way the testator signs any formal document, like a check, for instance. (I sign the wills I have made: William P. LaPiana.) The signature is then typed out underneath the signature line.

F   A   Q

Q: What does L.S., the abbreviation following the signature line, stand for?

A: Although you may have heard that L.S. is an abbreviation for "legal signature," that's not correct. It represents a two-word Latin phrase, *locus sigilli* ("the place of the seal"), and indicates where in the past the testator would have impressed his personal seal into a lump of wax. Today, signing one's name is enough, but the ancient custom of a seal lives on in those two letters.

So much for what should happen. Many disputed will cases concern signatures that do not follow the form just given. Turns out, the form of the signature doesn't matter; what's important is that the testator signs with the intention of adopting the document as her will. As comment j to § 3.1 of Restatement (Third) puts it:

> Signature by mark or cross is sufficient. . . . So also is a signature by term of relationship (such as "Dad," "Mom," or "Auntie"), abbreviation, nickname, a pet name, a first name, a last name, initials, or pseudonym, or even by fingerprint or seal. The name need not be spelled correctly. It need not be legible. . . . The crucial requirement is that it must be done with intent of adopting the document as the testator's will.

Of course, such informal signatures almost never appear on wills drafted by lawyers, who at least make sure that the testator's formal signature is typed underneath the signature line. Questions about the sufficiency of the signature more often arise when the testator or another nonlawyer has drafted the will. These documents can raise many questions about whether the document has met the requirements of the relevant statute. Indeed, the Restatement's long list of acceptable signatures is based on courts' rulings, which underscores how will execution statutes cannot be fully understood without knowing the cases that apply their laws to a wide variety of facts.

There is another possible question about the signature. What if the testator is too weak to sign or too ill to do more than indicate that yes, this is my will? As comment j notes, "[the signature] may be made with the assistance of another who guides the testator's hand."

Finally, where does the testator sign? It does seem obvious that the testimonium comes at the end of the will so that we can be sure that everything before the signature is meant to be the provisions of the will. Some statutes require the testator to sign "at the end" of the will. Courts have often held that if the testator did sign the will but some substantive provision (really almost anything other than the witnesses' signatures and related text) appeared after the signature, the entire will could be invalid. That result probably is not as likely today in jurisdictions that have a sign-at-the-end requirement; material appearing before the signature is likely to be given effect, with material following the signature simply ignored.

(c) Witnesses

The second half of the Restatement's description of an attested will concerns witnesses' signatures. All state statutes, as well as the UPC, require at least two witnesses. Who qualifies as a witness? UPC § 2-505 allows anyone "competent to be a witness" to act as one to a will signing; competence generally means that the witness understands what is going on and is able to describe what happened at some later time, specifically when the will is offered for probate. The UPC does not disqualify a witness who also receives a gift in the will (an "interested witness"). At least 20 states have followed the UPC's lead. Other states use **purging statutes** to qualify interesting witnesses by stripping them of their bequests or, if heirs, by limiting the amount of their bequests to what they would take of the testator died intestate. Clearly, it is easier all around if a beneficiary is not among the witnesses to the will.

(d) Execution Ceremony

Now that we understand who can be a witness, we have another statutory requirement to consider. What are the requirements for a proper will execution ceremony? First, the testator must sign the will in the presence of the witnesses or **acknowledge** the testator's signature to the witnesses. Acknowledging the signature means that the testator lets the witnesses know that the signature on the document is indeed that of the testator. The testator, therefore, can sign the will in solitude and then find witnesses under some statutes. Some statutes require the testator to sign or acknowledge in the presence of the witnesses and require the witnesses to sign in the presence of the testator and of one another. Therefore, if two witnesses are required, the testator and the witnesses must be in each other's presence while the ceremony of getting the will signed takes place.

What it means to be in each other's presence has been the subject of many judicial opinions. Take a simple example.

Example 3.1: Testator is ill in bed. Testator signs the will sitting up in bed while the witnesses watch. The witnesses then take the will to an adjacent room where they can sit at a desk and sign their names in comfort. Were the signatures made in the presence of Testator?

In answering that question, courts developed two tests. The **line of sight test** requires that the testator see the witnesses sign or that the testator could have seen them sign had the testator looked. The **conscious presence test** requires that the testator knows what is going on even if the testator cannot see what is happening. Thus, in Example 3.1, even if the testator cannot see what is going on in the adjacent room, the conscious presence test is satisfied if the testator is close enough to sense what is happening. As you no doubt realize, how these tests are applied is very much a question of the facts. The willingness of a court to apply either test to rescue a questionable execution ceremony from invalidity depends to some degree on the skill of the lawyer arguing for that result.

F   A   Q

Q: Because every state has its own will execution statute, do I have to make a new will whenever I move to a different state?

A: No. Most states have statutes that deal with **choice of law** (the UPC provision is § 2-506). These statutes are highly uniform and recognize as valid a written will executed in accordance with the state's own statutes, in accordance with the law of the place of its execution, or with the law of the testator's domicile at the time of execution.

The UPC section concerning execution, § 2-502, eliminates many of the difficulties we've been discussing. First, the only presence requirement applies when another person signs the testator's name at the testator's direction. The testator might make such a request if the testator is too weak to hold the pen. If the testator does make the request, the other person must sign in the "conscious presence" of the testator. Second, the testator need not sign in the presence of the witnesses; the acknowledging of the will or the signature is sufficient. Third, the witnesses need not be in each other's presence when they sign, nor do they need to be in the testator's presence. Finally, there is no requirement that the testator's signature appear at the end of the will. So long as the signature is there, it could

ATTESTATION AFTER THE TESTATOR'S DEATH

UPC § 2-502 does not require the witnesses to sign in the presence of the testator but does require that the witnesses sign within a "reasonable time" of witnessing the testator's signing of the will or the acknowledgment of the testator's signature. So may witnesses sign the will after the testator's death? The comment to § 2-502 says yes, but courts are divided. In *Estate of Saueressig*, 136 P.3d 201 (Cal. 2006), the California Supreme Court held that the removal of the "sign in the testator's presence" requirement in the latest revision of the California will execution statute did not authorize a witness to sign after the testator's death, both as a matter of law and as a matter of policy. A few months later, the Idaho Supreme Court in *Estate of Miller*, 149 P.3d 840 (Idaho 2006), held that when the legislature enacted UPC § 2-502 and removed the "sign in the testator's presence" requirement from Idaho law, the legislature really removed it and a court cannot put it back. Signing after death, in fact, is authorized by the statute.

In both cases, the wills were notarized and would be valid under new UPC § 2-502(a)(3)(B), and the facts are such that they both would be entitled to probate under UPC § 2-503.

be in the body of the will or only in the exordium if it is written in the testator's hand.

In 2008 an amendment to the UPC, § 2-502(a)(3)(B), added a new method of will execution: notarization. The testator must acknowledge his signature before a notary public or another individual authorized by law to take acknowledgments (a certificate appended to a document that certifies the identity of a person signing the document). The comment to the new provision says that this provision brings the law into conformity with what many laypeople ("and, sad to say, some lawyers") incorrectly believe to be the law. No matter how the ceremony is carried out, most lawyers who draft wills assume that the document will be executed and attested all at once, effectively in conformity with the strictest statutory requirements. That assumption is reflected in the **attestation clause** that comes right after the testator's signature in just about every professionally drafted will. A typical clause looks like this:

> The foregoing instrument was signed, published and declared by _____, the testator, to be [his *or* her] last will and testament, in our presence, and we, at [his *or* her] request and in [his *or* her] presence, and in the presence of each other have hereunto subscribed our names as witnesses this_____ day of _____ , 20_____ .

The signatures of the witnesses follow the attestation clause.

There is no execution statute that requires the use of an attestation clause. Its presence as part of the will raises a rebuttable presumption that the ceremony described in the clause has actually been carried out. That means, of course, that the ceremony should correspond to the narrative in the clause.

There is another way to raise an even stronger presumption that the execution ceremony has been properly carried out. The law of many states and UPC § 2-504 authorize the use of a **self-proving affidavit**. This is an affidavit made by the testator and the witnesses (in some states by only the witnesses) that recites the facts of the execution ceremony and also contains a statement that the testator was of the minimum age to make a will (usually 18), and that the testator also appeared to be of sound mind and not under any constraint or undue influence.

Once the affidavit is properly executed, the will is now a **self-proved will**. The advantages of having a self-proved will vary from jurisdiction to jurisdiction. At the very least, however, solemn form probate is much easier if the will is self-proved. Solemn form probate procedure usually requires the witnesses to testify to what happened at the execution ceremony at the time the will is offered for probate. Usually that is done by having the witnesses execute affidavits that contain the same information a self-proving affidavit contains. If there is a self-proving affidavit, whether incorporated into the attestation clause or as a separate document (usually physically attached to the will), the witnesses need not do anything at the time the will is offered for probate. Elimination of the need to locate the witnesses alone makes the extra effort involved in executing a self-proving affidavit worthwhile.

(e) Other Statutory Requirements

Some statutes have additional requirements for an attested will. One example is a **publication requirement**. "Publication" means that the testator informs the witnesses that they are signing the testator's will. The contents of the will need not be revealed, however, only the fact that the document is indeed the testator's will.

(3) Holographic Wills

The statutes of about half the states and the UPC recognize a way other than attestation (and notarization under the UPC) to create a valid will. This method involves the testator's handwriting. Wills that are created using this method are **holographic wills**. The fraud prevention function of attestation is supplanted by reliance on the testator's own handwriting. The lack of ceremonial execution, however, leaves open a rather large area of doubt. Remember that one of the reasons for having requirements for making a will is to help ensure that the document really embodies the decedent's testamentary intent, that it really is the device by which the person who signed it is making gifts at death. Often the problem with deciding whether a writing is a holographic will is really a problem of deciding whether the decedent intended to use the document to make gifts at death. Before we consider some of the problems with finding testamentary intent, let's take a general look at the statutes that validate holographic wills.

Restatement (Third) of Property discusses holographic will statutes in § 3.2. The comment to that section organizes the evolution of statutes authorizing holographic wills into three stages (although existing statutes exemplify all three stages). First-generation statutes require that the entire document be in the testator's handwriting and that it be signed and dated by the testator. Second-generation statutes are exemplified by the original UPC, which requires that the signature and the "material provisions" of the will be in the testator's handwriting but does not requiring dating. The third generation of statutes has its origin in the current UPC provision, § 2-502(b), which requires that the signature and the "material portions" of the document be in the testator's handwriting and does not require dating.

The original UPC required that the signature and the "material provisions" be in the decedent's handwriting. The problem with that formulation was what some courts did with it. The difficulty was especially acute when courts dealt with handwriting on preprinted will forms. Will forms are widely available. They almost always include the exordium in which the testator can fill in her name and details of residence. Then the dispositive provisions of the will may all contain printed material. For example, the **residuary clause** (the clause in the will that disposes of all probate property not otherwise disposed of) may start with "I give, devise, and bequeath the rest of my estate to" followed by a space in which the testator can write the names of the residuary beneficiaries.

Some courts using the "material provisions" standard denied probate to preprinted will forms filled in by the testator's handwriting because the words of giving ("give," "devise," "bequeath") are material and are printed rather than handwritten. Some courts went so far as to state that the printed material had to be completely ignored as if it had been washed off the page and the handwriting then searched for "material provisions." Commentators had a field day criticizing opinions that took that approach. They asked, and quite rightly, how the meaning of words can be understood apart from the context in which they appear. To put it more bluntly, if a will form has printed words that read "I give, devise, and bequeath" and following them the decedent has written "my estate in equal shares to my children," the handwritten words must be intended to give away the probate estate at death. Spending paragraphs of an opinion speculating on the meaning of the word "estate" — a large tract of land with a house on it, one's station in life, a particular societal group — should not blind one to the obvious. When on a printed form that is titled "Last Will and Testament" a person writes the word "estate" immediately after printed words of giving, the person is making a gift of the probate estate at death.

Third-generation statutes deal with the problem by replacing "material provisions" with "material portions." In fact, comment b to § 3.2 of Restatement (Third) of Property states that the UPC made the change from "material provisions" to "material portions" "to leave no doubt" about the validity of a holographic will in which "immaterial parts of a dispositive provision — such as 'I give, devise, and bequeath' — are not in the testator's handwriting."

Another question that comes up when dealing with holographic wills is that of testamentary intent. As we have seen, the formalities surrounding attested wills pretty much eliminate any doubt that a given document was meant by its author to make gifts at death. Even if there is no exordium or attestation clause, words of giving and the fact of attestation go a long way to making it clear that the document is intended to be a will. It's not that easy with holographs.

The classic case is the letter of instructions. Testator decides to make changes in her current will. She writes by hand and signs a letter to her lawyer explaining the changes she wants made in straightforward terms: "Instead of giving the savings bonds to Jenny, I give them to Henry. Instead of giving my Microsoft stock to Anthony, I give it to Betty." Testator mails the letter during the day and that night dies in her sleep. The letter duly arrives at the lawyer's office. Is it a holographic will (or a holographic codicil, an amendment to the existing will)? The answer is no. Why? Because the testator did not intend the letter to be the document that makes the gifts at death. She was expecting her lawyer to draft a new will or at least a codicil to her existing will. She was also expecting to review that codicil, to have the chance to have second thoughts and make changes, and eventually execute a new document. The letter lacks testamentary intent.

Another common problem is posed by letters to friends or family in which the writer discusses property and death. Whether the letter embodies testamentary intent depends on the facts. Words that express the idea of making a gift at death are important. Another significant fact is whether the writer tells the recipient to keep the letter or to put it in a safe place so it can be easily found after the writer's death. Telling the recipient to take such precautions is evidence that the writer is making gifts at death in the letter.

(4) Related Doctrines

So now we've seen the basic rules for making wills. Several doctrines also play an important part in making wills work.

(a) Integration

In order for multiple pages to be integrated into one will, they all have to be present when the will is executed and the testator must intend for them to be part of the will (Restatement (Third) of Property § 3.5). The few cases involving **integration** pretty much agree that just about any evidence that the pages were all present when the will was executed will do. Of course, no one should deliberately have the testator sign the last page of a pile of unnumbered pages, secure them with a rubber band and leave it at that. That's simply an invitation to a contest, and we'll discuss ways to avoid difficulties related to integration when we discuss avoiding will contests in Chapter 4.

(b) Incorporation by Reference

After all the words we've expended on proper execution of an attested will and the ins and outs of how much handwriting is necessary to create a valid holographic will, you will probably be less than thrilled, and indeed puzzled, by the doctrine of **incorporation by reference**. Under this doctrine, any writing can be part of a will if (1) the writing is in existence at the time of the execution of the will, (2) the will shows the intention to make the writing part of the will, and (3) the writing is sufficiently identified in the will. In other words, any writing, even if it's not signed by the testator, can be made part of a will.

First, why in the world does the doctrine even exist? This is probably an instance of courts trying to do the right thing in the face of testators' stubborn refusal to behave the way the law of wills wants them to behave. One of the most common scenarios involves gifts in wills of tangible personal property. We all care about our "stuff," especially if it has sentimental value. A mind-numbing inventory of every piece of tangible personal property the testator owns would not only make the will overly long but lead to complications as some of the items are given away, lost, sold, or thrown away and new ones take their place. A testator can try to get around the problem by instructing the executor to distribute the tangible personal property "in accordance with a memorandum I have prepared" or "as I have indicated in a list I have prepared" or something similar. Unless that list is a valid will, either because it has been attested or qualifies as a holograph in a jurisdiction that recognizes holographs, the gifts it makes are not binding on the executor, and the items in the list will pass under the residuary clause of the will. The executor could distribute the property according to the list, but the beneficiaries of the residuary clause will have a cause of action against the executor for failing to carry out the terms of the will.

If the list is part of the will, then the gifts it makes are valid gifts at death, and the executor must carry out the testator's instructions. A common problem, however, involves the requirement that the writing be in existence at the time

Sidebar

PERSONAL PROPERTY AND UPC § 2-513

One widely accepted innovation is UPC § 2-513, which authorizes the disposal of personal property other than money not otherwise disposed of in a will by reference to a written statement or list signed by the testator and referred to in the will. The list may be prepared before or after execution of the will, the testator can alter it at any time, and it need have no significance "apart from its effect on the dispositions made by the will." In other words, § 2-513 authorizes what the doctrines of incorporation by reference and independent significance do not. It provides a method for making gifts of personal property at death that accommodates what many testators want to do: change their minds about who gets their stuff without having to change the will.

the will is executed. Even if the writing is dated before the date of the execution of the will, any alterations in the list may have been made after that date and are not effective. The will might make reference to the writing, but the evidence might show that it was written after the execution of the will because the testator simply didn't get to it earlier. Sometimes the incorporation can be sustained because the testator executed a codicil, or amendment, to the will on a date that can be shown to be after the creation of the writing. As we'll see, executing an amendment to a will has the effect of republishing the will, which means it is treated as if it were executed when the amendment was executed. Therefore the writing would indeed be in existence at the time of the execution of the will.

Finally, you should know that three states, Connecticut, Louisiana, and New York, do not have statutes recognizing incorporation by reference, nor does any court-made law recognize the doctrine. In those states, the doctrine isn't generally available, although there may be cases that reach a result that amounts to incorporation on particularly appealing facts.

(c) Acts of Independent Significance

The doctrine generally called **acts of independent significance** is essential to the workings of wills. (UPC § 2-512 refers to the doctrine as "events of independent significance," and Restatement (Third) of Property § 3.7 calls it simply "independent significance.") Whatever you call it, the doctrine says that a will may dispose of property by reference to events or circumstances apart from the will, so long as those events or circumstances have some effect beyond simply determining the gift in the will.

All of that sounds terribly abstract, and it is. You can understand the doctrine as having two uses. The first is the unavoidable; wills can't work without it. Let's say the will makes a gift of "all of my tangible personal property including motor vehicles, clothes, household furnishings and appliances, to" whomever. At the time the will is executed, the testator owns a Honda motorcycle and a Buick automobile. The will is making a gift of those two items of tangible personal property. If the testator later sells the Honda and buys a Harley and sells the Buick and buys a Toyota, the gift in the will has been changed. Does that mean that the testator has to change the will every time the testator buys something new? Of course not. Acquiring new items of tangible personal property is done for lots of reasons, and probably the last on the list is to change the will. In the words used by UPC § 2-512 and § 3.7 of Restatement (Third) of Property, the event—acquiring new motor vehicles—has significance apart from its effect on the gift made in the will. The significance is the testator's desire to have a new bike and a new car.

This use of the doctrine is not limited to acquiring new stuff of a type given by the will. It also applies to people described as a class (by a common characteristic). A gift to "my children" will include children born after the will is executed. The assumption is that the testator makes the decision to have children for reasons that are not limited to creating more will beneficiaries. One hopes so, at least.

The less common use of the doctrine involves things done by persons other than the testator. This application of the doctrine even extends to wills of other persons. A gift to "the residuary beneficiaries of the last will of my brother, Simon" is valid. If Simon dies before the testator, then the identity of the beneficiaries is established at Simon's death. If the testator dies before Simon, Simon can dispose of the testator's gift through his own residuary clause. As we'll see in Chapter 10, this gives Simon a power of appointment. When we examine in Chapter 11 what happens when a will devises property to an existing trust, we'll see another use of this aspect of the doctrine.

(d) Going Beyond the Traditional Rules

Up to now we have been dealing with well-established law. Now we have to consider recent innovations in the law of execution of wills. We've already mentioned one of these, the amendment of UPC § 2-502 to add notarization to the methods for executing a will. Two other developments have lessened the rigidity with which courts apply the statutory requirements.

The first development was the application of the doctrine of **substantial compliance** to the requirements of executing a will. You might remember the doctrine of substantial compliance from your Contracts class. In essence, the idea is that close enough is good enough. Courts have probably taken some form of a substantial compliance approach to the formalities of will execution for a long time. One of the opinions in the New York slayer's case, *Riggs v. Palmer*, decided in 1889, mentions the "systematic statutory rules for the execution, alteration, and revocation of the will, which must be, at least substantially, if not exactly, followed. . . ."[1]

The modern history of the doctrine as applied to will execution requirements begins in 1975 with publication of a law review article by Professor John Langbein.[2] He argued that a will should be admitted to probate if there is clear and convincing evidence that purposes of the formalities were fulfilled. Twelve years later Langbein published another article based on his observations of the working of a statute adopted by the Australian state of South Australia, which allows the probate of a document if there is "no reasonable doubt" that the decedent intended the document to be the decedent's will.[3] In other words, the court can completely dispense with the formalities if it is satisfied that the decedent intended the document to make gifts at death. Langbein described this dispensing power as statutory enactment of a **harmless error rule**. After examining the Australian cases, Langbein concluded that the harmless error rule was superior to substantial compliance because of the difficulty courts had in deciding how close was indeed close enough. He argued that the only criterion for admission to probate where the will execution formalities had not been followed should be the existence of "clear and convincing evidence" that the decedent intended the document to be her will.

The harmless error concept has been adopted by Restatement (Third) of Property in § 3.3 and codified by the UPC in § 2-503. The Restatement section states a

Sidebar

GIFTS OF CONTENTS OF A CONTAINER

There is one other fairly common application of the doctrine of acts of independent significance, which is at best somewhat odd. The situation is usually called "gift of the contents of a container." In other words, the testator makes a gift in the will of "the contents of my safe deposit box" to someone. Such gifts are usually found to be valid, and the devisee takes the contents of the safe deposit box. The reasoning depends on the assumption that the testator puts things in and takes things out of the safe deposit box for reasons other than changing the gift in the will, although that is exactly the result. Identical reasoning upholds gifts of "the contents of my desk" or "the contents of the top left-hand drawer of my desk." Even so, it is certainly not good practice to make testamentary gifts of the contents of a container.

---

[1]22 N.E. 188, 191 (N.Y. 1889).
[2]John H. Langbein, *Substantial Compliance with the Wills Act*, 88 Harv. L. Rev. 489 (1975).
[3]John H. Langbein, *Excusing Harmless Errors in the Execution of Wills: A Report on Australia's Tranquil Revolution in Probate Law*, 87 Colum. L. Rev. 1 (1987).

general principle and the UPC section is of course a statute, but the basic concepts of the two formulations are exactly the same. A document should be admitted to probate as a will if there is clear and convincing evidence, which is the most stringent civil law evidentiary standard, that the decedent intended the document to be the decedent's will (or, in the words of the Restatement, "adopted" the document as a will).

Only a handful of states have adopted UPC § 2-503, and courts have refused to adopt the doctrine as a matter of decisional law, insisting that it is up to legislatures to make such a radical change in the law of wills. There are cases in which courts have used what amounts to harmless error doctrine on unique facts, but there are few cases applying UPC § 2-503. You will no doubt run across at least one or two in your studies, and very likely more will arise as time goes on.

B. Revocation

As you've just seen, it takes a good deal of time and thought to understand the law that governs the creation of a valid will. It should not surprise you that the law of revoking wills is just as complex. After all, it would be a shame if after going through the exercise of properly creating a valid will the testator discovered that some casual action or statement revoked the document.

Like the creation of a valid will, the revocation of a will is governed by statute. But before we start considering how those statutes work, you must remember that the testator does not have to include an express statement of revocability in the will in order to have the power to revoke it. As Restatement (Third) of Property puts it in comment a to § 5.1, "a will is inherently revocable throughout the testator's remaining lifetime." That revocation can come about in two ways: (1) by the testator's action or (2) through the legal consequences of what we've come to call "life cycle events."

(1) Revocation by Act of the Testator

Every revocation statute allows the testator to revoke a will by creating a writing that changes the will or by intentionally taking a physical action that destroys the will or at least part of it. But don't think that complications don't still arise in revoking existing testamentary arrangements — they certainly do!

(a) Writings and Codicils

If I have a will (Will #1) and I write a new will (Will #2), Will #2 should revoke Will #1. Sadly, it's not that obvious, or rather it is obvious *only if Will #2 expressly revokes Will #1*. Every revocation statute provides that a subsequent will can expressly revoke an existing will. The exordium, unless poorly drafted, expressly revokes all previous wills and codicils.

This universal practice of revoking existing wills and codicils in the exordium is a reaction to another provision of all revocation statutes. If Will #2 does not expressly revoke Will #1, Will #2 revokes Will #1 *only to the extent it is inconsistent with it*. The inconsistency rule has long been a cause of problems. What if Will #2 is identical to Will #1 except for a gift of a sum of money to a beneficiary not mentioned in Will #1? Does that mean Will #1 is revoked only to the extent the residuary gift is diminished by the new gift? If that's the case, then Will #2 is an amendment of Will #1. An amendment to a will is a **codicil**, and the codicil and will that it amends are together the last will and testament of the testator. (Nowhere in the UPC will you find the term "codicil." All documents that validly make a gift at death are "wills" in UPC-speak, § 1-201(57)). That means that both documents have to be offered for probate. Two execution ceremonies have to have been done correctly, and the witnesses to both instruments might have to be located. If the probate is in solemn form, the number of persons who have to receive formal notice might increase because formal notice must go to everyone who is adversely affected by the instrument offered for probate, and the codicil clearly adversely affects the residuary beneficiaries of Will #1.

When Will #2 is only partially inconsistent with Will #1, whether Will #2 completely revokes Will #1 is a matter of the testator's intent. Some courts have simplified determining that intent by adopting a presumption that Will #2 completely revokes Will #1 if Will #2 makes a complete disposition of the testator's estate. Under this presumption, Will #2 in our example in the previous paragraph completely revokes Will # 1 and is not a codicil. The UPC revocation statute, § 2-507, enacts this presumption, and it is also adopted by Restatement (Third) of Property in comment d to § 5.1.

Now you see why every well-drafted exordium expressly revokes prior wills and codicils and why the problem of the extent of revocation by inconsistency usually arises with homemade wills. What if the testator really wants to create a codicil? The clearest way to do that is to use an exordium that says the document is a codicil and identifies the will it amends. Here's a typical example:

I, __[testator's name]__ , residing in City of _____, County of _____, State of _____, hereby declare this to be a [first, second, etc.] codicil to my Will, dated [date].

It should go without saying, but let's be explicit about it anyway, that *a codicil must be executed in the same way as a will.* That means attestation (including attestation by notarization where that's possible), validity as a holograph where holographs are recognized, or meeting the clear and convincing evidence requirement of the harmless error rule where the harmless error rule is law.

Codicils have been around for a very long time and have been widely used. Not surprisingly, therefore, there's quite a bit of law about these amendments to wills. One doctrine relating to codicils was mentioned in the earlier discussion of incorporation by reference. Execution of a codicil to a will is a republication of the will, which means that the execution of the codicil is treated as a reexecution of the will. A writing referred to in the will but not in existence when the will was executed could still be incorporated by reference if a codicil to the will is executed after the writing is in existence.

Sidebar

CODICILS AND MODERN TECHNOLOGY

Codicils are far less common than they once were, thanks to technology. Once upon a time, not so very long ago, wills were created by typing the entire document on a typewriter (how exotic!) and making multiple carbon copies (ever seen carbon paper?) or photocopies. If a testator's changes were slight—changing the name of the nominated executor or eliminating a gift of a sum of money, for instance—creating a one- to two-page codicil was much easier than creating a new will. Today, the digital file containing Will #1 is opened, the changes are made, and Will #2 is saved and printed. Viola! New will without onerous effort.

Other doctrines dealing with codicils are relevant to the next part of our discussion of revocation, revocation by physical act. Before we go there, however, we have to note one more thing about revoking a will by a writing. So far we've discussed new wills and codicils. It is possible under just about all revocation statutes to revoke a will or a codicil by executing a writing that simply says: "I revoke my will" or "I revoke the first codicil to my will." Of course, the writing should also identify the will by adding "dated [insert date]."

A writing whose only function is to revoke a will or codicil must be executed as if it were a will. It must be attested or, where holographs are recognized, must meet the requirements for a valid holographic will. Where the harmless error rule is law, a court could decide that the document revokes a will or codicil if there is clear and convincing evidence that the author of the writing intended it to do so.

(b) Physical Acts

All revocation statutes recognize revocation by a physical act performed on the will (or on a codicil) with the intent to revoke it. The list of possible physical acts in UPC § 2-507(a)(2) is typical. Under that section, they include "burning, tearing, cancelling, obliterating, or destroying." Some statutes mention "cutting" or "mutilation," but all the statutes make it clear that the list is illustrative.

Revocation by cancellation—writing words such as "canceled," "void," or "revoked" on the will or crossing out words of the will—has been the method of revocation by physical act most likely to cause litigation, especially when it involves writing words on the will. Many courts have held that words of cancellation must touch the words of the will. According to these courts, if the testator writes "This will is void" in the margin of every page of the will, the will is not revoked. The phrase "this will is void" would have to be written across the words of the will to accomplish revocation. This rule probably comes from courts concerned with maintaining the integrity of the statutes that require a writing that revokes a will to be executed in the same way as a will.

Restatement (Third) of Property § 5.1 comment g states that the concern expressed in the requirement that words of cancellation touch the words of the will is best answered by recognizing the distinction between words written on the will and words in another document. According to the Restatement, therefore, writing "this will is revoked" in the margins of the pages of the will or even on the back of a page of the will can be a revocation. UPC § 2-507 agrees, and subsection (a)(2) states that "[a] burning, tearing, or canceling is a 'revocatory act on the will,' whether or not the burn, tear, or cancellation touched any of the words of the will."

There is another aspect of revocation by physical act on which the statutes differ. A large majority of revocation statutes, including UPC § 2-507, allow partial revocation of the will by physical act. Under these statutes, if the testator cancels part of the will, that part is revoked. For example, if a will contains a gift of money such as "I give $10,000 to my sister, Sally," and the testator crosses out the words on the will, or writes "void" over the words, or under the UPC and similar statutes writes in the margin "I revoke the gift to Sally" or "The gift to Sally is void," Sally does not take the $10,000. Instead, the $10,000 simply increases the value of the residuary gift. In the handful of states that do not recognize partial revocation, of course, absolutely nothing has happened. Assuming she survives the testator, Sally takes her $10,000.

Partial revocation by physical act really is changing the will without conforming to the requirements for executing a new will or a codicil to the will. After all, in the example in the previous paragraph, the testator has done with a simple cross-out what could have been done by executing a codicil revoking the gift to Sally. Note that the act of cancellation certainly is not an act of "independent significance" because its only significance is to change the will. Because partial revocation by physical act results in changing the will without observing the statutory requirements, courts have refused to recognize partial revocation by physical act unless it is expressly allowed by statute.

In almost all cases, performing a physical act on a *copy* of the will with intent to revoke accomplishes nothing. Except perhaps in a harmless error jurisdiction, where a court might treat the act as if it had been performed on a properly executed will or codicil, the physical act must be performed on the executed will with original signatures of the testator and witnesses. Note, however, that some courts have imposed a constructive trust (see Chapter 8) on the beneficiaries of such an ineffectively revoked will or codicil.

F A Q

Q: If partial revocation is not allowed, how can I tell if the physical act is sufficient to completely revoke the will?

A: The physical act must affect some critical part of the will. Canceling the residuary clause might be enough. Canceling boilerplate provisions or a number of individual gifts is probably not enough unless those gifts represent most of the value of the probate estate. If the testator wants to revoke the will but leave the text undisturbed for future reference, canceling the testator's and witnesses' signatures will revoke the will. Tearing the signatures from the will also works.

Some acts of physical revocation can result in the complete destruction of the will. The testator can burn the will completely and dispose of the ashes, or tear or mechanically shred the will and throw away the torn or shredded pieces. But if the will is found after the testator's death and there are words or marks of cancellation on it or if it is partially torn, how do we know that the testator performed the revocatory act? If the will was in the testator's possession at the time of death, there is a presumption that the testator preformed the act.

F   A   Q

Q: Since another person can sign the testator's name on the will at the testator's direction, can another person perform a revocatory act on the will for the testator?

A: Yes, and most statutes, like UPC § 2-507(a)(2), require the act to be performed in the testator's presence and at the testator's direction. The same problems with "presence" that we saw with execution exist here too. Consistent with its execution requirements, the UPC requires that the revocatory act take place in the testator's "conscious presence."

But what if the will was last known to be in the testator's possession and cannot be found after death? In that case, there is a presumption that the testator destroyed the will with the intent to revoke it. Restatement (Third) of Property § 5.1 comment i says that the presumption is not a strong one and does not require clear and convincing evidence to be rebutted. Some courts are more favorably disposed to the presumption and require some high standard of evidence to rebut it. As you no doubt realize, cases involving lost wills turn on the facts. If persons with some incentive to destroy the will can be shown to have had access to it, the presumption may be overcome far more easily than if those facts cannot be shown.

Sidebar

SAFEKEEPING OF WILLS

Given the rules and presumptions applicable to revocation by physical act, keeping the executed will safe is a serious matter. In some states it is possible to file a will with the court to be retrieved by the testator or by a family member or the nominated executor after the testator's death on presentation of a death certificate. UPC § 2-515 provides for deposit in court and gives rules for access during the testator's life. Another alternative is to leave the will in the possession of the nominated executor who should put it in a safe deposit box. UPC § 2-516 creates a duty to deliver the will to an appropriate person after the testator's death. The one place the will should not go is the testator's safe deposit box which is likely to be sealed after death and which may not be able to be opened without a court order or an administrative proceeding.

Can the lawyer who drafted the will store it for the testator? Although at one time it was thought that retaining a client's will was an unethical device to solicit the client's future business or the representation of the executor, today lawyers are free in almost every state to take custody of their clients' wills.

F   A   Q

Q: Can a lost will be admitted to probate?

A: Yes. Every jurisdiction allows the probate of a lost will that has not been revoked to the extent its provisions can be proved. That proof can come from a copy retained by the testator's lawyer or from any other copy that can be properly identified. Even if no copy is found, the provisions of the will can be shown from the drafter's notes or even from the testimony of the person who typed the will. (A few states have more demanding rules for proving the contents of a lost will.)

(c) Revival and DRR

Now that we've been through most of the ins and outs of revoking wills, we can consider the effect of revocation on prior wills of the testator.

Example 3.2: Testator properly executes Will #1. Testator then properly executes Will #2, which expressly or by inconsistency revokes Will #1.

Testator then revokes Will #2 either by a writing that does nothing but revoke Will #2 or perhaps more likely by an act of revocation performed on Will #2. What's the status of Will #1?

That question has three answers. Each has a different ancestry, but for our purposes, we can call them Rule 1, Rule 2, and Rule 3.

■ **Rule 1:** Will #1 is **revived**. It is now the testator's will; it has come back to life.

This common law rule goes back to the eighteenth century and rests on the idea that a will has absolutely no effect until the testator's death. That means that the revocation of Will #1 by Will #2, whether express or implied, does not happen until the death of the testator when Will #2 is entitled to admission to probate.

■ **Rule 2:** The revocation of Will #2 revives Will #1 *if that was the testator's intent.*

What counts as evidence of the required intent depends on the facts, and trying to predict what a court will do in a specific case requires careful research in the precedents in that particular jurisdiction. One generalization that can be made, however, is that simply revoking Will #2 without more is not evidence of the intent to revive Will #1.

■ **Rule 3:** The revocation of Will #2 has no effect on Will #1 no matter what the testator's intent.

Under Rule 3, Will #1 is revived only if the testator reexecuted it or executed a codicil that showed the intention of reviving Will #1, for example, by including an exordium that stated that the document was a codicil to Will #1.

The UPC revival provisions are in § 2-509(a) and are basically Rule 2. If Will #2 completely revokes Will #1, the revocation of Will #2 revives Will #1 if the testator so intends. The UPC provides that the required intent can be inferred from the circumstances of the revocation or shown by the testator's statements made at the time of revocation or afterward. Restatement (Third) of Property § 4.2(a) says the same thing.

What if Will #2 does not completely revoke Will #1 but is a codicil to Will #1? What happens if the codicil is revoked? Under UPC § 2-509(b) and Restatement (Third) of Property § 4.2 comment m, the presumption is that any part of Will #1 revoked by the codicil is revived automatically. The revoked provisions stay revoked, however, if that was the testator's intent. Just as in the case of showing intent to revive Will #1 when it was completely revoked by Will #2, the necessary intent can be shown by circumstances or the testator's declarations.

One thing that the UPC doesn't address is what happens to a codicil to a will if the will is revoked by a physical act but the codicil is not?

Restatement (Third) of Property § 4.1 comment m says that the codicil is not revoked by the revocation of the will. However, "if the codicil depends on the revoked will for its meaning," the codicil may be meaningless.

Example 3.3: Testator executes a codicil to her will that states: "I give $15,000 to the American Red Cross." Testator then revokes her will by physical act.

Example 3.4: Testator executes a codicil to her will that states: "Should my husband, Frank Fitzgerald, fail to qualify as executor or having qualified, ceases to act, I nominate my cousin, Joseph Green, as substitute or successor executor." Testator then revokes her will by physical act.

The codicil in Example 3.3 would not be revoked under the Restatement rule because it makes a devise, which can be given effect without the will. The $15,000 goes to the American Red Cross, and the rest of the probate estate passes in intestacy. The codicil in Example 3.4, however, is meaningless without the will. All it does is appoint a substitute or successor executor of a will that now does not exist. There are statutes, however, that revoke all codicils to a will when the will is revoked. The purpose of these statutes is to provide a bright-line rule.

Note that the results in these two examples depend on the wills being revoked by physical acts, not by subsequent wills. If you think about it, a subsequent will that revokes the existing will either expressly or by completely disposing of the testator's probate estate *will also revoke any codicils to the existing will because the will and the codicils together are the testator's will.* The only way to revoke the will but (possibly) not revoke a codicil to the will is to revoke the will by physical act.

There is yet another aspect of the revocation rules to consider, the doctrine known as **dependent relative revocation**. Restatement (Third) of Property refers to the doctrine as "ineffective revocation" and devotes § 5.3 to it. Calling the doctrine "ineffective revocation" makes sense because that what it's about. Under certain circumstances, an attempt to revoke a will or part of a will is found to be ineffective if that result better serves the testator's intent.

The doctrine operates in several typical fact patterns. We'll start with what is perhaps the most common and usually the easiest to understand. The testator's attested will is found after the testator's death in the testator's safe deposit box. One gift of a sum of money has been altered. (The material in italics is in the testator's handwriting)

$15,000

Example 3.5: I give ~~$10,000~~ to my cousin, Salma.

What's the effect of the testator's crossing out $10,000 and writing in $15,000? The first question we have to ask is whether the jurisdiction recognizes partial revocation by physical act. If it does not, absolutely nothing has happened, and Salma receives $10,000. If the jurisdiction does recognize partial revocation by physical act, the gift of $10,000 has been revoked. Is the testator's attempt to create a new gift of $15,000 effective? If this is a holographic will the answer is "yes." Because a holographic will gets its validity as a will, a document that makes gifts of probate property at death, from the fact that at least material portions (under the UPC formulation) are in the testator's handwriting, the testator can change the will simply by writing on it and does not need to sign again. (Restatement (Third) of Property § 3.2 comment f agrees.) Remember, too, that if the harmless error rule (UPC § 2-503) is the law, the new gift can be given effect if there is clear and convincing evidence of the testator's intent to make the new gift, even if the will is not a holograph.

But we've said this is an attested will whose validity comes from the testator's signature being witnessed. Here the testator didn't even initial the change, and there certainly are no witnesses. Result: the gift is revoked; no new gift is made; Salma receives nothing. That result is surely perverse. The testator wanted Salma to receive a gift greater than the original gift, and the result is she gets nothing.

The doctrine of dependent relative revocation (DRR) changes this result. Given the choice between allowing the revocation to stand and giving Salma nothing, and undoing the revocation and allowing Salma to receive the original gift of $10,000, it's easy for a court to decide to undo the revocation and allow the original gift to take effect. This is the heart of DRR: if a court finds that the testator's intent is better served by ignoring the revocation and allowing the original provision to stand, it will do so.

Now I'll bet your next thought is what happens if the will looks like this:

$1,000
Example 3.6: I give $~~$10,000~~ to my cousin, Salma.

In this case, a court would certainly be justified in refusing to hold the revocation ineffective. Remember that the choice is between giving Salma $0 and $10,000 when the testator wants her to receive $1,000. Allowing the revocation to stand is much closer to what we can pretty confidently presume the testator wanted.

Finally (and you knew this was coming), what if the will looks like this:

$5,000
Example 3.7: I give $~~$10,000~~ to my cousin, Salma.

Whether the revocation will stand generally depends on the facts. For example, if the value of the residuary gift is so large that the $5,000 decrease that will result from undoing the revocation will make a relatively insignificant change in the value of the residuary gift (remember, the revoked gift will be added to the property disposed of by the residuary clause), the revocation will be ignored. Restatement (Third) of Property § 5.3 comment d, illustration 8, says that where the ineffective new gift is exactly 50 percent of the revoked gift, the revocation is ineffective absent other evidence.

After the examples we've just seen, you might think that DRR has no role in jurisdictions that do not recognize partial revocation by physical act. Not so. DRR can do a lot more than undo the testator's revocations of part of an attested will.

Example 3.8: Testator, unmarried and without any descendants, had a perfectly valid will dividing the residuary estate among his three siblings. Two siblings received 10 percent of the residue each while the third sibling received 80 percent.

Sidebar

PARTIAL REVOCATION AND HOLOGRAPHIC CODICILS

What happens if the testator in Example 3.5 writes her initials next to the handwritten dollar amount? Could the change be a holographic codicil to the attested will? It is certainly possible to have a holographic codicil to an attested will, and it's equally possible to write the codicil on the will itself. The question is, is enough of the new gift in the testator's handwriting? Restatement (Third) of Property § 3.2 comment g, illustration 9, says that writing in the new amount and initialing is enough to create a holographic codicil. The same comment, however, collects cases that come to the opposite conclusion.

Testator then typed out a new will that gave the favored sibling 90 percent of the residuary estate and the other two siblings 5 percent each. That new will was never executed, but at some time Testator revoked the old will by physical act. After Testator's death, both the revoked will and the unexecuted document were found in the testator's desk. Did Testator die intestate?

The revoked will could be admitted to probate using DRR. If the revocation was allowed to stand, the testator would have died intestate and the three siblings would take equal shares of the probate estate. By undoing the revocation of the will, the testator's clear intent to give a far greater gift to the favored sibling was carried out.

So far the examples we've discussed of how DRR operates involve undoing a revocation because the testator did not create a valid replacement for the revoked will or gift in a will. The doctrine can also be used where the testator's action was based on a mistake of law or of fact. Mistakes of fact are probably more common than mistakes of law. An example of the former is the testator who cancels a gift of a sum of money to a person serving in the armed forces because the testator believes the person has died in combat. If the person is indeed alive, at the testator's death a court can ignore the revocation if that would better carry out the testator's intent. If it can be shown that the gift was revoked because the testator believed the person was dead, then ignoring the revocation is indeed what a court should do.

By the way, the examples illustrating DRR could just as easily be used to illustrate the operation of the harmless error rule (UPC § 2-503). All of the failed attempts to make gifts at death in those examples could be given effect through the use of the harmless error rule so long as the testator's intent to make those gifts can be shown by clear and convincing evidence. If harmless error becomes widely used—which requires that states add it to their statutes and that courts actually use it—then presumably the need for DRR will decrease. There is no need to use a doctrine that gives a second-best result when it is possible to give effect to the testator's intent.

(2) Revocation by Operation of Law

In some circumstances, the law will revoke the testator's will or parts of the will. Once common law, the relevant rules have been turned into statutes in the United States, and in turn those statutes have gone through generational changes, just as have the holographic will statutes. Today the scope and relevance of these statutes is much reduced except in one particular situation: the ending of the testator's marriage.

(a) Marriage and Birth of Children

Under the common law, the will of a woman was revoked on her marriage and the will of a man was revoked on marriage and the subsequent birth of issue. In the United States, these rules have been replaced almost everywhere by statutes that treat women and men identically. Many of these statutes revoke an existing will on the testator's marriage unless the will "provided for the contingency" of marriage. Decisional law generally held that the required provision had to expressly mention a future marriage. The results were often inane. A will written a few days before marriage that gave the entire probate estate to the future spouse but that did not mention the impending nuptials would be revoked the moment the couple was finished saying "I do." If the testator had descendants by a prior marriage and did not write a new will (or republish the premarital will by executing a codicil to it), on the testator's death the descendants and the surviving spouse share the probate estate in intestacy. That's not what the testator wanted.

These statutes have disappeared almost completely from the statute books, often to be replaced by much more sophisticated statutes (see Chapter 13). The same is true of statutes that revoked existing wills on the birth of children. They too have been supplanted by more nuanced statutes (again, see Chapter 13). Given the various statutory mechanisms (yes, Chapter 13) for preventing the disinheritance of a surviving spouse, some states have given up on any sort of revocation on marriage statute.

(b) Divorce

As if to counterbalance the withering away of the revocation on marriage statutes, statutes that revoke testamentary provisions for an ex-spouse have grown in importance. This development presumably is related to the frequency with which marriages in the United States end in divorce. It is also a reflection of the failure of divorced persons to change their wills (and nonprobate property arrangements) to take into account the divorce. These statutes are yet another example of a default rule and represent the legislature's judgment that divorced persons want to remove the ex-spouse as a beneficiary under the person's will.

Almost all states have statutes that address the effect of divorce (or dissolution of the marriage by annulment or declaration of invalidity) on the divorced person's will, and they all revoke any provisions for the ex-spouse, including appointment as executor or trustee. The will then operates as if the ex-spouse had predeceased the testator. The UPC provision, § 2-804, is quite comprehensive and deals with the effect of divorce on wills and on all sorts of nonprobate property arrangements and applies to any gift to or appointment as fiduciary of any "relative" of the ex-spouse. That provision means that a devise to "my spouse, or if my spouse does not survive to my spouse's descendants by representation" is completely revoked. The devise will end up as part of the residuary devise, or, if it is the residuary devise, it will pass through intestacy. Non-UPC statutes often do not extend to the relatives of the ex-spouse, and sometimes they do not apply to fiduciary appointments of the ex-spouse. UPC § 2-804 is a default rule, however, and yields to an express provision in the will, a court order, or a contract between the spouses made before or after the dissolution of the marriage. (We'll discuss the effect of divorce on nonprobate property arrangements in Chapter 6.)

SUMMARY

- To be valid, wills must conform to state statutory requirements, which are similar in their broad outlines but also contain important differences.

- Attested wills are signed by witnesses to the testator's signature. The signing formalities are meant to prevent fraud and to ensure that the document created by the testator really is intended to make gifts at death.

- The UPC breaks new ground by making acknowledgment of the testator's signature before a notary the equivalent of attestation.

- Many states and the UPC also authorize holographic wills, which are valid without attestation by witnesses so long as some portion of the text is in the testator's handwriting, which provides the guarantee of authenticity.

■ The harmless error rule, followed by the Restatement (Third) of Property and the UPC, authorizes ignoring the statutory formalities if there is clear and convincing evidence that the testator meant the document to be a will. This rule also applies to other documents that have to be executed with testamentary formalities, including codicils and documents revoking a will.

■ Revocation of a will must conform to state statutory requirements. All statutes allow revocation by a subsequent will, which expressly revokes or is inconsistent with the provisions of the prior will. A testator can also revoke a will by performing a physical act on the will with the intent to revoke. Statutes differ on whether the testator can partially revoke a will by a physical act.

■ An amendment to a will is a codicil. A codicil must be executed in the same way as a will. In a jurisdiction that recognizes holographs, a holographic codicil can amend an attested will and a holographic will can be amended by an attested codicil.

■ Statutes govern the effect of the revocation of a will that revokes a previous will.

■ The doctrine of ineffective revocation (dependent relative revocation) is used by a court to undo revocations of parts of wills or even of entire wills when that better serves the testator's intent.

■ Divorce will revoke the provisions in the testator's will benefiting the ex-spouse. Under the UPC, divorce also revokes provisions benefiting relatives of the ex-spouse.

CONNECTIONS

Revocation of Wills on Divorce and Nonprobate Property

Revocation on divorce also applies to nonprobate property devices under some statutes and court decisions, all of which is discussed in Chapter 6. The matter is complicated by the role of federal law designed to protect retirement savings, also discussed in Chapter 6.

Will Creation and Revocable Lifetime Trusts and Will Substitutes

Although revocable trusts are often used as will substitutes, the rules governing the creation, modification, and revocation of all types of trusts are different from those governing wills. In general, there is much less formality to the creation and revocation of trusts, all of which is discussed in Chapters 8 and 11.

Revocation of Wills on Marriage or the Birth Children

Although the doctrines of revocation of a will on marriage or the birth of children are anachronisms, they have been replaced by different devices for protecting at least some family members from disinheritance, both intentional and otherwise. These devices are discussed in Chapter 13.

Will Contests
and the Testator

4

Contested wills are no laughing matter, even though cartoonists and advertisers like to portray them humorously. Will contests may pit family

members against one another, destroy long-held beliefs about relationships or entitlements, and cost huge sums to litigate, which encourages parties to settle even when they believe that they are disregarding the testator's wishes by doing so. Wills are challenged most often for reasons that have to do with the testator — that the testator lacked testamentary capacity, for instance, or wrote the will under duress. Weighing the testator's circumstances against the relevant law in these types of challenges falls to courts and to juries. The emotional and financial stakes are high, making the role of all participants in the process that much more demanding.

A. CAPACITY

B. INSANE DELUSION

C. UNDUE INFLUENCE, FRAUD, AND DURESS

D. WHY DOES SOCIETY CARE?

E. HEADING OFF A CHALLENGE
    1. Precautions in the Will Itself
    2. Precautions Before, During, and After Execution

No matter how closely the execution of an attested will conforms to the state's statute or how clear it is that a holograph embodies testamentary intent, the document is not a valid will unless the testator had testamentary capacity, was not suffering from an insane delusion that led to the provisions of the will, and was free of undue influence.

Before we start investigating these concepts, realize that the legal meanings of competency, insane delusion, and undue influence are hammered out in litigation brought by those who will take the decedent's probate property if the will is held to be invalid. Those contesting the will just about always choose jury trials, and most commentators believe that trying these cases to juries means that emotion, as much as analysis and logic, will influence the eventual verdict. Some evidence for that belief comes from the large number of verdicts in will contests that are appealed. Appeals sometimes result in reversal because the verdict is found to be against the weight of the evidence or contrary to law.

Some commentators have argued that the particularly high number of successful appeals means that we should curtail jury trials of will contests or enact legislation that requires testators to leave some minimum amount at least to descendants (remember that in most states one cannot effectively disinherit one's spouse). These commentators also argue that the uncertainty of jury verdicts and the costs of litigating and appealing can lead the proponents of a will to settle with contestants, which in turn encourages the bringing of less than compelling cases in the hope of getting some kind of settlement. In effect, wills litigation has its share of **strike suits**, lawsuits of very little merit brought with the aim of coercing the other side into a settlement.

All this means that it is impossible to reduce what we discuss in this chapter to "rules" that will decide cases. There are widely accepted formulations; there are even lists of factors and definitive statements of what needs to be proved, who bears what burden of proof, and all sorts of presumptions. In the end, however, every case depends on its facts, and representing either side in a will contest requires exhaustive research and persuasive argument.

A. Capacity

Many state statutes require the testator to be of "sound mind" or "sound mind and memory." The UPC provision, § 2-501, requires that the testator be 18 years of age or older and "of sound mind." There is a fairly well-accepted idea of what that phrase means, and the way Restatement (Third) of Property puts it in § 8.1(b) is more or less the standard formulation: the testator "must be capable of knowing and understanding in a general way [1] the nature and extent of his or her property, [2] the natural objects of his or her bounty, and [3] the disposition that he or she is making of that property, and [4] must also be capable of relating these elements to one another and forming an orderly desire regarding the disposition of the property." To sum it up, then, the testator must understand what the will is giving away, how it's being given, and how the plan works as a whole. But what about those "natural objects of his or her bounty"?

That phrase is really at the heart of much of the difficulty in determining mental capacity. In comment c to § 8.1, the Restatement describes "natural objects of his or her bounty" as the testator's "closest family members." According to comment c, that group is not limited to genetic or adopted family members but can include stepchildren so long as the testator was "close" to them. The term does not include those collateral relatives who would take in intestacy just because they are heirs. The comment also notes that "non-traditional" family members such as domestic partners can certainly be natural objects of the testator's bounty.

The Restatement's discussion of the concept of natural objects of the testator's bounty is open-minded. You can certainly find opinions in which the "objects" are equated with the testator's heirs. That identification is particularly hard on the testator who is unmarried and without issue. If other descendants of the testator's parents survive the testator but receive nothing under the testator's will, they may find that the jury and the court are very sympathetic to their claim that the testator lacked mental capacity, especially if the beneficiary of the will is not a family member at all but a friend, neighbor, or caregiver. The same may be true if the testator was an only child and the disappointed heirs are first cousins or even more remote relatives.

F   A   Q

Q: Isn't there a conflict between testamentary freedom and judicial rulings that favor relatives over the will beneficiaries chosen by the testator?

A: Yes, there is something of a contradiction or a paradox here. Some opinions read as if any heir, no matter how distantly related or how little contact there was between the heir and the testator, is the natural object of the decedent's bounty. The conclusion, sometimes unspoken, is that being an heir confers some sort of claim on the probate estate, which somehow leads a court to be suspicious of a will that gives the probate estate to someone who is not a relative. Prejudice, preconceptions, and social conventions sometimes play a large role in will contests.

It is generally said, and the cases do bear this out, that the level of mental capacity needed to make a will is somewhat less than that needed to make an irrevocable lifetime gift. Restatement (Third) of Property agrees, and § 8.1(c) tells us why. To make an irrevocable lifetime gift, the donor must have the mental capacity to make a will "and must also be capable of understanding the effect the gift may have on the future financial security of the donor and of anyone dependent on the donor." In other words, if I give property away while I am alive, I can impoverish myself perhaps even to the point where the state will have to support me. What I give away in my will I no longer need (remember, you can't take it with you). You will also see the statement, which again is supported by a few cases that have considered the problem, that the mental capacity necessary to contract a valid marriage is less than that needed to make a valid will. Marriage is a "fundamental right" (at least for opposite-sex couples), and only the most necessary restraints on its exercise are constitutionally valid.

Mental capacity to make a will is a legal concept, and although the opinions of medical professionals might be valuable evidence in a will contest, they are not determinative. In fact, unless the medical expert actually examined the testator, as opposed to merely reviewing the testator's medical records, the medical evidence is of little use. The closer the medical examination is to the time of the execution of the will, the more persuasive the evidence is. It is not necessary to get a medical opinion on the testator's mental capacity whenever a lawyer writes a will for a client. The lawyer, however, must be satisfied that the client does meet the legal standard.

F   A   Q

Q: Does an incapacitated person whose property is under the control of a guardian or conservator also lack testamentary capacity?

A: Not necessarily. The level of capacity necessary to enter into contracts is greater than that needed to make a will for pretty much the same reason the level of capacity needed to make an irrevocable lifetime gift is higher than that needed to make a will. In addition, under some modern statutes dealing with adjudications of competency, there is no set standard for the appointment of a guardian or conservator. Instead, an incapacitated person is to receive the least amount of oversight possible. The guardian or conservator may have authority to deal with investments, but the incapacitated person will still deal with small sums of money for household expenses or small personal expenditures. The effect of an adjudication of incapacity under such a statute on the question of capacity to make a valid will depends on the nature and extent of the incapacity on which the adjudication is based.

Even if a person clearly lacks the mental capacity to make a valid will at time X, a will executed at a different time may still be valid if the will was made in a **lucid interval** (Restatement (Third) of Property § 8.1 cmt.m). A lucid interval is exactly that, a period of time in which the testator does indeed have the mental capacity necessary to make a valid will. It's all a matter of the facts of the particular case.

One last thing about will contests based on lack of capacity: the prevailing view is that the party claiming that the testator lacked capacity has the burden of proof. UPC § 3-407 agrees and also states that parties have the burden of persuasion as to matters on which they have the initial burden of proof.

B. Insane Delusion

A testator may have the mental capacity needed to make a valid will, but the will, or part of it, is invalid if it is the product of an **insane delusion**, sometimes called

monomania or **partial insanity**. Restatement (Third) of Property explains the principle in § 8.1 comment s:

> An insane delusion is a belief that is so against the evidence and reason that it must be the product of derangement. A belief resulting from a process of reasoning from existing facts is not an insane delusion, even though the reasoning is imperfect or the conclusion illogical. Mere eccentricity does not constitute an insane delusion.
>
> A person who suffered from an insane delusion is not necessarily deprived of capacity to make a donative transfer. A particular donative transfer is invalid, however, to the extent that it was the product of an insane delusion.

Insane delusion cases often involve claims by a disappointed relative, often a child, whom the testator falsely believed did not love the testator, was stealing from the testator, or deserved another type of unjustified grudge. It is difficult to carry the burden of proving that the testator's reasoning process is deranged. Consider the position of the child in the following example.

Example 4.1: Child serves as trustee of a trust created in the will of the first parent to die for the benefit of Surviving Parent. Surviving Parent is unhappy with the whole idea of the trust and doesn't understand why he cannot simply own the property outright. Child tries to explain, but Surviving Parent insists that there is something "wrong." When Surviving Parent dies, Child is left out of the will. Is the disinheritance of Child the product of an insane delusion?

Almost certainly not. The surviving parent's unhappiness with the trust arrangement is not itself "insane"; and even if the surviving parent blames unhappiness with the trust on the trustee and thus draws illogical conclusions based on imperfect reasoning, he is not suffering from an insane delusion. The result might be different if the surviving parent claimed that the child trustee was failing to follow instructions on how to manage the trust that the decedent was sending from beyond the grave. Even in that situation, the child would have to prove that the disinheritance was the product of that belief. Of course, even a belief that messages are being received from the dead might be "mere eccentricity." Insane delusion cases are not easy to prove.

C. Undue Influence, Fraud, and Duress

The basic idea of what constitutes undue influence is easy to understand. Applying it to concrete cases is another matter entirely. A will or a gift in a will is the product of undue influence if the testator's will is overridden so that the will expresses not what the testator wants but what the person who influenced the testator wants (Restatement (Third) of Property § 8.3(b)). The will then is literally not the will of the testator but the will of the person exercising undue influence.

I'm sure you can see that it is not easy to draw the line that separates acceptable influence — love for a spouse or partner, gratitude toward a friend, caregiver, spiritual advisor, or physician — from undue influence that makes a nullity of the testator's desires. Direct evidence of undue influence is not common, and undue influence cases, therefore, almost always involve circumstantial evidence.

It should not be surprising that the law of undue influence is almost exclusively case law. Understanding what sort of circumstantial evidence is necessary requires synthesizing a lot of cases, so we'll rely on that ready-made synthesis, Restatement (Third) of Property § 8.3. The party objecting to the admission of the will to probate on the grounds of undue influence must prove

- that the testator was "susceptible" to undue influence,
- that the person alleged to have exercised undue influence had an opportunity to do so,
- that the person alleged to have exercised undue influence "had a disposition to exercise undue influence," and
- that the will or part of the will appears to be the result of the alleged undue influence.

F   A   Q

Q: Will advanced age alone make a testator "susceptible"?

A: The answer used to be a qualified yes, but if there is any trend in the decisions, it is an increasing unwillingness to infer that a testator is susceptible simply because of advanced age. Courts are more likely today to require some specific proof of the testator's susceptibility, such as the existence of cognitive deficiencies or evidence of confusion and disorientation caused by medication for existing conditions. Indeed, courts used to talk about the testator being of "weakened intellect," which could easily be linked to the highly questionable generalization that increasing age is inevitably accompanied by senility.

Proving these elements is much easier when circumstances exist that raise a presumption of undue influence. What facts give rise to the presumption? Again, there is no truly definitive list, but the Restatement gives us a good summary. The first requirement for the presumption is a confidential relationship between the testator and the person allegedly exercising undue influence. In comment g to § 8.3, the Restatement breaks the concept of confidential relationship into three different sorts of relationships.

- A fiduciary relationship that arises in situations where the person allegedly exercising undue influence has formal fiduciary obligations to the testator, such as those an attorney owes to a client or a trustee owes to a beneficiary.
- A "reliant" relationship. This sort of relationship exists if the party objecting to the will can establish that the testator "was accustomed to be guided by the judgment of the alleged wrongdoer" or justifiably trusted that the alleged wrongdoer would act in the testator's interest. The relationship between a doctor and a patient, a financial advisor and a customer, and a member of the clergy and a congregant might fall under this heading. Courts sometimes describe this sort of relationship as fiduciary, especially if the relationship is one in which the testator trusts the alleged wrongdoer to act in the testator's interest. The obligation to act in someone else's interest rather than one's own is a hallmark of fiduciary obligation, and it is easy to understand how courts are often led to lump the two categories together.

■ A "dominant-subservient" relationship. The Restatement suggests that such a relationship might exist between a hired caregiver or an adult child and a testator who is very ill or feeble.

The general trend seems to be to identify more and more situations in which confidential relationships can arise. This trend is driven by increasing concern for elderly testators who are too ill or weak to live on their own and whose day-to-day needs are met by hired caregivers. Indeed, the predatory home healthcare aide is becoming a stock character in will contests based on undue influence. Persons objecting to a will often allege a confidential relationship between the caregiver and the testator based on a reliant relationship, the existence of a dominant-subservient relationship, and even a fiduciary relationship if the caregiver was the agent under the testator's **power of attorney** authorizing the caregiver to make decisions about the testator's property.

F   A   Q

Q: Can a testator's child be in a confidential relationship with the testator?

A: Yes, but not solely because of the parent-child relationship. Just as in establishing any confidential relationship, the facts must show that the child had fiduciary duties to the testator (most probably by being the agent under the testator's power of attorney), or that the testator relied or was dependent on the child.

Even if there is a confidential relationship between the testator and the person accused of exercising undue influence, the presumption of undue influence does not arise unless "suspicious circumstances" also exist. In comment h to § 8.3, the Restatement gives a long list of suspicious circumstances, which fall into several categories. The first has to do with the testator. Suspicious circumstances exist if the will was executed while the testator was "in a weakened condition" physically or mentally and thus susceptible to undue influence.

Another category involves the preparation of the will. Was the will a "rush job" hastily drafted and executed and done furtively? Did the person accused of exercising undue influence participate in procuring the will, for example, by selecting the lawyer who drafted it or, even more blatantly, drafting it himself (something made easier by drafting software readily available through the Internet)? If a lawyer drafted the will, did the testator talk to the lawyer without the alleged wrongdoer being present and did the testator express the testator's desires in the testator's own words? Handing over a memorandum drafted by the person accused of exercising undue influence and telling the lawyer to turn its provisions into a will or having the alleged wrongdoer present at the interview between the lawyer and the testator are classic "suspicious circumstances."

The final category involves the provisions of the will. Suspicious circumstances can exist if the challenged will is radically different from previous wills executed by the testator. Equally suspicious is the alteration of a pattern of disposition exhibited by previous wills and nonprobate property arrangements. Finally, and perhaps most problematically, the circumstances are suspicious if a reasonable person would regard the disposition of the decedent's property as unnatural or unjust, for example, where a will or nonprobate property arrangement was suddenly changed to disinherit a family member whom that same reasonable person would judge to be both loyal to the testator and deserving of a gift at death.

If you think about these possible "suspicious" circumstances, and particularly the final one, you might very well conclude (okay, I think you should conclude) that the law of undue influence is very much in the eye of the beholder. Where the disappointed family member sees a grabby caregiver or a conniving fellow family member, others might see a devoted helper — or, they might not, depending on their own experience and, if members of a jury, on how they respond to the advocacy of the lawyers who argue before them. Of course, what disappointed family member does not see him- or herself as loyal and deserving? It is no wonder that will contests often involve an enormous emotional investment on the part of the contending parties and that the loser at trial often appeals.

In any event, once the presumption has been established, the person offering the will for probate must come forward with evidence rebutting the presumption. The generally accepted rule, however, is that the presumption does not shift the burden of persuasion — the person attacking the will is not entitled to summary judgment unless the proponent of the will does not have evidence to rebut the presumption. That means that the jury must usually make the ultimate decision.

Yet another category of suspicious circumstance is related to the provisions of the will. Whenever a testator makes a devise to the lawyer who drafted the will, suspicions of undue influence are bound to arise, especially if the testator is not related to the lawyer. Lawyers often do draft wills for their spouses, partners, and other relatives. (And believe me, you will be asked not only by relatives but also by friends to draft their wills. In some instances, it may be very difficult to say no.) There is little likelihood of a challenge to the will if the lawyer is the spouse of the testator (unless, of course, the spouse has descendants from a prior marriage or relationship who are disinherited). A challenge is equally unlikely if the will gives the lawyer no more than he or she would receive in intestacy.

A presumption of undue influence will arise when a lawyer drafts a will for a client who is not a relative in which the testator makes a devise to the lawyer. If the gift is small in comparison to the probate estate, there will probably be no repercussions. A large gift, on the other hand, may be difficult to explain. If a client is absolutely determined to make other than a de minimis testamentary gift to her attorney or to a member of the attorney's family, the client must find a completely independent lawyer to draft the will.

Duress and fraud are relatively clear-cut. Duress involves obtaining a gift by threatening to do or actually doing a wrongful act so that the donor (testator) is coerced into making a gift the donor would not otherwise have made (§ 8.3 cmt. i). The difference between duress and undue influence, therefore, is the wrongful act, which the Restatement defines as a criminal act or one that the person doing the act had no right to do.

Fraud requires the making of a false representation knowingly or negligently, which leads the donor to make a gift that the testator would not otherwise have made. Failure to disclose a material fact is not fraud unless the person accused of wrongdoing has a confidential relationship with the donor (a concept that has the same meaning as it does in the undue influence context). Sometimes fraud is divided into fraud in the execution and fraud in the inducement. The former involves deceiving the testator into signing a will by representing that the document being signed is something else. The latter involves lying about a fact that leads the testator to make a gift that otherwise would not be made. Realize that it may be quite difficult to prove that a lie led to the challenged gift; but if the difficulties are overcome, the gift is void.

One difference between undue influence and fraud or duress involves the remedy. If a will or part of a will is the product of undue influence, then the contaminated transfer is simply void. Things are a bit more complicated if the wrongdoing prevents the testator from making or revoking a will. In that case, a valid document exists, but it does not dispose of the property in the way the testator wanted. As you might rightly conclude, the remedy in such a case is the imposition of a constructive trust. One of the most difficult questions about the use of the constructive trust as a remedy comes up when there are devisees under the instrument who took no part in the wrongful acts. There are many cases that state that the imposition of a constructive trust is the remedy for a wrongful act and, at least by extension, suggest that only a wrongdoer can be made trustee of a constructive trust.

Other cases and Restatement (Third) of Property § 8.3 comment *l* take the position that a constructive trust is a remedy for unjust enrichment and a constructive trust can be imposed on an innocent person who benefits from another's wrongdoing. For example, if some of the testator's heirs wrongly prevent the testator from executing a will that gives the testator's probate estate to a friend so that the testator dies intestate, obviously not all of the heirs are wrongdoers. Courts that are willing to use a constructive trust to remedy unjust enrichment and to follow the Restatement (Third) would impose a constructive trust on all of the heirs in favor of the beneficiary under the unexecuted will (§ 8.3 cmt. *l*, illus. 11).

Sidebar

CONSTRUCTIVE TRUSTS AND THE HARMLESS ERROR RULE

The harmless error provides an alternative to the use of a constructive trust in the case of wrongful prevention of the making or revoking of a will. Under the harmless error rule, a court can admit the unexecuted will to probate or treat the revocation as effective so long as there is clear and convincing evidence of the testator's intent. One of the arguments for adoption of the harmless error rule is its use in these situations. It provides a direct remedy — doing what the testator wanted by treating an instrument as valid or an attempted revocation as effective — rather than complicating the issue with questions of when a constructive trust is appropriate.

D. Why Does Society Care?

Before we leave this discussion it's worth asking why society cares about the testator's mental capacity or the possibility that a will or some part of it might be the product of insane delusion, undue influence, fraud, or duress. Why should society devote time and resources to squabbles among family members who are acting out their anger and resentment based on sibling rivalries or hatred for a stepparent or a simple invincible conviction of entitlement? If the answer is that we want to protect the testator, then being concerned with fraud and duress makes a good deal of sense. Wrongdoers should not profit from wrongdoing, and that goes for the person who deceives or threatens the testator as much as for the slayer.

Invalidating wills because of undue influence is a bit more difficult to explain. In theory, if the will reflects not what the testator wants but what another person wants, then the document is not the testator's will at all. The problems come when we try to put the theory into practice, so tangled is the determination of what influence is "undue" with ideas about what family members deserve and what sort of relationships testators, especially elderly testators, should have with nonfamily members. In addition, is it really possible for a person to have set ideas about making gifts at death that are then subverted by the influence of another person? Drawing the appropriate boundaries is extremely difficult.

Finally, we can even wonder about the requirement of mental capacity. The requirement that the testator have some level of mental capacity seems completely sensible. But there is a real question about how we can justify setting aside a person's expressed desires because the person lacks something we call mental capacity. As we noted, often challenges to a will based on the testator's alleged lack of capacity turn on how society judges the appropriateness of the gifts the testator has made in the will. Perhaps the best argument for the mental capacity requirement is that it protects the testator from undoing a carefully considered plan at a time when the testator cannot make valid judgments about that existing plan. Yet, how can we be sure what judgments are invalid? Short of a dementia so severe that the testator does not recognize family members and believes that the dead are still alive, it is difficult to say with any certainty when a testator is without the required level of mental capacity. What we can be sure of is that litigation over the validity of wills will be with us for as long as wills are written.

E. Heading off a Challenge

(1) Precautions in the Will Itself

The previous discussion should show you that there are many grounds on which a will can be attacked and that the law involved is at best imprecise. When you add to the legal framework the uncertainties of jury trial, you can see that many testators rightly fear that their will may not survive a determined attempt to prevent its admission to probate or that the beneficiaries will end up having to pay those objecting to the will to avoid the risks and expense of trial.

One thing that a lawyer preparing a will can do to help discourage challenges is to make sure that anyone examining the will can be sure that it has not been tampered with. Remember our discussion of integration in Chapter 3. It makes sense to do whatever is reasonably necessary to ensure that there can be no question about which pages of the will were present when the testator executed it. In fact, it's easy to take simple precautions that can avoid problems. First, the will should be internally coherent. That means that sentences should not end at the bottom of a page but rather should run on to the next. At least two lines of text should appear on the page with the testimonium and the attestation clause (although there is no rule requiring the signatures of the testator and witnesses to appear on a page that contains provisions of the will).

At the very least, the pages should be fastened together, usually with staples. Many lawyers also create a footer on each page that indicates the current page and the total number of pages. It could look like this: "_____Page 1 of 10." The testator places his initials on the line before the page number. In addition, the number of pages in the will can be included in the attestation clause so that the first sentence of the clause reads like this: "The foregoing instrument, consisting of ten (10) pages, was signed, published and declared . . ."

One last bit of practical advice related to integration of the will. If the will is stapled together, never, never, never remove any of the staples. The existence of staple holes leads suspicious minds (and when it comes to wills it seems that everyone has a suspicious mind) to wonder if someone took the will apart and inserted pages not present at the execution. For example, if you have to make a photocopy of the will after it has been stapled together (before or after execution), stand at the copier and do it one page at a time. Just don't stare into the green light.

One thing a testator can do to discourage a contest is to include a **no-contest clause** (sometimes called an **in terrorem clause**) in the will. While the wording of the clause can take different forms, the idea is always the same. Any beneficiary who contests the will loses whatever gift the beneficiary receives under the will. The purpose of the clause is to make the beneficiary do a cost-benefit analysis and answer the question of whether the risk of losing the gift under the will is worth taking the chance of receiving much more by successfully challenging the will. The testator wants the beneficiary to conclude that a bird in the hand is worth two in the bush.

No-contest clauses are widely used, but not always effectively. You will no doubt read cases in which the will includes a no-contest clause that is completely useless because the persons challenging the will receive nothing under the will. If there is nothing to lose, there is no reason not to bring a will contest (this kind of mistake is truly worthy of a "duh"). In other words, it is useless to include a no-contest clause in a will that completely disinherits a person who will take at least part of the testator's probate estate should the will fail.

Sidebar

ANTE-MORTEM OR LIVING PROBATE

Statutes in at least three states, Arkansas, North Dakota, and Ohio, allow a will to be admitted to probate before the testator's death. The idea of course is that the best way to settle questions of mental capacity, undue influence, and insane delusion is to have the testator available to testify. The beneficiaries named in the will and those persons who would be the testator's heirs were the testator to die at the time of the proceeding are given notice and an opportunity to appear. (Another model which has been suggested is to have the court appoint a guardian to represent those who would take were the will to be invalid.) The result is an order admitting the will to probate or denying probate. While there has been much scholarly discussion of this method of avoiding will contests, it has not been widely adopted, perhaps in part because is puts a difficult burden on those genuinely concerned about the testator's condition. Proving in court that a family member lacks capacity or is under undue influence is a good prescription for shattering family harmony once and for all.

Even if the no-contest clause is properly used, it may not accomplish the desired result. First, no matter how large the gift in the will, the beneficiary may wish to try for the larger reward that will come from successfully challenging the will. The more emotionally charged the situation, the more likely the beneficiary is to come to that conclusion. If setting aside the will is not so much a matter of economic gain as emotional satisfaction, it is unlikely that a no-contest clause will deter a litigant.

Second, courts construe no-contest clauses strictly. The reason for that says a good deal about our system for making gifts at death. On the one hand, the testator has wide latitude in making gifts at death. It really is true that the only person one cannot disinherit is a surviving spouse (at least outside of the community property states; see Chapter 13), and in some states the mechanism for ensuring that result is not at all robust. The testator has every right to disappoint potential heirs and the natural objects of the testator's bounty. On the other hand, no official body polices the boundaries that separate valid from invalid wills. Even in states with solemn form probate, the court itself will not investigate whether a will is the product of undue influence or whether the testator had the requisite mental capacity, except perhaps in the most egregious instances. The system counts on those who have an interest in challenging the validity of a will to prevent the admission to probate of defective instruments. Too-strict enforcement of no-contest clauses would defeat that reliance.

The most important generally accepted rule for mitigating the possible ill effects of no-contest clauses is to refuse to enforce them against beneficiaries who had probable cause for bringing a will contest. This is not the probable cause of the criminal law, of course. Bringing a will contest is not like obtaining a search warrant. Restatement (Third) of Property § 8.5 comment c describes probable cause as "evidence that would lead a reasonable person, properly informed and advised, to conclude that there was a substantial likelihood that the challenge [to the will] would be successful."

All in all, the law of no-contest clauses embodies an attempt to balance the testator's testamentary wishes against the need to prevent the admission to probate of wills that are the product of undue influence, fraud, or duress, or executed when the testator lacked mental capacity or suffered from an insane delusion.

(2) Precautions Before, During, and After Execution

Besides making sure the will's physical integrity is undoubted and including an effective no-contest clause, the lawyer can take other precautions before and after execution of the will to try to forestall a contest based on the usual grounds of lack of due execution, lack of capacity, undue influence, and insane delusion.

Lack of due execution. The lawyer should supervise the execution ceremony, making sure that it corresponds to the narrative in the attestation clause, and arrange for the execution of a self-proving affidavit immediately after the ceremony. If there is anything out of the ordinary about the execution ceremony, the witnesses should be asked to execute additional affidavits fully explaining what went on. For example, if the testator is blind, the witnesses should affirm that the will was read aloud to the testator and that the testator clearly indicated that the will states the testator's wishes.

Lack of capacity. Precautions should be taken if there is any doubt about the testator's capacity or if it is likely that someone will challenge the will on the grounds of lack of capacity. Depending on the seriousness of the possibility of challenge and the amount of wealth involved, the time and expense of multiple medical evaluations of the testator might be justified. Of course, testamentary capacity is a legal concept. Standard tests of cognitive capacity, however, can provide powerful evidence that the testator has testamentary capacity. Testimony from medical professionals interpreting standard neurological tests they have administered can be very persuasive.

F   A   Q

Q: Wouldn't videotaping the execution and the testator explaining the reasons for the will provisions help to prevent a contest?

A: Videotaping execution ceremonies and statements by the testator sounds like a great idea, but in many cases it isn't. If the testator is weak and ill, even though she may have capacity, a viewer of the video might easily conclude that the testator is simply too sick to make a valid will. In addition, the ability to manipulate digital video files makes it easy to doubt what one is seeing.

Undue influence. If the testator is disinheriting some family members in favor of others or in favor of unrelated persons, steps should be taken to remove the beneficiary as much as possible from the drafting process. The testator should be alone when discussing testamentary provisions with the drafter, who should not have any relationship with the beneficiary. In addition, the testator should explain, if possible in his own handwriting, why the testator has decided on the estate plan embodied in the will. One thing the drafter should avoid is including in the will itself any explanation of why a person is being disinherited. A detailed recital of whys and wherefores may only make disappointed family members even more unhappy and determined to vindicate themselves. In addition, the more detailed the recitation, the more likely the challengers can refute specific allegations or point out how the testator's perceptions were shaped by the person accused of wielding undue influence.

Insane delusion. Again, some contemporary statement by the testator of why the potentially controversial disposition is being made can go a long way to heading off a contest. Care must be taken, however, that the statement is rational and coherent and will not raise more doubts than it puts to rest.

SUMMARY

- The test of testamentary capacity is easy to state: the testator must understand what the will is giving away, how it's being given, and how the plan works as a whole, and must also know the identity of the "natural objects" of the testator's bounty.

- Identifying the natural objects of the testator's bounty becomes more complex as family structures continue to change.

- A testator suffers from an insane delusion if she holds a belief so contrary to evidence and reason that it amounts to derangement. If the will or part of the will is the product of an insane delusion, the will or that part is invalid.

- Undue influence exists when the provisions of the will represent the intent not of the testator but of another person. Proving the existence of undue influence is a matter of circumstantial evidence and involves many presumptions.

- Duress involves doing or threatening to do a wrongful act to coerce the testator into including a provision in the will.

- Fraud involves the knowing or negligent making of a false representation that leads the testator to include a provision in the will that otherwise would not be there.

- Carefully preparing the will so that its physical appearance raises no suspicions is an important step in ensuring that the will can withstand a challenge.

- In some cases, medical tests of cognitive ability can be an important tool for turning aside challenges based on lack of capacity, although testamentary capacity is a legal and not a medical concept.

CONNECTIONS

Will Contests and Execution of Wills

A challenge to a will usually includes an allegation of lack of due execution, the requirements for which are explained in Chapter 3, as well as allegations of lack of capacity and undue influence (and, less commonly, insane delusion) discussed here in Chapter 4.

Wills Contests (Capacity) and Will Substitutes

While the level of mental capacity needed to execute a valid will is more or less understood, it is not necessarily what is needed to create valid will substitutes, including revocable trusts and other nonprobate property devices. See Chapters 6 and 11.

Will Contests and Intestacy I

Only someone who can benefit from the denial of probate of a will can bring a will contest. In many instances, those who can benefit are the testators' heirs determined under the intestacy statute discussed in Chapter 2.

Wills Contests and Intestacy II

One element of the classic statement of testamentary capacity requires the testator to know the identity of the natural objects of the testator's bounty. Those persons are often identified with the testator's heirs, which makes relevant the intestacy statutes discussed in Chapter 2. Equally relevant is the changing law of families, especially regarding the recognition of same-sex relationships and the challenges to traditional notions of who is a child posed by assisted conception, also discussed in Chapter 2.

Wills: How They Work

While some wills are executed only a short time before the testator's death, many are executed long before that. From the time a will is executed until the time the testator dies, property can change, devisees can be born or die, and debts or expenses can increase or decrease. It's not surprising, then, that the law of wills includes both statutory and case law to deal with the problems caused by the inevitable passage of time. Most of these provisions are default rules that operate when the will itself does not provide a solution. But courts still find it difficult sometimes to apply these rules neatly. Knowing how to research and how to accurately interpret common law precedent are key skills for estate lawyers to build.

O V E R V I E W

A. TYPES OF GIFTS AND THE CONSEQUENCES OF CLASSIFICATION

1. Specific, General, Residuary, and Demonstrative
2. Ademption
3. Abatement

B. THE INTERESTS OF THE DEVISEES

1. Expectancies
2. Failure of an Individual Devisee to Survive the Testator
3. Class Gifts
4. Anti-Lapse Statutes
5. Conditional Gifts

A. Types of Gifts and the Consequences of Classification

After reviewing three types of gifts that can be made in a will and introducing a fourth, we'll talk about the consequences of classifying a gift. The consequences are important because what kind of gift a beneficiary is given may determine whether the beneficiary will receive anything at all.

(1) Specific, General, Residuary, and Demonstrative

Three types of devises (or gifts) that can be made in a will are

- a **specific devise** of a specified article of personal property or a specified tract of real property,
- a **general devise** of a sum of money or quantity of property, and
- a **residuary devise** of what's left of the probate estate once the specific and general devises are made.

Example 5.1: [*Specific devise*] I give the gold pocket watch that belonged to my grandfather to my son, Samuel, but if he does not survive me this devise will lapse and become part of the residuary devise.

Example 5.2: [*General devise*] I give and bequeath $10,000 to my friend [name], if [name] shall survive me, but if [he or she] does not survive me this devise will lapse and become part of the residuary devise.

Example 5.3: [*Residuary devise*] I give, devise, and bequeath all the rest, residue, and remainder of my property, both real and personal, wheresoever situated ("my residuary estate") as follows:

(A)   To my spouse, [name], if [name] survives me and if not
(B)   To my descendants who shall survive me, by representation.

That list, however, is not quite complete. There is a fourth type of devise, the **demonstrative devise**. A demonstrative devise is a gift that is usually of a sum of money or quantity of property, in other words the subject matter of a general devise, which is to be paid at least in the first instance from a specified source.

Example 5.4: I give $10,000 from my bank account at Big Bank and Trust *or* I give $10,000 from the sale of my stock in ABC Corp.

So long as the language in the will does not state that the gift is to come only from the designated source (in which case it would be a specific devise), if the designated source is insufficient, the gift will come from the other assets of the probate estate. Demonstrative devises are not particularly common, and cases dealing with them are few and far between.

(2) Ademption

Specific devises are subject to **ademption by extinction**. If the subject of the specific devise is not included in the decedent's probate estate, the gift is gone. A straightforward example is a specific devise of a single piece of personal property: "I give my gold Rolex watch to my nephew, Ned." When the will is executed, testator does indeed own a gold Rolex. By the time of the testator's death, however, there is no gold Rolex to be found among the testator's possessions. Does Ned receive anything?

The most widely accepted answer is that Ned loses out; the specific devise has adeemed by extinction. The prevailing view is that the reason the watch is no longer part of the probate estate is irrelevant (with some exceptions that we'll get to in a minute) and that the testator's intent is also irrelevant. The view is known as the **identity theory of ademption**. If the exact property that is the subject of the specific devise is not included in the probate estate, the gift fails.

Statutes sometimes modify this result. For example, if the article was lost or stolen and proceeds of insurance on the article have not been collected by the time of the decedent's death, the devisee is entitled to the proceeds. Often if the article was sold by a conservator or guardian of the testator, the devisee is entitled to the value of the article. The idea behind that provision is the testator did not make the decision to dispose of the item of personal property and that the gifts in the will should be under the sole control of the testator.

Driven by the desire to do equity in a specific situation by preventing ademption, courts have found ways to modify the bright line of the identity rule. First, there is a presumption against classifying a gift as a specific devise so that ademption cannot occur. Sometimes this leads to what looks like hairsplitting. Perhaps the most common example is the treatment of language like this:

Example 5.5: I give 1,000 shares of Microsoft to my niece, Nora.

Courts tend to find that Example 5.5 is not a specific devise. If there are not 1,000 shares of Microsoft included in the probate estate, the executor will either have to buy 1,000 shares and distribute them to Nora or distribute to her the value on the date of the testator's death of 1,000 shares of the corporation. The only way to make a specific devise of a specified number of shares of stock in a corporation is to include language that indicates that the gift is of a particular 1,000 shares.

Example 5.6: I give my 1,000 shares of Microsoft to my niece, Nora.

The inclusion of "my" in Example 5.6 makes all the difference. Traditionally, the inclusion of the possession pronoun means that the testator intends to make a gift of the shares the testator owns. If those shares are not included in the probate estate at death, the gift adeems.

Another technique courts use to prevent ademption is to decide that the specifically devised property underwent a **change in form rather than substance**. It simply

Sidebar

GIFTS OF SHARES OF STOCK

Problems arising from gifts of a specified number of shares of stock do not arise as often as they once did, probably because the way individuals invest has changed during the last thirty years or so. Today investments in corporate stock are overwhelmingly likely to be held in brokerage accounts, not distributed to purchasers as share certificates. The brokerage firm owns very large numbers of shares in many companies under what is known as a "street name," usually the name of the partnership that does the actually buying and selling. Any one customer's investment is really an electronic entry in the brokerage firm's records. The disappearance of the share certificate seems to have disconnected investors from their investments so that they think not about "my 1,000 shares of Microsoft" but about "my stock portfolio." Styles of investing have changed too. Past investors were more apt to hold "blue chip" stock for a very long time than they are today, when active trading is more the norm.

is not possible to create a general rule about when disposing of the subject of a specific devise and replacing it with different property is a change in form and not substance. This is yet another area in which questions about specific facts can be answered only by thorough research in the decided cases. A typical example you'll find there involves the acquisition of one corporation by another.

Example 5.7: Testator's will devises "my 500 shares of PastryCo Corporation" to Devisee. PastryCo is acquired by BakeryCo, and Testator receives 300 shares of BakeryCo in exchange for her shares in the acquired corporation. If Testator does not change the specific devise, the devisee of the PastryCo shares will receive the BakeryCo shares.

Restatement (Third) of Property rejects the identity theory of ademption in favor of an **intent theory of ademption** (§ 5.2 cmt. b). Under this theory, if a specifically devised item is not in the probate estate at death, the gift adeems unless the devisee can show that ademption would be contrary to the testator's intent. The party opposing ademption (almost always the specific devisee) bears the burden of proof and must show that ademption would be contrary to the testator's intent by a preponderance of the evidence.

Example 5.8: Testator's will devises one piece of jewelry to Son and another piece of jewelry to Daughter. The two items are approximately equal in value. The item devised to Son is stolen and not recovered. Does the devise adeem?

According to the Restatement, the gift would not adeem, and the son would be entitled to the value of the jewelry. The testator's plan is to make gifts of roughly equal value to the son and daughter. Allowing one gift to adeem distorts the testator's plan for making gifts at death.

The UPC ademption provision, § 2-606, codifies the Restatement's intent theory. It includes, however, a controversial provision that provides that the devisee of specifically devised property that is not in the probate estate at death is entitled to "any real property or tangible person property owned by the testator at death which the testator acquired as a replacement for" the specifically devised property (§ 2-606(a)(5)). This provision has been the object of criticism, much of which has been aimed at the idea of replacement. Some of the critics seem to assume that the provision requires tracing of the proceeds of sale of the specifically devised property into whatever the testator acquired with the proceeds. The comment to § 2-606 is emphatic that tracing is not what's involved. Rather, the provision "should be seen as a sensible 'mere change in form' principle." The example in the comment involves a specific devise of a 1984 Ford. By the time of the testator's death, the testator has sold the Ford, acquired another car, sold that one, and dies owning a third automobile. The devisee receives the car the testator owned at death.

The identity theory of ademption has no room for accommodating what we presume to be the testator's intent in a situation like the specific devise of an identified automobile. The Restatement approach, turned into a statute in UPC § 2-606(a)(5) and (a)(6), probably makes it more likely that the testator's intent will be carried out, but at the price of delaying administration of the estate as the executor tries to sort matters out. If the specific devisee and the devise of the residuary estate cannot agree, of course, a careful executor will certainly seek the advice of the appropriate court, which means more delay and expense. Remember that the fees charged by the executor's lawyer almost certainly will be paid by the estate, further diminishing the residuary gift. The price of abandoning bright-line rules in favor of a search for intent can be expense and delay.

Ademption by satisfaction is yet another variety. If the testator gives a lifetime gift to a devisee, the gift can take the place of the devise. The only requirement is a written acknowledgment that the gift is given in place of the devise in the will. The doctrine of ademption by satisfaction has been codified in most states. Many states have adopted the UPC provision, § 2-609, which provides three different ways to ensure that ademption is the result of the gift: (1) a statement in the will that the value of property given as a lifetime gift is to be deducted from the value of the devise, (2) a writing by the testator made contemporaneously with the gift indicating that the value of the gift is to be deducted from the devise, or (3) a writing by the devisee acknowledging that the devise has abated to the extent of the value of the gift. The parallel to the doctrine of advancements (see Chapter 2) is clear.

Sidebar

ADEMPTION AS EXEMPLAR

Ademption is a classic example of the challenges involved in understanding the law of wills and trusts. A very common occurrence (the failure of the probate estate to include some item of specifically devised property) is governed by a long-accepted rule (ademption by extinction), which in turn has a traditional gloss (the identity rule). Relentless application of that rule leads to results that are clearly contrary to testators' intent, so it is modified (by the change in substance rather than form rule).

Then Restatement (Third) of Property and the UPC take a more intent-oriented approach that requires courts to answer questions that were once resolved by applying a bright-line rule. The result is often a debate about whether the goal of better serving the testator's intent is worth the increased possibility of complications requiring the intervention of a court. Resolving the debate depends on carefully evaluating the cases that arise under the newer approach and other information including attempts to understand what happens in the vast majority of instances that never reach the courtroom, let alone the appellate courts.

(3) Abatement

Abatement, a reduction of the estate's gifts, is made necessary when the estate cannot pay all of its debts and expenses plus all of its heirs or devisees. Statutory default rules govern abatement in just about every state. Although these rules are remarkably uniform, they deal with a subject that is sometimes not easy to grasp, principally because the entire problem comes from the usual practice in distributing probate property to the heirs or the devisees under a will, a practice that is seldom directly addressed in statutes but which is crucial to understanding what abatement is all about.

To explain the idea, let's look at an intestacy example in which heirs are entitled to their proportionate share of each item of property making up the estate.

Example 5.9: Decedent dies intestate, and the heirs are decedent's three children. The probate estate consists of cash, real property, and stocks and bonds. Each child is entitled to *one-third of each item*. They will be tenants in common in the real property with equal one-third shares, they each get one-third of the cash, and they should get one-third of the stock in each company and one-third of each bond.

Of course, dividing the stock investments and bonds might be impractical, and the administrator may have statutory authority, or more likely will have to ask the appropriate court to approve, a **non–pro rata distribution** under which the three heirs receive property of equal value but not necessarily one-third of each item in the probate estate.

So what does all this have to do with abatement? Consider the payment of the debts and expenses of the decedent out of the probate estate. Since the three heirs are entitled to the entire probate estate, they will each pay one-third of the debts and expenses out of the one-third share of the probate property.

What happens, however, if the decedent died testate? If the debts and expenses are paid and then the estate is distributed, the residuary devisees will bear the cost.

Example 5.10: The probate estate is worth exactly $1,000,000. Decedent's debts and expenses total $100,000. The will makes the following gifts:

- Specific devises:
  - diamond ring to A, value $10,000
  - gold watch to B, value $5,000
  - painting to C, value $5,000
- General devises:
  - $20,000 to D
  - $30,000 to E
  - $50,000 to F
- Residuary devise to G value: $1,000,000 minus $100,000 debts and expenses, minus $120,000 of specific and general devises, leaving $780,000

What happens if something unexpected happens before the testator's death and the debts and expenses are much larger than $100,000? Perhaps the testator owed back taxes or had an outstanding judgment against her for a large amount. What if the debts and expenses total $800,000?

F   A   Q

Q: What are an estate's "debts and expenses"?

A: Debts include all of the decedent's outstanding debts — credit cards balances, unpaid utility bills, student loans, other loan balances (but usually not a mortgage on real property), income taxes for the year of death, unpaid medical bills — and expenses related to the administration of the estate — the executor's commissions, legal fees, and the cost of the decedent's funeral arrangements. Not included are federal and state estate taxes. Those are subject to special federal and state apportionment rules and are beyond our scope here.

The rule — and this time it really is a rule you can apply everywhere — is that *unless the will provides otherwise or the testator's intent would be unfulfilled* (that means, of course, this is a default rule), the debts and expenses are paid first from the residuary estate. In Example 5.10, the residuary estate, before the debts and expenses, totals $880,000 ($1,000,000 minus $20,000 of specific devises and $100,000 of general devises). The residuary devisee, G, will receive $80,000 if the debts and expenses total $800,000.

What happens if the debts and expenses total $930,000? The residuary devise will be completely consumed in paying the debts and expenses, and $50,000 will remain unpaid. The rule is that the general devises must be used to pay the shortfall, and those who receive the general devises contribute proportionately. In our example, the general devises total $100,000 with D receiving 20 percent of that amount, E 30 percent, and F 50 percent. The three general devises must contribute to the $50,000 shortfall in those proportions: D has to contribute $10,000 (.20 × 50,000), E has to contribute $15,000 (.30 × 50,000) and F $25,000 (.50 × 50,000). As a practical matter, of course, the executor will simply deduct those amounts from what is otherwise due the three recipients of the general devises.

What if the debts and expenses are greater still and total $990,000? The residuary devise and the general devisees total $980,000. The only thing that can be done is get the recipients of the specific devises to contribute to the $10,000 shortfall. Once again they contribute proportionately. The total value of the specific devises is $20,000, of which A receives 50 percent and B and C 25 percent each. Therefore A owes $5,000 and B and C $2,500 each. They will have a choice. They can sell the items devised to them and contribute the cash to the estate, or they can simply write a check to the executor for the amount and keep the devised property. In essence they are buying the property specifically devised to them by paying the proportional share of the decedent's debts and expenses for which the property devised to them is liable.

As you can see, the idea is that those who receive probate property contribute proportionately to the payment of the debts and expenses within each class of devise. The residuary devise is the first to be tapped for payment, then general devises, then specific devises. Where demonstrative devises fit in this scheme depends on whether the property or fund from which they are to be paid has adeemed. If it has not, then the demonstrative devise is classed with specific devises. If ademption has occurred, the demonstrative devise is classed with the general devises.

This pattern of abatement is all but universal. It is endorsed by Restatement (Third) of Property § 1.1 comment *f* and is incorporated into UPC § 3-902. Remember that this is statutory law and a default rule, so that the words of the will can expressly override the statutory scheme. In most states, the statutory order of abatement can also be overridden if doing so will fulfill the testator's intention, even if the will does not expressly override the statute. UPC § 3-902(b) says exactly that.

Example 5.11: Testator owns a controlling interest in the shares of a closely held corporation. Her daughters work in the business and are committed to keeping it going after Testator's death, but her son is not interested. Testator's will makes specific devises of an equal number of shares to each daughter and a general devise of cash to her son in an amount roughly equal to the value of one of the specific devises. Over time the value of the business increases, and Testator rewrites her will several times, each time increasing the value of the general devise so that it remained roughly equal to one of the specific devises. At Testator's death, the debts and expenses exceed the value of the residuary devise, and a large portion of the general devise to the son would be consumed in paying the remaining balance of the debts and expenses.

A court would almost certainly hold that the general devise to son should be treated for abatement purposes as if it were a specific devise so that son and both daughters would have to contribute proportionately to paying the debts and expenses. The testator's purpose in making the general devise was to equalize the treatment of son and daughters, and that purpose would be defeated if the devise to son were solely responsible for paying debts and expenses.

B. The Interests of the Devisees

In this section we're going to discuss rules that apply to the devisees of the will. Some of these rules concern identifying the beneficiaries when they are described using general terms like "children," "brothers," or "sisters." Others deal with what happens when a devisee does not survive the testator, and we'll discuss exactly what it means to "survive."

(1) Expectancies

A devisee (beneficiary) of a will receives nothing unless he survives the testator. While the testator is alive, the beneficiary, just like an heir apparent, has an expectancy, which is not an interest in property. Even so, Restatement (Second) of Torts § 774B recognizes a cause of action for intentional interference with an expectancy under a will or in intestacy or with a gift. Although many states agree and have a steady stream of cases moving through their courts, the law is not uniform. One of the biggest differences is whether the plaintiffs must first pursue a remedy in the probate court by trying to prevent probate of the will. For example, testator's heirs are convinced that the will offered for probate, which makes a large gift to X, was procured by X's exercise of undue influence. If the will is not admitted to probate, they will inherit the probate estate. In some states, the heirs cannot bring a tort action unless they oppose probate of the will, although in some jurisdictions they might be able to bring both causes of action simultaneously. In others, the tort action can be brought only if the claim could not have been asserted in a probate contest.

F   A   Q

Q: Why would disappointed heirs or devisees under a prior will prefer a tort action to objecting to probate of what purports to be the testator's last will?

A: Statutes of limitations can differ, making the tort action available even if a will contest is not. The remedies also differ. Successfully opposing probate of the will results in no probate of the will. The probate estate will pass in intestacy or under the provisions of the testator's last valid will. Success in the tort action can mean the award of punitive and consequential damages and, in some cases, perhaps even an award of attorneys' fees. The tort recovery might be worth more than success in the probate contest.

(2) Failure of an Individual Devisee to Survive the Testator

One of the most basic (and obvious) rules of the law of wills is that a devisee must survive the testator to receive the devise (Restatement (Third) of Property § 1.2). If the devisee doesn't survive, the gift fails. The technical term is **lapse**. For now we are going to deal only with devises to a single individual.

(a) Lapse and Pre-Residuary Gifts

The lapse of a pre-residuary devise to an individual — in other words, a specific, general, or demonstrative devise — results in the property that is the subject of the devise being added to the residuary devise, unless the will makes a disposition of the devise should the devisee not survive. We'll see in a bit that statutes might have an effect here, but for now you need to understand that when an individual devisee of a pre-residuary devise does not survive the testator, the subject of the devise is added to the residue unless the will provides otherwise.

(b) Lapse and Residuary Gifts

What if the residuary devise lapses? If the residuary clause reads "I give the residue of my estate to Trey" and Trey does not survive the testator, the only place for the residuary devise to go is to the testator's heirs (unless a statute intervenes, as we'll see). Any portion of the probate estate that is not disposed of by will must pass under the intestacy statute (recall the discussion of partial intestacy in Chapter 2).

Unfortunately, things get a bit more complicated if the residuary devise is given to two or more devisees. If one of them does not survive the testator, under the common law that devisee's portion of the residuary devise passes in intestacy to the testator's heirs. This common law rule is known as the **no-residue-of-a-residue rule**. Any part of the residuary devise that fails passes in intestacy. Not so sensible a rule, given the fact that there is still at least one residuary devisee capable of taking the devise. The testator wrote the will to avoid the intestacy statute, right? Well yes, but for historical reasons (all together now, "Because the Normans conquered England!"), the rule is that if any part of the probate estate is not disposed of by the will it goes to the heirs.

Today this rule is definitely the minority rule in the United States. It is rejected by Restatement (Third) of Property (§ 5.5 comment o) and by the UPC (§ 2-604), and in a sizeable majority of states it has been undone by statute or court decision. In those states, any part of the residuary devise that fails passes to the residuary devisees entitled to take. Consider the following residuary clause.

Example 5.12: "I give the residue of my estate in the following shares: 20 percent to A, 30 percent to B, and 50 percent to C." A does not survive Testator.

Where the no-residue-of-a-residue rule is abolished, A's 20 percent of the residue goes to B and C in proportion to their shares of the residuary devise. B will get 37.5 percent (3/8) of the residuary estate and C will get 62.5 percent (5/8).

(c) What Does "Survival" Mean?

Before we continue with our investigation of what happens when a devisee does not survive the testator, we have to consider what it means to "survive." Hardly seems worth worrying about, doesn't it? Either you survive the testator or you don't. If only. What happens if testator and a devisee under the will are involved in an airplane crash that kills them both? It will almost certainly be impossible to figure out who died first. A fatal motor vehicle accident or fire or any other event that results in fatalities could raise the same question.

Many wills contain language that deals with this possibility. Very often a devisee receives the devise only if she survives the testator for a certain period of time; 30 or even 60 days is pretty common. There are two reasons for including such a provision in a will. The first is to try to ensure that the devisee will actually be able to enjoy the property. It makes little sense to pass property to the estate of a devisee who has survived the testator but then dies before distribution. The devisee will never get to enjoy it, and the property will be subject to the devisee's debts and the expenses of administering the devisee's estate. Assume that the devisee is the testator's spouse; if the spouse does not "survive," the devise goes to the couple's children. If one spouse dies and then the other dies very shortly thereafter, sure the children will receive the first spouse's property, but it will have been administered twice.

The second reason is that such a provision eliminates the need to determine who died first when the circumstances are ambiguous. Assume that the spouses in our previous example do die in a traffic accident, and each spouse's will gives the residuary estate to the other spouse if the spouse "survives me by 30 days, and if not, to our descendants by representation." If both spouses are dead when the EMTs arrive at the accident scene or if one spouse is dead and the other dies in the hospital a short time later, each spouse will have predeceased the other, and each spouse's probate estate will go directly to their descendants.

All this is fine if there is a will and the will deals with the question, but what if the will is silent or the decedent dies intestate? If the decedent and a presumptive heir die in the same accident, how does the administrator decide if the presumptive heir became an heir by surviving the decedent? The same problem can happen with nonprobate property. If the beneficiary of an insurance policy on the life of the decedent is "my spouse, and if my spouse does not survive me, my children in equal shares," what should the insurance company do if the insured and the spouse die in the same accident? Unless the insurance contract has a provision requiring survival for a certain period of time (and it almost certainly doesn't), how can the insurance company decide whether it should pay the spouse's estate or the children? Think about real property held by joint tenants with right of survivorship. The deed will not have a provision dealing with the "who died first" problem.

The answer to the insurance company's dilemma is found in the statute book. Every jurisdiction has a statute that answers the question of who survives, and these statutes are closely based on the Uniform Simultaneous Death Act (USDA) either in its original or revised version. Both versions are default statutes. And both versions give more or less the same results. If the testator and a devisee die in circumstances in which the statute applies, they each predecease the other. In our spousal example, that means that each died before the other and each spouse's probate property will pass directly to the descendants without passing through the other spouse's estate. Property held as joint tenants with right of survivorship (or as tenants by the entirety) is distributed one-half to the probate estate of each joint tenant. Generally, beneficiaries of contract-based nonprobate property arrangements are treated as dying before the owner of the property, so, for example the beneficiary of a life insurance policy is deemed to have died before the insured, which means the death benefit will go to contingent beneficiaries or, if none were designated, to the owner of the policy. So what is the difference between the original and the revised USDA? The original version applies when there is "no sufficient evidence" of who died first. Those three words gave rise to some grotesque cases in which the concept of "sufficient evidence" was strained to the breaking point. For example, testator and devisee die in a fire. Autopsies show that the testator's lungs are scorched but that the devisee's lungs are unmarked. Conclusion: the testator "survived" because the testator was breathing while the fire was raging but the devisee had ceased to breathe and therefore was dead before that time. In addition, survival for only a few hours is of course enough. The original USDA can result in a devisee receiving property that the devisee will never really enjoy.

Under the revised USDA, in order for a person to have survived an event it must be shown by clear and convincing evidence that the person survived the event by 120 hours. The 120 hour requirement puts an end to the bizarre applications of the "no sufficient evidence" requirement and also eliminates the problem of the survivor dying too quickly to ever enjoy the property. The revised USDA is incorporated into the UPC in §§ 2-104 and 2-702, and the 120 hour requirement applies whenever a person is required to survive an event. In order to be an heir, for example, one must survive the decedent by 120 hours.

(3) Class Gifts

So far we've talked about devises to individuals. Now we're going to consider gifts groups, which are called **class gifts**. There are two kinds of class gifts: multigeneration and single generation.

(a) Multigeneration Class Gifts

A **multigeneration class gift** is a gift to a group that by its very nature can have members from more than one generation. The classic example is a devise to "my descendants." There are two distinguishing characteristics of such a gift. First, only those members of the class who are alive when the property is ready to be distributed can share in the gift (Restatement (Third) of Property § 15.3). For a devise in a will, that time is the testator's death (or 120 hours after the death if UPC § 2-702 applies). This is the rule that applies to all gifts in a will. (In Chapter 7, we'll see that things can be a bit different for gifts in trusts.)

The second characteristic is that unless the will expressly says otherwise, the members of the class take by representation (Restatement (Third) of Property § 14.4). Any descendant who has a living ancestor between himself and the testator will not receive any of the property that makes up the devise, just as that person would not be an heir were the testator to die intestate. The only way this sort of gift can lapse is if no one in the class survives the testator.

F   A   Q

Q: Which system of representation is used for a devise to a multigeneration class?

A: The will can define which system to use. If the will is silent, many jurisdictions have statutes that define "representation" when the word is used in a will or trust, and the system is most likely the one that is used for distributions in intestacy. That's the position of Restatement (Third) of Property § 14.4 comment c and UPC § 2-708. If there is no statute, there will be decisional law creating a default rule, and the court could certainly decide to follow the Restatement. If the will's attempt to define representation uses ambiguous language, a court will have to construe the language.

(b) Single-Generation Class Gifts

Identifying a gift to persons in a **single-generation class** depends on identifying the intent of the creator of the gift, and that means looking first for constructional rules. As you no doubt realize by now, that means that the answer to the question "Is this a class gift?" depends on the jurisdiction. Fortunately, Restatement (Third) of Property gives us some widely accepted rules that we can summarize as follows.

A single-generation class gift is a gift to a group that is described by a common characteristic, and everyone who shares that characteristic is a member of the same generation. Examples are "my children," "my nieces and nephews," and "the children of my sister Susan." In addition, the testator must intend that the members of the group take as a group. Taking as a group means first that the membership of the class can fluctuate until the time for distribution of the property being given, and that when the time for distribution comes, the members of the group who are living at that time take in equal shares. Once we've classified the gift as a single-generation class gift, the only way the gift can lapse is if there are no living class members at the time the property is to be distributed (and for a devise in a will, that time is the testator's death, although under the UPC the critical time is 120 hours after the testator's death unless the will provides otherwise).

- If the beneficiaries are described by a group label, then the gift is presumptively a class gift. Example: "I give $100,000 to my grandchildren." (§ 13.1(b))
- If the beneficiaries and their relative shares are expressly identified, the gift is not a class gift. Example: "I give $100,000 half to my niece Dolores Sanchez and half to my Nephew Norberto Sanchez." (§ 13.2(b)(1))
- If the beneficiaries are described by their names alone or by a group label and either by name or by the number of beneficiaries who fit the label at the time the will is written, then the gift is presumptively not a class gift. Example: "I give $100,000 to my niece and nephew Dolores Sanchez and Norberto Sanchez" or "I give $100,000 to the two children of my sister Josefina Sanchez." (§ 13.2(b)(2))

Notice that the first and third rules are presumptions, and as far as the Restatement is concerned, presumptions involving class gifts shift the burden of proof to the person trying to rebut the presumption (Reporter's Note to Division V). That means as a practical matter the presumptions would be rarely rebutted. Once we have a class gift, the number of beneficiaries can fluctuate up until the time of the testator's death, and the share each beneficiary takes depends on how many class members survive the testator (taking into account the 120 hour rule of the UPC if applicable and any will provision dealing with survivorship).

(c) Gifts Defined by Relationship

You've no doubt noticed that the class gift examples involved family members. The same questions about who is a child that we considered when we studied the intestacy statutes (see Chapter 2) arise when we're dealing with gifts in wills. The difference is that the testator's intent determines the meaning of the terms used in the will, although statutes and courts have created constructional rules that really are strong presumptions about intent.

(d) Adoption

We saw in Chapter 2 that in today's world the inheritance rights of adopted persons are the same as those of persons born into the adopting family. That is pretty much the result when dealing with class gifts in wills. Unless the will provides otherwise, construction will include the testator's adopted children and the adopted children of the testator's descendants in a class gift to the testator's children or descendants. Sometimes this constructional rule is modified depending on when the will was executed, on the theory that the complete integration of adopted persons into the adopting family is a relatively recent development. Wills executed before whatever date a court or a statute decides marks the acceptance of the complete integration rule are construed not to include adopted persons (other than the testator's own adopted children) in relationship-based class gifts.

Some courts and statutes do not apply the complete integration rule to persons adopted as adults. The point of the exception for adult adoptions is to remove the incentive to adopt an adult in order to give that person a share in a gift created by a relative of the adoptive parent.

Example 5.13: Testator's will devised the residue to Trustee, in trust, to pay the income from the trust property to Testator's Child for life. On Child's death, the trust ends and the trust property is to be distributed to Child's "descendants by representation" and, if there are none, to Child's siblings. Child is married but childless. Child is concerned that the surviving spouse will not be able to make ends meet without the trust income that the couple has enjoyed for their entire marriage. Child then adopts the spouse, hoping to make the spouse Child's own descendant and thus the person who will receive the trust property on Child's death.

In the absence of a statute, courts faced with this and similar situations have come to different conclusions, but courts that find that the adopted spouse is not a descendant of Child usually decide that Testator did not intend to include Child's spouse in the gift, adoption or not. A court faced with this question could study UPC § 2-705(f) or Restatement (Third) of Property § 14.5(2), which both exclude from class gifts a person adopted before the age of majority, with exceptions for adoptions by stepparents and foster parents.

As we saw in Chapter 2, under a handful of statutes (including UPC § 2-119), adopted-out persons can be heirs of members of their genetic families under certain circumstances. Where such statutes are in force, there also are statutes that create a default rule allowing adopted-out persons to participate in relationship based class gifts in wills and trusts under the same circumstances that would allow them to inherit.

(e) Non-Marital Children

Statutory provisions dealing with the inclusion of non-marital children in class gifts generally mirror provisions for giving such children intestate succession rights. A gift in a woman's will to "my children" will include all of a woman's children (except those adopted out, unless a statutory exception applies). In the will of a man, the gift will include all of the man's children who would be entitled to inherit from him, including his non-marital children whose paternity is established before or after his death.

Because we are dealing with wills and not the default provisions of the intestacy statute, it is possible to draft the will to exclude non-marital children. If a parent wishes to exclude his or her non-marital children, the will could list the children who are to be included in the gift and also include children born after the will is executed.

Just as with adopted persons, there is the question of who takes under a class gift in the will of a testator who is not the parent of the non-marital child. In other words, does a devise to "my descendants by representation" include the non-marital children of descendants from whom those children would be entitled to inherit or to a gift to children in their parents' wills? Just about every state has case law on the subject. We can make two broad generalizations. First, if the will says nothing about the subject, whether non-marital children are included often depends on when the will was executed, just as it does with adopted children. Before time X, non-marital children are not included because society generally considered them not to be related to their parents' relatives; and after time X, they are included because by that time society came to the opposite view. The dates differ from state to state, but the approach is a common one. Second, if the gift is to "lawful descendants" or the gift is limited to class members "born in wedlock," non-marital children do not share in the gift.

(f) Children of Assisted Reproduction

With the exception of the UPC, the existing statutes that deal with children of assisted reproduction address only the question who is the child's parent. There is almost a complete absence of law on whether these children participate in relationship-based class gifts in the wills and trusts of persons other than their parents. Restatement (Third) of Property § 14.8 provides that children of assisted reproduction, even when conceived posthumously, participate in class gifts as children of both parents. The UPC codifies the Restatement rules. Under § 2-705, a child of assisted reproduction is related to all of the parents' relatives and would take in a gift to descendants or children of a named person who is an ancestor of the parents. For example, a gift to "my nieces and nephews" in the will of one of the husband's siblings includes the posthumously conceived child. The only qualification involves the class closing rules, which you'll read more about in the discussion of class gifts of future interests in Chapter 7.

(g) Lapse and Class Gifts

Classifying a gift as a single-generation class gift is of the greatest importance when it comes to dealing with lapse of a gift in a will. No matter which members of the class are alive when the will is written, how many are born before the testator's death, or which ones die during the testator's lifetime, the gift belongs in equal shares to the class members who survive the testator. Surviving the testator might be a question of meeting survival requirements in the will or being presumed to survive by application of the simultaneous death statute. The single-generation class gift, therefore, contains its own adjustment for lapse. And as we've already seen, a multi-generation class gift requires survival to the time of distribution, which for a devise is the testator's death. The only difference from a single-generation gift is that the class members take by representation, as we've seen.

(4) Anti-Lapse Statutes

Lapse is a harsh result or, at least, is seen by state legislatures as something to be avoided. Every state (except Louisiana) has an **anti-lapse statute** that prevents lapse of a gift under certain circumstances. The question, of course, is *what* circumstances, and that's where things get interesting.

Although the anti-lapse statutes of jurisdictions in the United States differ, they do share some characteristics.

- *Anti-lapse statutes are default statutes.* They apply only if the will does not provide otherwise.
- *Anti-lapse statutes, with very few exceptions, apply only to certain devisees.* Usually these are devisees related to the testator, although the definition of who is related varies. The UPC anti-lapse statute, § 2-603, applies to devises to the testator's grandparents and descendants of the grandparents.
- *Once the anti-lapse statute applies to a lapsed devise, the property that is the subject of the devise passes to the issue of the deceased devisee by representation.* If no issue of the devisee survives the testator, the gift will lapse. There are a very few statutes that give the lapsed gift to the estate of the deceased devisee: if the devisee died intestate, the property passes to the heirs; and if the devisee had a valid will, the property will almost certainly pass through the residuary clause since it is highly unlikely that the deceased devisee will make a specific devise of the lapsed gift.
- *Most anti-lapse statutes, including UPC § 2-603, apply to single-generation class gifts as if the gift were to the class members as individuals.* For example: "I give $100,000 to my brother and sisters." When the testator executes the will, she has five living brothers and sisters. One of them predeceases the testator, leaving

Sidebar

CLASS GIFTS, VOID GIFTS, LAPSED GIFTS, AND ANTI-LAPSE STATUTES

The common law makes a distinction between devises that are void because the devisee is dead at the time the will is executed and devises that lapse because the devisee is alive at the time the will is executed but dies before the testator. Restatement (Third) of Property § 5.5 comment a says that the distinction "is of no consequence" in modern law and that an anti-lapse statute should apply to both lapsed and void devises — and UPC § 2-603 does. You should be aware, however, that some anti-lapse statutes do indeed maintain the distinction, often as applied to single-generation class gifts. The reason is a belief that a testator who makes a devise to "my brothers and sisters" knows whether a sibling is living at the time of the execution of the will, and if the testator wanted to make a gift to the issue of a predeceased sibling the testator would do so directly. Therefore the anti-lapse statute does not apply to a sibling who is dead at the time the will is executed.

issue who survive the testator. If the anti-lapse statute applies to class gifts and to gifts to siblings (as it almost certainly does), the $20,000 (1/5 of $100,000) that would have gone to the predeceased sibling is distributed to the sibling's descendants by representation. Note that we're talking about *single-generation* class gifts. Anti-lapse statutes usually don't apply to multigeneration class gifts, although there is surprisingly little authority. If one has to give a reason, it's probably because the idea of representation overwhelms the policy of preventing lapse. In fact, UPC § 2-603 expressly excludes devises to issue, descendants, heirs, next of kin, relatives, family, "or a class described by language of similar import."

The single most important issue that is raised by anti-lapse statutes is caused by their being default statutes. What it takes to override the anti-lapse statute and cause the gift to the deceased devisee to lapse has become a controversial question. Traditionally, an express requirement of survival is enough to prevent application of the anti-lapse statute.

Example 5.14: "I give $10,000 to my sister, Jiao, if she shall survive me."

The addition of "if she shall survive me" to this general devise is still enough in many states to prevent application of an anti-lapse statute that would otherwise apply to a gift to a sibling, and if Jiao does predecease the testator, the $10,000 will become part of the residuary devise.

Sometimes it is not so easy to determine whether words having something to do with survival override an otherwise applicable anti-lapse statute. There are many, many cases, and it's not necessary for us to examine them — if we did, this discussion would go on for the rest of the book. Just remember that this is another one of those questions that can be answered only by careful research in the case law.

One of the most controversial provisions of the UPC deals with the question of what language is necessary to override the anti-lapse statute. UPC § 2-603(b)(3) makes it clear that "words of survivorship" such as "if he survives me" or a devise to "my surviving children" are not sufficient to prevent application of the anti-lapse statute. What is necessary is language or evidence that shows the testator deliberately set out to prevent application of the anti-lapse statute. Language that disposes of the devise if the devisee does not survive the testator or language in the residuary clause that includes in the residuary devise "all failed and lapsed gifts" is sufficient. The necessary evidence could be evidence from outside a will such as a memorandum or letter from the attorney who drafted the will to the testator stating that the survivorship provision was included to defeat the anti-lapse statute.

Sidebar

CONDITIONS OF SURVIVAL AND THE ANTI-LAPSE STATUTE

The UPC's elimination of the traditional rule that an express requirement of survival is sufficient to prevent operation of the anti-lapse statute has proven to be controversial. The UPC approach received a big boost with the decision in *Routolo v. Tietjen*, 890 A.2d 166 (Conn. App. 2006), *aff'd on opinion below*, 916 A.2d 1 (Conn. 2007), which held that an express requirement of survival was not sufficient to override the anti-lapse statute. The court's reasoning was based on the same factors cited by the drafters of the UPC: the remedial nature of the statute and the likelihood that survivorship provisions are included because they appear in widely used forms and not as a result of an informed decision by the testator.

The reason for this provision is twofold. First, the anti-lapse statute is remedial and designed to carry out the testator's presumed intent and therefore should not be defeated without a clear indication that the testator did not want the anti-lapse statute to operate. Second, the drafters of the UPC clearly believe that survivorship language is often included because the attorney drafting the will used a form that included a survivorship provision and never discussed its effect with the testator.

As you can see, figuring out what happens to a devise when the devisee dies before the testator can take a bit of work. We have to think about whether the devise is a single-generation class gift; whether the anti-lapse statute applies; and, if the devise is the residuary devise and there are more than one devisee, whether the no-residue-of-a-residue rule is the law or not. The following flowcharts depict three different scenarios involving a devisee who fails to survive the testator.

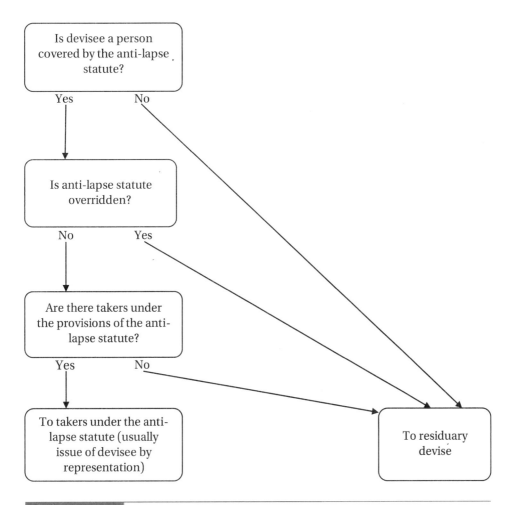

FIGURE 5.1 NON-RESIDUARY DEVISEE FAILS TO SURVIVE

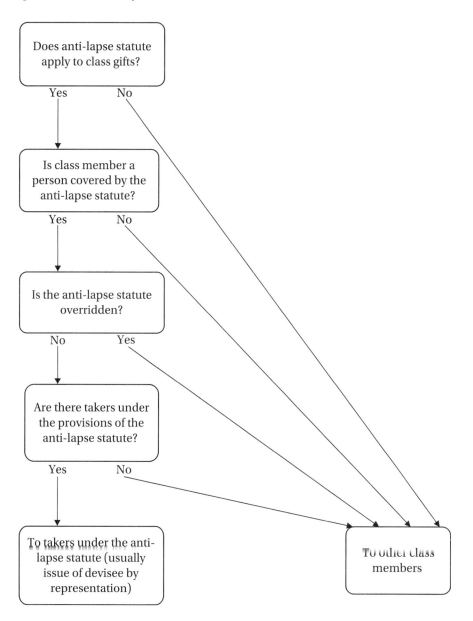

FIGURE 5.2   MEMBER OF SINGLE-GENERATION CLASS GIFT FAILS TO SURVIVE

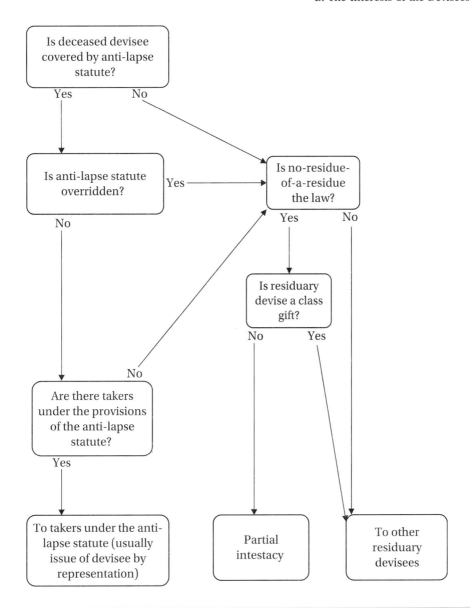

FIGURE 5.3 **ONE OF MULTIPLE RESIDUARY DEVISEES FAILS TO SURVIVE**

(5) Conditional Gifts

(a) True Conditional Wills

Many cases involve wills that contain language that appears to make the will conditional on the happening of some event, usually death from a specified peril or during a particular period of time. The classic is "I am going on a journey and may not return; in case I do not I give . . . ." Courts almost always interpret such language as stating the occasion for making the will and not as creating a true condition, especially if the alternative is intestacy. The always cited case is an opinion by Justice Oliver Wendell Holmes, *Eaton v. Brown*, 193 U.S. 411 (1904).

F   A   Q

Q: How did *Eaton v. Brown* avoid the federal abstention doctrine in probate and end up in the Supreme Court?

A: The decedent in *Eaton* was domiciled in the District of Columbia, which for many years did not have courts of its own and relied instead on the federal courts. The highest court of the District for these purposes was the U.S. Supreme Court.

(b) Other Conditions and Public Policy

Many other types of conditions can attach to gifts in a will. Not surprisingly, then, the limits on what a testator can do are set by public policy. A condition requiring the devisee to do something unlawful certainly would be unenforceable. Requiring the devisee to do something lawful can also be contrary to public policy. The classic example is conditioning a gift on the devisee's divorcing the devisee's spouse. Marriage is regarded as too important to the functioning of society to allow someone to create an economic incentive to end a marriage. Conditions that disrupt family life, such as conditioning the gift on the devisee's not having contact with closely related family members, are also almost certainly invalid.

Some conditions are unenforceable because a court will not deal with them. A requirement that the devisee believe in or "remain true to" a specific religion is unenforceable. If those persons who would take the gift if the condition is not fulfilled bring suit to obtain the property, the court will not examine the devisee's conscience to determine the devisee's religious beliefs, nor will it determine what a particular religion requires someone to believe. On the other hand, conditions involving marrying within a religious faith can be valid if they are properly worded. Those of you who have studied *Shapira v. Union National Bank*[1] know that the condition that the testator's youngest son marry a Jewish woman, "both of whose parents were Jewish," was upheld in part because whether the testator's son married the right woman could be determined objectively — the will's condition was met as long as the bride's parents were married in a Jewish ceremony.[2] On the other hand, if fulfilling the condition required the testator's son to marry a woman who was a "believing" or even "observant" Jew, a court would probably invalidate the condition for the same reasons it would not uphold a condition requiring a devisee to hold specific religious beliefs.

---

[1]315 N.E.2d 825 (Ohio Com. Pleas 1974).
[2]Presumably the parents' *ketubah* (marriage contract) would be sufficient proof of their being Jewish.

C. Contracts and Wills

Contracts and wills do not play together well in either of the arenas in which they usually interact. One involves contracts to make a will. These involve a promise to make a will in favor of the promisee in exchange for the promisee's doing something for the promisor. The classic situation is the young person who moves in with an elderly relative and promises to care for the older person. Older cases often involve the younger person's promise to run the family farm in exchange for a promise by the elderly owner of the farm to make a will giving the farm to the younger person. When death comes to the promisor, however, the will does not make the promised gift and the disappointed promisee sues.

If the contract was valid to begin with, the promisee does have a cause of action, although if the contract was subject to the Statute of Frauds and therefore had to be in writing, the promisee is limited to a quantum meruit recovery on an oral contract. UPC § 2-514 requires a contract to make a will to be in writing, but the comment to the section states that the section does not preclude a recovery in quantum meruit for the value of the services the promisee provided to the testator.

In some circumstances, the promise can never be valid. The most obvious is a promise by one spouse to another to leave some part of the first spouse's probate estate to the second spouse in return for the second spouse's promise to care for the first spouse. The contract fails for lack of consideration because spouses have a legal duty to support each other. On the other hand, such an agreement between unmarried cohabitants can support a recovery in quantum meruit. There are cases barring recovery by a surviving unmarried cohabitant if the consideration for the contract included sexual services. Newer cases tend not to draw that distinction.

The second way contracts and wills interact involves a promise not to revoke a will. A contract not to change a will sometimes was implied when spouses wrote **reciprocal** or **mutual wills** in which each spouse leaves the probate estate to the survivor, and on the death of the survivor the probate estate passes to the same devisee or devisees. The presumption more frequently applied when a married couple made a **joint will**, which is one will executed by both spouses that leaves all of the property to the survivor and on the death of the second to someone; in the second marriage situation, that "someone" is usually the children or descendants of both spouses. Such a will would begin with an exordium that reads something like this:

> We, [name of spouse] and [name of spouse], declare this to be our last will and testament, hereby revoking all wills and codicils heretofore made by us.

Today, however, many jurisdictions have statutes modeled on UPC § 2-514 that require all contracts that have to do with wills to be in writing and signed by the person intending to be bound. The UPC provision also provides that executing joint or mutual wills does not give rise to any presumption of a contract not to revoke.

Q: Why would anyone make a contractual will?

A: The paradigmatic situation involves a married couple who have children from prior marriages. They want the survivor to enjoy all of the property of the deceased spouse, but at the surviving spouse's death they want the survivor's property to pass equally to each spouse's descendants. They therefore agree not to change the reciprocal or joint will after the first spouse's death. Almost all contractual will cases deal with this scenario.

If a person really is bound by a contract not to change an existing will, problems can arise very easily. Can the survivor turn probate property subject to the will into nonprobate property that is not subject to the will? It depends in the first place on the provisions of the contract. A well-drafted agreement will include a promise by the parties not to attempt to frustrate the contract by creating nonprobate property. If the contract does not address the question, a court that is hostile to contracts not to revoke is likely to find that the survivor could indeed create nonprobate property.

Another question that arises with contracts not to revoke is the extent of the survivor's control over the property. Can the surviving testator make gifts during life and thus diminish the value of the property subject to the contractual will? Can the survivor consume the property? A classic situation is the surviving spouse who decides that an extravagant vacation is just what he needs, even though while both spouses were alive they lived frugally. Courts are generally reluctant to police the lifestyle of the surviving testator. When the beneficiaries of the contractual will have gone to court to prevent the surviving testator from spending or making gifts, they have sometimes been turned away because they have no cause of action until the surviving testator dies in breach of the contract. All in all, contracts not to revoke a will cause lots of problems. As we'll see when we study trusts in greater detail, a testator who wishes to control what happens to probate property after the death of the person to whom the property is given should create a trust.

D. Interpretation and Construction

Deciding what the words of a will (or a trust or other documents that make gifts during life or at death) mean traditionally involves two different processes: **interpretation** and **construction**. The first involves finding the intent of the testator by examining the text of the will and extrinsic evidence. The second involves deciding what the testator intended by applying to the words of the document rules that have developed over time. It is also traditional to say that interpretation comes before construction and that construction is resorted to only when interpretation does not work because of a lack of extrinsic evidence or the application of rules that bar the consideration of extrinsic evidence. If only it were that simple. Restatement (Third) of Property § 11.3 comment c argues that interpretation and construction are part of a single process. According to the Restatement, constructional rules have to be considered along with evidence of actual intention—which may be of greater or lesser weight depending on the circumstances. And because extrinsic evidence of intent may itself contain "conflicting elements," constructional rules and preferences may tip the balance one way or the other.

The principal difficulty is that the huge number of cases in which courts have been asked to assign meaning to words in a will cannot be easily categorized and neatly packaged as illustrations of a consistently applied set of principles and rules. Sometimes lawyers for one side in a contested matter are such skilled advocates that they convince a court to apply the rules in ways that are not at all congruent with the precedents. Those cases in turn give birth to a line of authority that can't be reconciled with most of the other existing authority. The entire question is further complicated by the nature of wills and trusts litigation. Often cases about the meaning of the words of a will or trust are not really contested cases. The parties who have interests in the property disposed of by the will or trust have all agreed on what the document should mean and they want a court to confirm that meaning. Why? Well, for many reasons. One involves the hope the Internal Revenue Service will be more likely to accept an interpretation that results in favorable tax treatment if a court has issued a decree confirming that interpretation. Another reason comes up when we're talking about a trust in which minors or incapacitated persons, or even persons not yet born, might be an interest in the trust property. The only way to make the agreed-on meaning binding on these persons is to embody that meaning in a court decree. Of course, the court will not approve an interpretation or a construction of the words of the will just because the parties before the court have agreed on it. If the words are ambiguous and some meaning has to be agreed on, however, a court will almost always pay careful attention to an agreement reached by the parties before the court, so long as the court believes it is fair. The matter will be settled more cheaply and expeditiously than it would if there were an adversarial proceeding.

Finally, and perhaps most importantly, courts often are convinced of the "right" answer; they are certain — or perhaps to put in a more lawyerly way, they have clear and convincing evidence — of the testator's intent. Imagine yourself a judge of a trial court or even of an intermediate appellate court in just that situation. You feel constrained by the existing jurisprudence in your jurisdiction, which talks about all sorts of rules and principles governing the use of extrinsic evidence and also provides a wide range of constructional preferences and rules. Do you strike out into new territory by deciding to heck with the rules and write an opinion that says the will means what we're confident it means? That almost certainly invites an appeal to and perhaps reversal by a higher court. You should be able to understand the attraction of writing an opinion that uses the existing rules to get to the right result, even if your opinion is not completely consistent with some of the existing case law. The result is that it is extremely difficult even in a single jurisdiction to formulate "rules" for the interpretation and construction of wills.

You're entitled to expect more than professorial caution about saying anything that is not either absolutely correct or clearly labeled as a grand new theory explaining everything. So we're going to try to have a discussion of interpretation and construction that will introduce you to the rules and concepts you need to begin to understand your class discussions and the cases you will read, either for class or in the world of practice.

Before we begin our tour of the techniques courts use to find the meaning of the words in a will, you must understand that neither process is supposed to fix mistakes in wills. The testator is presumed to be the author of the will. Even if the lawyer drafting the will makes a mistake in putting what the testator wants into words — getting the name of a devisee wrong or not properly identifying an item of personal property or a piece of real property—the testator is presumed to have read the will, understood it, and, by signing it, made the document the testator's will. As we'll see, however, the "mistakes cannot be fixed rule" is not a rule at all.

The first and most frequently cited "rule" of interpretation and construction is that the purpose of both operations is to find and carry out the testator's intention. That intention, in turn, is supposed to come from the words of the will. The phrase most often used is "the four corners of the will," which simply means from the text of the will itself. This rule is most often applied strictly when the question is the meaning of a word that is a legal term of art. The clearest example is a devise to the testators "heirs." Even though extrinsic evidence—the testimony of the lawyer who drafted the will, statements by the testator to disinterested persons—clearly shows that the testator did not understand the provisions of the intestacy statute, it is quite unlikely that a court will interpret the word to mean anything other than those persons entitled to take the testator's probate estate should the testator die without a will. Another example is a devise to the "children" of a named person. One of the children predeceases the testator, but issue of that child survive the testator. The child is not covered by the applicable anti-lapse statute, so the issue will receive nothing. Even though extrinsic evidence shows that the testator wished to benefit the descendants of the named person, many courts will not go beyond what they consider to be the absolutely clear meaning of the word "children."

Even the strictest ban on extrinsic evidence is often modified by yet another rule that states that the meaning of a will has to be understood as a whole and in light of all the "facts and circumstances" surrounding its drafting. For example, the will makes a devise to "my nieces and nephews." If the testator is survived by children of the testator's siblings, it will be difficult for the children of the testator's spouse's siblings to argue that they should be included in the gift. Like "children," "nieces and nephews" has a fixed meaning. If, however, the testator was an only child, that circumstance coupled with evidence that the testator referred to the children of the testator's spouse's siblings as "my nieces and nephews" would probably be enough to give the devise to the children of the testator's brothers- and sisters-in-law.

A court examining the meaning of "nieces and nephews" might also approach the question by asking if the will is "ambiguous." If the answer is yes, then the court is able to use extrinsic evidence at least of the fact and circumstances kind. Of course, deciding whether there is an ambiguity in the first place often requires the use of extrinsic evidence. How else is the court to learn that the testator was an only child and has no nieces and nephews related by blood or adoption into the testator's extended family? You can find a number of appellate cases, sometimes from the highest court of the jurisdiction, clearly holding that extrinsic evidence may be used to determine if the will is ambiguous.

Many courts, however, make the admissibility of extrinsic evidence depend on the type of ambiguity. The traditional rule is that extrinsic evidence can be used to explain a **latent ambiguity** but not a **patent ambiguity**. An example of a latent ambiguity is the "nieces and nephews" example from the previous paragraph. The words of the will make perfect sense; they are problematic only when we know that the testator was an only child.

A patent ambiguity exists when the words of the will don't make sense. A classic example is a residuary clause that gives "25 percent of my estate to the following:" and then lists only three devisees. A court tied to the traditional rules would say that the remaining 25 percent passes in a partial intestacy to the testator's heirs. Why? Because a court cannot add words to a will. At least that's the traditional rule. Courts less tied to these older views would probably be willing to admit extrinsic evidence of what the testator intended to do with that remaining 25 percent.

Even courts whose cases repeat the most rigid rules excluding extrinsic evidence almost certainly agree with some out-and-out exceptions to those rules. These exceptions have the sanction of tradition, but they are exceptions none the less, and their long history only shows that the rigid ban on extrinsic evidence has never really been that absolute. One of these exceptions is old enough to be expressed as a "maxim" of the law, in Latin no less: *falsa demonstratio non nocet*; or a mere erroneous description does not void the gift. A famous example involves a devise of a house and the land on which it stands described by the street address. However, the house number is wrong—the testator owned property on the named street but the house number was not that stated in the will. The court held that the "mere errone-ous description" did not undo the gift. The erroneous house number is ignored. The devise now refers to the property on the named street, which is sufficient to make a gift of the house and land at the proper street address.

This result is of course "impossible" under traditional law. The will is being rewritten! A mistake is being fixed by using extrinsic evidence! Now it's perfectly clear that the erroneous street address could be classified as a latent ambiguity that could be resolved by acceptable extrinsic evidence. That discussion, however, would involve the court in a more searching discussion of the use of extrinsic evidence. The court would be dealing with something more controversial than the "straightforward" application of a long-standing maxim. Indeed, resting a decision on a "rule" that is supposedly as ancient as the ban on fixing mistakes in wills allows the court to avoid talking about mistakes at all.

Our house number example illustrates another "rule." It is often said by com-mentators and courts that excluding words from a will is more acceptable than adding words to a will. Excluding the incorrect house number is considered to involve less tam-pering with the text than adding something the testator left out. This is a perfect example of how nonsensical this discussion can be. Okay, we excise the incorrect house number and decide we're only going to look at the street name, and lo and behold we decide that the will must be referring to the house that the testator owned on that particular street. Is this different from "adding" the correct house number to the will? The traditional answer is an enthusiastic yes, although that is not really a sensible answer. Whether the court is adding or subtracting lan-guage from the will, it is fixing a mistake no matter what the traditional rule says.

A similarly ancient "rule" is the "personal usage exception" to the consideration of extrinsic evidence. Let's say that testator's will makes a devise to "Harry Hackwood." There is a person named Harry Hackwood who claims to be enti-tled to the devise, even though he never knew the testator. Extrinsic evidence, however, shows that the testator had a friend named Harold

> ### S i d e b a r
>
> **EXTRINSIC EVIDENCE AND DEAD-MAN'S STATUTES**
>
> There is a distinction between what sort of extrinsic evidence can be considered and what might be actually admissible. Some states have statutes that prevent the admission of testi-mony about a transaction between the dece-dent and a witness in an action against the estate of the decedent. Known as dead-man's statutes, these provisions vary widely in their details, but in some instances they can greatly complicate the admission of testimony about the testator's statements of intent. Dead-man's statutes are rules of competency and do not supplant other rules such as those dealing with hearsay and the attorney-client privilege. Restatement (Third) of Property § 10.2 comment *h* says that "to the extent appropriate" all of these rules should be construed to allow direct evidence of the testator's intention.

Hackwood whom the testator referred to as "Harry." A court would almost certainly decide that the will referred to Harold because the testator referred to him as Harry, and because, of course, Harold had a connection to the testator and the person actually named Harry did not. Again, the court is fixing a mistake in the will by substituting the correct name of the devisee. And once again, the shelter of a long-established "exception" means the court does not have to face up to what it is actually doing.

RESTATEMENT (THIRD) OF PROPERTY AND INTERPRETATION AND CONSTRUCTION

The Restatement's discussion of what it calls a single process of construction does not honor much of the traditional learning. For example, comment *a* to § 11.1 states that "no legal consequences attach to the distinction" between latent and patent ambiguities, even though many courts still repeat the "rule" that extrinsic evidence cannot be used to resolve a patent ambiguity. The goal of the Restatement is to resolve ambiguities in accord with the testator's intent, and to that end the comments to § 11.2 draw on extrinsic evidence to resolve all sorts of ambiguities. Similarly, § 11.3(c) states that the most basic constructional preference is for a meaning "in accord with common intention."

The other part of determining the meaning of the words in a will, construction, is just as tangled a mess. Remember that construction is limited to examining the words of the will without the use of extrinsic evidence. Different authorities recognize varying lists of rules of construction, some of which we should actually describe as techniques. One of the most common is to read problematic words in the will in the context of the entire will. If the question is whether a devise is actually a class gift, an answer of no is supported by other language in the will that unquestionably creates a class gift. The reasoning is that the testator knew how to create a class gift, so the testator could not have intended to create a class gift by using ambiguous language.

We could multiply examples for pages, but it would not be much use. You should be able to identify the use of constructional rules and preferences in opinions. Just keep in mind that they can be manipulated as easily as the "ban" on extrinsic evidence.

E. Reformation

Unlike interpretation and construction, **reformation** of a document changes its provisions to make them say what the creator of the document intended them to say. While courts have long been willing to reform lifetime documents like contracts and deeds (and including lifetime donative documents like trusts created by living persons and deeds made without consideration from the grantee), they have been completely unwilling to change the provisions of wills (and that includes the terms of trusts created in wills). Remember that interpretation and construction are not supposed to change the provisions of a will even to make them conform to the testator's intent, although that can be, and some would say often is, the result.

Given its emphasis on carrying out the testator's intent, you should not be surprised that Restatement (Third) of Property § 12.1 states that a "donative document" including a will can be reformed even if it is unambiguous, so long as two elements are established by clear and convincing evidence. The first is that "specific terms" of the document were affected by "a mistake of fact or law." The second is the donor's (testator's) intention. When it comes to deciding whether these elements have been established by the required clear and convincing evidence, the decision maker (usually a court, of course) may consider "direct evidence of intention contradicting the plain meaning of the text" as well as other evidence. (This provision of the Restatement is codified in UPC § 2-805.)

The reformation remedy would apply to many of the situations we've already discussed. Incorrect identification of a person or property is likely a mistake of fact and can be corrected without worrying about what sort of ambiguity exists, so long as the evidence is clear and convincing. Misuse of legal terms can also be fixed. Remember our example of a devise to the testator's "heirs." Under traditional law, the subject of the devise will go to those who would take the testator's property had the testator died in intestate, no matter what evidence shows that the testator was mistaken as to the identity of the "heirs." Under the reformation doctrine, so long as there is clear and convincing evidence of the testator's intent—for example, an affidavit from the lawyer who drafted the will stating the testator's idea of who the heirs would be—a court can reform the language of the document to give the devise to the devisees the testator intended.

The Restatement and UPC concept of reformation involves sweeping away lots of distinctions and rules that have been around for a very long time and that are supposed to protect the almost sacred words of a properly executed will. Courts that have squarely faced the question of adopting the Restatement's idea of reformation often decline because of the possibility of allowing all sorts of challenges to wills based on assertions of what the testator "really" wanted. In addition, at least one state high court has flatly rejected the idea that the clear and convincing evidence standard would prevent such problems.[3] But that's only one court. Other courts may look at the problem differently, and of course the incorporation of the reformation and modification principles into the UPC means that legislatures may be faced with the question of changing existing law before the courts address the question. Stay tuned.

SUMMARY

- Four types of gifts ("devises" under the UPC) can be made in a will: specific, general, residuary, and demonstrative. The type of gift is important when there are changes in the testator's probate property after execution of the will.

- If property that is the subject of a specific devise is not in the probate estate at the testator's death, the gift adeems (or fails). There are very limited exceptions to that rule, but the UPC does expand those exceptions.

- The type of devise also determines in what order probate property is used to pay the testator's debts and expenses. Default statutes order liability for the payment of debts and expenses: first from the residuary devise, then from the general devises, then from the specific devises. If the property from which a demonstrative devise is to be paid has not adeemed, the devise is treated like a specific devise; otherwise it is treated like a general devise.

- If a beneficiary fails to survive the testator, the beneficiary's devise lapses (or fails). All states (except Louisiana) have default statutes that prevent lapse in some cases, usually only involving certain relatives of the testator.

---

[3]Flannery v. McNamara, 738 N.E.2d 739 (Mass. 2000).

■ Class gifts are gifts to a group identified by a group characteristic. A multigeneration class gift is distributed by representation, and a single-generation class gift is distributed to the class members who survive the testator. Anti-lapse statutes usually apply to a single-generation class gift as if it consisted of a gift to each class member. If the will is silent, determining who is a child for purposes of a class gift is often done by applying the same rules that apply in intestacy.

■ Conditional wills govern the disposition of the testator's probate estate only if a certain event comes to pass. While properly structured conditions are usually valid, the law may be changing.

■ Contracts to make a will are difficult to enforce, but the disappointed promisee sometimes can recover on a quantum meruit basis from the decedent's estate.

■ Contracts not to revoke a will are fraught with problems. While contracts not to revoke a will were often implied from the terms of joint, mutual, or reciprocal wills, modern statutes require a signed writing to establish the contract.

■ The law governing the construction and interpretation of wills is changing to allow the use of extrinsic evidence of the testator's intent and to allow courts to modify or even reform wills to make them accomplish the testator's intent more closely.

CONNECTIONS

Lapse and Nonprobate Property
Chapter 6 discusses how the law governing nonprobate property deals with the analogue to lapse. Only the UPC deals with the problem in a systematic way by creating an anti-lapse statute applicable to designations of beneficiaries of nonprobate property.

Class Gifts and Future Interests
The rules applicable to class gifts in wills are relevant to class gifts of future interests, discussed in Chapter 7. The rules governing the inclusion of adopted and non-marital children in a class defined by family relationships is usually governed by the law in effect at the time the trust creating the future interests was itself created.

Interpretation and Construction and Trusts and Future Interests
The law of the construction and interpretation of trusts and future interests (which are usually created in trusts) are discussed in Chapters 7 and 8. The basic concepts as well as the current trends are the same as those discussed in this chapter. There are some differences, however, and there are generally accepted rules that apply only to future interests.

Nonprobate Property Other than Revocable Trusts

Will substitutes try to do what only a will can do — make a gift at death of property that the decedent retains absolute ownership over during life. Until relatively recently, "try" was usually the best will substitutes could do; the law considered most of them invalid. Today, however, contractual will substitutes have a new spring in their step. Case and statutory law are validating more and more of them. The law governing contractual will substitutes is not as settled as the law governing wills, however, and although the UPC creates a comprehensive law of contractual will substitutes, not every jurisdiction has adopted these or similar rules. Not yet, anyways. Looking ahead, the question looms: might will substitutes create a world in which wills become superfluous?

O V E R V I E W

A. The Invalid Will Substitute

The only way to make a gift at death of probate property is by creating a document that conforms to the requirements of the Statute of Wills (remember "Statute of Wills" is simply shorthand for whatever the relevant jurisdiction requires to make a valid will). A less technical way to put that thought is to say that if I want to determine where the property I own solely in my own name goes when I die, I have to write a valid will. If you attempt to do the same thing by using a document or some arrangement that is not a will, all you end up doing is creating an **invalid will substitute**.

The traditional dividing line between an invalid will substitute and an arrangement other than a will that does indeed govern where my property goes when I die is whether the intended beneficiary receives some sort of interest while I am alive. Here's an example from the basic property law course. I own Blackacre and I want Darling to own it when I die. I can do a deed conveying Blackacre to Darling, reserving a life estate to myself. I go on living on Blackacre or using the land in some other way until I die, at which time Darling owns Blackacre in fee simple absolute. Why is this not an invalid will substitute? At the time of the deed, Darling does indeed receive an interest in the property, the remainder; Darling receives an interest in the property while I'm alive, even though it is a future interest and Darling has no present right to Blackacre. If, however, I executed a deed that purported to give Blackacre to Darling on my death, I have created an invalid will substitute. Darling takes nothing until I die. The only way to do that is by creating a valid will (at least in states that do not have statutes making such deeds valid).

Let's look at this invalid will substitute thing another way. The dividing line between an invalid will substitute and a valid arrangement disposing of my property at my death is whether the intended beneficiary receives some interest while I am alive. That means that the only way I can retain complete control of my property and still decide where it goes at my death is to create a valid will. At least that was the law for a very long time. Beginning in the mid-nineteenth century, the rigid approach to invalid will substitutes began to change until, by the beginning of the twenty-first century, a wide array of once invalid methods for transmitting property at death while keeping complete control of it while alive worked just fine. There are, however, several valid will substitutes that have always worked to transfer property on death in addition to the legal life estate and remainder. These will substitutes all involve some form of joint ownership. We'll talk about those first, and then deal with the modern will substitutes based on contract concepts.

B. Jointly Held Property

A will substitute you no doubt encountered in your property class is the joint tenancy with right of survivorship in real property. Two or more persons can jointly own real property. When one joint tenant dies, his interest simply vanishes, and the surviving joint tenant or tenants continue to own the property. If there were only two joint tenants to begin with, the survivor is now the sole owner of the property in fee simple absolute. Spouses or unmarried partners often hold their home as joint tenants with right of survivorship, no matter who provided how much of the purchase price or in what proportions they make payments on any mortgage. In this arrangement, the survivor of the couple is the sole owner of the home. The jointly held property, remember, is not probate property, does not pass in intestacy, and cannot be disposed of in the decedent's will.

F   A   Q

Q: What distinguishes joint tenancies, tenancies in common, and tenancies by the entirety?

A: Joint tenancies with right of survivorship always create nonprobate property. The interests of tenants in common, however, are always probate property. If A and B own Blackacre as tenants in common, their undivided half interests are part of their respective probate estates. Tenancies by the entirety exist only between married couples and are also nonprobate property. The surviving spouse is the sole owner of the property. A tenancy by the entirety cannot be unilaterally severed and ends only on the death of one spouse or the dissolution of the marriage.

What makes the joint tenancy with right of survivorship a not quite perfect will substitute is the ability of either joint tenant to sever the joint tenancy and turn the arrangement into a tenancy in common, under which each owner's interest is that person's probate property. If I own Blackacre and want Darling to own it when I die, I could execute a deed making myself and Darling joint tenants with right of survivorship in Blackacre. (In some states, I might have to execute a deed to a straw, who then would execute the deed to me and Darling.) If I die first, Darling will be the sole owner of Blackacre, as I wished. But once the deed is effective, Darling is the owner of an undivided one-half of Blackacre. Darling can then sever the joint tenancy, meaning that if I die first Darling will not be sole owner of Blackacre, but if Darling dies first, one-half of Blackacre will be part of Darling's probate estate and pass in intestacy or under Darling's will. The price of using the joint tenancy with right of survivorship as a will substitute is my loss of total control over Blackacre.

Joint and survivor bank accounts are similar jointly held property arrangements with rights of survivorship that create nonprobate property. On the death of one joint account holder, the survivor is the sole owner of account. While both the account holders are alive, the bank will honor

Sidebar

TENANCY BY THE ENTIRETY

Tenancy by the entirety exists only between a married couple. In some states, a married couple can hold only real property in a tenancy by the entirety; other states allow tenancy in the entirety to include personal property. Like the surviving joint tenant of a two-person joint tenancy with right of survivorship, the surviving tenant by the entirety has absolute ownership of the property. Unlike a joint tenant, however, a tenant by the entirety cannot unilaterally sever the tenancy. Joint tenants own undivided shares of the property; tenants by the entirety have a shared undivided interest in the whole. The tenancy by the entirety ends when the marriage does, by death or dissolution. In most states, and under UPC § 2-804(b)(2), the default rule is that a tenancy by the entirety becomes a tenancy in common on divorce.

Another reason to hold property by the entirety has to do with protection from creditors' claims. Depending on the jurisdiction, property held in tenancy by the entirety is more or less unavailable to the creditors of one spouse. The degree of protection varies, however.

checks signed by either one, even if one of them contributed none of the funds in the account. In most states, however, the holders own the funds in the account in proportion to their contributions. That means if A and B are joint holders of a bank account but A contributed all of the money in the account, B can indeed write checks on the account but A is entitled to recover the funds. That's how UPC § 6-211 deals with jointly held accounts. The UPC does not deal with *how* A can recover the funds, leaving that, in the words of the comment to § 6-211, to "general law."

Brokerage accounts holding investments in stocks, bonds, and other financial instruments can also be held jointly with right of survivorship, so long as the brokerage firm will allow such an arrangement. Similarly, stock certificates can be held jointly with right of survivorship if the corporation will recognize such a registration of the shares. All of these arrangements are effective to create nonprobate property, but like jointly held bank accounts, even if the parties own the property in proportion to their contributions while they are alive, either party can get their hands on the property and the other may or may not be able to do anything about it, depending on the "general law."

F   A   Q

Q: Is a joint and survivor bank account a "joint tenancy"?

A: Almost never. "Joint tenancy" means that the tenants have undivided (traditionally equal) interests in the property and can sever the tenancy and create a tenancy in common; their ownership interest is a **moiety**. The ownership interest of the joint holders of a joint and survivor bank account (or other joint account like a brokerage account) is almost always defined by their contributions to the account. "Almost" because in New York, at least, joint accounts are joint tenancies and the account holders own undivided equal interests.

F   A   Q

Q: What sort of "general law" might prevent one joint holder of an account from recovering withdrawals by another holder that exceed that holder's proportionate share?

A: Possibilities include the running of a statute of limitation on the claim and laches preventing the pursuing of a claim in equity. Especially if the claim is made by the guardian of the contributing joint holder or the personal representative of the contributing joint holder's estate some time after the withdrawal was made, a court could find that the contributing joint holder ratified the noncontributing joint holder's actions by not doing anything after learning of the disproportionate withdrawal.

Because any joint holder of an account can take the property out of the account, even if that person never deposited anything into the account, a joint account is far from being a perfect substitute for a will. Just as with a joint tenancy in real property, the price of avoiding probate is giving the intended recipient of the gift at death access to the property while the owner is alive.

C. Contract-Based Will Substitutes

As we've seen, to be a true substitute for a will, an arrangement creating nonprobate property should leave the owner of the property in total control of the property during life and give the intended recipient of property nothing until the death of the owner. We've also seen that such an arrangement fits the definition of an invalid will substitute because it indeed tries to do what a will does without the formalities of a will.

In spite of the traditional law, many such arrangements are perfectly valid today. These arrangements are recognized as valid contracts between the property owner and a party who in one way or another has custody or control of the property. The contract specifies to whom the non-owning party will deliver the property on the owner's death. The owner can change the contract at any time (so long as the owner has the necessary capacity), and the beneficiary specified in the contract has absolutely no interest in the property subject to the contract until the owner dies. Then the other party to the contract is bound to deliver the property to the beneficiary, once the beneficiary presents the owner's death certificate and properly indentifies herself as the named beneficiary.

> **Sidebar**
>
> **CONVENIENCE ACCOUNTS**
>
> Let's say you become too ill to manage your checking account and pay your bills. You'd like someone besides you to be able to sign checks. When you go with that someone else to the bank to make arrangements, the odds are the bank will offer you a joint and survivor account, which means that if you die first the other person ends up with the money in the account, even though you didn't mean to make a gift at death to that person. All is not lost if your estate can show that you intended instead to create a **convenience account** on which the other person could draw checks solely to pay your bills and expenses. A great deal of litigation concerns whether a joint account is actually a convenience account, all of which could be avoided if the bank had counseled you to give your friend a power of attorney (Chapter 14), which would allow the other person to sign checks without giving that person any interest at all in the account.

The paradigmatic contractual will substitute is the life insurance contract. The insured is almost always the owner of the contract and designates the beneficiary. The owner can change the beneficiary designation, and a designated beneficiary has no interest in the contract or the insurance proceeds until the insured's death. The proceeds are not probate property, and the insured's will has no effect on them, unless, of course, the insured's estate is the designated beneficiary, in which case the proceeds will be paid over to the executor or administrator.

An annuity contract is similar to a life insurance contract. (Note that "annuity" refers to any fixed sum paid at a regular interval.) In return for the payment of premiums (sometimes a lump-sum payment), the company that sells the annuity (almost always an insurance company) guarantees the beneficiary a fixed amount paid at stated intervals — monthly, quarterly, or yearly, for example — sometimes for life, sometimes for a fixed number of years. The person paying the premiums may be the beneficiary or that person may designate someone else as beneficiary of all of the periodic payments or of any portion remaining unpaid at the first beneficiary's death. Either way the arrangement is a contractual will substitute if the beneficiary receives something after the death of the owner of the annuity contract.

A very common contractual will substitute, and one of the oldest, is a **payable-on-death (POD)** bank account, often called a **Totten trust** after *Matter of Totten*,[1] the

---

[1] 71 N.E. 748 (N.Y. 1904).

New York Court of Appeals case that validated the arrangement as a "tentative trust." The ins and outs of the opinion and the peculiarities of New York law are not relevant to our discussion. The important thing is that the validity of these accounts was accepted in other states both by court decision and legislation, and today they are very common. The UPC validates them as a POD account in §§ 6-201(8) and 6-203.

A much newer but important statutory will substitute is **transfer on death** (**TOD**) security registration. Forty-eight states and the District of Columbia have adopted the Uniform TOD Securities Registration Act, which has also been incorporated into the UPC (§§ 6-301 to 6-311). Under the act, a share certificate "or other interest in property, or in an obligation of an enterprise or other issuer" and a security account can be registered in the name of its owner with a designation of a beneficiary to take the property at the owner's death. Under the act, any brokerage account, no matter how great its value, can be turned into nonprobate property by registration in TOD form. The extent to which contract ideas have taken over the making of a gift at death is made clear by a provision in the act that states that "a registration governed by the law of a jurisdiction in which this or similar legislation is not in force or was not in force when a registration in beneficiary form was made is nevertheless presumed to be valid and authorized as a matter of contract law" (UPC § 6-303).

All sorts of retirement savings arrangements make up another group of common valid will substitutes. Individual retirement accounts (IRAs) (which come in several different varieties), Keogh plans, and other types of deferred compensation arrangements allow employees to save a portion of their wages, which is not subject to federal income tax (or to state income tax in some states). The money saved is invested, and the earnings are not subject to income tax until it is withdrawn (although withdrawals from one variety of IRA are not subject to income tax). The owner of the account can name a beneficiary who will own the account should the owner die before beginning to withdraw the accumulation or if anything is left in the account if the owner dies while gradually withdrawing the money. These accounts are creatures of the federal tax system and are governed by the Internal Revenue Code. They hold large amounts of wealth and represent a truly enormous amount of nonprobate property. We'll deal with these tax-favored saving devices in greater detail at the end of this chapter. For now we can simply add them to the list of contractually based will substitutes.

Other sorts of contractually based will substitutes have been validated by court decisions and by statutes. The UPC even has a provision, § 6-101, that validates as a proper will substitute "a provision for a nonprobate transfer on death" in a long list of arrangements, including bonds, mortgages, promissory notes, conveyances, deeds of gifts, or "other written instrument[s] of a similar nature." Once this provision is enacted in a state, you are perfectly justified in asking "What's left?" for the poor old will.

There is another will substitute whose validity is quite recent. For generations, one of the classic invalid will substitutes has been a deed that purports to take effect only on the death of the grantor. No interest passes to the grantee under this grantor's death; the deed is not a will, so Q.E.D.—invalid will substitute. Despite the number of cases involving this sort of deed, its status as an invalid will substitute did not prevent attempts to use it to pass property at death. Finally, states began to make these deeds valid by legislation. At least eight states have such statutes, and in 2009 the Uniform Law Commission approved the Uniform Real Property Transfer on Death Act. Under the act, a TOD deed is a valid will substitute. It must be recorded before the death of the transferor, but it is revocable until death and need not be delivered to the beneficiary during the transferor's life. The act has been incorporated into the UPC as §§ 6-401 to 6-417.

We can add to the table of probate property from Chapter 1 and show what kinds of arrangements can turn these classic forms of probate property into nonprobate property. In Table 6-1, the types of nonprobate property in *italics* are "imperfect" will substitutes; while validly passing the property on death, any parties to the arrangement other than the property owner who created it can have access to the property while the original owner is alive.

TABLE 6.1	Changing Probate Property into Nonprobate Property	
Property	**What the Decedent Cannot Do**	**Will Substitute**
Checking account	Sign a check	*Joint account* or POD account
Savings account	Sign a withdrawal slip	*Joint account* or POD account
Stock certificate	Sign a stock power	*Jointly held* or TOD registration
Brokerage account	Give instructions to a broker	*Joint account* or TOD account
Motor vehicle	Sign the certificate of transfer	None
Real estate	Sign a deed	*Joint tenancy, tenancy by the entirety*, or TOD deed (UPC and 7 states)

D. Problems of Coordination with Wills Rules

Even though so many will substitutes "work" to get property to beneficiaries outside of the probate system, the relative newness of these devices means that there is some uncertainty about how they work in situations that the law of wills has addressed for a long time.

(1) Capacity and Protection against Wrongdoing

There appear to be few cases that deal with the level of capacity needed to create a valid will substitute. Restatement (Third) of Property § 8.1 comment e says that the standard for capacity to make a revocable will substitute is the same as that needed to make a valid will. In other words, so long as the designation of the beneficiary of a POD bank account or TOD securities account, a life insurance policy, or an annuity contract can be changed by the owner of the account or policy, the designation is valid if the owner understands the nature and extent of her property, who the natural objects of her bounty are, how the disposition is being made, how these elements relate, and is capable of forming an "orderly desire regarding the disposition of the property."

The use of the will standard is completely sensible. Making a revocable beneficiary designation has exactly the same effect as making a will. The beneficiary is entitled to nothing while the owner lives, and the owner's own resources are not diminished. Of course, making an irrevocable gift requires a higher standard of capacity because, as comment d to Restatement (Third) § 8.1 says, making an irrevocable gift depletes the financial resources of the person making the gift (the donor); therefore the donor must not only have the mental capacity necessary to make a will but also "be capable of understanding the effect that the gift may have on the future financial security of the donor and or anyone who may be dependent on the donor."

Undue influence, duress, or fraud invalidates an otherwise valid will substitute, just as it does a will. (Restatement (Third) of Property § 7.2 cmt. f.) The cases are few, but that probably only reflects the relatively recent widespread use of most contractual will substitutes.

(2) Death of the Beneficiary before Distribution

We know that if a devisee under a will dies before the testator, the gift lapses unless an anti-lapse statute prevents that outcome. In addition, the lapse of a part of the residuary devise implicates the no-residue-of-a-residue rule, which in most states has itself been undone by court decision or statute. We also know that the death of a joint tenant, a tenant by the entirety, or the joint holder of a joint account with survivorship provisions simply triggers the survivorship provision, and the survivor or survivors now own the property.

The law governing contractual will substitutes under which the designated beneficiary has no interest until the death of the owner of the property is not as well developed. General contract law principles generally provide that the interest of a third-party beneficiary of a contract passes through the beneficiary's estate if the beneficiary dies before the completion of the contract. That result can be altered by the contract. Most life insurance contracts provide that the designated beneficiary will receive the proceeds on the death of the insured only if the beneficiary is living at the insured's death. The contracts also allow the owner of the policy (remember, usually that's the insured) to name a contingent beneficiary to take the proceeds should the primary beneficiary not survive the insured. If there is no beneficiary who survives the insured, the proceeds are paid to the owner of the policy. If the insured was the owner, the proceeds are paid to the owner's estate.

Statutory provisions validating contractual will substitutes often include provisions dealing with the death of the beneficiary before the death of the owner. The Uniform TOD Securities Act provides that if at the death of the owner no beneficiary is living, the securities belong to the estate of the deceased owner. (UPC § 6-307.) If there are no surviving beneficiaries of a POD account, the UPC says the sums on deposit in the account belong to the estate of the deceased account owner. (§ 6-212(b)(2).) These provisions, and others like them, turn what was nonprobate property into probate property governed by the owner's will (or by the intestacy statute as applied to the decedent's probate estate).

In order to prevent that result, which is presumably not what the property owner intended, the UPC includes a comprehensive anti-lapse statute for contractual will substitutes, UPC § 2-706. Like the UPC anti-lapse statute applicable to wills (§ 2-603), § 2-706 applies to beneficiaries who are grandparents or descendants of grandparents or stepchildren of the deceased owner of the property. If the beneficiary does not survive the owner of the property by 120 hours, the beneficiary's issue take by representation the property to which the beneficiary would have been entitled. Also, like the testamentary anti-lapse statute, § 2-706 is a default statute and the inclusion of a simple requirement of survival as part of the beneficiary designation is not sufficient indication of an intent to override the statute.

Unless it has adopted UPC § 2-706, it is unlikely that a state will have an anti-lapse statute generally applicable to contractual will substitutes.

(3) Revocation

We spent a lot of time in Chapter 3 exploring the ways in which a will can be revoked. Revocation of nonprobate property arrangements depends on what sort of arrangement we're talking about. Revocation of joint property arrangements with right of survivorship involves ending the joint arrangement either by unilateral severance (joint tenancies), withdrawal of one's proportionate share of a joint account, or, in the case of a tenancy by the entirety, by jointly making a deed to a straw who then conveys the property back to the married couple in some other form of ownership. Contractual will substitutes can be ended by the property owner, of course. The owner of a life insurance policy (who is usually the insured) can freely change beneficiaries. The owner of a brokerage account with a TOD designation can change the beneficiary designation or withdraw the assets from the account and start over.

All of these methods are the equivalent of revoking a will by writing a new will or revoking it by physical act, although tearing up a life insurance policy or an agreement establishing a joint account will not "revoke" the policy or the account agreement. Because a contractual will substitute involves a third party — the insurance company, the brokerage firm, the bank — the property owner's destruction of the paper recording the contract does not mean that the contract is revoked. The paper recording the agreement is not the contract itself in the way a properly executed will is the embodiment of the testator's intent. Nor will tearing, burning, canceling, or obliterating a deed creating a joint tenancy or tenancy by the entirety destroy the tenancy.

There are, however, parallels between the revocation of wills and the revocation of contractual will substitutes. We'll deal with revocation by operation of law and revocation by a provision in the property owner's will.

(a) By Operation of Law

Back in Chapter 3 we mentioned statutes that revoke wills or parts of wills when the testator marries or has children whether by birth or adoption. We'll discuss those statutes in detail in Chapter 13. We can say now, however, that the UPC versions of these provisions (§§ 2-301 (spouses) and 2-302 (children)) are limited to wills and do not apply to contractual will substitutes, which is most likely to be true of non-UPC statutes as well.

The dissolution of a marriage will revoke will provisions for the ex-spouse (and, under UPC § 2-804, will provisions for the ex-spouse's family). While the UPC revocation on divorce provision applies to a wide variety of contractual will substitutes and to revocable trusts as well, some states with statutes not based on the UPC often lack statutory provisions addressing the effect of divorce on will substitutes. Those states may have decisional law, however, revoking beneficiary designations of an ex-spouse (but rarely those of the ex-spouse's family members) at least for some contractual will substitutes.

The same goes for the slayer's rule. The UPC provision, § 2-803, applies to any provision for the slayer in any sort of contractual will substitute. Once again, states that have not adopted UPC § 2-803 may not have as comprehensive a statutory scheme, but even if there is no applicable statute, a court would certainly prevent the slayer from profiting from the crime no matter how the slayer might otherwise benefit.

(b) By a Provision in the Property Owner's Will

Can the owner of property subject to a will substitute revoke the arrangement or change the beneficiary by a provision in the owner's will? The short answer is that it depends what kind of will substitute we're talking about. A will cannot change a deed that has created a joint tenancy with right of survivorship or a tenancy by the entirety because the decedent's interest vanishes at the moment of death.

It would be highly unusual for an agreement creating a contractual will substitute to allow the will of the owner to modify the agreement. Restatement (Third) of Property § 7.2 comment e says that institutions holding property subject to contractual will substitutes should respect the intent of the owner of the property and enforce a change of beneficiary made by will if the institution has not distributed the property, but few judicial decisions have upheld a change of beneficiary by a provision in the property owner's will. In fact, there are many decisions in which courts have refused to give effect to attempts to change a beneficiary designation in a will, especially when the will substitute involved is a life insurance policy. The reason given is the need for the insurance company to rely on the beneficiary designation on its records so that payment can be made quickly and cheaply without worrying about a later claim from the beneficiary named in the will.

In spite of this general reluctance to give judicial sanction to testamentary attempts to change beneficiaries, there are cases that give effect to will provisions that revoke or change the beneficiaries of POD bank accounts. Some states have statutes validating such changes in POD accounts and other contractual will substitutes like TOD security accounts. The statutes almost uniformly require that the will expressly refer to a specific account in order to effect the change.

(4) Rights of Creditors

The rights of a decedent's creditors are clearly spelled out in the law of wills. The decedent's probate estate is liable for the decedent's debts, the rules of abatement govern how the devisees under the will bear the burden of paying those debts, and the probate system establishes how and when creditors must make their claims. The law that applies to contractual will substitutes, however, is not nearly as clear about the rights of creditors.

Some things can be said with certainty. Proceeds of life insurance on the decedent's life are not subject to the decedent's creditors unless the beneficiary is the estate of the deceased insured. POD accounts are usually subject to the debts of the depositor of the funds. As we'll see in the next section, retirement savings are not subject to the debts of the owner. Property held in TOD form (securities and brokerage accounts) are liable for the debts of the deceased owner under § 9(b) of the Uniform TOD Securities Act.

The UPC has a comprehensive scheme for dealing with claims against the decedent's estate and nonprobate property, including contractual will substitutes. Section 6-102 makes property subject to arrangements that result in valid transfers at death liable for the debts of the decedent's estate so long as the decedent could have revoked the arrangement and used the property for her own benefit and so long as no statutes provide otherwise. This last provision preserves the exemption for proceeds of insurance on the decedent's life and the exemption of retirement savings, which we'll discuss in a bit. In addition, the nonprobate property is liable only to the extent the probate property is insufficient.

Sidebar

THE UPC AND CREDITORS' CLAIMS AGAINST WILL SUBSTITUTES

UPC § 6-102 sets forth procedures for implementing its provisions, which parallel the abatement rules. The section also gives a creditor the right to start a proceeding against the recipient of the nonprobate property if the decedent's personal representative declines to do so. The proceeding must be begun within one year of the decedent's death, which provides finality for the recipients of the nonprobate property. In short, having broadly validated all sorts of nonprobate property arrangements, the UPC has had to reinvent the debt payment part of the probate system to accommodate this new world in which the value of property passing on death through valid will substitutes can greatly exceed that passing under wills.

E. Retirement Savings

Accounts that hold retirement savings are from a property law point of view simply one more example of contractual will substitutes. What makes these accounts different from other contractual will substitutes is the extent to which they are governed by federal law. Complex federal tax rules apply to these accounts, but for now we're interested in federal provisions that deal with the rights of creditors and revocation by operation of law.

These provisions are part of the Employee Retirement Income Security Act (ERISA). ERISA applies to all employment benefit plans, and that includes retirement savings arrangements sponsored by employers and group term life insurance provided to employees. For our purposes, there are two very important provisions in ERISA. The first is the "non-alienation provision," which prevents the employee's creditors from reaching the employee's retirement accumulations and using them to satisfy the employee's debts. The second is the preemption provision. ERISA preempts all state laws that "relate to" any employee benefit plan subject to ERISA. The preemption provision means that the anti-alienation provision overrules any state law allowing creditors to reach an employee's retirement savings or other benefit plan to satisfy the employee's debt.

The supremacy of the anti-alienation provision is not controversial. The policy that protects assets accumulated to provide income in retirement is a strong one. In fact, states have long provided protection from creditors for retirement vehicles not covered by ERISA, most importantly IRAs. Most of these accounts are not employee benefit plans and are not therefore subject to ERISA, but they are as immune from creditors under state law as are plans subject to ERISA. One other consequence of ERISA preemption, however, is far more contentious.

S i d e b a r

ERISA, CONSTRUCTIVE TRUSTS AND REVOCATION ON DIVORCE

Some courts, both state and federal, tried to implement the revocation on divorce policy by crafting a federal common law of revocation on divorce. That project came to an end in early 2009 with the U.S. Supreme Court's decision in *Kennedy v. Plan Administrator for DuPont Savings & Investment Plan*, 129 S. Ct. 865 (2009). The Court held that if the governing documents of a plan subject to ERISA do not provide for a common law waiver of benefits, no such wavier can be effective. The Court held open the possibility that once the proceeds are paid to a designated beneficiary who made a wavier — in *Kennedy* the wavier was contained in the property settlement, which was part of the decedent's and the beneficiary's divorce — a state court could enforce the waiver. Presumably the remedy would be a constructive trust imposed on the designated beneficiary. Look for more developments in the state courts.

As we've seen, UPC § 2-804 and statutes like it revoke the beneficiary designation of an ex-spouse (and family members of an ex-spouse under the UPC provision) for a wide variety of contractual nonprobate property arrangements. Some of these arrangements are employee benefit plans subject to ERISA. The question is whether ERISA's preemption provision prevents the operation of a state law revocation on divorce provision. In *Eglehoff v. Eglehoff*,[2] the U.S. Supreme Court answered that question and held that the ERISA preemption provision prevented the operation of the State of Washington's revocation on divorce statute. The decedent's ex-spouse, therefore, was entitled to the proceeds of the group term life insurance provided by the decedent's employer. She was the designated beneficiary on the records of the employee benefit plan, and the only way to change that designation is to follow the requirements of the plan. The preemption provision means that no state law can change that provision of the plan.

SUMMARY

- Traditionally, a device for passing property at the death of the owner is an invalid will substitute if no interest passes to the intended transferee during the lifetime of the owner of the property.

- Jointly held property with right of survivorship is a valid form of will substitute because the intended transferee does indeed have an interest in the property during life. Although joint accounts are valid will substitutes, they are often created solely for convenience and not as a device for transferring property at death.

- Contract-based will substitutes are classic invalid will substitutes because the beneficiary has no interest in the property while the owner of the property is alive. Today, however, a wide variety of such devices have been validated by decisional law and by statutes. The UPC validates just about every possible variety of contractual will substitute.

- Although today a vast amount of wealth is held in contractual will substitutes, the law governing the workings of these devices is in many cases unsettled. The UPC, however, does fully address the workings of contractual will substitutes.

- One category of contractual will substitutes, those that are part of an employee's employment benefits — usually vehicles for retirement savings as well as employer provided group term life insurance — are subject to ERISA, whose

---

[2]532 U.S. 141 (2001).

preemption provision overrules what state laws there are governing revocation of beneficiary designations and other matters.

CONNECTIONS

Will Substitutes and Future Interests

The concept of an interest passing to the intended recipient of a gift at death during the life of the property owner is closely related to the concept of the future interest, which is the subject of Chapter 7. One of the distinguishing features of the Anglo-American legal system is the existence of interests that are property but that do not involve possession or enjoyment of the property involved.

Will Substitutes and How Wills Work

The law of how wills work is discussed in Chapter 5. Many of the rules and concepts discussed there, such as acts of independent significance, incorporation by reference, and ademption, are not applicable to contractual wills substitutes or joint holding of property. The law of wills fully addresses the death of the beneficiary before the death of the testator and revocation, questions that arise with contractual will substitutes as well. With the exception of the UPC's anti-lapse provisions, the law applicable to contractual will substitutes usually addresses these problems differently from the law of wills. ERISA preemption, of course, is a problem unique to certain will substitutes.

Will Substitutes and Revocable Trusts

Revocable trusts are also valid will substitutes and can be used to turn any property into nonprobate property, making them the most powerful of all will substitutes. They are also the most complex because they truly straddle the worlds of the will and the trust. Chapter 11 discusses this odd creature in detail.

Will Substitutes and Protection of the Surviving Spouse

By diminishing the probate estate, will substitutes can have an important effect on the statutory mechanisms that attempt to prevent the disinheritance of a surviving spouse. As discussed in Chapter 13, both statutes and judicial doctrines have developed to meet the challenge for spousal protection posed by will substitutes.

Wealth Transfer Taxes and Will Substitutes

Limiting the federal estate tax to a decedent's probate property would make the tax meaningless. The estate tax provisions of the Internal Revenue Code include provisions designed to subject will substitutes to taxation in the estate of the person who created them. Those provisions are discussed in Chapter 17.

Revocation on Divorce

Statutory revocation on divorce provisions, including UPC § 2-804, often apply to wills, to contractual will substitutes, and to revocable trusts. These provisions as applied to wills are discussed in Chapter 5, as applied to will substitutes (other than revocable trusts) in this chapter, as applied to revocable trusts in Chapter 11, and as applied to powers of appointment in Chapter 10. The application of these state law provisions to will substitutes that are employment benefits subject to ERISA is preempted by the ERISA preemption provision.

Future Interests

7

Future interests are one of the distinguishing features of Anglo-American law. The owner of a future interest does not possess or enjoy property

now but only the possibility, more or less certain, that he or she will possess or enjoy property in the future. The complications come when we try to classify a future interest based on what event determines whether the future interest will turn into possession. The differences between the various types of conditions are purely differences of form, not substance, making the language used key. But since language is often not perfectly clear, courts use constructional rules to sort out future interests. Although many attempts have been made to simply all of this, the traditional law is still widely used.

A. WHAT IS A FUTURE INTEREST?

B. CLASSIFICATION OF FUTURE INTERESTS

1. Remainders, Reversions, and Executory Interests
2. Transmissibility

C. COMMON CONSTRUCTIONAL RULES

1. The Preference for Early Vesting
2. Express Conditions of Survival
3. Express Conditions of Death Without Issue
4. Express Conditions of Reaching a Specified Age
5. Class Gifts

A. What Is a Future Interest?

A **future interest**, a form of intangible property, is the possibility of coming into possession or enjoyment of certain property when the interest of whoever currently possesses or enjoys the property comes to an end. That person has a **present interest** in the property. You can think of a future interest as a claim check like the sort you get when you check your coat at a club or restaurant. When you're ready to leave, you present the check and get your coat back. The difference is that when you "cash in" a future interest, usually you are not getting your own property back but you're getting an interest in what was the property of the person who created the future interest.

Sometimes the property you're going to get is held by a trustee, and your claim check is a future interest created in a trust, making it an **equitable interest**. Sometimes the property is in the possession of the person with the preceding interest, and your future interest is a **legal interest**. You're probably already familiar with one sort of legal future interest: a remainder following a life estate in land. We've already discussed the legal life estate and remainder when we looked at nonprobate property in Chapters 1 and 6. I own Blackacre and want Darling to own it when I die, so I make a deed conveying Blackacre to Darling but reserving for myself the right to use and occupy Blackacre for my life. I have a life estate, and Darling has a remainder. Darling has a claim check that can be cashed in for full fee simple absolute ownership of Blackacre when I die and my life estate is over. Of course there is no trustee involved. That's because the life estate and remainder are legal interests.

Why? Because matters involving land were decided in the law courts. Matters involving trusts were decided in the equity courts. Today we don't give much thought to the difference between law and equity, except perhaps when we're trying to figure out whether litigants can demand a jury trial, but one difference is still of great importance. You no doubt learned that when I have my legal life estate in Blackacre and Darling has the remainder, if someone wants to have fee simple title to Blackacre, that person must acquire the life estate and the remainder; he will have to bargain with me and with Darling. As you've also probably learned, fee simple absolute ownership is a bundle of sticks, and the legal life estate and remainder arrangement divides those sticks between the life tenant and the remainder person. If I want fee simple absolute ownership, I must acquire all of the sticks.

There's another way to arrange things so I can enjoy Blackacre for life and Darling can own Blackacre after my death. I can create a trust by conveying Blackacre *to the trustee* who, according to the terms of the trust, must administer the trust so that I can enjoy Blackacre for life. When I die, the trust terms require the trustee to convey fee simple ownership of Blackacre to Darling. I have an equitable life estate (a present interest) in the trust property, and Darling has an equitable remainder (a future interest). The person who wants to acquire fee simple absolute ownership of Blackacre must bargain *with the trustee*. The trustee has *legal title* to Blackacre and can indeed convey a fee simple title, although only if such a conveyance does not violate the trustee's fiduciary duties to the beneficiaries, something we'll talk about in Chapter 16. Figure 7.1 shows a graphical representation of this difference.

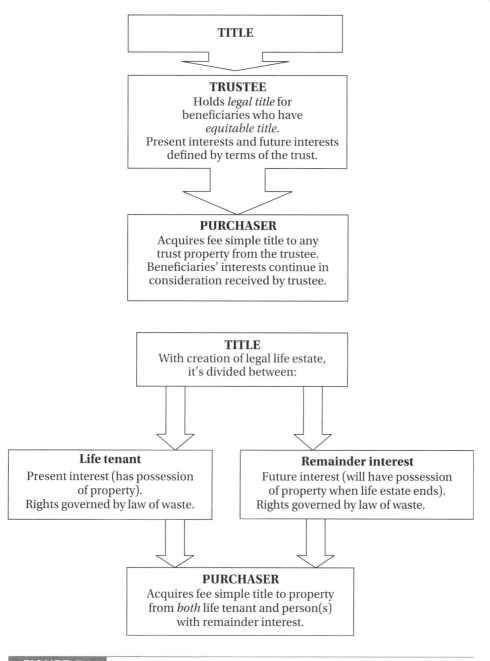

FIGURE 7.1　LEGAL VERSUS EQUITABLE INTERESTS

So there is at least one very practical difference between legal and equitable interests. There is another that you have to understand to make sense of the way present and future interests are discussed. The term **possession** or **enjoyment** is a term of art that refers to the result of cashing in a future interest at the time it turns into a present interest. The holder of a legal present interest has *possession* of the property involved—she has the right to occupy Blackacre. The holder of an equitable present interest has *enjoyment* of the trust property—the holder of the present interest gets to use the trust property, say by living on Blackacre, or the income from the trust property is distributed to the holder of the present interest or expended for her benefit by the trustee (paying bills, satisfying other obligations, and so on). The holder of a remainder interest that can be cashed in at the end of the preceding interest (including when a trust ends) will have *possession* of the property involved.

B. Classification of Future Interests

Classifying future interests is not actually as important as it might seem. What is important is knowing under what circumstances the holder of a future interest will come into possession or enjoyment of the property. That knowledge depends not on classifying the future interest but on understanding what the language creating the future interest means. Much of the learning involved in classification is ultimately related to old English law governing future interests in land. That law is pretty much obsolete, but the classification system that grew from it is still widely used, although as we'll see, Restatement (Third) of Property radically simplifies the traditional system.

Because we are concentrating on future interests created by trusts, we're going to spend our time on three types of future interests: reversions, remainders, and executory interests. We're not going to spend time on three types of future interests that are created when real property is conveyed in such a way that a fee simple absolute is not conveyed to the grantee of the deed. You probably studied these **base fees** in your property course. A quick refresher:

- The **fee simple defeasible** is created when the grantee's possession lasts only so long as the land is used in a specified way. The classic example: Grantor conveys Blackacre to the School Board (the grantee) for so long as the grantee uses the land for school purposes. The grantor has retained a **possibility of reverter**. When the specified use ceases, fee simple title to the land immediately goes to the holder of the possibility of reverter, who may be the grantor or whoever has received the possibility of reverter from the grantor.
- The **fee on a condition subsequent** is created when the grantee has possession of the land so long as something *does not* happen. The classic example: Grantor conveys Blackacre to grantee, but if alcoholic beverages are ever sold on the land the grantor may reenter the land and regain possession from the grantee. Having eliminated the grantee's interest, the grantor will then have title in fee simple absolute, which the grantor must enforce by bringing an action to recover possession. In this case, the grantor retains a **right of entry**. Just like the possibility of reverter, the right of entry may pass from the grantor to one or more other persons, and whoever has the right of entry at the time the forbidden thing comes to pass has the right to bring an action to recover possession.

The future interests created in the grantor when the grantor creates one of the base fees—the possibility of reverter and the right of entry—are two of the three sorts of future interests that can be held by the person who transfers property to others. The third is the reversion, which can be created in the transferor when the transferor accomplishes a transfer that creates certain other types of future interests in transferees.

We'll discuss reversions, but first we're going to examine the three types of future interests that are created in transferees who are the beneficiaries of the trust created by the transferor (or the persons who take possession of the property when the legal life estate ends). These are remainders, which can be further classified as contingent remainders and vested remainders, and executory interests.

(1) Remainders, Reversions, and Executory Interests

A **remainder** is a future interest created in a transferee that will turn into possession or enjoyment of the property in which the future interest exists (and remember that in the modern world that means the property in the trust the creation of which created the remainder), if it ever does, when the preceding interest in the property ends, so long as that preceding interest and the remainder were created at the same time. The "at the same time" requirement is far less important than it once was. Remember that today almost all future interests are created by creating trusts. The trust is created at a given moment, and all of the present and future interests are created at that time.

The person who has the remainder (the **remainder person**) sits around and waits for the preceding interest to end; when it does, it's time to cash in the claim check, assuming that the claim check can be cashed in. As we've already noted, it is possible for the settlor of the future interest to attach conditions to it that may or may not be fulfilled when the time comes for the remainder person to cash in the claim check. Figure 7.2 illustrates this basic idea.

Remember that the transferor creates the present and future interests by creating a legal life estate and remainder (by a deed of real property to A for life, then to B) or by conveying title of any sort of property to the trustee of a trust created by the transferor (or by anyone else, for that matter). The terms of the trust will create the present and future interests in the trust beneficiaries.

Remainders come in several different varieties, and we'll explore those varieties next.

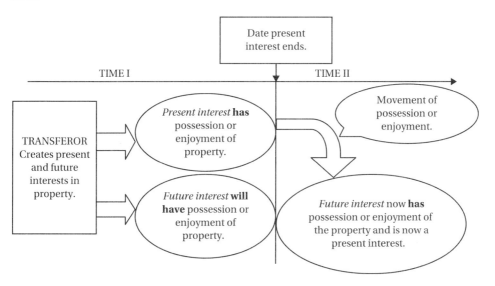

FIGURE 7.2   MOVEMENT OF POSSESION OVER TIME

POSSESSION OF TRUST PROPERTY

Usually, we think of the trustee has having possession of trust property. In some cases, however, a beneficiary will have possession and enjoyment of trust property. For example, the trust property includes artwork. A beneficiary with a present interest in the trust might very well have possession of the artwork and display it in her residence. Because the artwork does not produce income in money (unless the trustee can rent it out for display somewhere), the only way to presently enjoy the artwork is to look at it. The same can be true of just about any kind of tangible personal property held in trust (jewelry is another common example).

(a) Described by the Nature of Eventual Possession

One thing that distinguishes remainders is what sort of ownership the remainder person gets when the claim check is cashed in—in more traditional terms, when the remainder "falls in" or **vests in possession** or **enjoyment** on the **distribution date**, which is the time when the previous interest in the property comes to an end. The remainder person will have either enjoyment of the property for a limited time (or possession for a limited time if it's a legal remainder) or full fee simple ownership. The limited time could be for the remainder person's life or for a term of years or until the occurrence of an event. Remainders that come into possession before a trust ends are likely to be remainders in an equitable life estate or in an income interest, and remainders that come into possession when a trust ends will be remainders in fee simple. To put it in technical doctrinal terms, when the trust ends the trustee will pass legal title to the trust property to the remainder person, and the remainder person's equitable title as beneficiary and the legal title received from the trustee will merge into fee simple absolute ownership.

Example 7.1: O conveys Blackacre to A for life, then to B for life, then to C.

Example 7.2: O conveys property in trust to T as trustee to pay the income from the trust property to A for life, then to pay it to B for life, then to end the trust and distribute the trust property to C.

In Example 7.1, A has the legal life estate in Blackacre, B has a remainder in a legal life estate, and C has a legal remainder in fee simple.

In Example 7.2, A has an equitable life estate or the life income interest in the trust, B has a remainder in an equitable life estate or life income interest, and C has an equitable remainder in fee simple.

Both B and C have remainders because they will enjoy the property (Blackacre or the trust property) when the preceding interest ends and all of the interests were created at the same time.

We're going to spend most of our time with the remainder in fee simple, the remainder that comes into possession when all of the other interests in Blackacre are finished or when the trust ends. Because these remainders in fee simple often are designed by the person creating the trust to come into possession at some time in the future, they are often fancied up with provisions that are designed to deal with the difficulty of trying to predict what will happen between the creation of the remainder and its eventual vesting in possession on the distribution date.

Tailoring a remainder so that it accomplishes its creator's intent and gets property to the right persons usually involves the creator putting conditions on the remainder. Whether these conditions are fulfilled determines whether the remainder will vest in possession or enjoyment.

(b) Described by Type of Conditions Attached

No Conditions — Indefeasibly Invested. It is not necessary to attach conditions to a remainder. If there are no conditions governing whether the remainder will vest in possession or enjoyment, the remainder is **indefeasibly vested**. To use our goofy analogy, the claim check will never become worthless. When the preceding interest ends, whoever has the claim check will be able to turn it in and get possession or enjoyment of the property in return. How can you tell whether a remainder is indefeasibly vested? The answer comes from examining the words that create the remainder. If the settlor of the trust (or the grantor of the deed creating the legal life estate and remainder) includes no language that could result in the remainder not vesting in possession, the remainder is indefeasibly vested. Here's an example.

Example 7.3: O conveys property in trust to T as trustee to pay the income from the trust property to A for life, then to end the trust and distribute the trust property to C.

Nothing qualifies the remainder created in C. No matter what happens, at A's death (the distribution date), the person who has the remainder (it may be C or it may be someone who acquired the remainder from C because, as we'll see, this remainder can pass through C's estate if C dies before the distribution date) will vest in possession and will have fee simple ownership of the trust property. This will make more sense after we examine the ways in which a remainder can be qualified so that it is not indefeasibly vested. If you take another look at Figure 7-2, possession and enjoyment is certain to flow through the arrow to the remainder interest.

Subject to Conditions. In the traditional system of classification, conditions that can be attached to remainder come in two forms: conditions precedent and conditions subsequent. The form of the condition is important for two reasons: it dictates the classification of other future interests created by the trust, and it governs the application of the Rule Against Perpetuities to all of the interests created. The *form* of condition *does not* tell us whether the remainder or other future interest will actually vest in possession or enjoyment. Whether that happens depends on the *substance* of the condition. We're going to deal with form and classification first and then with substance.

Classifying a condition as precedent or subsequent is purely a matter of the language used to create the condition. A **condition subsequent** is created by language that indicates that the remainder will vest in possession or enjoyment *unless something happens.* Here's a classic example with the language that creates the condition subsequent *italicized.*

Example 7.4: O conveys property in trust to T as trustee to pay the income from the trust property to A for life, then to end the trust and distribute the trust property to C, *but if C does not survive A*, T is to distribute the trust property to D.

The *substance* of the condition is that C must be alive when A dies if C is to have possession of the trust property and that C must not be alive at A's death if D is to have possession. The *form* of the condition creates a condition subsequent because of the way the language is put together. The remainder is given to C, but then the language goes on take the remainder away, to **divest** it, if C does not survive A. Of course, the language in this example is completely unambiguous. The remainder is created ("pay the trust property to C") and then comes the "but if"—take the remainder away if C does not survive A and give it D. In the real world, the language often is not so clear. Determining whether language creating a condition creates a condition subsequent involves deciding whether the language creating the condition should be preceded by a "but if," which is another way of asking whether the language gives something and then takes it away should the condition come to pass.

Because classification is a matter of the form of the condition, we can say that any remainder subject to a condition subsequent is **vested subject to divestment**. (Remember that should the condition happen, it divests the otherwise vested remainder.) And that means that the future interest that will vest in possession or enjoyment if the condition happens (D's interest in Example 7.4) is an **executory interest**. The distinguishing feature of the executory interest is that it will vest in possession or enjoyment *by divesting an otherwise vested interest.*

Executory interests have a long and complex history that is an integral part of the law of trusts. The details of that history are irrelevant to modern trusts, but one tiny part of it still requires a mention. The sort of executory interest we're discussing, the sort that waits around to see if a remainder is divested by the occurrence of a condition subsequent, is a **shifting executory interest**. It's "shifting" because the interest that has to be divested if the executory interest is going to vest in possession or enjoyment of the property is a transferee, someone in whom an interest was created, in this case the remainder vested subject to divestment. The other type of executory interest is a **springing executory interest**. It's described as "springing" because the occurrence of the condition subsequent will divest the person *who created the executory interest* rather than another transferee. This sort of executory interest is seldom seen in the modern world. About the only instance worth thinking about is a conveyance by the fee simple owner of Blackacre giving possession to the grantee at some time in the future should the condition subsequent come to pass. Here's the example everyone uses: O conveys Blackacre to his child C when C marries. The condition subsequent that will divest O is C's marriage. C has a springing executory interest.

Now, our next question. What makes a condition attached to a remainder a condition precedent? A **condition precedent** is a condition that must be fulfilled *before the remainder can vest in possession or enjoyment.* Here's a classic example with the language that creates the condition precedent *italicized.*

Example 7.5: O conveys property in trust to T as trustee to pay the income from the trust property to A for life, then to end the trust and distribute the trust property to C *if C survives A,* and if C does not survive A, T is to distribute the trust property to D.

The *substance* of the condition is that C must be alive when A dies if C is to have possession of the trust property and that C must not be alive at A's death if D is to have possession. The *form* of the condition creates a condition precedent because of the way the language is put together. Before C's remainder can vest in possession, C must survive A. Another way to put it is that the interest in C will not vest in possession *unless* C survives A. This is the opposite of language creating a condition subsequent. That language gives the remainder to C and then *takes it away* if the condition occurs. Just as in Example 7.4, the language in Example 7.5 is completely unambiguous. The remainder is created in C, but it will vest in possession *only* if C survives A. Just as with conditions subsequent, determining whether language creates a condition subsequent involves determining whether the language creating the condition should be preceded by an "unless," which is another way of asking whether the condition must happen before the remainder can vest in possession or enjoyment.

Because classification is a matter of the form of the condition, we can say that any remainder subject to a condition precedent is **contingent**. And that means that the interest that will vest in possession or enjoyment unless the condition happens (D's interest in Example 7.5) is an **alternate contingent remainder**, and we can describe both C's interest and D's interest as alternative contingent remainders.

Besides making the interest in the other transferee an alternate contingent remainder, the existence of a condition precedent has another consequence for the traditional law of future interests. If the creator of the interests creates a remainder subject to a condition precedent, the creator has a **reversion**. This makes perfect sense in an example like the following.

Example 7.6: O conveys property in trust to T as trustee to pay the income from the trust property to A for life, then to end the trust and distribute the trust property to C if C survives A.

O has created a contingent remainder in C because the language "if C survives A" is a condition precedent. The only way the remainder will vest in possession on A's death is if C survives A, and unless that happens, the remainder will not vest in possession. When C does dies before A, what happens to the trust property on A's death? The trust property goes back to O, the creator of the present and future interests in the trust property. The reversion is the interest that will vest in possession when the contingent remainder fails because the condition precedent is not fulfilled.

Now look again at Example 7.5. Yes, C and D have alternative contingent remainders because C's remainder is subject to a condition precedent. If the condition does not happen, if C does not survive A, then it is certain that D's remainder will eventually vest in possession (realize that there is no express condition that D must survive A). Since either C will survive A or not, there is no circumstance under which the trust property goes back to O on A's death. *But O still has a reversion when the trust is created.* The reason is buried in the history of the law of future interests, and we're not going to worry about it here. Just remember what some have called the "rule of reversions": when a transferor creates contingent remainders, the transferor *always* has a reversion.

We can't overemphasize that the difference between a condition subsequent and a condition precedent *is purely one of form.* Look at Examples 7.4 and 7.5. Whether it's vested subject to divestment or contingent because of a condition precedent, the remainder created in C is never going to vest in possession unless C survives A. The substance of the two conditions is exactly the same. C doesn't care how that condition is expressed; all C cares about is surviving A, and all D cares about is C not surviving A. Sure, the form of the condition determines the classification of the remainder to which it's attached, the classification of other future interests in the property involved, and whether the transferor who created the interests retained a reversion, but the practical effects of classification are exactly zero. Well, not exactly. We'll see in Chapter 12 that vested remainders subject to divestment satisfy the requirements of the Rule Against Perpetuities but that contingent remainders and executory interests may be invalidated by the Rule.

Q: Since you have to be alive to possess a legal or equitable life estate, is every remainder in a life estate contingent?

A: No. Being alive is an inherent quality of a life estate or life income interest and is not treated like a condition precedent. Of course, a remainder in a life estate, although vested, will never vest in possession if the holder of the remainder is not living at the time the previous interest ends. The technical way of describing this fact is to describe the remainder in a life estate as *vested subject to limitational defeasance.* Usually such a remainder is described simply as vested, and that's that.

Figures 7.3 and 7.4 illustrate how even though the future interests created in Examples 7.4 and 7.5 are classified differently, the end result is exactly the same

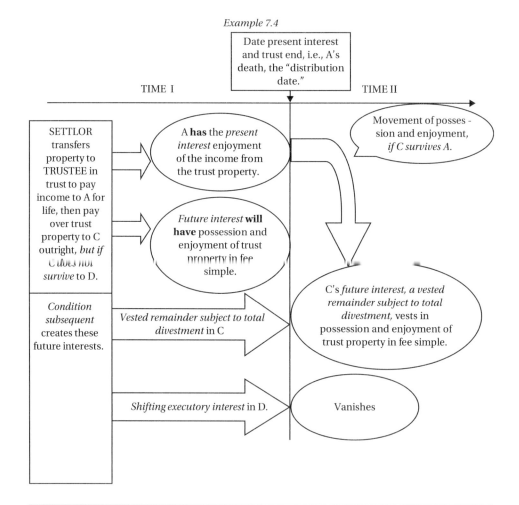

FIGURE 7.3   VESTED REMAINDER SUBJECT TO DIVESTMENT VESTS IN POSSESSION

Example 7.5

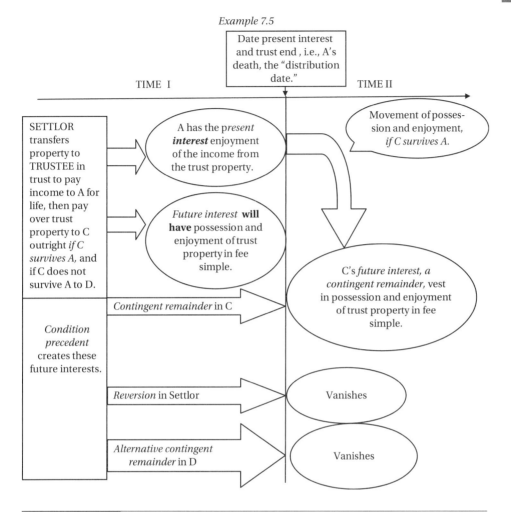

FIGURE 7.4   **CONTINGENT REMAINDER VESTS IN POSSESSION**

when C survives A. Of course, in both examples, if C does not survive A, D's interest will eventually vest in possession of the trust property. The only difference between the two examples is in getting to that result. In Example 7.4, C's death during A's lifetime means that the condition subsequent has indeed happened, C's vested remainder subject to divestment is indeed divested and vanishes, and D's executory interest becomes an indefeasibly vested remainder. In Example 7.5, C's death during A's lifetime means that the condition precedent has not been fulfilled, C's contingent remainder vanishes, D's alternate contingent remainder is now indefeasibly vested, and O's reversion vanishes too because there no longer is a contingent remainder in the trust property.

Before we leave the topic of remainders, we have to consider one other circumstance in which a remainder is contingent

Unascertained Persons. A remainder is contingent because it is created in unascertained persons, persons not yet born. Unless you can point to a person and say, that person has the remainder, the remainder is contingent. The remainder can be given to a single individual or to a group. Look at these three examples.

S i d e b a r

DEAD AS THE DODO, PART 1 —
DESTRUCTABLILITY OF CONTINGENT
REMAINDERS

There are some features of the law of future
interests that are extinct yet are almost always
part of a student's training, so we'll deal with
them in sidebars. The first is the doctrine of the
destructibility of contingent remainders. The
doctrine applied only to legal interests, interests in land, so it had nothing to do with future
interests created in trusts. The doctrine states
that if a contingent remainder is not ready to
vest in possession when the preceding interest
(which must be a "freehold interest," that is, an
interest other than a term for years) terminates,
the remainder is destroyed. If O conveys land to
A for life, then to B if B attains 21 years of age,
and B is not yet 21 at A's death, the remainder is
destroyed and whoever held the reversion at
that time would have a fee simple absolute in
the land. The reasoning is based on ancient
ideas about seisin, the name given to the right
to possess land. The details are not worth going
into here (you can find them in almost any
student work on future interests), but as a
practical matter it really is extinct as the dodo.
Restatement (Third) of Property § 25.5 simply
says that the destructibility rule is not recognized as part of American law.

Example 7.7: O conveys property in trust to T as trustee to pay the income from the trust property to A for life, then to end the trust and distribute the trust property to A's first-born child.

Example 7.8: O conveys property in trust to T as trustee to pay the income from the trust property to A for life, then to end the trust and distribute the trust property to A's first-born child if that child attains 21 years of age, and if not, T is to distribute the trust property to B.

Example 7.9: O conveys property in trust to T as trustee to pay the income from the trust property to A for life, then to end the trust and distribute the trust property to A's first-born child, but if that child does not attain 21 years of age, T is to distribute the trust property to B.

In all three examples before A's first child is born, the remainder in that child is contingent because it is created in an unascertained person. What happens to the future interests created at the creation of the trust depends on the language of the trust terms. In Example 7.7, there is no condition attached to the remainder, so once A's first child is born the remainder is indefeasibly vested. In both Examples 7.8 and 7.9, the child must reach age 21 if the remainder is to vest indefeasibly, but in 7.8 that require-ment is expressed as a condition precedent and in 7.9 it's expressed as a condition subsequent. Table 7.1 sums up what happens in each example when A's first child is born and later reaches 21 years of age.

Remember, *interests change over time.* Figure 7.5 shows a decision tree that illustrates how a contingent remainder created in an unborn person can change when that person is born (things are a bit different when the remainder is created in a group of persons; that makes the remainder a class gift, and we'll talk about that at the end of this chapter). If the contingent remainder in our decision tree is accompanied by an *alternative contingent remainder*, the alternate contingent remainder will

- *vanish* if the other remainder is now *indefeasibly vested,* or
- become a *shifting executory interest* if the other remainder is now *vested subject to divestment* (i.e., the other remainder is still subject to a *condition subsequent*).

Finally, when the contingent remainder in the decision tree ceases to be a contingent remainder, the accompanying *reversion* will *vanish.*

TABLE 7.1	Interests in A, C, B, and O		
Event	**Example 7.7**	**Example 7.8**	**Example 7.9**
Creation of trust	A = present interest C = contingent remainder (unascertained) B = alternate contingent remainder O = reversion	A = present interest C = contingent remainder (unascertained) B = alternate contingent remainder O = reversion	A = present interest C = contingent remainder (unascertained) B = alternate contingent remainder O = reversion
Birth of C	A = present interest C = indefeasibly vested remainder B = interest vanishes O = interest vanishes	A = present interest C = contingent remainder (condition precedent) B = alternative contingent remainder O = reversion	A = present interest C = vested remainder subject to total divestment (condition subsequent) B = shifting executory interest O = interest vanishes
C turns 21	Nothing changes	A = present interest C = indefeasibly vested remainder B = interest vanishes O = interest vanishes	A = present interest C = indefeasibly vested remainder B = interest vanishes O = interest vanishes

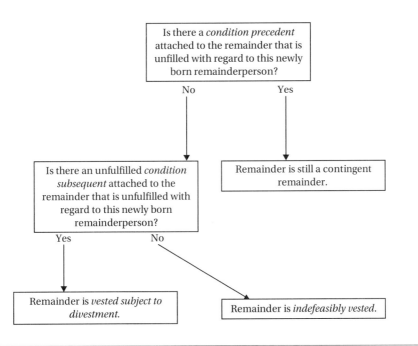

FIGURE 7.5 WHAT HAPPENS ON BIRTH OF A REMAINDER BENEFICIARY

F A Q

Q: What does "vested" mean?

A: It depends (don't get frustrated; I'm not making this up). The meaning of vested depends on the context in which it is being used. When we're talking about *classification* of a future interest, "vested" means the future interest belongs to someone you can point to — it is not subject to a condition precedent and at least one remainder person is in being (not unascertained). Outside of classification, "vested" might mean vested in possession or enjoyment. When that's the case, the holder of the future interest has possession or enjoyment of the property in which the future interest was created. Finally, a future interest can be "vested in interest." That means that we know who will get the property when the interest vests in possession or enjoyment and the minimum share of the property that person will get. In other words, if there is more than one holder of the future interest, we know the maximum number there can be. Vested in interest is the "vesting" that's relevant to the Rule Against Perpetuities.

(2) Transmissibility

Before we talk about the rules courts use to sort out what kind of conditions are created by language that is not completely clear, we have to think about one more aspect of future interests. Future interests are alienable; they can pass from the person or persons in whom they were created to other persons. Alienation during the lifetime of the person in whom the interest is created is possible, although as we'll see when we talk about the rights of the creditors of trust beneficiaries in Chapter 9, the person creating the future interest can pretty much prevent its alienation during the lifetime of the holder of the interest. What we're concerned with here is alienation at death, which is usually referred to as **transmission**. A future interest that can be transmitted at the death of the holder of the interest is said to be **transmissible**.

F A Q

Q: How can a person who has a transmissible future interest turn it into nonprobate property?

A: Because a future interest is property, it can be trust property; a trustee can hold equitable title to it. Therefore the easiest way to make a future interest nonprobate property is to convey it to the trustee of a revocable lifetime trust.

If the holder of a future interest can transmit it at death, then the future interest is simply part of the holder's probate estate like any other property that has not been turned into nonprobate property. If the holder dies intestate, it will go to the heirs; and if the holder has a valid will, the future interest could be the subject of a specific devise — "I give my remainder interest in the trust created by O on such-and-such a date with T as trustee to my cousin, C." If the future interest is not mentioned specifically, it will be part of the residuary devise. When the interest is transmitted, the person who ends up holding it is the original holder's **successor in interest**.

There really is a simple rule you can apply in deciding whether a future interest is transmissible at death. *If the death of the holder of the future interest does not resolve a condition in such a way as to destroy the interest, the interest is transmissible and will continue to be until the condition is resolved.* To illustrate that, let's take another look at Examples 7.8 and 7.9.

Example 7.8: O conveys property in trust to T as trustee to pay the income from the trust property to A for life, then to end the trust and distribute the trust property to A's first-born child if that child attains 21 years of age, and if not, T is to distribute the trust property to B.

Example 7.9: O conveys property in trust to T as trustee to pay the income from the trust property to A for life, then to end the trust and distribute the trust property to A's first-born child, but if that child does not attain 21 years of age, T is to distribute the trust property to B.

Two things to note: (1) B's interest is transmissible. B's death before A doesn't change anything as far as the future interests are concerned. (2) *The end result is the same.* In both examples, B's successors in interest end up with the trust property. It doesn't matter that in one example B has an alternate contingent remainder and in the other an executory interest. In neither example does B's death resolve a condition. If that's the case, then B's interest is transmissible. Remember that whether a future interest is transmitted at the death of the holder of the interest does not depend on the classification of the interest. Contingent remainders can be transmitted at death and vested remainders subject to divestment can fail at the death of the holder. *What matters is whether the death of the holder resolves a condition.* The differences between these two examples are shown in Table 7.2 and presented graphically in Figures 7.6 and 7.7.

Sidebar

PROBLEMS WITH TRANSMISSISBILITY

Transmissible future interests are unpopular for three reasons. First, they are transmissible, which means that the interest will pass under the holder's will or through intestacy. The settlor of the interest might not have realized that the person in whom the interest was created was also being given control over who might ultimately cash in the claim check and get the property. Second, because the transmissible future interest is property, it is part of the holder's **gross estate** to which federal and perhaps state estate taxes apply. Third, if the interest does vest in possession, getting the property to the person entitled to it may be complicated, for reasons that we'll leave for your casebook to explain.

TABLE 7.2	"As Time Goes By I"		
		Future Interests	
Time	Event	Example 7.8	Example 7.9
1	Trust created; A has no children	A's first child = contingent remainder (unborn) B = alternative contingent remainder O = reversion	A's first child = contingent remainder (unborn) B = alternative contingent remainder O = reversion
2	A's first child born	A's first child = contingent remainder (condition precedent) B = alternative contingent remainder O = reversion	A's first child = vested remainder subject to total divestment (condition subsequent) B = executory interest Reversion vanishes
3	B dies	A's first child = contingent remainder (condition precedent) B's successors in interest = alternative contingent remainder O = reversion	A's first child = vested remainder subject to total divestment B successor's in interest = executory interest Reversion vanished at time 2
4	A's first child dies before reaching 21	A's first child's interest vanishes B's successors in interest = vested remainder Reversion vanishes	A's first child's interest vanishes B's successors in interest = vested remainder Reversion vanished at time 2
5	A dies	B's successors in interest vest in possession of the trust property	

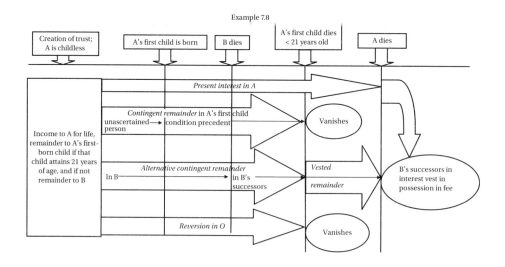

Example 7.8

FIGURE 7.6   TRANSMISSION OF AN ALTERNATIVE CONTINGENT REMAINDER

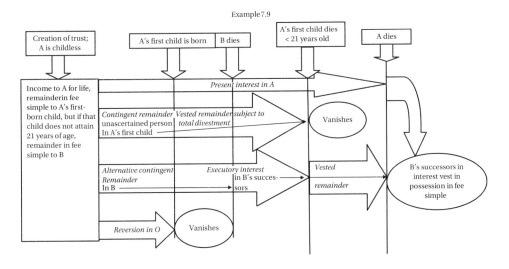

Example 7.9

FIGURE 7.7   TRANSMISSION OF AN EXECUTORY INTEREST

C. Common Constructional Rules

As we've seen, it's relatively easy to classify future interests when the language creating them is unequivocal—conditions precedent always involve an "if," and conditions subsequent are always introduced by "but if." Language and persons whose drafting creates future interests are not always that cooperative, and we've seen how complex the construction of the language of wills can be. The construction of language creating future interests can be equally complex. What we're going to deal with here are rules that courts apply to commonly occurring problems.

(1) The Preference for Early Vesting

The most important constructional rule growing out of the truly enormous number of cases dealing with the construction of future interests is a preference for construing language so that the future interests created by the language are vested. To put it another way, language is not construed to create a condition precedent. Under the classic common law, there were really two basic reasons for this rule. First, it prevented the application of the rule of the destructibility of contingent remainders. Second, because vested remainders are not subject to the Rule Against Perpetuities, the application of this rule of construction meant that fewer interests were invalidated by the Rule. The first reason is no longer meaningful. The second is losing its significance as more states abolish or severely limit the sting of the Rule Against Perpetuities. This constructional preference, however, is still widely used by courts.

(a) No Implied Requirement of Survival

The most important corollary of the preference for early vesting is a rule that survival to the time of vesting in possession or enjoyment, the distribution date, is not required unless expressly stated. In other words, a condition precedent of survival to the distribution date is never implied. (There is an overwhelmingly important exception to this rule, which we'll discuss when we talk about class gifts.)

The refusal to imply such a condition of survival means that transmissible interests are more likely to be created. This may keep the property in the family line of the first holder of the interest if that person's probate estate does pass to his family, and if that first holder is related to the creator of the interest, then the effect is to keep the property in the family of the creator of the interest. Here's a very simple example.

Example 7.10: O conveys property in trust to T as trustee to pay the income from the trust property to A for life, then to end the trust and distribute the trust property to A's children, B, C, and D.

Let's assume that O is A's parent. Then assume that B dies before A with a will that gives B's entire estate to B's children and C dies before A, intestate and unmarried and survived by two children. Because there is no language requiring any of A's children to survive to the distribution date—A's death—B's vested remainder passed through B's will to B's children and C's vested remainder passed by the intestacy statute to C's children. When A dies, the trustee distributes one-third of the trust property to D, one-third to B's children, and one-third to C's children. The property not only has stayed in O's family line, but three branches of A's family have benefited equally. Of course, B's will could have given the remainder to anyone, including a surviving spouse, nonfamily members, or charity. Similarly, if C had been survived by a spouse, the spouse would have taken some part of the remainder, and perhaps O would not want a grand-child-in-law to receive some the trust property. In short, the no implied conditions of survivorship to the distribution date rule is a crude way of ensuring that property stays within a family line.

(b) Acceleration

Another important effect of construing interests to be vested when that is possible comes from another rule: vested interests accelerate into possession, but contingent interests do not. **Acceleration** simply means that a remainder vests in possession whenever the preceding interest ends, even if it ends prematurely. How could that happen? Take the following example.

Example 7.11: O devises property in trust to T as trustee to pay the income from the trust to O's surviving spouse S for life, then to end the trust and distribute the trust property to O's children who survive S.

Sometime after O's death, S decides that he doesn't want the income from the trust any longer and releases the income interest. If the remainder in O's children were vested, then the children alive when S releases the income interest would divide up the trust property. The vested remainders would accelerate into possession. In the example, however, the remainders are contingent because there is a condition precedent of surviving S. The traditional rule is the contingent remainders cannot accelerate. Some courts, however, decide the question by deciding whether the settlor of the trust intended the remainders to accelerate.

(c) Gifts to Heirs

We all know by now that "heirs" are the persons who take a decedent's probate estate when the decedent dies intestate. The intestacy statute tells us who the heirs are. Because the identity of a person's heirs is not known until that person's death, *a remainder created in the heirs of a living person is always contingent* because it is in unascertained persons and there is a condition precedent of surviving the named person. Easy. And because of the preference for early vesting, the moment the named person dies, the heirs have indefeasibly vested remainders. Also easy.

This is all fine and dandy when the death of the named person is also the distribution date. The heirs are ascertained, and they are entitled to the property. But what if the death of the named person happens before the distribution date? Example 7.12 gives a classic example.

Example 7.12: O devises property in trust to T as trustee to pay the income to O's surviving spouse S for life, then to end the trust and distribute the trust property to O's sister M if she survives S and, if she does not, to M's heirs.

There's nothing problematic here so long as M survives S. But if she doesn't, at her death her heirs get vested remainders in the trust property (until M's death they have an alternative contingent remainder). That means that should any of M's heirs die before S, their remainders are transmissible. The likelihood that the estates of the heirs owe estate tax increases because the gross estate for tax purposes now includes the remainder interest. As with any transmissible interest, the holder may not realize that she is disposing of it by will or through intestacy, and whether the holder knows that or not, the creator of the interest may never have intended the holder to dispose of it should the holder die before the interest vests in possession or enjoyment.

These problems are the same for all transmissible interests, but in the case of a remainder in "heirs," many state legislatures have stepped in to "solve" the problem. This solution rests on two assumptions: (1) the settlor of the remainder in the heirs of the person who could die before the

---

Sidebar

REMAINDERS IN HEIRS IN THE ABSENCE OF A STATUTE

If a state has not adopted UPC § 2-711 or a similar statute, courts can reach the same result by using some well-established constructional rules that identify situations in which it is assumed that the creator of the interest in the heirs of a designated person who has died before the distribution date actually intends the designated person's heirs to be determined as if the named person had died at the distribution date. It would take more time to explain and illustrate these rules than their significance warrants. You may come across cases that use these rules, however, so realize that they do exist.

Sidebar

DEAD AS THE DODO, PART 3—THE DOCTRINE OF WORTHIER TITLE

This is the second dodo that deals with interests created in heirs. The doctrine, which was at the start a rule of law, gave concrete effect to the notion that to acquire property by inheritance was "worthier" than acquiring by conveyance. In addition, the feudal lord received the equivalent of an estate tax only when the heir inherited land. Originally applying only to land, the doctrine reflected these two considerations by nullifying any attempt by a grantor to create an interest in his heirs. The attempted creation of a life estate in the grantor, remainder to the grantor's heirs, failed to create the remainder and left the grantor with a reversion.

In England, the doctrine of worthier title was abolished by legislation in 1833. In the United States, it lingered at the fringes of the law until 1919. In that year the New York Court of Appeals decided *Doctor v. Hughes,* 122 N.E. 221 (N.Y. 1919). In the course of deciding the case, the doctrine was transformed from a rule of law into a rule of construction. The result was an invitation to litigate any creation of a remainder in the grantor's heirs if someone would profit by the interest being a reversion. New York overruled the case and abolished the doctrine by legislation in 1967. Most other states have abolished the doctrine either by statute or court decision. As with the Rule in Shelley's Case, Restatement (Third) of Property § 16.3 "repudiates" the doctrine of worthier title.

distribution date does not want the heirs to have control over where the trust property goes and (2) the creation of future interests potentially subject to the estate tax is a bad thing. The solution is accomplished by adopting a statute that directs the heirs to be ascertained as if the named person died at the distribution date. (The UPC provision is § 2-711.) A remainder created in a named person's heirs, therefore, is still contingent, but the condition precedent is being alive at the distribution date. In Example 7.12, the trust property would be distributed to M's heirs determined *as if she has died when S died.* No one has a transmissible interest, and whoever gets the property will be an heir and therefore a relative of the named person, thus preventing property "going astray" to nonfamily members.

(2) Express Conditions of Survival

In spite of all the time devoted to examining the features of transmissible interests, many trusts do indeed attach express conditions of survival to remainder interests, no doubt at least in part because the intent is not to create transmissible interests. The problem is that it is far too easy to use the word "surviving" in ways that leave uncertain the time to which survival is required. The generally accepted rule is to construe the survival requirement to mean survival to the distribution date.

Example 7.13: G devises property in trust to T as trustee to pay the income to A for life and then to end the trust and distribute the trust property to B, but if B does not survive A to B's surviving children.

Interests created: A = *present interest* (life income interest)

B = *vested remainder subject to divestment* ("but if" indicates a condition subsequent)

B's "surviving" children = *executory interest*

The question is, whom do B's children have to survive? Do they have to survive B or do they have to survive A if B dies before A? Let's assume that at G's death there are two children of B living, C and D. B predeceases A, and then C dies survived by two children. A then dies, at which time

B's only surviving child is D. The constructional rule says that if an express condition of survival is ambiguous regarding to what time survival is required, the language is construed to require survival to distribution date. In Example 7.13, therefore, all of the trust property is distributed to D.

F   A   Q

Q: Isn't there something wrong with applying the usual constructional rule to Example 7.13 if it results in the children of the child who died after B but before A receiving nothing?

A: Some courts would indeed say "yes, there is" and might construe "children" to include grandchildren (although that's an uncommon approach) or they might simply reverse the usual rule and construe "surviving" to mean surviving G.

---

(3) Express Conditions of Death without Issue

Example 7.14: G devises property in trust to T as trustee to pay the income to A for life and then to end the trust and distribute the trust property to B, but if B dies without surviving issue, to C.

Interests created: A = *present interest* (life income interest)

> B = *vested remainder subject to divestment* ("but if" indicates a condition subsequent)
>
> C = *executory interest*

The question is when do we decide if B has died "without surviving issue"? If B is alive at A's death, does the condition subsequent disappear and along with it C's executory interest? Or do we have to wait in that circumstance to see if B dies without issue *after* A's death? If we take the later construction, the shadow of possible divesting will always darken B's ownership of the property, making it difficult for B to sell the property since any title B delivers will also be subject to possible divestment. The usual construction is to resolve the condition subsequent at the distribution date, in Example 7.14, A's death. If B is alive at that time, the trust property is distributed to B and C's interest vanishes. If at A's death B is dead and there are no living issue of B, the property will be distributed to the holder of the executory interest. Remember that if C dies while A and B are still alive, the executory interest passes through C's estate because C's death does nothing to resolve to condition subsequent.

Sidebar

DEAD AS THE DODO, PART 4—INDEFINITE FAILURE OF ISSUE

All this talk about dying without issue requires another trip to the museum of extinct concepts. The common law definition of "to die without issue" is what's known as **indefinite failure of issue**. Indefinite failure of issue means that all of a person's descendants are dead. Indefinite failure of issue, therefore, occurs when a family line dies out. That means no matter how many descendants of a person are living at the person's death, he will "die without issue" if there are no descendants living at any time in the future. So if a condition precedent or subsequent involves "dying without issue" and dying without issue means indefinite failure of issue, it could be a very long time before the condition is resolved. That wait increases the possibility that the Rule Against Perpetuities will somehow be violated. For now you just have to know that the indefinite failure of issue construction is not part of American law, sometimes by statute, sometimes by court decision, and to die without issue means to have no descendants living at one's death.

(4) Express Condition of Reaching a Specified Age

Express conditions involving a requirement that the beneficiary reach a certain age are very common. It is easy to think of reasons why such a requirement is widely used. One reason is the fear that a relatively young person lacks the maturity to manage wealth prudently, even if that person is no longer a minor. Another reason more relevant to the creation of future interests is the simple fact that a minor cannot make a will. If a minor dies with a transmissible interest, it will most likely pass to the minor's surviving parents or parent as the minor's sole heirs. A transferor might prefer that in such a situation that other persons in the minor's generation benefit from the property at the distribution date.

Whatever the reasons, contingencies related to age are frequently attached to future interests, and there are well-established rules of construction that apply when courts have to find the meaning of the words used to state the condition. The most widely accepted rules have their origin in a decision of the English Court of Chancery made in 1677. In Clobberie's Case,[1] the Lord Chancellor[2] held that a bequest of a sum of money to a woman "at her age of twenty-one years, or day of marriage, to be paid unto her with interest" was not contingent on the woman reaching the age of 21, but rather was vested. That means that if she died before reaching age 21, the money passed to her estate. According to the report of the case, Chancellor Finch then uttered two dicta. The first was that "if money were bequeathed to one at his age of twenty-one years," reaching the stated age is condition precedent. The second was that "if money be given to one, to be paid at the age of twenty-one years," the age requirement is not a condition precedent and if the donee dies before that age the money goes to the deceased donee's estate.

The first and third rules in Clobberie's Case, that is, the holding and the second dictum, are widely followed. Under the holding, a gift of the income of property to a person with the property itself to be paid over at a stated age is a gift of all the property. Survival to the stated age is not required. The third rule ("to be paid at") is often described as creating a gift with possession postponed. The second rule — the use of the word "at" means that the age requirement is a condition precedent — is not as widely accepted as the first and third rules. The best that can be said is that the cases are divided.

(5) Class Gifts

We've already met class gifts in Chapter 5. There we were dealing with class gifts in wills, and most of the discussion was about single-generation class gifts — gifts to "my children" or to "my brother and sisters." We did note, however, that class gifts can also be multigenerational — gifts to "my descendants" or to "my issue." One of the distinguishing characteristics of multigenerational class gifts is that the only class members entitled to share in a devise under a will are those who are living when the testator dies. So far so good, and so far we've only been talking about immediate gifts, more properly gifts of present interests. The property is distributed when the testator dies, which is the moment when the gift is made. What happens when future interests in a trust are class gifts?

---

[1] 2 Vent. 342, 86 Eng. Rep. 476 (1677).
[2] The Lord Chancellor was Heneage Finch, who later became the first Earl of Nottingham and who decided the Duke of Norfolk's Case, which set the Rule Against Perpetuities on its modern course of development.

(a) Future Interests and Class Gifts

When it comes to discussing class gifts and future interests, the most important thing you have to know is illustrated by the following example.

Example 7.15: O devises property in trust to T as trustee to pay the income to O's surviving spouse S for life, then to end the trust and distribute the trust property to O's descendants [or issue, doesn't matter].

The remainder in Example 7.15 is a multigeneration class gift. When we discussed multigeneration class gifts in wills, all we had to understand was that whatever property was given to the class members would be distributed by representation. Which system of representation to use could be set out in the will or determined by a statutory default rule. We didn't give much thought to the requirement that a devisee survive the testator, except to note that anti-lapse statutes do not apply to multigeneration class gifts. When the gift to the multigeneration class is a future interest, however, there is a very important and universally accepted rule you must know: *a gift of a present or a future interest to a multigeneration class carries with it an implied condition of survival to the distribution date.* This is the one important exception to the preference for early vesting and the no implied condition of survival rule. In Example 7.15, therefore, O has created a contingent remainder because there is an implied condition precedent of survival to the distribution date, the death of S. What does that mean for child B who survives O but dies before S? At B's death, B's contingent remainder simply vanishes because B has failed to fulfill the condition precedent of surviving S.

Most of what we said in Chapter 5 about multigeneration class gifts of present interests in wills — a gift of the residue to "my descendants," for example — applies to a class gift of a future interest in a trust, whether the trust is created by will or by during the lifetime of the settlor of the trust:

- The class takes by representation even if the words "by representation" or "per stirpes" or something similar do not appear.
  - In that case, a statute may define the representational scheme to use.
  - If there is no statute, decisional law probably holds that the same system used by the jurisdiction's intestacy statute should apply.
- If the words "by representation" or "per stirpes" or something similar do appear, the document may also define the system of representation to which those words correspond.
  - If the document doesn't include a definition, a statute may define what system is meant "by representation" and "per stirpes."
  - If there is no statutory definition, case law will probably tell us which system corresponds to which terms.

We can also have the gift of a future interest to a single-generation class.

Example 7.16: O transfers property in trust to T as trustee to pay the income to O's surviving spouse S for life, then to end the trust and distribute the trust property to O's children.

At the time of the creation of the trust, any living children of O have indefeasibly vested remainders. There is no condition precedent, and the children are ascertained. If a child, we'll call the child B, dies after creation of the trust and before the distribution date, which is S's death, the interest passes through B's estate to B's successors in interest. The interest is clearly transmissible; there is no condition attached to the remainder, so the death of remainder person can't change anything. At the date of distribution, whatever fraction of the trust property belongs to B's remainder interest will be distributed to B's successors in interest and can include the successors in interest of B's successors in interest.

If Example 7.16 involved a testamentary trust created in O's will, the only additional consideration would be the possible application of the anti-lapse statute if a class member, like child B, died before O. As we learned in Chapter 5, it is highly likely that unless the will overrides the anti-lapse statute, (1) the anti-lapse statute will apply to gifts to children of the testator, (2) the anti-lapse statute will apply to a class gift to a single-generation class as if it were a gift to the class members as individuals (but maybe not to class members who died before execution of the will), and (3) the anti-lapse statute will give the lapsed gift to the issue of the deceased beneficiary by representation. So in Example 7.16, the death of B before O means that B's remainder interest will end up in the hands of B's issue who survive O, using whatever scheme of representation the anti-lapse statute uses. If there are no issue of B who survive O, the usual class gift rules will take over and B's other children living at O's death will take the remainder interest.

There are a few other things about class gifts of future interests that we have to talk about before we can leave the topic. The first is classification of class gifts of future interests.

Example 7.17: O devises property in trust to T as trustee to pay the income to O's child A for life, then to end the trust and distribute the trust property to A's children.

If when O dies A has never had children, the remainder is contingent because it is created in unascertained persons. Once A does have a child, the remainder is vested (there is no condition precedent here), but it is not indefeasibly vested. (And the birth of the child means that O's reversion disappears.) After all, A can have more children who will have a share of the remainder. Therefore, while A can have more children, the existing children of A have a **vested remainder subject to partial divestment**. The next child of A to be born will also have a vested remainder by taking one-half of the interest of her older sibling. Another way to describe the interest the living children of A have is to call it a **vested remainder subject to open**. "Open" means that more class members can come into existence. These unborn class members have executory interests because their interest will divest an existing vested interest.

F   A   Q

Q: In Examples 7.17 and 7.18, what happens if A does have a child who dies before O? Will the anti-lapse statute apply?

A: Yes it will, so long as the child's death does not mean that the child's interest has vanished. In Example 7.17, there is no condition precedent attached to the remainder so the anti-lapse statute could apply if the requirements for its application are met. In Example 7.18, the anti-lapse statute can apply only if the child of A reached 21 years of age before the testator's death. If the child died before that age, the child's interest vanished and the anti-lapse statute cannot apply.

Nothing prevents the creator of the future interest from adding a condition precedent to the mix.

Example 7.18: O devises property in trust to T as trustee to pay the income to O's child A for life, then to end the trust and distribute the trust property to A's children who attain the age of 21.

The addition of "who attain the age of 21" creates a condition precedent. How the addition of the condition affects the future interests compared with Example 7.17 is shown in Table 7.3.

TABLE 7.3	"As Time Goes By II"	

		Future Interests	
Time	**Event**	**Example 7.17**	**Example 7.18**
1	O dies and creates trust; A has no children	Unborn children = *contingent remainder* O's successors in interest = *reversion*	Unborn children = *contingent remainder* O's successors in interest = *reversion*
2	Child X born to A	X = *vested remainder subject to partial divestment (subject to open)* Unborn children = *executory interest* *Reversion* vanishes	X = *contingent remainder* (condition precedent) Unborn children = *contingent remainder* O's successors in interest = *reversion*
3	Child Y born to A	X, Y = *vested remainder subject to partial divestment (subject to open)* Unborn children = *executory interest* *Reversion* vanished at time 2	X, Y = *contingent remainder* (condition precedent) Unborn children = *contingent remainder* O's successors in interest = *reversion*
4	Child Z born to A	X, Y, Z = *vested remainder subject to partial divestment (subject to open)* Unborn children = *executory interest* *Reversion* vanished at time 2	X, Y, Z = *contingent remainder* (condition precedent) Unborn children = *contingent remainder* O's successors in interest = *reversion*
5	X dies at 18	X's interest transmitted in intestacy to A and other parent (B) Y, Z = *vested remainder subject to partial divestment (subject to open)* Unborn children = *executory interest* *Reversion* vanished at time 2	X's interest vanishes Y, Z = *contingent remainder* (condition precedent) O's successors in interest = *reversion*

TABLE 7.3	*(Continued)*		

		Future Interests	
Time	**Event**	**Example 7.17**	**Example 7.18**
6	Y turns 21	Y, Z, A, B = *vested remainder subject to partial divestment (subject to open)* Unborn children = *executory interest* *Reversion* vanished at time 2	Y = *vested remainder subject to partial divestment (subject to open)* Z = *contingent remainder* (condition precedent) Unborn children = *contigent remainder* *Reversion* vanishes
7	Z turns 21	Y, Z, A, B = *vested remainder subject to partial divestment (subject to open)* Unborn children = *executory interest* *Reversion* vanished at time 2	Y, Z = *vested remainder subject to partial divestment (subject to open)* Unborn children = *contingent remainder* *Reversion* vanished at time 6
8	Y dies at age 25 with a will leaving probate estate to spouse H	H, Z, A, B = *vested remainder subject to partial divestment (subject to open)* (Y's interest transmitted) Unborn children = *executory interest* *Reversion* vanished at time 2	H, Z = *vested remainder subject to partial divestment (subject to open)* (Y's interest transmitted) Unborn children = *contingent remainder* *Reversion* vanished at time 6
9	A dies	Trust ends; trust property distributed 1/3 to H, 1/3 to Z, 1/6 to A's estate, and 1/6 to other parent	Trust ends; trust property distributed 1/2 to H, 1/2 to Z

There are several things to note:

- In Example 7.18, X's death before fulfilling the condition precedent means X's interest vanishes; but when Y dies *after* fulfilling the condition precedent, Y's interest is transmissible and passes through Y's testate estate to H. Because there is no condition precedent in Example 7.17, X's interest is transmissible no matter what X's age.
- In Example 7.18, when Y fulfills the condition precedent, the reversion vanishes because now there is a vested remainder. In Example 7.17, because there is no condition precedent, once a child is born to A the reversion vanishes.
- In both examples so long as A is alive, A is presumed to be able to have children so the class remains open so all the children in Example 7.17 and the children in Example 7.18 who have fulfilled the condition precedent have remainders that are vested subject to partial divestment (or subject to open).

F   A   Q

Q: Is there such a thing as a "contingent remainder subject to open"?

A: Yes, but really no (sorry). Any remainder in a class that can increase in number, in other words, which more persons can join, usually by being born, is "open." However, a contingent remainder in a class that is not closed is never described as "subject to open." Why? Well, it just isn't done. There is a good reason for avoiding the term, however. It is very useful to think of "vested subject to partial divestment" and "subject to open" as the same thing. Since a remainder in a class is contingent when none of the class members have vested interests, they can't be subject to partial divestment and therefore the contingent remainder is not "subject to open." If you keep the term "open" away from continent remainders, you have less of a chance of being confused about whether a member of a class has a vested remainder.

(b) Closing the Class

Clearly, it is very important to know when no more persons can join the class. When no more members can join the class, the class is "closed." Classes can close in two ways: (1) *physiologically*, when no more class members can be born; and (2) by *the rule of convenience*, which states that when a class member is entitled to possession of the property that is the subject of the class gift, the class must close so that the minimum amount that can be distributed to the class member entitled to payment can be calculated.

Closing the Class Physiologically. If a gift is made "to the children of A," then the class closes physiologically when A dies and is no longer capable of having children. Of course, that statement has always been less than literally true. When A is male, there is always a possibility that a child of A is *in ventre sa mere* at A's death. If that child is later born alive, her existence relates back to the time of conception and thus she can participate in a class gift to the children of A.

In determining when a class closes physiologically, the possibility of adopting children must be taken into account. Generally speaking, an adopted child is "born" for purposes of a class gift when the child is adopted. The new Restatement goes even farther. Restatement (Third) of Property § 15.1 comment i states that "by analogy to a child in gestation," a child in the process of being adopted is a child for purposes of determining class membership while the adoption is in process. The child is therefore included in the class gift "if the adoption is concluded within a reasonable time." The UPC codifies this rule in § 2-705(g)(3).

F   A   Q

Q: What does the possibility of posthumous conception do to the class closing rules?

A: We have next to no law on the question, although since 2008 the UPC has dealt with the question of who is a class member in the same way it deals in §§ 2-115 to 2-121 with the question of who is a child for purposes of intestate succession. Once parentage is established, a child of assisted conception is a class member in the same way as children conceived through sexual intercourse. The only exception applies if the distribution date is the date of death of the child's parent (UPC § 2-705(g)(2)). If that's the case, then to be treated as living at the parent's death, the child must be in utero not later than 36 months after the deceased parent's death or born no later than 45 months after the deceased parent's death (a requirement that parallels the requirement for treating a posthumously conceived child as an heir of the genetic parent (UPC §§ 2-120(k), 2-121(h)).

Closing the Class by the Rule of Convenience. The common law takes a ruthlessly practical view of human nature. The rule of convenience is a manifestation of that view because it is based on the simple assumption that once a person has property, he will not give it back. Because the members of a class take the property that is the subject of the gift in equal shares, once at least one class member is entitled to a share of the property, the minimum size of that share must be known. That calculation requires the closing of the class so that the share will not be diluted in the future. Here's a straightforward example.

Example 7.19: T devises $50,000 "to the children of my sister, B." B is living at T's death and has two living children and no children who died before T.

The class of B's children closes on T's death because T's executor needs to know how much to give the two living children. In other words, if the class did not close on T's death so that after-born children of B would be entitled to share in the $50,000, how would T's executor know how much to distribute to the two children of B who are entitled to a share in the gift? If the executor gives them each $25,000, you can be sure that if B does have another child, the executor will have a difficult time getting the older children to give some of their gift back so that their new sibling can share in the gift. As we said, the common law is ruthlessly practical. If the executor decides to distribute less than the entire $25,000 to the two children of B to take into account the possibility of B having more children, how much should the executor hold back and for how long? Will the executor ever be able to close the estate before B's death? Respect for the practicalities leads to the formulation of a rule that allows the executor to wrap up the administration of T's estate as expeditiously as possible.

Things are a little more complicated when the class gift is a future interest that will vest in possession after the termination of a life estate or a life income interest in a trust. The class might be closed physiologically at the time the future interest in the class is created, of course, but if it is not, *the rule of convenience cannot apply until the life income interest ends.* In other words, *the rule of convenience cannot close the class before the distribution date.* It should be obvious why that statement is always true. While the trust property is paying income to the life income beneficiary, the trustee cannot distribute the trust property to the remainder beneficiaries. (And while the life tenant is in possession of Blackacre, the remainder persons cannot be.) They cannot cash in their claim check until the life income interest is finished. Here's an example.

Example 7.20: O devises property in trust to T as trustee to pay the income to A for life, then to end the trust and distribute the trust property to the children of B who attain 25 years of age.

The class of B's children will close physiologically when B dies. If B survives A and a child of B is 25 years old when A dies (that's the distribution date), the class will close by the rule of convenience. That child has fulfilled the condition precedent, is entitled to come into possession of her share of the trust property, and the trustee must be able to calculate the minimum share to which the child is entitled. Other living children of B under the age of 25 are in the class and will share in the trust property if they reach 25. Children of B born after the class closing are out of luck. If the class of B's children is not closed physiologically at A's death, it will also close by the rule of convenience if a child of B died after reaching 25 but before A. By fulfilling the condition precedent, that child acquired a vested remainder that was transmissible, and on A's death that child's successors in interest can demand payment of their share of the trust property, thus closing the class. Of course, if B survives A and at A's death no child of B has ever reached 25 years of age, the class can close by the rule of convenience when a child of B turns 25 before B's death.

As you can see, knowing when the class closes is absolutely necessary to knowing how to distribute the property that is the subject of the class gift. In addition, as we will learn, the application of the Rule Against Perpetuities to class gifts requires knowing when the class closes.

There are two more rules involving class gifts that deal with unusual situations. Here's the first.

Example 7.21: T devises $50,000 "to the children of my sister, B." At the time of T's death, B has never had any children.

This is a class gift to an "empty class." The rule is that the class remains open until it closes physiologically at B's death, even though that makes things difficult for the personal representative. The same rule applies to a gift of a future interest to an empty class.

Another traditional rule concerns "specific sum" class gifts — that is, gifts of a specific sum to each member of a class.

Example 7.22: O devises "$10,000 to each of the children of my nephew, N."

If at T's death N is alive but N has never had children, the class closes at T's death and the gift fails. If N had living children at T's death, or if a child of N had predeceased T but was covered by an anti-lapse statute, the class would close by the rule of convenience at T's death, and a child born to N after T's death would not share in the gift.

D. A New System of Future Interests?

Anything has to be better than this collection of arbitrary anachronisms, right? It is quite true that a good deal of future interest law comes from a past that is quite dead. It should not surprise you, then, that both Restatement (Third) of Property and the UPC have tried to reform the law of future interests. The Restatement project is fairly modest, the UPC provisions quite radical.

(1) Restatement (Third) of Property

Division VII of Restatement (Third) of Property simplifies the classification of future interests. The number of present interests is reduced to four. Three are old friends:

the fee simple absolute, the life estate, and the term of years. The fee simple deter-minable, the fee on a condition subsequent, and a third variety of the "base fee," the fee simple subject to an executory limitation, are all lumped under one classification, the "fee simple defeasible." The three interests that can remain in a transferor—reversion, possibility of reverter, and the right of entry—are all reversions.

The distinction between contingent remainders and executory interests is abolished, and both interests become "contingent remainders." Finally, there is no distinction between a vested remainder subject to divestment and a contingent remainder. Remainders are either certain to vest in possession and are "vested" or it is uncertain whether they will vest in possession and they are therefore "contingent." The Restatement system, therefore, makes no distinction between conditions precedent and conditions subsequent. Either condition will create a contingent remainder. Finally, if a remainder is in a class that can increase, it is "subject to open" whether it is vested or contingent.

Time will tell how influential this new system of classification turns out to be.

(2) The UPC Provisions, § 2-707

The Restatement provisions creating a new sys-tem of classification for future interests are nowhere near as radical as a single section of the UPC. Section 2-707 creates a whole new world of future interests in trusts. Under UPC § 2-707(b), "[a] future interest under the terms of a trust is contingent on the beneficiary's sur-viving the distribution date." In other words, under UPC § 2-707 *every future interest created in a trust is subject to a condition precedent of survival to the distribution date.* This is a rule of construction, however, and under UPC § 2-701 it must give way to a contrary intention on the part of the settlor of the interest. The comment to the section gives two examples of language that creates a transmissible interest; " 'income to A for life, remainder in corpus to B whether or not B survives A' " and " 'income to A for life, remainder in corpus to B or B's estate.' " The examples, however, indicate that the drafters of the UPC at least believe that the contrary intention must be very clear and must expressly negate the requirement of survivorship to the distribution date.

Having made all future interests in trusts contingent on survival to the time of distribution date, UPC § 2-707 goes on to create an anti-lapse statute for such interests. Example 7.23 represents the simplest case.

Example 7.23: O conveys property in trust to T as trustee to pay the income to C for life and then to end the trust and distribute the trust property to X.

Under traditional future interests law, the preference for early vesting and the accompanying no implied conditions of survival rule mean that X has a vested remainder, and if X dies before C the remainder simply passes through X's estate; in other words, the remainder is transmissible. Under UPC § 2-707, if X dies before C, on C's death the trust property passes by representation to X's descendants who survive C. If no descendants survive, the property passes under the residuary clause of O's will if the trust involved was created by a nonresiduary gift in the will; if that rule doesn't apply, the property passes to O's heirs determined as if O had died at the time the property comes into possession.

F   A   Q

Q: Why is UPC § 2-707 limited to interests in trusts? Why exclude legal remainders?

A: Remember that if A has the legal life estate in Blackacre and B has the remainder, a prospective purchaser of fee simple title to Blackacre has to acquire both the legal life estate and the remainder to reassemble the complete bundle of sticks. If the remainder is contingent, not only will the prospective purchaser also have to acquire the reversion, it will be difficult to acquire the remainder interest because the prospective purchaser cannot be sure that every person with a contingent remainder interest had agreed to sell. Some contingent remainder persons may be not yet born, and some who are alive may be minors. In either case, it will be necessary to have some kind of court proceeding to make sure that the interests of the minors and the unborn can be property conveyed. The result is that it will be difficult to sell the real property involved, even if that is the economically wise thing to do. The drafters of the UPC provision decided that the difficulties caused by making all legal remainders contingent on survival to death of the life tenant far outweighed any advantages to be gained by eliminating transmissible interests.

There is much more to UPC § 2-707 than the simple example above. The statute carefully provides rules for situations where there is more than one gift of the property. The statutory scheme is necessarily complex, but it does work. The provision has not proved popular, however, and has been enacted in only ten states and in some of those in modified versions.

Whether UPC § 2-707 is a good idea is a difficult question to answer. It does work a radical change and probably will lead to many unforeseen results before the old law completely passes from the minds of practitioners and judges. On the other hand, it eliminates all transmissible interests except those deliberately created. Trust property will not be disposed of unknowingly through the residuary clauses or intestate estates of beneficiaries who do not understand that among their assets is a future interest. The beneficiary who does understand, however, is deprived of the opportunity to select the person to enjoy the trust property if the beneficiary cannot. If the settlor of the trust wants to give the beneficiary that control, however, as we have noted and will examine in detail in Chapter 10, the way to do it is to create a power of appointment.

SUMMARY

- A future interest is a property interest that may or may not give the holder of the future interest the possession or enjoyment of the property to which the future interest is related.

- Future interests are subject to a complex system of classification, which is based on whether the future interest is retained by the settlor of the arrangement or created in transferees; on what type of estate the holder of the future interest might eventually acquire; and on what types of conditions, if any, are attached to the future interest.

■ A future interest can be transferred at death by the holder of the interest so long as the death does not resolve a condition in such a way that the interest vanishes.

■ Courts have a battery of constructional rules at their disposal when they are called on to give meaning to unclear language creating a future interest. The most important of these is a preference for early vesting and the corresponding refusal to imply a condition of survival to the distribution date.

■ Class gifts of future interests are subject to some special rules, the most important of which is that multigeneration class gifts are subject to an implied condition of survival to the distribution date. It is very important to know when a class gift closes. Classes can close physiologically when no more class members can come into being or by the rule of convenience when a class member is entitled to distribution.

■ The future interest provisions of Restatement (Third) of Property create a simplified system that classifies interests remaining in transferors as reversions and interests created in transferees as remainders, which in turn are either vested or contingent.

■ UPC § 2-707 radically alters the traditional law of future interests by making every interest in a trust contingent on survival to the distribution date.

CONNECTIONS

Future Interests and Wills

Remember that the discussion of the interests of the beneficiaries of wills in Chapter 3 deals with devises of present interests, devises that come into possession at the testator's death. In other words, the distribution date for such gifts is the testator's death. A will creates future interests when the will creates a testamentary trust. Creation of trusts is discussed in Chapter 8.

Present Interests and Beneficiaries of Trusts

Some beneficiaries of trusts have present interests. In all the examples in this chapter, the beneficiary who has a present interest in the trust has a mandatory income interest because the trustee is directed to distribute all of the trust income to the beneficiary. There are other sorts of present interests in trusts, which are discussed in Chapter 9.

Future Interests and Beneficiaries of Trusts

Some beneficiaries of trusts have future interests. Whether the beneficiaries will actually receive trust property depends on whether they can cash in their claim checks, whether their interests will vest in possession or enjoyment. Knowing whether that will happen requires understanding the rules for construing the words that create future interests. Constructing the right kind of future interests to give the beneficiaries what the person who creates the trust wants them to have equally requires a thorough knowledge of what words create what sorts of interests.

Transferability of Future Interests and Creditors

The basic rule of transferability of future interests at death is that if the death of the holder of the future interest does not resolve a condition that makes the interest disappear, the interest is transmissible. The settlor of the future interest can prevent lifetime transfer of the interest to keep the interest out of the hands of the creditors of the holder of the interest. The law that governs the prohibition of lifetime transfers of all interests in trust, whether future or present, is discussed in Chapter 9.

Classification of Future Interests and the Rule Against Perpetuities

How a future interest is classified determines whether it can be invalidated by the classic common law Rule Against Perpetuities. The Rule is the subject of Chapter 12. Realize, however, that the classic common law Rule is diminishing in importance, which in turn makes the traditional scheme for classifying future interests of less significance.

Trusts: Creation, Modification, and Termination

If wills and trusts were clothing, wills could be tuxedos and trusts blue jeans. How so? Valid wills typically must comply with the formalities

of the Statute of Wills. They're dressed up, formal, and sitting atop too-tight shoes on their way to their brother's wedding. Trusts, on the other hand, are created when a property owner manifests only an intention to create these instruments, and this intention can be expressed informally. Sure, trusts have got some basic requirements: property, a trustee, and at least one beneficiary. And yes, the law has more than just that to say about the elements of a valid trust (though the requirements are less demanding than they once were). But compared to wills? Trusts are dressed down, informal, and ready for a Saturday afternoon.

A. WHAT IS A TRUST?

B. TRUST CREATION

1. Intention to Create a Trust
2. Mechanics of Creation
3. All about Trustees
4. Necessity of Trust Property
5. Need for Beneficiaries

A. What Is a Trust?

We've already had a good deal to say about trusts, and we'll have much more to say. Before we go on, however, it's time (or perhaps past time) to make sure we know what we're talking about when we utter that magic word, "trust." It's worth quoting Restatement (Third) of Trusts § 2: a trust "is a fiduciary relationship with respect to property, arising from a manifestation of intention to create that relationship and subjecting the person who holds title to the property to duties to deal with it for the benefit of charity or one or more persons, at least one of whom is not the sole trustee."

Almost every concept in that definition will be discussed in this and the following chapters. For now, however, let's make the idea of a trust more concrete by using a metaphor. We're going to think of a trust as a box with a lid and a spout coming out of one side. (Instead of a box, you can envision a coffee urn, a samovar, or a keg, just so long as you've got a vessel with a lid and a spout.) The spout has a valve on it so the flow through the spout can be regulated.

The person who creates the trust, the **settlor**, builds the box. The instructions for building the box can be contained in a will. If that's the case, the trust is a **testamentary trust**. The settlor can also create a trust during life, and such a trust is a **lifetime** or **inter vivos trust** (use of the Latin term is diminishing). The instructions for building that box can be contained in a variety of written documents, and if the box is going to hold personal property, the instructions can be oral. The purpose of the box is to hold property, and the property is placed in the trust — in formal terms, the trust is **funded** — by opening the lid and putting the property in. Opening the lid to put property into the trust is accomplished by the **trustee** taking title to the property. If you read the Restatement definition carefully, you'll see that a trust is defined not as a "thing" but as a relationship with respect to property. The relationship is between the trustee who holds title to the property and the **beneficiaries** for whose benefit the trustee manages the property. The box really is a metaphor for a relationship that involves the property, the trustee, and the beneficiaries. Therefore, when property becomes trust property, it gets put in the box through the open lid by giving the trustee title to the property.

F   A   Q

Q: What do we call the person who creates a trust?

A: Restatement (Third) of Trusts and the Uniform Trust Code (§ 103(15)) use the term already introduced, "settlor," which comes from the English usage in which a trust is often referred to as a settlement. The Internal Revenue Code uses the term **grantor**, which is related to the practice of creating a trust of real property by granting property by deed to the trustee. Because taxation is so important in the modern world, use of "grantor" in connection with all trusts has become quite common. A somewhat more modern usage is **creator**. This is a perfectly good term (and used in some state statutes), even though it can seem a bit pretentious (since "Creator" with a capital "C" refers to ideas and concepts of somewhat greater depth and complexity than the law of trusts). **Trustor** is a somewhat uncommon term, but it is used from time to time.

Once the box is constructed, the trustee has title to the trust property, and the beneficiaries are named, the day-to-day operations of the trust begin. These operations involve getting the benefits of the trust property to the beneficiaries. The benefits to which the beneficiaries are entitled come in two varieties. Beneficiaries who are entitled to benefits at any given time — that is, those who have a present interest in the trust property — almost always benefit from what flows out of the box's spout. The property that flows out of the spout is the income produced by the trust property. We have a good deal more to learn about trust income, but for now realize that the most common sorts of income and their sources are these:

TABLE 8.1

Type of Trust Property	Income Produced
Equity investments (common and preferred stock)	Dividends
Real estate	Rents
Debt instruments (bonds, CDs, bank accounts)	Interest

While anything that qualifies as property can be held in trust (we'll have more to say about that too), it's probably a safe bet that most of the trust income produced by trusts in the United States falls into one of the three categories in the table.

The income flows through the spout, which, as I hope you remember, includes a valve. The trustee controls the value and manages it according to the settlor's directions. These directions are the **terms of the trust**. Sometimes the trustee is instructed simply to leave the valve open so that all of the trust income is distributed to the beneficiaries at some interval — monthly or quarterly, for example. Sometimes the trustee is given the authority to turn the valve on and off or to open it part way and to vary the amount of opening. If there is more than one beneficiary of the income, the trustee can also be given the authority to direct the flow of income from the spout to

WHAT'S WITH THE DIFFERENT TERMS FOR TRUST PROPERTY?

"Trust property" is perfectly clear and is becoming more widely used. An older term with an English flavor is **trust res** (*res* is Latin for "thing"). The Internal Revenue Code talks about the **trust corpus** (*corpus* is Latin for "body"). The Latin terms are somewhat old fashioned, and "trust property" is widely used along with another modern term, **trust principal**. "Principal" and "income" are accounting terms, and "trust principal" is usually used when the discussion involves distinguishing between income and principal. That's why a trust in which the trustee has authority to distribute trust property to current beneficiaries is often said to be discretionary as to principal.

beneficiaries the trustee selects. If the trustee has the authority to open and close the valve or to direct the flow of income among the beneficiaries, the trust is a **discretionary income trust** (and we'll have more to say about those trusts, too).

The second way beneficiaries are entitled to benefit from the trust is through their interest in the trust property itself. The settlor can give the trustee authority to open the lid of the box and take property out and give it to the beneficiaries. The trustee can be directed to do that on regular intervals or, and what is far more usual, when the trustee sees fit. If the trustee does indeed have the authority to open the lid and remove trust property for distribution to the beneficiaries, the trust is a **discretionary trust as to principal**.

So far we've been talking about current beneficiaries who receive the benefit of income and principal (no matter what degree of trustee discretion is involved). "Current beneficiaries" are not necessarily the same as "income beneficiaries" because some income beneficiaries may be entitled to benefit only from the trust's income at some time in the future. Such beneficiaries can have remainders in income, which they can begin to enjoy once a condition precedent is fulfilled (like reaching a certain age or being born). Usually, however, when we contrast the interests of current beneficiaries and future beneficiaries, we are contrasting current beneficiaries with **remainder beneficiaries**, persons who have remainders in fee simple that may eventually come into possession giving them fee simple ownership of the trust property. (See, all that future interest stuff really has some real-world significance.)

At some time in the future, the trust will end, or **terminate** (although as we will see, one of the striking developments in the law of trusts at the end of the twentieth century is the possibility of a perpetual trust). At the time appointed by the settlor, the trustee will take all of the trust property out of the box and distribute it to the remainder beneficiaries, who will own the property outright. At that time, the box will dissolve and be no more. The trust relationship will be over.

So now we've seen two ways that property can come out of the trust box. Income can flow through the spout or, if the trustee has authority to open the lid, trust property can be distributed to current beneficiaries in accordance with the settlor's instructions. The trustee will also open the lid for the last time at the termination of the trust, and the trust property will be distributed to the remainder beneficiaries. There is another way for trust property to leave the trust box, but it does not involve opening the lid and distributing property to beneficiaries.

To understand this second way in which property can leave the box, we have to elaborate the metaphor a bit. Now we have to imagine that the trustee has a pair of magic gloves that allow the trustee to reach right through the side of the trust box and take property out. This is trust property that the trustee has decided to sell rather than distribute to beneficiaries. The proceeds of sale are also trust property, and the trustee can reach through the side of the box and put the proceeds in. If the trustee uses the proceeds to buy property, the property bought is trust property and goes into the box. One of the great challenges a trustee faces is how to make decisions about selling trust property and buying different property—in other words, how to invest the trust property to make its value increase and still treat the current and the remainder beneficiaries impartially. We'll talk about this in greater detail. For now, you must understand the difference between distributing trust property to beneficiaries (opening the lid) and investing and reinvesting trust property (reaching through the side of the box). And now to discussing all of this in much greater detail.

But not quite yet. We better deal with some important terminology before we go any further. Almost all of this chapter is devoted to **express trusts**. An express trust is created when a person manifests the intent necessary to do so, something we're going to deal with immediately after this short diversion. The other two types of trusts are resulting trusts and constructive trusts. They are not created by a person's manifestation of intent to create a trust, but instead come into existence through a legal implication in appropriate circumstances. To use our box metaphor, these two types of trusts are boxes built not by persons but by the law (acting through courts with equity powers). Both resulting and constructive trusts interact with express trusts, so we'll discuss them here to the extent necessary.

This is also a good time to describe briefly how express trusts can be classified. One way, as we've already said, is by how a trust is created: either in a will (testamentary trust) or by a living person (lifetime trust). Another way is according to who the beneficiaries of the trust are. A **charitable trust** is for the benefit of charity, and we'll discuss that sort of trust in Chapter 15. A **private trust** benefits private individuals. It is possible to create a trust to benefit charity and private individuals, and we'll say a bit about those too in Chapter 17.

B. Trust Creation

To keep with our metaphor, the first step in using a trust to make gifts is building the box. The trust family divides into two basic branches. The first contains trusts created by living settlors (lifetime trusts), and the second, trusts created in wills (testamentary trusts). While the same law of trusts governs both branches of the family, occasionally different rules apply depending on how the trust was created.

F   A   Q

Q: When is a testamentary trust created?

A: A testamentary trust is created at the moment of death, and the beneficiaries' interests come into existence then. However, the trustee will receive letters testamentary only when the will is admitted to probate, and it will be some time after that before the executor actually funds the trust by distributing to the trustee the probate property devised to the trustee by the will. Once the trust is funded, the beneficiaries may be entitled to "make-up" distributions for the period before the trust was funded or the executor may have made distributions to them during that time from the property devised to the trustee.

F   A   Q

Q: How does a will create a trust?

A: A well-drafted will creating a trust will make a devise to the trustee named in the will to be held in trust on terms set forth in the will. The devise can be a specific devise of an item of property, a general devise of a sum of money, or a devise of the residue of the probate estate. Of course, a testamentary trust is created by the manifestation of the testator's intent to create a trust. In a will that does not expressly create a trust, that intent can be found through interpretation and construction of the will's language.

(1) Intention to Create a Trust

To create a trust, the would-be settlor needs only the intention to do so. This really distinguishes the law of trusts from the law of wills. You'll remember that unless a jurisdiction has adopted the harmless error rule by enacting UPC § 2-503 or a similar statute, all the intent in the world does not make a document a will unless the requirements of the Statute of Wills have been fulfilled or the document is a valid holograph. (Recall that U.S. courts have been reluctant to hold that the harmless error rule or something like it is part of the common law.) The law of trusts is the exact opposite. So long as there is intention to create a trust, a trust indeed is created (with some exceptions, noted below). That last sentence is a bit of a fudge because "intent to create a trust" involves more than announcing to the world "I now create a trust." Remember that we're talking here about creating our metaphorical box and that the box is a metaphor for the trust relationship, which in turn involves a trustee, beneficiaries, and property. So the intent to create a trust involves not only saying "I create a trust" but also identification of the trust property, the beneficiaries, and the purposes of the trust. Those requirements, however, have become much less demanding than they once were.

(a) Capacity of Settlor

It should go without saying that a person intending to create a trust has to have sufficient capacity. Here again, there is a dramatic difference between the law of trusts and the law of wills. There is one standard of capacity for the making of a will, because, well, a will is a will is a will. The capacity necessary to create a trust, however, depends on the type of trust and the terms of the trust. Creating a testamentary trust requires the same relatively low level of capacity necessary to make a will (comment to UTC § 402, Restatement (Third) of Trusts § 11(1)). Creating an irrevocable lifetime trust requires the same capacity necessary to make an outright transfer of the property, which usually means the capacity to make a gift (Restatement (Third) of Trusts § 11(3)). To create a lifetime revocable trust, however, the settlor needs only the level of capacity necessary to make a will because the settlor can resume fee simple ownership of the property and revocable trusts are usually created as will substitutes (fully discussed in Chapter 11) (Restatement (Third) of Trusts § 11(2)).

(b) Language and the Creation of Trusts

Words being what they are, courts sometimes draw fine lines between language that creates a trust and language that simply expresses a wish that someone will do something with property. Drawing these lines is complicated by the well-accepted principle that manifesting the intent to create a trust does not require the use of the words "trust" or "trustee" (Restatement (Third) of Trusts § 13 cmt. b). Courts must usually decide whether the questionable language shows the intention to create a trust or is merely **precatory**—that is, it expresses only a nonbinding wish that the transferee of the property do something with it.

What this all means is that (1) if you're drafting language for a client who does not want to create a trust, state that the "desire" or "request" or "wish" is precatory and not binding on the transferee of the property involved; and (2) if you're trying to determine what someone else's poor drafting means, you're going to have to immerse yourself in the cases in the relevant jurisdiction.

(2) Mechanics of Creation

In one sense, there are no mechanics of creating a trust worth talking about. Because intent can be expressed in so many ways and because there is nothing like the Statute of Wills for lifetime trusts, there are no requirements for the form a lifetime trust must take—except in one case: where real property is involved.

(a) Distinction between Real and Personal Property

Once again we have to consider the Statute of Frauds, which since its enactment in 1677 has influenced the formal requirements for executing a will. Section 7 of the statute requires that all trusts of lands "shall be manifested and proved by some writing, signed by the party who is by law enabled to declare such trust, or by his last will in writing." Otherwise, as the statute says, the trust "shall be utterly void and of no effect." This requirement of a writing for trusts of land is the law of most of the United States, but as comment a to Restatement (Third) of Trusts § 22 notes, the requirement is expressed in a variety of statutes, and in some states it is even part of the common law of the jurisdiction. And needless to say, there are jurisdictions in which the requirement is *not* the law. On the whole, you can be pretty confident that creating a trust that holds land as trust property requires a signed writing.

F   A   Q

Q: If the settlor validly creates an oral trust of personal property, can the trustee sell the personal property and buy real property with the proceeds?

A: Yes, strangely enough. The whole Statute of Frauds thing applies only to the *creation* of the trust. Of course, if it can be shown that the trust terms do not authorize the trustee to invest in real property (more likely in the modern world that they expressly forbid the trustee from making such an investment), then the trustee would be committing a breach of duty to invest in real property.

Trusts that hold personal property as trust property at the creation of the trust need not be in writing. But just because a person can create an oral trust doesn't mean that it's advisable to do so. It's a lot more difficult to prove a trust exists when there's no writing that states the terms of the trust — who the beneficiaries are and what their respective interests are and what the trustee is supposed to do. The UTC requires clear and convincing evidence to prove the creation of an oral trust and its terms (§ 407). There are non-UTC statutes that require this high level of proof, and many cases that do so as well, but it is not a universal rule. Again, the UTC agrees with the UPC and the third series of Restatements of Property and Trusts that the way to ensure that intent is carried out in the absence of compliance with formalities (or of any formalities at all) is to require proof by clear and convincing evidence.

THE UTC AND FORMALITIES OF TRUST CREATION

The UTC mirrors the lack of agreement among U.S. jurisdictions on whether trusts of land must be in writing and on the source of that rule. UTC § 401 says that a trust may be created by a transfer of property to someone as trustee during the lifetime of the property owner, by will, or by some other disposition at death or a declaration by the owner of property that the owner holds the property as trustee. Whether the transfer has to be in writing is left to other law.

Also left to other law is the question of when the required writing must be signed. In some jurisdictions, the "when" question is a matter of common law, and the provisions of Restatement (Third) of Trusts § 23 may very well state the governing rules.

All in all, given the lack of uniformity on the writing requirement and the resulting signature requirement, the drafters of the UTC made a wise choice not to try to create a uniform provision.

(b) What Sort of Writing Is Needed?

Every testamentary trust, of course, is set out in writing because it is part of a will that must be in writing (putting aside the very narrow exceptions for oral wills; see Chapter 3). There are basically two ways to create a lifetime trust in writing. The settlor can make a written **declaration of trust** that states that the settlor holds certain property as trustee and states the purposes of the trust and identifies the beneficiaries. The only formality involved is that the declaration of trust must be signed by the settlor. The settlor can also transfer property to another person as trustee through the use of a **trust agreement** in which the transferor says "I'm transferring this property in trust to X as trustee."

When a writing is required by the Statute of Frauds or another provision of the law of the jurisdiction, there are widely accepted rules about who must and sign and when. The signature of the creator of the trust will do, and if the trust is created by a trust agreement, the signature of the trustee will suffice. The settlor can sign a declaration of trust making the declaration or at any time before transferring the property involved to someone else. The settlor can sign the trust agreement before or at the time of the transfer of the property to the trustee. The trustee under a trust agreement can sign before or after the time of transfer of property to the trustee or at any time after the transfer but before the property is transferred to yet another person. Restatement (Third) of Trusts § 23 sets out these widely accepted principles.

By now you've no doubt figured out that the "traditional" law of the formalities of trust creation is not at all uniform. This lack of uniformity is not just a matter of different versions of the Statute of Frauds. A few states use far more elaborate rules for the creation of lifetime trusts, including requirements that all lifetime trusts be in writing and executed in conformity with statutory requirements. The execution requirements often require that the settlor and the trustee sign the writing creating the trust and acknowledge their signatures before a notary public; often the acknowledgment is required to be in the form required for a deed of real property. The more formal the execution requirements, the more this aspect of the law of trusts resembles the law of due execution of wills.

(c) Secret Trusts and Semi-Secret Trusts in Wills

You've probably got yourself convinced that you don't have to worry too much about the formalities of creating a testamentary trust — a testamentary trust is created in a will so it must be in writing (absent the rarely encountered oral will), and unless the will is a holograph, it has be executed with whatever formalities are required by the law of the jurisdiction.

Now I have to disturb your nice settled conceptions. There is one nasty little aspect of the creation of testamentary trusts that often drives students crazy. First, imagine a testator whose will includes a devise to X, who has promised the testator to hold the property in trust for whatever purpose the testator has explained to X. This is a **secret trust**. We know that the testator has not created a testamentary trust — the words of the will say nothing about the trust; and even if the terms of the trust exist in some written document, they cannot be incorporated by reference into the will because the will does not mention any document. One alternative would be to allow the devisee to keep the property, but that doesn't seem right, does it? The devisee agreed to do what the testator wanted and certainly should not be rewarded for breaking that promise.

Now imagine that the will reads "I give my residuary estate to X to distribute in the manner I have expressed to him." The situation where the language of the will shows that the devisee is supposed to do something with that property that benefits others and not to keep the property for himself is known as a **semi-secret trust**. There still is no testamentary trust — the terms of the will do not appear in the will, and there is no reference to any document that could be incorporated by reference. And once again, it seems wrong to allow the devisee to keep the property. The language of the will shows that the testator did not intend the devisee to have the property for her own. In addition, of course, the devisee probably agreed to do what the testator asked.

Restatement (Third) of Trusts § 18 says that the result in both cases is the same. So long as there is admissible evidence of the testator's intent in making the gift, the devisee can be required to carry out the testator's intent. The remedial device that is used is a constructive trust, which as we'll see in the next section is a powerful equitable remedy. However, there is one little problem. As the reporter's note to Restatement (Third) of Trusts § 18 comment c admits, the blackletter of § 18(1), which says that a constructive trust is the remedy in both the secret trust and semi-secret trust scenarios, "probably does not reflect the current weight of authority in the 'semi-secret trust' situation. . . ." The majority view in U.S. jurisdictions is that property that is the subject of the devise creating a trust but without setting out the terms of the trust is not disposed of by the devise. If the devise is specific or general, it will pass through the residuary devise; and if the devise is of the residuary estate, the property goes to the testator's heirs.

This result is the holding of a very influential opinion of the Massachusetts Supreme Judicial Court, *Olliffe v. Wells*.[1] The testator left her residuary estate to an individual, but not for his own use. The will said the devisee was supposed to distribute the estate in a way that he determined would best carry out the "wishes" the testator expressed to him. The court held that the will gave the devisee only the legal title to the property. Because the will did not give away the beneficial interest in the property (in other words, the devisee was a trustee and not a beneficiary), the beneficial interest must have passed in intestacy to the testator's heirs. (The technical device that gives that result is a resulting trust, which we'll discuss at the end of this chapter.) The holding in *Olliffe v. Wells* was contrary to most of the existing precedents (almost all of them English), but it can be understood as a very formalistic decision taking a very rigid approach to doctrine, perhaps made necessary by the difficult facts of the case. *Olliffe* has been very widely followed, much to the chagrin of many commentators (and the American Law Institute (Restatement (Second) of Trusts § 55 comment e agrees with Restatement (Third) that a constructive trust should be imposed on the devisee for the benefit of the beneficiaries of the semi-secret trust).

(d) Constructive Trusts

We've mentioned constructive trusts several times before now, and the time has come to look at the constructive trust a little more closely. Not that closely, however. As promised at the beginning of this chapter, our subject is express trusts, trusts that are intentionally created by the settlor. A **constructive trust** is a remedial device imposed by a court of equity on a person who holds title to property but who should not be allowed to keep it. The remedy works through the legal fiction of treating the person not as the beneficial owner of the property but as a trustee who has only legal title. The persons who should have title to the property are the beneficiaries of the trust, and the trustee's duty is to convey legal title to the beneficiaries so they become the outright owners of the property (giving them both legal title and beneficial or equitable title).

It's pretty obvious that the real heart of the use of the constructive trust is deciding when the person who has title to the property shouldn't and when the property should be sent elsewhere via the constructive trust. This is where things get a bit murky. If the person who holds title did something wrong to get the property, it is easy to conclude that a constructive trust is an appropriate remedy. The most obvious example is a slayer in a jurisdiction that does not have a comprehensive slayer's statute. Surely someone who commits homicide should not profit from the crime by obtaining the victim's property by inheritance, beneficiary designation, or under a will. Assuming the will or beneficiary designation is valid and that the slayer really is an heir, fee simple title to the property does indeed belong to the slayer. If as a result

---

[1] 130 Mass. 221 (1881).

of an action brought by those persons who would take the victim's property the appropriate court holds that the slayer is not entitled to the property, the constructive trust is the proper remedy. The court cannot invalidate a valid will or beneficiary designation, and it certainly cannot rewrite the intestacy statute, but it can impose a constructive trust on the property and order the slayer as constructive trustee to convey the property to those who should have it.

F A Q

Q: What happens if the constructive trustee does not comply with the order creating the constructive trust?

A: The constructive trustee would be in contempt and could be fined or even imprisoned. In case of a slayer, of course, the constructive trustee may already be imprisoned. Being in contempt, however, could lead to a denial of privileges based on good behavior, including the accrual of time reducing the sentence. The constructive trust does not involve an empty threat.

There are far less reprehensible types of wrongdoing that would justify the imposition of a constructive trust. The most frequent use of the constructive trust in the world of donative transfers is to remedy a failure to comply with a promise not to change a will executed pursuant to a contract (Restatement (Third) of Trusts § 1, reporter's note to cmt. e). If the party bound by the contract executes a new valid will that is admitted to probate, a constructive trust will be imposed on the beneficiaries requiring them to deliver the property to the beneficiaries of the will the testator promised not to change. Even if those beneficiaries have done absolutely nothing wrong, they received the property because of the testator's wrongdoing and therefore have been unjustly enriched. But what about beneficiaries who are unjustly enriched, but through no fault of anyone's wrongdoing?

Here's an example. Testator wants to revoke the codicil to testator's will. Testator shows a photocopy of the signed and attested codicil to a friend who is a retired lawyer. The friend assumes that the paper the testator has is the original codicil, not a copy, and tells the testator, "Just tear it up, that will revoke it." The testator does so, but the codicil is not revoked because a revocatory act must be performed on the original document, the one with the original signatures of the testator and the attesting witnesses. At the testator's death, the codicil is entitled to probate; it was validly executed and it's not revoked (and we'll assume there's no question of lack of capacity, insane delusion, or undue influence). A court might be persuaded to impose a constructive trust on the beneficiaries of the codicil requiring them to deliver their devises to the will beneficiaries who would have taken the property had the codicil been revoked. (That's what happened in *Estate of Tolin*, 622 So. 2d 988 (Fla. 1993), from which this example is drawn.) The faulty revocation came about because of a mistake, no wrongdoing involved. (Realize that if the harmless error rule is the law, the court could decide that the evidence of the testator's intent to revoke the codicil was clear and convincing and decide that it was indeed revoked.)

The position of Restatement (Third) of Trusts is very clear. Section 1 comment e states that "a constructive trust is imposed . . . to redress a wrong or to prevent unjust enrichment." The reporter's note to the comment has quotations from cases and treatises saying the same thing. On the other hand, one can find lots of cases that link the imposition of a constructive trust to wrongdoing by the person holding title to the property or at least wrongdoing by someone (like the testator who breaks a contract not to revoke a will). Be alert to developments in this area of law; there does seem to be a trend toward finding unjust enrichment sufficient justification by itself to impose a constructive trust.

(3) All about Trustees

(a) Becoming Trustee

The legal doctrine governing the selection of a trustee is pretty straightforward. Only natural persons and banks with trust powers can be trustees (or personal representatives, for that matter). At least that's the traditional learning. Section 33(2) of Restatement (Third) of Trusts states that a partnership, unincorporated association, or other "entity" (for example, an LLC) can be a trustee if it "has capacity to take and hold property for its own purposes." On the whole, however, it is still true that the vast majority of trustees are either natural persons or banks that have the appropriate authority under the applicable law. You should also keep in mind another limitation that applies to personal representatives as well. Some states prohibit out-of-state corporations and residents of other states from acting as trustees.

Becoming trustee involves accepting the trusteeship, which can happen in a variety of ways. An express acceptance happens when the trustee signs the agreement with the settlor creating the trust. (Every well-drafted trust agreement will have language that says that the trustee "accepts the trust" by signing the agreement.) In many states, a testamentary trustee must request letters of trusteeship from the appropriate court at the time the will is offered for probate; asking for letters is an express acceptance.

Acceptance need not be express; conduct can constitute acceptance as well. Restatement (Third) of Trusts § 35(1) says simply that either words or conduct can constitute acceptance of a trusteeship, and UTC § 701(a)(2) expands on the idea of acceptance by conduct, listing "accepting delivery of the trust property, exercising powers or performing duties as trustee, or otherwise indicating acceptance of the trusteeship." However, if I know I've been named trustee, do nothing that amounts to acceptance by conduct, and never say anything about whether I accept, after a reasonable time I am deemed to have rejected the trusteeship (UTC § 701(b); Restatement (Third) of Trusts § 35 cmt. b).

This is a good time to note an important feature of the UTC that is well illustrated by § 701 on accepting trusteeship. Subsection (a)(1) states that a designee can accept by "substantially complying with a method of acceptance provided in the terms of the trust." As we just saw, subsection (a)(2) deals with acceptance by conduct, but it limits the applicability of acceptance by conduct to situations where "the terms of the trust do not provide a method [of acceptance] or the method provided in the terms is not expressly made exclusive." This provision illustrates the UTC's approach to some of the default rules it contains. These rules operate not only when the trust does not contain terms dealing with the subject but also when trust does contain terms dealing with the matter but the trust terms do not expressly make the provision *the only way* to deal with the matter. So here, if the trust does contain a provision on how a designated trustee is to accept the trusteeship (for example, by signing the trust agreement) so long as that method is not expressly stated to be the only way the trusteeship may be accepted, acceptance by conduct is possible.

(b) Voluntarily Ceasing to Be Trustee

Once having accepted the trusteeship, the trustee might serve until death (or, if a corporate trustee, until the corporation changes in some significant way, as in a buyout or merger). On the other hand, any trustee may want to lay down the burden sometime. It's not as easy, however, as simply saying, "Sorry, I don't want to do this anymore." Part of the responsibility that comes with being trustee is faith in the trustee and reliance on the trustee's skill and care on the part of the beneficiaries. The trustee cannot just walk away from all that responsibility.

In some states, a trustee may have to ask the appropriate court for permission to resign. This is the common law rule. Even where the common law has been modified, it might still be the rule for trustees of testamentary trusts. Having accepted letters of trusteeship from the court, the court must in effect take them back. Otherwise, the trust may contain provisions governing the resignation of a trustee. The Restatement (Third) of Trusts § 36 says that in addition to resigning in accordance with the provisions in the trust, a trustee may resign with the consent of all the beneficiaries or with court approval. UTC § 705(a) allows a trustee to resign after giving proper notice to at least certain beneficiaries and the living settlors (if any). This is a default rule that operates in addition to any provision in the trust.

Even in states that allow trustees to resign without a court proceeding, a trustee might want to go to court to make sure that a definite end to his trustee responsibilities is effected. While procedures differ from state to state, the basic idea is the same everywhere: (1) the trustee brings to the appropriate court the trustees's account; (2) process will issue to everyone who has an interest in the trust; (3) those interested may be heard; (4) any objections are dealt with; and (5) when the court is satisfied with the trustee's performance of his duties, it will issue a decree settling the account and absolving the trustee of all further responsibility.

(c) Involuntarily Ceasing to Be Trustee

A trustee may want to continue as trustee, but the beneficiaries may not be happy with the trustee's performance. How can disaffected beneficiaries get rid of a trustee in whom they have lost confidence? The first place to look is in the terms of the trust since settlors often include a mechanism for removing the trustee. The procedure for effecting removal can take different forms. The settlor can require a vote to remove by a majority of the beneficiaries or by some supermajority greater than 50 percent plus 1; she can limit voting to adult beneficiaries, beneficiaries who reach a certain age, or current beneficiaries as opposed to those who hold remainder interests. As with so many other aspects of the law of trusts, the settlor has great latitude in creating a removal mechanism.

Sidebar

CO-TRUSTEES

Settlors somewhat frequently designate co-trustees, though the reasons vary (e.g., a corporate co-trustee might be designated to handle administrative tasks and a family member trustee to deal with beneficiaries). Under the common law, multiple trustees of trusts (other than charitable trusts) must act unanimously. That requirement can certainly cause friction and perhaps paralysis requiring the intervention of a court. Even though Restatement (Third) of Trusts § 39 and UTC § 703 (a) allow co-trustees to act by majority decision, it is worth heeding this advice: "Cotrusteeship should not be called for without careful reflection" (UTC § 703 cmt.).

What happens if the trust terms do not include any mechanism for removal of a trustee by the beneficiaries? In that case, a court will have to remove the trustee on the motion of some interested person. In addition, a court can remove a trustee on its own motion. The court's decision whether to remove a trustee is based on the facts, and usually the trial court's decision receives strong deference from an appellate court. You might wonder what sorts of facts provide grounds for removing the trustee. It's impossible, of course, to list all of the possibilities, but they fall into two broad categories. Either the trustee has violated the fiduciary duties owed to the beneficiary (discussed in Chapter 16) or the trustee is an individual who is incapable of carrying out those duties because of serious illness, loss of capacity, substance abuse, or commission of a crime, especially a crime involving dishonesty. If you ever have to deal with the question of whether a trustee can be removed, you'll be reading lots of cases from the relevant jurisdiction as well as looking for relevant statutes.

BENEFICIARIES' RIGHTS AND TRUSTEE REMOVAL

The rise of the "beneficiaries' rights movement" is putting pressure on the traditional law of trustee removal. Some beneficiaries (and some commentators) believe that many trustees pay little attention to what the beneficiaries need and want. These beneficiaries have become more aggressive in challenging trustees, even banding together to create what amount to special interest groups. Some of the complaints are clearly related to the great wave of bank mergers, which has replaced small local bank trustees with much larger institutional trustees that may take a less personal approach to trust administration.

UTC § 706 deals with trustee removal. The comment to the section notes that the "trustee removal may be regulated by the terms of the trust," so § 706 is a default rule. The provisions of § 706 include one important innovation: subsection (a) allows a co-trustee, a beneficiary, or *the settlor* of a trust to petition a court to remove a trustee. What's the big deal? Under the common law, the settlor of a lifetime irrevocable trust has no right to oversee the administration of the trust, nor does he have any standing to ask a court to remove a trustee or even to order the trustee to submit an accounting. The common law notion is that having built the trust box, the settlor simply walks away and leaves things to the trustee and the beneficiaries. By giving the settlor of an irrevocable lifetime trust standing to ask a court to remove a trustee, the UTC is breaking new ground. We'll see in Chapter 15 that "settlor enforcement" has become an extremely controversial subject when the trust in question is charitable.

Another aspect of trustee removal that is even more controversial than settlor standing is whether what is usually described as "friction" between the trustee and the beneficiaries is grounds for removal of the trustee. The traditional answer and the answer of both the Restatement and the UTC is no. "Friction between the trustee and the beneficiaries is ordinarily not a basis for removal" (UTC § 706 cmt.). Comment e(1) to § 37 of Restatement (Third) of Trusts says the same thing in almost exactly the same words. Both the UTC and the Restatement agree, however, that if the "friction" is so bad that communication between the beneficiaries and the trustee "breaks down" (i.e., they won't even talk to each other), removal might be appropriate, especially if the trustee is causing the problem.

(d) Replacing Trustees

Once a trustee is removed, what happens? Once again, we look first to the terms of the trust. The settlor may have selected a **successor trustee** who is to take office when the original trustee ceases to act. The trust terms can also provide for the beneficiaries or some of them (usually those who are adults) to select a new trustee. Some trusts with co-trustees provide that the remaining trustees select a successor if one of their number ceases to act. If the trust makes no provision for replacing a trustee, the appropriate court can select the replacement. The court's authority to do so is basic blackletter law, followed both by Restatement (Third) of Trusts § 34 and UTC § 704.

The law of trustee replacement really is a reflection of a core principle of the law of trusts: a trust will not fail for lack of a trustee (Restatement (Third) of Trusts § 31). The appropriate court always has the power to appoint a trustee to carry out the duties given the trustee by the terms of the trust and the law of general fiduciary duties. The only qualification is also blackletter law and also appears in § 31 of the Restatement. The only circumstance in which a court cannot appoint a trustee is if, in the words of § 31, "the trust's creation or continuation depends on a specific person serving as trustee. . . ." But as comment b to § 31 notes, such cases are "most unusual."

(e) Compensating Trustees

Both Restatement (Third) of Trusts (§ 38(1)) and the UTC (§ 708(a)) say the same thing: if the terms of the trust do not set the trustee's compensation, the trustee is entitled to "reasonable compensation." That means that a court may have to set the amount of compensation by taking into account a range of factors including, according to the comment to UTC § 708, "the custom of the community; the trustee's skill, experience, and facilities; the time devoted to trust duties; the amount and character of the trust property; the degree of difficulty, responsibility and risk assumed in administering the trust"; and how well the trustee has performed.

Some jurisdictions have statutes that set trustee commissions, usually as a percentage of the value of the trust property. Some statutes use a sliding scale with a smaller percentage allowance on larger sums, and some use different percentages for income paid out and the value of the trust property. In addition, corporate trustees almost always charge fees according to their published fee schedules. In the end, however, the amount of trustee compensation can always be reviewed by the appropriate court.

(f) Passive Trusts and the Statute of Uses

One more critical part of being a trustee is that the trustee must have duties to perform. Why? Well, because the Normans conquered England. And because Henry VIII isn't just a character on Showtime's *The Tudors*. Of course, there's more to it than that. But here's the abridged version.

Once upon a time in medieval England, some creative lawyers cooked up and some equity court judges approved a device called a "use," by which a landowner transferred his fee simple estate in the land to a group of persons "for the use of" the landowner and his heirs. While alive, the original landowner (the "cestui que use") could go on occupying and using the land as before; on his death, the transferees (the "feoffees to uses") were to follow his written instructions detailing what to do with the land. The whole thing was brilliant — no one inherited anything, and therefore no taxes were paid. Needless to say, uses became very popular.

By the time Henry VIII came to the throne in 1509, tax revenues had greatly diminished. Henry's solution? To pressure Parliament to pass the Statute of Uses, which it did in 1535. The statute solved Henry's problem by "executing" every use. In modern terms, it gave the legal estate created in the feoffees to uses back to the cestui que use. Alas! But wait. Dry your eyes! The courts carved out some pretty big exceptions to the Statute of Uses. The most important one for our purposes was that if the feoffee to uses had active duties to perform, the use was not executed. Thus was born the modern trust.

This idea that a trustee must have active duties to perform to prevent the trust from becoming "passive" — collapsing into legal ownership in the beneficiaries — is still with us. In most U.S. jurisdictions, the Statute of Uses is the law, either through "reception" of big parts of English law at the time of independence or through courts holding that its principles are part of the common law. In addition, although the Statute of Uses dealt only with real property, U.S. jurisdictions where the principles of the statute are part of the law often extend those provisions to trusts of personal property.

The nature of a trustee's duties in the modern trust, however, makes it highly unlikely that a trust will fail because it is passive. At a minimum, the trustee must collect and distribute income to the beneficiaries. In addition, the terms of a trust almost always say that the income is to be distributed *net* of expenses, which means that the trustee has to pay whatever expenses there are — and bingo, there's your active duty. Far more significant is the trustee's duty to make the trust property productive. As we'll see in Chapter 16, modern notions of a trustee's responsibility to properly invest trust property probably preclude any notion that a trustee can ever have nothing to do.

(4) Necessity of Trust Property

What does a trust need besides a trustee? One thing is trust property, something in the trust box. After all, a trust is a relationship with respect to property. (Plus, without trust property, the trustee will have no duties, and the trust will fail as passive.) Even though modern statutes allow a settlor to create a trust to be funded at some time in the future (as we'll see when we deal with "pour-over" wills in Chapter 11), questions about whether there is trust property do come up.

(a) What Can Be Trust Property?

Any property interest that can be transferred can be held in trust. That means, of course, that there are two questions to be answered: is the interest "property" and can it be transferred? As you know, "property" is a very broad concept. Future interests are property and can certainly be held in trust, even if the possibility that a particular interest will vest in possession is remote. The future interest as trust property also illustrates the second part of the requirement — transferability. Under classic common law, some future interests were not transferrable during life and therefore could not be held in trust. Those rules are pretty much ancient history everywhere, but as we'll see in Chapter 9, a settlor can prohibit the transfer of a beneficiary's interest in a trust. One of the effects of such a prohibition is that the beneficiary's interest cannot be held in trust.

A beneficiary designation can also be held in trust. Let's say that I am the owner of an insurance policy on my life. I can create a trust and make the trustee the beneficiary of the insurance policy. Even though it may be many years before I die and the benefit under the policy can be paid, and even though the trust holds no other property, a valid trust has been created. The trust property is a **chose in action**, the trustee's right to sue to enforce the insurance company's promise to pay the death benefit.

F A Q

Q: Is there a difference between funding a trust with a life insurance policy and making the trustee beneficiary of the policy?

A: Yes. If I own a policy on my life and do what the insurance company requires to change ownership of the policy from myself to the trustee, the policy is now trust property. The trustee can do what an owner can do, including change the beneficiary and borrow against the policy if the policy allows. Designating the trustee as beneficiary means just that; I continue as owner and can do whatever an owner can do, but so long as the trustee is beneficiary, there is trust property, as we've seen.

F A Q

Q: Okay, I get the difference between the insurance policy as trust property and the trustee as beneficiary, but why do you keep talking about the trustee as beneficiary? Isn't the *trust* the beneficiary?

A: Good question, difficult answer. The traditional answer is that a trust is not an entity (like a corporation, for example). Remember we started out talking about the trust as a relationship with regard to property. That definition means that the trust really isn't a "thing." However, it is becoming more and more common both in opinions and statutes to refer to the trust as an entity. The older language tends to endure in formal documents like a beneficiary designation. (For a discussion with references to cases, statutes, and treatises, see Restatement (Third) of Trusts § 2, reporter's note, cmts. a and i.)

(b) What Cannot Be Trust Property

Something that clearly cannot be trust property is an expectancy, a mere hope or expectation of receiving property in the future. The classic example is the possibility that I will inherit from X if X dies intestate and I survive X or the possibility that I will receive a devise made to me in the current will of a living person. Such expectancies simply are not regarded as property and therefore cannot be held in trust. (You want "proof"? Restatement (Third) of Trusts § 41 comment a: "By all traditional and current concepts of property, expectancies are not property interests.")

Something else that cannot be held in trust is property that has not yet come into existence, like future profits. If I declare myself trustee of the royalties I am going to earn on the sales of this book while I'm still working on the manuscript, there's no trust (Restatement (Third) of Trusts cmt. b). However, if I declare myself trustee of my rights under the contract with the publisher, which of course include the receipt of royalties calculated in a specified way, or if I create a trust and assign my rights under the contract to the trustee of the trust, the trust has been funded. The trust property is once again a chose in action, this time the right to sue to enforce the contract (Restatement (Third) of Trusts § 10 cmt. g).

The truth is that problems arising from doubts about whether there is trust property are not particularly common. With an expansive modern notion of property and prohibitions on transfer usually created only by express provisions, there just isn't much chance of creating a trust that fails for lack of property even if you try. We've spent some time with property that doesn't exist yet because it's a topic you're likely to run up against in the classroom, and thinking about it does remind us of how many ways the intention to create a trust can be fulfilled. How different from the world of the Statute of Wills.

(c) Getting the Property into the Trust

Getting the property into the trust box is often called funding the trust. Remember that a trust is a relationship with regard to property, so property there must be, at least eventually. Sometimes this requirement for the creation of the trust is described as a requirement that the trust property be delivered to the trustee. Restatement (Third) of Trusts always uses the term "transfer" to the trustee. The change in terminology is intended to keep the intricacies of the law of delivery from unnecessarily complicating the law of trust formation. It's clear, for example, that the law of delivery has nothing to do with a written declaration of trust that says the settlor declares herself trustee of the property listed in the declaration, which is totally sufficient to make the listed property trust property.

If the trust is created by trust agreement, a statement that the settlor transfers to the trustee the property listed on a schedule annexed to the trust agreement is sufficient to make the property trust property. In some jurisdictions, it's not only possible but common to fund a revocable lifetime trust by a blanket assignment of all of the settlor's property to the trust. Talk about informal. You should contrast this informality in the creation of lifetime trusts with the creation of testamentary trusts. The testamentary trust is created by a devise in a will to the trustee. There is no problem in establishing the transfer of the property to the trustee. The will makes the transfer of whatever probate property funds the trust.

F   A   Q

Q: Wouldn't a settlor have to execute and record a deed to make real property trust property?

A: Absent an applicable statute that requires recording a deed to the trustee, the answer is no. The Statute of Frauds requires a trust of real property to be in writing and a conveyance of land to be in writing. Recording the deed, of course, gives notice to third parties and is clearly the only sensible thing to do, but as between the settlor and trustee, the real property is trust property.

Restatement (Third) of Trusts § 16 comment b confirms the widely recognized principle that a writing creating a trust that shows that the settlor intends to transfer specified property is sufficient to create a trust of that property. (The Restatement is silent on the use of blanket assignments, but they are indeed used.) The same comment also says: "Good practice certainly calls for the use of additional formalities and the taking of appropriate further steps, such as changes of registration, or the execution and recordation of deeds to land." That is probably as close as the Restatement comes to an under(re)statement.

What sort of property has written title or registration that should be changed? All sorts, but some common examples are motor vehicles, boats, airplanes, stock certificates, bank accounts, certificates of deposit, and brokerage accounts. We'll do one example. It's possible to hold all sorts of financial investments in a brokerage account: stocks, bonds, certificates of deposit, mutual funds and exchange traded funds, and even options. Clearly large amounts of wealth can be held in a brokerage account, and for many people such an account holds most of their financial investments (other than their retirement savings). Sally Settlor has such an account, and she wants to make it the property of the revocable lifetime trust she's created with herself as trustee because she wants to make the brokerage account nonprobate property. Right now the title to the account—that is, the title on the records of the brokerage firm and that appears on the statements she receives—reads "Sally Settlor." After she completes whatever paperwork the brokerage firm requires to change the title to a trustee, the title will read something like this: "Sally Settlor, ttee, u/a/d 7/1/2011 f/b/o Sally Settlor." We can translate that as follows: "Sally Settlor, as trustee under agreement dated July 1, 2011, for the benefit of Sally Settlor." When Sally dies, the successor trustee simply takes over, assuming the trust has been properly drafted to name a trustee to succeed Sally when she dies. The brokerage firm will require some sort of proof that the successor trustee is indeed the successor trustee, and a copy of the trust terms naming the successor trustee will usually be sufficient (the brokerage firm might insist on seeing the original trust instrument or might accept a copy certified by an attorney). If the trust terminates at Sally's death and simply distributes property outright to the beneficiaries, the trustee will do exactly that. If the trust is to continue, the successor trustee will take over and the title of the account will now show the name of the successor trustee, but the rest of the information probably will not change—in other words, the trust will still be identified as for the benefit of Sally.

(d) Failed Gifts Enforced as Trusts

There's another circumstance in which delivery, gifts, and trusts get tangled up together. We've already said that making a lifetime gift requires delivery of the property that is being given away. The intricacies of the law of delivery can indeed cause a gift to fail. More than one disappointed donee of a failed lifetime gift has argued that the estate of the "donor" should give up the property involved to the "donee" because whatever it was that the donor did during life was really a declaration of trust under which donor became trustee of the property for the benefit of the donee. The "donee" is now not a donee of an outright gift of the property but the beneficiary of a trust of the property. The requested remedy? A constructive trust, of course, imposed on the personal representative of the deceased settlor of the trust for the benefit of the intended donee of the failed gift.

Restatement (Third) of Trusts § 16(2) says quite clearly that if a lifetime outright gift fails because the property owner "fails to make the transfer that is required," a constructive trust *cannot* be used to give effect to the intention to make a gift. Now this might seem a bit strange given the basic theme of giving effect to the intent of the transfer, which is such an important feature of the Restatements (Third) of Property and of Trusts. Sure enough, comment d to § 16 discusses circumstances under which it should be possible to do what the blackletter says cannot be done. The key to this ambivalence, you should not be surprised to learn, is the basic informality of the law of trusts. With no prescribed formali-ties for creating a trust, careful inquiry into the intent of the person who said or did something with regard to property can often find facts that support the conclusion that she did intend to create a trust by declaration. As comment d says: "The settlor need not even know that the relationship that is being created is called a trust, as long as the intended relationship and rights and duties are those the law treats as a trust."

Could there be a better illustration of the great gap between the law of wills and the law of trusts? The Statute of Wills is all about making sure that a writing can be easily identified as embodying testamentary intent. Holographic wills, of course, often raise the same problems of determining intent that are involved in determining whether a writing creates a trust, and the harmless error rule extends the inquiry to documents that involve no handwriting at all. But the law of trusts really is the "winner" here.

(5) Need for Beneficiaries

The third element necessary to the creation of a trust is at least one beneficiary. Part of the trust relationship is the trustee's fiduciary duty to deal with the property for the benefit of some person or for charity. Putting aside charitable trusts until Chapter 15, it is obvious that beneficiaries are an indispensible element of the trust relationship. Why? Well, try this from comment a to § 44 of Restatement (Third) of Trusts. "The creation of a trust . . . requires that there be a person to receive and hold the beneficial interest in the trust property — an identifiable person by whom or on whose behalf the trust . . . can be enforced." To put it more informally, there must be someone who can keep the trustee honest; the fiduciary obligation must be owed to someone who can ask a court to enforce it should the trustee misbehave. If there is no beneficiary, then there is no trust.

(a) Who Can Be a Beneficiary

Who can be a beneficiary of a trust? Section 43 of Restatement (Third) of Trusts says that the test is whether the person designated as beneficiary can "take and hold legal title to the intended trust property." Clearly, any natural person can be a trust beneficiary, and the vast majority of private (as opposed to charitable) express trusts are created for beneficiaries who are natural persons.

One puzzling aspect of this "who can be a beneficiary" concerns the following common scenario. The settlor by trust agreement transfers property to trust to pay the income from the property to the settlor's grandchildren until all of the settlor's children are dead, when the trust is to terminate and the trust property distributed to the grandchildren; but at the time of the transfer, the settlor's children have never themselves had children? In other words, is a valid trust created if the only beneficiaries are unborn persons? For once a simple answer: yes. So long as it is possible for beneficiaries to come into existence before any rule of law would terminate the trust (more on that when we talk about the Rule Against Perpetuities in Chapter 12), the trust has beneficiaries and is valid (UTC § 402(b)). If the beneficiaries never come into existence, you know what happens—the trust property will be distributed to whoever has the reversion that was created when the transferor created a contingent remainder. The doctrinal device that makes this happen is called a resulting trust, and we'll discuss that at the end of this chapter.

F   A   Q

Q: How can unborn beneficiaries enforce the trustee's duties?

A: A court can always appoint a **guardian ad litem** to represent unborn—or minor or incapacitated—beneficiaries in a proceeding against a trustee. In the example of a trust for unborn grandchildren, the grandchildren's parents could ask a court to appoint someone to carry on the litigation. In most instances, the court will appoint a lawyer to do just that. In addition, the person who has the reversionary interest could bring the appropriate proceeding. After all, if no grandchildren are ever born, the trust property will pass to the reversion rather than the remainder beneficiaries, and therefore whoever holds the reversion has the same interest in making sure the trustee behaves that the remainder interest does.

You probably noticed that in the previous example the beneficiaries were members of a class—the settlor's grandchildren. What we have here in fact is a class gift, and there is no problem with members of a class as beneficiaries of a trust so long as the members can be ascertained before the trust is required to terminate by any applicable rule of law. Here's an example of a sort we've seen before: Settlor transfers property to Trustee in trust to pay the income to settlor's daughter, D, for life, remainder to D's issue who survive D, by representation. You know that Settlor has created a present interest in the income and a contingent remainder in fee simple in D's issue because there is a condition precedent of surviving to the distribution date, which is D's death. D, of course, is a beneficiary, and so are the contingent remainder persons. Membership in the class can be ascertained when the time comes to distribute the trust property to the class members. No problem.

You no doubt can think of many **definite classes** whose members can be ascertained without any difficulty. We've seen many examples in our various discussions of class gifts: children, grandchildren, nieces, nephews, and so on. Definite classes are not limited to family relationships. "Members of the settlor's high school graduating class" is a definite class.

(b) Indefinite Groups

Trusts do fail, however, for lack of definite beneficiaries. A common example is a transfer by the settlor to the trustee to pay the income from the trust property to the settlor's "friends" for a certain number of years and then to distribute the trust property to a charity. Absent a court interpreting the word "friends" in a way that makes it refer to a definite group, the gift of the income interest fails and the charity takes the property immediately.

A slightly different problem arises when a trustee is given power to make distribution of property among the members of an indefinite class as the trustee shall select. The traditional, and by far the prevailing, rule in the United States is that if a trustee is given the power to make distributions to the members of an indefinite group, there is no trust created, and property belongs to the settlor (or to the settlor's successors if the arrangement is created by will).

This treatment of the power to select beneficiaries from among an indefinite group as an invalid attempt to create a trust has been the subject of scholarly discussion for more than 100 years. The reasoning supporting the traditional result is very simple. The trustee has a duty to distribute the property among those persons she selects from an indefinite group. There is no one who can be identified as a beneficiary; therefore, no one can invoke the authority of a court if the trustee refuses to select recipients and distribute the property. There is no trust. *Q.E.D.*

F A Q

Q: Are "family" or "relatives" a definite or indefinite class?

A: Restatement (Third) of Trusts § 45 comments d and e sum up the general law on this one. First, it's easier to show that "relatives" refers to a definite class; if the settlor's intent is not clear, courts have a constructional rule that says "relatives" means "heirs." "Family" is a more difficult case. If it's possible to show whom the testator intended by using the term — the spouse and descendants of a named person ("my daughter's family"), for instance — then a definite class exists. Absent such evidence, the gift will fail unless it can be shown that the settlor's intent was to designate the named person's *relatives*, in which case we're back to where this answer started.

The criticism of the seemingly obvious result has to do with the power to select. As we'll see in Chapter 10, if the power to select were not given to a trustee — in other words, if the person with the power to select did not have fiduciary duties to the potential recipients of the property — it would be a **power of appointment**. The "trustee" could then make the selection without having to worry about fiduciary duties.

In § 46(2), Restatement (Third) of Trusts says that in this situation the trustee does indeed have a power of appointment, and UTC § 402(c) agrees. Both provisions also state that if the trustee does not exercise the power in a timely fashion, the power fails and the property involved goes to those who take the property had the will not created the power (usually either to the residuary devises or in a partial intestacy). As with so many innovation provisions in the Restatement and UTC, we'll see how courts and legislatures react.

Another way in which the problem of indefinite beneficiaries can come up appears next under its own subheading, not only because it is important but because it helps to illustrate another doctrine that is often involved in indefinite beneficiary problems.

(c) Animals and Honorary Trusts

Many pet owners think ahead about how to make sure their animal companions are properly cared for if they survive their human companions. As far as the law is concerned, domestic animals are personal property and certainly can be devised in a will. It's perfectly possible therefore for a testator to give his dog or cat (or horse or any other domestic animal) to a devisee who is willing to care for the animal. So far so good. What happens, however, when the testator wants to make sure that the animal is well cared for and that doing so is not a burden on the devisee?

The testator could easily make a devise of a sum of money to the devisee to use for the care of the animal. If the language describing the purpose of the devise is precatory, there's no problem. If the language in the will, however, shows the intention to create a trust for the animal — "I give X the sum of $10,000 in trust to be used for the care of my cat Muffin for the remainder of her life" — we've got a problem. How can the trustee's duties be enforced? Muffin may be skilled when it comes to mice roundups, but she cannot bring an action in court. And even though some advocates have tried, no court has been willing to grant standing to an animal and then appoint a guardian ad litem to carry on the action. The trust fails, and the money almost certainly will end up as part of the residuary devise. The testator's intent is frustrated, and the devisee who agreed to take the animal, usually out of friendship for the testator, is going to be out of pocket. While routine care of an animal may not require much in the way of expenditures, veterinary care is expensive.

The trust itself can be upheld, however, if the trustee is willing to carry out its terms. The trustee's willingness to do what the testator asked makes this an **honorary trust**, which will make the gift of the property to the trustee valid. If all of the trust property has not been expended for the trust purpose at the time the trust ends — the death of Muffin in our example — the property will pass to the testator's successors in interest, in most cases the residuary beneficiaries of the will. Restatement (Third) of Trusts § 47 analyzes this situation as involving a power in the trustee to use the property for the designated purpose. The trustee's fiduciary duties are owed to the persons who take any property not used to in accomplishing the purpose for which the gift was made. This is exactly how the Restatement deals with the power to select among indefinite beneficiaries and uses the term **adapted trust** to refer to both.

A trust created for the care of an animal is an example not only of an honorary trust, but also of what's called a **purpose trust**, a trust that does not have definite beneficiaries but that was created to carry out a purpose (other than a charitable purpose, which we'll discuss in Chapter 15). A trust for a specific animal is a trust for a specific noncharitable purpose. Even though such an arrangement can be an honorary trust, which means that the property involved can be devoted to the purpose, there's another problem with the validity of such trusts — they violate the Rule Against Perpetuities. This is not the time to get into a detailed discussion of the Rule; we're saving that for Chapter 12. You probably at least have heard, however, that the Rule requires certain things to happen within "lives in being plus 21 years and a period of gestation." As applied to a trust for any specific noncharitable purpose, that's a problem. So long as the purpose can be fulfilled, the trust would go on and on, with successor trustees taking over as trustees die or resign. Since there is no human life involved, the relevant time period is the 21 years. Restatement (Third) of Trusts § 47(2) limits the duration of these trusts to 21 years, at which time the trust must end if it hasn't already and whatever property is left goes to whoever holds the reversionary interest (probably the residuary devisees of the will that created the arrangement).

PURPOSE TRUSTS

The validity of the purpose trust is a hot topic in trust law. Several jurisdictions whose law is part of the common law tradition have adopted legislation validating purpose trusts in an attempt to attract business for money managers based in these jurisdictions. These locations — Bermuda, the Isle of Man, Jersey and other of the Channel Islands, and others — often impose no taxes on income, or at least on the income of nonresidents. The combination of no taxes on the income generated by the trust property and no rights in meddlesome beneficiaries who might want to have a say in how the trust is administered has turned out to be very attractive to some very rich (and secretive) settlors. All of these statutes deal with the problem of enforcing the trustee's duties by allowing the settlor to name a "trust protector" who has the power to call the trustee to account. Of course, the trust must also create some mechanism for succession to the office of trust protector. U.S. jurisdictions have not been very hospitable to this sort of purpose trust, but a few have legislation dealing with trust protectors.

The UTC validates trusts for animals in § 408 and other purpose trusts in § 409. A handful of states that have not enacted the UTC have statutes that validate trusts for animals. These statutes are usually similar to UTC § 408, setting a time limit (usually 21 years or the animal's life) and allowing a court to reduce the amount of the trust property if the court finds that value of the trust property exceeds what is necessary to carry out the purpose for which the trust was created. Like the UTC, these statutes also provide that the trust may be enforced by a person named in the trust or by someone appointed by a court.

(d) Merger

Before we leave beneficiaries as a necessary component of a trust, we have to briefly consider another doctrine related to the beneficiaries' role. This is the doctrine of **merger**: "If the legal title to the trust property and the entire beneficial interest become united in one person, the trust terminates" (Restatement (Third) of Trusts § 69). Another way to state the same principle is that if the separation of legal and equitable title no longer exists, the trust doesn't either.

How could this happen? Settlor creates a trust to pay the income to the settlor for life, then to pay the income to settlor's son until age 40, at which time the trust ends and the trust property is to be distributed to the son. Settlor is the trustee and at settlor's death the son becomes trustee when the son is 35 years old. The son holds the legal title to the trust property and all of the beneficial interest. Remember that son's remainder is vested, and if he dies before age 40 the trust property will be distributed to his estate. Under these circumstances, the trust ceases to exist and the son becomes the outright owner of the trust property as soon as he becomes trustee on his father's death.

Merger is rare in the modern world. The modern rule is that so long as there are more than two persons involved (one as trustee and one as beneficiary), the trust will not self-destruct. In other words, if you put all of the trustees and all of the beneficiaries into one room and there are at least two persons in the room, the merger doctrine will not operate. All of the persons in the room can be both trustees and beneficiaries because each one is trustee not only of her own interest but also of the interests of the other trustee/beneficiaries. If there are only two people in the room, the sole trustee who is also the only beneficiary of the trust for life and a beneficiary who is not a trustee, the trust will not self-destruct even if the beneficiary has a contingent remainder that is dependent on a condition precedent that is extremely unlikely to occur or is unborn and therefore unascertained.

Finally, don't confuse merger with the destruction of a passive trust through the operation of the Statute of Uses. The merger doctrine applies when all of the beneficial interests in the trust property are held by one person who is also the sole trustee. A trust can have many beneficiaries, none of whom are trustees, but still be destroyed by principles of the Statute of Uses if the trustees have no duties to perform.

C. Construction of the Terms of the Trust

Construction of the terms of a trust proceeds on principles like those involved in the construction of a will, which we discussed in Chapter 5. The similarity is especially strong when dealing with a testamentary trust. Because lifetime trusts are not bound up with the formalities of the Statute of Wills and the resulting fixation on the inability to change the words of a document executed with testamentary formalities, courts have traditionally been more willing to fix mistakes in identification of persons and property in lifetime trusts than they have been when dealing with wills. Where the distinction between latent and patent ambiguities is still followed, courts may be more zealous in enforcing the distinction when dealing with testamentary as opposed to lifetime trusts.

Construction questions involving trusts often involve future interests. Many of these questions have to do with whether trust terms create a condition subsequent or a condition precedent. As we saw in Chapter 7, there are constructional rules that are widely used to help answer these questions. Traditionally, most of these problems are classified as patent ambiguities, and there is no question of using extrinsic evidence to help decide what the settlor meant. The constructional rules are applied, and that's that, although even if the trust is a testamentary trust, the usual admonition to read the entire document in light of the circumstances often allows the consideration of extrinsic evidence without actually saying that's what's going on.

Restatement (Third) of Trusts follows Restatement (Third) of Property on questions of construction and interpretation. We never did pay much attention to the "donative transfers" part of the title of the Property Restatement, but now we have to note that a lifetime trust does involve a donative transfer of some interest in the trust property to the beneficiaries of the trust. It makes sense, then, that the rules of that Restatement, which we discussed in Chapter 4, apply to trusts.

D. Revocable or Irrevocable?

Once an irrevocable trust is created, it is very difficult to undo what has been done. The default rule of the common law is that a trust is irrevocable unless the settlor says otherwise. In every state that has enacted UTC § 602(a), the default rule is the opposite of the common law rule: a trust is revocable unless the settlor expressly provides otherwise. (A default rule of revocability is also the law in a handful of states that have not adopted the UTC provision.) The UTC's reason for reversing this long-standing default rule is simply stated in the comment to § 602. A professionally drafted trust will expressly state whether the trust is revocable or irrevocable. A trust that is silent on the subject was likely drafted by a nonprofessional who intended the trust to be a will substitute and therefore revocable, just as a will is. Restatement (Third) of Trusts takes the same approach. The blackletter of § 63(2) says that if the settlor does not expressly state the trust is revocable, whether the trust is revocable or not is a question of interpretation. No matter what the default rule is, once a trust is irrevocable, changing any of its terms requires threading your way through a complex body of rules that on the whole make accomplishing any change a difficult task. And those changes *do not* include revoking the trust; the settlor is not going to get the trust property back. The only possibilities are termination or modification.

F   A   Q

Q: What's the difference between termination and revocation?

A: Revocation of a trust means that the settlor takes the trust property back. The trust box is dismantled, and everything goes back to the way it was before the trust was created. The beneficiaries' interests disappear. If the trust is irrevocable, however, the only way it can be ended is by termination. If a trust is terminated, the trust property is distributed *to the beneficiaries.* The beneficiaries may agree on the terms of the distribution or a court can make an order setting out the distribution to be made. In either case, the settlor may receive part of the distribution to the extent the settlor is a beneficiary, even if only because the settlor has a reversion.

E. Modification and Termination of Trusts

(1) Termination According to the Trust Terms

Trusts terminate all the time. They come to an end because the trust terms require it. The income interests are over, often because the income beneficiaries are dead, and the trust property then passes outright to the persons who hold the remainder interests. Sometimes the trustee has discretionary power to distribute all of the trust property and terminates the trust by doing so. A beneficiary might have the power to require the trustee to distribute all of the trust property to the beneficiary or to other persons, and the exercise of that power terminates the trust. These are all ways in which a trust comes to a "natural" end in accordance with the terms of the trust. Trusts can also be modified according to their terms. A trustee may have the power to add beneficiaries or change the terms governing a beneficiary's interest. For example, the trust terms may require the trustee to withhold distributions from a beneficiary who fails a drug test. If the trust has a single-income beneficiary, the trust terms might require that the trust be modified to make it a **supplemental needs trust** if the beneficiary becomes disabled (the beneficiary's interest in such a trust is not counted as a "resource" when determining if the beneficiary qualifies for government benefits).

Other situations in which a trust will terminate because of its terms probably don't happen very often. They include the trust purposes becoming unlawful, contrary to public policy, or impossible to achieve. There are probably few cases where a trust that is lawful and in conformity with public policy later ceases to be so. "Impossible to achieve" is a bit easier to imagine. One example is a trust created solely to provide for the college education of the beneficiary. If the beneficiary doesn't go to college and it is certain she never will, the trust terminates because its purpose cannot be achieved.

   The various ways in which trusts end more or less in accord with the trust terms
are well established in the common law, clearly recognized in Restatement (Third) of
Trusts §§ 61 and 63, and codified in UTC § 410(a) as well in non-uniform statutes in
some states.

(2) Reformation and Rescission

Now we come to termination and modification that does not involve carrying out the
trust terms in some way but rather depends on the intervention of a court to change
the trust terms. **Rescission** means to undo the creation of the trust. The grounds for
rescission are the same as those for undoing a gratuitous transfer not in trust: fraud,
duress, undue influence, and mistake on the part of the settlor. A lifetime trust is
governed by the law that generally governs lifetime transfers. Testamentary trusts are
governed by the law that applies to wills. As we've seen, the law of undue influence on
testators is voluminous, and while there are variations from jurisdiction to jurisdiction, there are always lots of cases to read. In most jurisdictions, the law that applies
to lifetime transfers is probably not as well developed as, and may be somewhat
different from, the law applicable to testamentary transfers.
   Reformation means to change the terms of a trust to make them correspond to
the settlor's intent in creating the trust. In accomplishing a reformation, the court
uses the tools of interpretation, often including what is traditionally regarded as
extrinsic evidence and evidence of mistake on the part of the settlor to discover
and then properly state the settlor's intent. The courts have been more willing to
reform lifetime trusts. Reformation of testamentary trusts has been limited by the
restrictive rules that apply to wills in general, including the oft repeated refusal to
correct mistakes in wills. As we saw in Chapter 5, that traditional view has not always
been strictly followed. The third series of Restatements as well as the UPC in § 2-805
take a much more liberal approach to reforming wills and trusts, including the remedying of mistakes. UTC § 415 takes an equally liberal approach to reforming testamentary trusts, putting them on a par with
lifetime trusts. The UTC provision, like all of the
intent enforcing provisions of the Restatements
Third and the UPC, requires clear and convincing
evidence of the intent that the reformation is to
serve. The Restatements and the UPC and UTC
reformation provisions are still new enough that
we cannot be sure how courts will react either to
the invitation in the Restatements that they adopt
the new approach to reformation as a matter of
common law or to the codifications of the
principle in the UPC and UTC.
   One sort of reformation is fairly widely
accepted in case law and in some statutes. In
many cases, courts have reformed trusts to
make them more tax-efficient. Most of us
would agree that settlors probably wouldn't
mind changes that minimize taxes paid without
significantly changing beneficiaries' interests.
Restatement (Third) of Property § 12.2 sanctions
modifications of a "donative document," which

Sidebar

TAX-DRIVEN MODIFICATION AND THE IRS

Just because a court approves a modification
of a trust to carry out the settlor's tax objectives
does not mean that the Internal Revenue Service will agree. Under the holding in *Commissioner v. Estate of Bosch*, 387 U.S. 456 (1967),
the IRS is bound by a construction of the trust
language or a modification of the trust terms
only if the construction or modification has
been approved by the highest court of the state
where the action is brought. *Bosch* also
demonstrates that these types of proceedings
are seldom truly adversarial. The beneficiaries,
the trustee, and any guardians ad litem are
usually only too happy to have a decision that
reduces the tax burden on the estate or trust,
and the state court is likely to be helpful.

of course includes wills and trusts, to achieve the donor's (and that includes a testa-tor's or a settlor's) tax objectives. The rule is codified in UPC § 2-806 and UTC § 416.

(3) Modification by Equitable Deviation

There is one long-standing doctrine that allows courts to modify the administrative terms of a trust. Many of the reported cases involve restrictions on the trustee's power to make investments, sometimes by requiring that the trustee retain property placed in trust by the settlor. The classic case involves the settlor's prize investment, perhaps shares in a corporation the settlor founded, and a direction to the trustee never to sell the investment. The ways of the world being what they are, the investment's value begins to decline. The situation is really grave if the enterprise started by the settlor can no longer compete in the marketplace and is headed for bankruptcy. If the trustee asks the appropriate court to allow the trustee to deviate from the terms of the trust in order to sell the investment, traditionally the request is likely to be granted *if* the situation is so severe that if the trustee is not allowed to deviate from the trust terms the very existence of the trust will be in danger and *if* the situation is due to circumstances neither foreseen nor anticipated by the settlor.

Restatement (Third) of Trusts and the UTC make important changes in the doc-trine of equitable deviation. The blackletter of Restatement (Third) of Trusts § 66(1) says that a court may modify "an administrative or dispositive provision" or direct or permit the trustee to "deviate" from either sort of provision, "if because of circum-stances not anticipated by the settlor the modification or deviation will further the purposes of the trust." As you can see, this formulation goes beyond the traditional view of equitable deviation, both because it explicitly includes dispositive provisions and because of the much less demanding standard for invoking the doctrine. Con-cluding that in light of unanticipated circumstances the requested deviation will "further the purposes of the trust" should be easier than deciding that the very existence of the trust is in danger. UTC § 412 codifies the Restatement provisions. Subsection (a) allows a court to modify the administrative or dispositive terms of a trust if that "will further the purposes of the trust" because of "circumstances not anticipated by the settlor." Subsection (b) allows a court to modify the administrative terms of a trust if continuing to administer the trust under the existing terms "would be impractical or wasteful or impair the trust's administration." The comment to § 412 notes that when it comes to administrative terms, subsections (a) and (b) do overlap; situations that justify a modification of administrative terms under (a) will most likely justify modification under (b) as well. The difference, of course, is that modification under (b) does not require the existence of circumstances not antici-pated by the settlor. The traditional, Restatement, and UTC versions of the doctrine are summed up in Table 8.1.

There is one situation in which a court will terminate a trust even under tradi-tional law. When the costs of administering a trust are so large in comparison to the value of the trust property that there is very little left for the beneficiaries, the trust has become "uneconomic" and subject to court-ordered termination. Of course, you can fit the termination of the uneconomic trust into the traditional doctrine of equitable deviation if you look at the loss of value as a circumstance not anticipated by the settlor. Restatement (Third) of Trusts treats the termination of the uneconomic trust as an application of the general rule of § 66(1), allowing the court to modify the trust terms in light of unanticipated circumstances (cmt. d).

TABLE 8.2	Equitable Deviation			
What may be changed	**Restatement (Third) § 66(1)**	**UTC**		**"Traditional" law**
		§ 412(a)	**§ 412(b)**	
Administrative provisions	Yes	Yes	Yes	Yes
Unanticipated circumstances required?	Yes	Yes	No	Yes
Threshold	Further trust purposes (medium difficulty)	Further trust purposes (medium difficulty)	Terms impractical, wasteful, or impair administration (lowest difficulty)	Existence of trust imperiled (highest difficulty)
Dispositive provisions	Yes	Yes	No	No (with case-by-case exceptions)
Unanticipated circumstances required?	Yes	Yes	n/a	n/a
Threshold	Further trust purposes (medium difficulty)	Further trust purposes (medium difficulty)	n/a	n/a

F A Q

Q: Why does UTC § 414(b) give the court the power to remove the trustee of an uneconomic trust and appoint another as well as the power to terminate the trust?

A: One cost of administration is the trustee's commissions. If the beneficiaries can find someone willing to serve as trustee for no commission (perhaps even one of the beneficiaries), the trust may be uneconomic no longer. A trustee may be reluctant to resign (and give up the commissions), however, and usually a court can remove a trustee only for wrongdoing or if there is a truly irreconcilable conflict with the beneficiaries. The statute therefore gives the court the power to remove the trustee if doing so will allow the trust to continue on a sensible economic basis.

The UTC confirms this traditional rule in § 414(b), which gives the court the power to modify or terminate a trust (or remove a trustee and appoint a new trustee) if the court concludes that the value of the trust property does not justify the cost of administration. UTC § 414(b) goes well beyond the traditional rule and gives the *trustee* the power to terminate a trust consisting of property worth less than $50,000 on notice to the beneficiaries if the trustee concludes that the value of the trust property does not justify the costs of administration. The point of this provision is that if the costs of administration make continuing the trust uneconomical, using trust property to pay for a court proceeding to terminate the trust may leave nothing at all for the beneficiaries.

F   A   Q

Q: What besides the trustee's commission could be a "cost of administration"?

A: Accounting services, for one. The income tax rules applicable to trusts and estates are complex, and paying a properly qualified accountant to prepare the returns can be expensive. Another common administrative cost is bank and brokerage firm service charges, which can add up to a sizeable expense. And of course, don't forget legal fees!

(4) Termination or Modification by Consent

The first principle you need to know is that if the settlor and the beneficiaries of an irrevocable trust agree, the trust can be modified or terminated. This makes sense intuitively; the settlor created the trust to benefit the beneficiaries on the terms the settlor wrote into the trust. If the settlor and the beneficiaries agree to end the whole thing, who else should have anything to say about it? You are no doubt ready to answer "the trustee," but you'd be wrong. Unless the terms of the trust require the trustee's consent to terminate or modify the trust or the trustee is also a beneficiary, the trustee cannot prevent the settlor and the beneficiaries from taking either of those actions. Just because the trustee received commissions for being trustee does not give him a say in whether the trust can be terminated by consent.

If the settlor withholds consent, of course, the beneficiaries' consent won't accomplish a thing. The ability of the settlor to keep the trust in existence with its terms as the settlor created them (unless a court will invoke equitable deviation) is a distinguishing characteristic of the American law of trusts. But what if the settlor is dead, which is always the case when we're dealing with a testamentary trust? Then the traditional law is quite clear. Even if all of the beneficiaries are adamant in their desire to end or modify the trust, they cannot have their way if doing so would defeat a "material purpose" of the settlor in creating the trust.

"Material purpose" is a term of art, and its use in this context is based on an 1889 decision of the Massachusetts Supreme Judicial Court, *Claflin v. Claflin*.[2] The case involved a testamentary trust created by a father for one of his sons. The trustees were to pay the beneficiary the sum of $10,000 when he reached age 21, another $10,000 on reaching age 25, and the balance on reaching 30 years of age. When the beneficiary

---

[2]20 N.E. 454 (Mass. 1889).

was older than 21 but not yet 25, he asked the court to compel the trustees to distribute the entire trust property to him. His argument was simple: his interest in the trust property was indefeasibly vested. The court agreed. "There is no doubt," the court wrote, "that [the beneficiary's] interest in the trust fund is vested and absolute, and that no other person has any interest in it."[3]

Even though there was substantial English precedent approving the termination of a trust in this situation and giving the beneficiary outright ownership of the trust property, the Massachusetts court refused to follow those precedents. They based their decision on the principle that the settlor could dispose of his property "with such restrictions and limitations, not repugnant to law, as he sees fits, and that his intentions ought to be carried out, unless they contravene some positive rule of law, or are against public policy."[4] Requiring the trustees to distribute the property to the plaintiff in stages culminating at age 30 is not against public policy, nor is it an impermissible restriction on the rights the plaintiff does have in the property. Nor are the terms of the trust "altogether useless, for there is not the same danger that he will spend the property while it is in the hands of the trustees as there would be if it were his own."[5] The blackletter of Restatement (Third) of Trusts § 65 states the *Claflin* doctrine and says that a court can authorize termination or modification of a trust only if the court determines "that the reason(s) for termination or modification outweigh the material purpose."

But what is a "material purpose"? If the Massachusetts Supreme Judicial Court's language in the *Claflin* opinion really states the "*Claflin* doctrine," then it is difficult to imagine what sort of trust terms could be "utterly useless." You've probably concluded, and you'd be right, that the *Claflin* doctrine as it has usually been applied is a powerful break on the termination or modification of irrevocable trusts on the basis of beneficiary consent. Given what you know now about the general approach of the third series of Restatements, you probably also have concluded that Restatement (Third) of Trusts takes a more relaxed view of what is and isn't a material purpose of a trust, and once again you're right. Comment d to § 65 says that "material purposes are not readily to be inferred."

As you can see, there's lots of room to argue about the material purpose of a trust. Winning the argument requires thorough research in the law of whatever jurisdiction in involved. There is, however, one particular trust term that is both very common and whose status as a material purpose is the subject of a good deal of discussion. As we'll learn in Chapter 9, a settlor can include in the trust terms a **spendthrift provision**. Such a provision prevents a trust beneficiary from transferring his interest and also prevents a creditor of the beneficiary from seizing the interest to satisfy the beneficiary's debt. (Remember that the trust involved in *Claflin* did not contain a spendthrift provision.) At least one purpose for including such a provision in the trust terms would seem to be to protect the beneficiary from her own improvidence in money matters. Many courts have found that the termination of a trust that includes a spendthrift provision would indeed be inconsistent with a material purpose of the trust. That result should not surprise you. If keeping money out of the hands of the beneficiary of the trust in *Claflin* until he reached age 30 is a material purpose, certainly protecting the trust property from the beneficiary's creditors is even

---

[3]*Id.* at 455.
[4]*Id.* at 456.
[5]*Id.*

S i d e b a r

DECANTING

At least ten states have **decanting statutes**, which allow a trustee who has discretionary power to invade principal to create a new trust by exercising the power to invade (known as "decanting" the existing trust). These statutes usually give the trustee a great deal of discretion in establishing the terms of the new trust, requiring only some degree of protection for current beneficiaries (e.g., that their interests are not diminished by the creation of a new trust). Decanting is another method of terminating or modifying an existing trust and seems to be growing in importance.

more protective and therefore surely qualifies as a material purpose. Comment e to Restatement (Third) of Trusts § 65, however, tries to take the spendthrift provision down a notch, declaring that such a restriction is not "in and of itself" sufficient to prevent termination.

The UTC deals with termination and modification by consent in § 411. The section codifies the Restatement (Third) of Trusts provisions including the demotion of a spendthrift restriction from automatic "material purpose" status, but the provision, § 411(c), is in brackets. The brackets weren't there when the UTC was promulgated in 2000 but were added in 2004. Several states that adopted the UTC omitted § 411(c) because the provision turned out to be quite controversial. Not only is there authority that says that a spendthrift provision does constitute a material provision, but there is also a good deal of sentiment that that position is correct. This controversy is one of several that surround spendthrift provisions, and we'll discuss others in Chapter 9. Finally, § 411(e) codifies Restatement (Third) of Trusts § 65 comment c, which we noted allows the court to terminate or modify the trust even when all the beneficiaries do not consent. Under the UTC, the court may approve the requested termination or modification if the request could have been granted had all the beneficiaries consented and if the interest of any beneficiary who does not consent "will be adequately protected."

We can end this discussion of terminating and modifying trusts with one more important note about the UTC provisions. All of the sections we've discussed that give a court the power to modify or terminate a trust — §§ 410 (termination according to the trust's terms), 411 (termination or modification by consent), 412 (equitable deviation), 414 (termination of uneconomic trust), 415 (reformation to correct mistakes), and 416 (modification to achieve settlor's tax objectives), as well as the court's power to modify or terminate a charitable trust in § 413 (which we'll discuss in Chapter 15) — *cannot* be overridden by the terms of the trust. Under UTC § 105(b), these are mandatory terms and not default rules.

(5) Representation

As we've seen, consent by the beneficiaries is critical to termination and modification. We've also seen that beneficiaries can be minors, or under another sort of disability, or even unborn. The one thing these latter beneficiaries have in common is that they cannot give consent. The concept of **representation** is the way around this problem. Representation, in turn, comes in two varieties. A minor, unborn, or incapacitated person can be represented by a fiduciary. The fiduciary could be a guardian or conservator appointed by a court. Generally this sort of fiduciary deals with all of the property interests belonging to the represented person. A court can also appoint a guardian ad litem to represent the beneficiary only in a particular proceeding.

The other sort of representation is **virtual representation**. No, this sort of representation has nothing to do with representation via an avatar in some massive multiplayer game. The idea is that another beneficiary who is an adult and has capacity can represent beneficiaries who are unable to represent themselves and have the same interest as a beneficiary who is a competent adult. A straightforward example is an irrevocable trust that pays income to the settlor's spouse for life, remainder to the descendants of the settlor and the spouse, by representation. The interests in the trust are, of course, the income interest, the remainder interest in the trust, and the reversion in the settlor. Because the remainder is in a multi-generation class, vesting in possession is contingent on survival to the distribution date, which is the death of the income beneficiary. Any proceeding relating to the trust that is begun before the distribution date and that requires the participation of the beneficiaries cannot go forward unless there is some way to deal with the fact that the identity of remainder beneficiaries who will receive the trust property when the trust terminates at the death of the income beneficiary can be determined only at the distribution date.

The solution is to use virtual representation. If all of the persons who would receive the trust property were the distribution date to occur at the time the pro-ceeding is begun are competent adults, then those persons can represent the remainder interest, no matter who the recipients of the trust property are when the distribution finally rolls around. In our example, if all of the children of the settlor and the income beneficiary are competent adults and there are no minor descen-dants of deceased children, then the participation of the adult, competent children will adequately represent the remainder interest. They would be the recipients of the trust property were the trust to end now, and therefore their interest is the same as that of whoever actually receives the trust property at the death of the income beneficiary. That means that if the children have minor children, there is no need to appoint a guardian ad litem to represent the minors, thus saving time and money. Of course, the persons who will receive the trust property in the future may not yet be born. Once again, the living adult competent children can represent these possible recipients of the trust property. This sort of virtual representation is called **vertical representation**; competent adults represent, and their actions will bind, those who would take the same interest should the distribution date occur after the death of those who represent them.

Things get a bit more complicated if there are minor children of a deceased child who would receive a share of the trust property were the distribution date to occur when the proceeding is begun. Traditionally, even though they have the same interest as their adult, competent aunts and uncles, their interest cannot be represented by them. A guardian ad litem would have to be appointed to represent the minors' interest. Under some statutes, however, virtual representation is possi-ble. This sort of virtual representation is called **horizontal representation** because the persons represented would indeed be entitled to receive a share of the trust property were the distribution date to occur just before the commencement of the proceeding.

Some states have case law dealing with representation, and some have codified the concept. Even in states with statutes, the working of those statutes in particular situations is often the subject of numerous cases. UTC § 304 and UPC § 1-403 allow both sorts of virtual representation, requiring only that the interests of the represen-tatives and the represented be "substantially identical" and only to the extent that there is no conflict of interest between them.

We've discussed representation now because it makes sense to do so in the context of obtaining the consent of the beneficiaries for the termination or modification of a trust. I have to warn you, however, that this is an instance of organizational convenience prevailing over substance. The truth is while the concept of virtual representation, both vertical and to a slightly less degree horizontal, is well accepted in proceedings to approve a trustee's account or to remove a trustee, Restatement (Third) of Trusts, the UTC, and the UPC break new ground by allowing the use of virtual representation in a proceeding to terminate an irrevocable trust. As with so many innovative provisions of the Restatements Third, the UTC, and the UPC, we will have to see how courts deal with use of virtual representation in modification and termination proceedings.

F. Resulting Trusts

We'll end this chapter with a brief discussion of **resulting trusts**. The first sort of resulting trust is like a constructive trust because it too is a type of remedy. The difference between this sort of resulting trust and the constructive trust is that this first type of resulting trust is used in only fairly narrow circumstances. The second sort of resulting trust really is part and parcel of the law of express trusts. As you'll see, the law of express trusts really isn't complete without this second type of resulting trust.

(1) Purchase Money Resulting Trusts

Under common law, a purchase money resulting trust arises when a person buys property with money supplied by another person and takes title to the property. By operation of law, a resulting trust arises in favor of the person who provided the money for the purchase. There are two exceptions to this rule: first, if the person providing the purchase money in some way demonstrates an intention *not* to create a resulting trust; second, if the purpose of the transfer is to do something illegal, such as defrauding creditors, there is no resulting trust if letting the purchaser keep the property is less offensive than giving relief to the person who provided the money and was trying to accomplish an illegal end.

There is another exception to the rule that a resulting trust arises when one person using money supplied by another person buys property and takes title to it. If the buyer is a "natural object of the bounty" of the person supplying the money, no resulting trust arises unless the person supplying the money did not intend for the purchaser to benefit from the property. In other words, when the purchaser and the person supplying the money are related, the presumption is that the person supplying the money is making a gift to the purchaser.

These traditional rules are set forth in Restatement (Third) of Trusts § 9. The UTC does not deal with resulting trusts, remember. It is a statute about express trusts. That does not mean that there are no statutes dealing with the subject. The reporter's notes to § 9 identify and discuss some of those statutes, which sometimes abolish the purchase money resulting trust.

(2) Other Resulting Trusts

It's a shame there really isn't a better title for this final section than "other" resulting trusts because it's this sort of resulting trust, one that is not a purchase money resulting trust, that's important for the law of express trusts. Remember the reversion, that future interest that is left in a transferor who transfers less than the transferor's entire interest? Of course you do (and if you don't, take a quick look at Chapter 7). You should also remember that whenever a transferor creates contingent remainders, a reversion is indeed left in the transferor. When we discussed those rules, we didn't say anything about what happens when the reversion actually is entitled to possession of the property involved in the transfer. It was enough at the time for you to understand, for example, that if the settlor transfers property to X as trustee to pay the income from the trust property to A for life, remainder to B if B survives A, if it turns out that B does not survive A, whoever has possession of the reversion is entitled to the trust property.

Here's the problem. We didn't emphasize this when we talked about the reversion as a future interest, but now you can see that the reversion, which is an interest in the trust property, *is not created by the terms of the trust.* It arises by operation of law because the settlor did not give away all of the interests in the transferred property. When A dies and the trust terminates, therefore, the trust terms are silent on what is supposed to happen. The trustee is not supposed to have beneficial ownership of the trust property; that's not what being trustee is about. To deal with this situation, the law says the trustee holds the property on a resulting trust for the benefit of whoever has the reversionary interest, which is entitled to possession of the trust property. In this context, the resulting trust is simply the technical device that allows the trustee to get title to the trust property into reversionary interest, and it arises, therefore, only when the reversionary interest is entitled to possession. (This "get the property to the reversion" type of resulting trust is discussed in § 7 of Restatement (Third) of Trusts.)

There is one other situation in which a resulting trust can be associated with an express trust. If an express trust fails in whole or in part, or if the purpose of the trust has been accomplished and there is still trust property that has not been used in accomplishing that purpose, the trust property is held by the trustee on a resulting trust for the settlor. This kind of resulting trust is the subject of § 8 of the Restatement, which states the rule just as we've done here. While the comments to § 8 give several examples of this use of the resulting trust, one of the examples will make sense to you now.

Remember the testamentary semi-secret trust void because the will on its face devises legal title to the property but not the beneficial interest? This is an example of an express trust that fails at the moment of its attempted creation. The named trustee holds the property on a resulting trust for the testator's successors in interest, which are usually either the residuary devisees if the semi-secret trust is created in a pre-residuary devise or the testator's heirs if the semi-secret trust was created by the devise of the residue to the named trustee.

SUMMARY

- A person may create a trust during life (a lifetime, or inter vivos, trust) or by will (a testamentary trust).

- A person creates a trust by manifesting the intention to do so. While trusts of real property must be in writing, traditionally it is possible to create an oral trust of personal property. In some states, statutes dictate that the creation of all trusts require certain formalities, including that they be in writing.

- Every trust requires a trustee, beneficiaries, and trust property, although no trust will fail for want of a trustee; if necessary, a court will appoint a trustee.

- A natural person or a bank with trust powers may be trustee. Once a trustee accepts the responsibility of being trustee, voluntary resignation must be approved by the appropriate court. A trustee can be removed by a court for failing to properly carry out the trustee's duties.

- Anything that is property can be trust property. The most common exclusions are expectations and future profits.

- A trust must have beneficiaries. The two most common problems in this area are trusts for indefinite groups and trusts for animals.

- If one person becomes sole trustee and sole beneficiary of a trust, the trust will merge out of existence.

- Trusts are either revocable or irrevocable. The traditional default rule is irrevocability. The UTC reverses the default as do non-uniform statutes in some non-UTC states.

- Under traditional law, it is very difficult to modify or terminate an irrevocable trust without the settlor's consent. Modification of administrative terms at the request of the trustee (equitable deviation) is possible if carrying on under the existing terms will endanger the very survival of the trust. Modification of the dispositive terms of the trust or the termination of the trust at the request of the beneficiaries is possible without the settlor's consent only if doing so will not defeat a material purpose for the creation of the trust. Traditionally it is very difficult to show that a material purpose will not be defeated by a modification or termination.

- Under Restatement (Third) of Trusts and the UTC, modification at the request of the beneficiaries or the trustee and termination at the request of the beneficiaries without the settlor's consent is easier than under traditional law because of a lower threshold for modification and a bit more reluctance to find a material purpose.

- Resulting trusts are of two types. Purchase money resulting trusts arise when one person buys property with funds supplied by another. Resulting trusts arise by operation of law when the trust terms do not completely dispose of the trust property.

CONNECTIONS

Creation of Trusts and Creation of Wills

Wills often create testamentary trusts, but the language of the will need not use the word "trust." All that is necessary is that the language of the will indicates the testator's intent to create a trust. Finding that intent is subject to the usual rules for the interpretation and construction of wills discussed in Chapter 5.

Creation of Trusts and Future Interests

Every trust creates future interests (Chapter 7). Sometimes the vesting in possession of the future interest will give the holder of the future interest a present interest in the trust, like an interest in the trust income. Sometimes the future interest is a remainder in fee simple absolute, and its vesting in possession will give the holder possession of trust property free of trust. In other words, the interest will vest in possession when the trust ends. Properly drafting a trust requires a thorough knowledge of how to create future interests that give the beneficiaries what the settlor wants them to have.

Creation of Trusts and Powers of Appointment

One way to dispose of trust property in the future is to give someone, usually a beneficiary, a power of appointment (Chapter 10). The use of powers of appointment creates flexibility in the future disposition of trust property by allowing someone on the scene to determine who will get trust property.

Representation and Trustee's Duties

When a trustee accounts to the beneficiaries of the trust (Chapter 16), vertical and sometimes horizontal representation apply in obtaining the approval of the accounting by the beneficiaries.

Termination of Trusts and Spendthrift Limitations

A restriction on the ability of a beneficiary to alienate her interest in the trust will keep the beneficiary's creditors away from the trust property (Chapter 9). Such a limitation on the beneficiary's interest is usually a material purpose of the trust and will prevent termination of the trust by the consent of the beneficiaries.

Trusts: Beneficiaries' Interests

9

Your former property professor has made you a beneficiary of a very well-endowed trust. Don't ring up the local Lexus dealer just yet. First ask yourself, what are my interests? Present? Future? Based on trust income or trust principal? Can I get money whenever I need it, as long as I make a big fuss over the trustee's cat, Chompers? Will I have to fork over any of my trust benefits to Mona Lisa's Pizzeria, just because I owe them a buck or two? Look for the answers you seek first in the trust terms and then in the applicable law. And take heart! The law hates to frustrate a settlor's material purpose in creating a trust, which usually means strong protections for the trust beneficiaries, particularly against third-party claims.

O V E R V I E W

A. BASIC TRUST ACCOUNTING PRINCIPLES: PRINCIPAL, INCOME, AND UNITRUSTS

1. What Is Income and What Is Principal
2. The Unitrust

B. TRUSTEES AND BENEFICIARIES' INTERESTS

1. Mandatory Trusts
2. Discretionary Trusts

C. RIGHTS OF CREDITORS OF THE BENEFICIARIES

1. What a Creditor Can Get in General
2. Discretionary Trusts
3. Spendthrift Trusts
4. Self-Settled Asset Protection Trusts
5. Government as Creditor and Provider of Support

A. Basic Trust Accounting Principles: Principal, Income, and Unitrusts

To understand what it means to be the beneficiary of a trust, we have to first understand the rules that give practical meaning to having a present or a future interest in a trust. The basis of those rules is the distinction between income, what the trust property produces, and principal, the trust property itself. With one important exception that has developed since the early 1990s, what beneficiaries are entitled to and what trustees are directed to give to beneficiaries is defined in terms of principal and income.

(1) What Is Income and What Is Principal

Income is what trust property produces; it is the return that is received from the investments the trustee makes with the trust property. Just about any kind of property can be trust property. However, most of the property held in U.S. trusts falls into one of three categories: equity investments in corporations (shares of common and preferred stock), debt instruments (corporate and government bonds, bank deposits including certificates of deposit), and real estate. These are shown in Table 9.1.

F   A   Q

Q: What's the difference between preferred stock and common stock?

A: The difference is in the dividend one receives as an owner of the stock. Dividends on common stock are set by a vote of the corporation's board of directors and usually vary with the profitability of the corporation. The dividend on preferred stock is set when the stock is sold to the public and does not vary, which makes it more like a bond.

TABLE 9.1	Types of Trust Property and Income
Type of property	**Income from that property**
Shares of stock	Dividends
Debt instruments (including bank accounts)	Interest
Real estate	Rent

Trust **principal** is the property that produces the income. To use the box metaphor from Chapter 8, the trust property is what's put into the box to initially fund the trust and the property that the trustee acquires from the proceeds of selling trust property. The income, then, is what flows out through the spout to the current beneficiaries. In many trusts, the trustee has what's called the **power to invade principal**: he may open the lid of the box, take out trust property, and give it to a beneficiary.

Deciding on what is income and what is principal is often not difficult at all. Property that the settler of the trustee conveys to the trustee "in trust" is clearly trust principal, as are the proceeds of sale of that property. And most of the time, interest payments, dividends, and rent checks are clearly trust income just because they are interest, dividends, and rent. On the other hand, when trust principal is sold, the proceeds remain trust principal. You might think,

then, that if trust property consisted only of financial assets like stock, bonds, and other debt arrangements and real estate, questions about how to allocate property received by a trust between principal and income would almost never arise. But they do, and more often than you might think.

For example, you probably know what a **stock split** is. A corporation's board of directors can decide to increase the number of shares owned by the shareholders by giving them new shares based on how many shares they own. Probably the most common is a two-for-one split in which each shareholder receives two shares in exchange for every share the shareholder owns, doubling the number of shares owned by the shareholders. If the shareholder is a trust, the new shares are trust principal just the way the old shares were — the trust doesn't own any greater interest in the corporation; its ownership interest is simply represented by more shares. The same rule applies to stock splits that are less generous — three new shares for every two shares owned for example.

F   A   Q

Q: When a trust sells property for more than the trust's basis in it, is the capital gain income or principal?

A: It's trust principal, even though it's income for income tax purposes. Generally, a trust pays income tax on the *taxable* income it does not distribute to beneficiaries, so usually a trust pays the income tax on the capital gain income. This is just one example of how the rules for the tax system do not agree with property law rules (discussed in more detail in Chapter 17).

On the other hand, sometimes a corporation will pay what the corporation calls a "dividend" not in cash but in shares. Usually this means that the shareholder receives some small fraction of a share for each share the shareholder owns. Should these shares be allocated to income or principal? Sometimes the terms of the trust will tell the trustee what to do. Most often, though, the trustee will rely on the default rules in the state law that governs the administration of the trust. Every state has statutes that provide rules for allocating property and money received by the trustee to income or principal. These statutes are usually based on the Uniform Principal and Income Act (UPAIA), which was first offered to states for adoption by the Uniform Law Commission in 1931. The uniform act was revised in 1962 and revised again, quite extensively, in 1997. It provides comprehensive rules for determining whether property or money received by a trust is income or principal. Court decisions settle matters that aren't covered by the statutory rules. Remember, the various principal and income statutes are default rules, and the settlor of a trust can include in the trust document rules for allocations between principal and income. The dividend paid in stock, by the way, is principal under the UPAIA (§ 401(c)(1)).

One of the reasons the uniform acts dealing with principal and income have been widely adopted, in addition to their intrinsic merits, is that a well-drafted default rule for making allocations between principal and income is very popular with trustees. One of the trustee's duties, which we will discuss much more thoroughly in Chapter 16, is to treat all of the beneficiaries of the trust impartially. That includes, of course, properly balancing the interests of the current and future beneficiaries of the trust. Deciding what is principal and what is income certainly affects the balance of benefit between the current income beneficiaries and the future remainder beneficiaries (whether their interests are in future income or in receiving outright ownership of the trust property when the trust terminates). If the trust provisions do not provide answers to questions of allocation between principal and income, and many trusts do not, then a trustee very much would like to rely on a statute that gives the answer. Although in some probably unusual cases the statutory solution may be inappropriate, in most cases the trustee will be able to rely on the answer provided by the legislature.

> ## Sidebar
>
> ### UNPRODUCTIVE PROPERTY STATUTES
>
> Some state statutes (but not the UPAIA) try to be fair to income beneficiaries when the trustee has invested in property that produced little or no income. These statutes require that when the trustee sells the property, some part of the proceeds, which would otherwise be principal, be allocated to income. The application of these statutes sometimes leads to litigation, and it's fair to say that they are being replaced by statutes that give trustees discretion to deal with the possible problems created by investing in property that does not produce income.

(2) The Unitrust

The traditional distinction between principal and income is on the way out, for two reasons. The first has to do with a profound change in the legal standard governing how trustees are to invest trust property and is discussed in Chapter 16. For now we need to note only that this change might require a trustee to invest in property that does not produce a lot of what is traditionally thought of as income. The second reason has to do with the economic environment beginning around 2000 or so. During that period, not only have interest rates, and especially long-term interest rates (for loans longer than ten years), been at historic lows, but the dividend yield on the common stock of publicly traded corporations also has been at all-time lows. All this means that at least some trustees have had a difficult time investing trust property to produce sufficient traditionally defined income to meet their obligations to the income beneficiaries.

The answer has been the redefinition of what the income beneficiary of a trust is entitled to receive. Instead of the traditionally defined trust income, the income beneficiary (more accurately the current beneficiary) is entitled to a fixed percentage of the total value of the trust as determined once a year. This kind of trust is called a **unitrust**. Here's how it works. The trust document reads something like this: "The trustee shall distribute yearly to the income beneficiary in at least quarterly installments an amount equal to 3 percent of the value of the trust property on [the valuation date]." If on the valuation date the trust property is worth $2,000,000, over the coming year the trustee will distribute to the income beneficiary $60,000 (.03 × 2,000,000).

The advantage the unitrust has over a trust administered under the traditional principal and income rules is the freedom it gives the trustee to make investment decisions. The trustee of a trust administered under those traditional rules has to try to invest the trust property to earn a sufficient amount of income to give the income beneficiary the level of benefits from the trust that the settlor intended. At the same time, the trustee has to try to invest at least some of the trust property in investments that will grow in value over time so that the remainder beneficiaries will also get something from the trust. To understand the problem a little better, try to put yourself in the position of a trustee who has $5,000,000 of trust property to invest. All of the income is to be paid to the settlor's daughter, and on her death the trust ends and the trust property is to be paid to the daughter's issue. To produce a steady and dependable stream of income, the trustee invests the entire $5,000,000 in bonds that will pay interest. How much income will be produced depends on the bonds' interest rate. When the trustee buys the bonds, of course, the trustee is loaning the trust property to the issuers of the bonds in exchange for the payment of interest. When the bonds mature, often 20 or more years after the loan is made, the loan will be repaid and the trust will get $5,000,000. Twenty years from now, we can be sure that $5,000,000 will not buy as much as it does today. The trustee hasn't lost any of the trust property, but how happy will the remainder beneficiaries be if the trust does indeed end when those bonds are paid off and they receive $5,000,000, which buys only some fraction of what it bought 20 years before (in fact, in 2010 a dollar bought about 60 percent of what it did in 1990).

Sidebar

UNITRUST CONVERSION STATUTES

Some state statutes allow a trustee to convert a trust that uses the traditional definition of income to a unitrust. The conversion might be possible with the consent of the beneficiaries (using virtual representational principles described in Chapter 8), or court approval might be necessary. The statutes might also allow a conversion from a unitrust definition of income to the traditional definition of income.

Sidebar

THE POWER TO ADJUST

The UPAIA created a new tool for trustees to use to fulfill their duty to treat all trust beneficiaries impartially. Under § 104, a trustee who is administering a trust that makes the traditional distinction between principal and income may "adjust between principal and income," that is, treat some of the trust principal as income or vice versa. The adjustment must be necessary for the trustee to fulfill the duty to administer the trust "impartially, based on what is fair and reasonable to all of the beneficiaries," except to the extent the terms of the trust provide otherwise (§ 103). One other prerequisite for the exercise of the power to adjust is that the law that governs the trustee's duty to invest the trust property must use the prudent investor standard: the trustee must invest the trust property as a whole rather than treating each investment as separate and distinct from every other investment.

If the trust is a 3 percent unitrust, however, in the first year the trustee will pay $150,000 to the daughter. If five years later the trust is worth $6,000,000, the daughter will receive $180,000. As long as the trust keeps growing, both the current beneficiary and the remainder beneficiaries will be better off. The trustee now invests not to produce a stream of income and growth in the value of the trust investments, but only to make the value of the investments taken as whole increase in value. This is often called investing for total return, and a unitrust is therefore sometimes referred to as a **total return trust**.

B. Trustees and Beneficiaries' Interests

We've talked about the trustee's duty to administer the trust impartially. What we haven't talked about is the nature of the beneficiaries' interests in the trust property and the ways in which the settlor of a trust can give to the trustee greater or lesser control over the beneficiaries' interests. Classifying trusts according to the nature of the beneficiaries' rights to enjoyment of the trust property creates two categories: **mandatory trusts** in which the trustee has no control over the beneficiaries' rights to enjoy the trust property and **discretionary trusts** in which the trustee has some degree of control of what the beneficiaries receive from the trust. Many trusts are a blend of the two.

(1) Mandatory Trusts

In a mandatory trust, the trust terms created by the settlor tell the trustee what to give to the beneficiaries. The most common type of mandatory trust is a trust in which the trustee is directed to pay all of the trust's income (which could be defined as a unitrust amount) to one or more beneficiaries. If there is more than one income beneficiary, the trust terms tell the trustee how much to give to each.

Example 9.1: T devises property to Big Bank in trust to pay the income to T's daughter D for life, remainder to D's issue.

Example 9.2: T conveys property to X in trust to pay the income in equal shares to T and T's spouse or all the income to the survivor of them, and on the death of T and T's spouse to terminate the trust and distribute the property to T's issue.

Example 9.3: T devises property to Bigger Bank in trust to pay a unitrust amount of 3 percent annually to T's surviving spouse for life, remainder to T's issue.

These are all mandatory trusts. The trustee has no decisions to make about who gets the income (or the unitrust amount), or about who gets the remainder, for that matter, when the trust is over. Sometimes the trustee is also told how to distribute trust principal before the trust ends.

Example 9.4: T devises property to X in trust to pay the income to T's child, C. When C attains the age of 25, X is to distribute 1/3 of the trust property to C; when C attains the age of 30, X is to distribute 1/2 of the remaining trust property to C; and when C attains the age of 35, X is to distribute all of the remaining trust property to C.

As we've seen, the trustee of a mandatory trust can influence what the beneficiaries receive from the trust not only by selecting trust investments but also by allocating what the trust receives between income and principal. Remember that the trustee must administer the trust impartially and cannot manipulate investments or allocations to principal and income to favor some beneficiaries over others. We will discuss this in greater detail in Chapter 16.

(2) Discretionary Trusts

Settlors who create discretionary trusts write trust terms that give the trustee the authority to make decisions that affect what the beneficiaries receive from the trust. A very common example is a trust that gives the trustee discretion to distribute trust income (or a unitrust amount) among a group of beneficiaries.

Example 9.5: T devises the residue of T's estate to Big Bank in trust to pay the trust income in such amounts as the trustee determines to one or more of T's issue living from time to time.

Here the trustee has discretion to determine the amount of income each beneficiary receives. This sort of discretionary trust is sometimes called a **spray trust**. The term is a metaphor, really, in which the income produced by the trust is envisioned as a stream coming from a hose. The trustee controls the hose and can manipulate it to spray the income stream over the beneficiaries as the trustee decides.

Example 9.6: T devises the residue of T's estate to Big Bank in trust to pay so much of the trust income as the trustee decides to one or more of T's issue living from time to time in whatever amounts the trustee determines. Any income not distributed is added to and becomes part of the trust principal at the end of the year.

This sort of discretionary trust is sometimes called a **sprinkle trust**. This is another metaphor. Again, the trustee is in control of the income stream, but rather than simply spraying it over the beneficiaries, the trustee can determine how much of the income to distribute. You can imagine the trustee directing the stream into a sprinkling can, "watering" which beneficiaries the trustee chooses for how long the trustee chooses, and whatever is left in the sprinkling can at the end of a given year is added to principal.

Example 9.7: T devises the residue of T's estate to Big Bank in trust to distribute so much of the income *and principal* as the trustee decides to one or more of T's issue living from time to time in whatever amounts the trustee determines. Any income not distributed is added to and becomes part of the trust principal at the end of the year. (This is a *sprinkle trust* as to both income and principal.)

Example 9.8: T devises the residue of T's estate to Big Bank in trust to pay the trust income in such amounts as the trustee determines to T's issue living from time to time and make distributions of principal in whatever amounts the trustee determines to one or more of T's issue living from time to time. (This trust is a *spray trust* as to income and a *sprinkle trust* as to principal.)

It's also possible to combine mandatory and discretionary elements.

Example 9.9: T devises the residue of T's estate to Big Bank in trust to pay the trust income to T's surviving spouse and to make distributions of principal in whatever amounts the trustee determines to one or more of T's issue living from time to time. (This is a *mandatory trust* as to income and a *sprinkle trust* as to principal.)

All of these examples of discretionary trusts have one thing in common. In none of them did the settlor give the trustee any instructions on how to exercise the decision-making authority given to the trustee.

(a) Extended Discretion

The absence of instructions from the settlor on how the trustee is to exercise that decision-making authority means that the trustee has **simple discretion**. The trustee is required to exercise reasonable judgment in making decisions. The trustee also must not act on an improper interpretation of the trust terms (Restatement (Third) of Trusts § 50 cmt. b). Sometimes the settlor will add language to the trust terms that attempts to make it *really* clear that the trustee has the last and only word on making distributions of income and principal to the beneficiaries. The trustee can be given "sole and absolute discretion" or "sole and unlimited discretion" or even "sole and uncontrolled discretion" to make decisions. The addition of these adjectives or others like them gives the trustee what Restatement (Third) of Trusts § 50 comment c calls **extended discretion**.

No formulation designed to give a trustee extended discretion means exactly what it says. Restatement (Third) of Trusts says flat out that words like "uncontrolled" or "absolute" or "sole and unlimited" modifying "discretion" "are not interpreted literally" (§ 50 cmt. c). No trustee can ever be the only judge of the propriety of the decisions the trustee makes. Remember that a trust is a relationship between the trustee, the trust property, and the trust's beneficiaries and that the trustee's behavior in that relationship is governed by the trustee's fiduciary duties (Chapter 16). For now, realize that if those duties cannot be enforced, then the trust does not exist. According to Restatement (Third) of Trusts, no court will allow a trustee to act in bad faith or in a way or for a reason other than to accomplish the purposes for which the trustee was given the discretionary power by the settlor. The Uniform Trust Code codifies the rules applied to extended discretion in § 011(a), which says that notwithstanding any sort of language giving extended discretion "the trustee shall exercise a discretionary power in good faith and in accordance with the terms and purposes of the trust and the interests of the beneficiaries."

(b) Standards

Not every trust gives its trustee simple discretion, let alone extended discretion. Settlors often include among the provisions language that directs the trustee when to give income or principal or both to the beneficiaries. This language creates *standards* for the trustee's exercise of discretion. Language creating a spray or sprinkle trust can be coupled with language that directs the trustee to exercise the power to spray or sprinkle while taking into account the beneficiaries' needs for "support," for "maintenance in their accustomed standard of living," or for help handling an "emergency," which could include, for example, a serious illness that prevents the beneficiary from working and results in large medical bills. Trusts that couple discretion with standards related to the beneficiaries' need for financial resources to make possible the beneficiaries' lifestyle are called **discretionary support trusts**.

It is possible to add a support standard to a mandatory trust. That kind of trust is created by using language that directs the trustee to distribute to the beneficiary as much of the income, and perhaps of the principal as well, as is necessary "for support" without including any language that gives the trustee discretion in deciding how much income or principal is necessary for the beneficiary's support (Restatement (Second) of Trusts § 154). This sort of trust is a **support trust** and has long been recognized by the law of trusts as a particular kind of trust. Discretionary support trusts, however, have not traditionally been treated as a distinct type of trust. What that means for the beneficiaries will be clear when we talk about the rights of creditors of the beneficiaries in the next section.

One question that sometimes arises about the nature of a beneficiary's interest in a discretionary support trust is whether the trustee may consider the beneficiary's "other resources" when determining whether the beneficiary needs a distribution from the trust for "support."

Sidebar

INCENTIVE TRUSTS

Trusts that contain very specific standards that require a beneficiary to behave in certain ways to receive a distribution from the trust are known as **incentive trusts**. Examples are requiring a beneficiary to obtain an undergraduate degree, perhaps even from a certain college; to take and pass a test for illicit drugs; or to submit to the trustee proof of employment, such as a W-2 form. While these trusts are well within the limits of current law, they do raise policy issues about the extent of "dead hand" control over the living.

If the settlor does not include this in the trust terms, what is the trustee to do? Courts usually conclude that the trustee is *not* to take into account a beneficiary's other resources (determined, for example, from the beneficiary's income tax return). Restatement (Third) of Trusts § 50 comment e, however, takes the opposite position. In the absence of direction from the settlor, the presumption is that the trustee is to take the beneficiary's other resources into account. The presumption, however, is hedged with several qualifications and modifications. All in all, when the trust terms do not address the question, litigation is often the result.

From the beneficiaries' point of view, the settlor's inclusion in the trust terms of standards, whether they are coupled with a grant of discretion to the trustee, gives the beneficiaries a better chance of making sure that the trustee administers the trust in the way the settlor intended. Another way to look at it is that the inclusion of a standard makes the settlor's purpose in creating the trust somewhat clearer. That in turn makes it somewhat easier for the beneficiaries to argue to a court that the trustee is not properly carrying out the terms of the trust created by the settlor. On the other hand, a trustee might certainly prefer to have extended discretion and a relatively easier job of defending decisions about distributions.

C. Rights of Creditors of the Beneficiaries

Generally, it's a good thing to be the beneficiary of a trust. We can be pretty sure that trust beneficiaries (except perhaps those who are beneficiaries of particularly intrusive incentive trusts) like to receive a check now and then just for being a beneficiary. However, there may be other people who are almost as pleased as the beneficiary to know that the beneficiary has a source of income that does not depend on the beneficiary's willingness or ability to earn it: the beneficiary's creditors.

(1) What a Creditor Can Get in General

The beneficiary of a trust has an equitable interest, and that fact makes collecting a judgment against a debtor's interest in a trust somewhat different from collecting it against assets to which the debtor has legal title. Generally the law recognizes that because the trust beneficiary's interest is equitable only, a court with equitable jurisdiction may give the creditor access to the beneficiary's interest. The equity court won't do that unless the creditor can show that the creditor's remedies at law are inadequate.

Even if the creditor gets over that hurdle, in many jurisdictions the procedure for turning the debtor-beneficiary's interest into cash isn't necessarily like the procedure followed when enforcing a judgment against property to which the beneficiary has legal title. When a creditor levies on a legal interest, the result is a judicially ordered sale of the property with the proceeds going to satisfy the debt. That might not work so well when the debtor's property is an equitable interest in a trust. Think about levying on an income interest. Anyone willing to buy the income interest probably would not be willing to pay a great deal of money "up front." In addition, the income stream itself might produce in a relatively short time enough money to pay the debt. So even in those states where the creditor may proceed as if the beneficiary's interest were a legal interest — that is, by demanding a forced sale — Restatement (Third) of Trusts § 56 comment e says that the court can direct that the debt be satisfied out of future distributions of income, at least when that will not take an unreasonably long time. In addition, the creditor might not get the entire income stream. The same comment e says that the appropriate court may allow some of the income to be paid to the debtor-beneficiary for the "actual needs" of the beneficiary and his family. "Actual needs" is not a particular generous standard as far the Restatement is concerned and is supposed to take into account the beneficiary's other resources. Several states have statutes that preserve some part of a present interest in the trust for the debtor.

The same rules apply to future interests in trusts, primarily remainder interests. Actual possession of the trust property will occur sometime in the future. If a forced sale of the interest does occur, it is likely to be at a price that is quite small compared to the value of the property that will eventually come into possession. Restatement (Third) of Trusts § 56 comment e says that if the interest is not sold, the court may give the creditor a lien on the interest. That means, of course, that if the remainder never vests in possession because of the way a condition precedent or subsequent ends up being resolved, the creditor will get nothing. On the other hand, the sale of the remainder probably would have brought very little anyway.

The UTC deals with all of this in § 501, which simply states that in situations where a creditor can reach a beneficiary's interest in a trust (and we'll see in a minute how easy it is to create a "situation" where that is not the case), the creditor (or a person to whom the beneficiary has validly assigned her interest) may attach "present or future distributions to or for the benefit of the beneficiary or by other means." In addition, the court can order the trustee to deliver all or part of currently due or future payments of income or principal to the creditor. What UTC § 501 does not contemplate is an outright sale of the beneficiary's interest.

Q: Why wouldn't the sale of a remainder interest bring a good price?

A: What the interest is worth at the time of sale (the present value) can be very difficult to determine. It depends on how long the wait before the interest vests in possession, how certain it is that the interest will vest in possession, and finally on a guess about interest rates during the time between now and when the remainder will vest in possession, if it ever does. In addition, because of the widespread use of spendthrift clauses, there really is no market for future interests in the United States.

(2) Discretionary Trusts

All this discussion of how a creditor of a trust beneficiary can enforce a judgment against the beneficiary's interest is a bit misleading unless we're talking about *mandatory* interests. A creditor may not be displeased to be told by the equity court that the trustee must pay all or some portion of the income that must be paid to a beneficiary to the creditor until the creditor's judgment is satisfied. It might not be as good as getting the entire amount of the judgment at once through the sale of property to which the debtor has legal title, but it is certainly better than nothing. But think about the creditor of a beneficiary who has a *discretionary* interest in the trust. The beneficiary gets nothing until and unless the trustee exercises discretion and decides to make a distribution to the beneficiary. The rights of creditors of beneficiaries of discretionary trusts are quite limited. First, the beneficiary of a purely discretionary trust, one that does not attach any standard to the trustee's exercise of discretion, whether the discretion is "simple" or "extended" in Restatement (Third) of Trust terms, does not have any property interest of any kind that can be reached by a creditor. The beneficiary is entitled to nothing unless and until the trustee decides to make a distribution. (Remember that a remainder interest in a discretionary trust could be reached by creditors of the remainder beneficiary subject to the qualifications we've just discussed.) Under widely accepted law, the only remedy the creditor has is to ask a court to order the trustee to pay the creditor before the trustee distributes to the beneficiary. That means that if the trustee does decide to make a distribution, the property that makes up the distribution must go to the creditor. Using this "cutting off" procedure means the creditor can prevent the beneficiary from receiving any distributions. That would certainly give the beneficiary an incentive to make an arrangement with the creditor (e.g., agreeing to give half of what the trustee decides to distribute).

Sidebar

REMAINDERS AND DIVORCE

Modern divorce law of non-community property states generally provides for the **equitable distribution** of the couple's property, which means that all property owned by both spouses is allocated to them on an equitable basis. If a spouse is the remainder beneficiary of a trust, the divorce court must answer the question of whether the remainder is property subject to distribution. The answer is almost always yes, but because the interest may be difficult to value, the court may postpone division between the spouses until the remainder actually vests in possession, which is analogous to the way a creditor of the remainder beneficiary may reach the remainder to satisfy the debt.

This "cutting off" procedure does not necessarily mean that the creditors will ever be paid, but at least it may give them leverage. But even that small benefit might be illusory. The law in some states, and certainly in England, limits the cutting off order to payments made directly to the beneficiary. The trustee can still make payments *for* the beneficiary, if the trust allows such payments, without any interference on the part of the creditors. The terms of many trusts do authorize the trustee to make payments "to or for" the beneficiary. That means that the trustee can pay the beneficiary's bills directly to those who submit them. Therefore a trustee subject to a cutting off order in favor of creditor A can directly pay the beneficiary's bill from creditor B without creditor A being able to do anything about it. Clearly, the leverage given by the cutting off order has all but disappeared if the trustee can and will make payments "for" the beneficiary's benefit.

Neither Restatement (Third) of Trusts nor the UTC has any sympathy for the distinction between "to" and "for" the beneficiary. Comment c to Restatement (Third) of Trusts § 60 says that once the trustee is served by a proper cutting off order, the trustee is "personally liable to the creditor for any amount paid to or applied for the benefit of the beneficiary" in disregard of the creditor's rights. As we've seen, UTC § 501 allows the beneficiary's creditor to attach "present or future distributions to or for the benefit of the beneficiary."

Even if a trustee has extended discretion, however, the beneficiary can require the trustee to exercise discretion properly. If the trust includes a standard governing the trustee's exercise of discretion, the beneficiary can require the trustee to make distributions in accordance with the standard. Recall the discretionary support trust we discussed as part of the general discussion of beneficiaries' interests and trustees' discretion. Surely the beneficiary of a discretionary support trust can go to court to enforce the trustee's duty to make distributions for the beneficiary's support (whether or not the trustee has to take into account the beneficiary's other resources). When it comes to creditors the question is, can the creditor of the beneficiary of a discretionary trust "stand in the shoes of the beneficiary" and ask a court to require the trustee to make a distribution?

If the trustee has discretion with no standard attached, courts have made it all but impossible for the creditor of a beneficiary to compel a distribution. The general assumption is that no settlor would expect the trustee to exercise a purely discretionary power to distribute to benefit anyone other than the beneficiary, even if that "other" is the beneficiary's creditor. Courts have often taken a different approach if the trust is a discretionary support trust. Creditors who are owed for necessaries have been able to compel the trustee to make a distribution. Courts have been most open to this argument when the creditor is a governmental agency that has provided medical care or other welfare benefits to the beneficiary. But classifying trusts as discretionary support trusts has proven to be a difficult task, and there is a good deal of litigation about the issue.

Restatement (Third) of Trusts has attempted to put an end to litigation over classifying a discretionary trust as a discretionary support trust by declaring that the creditor of the beneficiary of any discretionary trust is as entitled as the beneficiary is "to judicial protection from abuse of discretion by the trustee," but what might be an abuse of discretion in refusing a distribution to a beneficiary may not be when the question is making a distribution to a creditor (§ 60 cmt. e). Whether the creditor can compel a distribution depends on the terms of the trust and the circumstances.

	Restatement (Third) § 60	UTC § 504	Generally accepted traditional law
TABLE 9.2	**Discretionary Trusts and Creditors**		
Distinction between discretionary and discretionary support trusts	No; comment a	No; § 504(b)	Yes
Can creditor compel distribution according to standard?	Yes, with qualifications; comment e	No; § 504(b), with exception for support obligations to spouse, ex-spouse, and children (§ 504(c))	Yes, if discretionary support trust and if creditor has provided necessaries
"Cutting off" procedure available?	Yes; comment c	Yes; § 501	Yes
Exception for distributions "for" the beneficiary?	No; comment c	No; § 501	Yes in England; some U.S. authority as well

The UTC agrees with the Restatement in making no distinction between discretionary trusts and discretionary support trusts. It takes a very different position, however, on the rights of creditors. Under § 504(b), a creditor cannot compel the trustee of a discretionary trust to make a distribution to satisfy a beneficiary's debt, even if the discretion is subject to a standard or the trustee has abused the discretion. Subsection (c) creates an exception for support claims by the beneficiary's spouse, former spouse, or children. When the exception applies, the court is limited to ordering payment to the spouse, former spouse, or children in an amount not greater than what the trustee would have had to distribute to the beneficiary under the terms of the trust.

Table 9.2 summarizes the various rules and their treatment of creditors.

(3) Spendthrift Trusts

The settlor who wishes to keep trust property out of the hands of the beneficiaries' creditors is not limited to creating a discretionary trust. If the settlor creates a support trust, the only creditors of the beneficiary who can reach the beneficiary's interest are those who are owed for necessaries — food, clothing, shelter, medical care. In addition, the beneficiaries of a support trust cannot assign away their interests in the trust. The purpose of the trust is to support the beneficiaries, and that purpose would be frustrated if the beneficiaries could give away their interests.

But the support trust is not the only alternative. In most states it is possible for the settlor to prohibit any payment from the trust to satisfy the beneficiary's debts or any payment to someone to whom the beneficiary has assigned the beneficiary's interest, whether the beneficiary's interest is mandatory or discretionary. A trust whose terms include a restraint on voluntary or involuntary alienation or both is known as a **spendthrift trust**. Its purpose is to protect the beneficiary from her own improvidence and to make sure she can always rely on the trust to pay for goods and services, even though the beneficiary is completely broke and deeply in debt.

The validity of these sorts of restraints on the beneficiary's interest was in doubt until the third quarter of the nineteenth century when the U.S. Supreme Court and state high courts began to hold that such restraints were enforceable. Courts usually reasoned that since the settlor of a trust can do whatever he likes with his own property, the settlor can limit the beneficiary's interest by forbidding voluntary or involuntary alienation.

F   A   Q

Q: Can the interest of a beneficiary of a spendthrift trust be reached by creditors in a bankruptcy proceeding?

A: No. The federal Bankruptcy Code § 541(c)(2) respects state law recognizing spendthrift trusts.

Sidebar

SPENDTHRIFT TRUSTS AND THEIR GREATEST CRITIC

Although spendthrift trusts are widely accepted, they are not without their critics. Perhaps the most vociferous was John Chipman Gray, professor of law at Harvard Law School; a founder of Ropes & Gray, still one of the United States' leading law firms; and the principal creator of the modern Rule Against Perpetuities through the influence of his 1886 treatise on the Rule. In his 1883 treatise *Restraints on the Alienation of Property*, Gray railed against the then new spendthrift trust doctrine. Gray believed the spendthrift trust not only was insupportable doctrinally — as an impermissible restraint on alienation — but also was wretched policy. Gray was appalled that spendthrift trusts might actually promote irresponsibility by eliminating the consequences of beneficiaries' bad judgment, mistakes, and out-and-out foolishness.

State laws governing spendthrift trusts vary greatly, but one thing on which all agree is that when it comes to creating a spendthrift trust, all that is necessary is that the trust terms manifest the settlor's intent to restrain alienation. Most published forms use language that expressly prohibits voluntary or involuntary alienation by the beneficiary. Spendthrift trusts are also recognized in the blackletter of Restatement (Third) of Trusts § 58 and in UTC § 502. Both the Restatement and the UTC require the trust to forbid both voluntary and involuntary alienation (§ 58 cmt. b(2) and § 502(a)). Both also state that identifying the trust as "a spendthrift trust" in the trust terms is sufficient; "alienation" need not be mentioned (§ 58 cmt. b(3) and § 502(b)).

When it comes to exceptions to protection from creditors, the blackletter of Restatement (Third) of Trusts § 59 states the most widely accepted: claims for support by a beneficiary's children, spouse, and ex-spouse and claims by those who have provided necessaries or services for the protection of the beneficiary's interest in the trust (i.e., the beneficiary's lawyer). Comment a(1) says that "implicit" in the blackletter is an exception for claims by government under federal law or state statutes. Comment a(2) names another exception, one that the ALI has supported for decades: a tort victim who has a judgment against the beneficiary/tortfeasor (Restatement (Second) of Trusts § 157 cmt. a; Restatement (Third) of Trusts § 59 cmt. a(2)). But this suggestion has gone nowhere.[1]

UTC § 503 lists the code's exceptions to a valid spendthrift restrictions. These include the beneficiary's child, spouse, or former spouse who has a judgment for support or maintenance; a judgment creditor who has provided services for protection of the beneficiary's interest (yes, lawyers); and, making explicit what the Restatement says is implicit, claims by the state or by the United States to the extent provided by a state statute or federal law. The comment to the section explains the omission of two of the Restatement's exceptions: (1) creditors who have supplied necessaries ("most of these cases involved claims by government entities" and are better handled by specific legislation); and (2) tort claimants (the drafters specifically "declined to create an exception for tort claimants"), which reflects the sensible conclusion that such a provision would not be popular, would not be included in state adoptions of the section, and might make not only § 503 but the entire UTC less likely to be adopted by the states.

(4) Self-Settled Asset Protection Trusts

One rock bottom basic principle of the law governing the rights of creditors in interests their debtors have in trusts is this: the settlor cannot be a beneficiary of the trust the settlor creates and expect the settlor's interest as beneficiary to be safe from the settlor's creditors, no matter how extended the trustee's discretion to make distributions to the settlor/beneficiary or how strong the spendthrift provision included in the trust terms. In other words, there is no such thing as a **self-settled spendthrift trust**, a trust which provides spendthrift protection to an interest retained by settlor as a beneficiary of the trust. (Restatement (Third) of Trusts § 58(2); UTC § 505(a)(2)). This prohibition on trying to put your own property beyond the reach of your creditors while retaining the possibility of enjoying the economic benefit of that property extends to discretionary trusts. The rule for discretionary trusts is that the settlor/beneficiary's creditor may reach the maximum amount of property that the trustee can distribute to or for the beneficiary. If the trustee could distribute all of the trust principal to or for the beneficiary, then the beneficiary's creditor can execute the creditor's judgment against all of the trust property (Restatement (Third) of Trusts § 60 cmt. f; UTC § 505(a)(2)).

---

[1] *See* Family Trust Preservation Act, Miss. Code Ann. § 91-9-903 (passed to override Sligh v. First Natl. Bank, 704 So. 2d 1020 (Miss. 1997), in which tort victim was allowed to collect from tortfeasor/beneficiary's spendthrift trust).

F   A   Q

Q: Why did the self-settled asset protection trust appear when it did?

A: Competition is one reason. Well before Alaska passed its statute in 1997, foreign jur-isdictions like the Cook Islands, Bermuda, the Cayman Islands, and some others allowed settlors to create asset protection trusts. Statutes in these jurisdictions make it very difficult to enforce foreign judgments against trust assets held there. The Alaska statute was motivated in part by the desire to create a U.S. alternative to foreign trusts and to keep the assets and the business of administering them in the United States.

These rules have long been accepted almost without question. In 1997, however, the world began to change. In that year, Alaska enacted legislation that allowed a settlor to create a discretionary trust of which she is a beneficiary that cannot be reached by the settlor's creditors. At least 12 states now have legislation authorizing what are usually called **self-settled asset protection trusts**, discretionary trusts that cannot be reached by the creditors of the settlor who is also a beneficiary. The pro-tection provided to the settlor is usually quite comprehensive. About the only limit under these statutes is that the transfer of property to the trust cannot be a **fraud-ulent transfer**, an attempt to give property away for less than full and adequate consideration when the transferor's debts exceed the transferor's assets. In some instances, the debt need not yet be legally enforceable. The easiest example is where the transferor has been involved in a serious motor vehicle accident and faces a good chance that he will be sued for negligence. The law of fraudulent transfers is complex, but if the settlor of an asset protection trust creates the trust before there is even the possibility of serious potential liability, the trust will accomplish its purpose.

(5) Government as Creditor and Provider of Support

When government has claims against an individual for providing support, state and federal statutes that create exceptions to spendthrift protection come into play. The same rules generally apply when the question is whether the trust beneficiary will qualify for governmental benefits for which there is a means test. In other words, a person is eligible for benefits only if that person's assets and income do not exceed a certain level. The most important of these programs is Medicaid, a joint state and federal program that provides medical care for the indigent.

Federal law provides the basic rules. Under those rules, any part of a trust created with assets that belonged to the applicant by the applicant, the applicant's spouse, or by a person (such as a guardian or an attorney-in-fact) or court with legal authority to act for the applicant or the applicant's spouse is "self-settled." Property of a self-settled trust is counted as an asset of the applicant for determining eligibility to the maximum extent assets can be distributed to the applicant. Therefore, even if the trust gives the trustee extended discretion to distribute income and principal to the beneficiary/applicant, all of the self-settled trust is an asset of the applicant and will be taken into account in determining eligibility. If the government has already provided services and is seeking reimbursement, the same rules apply. In short, it is not really possible to use a trust to shelter one's own assets from governmental claims for support. Nor is it possible to use a trust to keep some interest in your own property yet not have that interest counted as yours when you want the government pay for your support.

The most important exception to the self-set-tled trust rule for our purposes involves a trust created with the property of a disabled person by a parent, grandparent, or guardian of the disabled person, or by a court acting on the disabled person's behalf. Property in the trust is not counted as an asset of the disabled person so long as during the beneficiary's life the trust property can be used only to supplement governmental benefits and, on the beneficiary's death, the trust property is applied first to repaying the governmental entity that provided the benefits. Such a trust is often called a **payback trust**. If the victim of an accident or of professional malpractice receives a recovery in tort, the proceeds can be placed in this sort of trust and will not affect the injured person's eligibility for government benefits. The trust can then be used to pay for things government programs will not. If the disabled person is living at home, the trust could be used to pay for modifications to the living space to make it wheelchair accessible or even to buy a new house. This sort of trust is also called a **first-party supplemental needs trust** because although it is created by the recipient of governmental benefits, the trust property can be used only to supplement those benefits (so long, of course, as the payback provision is there).

Someone receiving governmental benefits like Medicaid can be the beneficiary of a trust created by someone else without the risk of disqualification so long as the trust is a **third-party supplemental needs trust.** Defined by statute in some states, such a trust includes provisions expressly stating that the trustee is to make distributions to the disabled beneficiary only to supplement the governmental benefits the beneficiary is receiving, for instance, by providing anything from pocket money to vacations with family members. So long as the trust qualifies, the beneficiary's interest in the trust will not be a resource that will be counted in determining whether the beneficiary is eligible for benefits. At the beneficiary's death, there are no limits on who receives any remaining trust property. In states without such statutes, the drafter must be guided by existing cases in drafting a trust that does not give the beneficiary any interest that can be characterized as a resource.

SUMMARY

■ Trust beneficiaries may hold present or future interests, or both. One important way these interests are distinguished are by whether the beneficiary's interest is in the trust's income, what the trust property produces, or in its principal, the trust property itself.

■ The terms of the trust can give the trustee greater or lesser control over the beneficiaries' interests. In any event, the trustee's exercise of discretion is always subject to supervision by the court.

- A support trust gives the beneficiary so much of the income and/or principal as is necessary for the beneficiary's support. A support trust is immune from most claims of the beneficiary's creditors. In addition, the beneficiary cannot voluntarily transfer the beneficiary's interest.

- The beneficiary of a purely discretionary trust does not have a property interest that a creditor can attach. While Restatement (Third) of Trusts allows a creditor to compel a distribution by the trustee if the beneficiary could do so (with some limitations), both the UTC and generally accepted law do not.

- The distinction between a discretionary trust and a discretionary trust containing a standard for distributions related to the support of the beneficiary has been a source of much litigation. Generally accepted traditional law allows a creditor who has provided "necessaries" to the beneficiary to be paid from a discretionary support trust. Both Restatement (Third) of Trusts and the UTC reject the distinction and treat all discretionary trusts alike when it comes to the claims of creditors of the beneficiary.

- A spendthrift trust prohibits involuntary alienation of the beneficiary's interests, thus immunizing the beneficiary's interests from creditor's claims. The settlor can also prohibit voluntary alienation of the beneficiaries' interests. Both Restatement (Third) of Trusts and the UTC require that a spendthrift trust contain both prohibitions.

- The few exceptions to spendthrift protection are almost always limited to claims for support by spouses, ex-spouses, and children of beneficiaries and claims of creditors who have supplied necessaries to the beneficiary.

- Self-settled asset protection trusts allow settlors to create trusts that cannot be reached by creditors by naming themselves as discretionary beneficiaries. These trusts are both controversial and heavily promoted by the handful of states that allow them.

- A self-settled trust established for a disabled person protects the person's interest in the trust from being considered an asset for determining eligibility for governmental benefits, so long as the trust terms provide that on the beneficiary's death the trust property is used first to reimburse the government for the care given the beneficiary.

CONNECTIONS

Spendthrift Restrictions and Future Interests

Beneficiaries often have future interests in trusts (Chapter 7). Although future interests are transferable in the modern world, a valid spendthrift restriction will prevent transfer of the interest.

Spendthrift Restrictions and Disclaimers

Modern disclaimer statutes (Chapter 2) allow the disclaimer of trust interests subject to a valid spendthrift restriction, subordinating the right of the settlor to prevent assignment of the interest to the beneficiary's right to reject the interest.

Spendthrift Restrictions and the Termination of Trusts

A trust cannot be terminated by the consent of the beneficiaries if doing so would frustrate a material purpose of the settlor in creating the trust (Chapter 8). Courts have very often held that spendthrift restrictions are a material purpose, thus making it impossible to terminate a spendthrift trust on the consent of the beneficiaries.

Trustee Powers of Distribution and Wealth Transfer Taxes

Because of the adverse tax consequences of holding a power to give property to yourself, beneficiary/trustees are often limited by a standard related to the health, education, maintenance, and support of the trust beneficiaries (Chapters 10, 17). While this standard prevents adverse tax consequences to the trustee who is also a beneficiary, it creates a support standard that may make the beneficiaries' interests vulnerable to their creditors, at least to those who have provided support, which can include the government.

Powers of Appointment

10

Powers of appointment are powerful estate planning tools because they allow a property owner
to put future decisions about the ultimate dispo-

sition of the property into the hands of a person who is likely to be alive at that future
point. How the settlor of the power establishes its parameters is critically important
because they determine whether the property is treated as if it were the property of the
person making the decision, a key issue in resolving litigation. The crucial question is
always: "What kind of power of appointment is this?" Most of this chapter is devoted
first to explaining how to answer that question and second to explaining what the
answer means for all the various problems that can be created by the use of powers of
appointment.

A. TERMINOLOGY AND CLASSIFICATION

B. EFFECTS OF CLASSIFICATION

    1. Rights of Creditors
    2. Tax Effects

C. CREATION OF POWERS OF APPOINTMENT

D. EXERCISE OF POWERS OF APPOINTMENT

    1. Intent to Exercise and Residuary Clauses
    2. Blanket Exercise and Blending Clauses
    3. Blending Clauses, Capture, and Allocation

E. MISCELLANEOUS QUESTIONS

1. Failure to Appoint and Takers in Default
2. Choice of Law
3. Anti-Lapse Statutes and Powers of Appointment
4. Contracts to Appoint
5. Complications in Understanding Special Powers

What is a **power of appointment**? It is a power given by the owner of property to someone (who can be the owner) to dispose of property, to "say where it goes," at some time in the future. The power is held in a **nonfiduciary capacity**, which means that the person who has the power can exercise it more or less as she wants within the limits set by the person who gave the power. Unlike a fiduciary, the person who has the power does not have to act selflessly for someone else's benefit. Now this is all really abstract, and the rest of this chapter is devoted to making this description more concrete.

But before we start that project, an example of a power of appointment might be useful.

Example 10.1: Testator devises her residuary estate to Big Bank in trust to pay the income to her Daughter for life and on Daughter's death to distribute the trust property as Daughter shall appoint in her will.

A well-drafted power of appointment will have a lot more to say than that, but we're keeping this simple for now. Daughter can decide what happens to the property in the trust created by her mother after Daughter's death. Why do that? Mother probably realizes that she has no idea what sort of world her grandchildren and more remote descendants will be living in, what their needs will be, or how much property will be in the trust at Daughter's death. Daughter will have far more information about those matters when the time comes for her to make her testamentary plans. A power of appointment is a way to deal with the uncertainties of the future by allowing someone with knowledge of what the future is like to make decisions about how best to use the property that the creator of the power once owned. That makes the power of appointment an extremely important estate planning tool and one that is very widely used.

A. Terminology and Classification

Understanding powers of appointment has to begin with understanding the associated terminology. So:

- The person who creates a power of appointment is the **donor**.
- The person in whom the power of appointment is created is the **donee**.
- The property over which the donee has the power is the **appointive property**.
- The persons to whom the donee can appoint the appointive property are the **objects of the power** or the **permissible appointees**.
- The persons designated by the donor to take the appointive property if the donee does not exercise the power are the **takers in default** (in default of

exercise of the power). (The donor doesn't have to name takers in default, but, as we'll see, it's a very good idea to do so.)

The terminology applicable to powers of appointment themselves is related to how the powers are classified. Powers are classified according to when and how the donee may exercise them and by the permissible objects of the power.

By Time or Manner of Exercise. **Inter vivos** (or lifetime) powers may be exercised by the donee during his lifetime by a written instrument or some act that "would be formally sufficient under the applicable law to transfer an interest in the appointive assets to the appointee in the donee's lifetime if the donee owned the appointive assets." (Restatement (Third) of Property § 17.1 cmt. e). Lifetime powers can be further classified as **presently exercisable**—the donee can exercise the power right now—and **postponed powers**—the donee can exercise the power while alive but just not at the moment; the donee may have to reach a stated age, or marry, or meet some other condition before he can exercise the power. **Testamentary powers** can be exercised only by the donee's will. How the will is supposed to exercise the power, that is, what words the donee has to use, is a complicated matter, as we'll see.

By Permissible Objects. If the permissible objects include the donee, then the power is a **general power of appointment**. "Including the donee" requires some further explanation. It really is more accurate to say that if the donee can take direct economic advantage of the appointive property for himself, then the power is general. A donee can take that economic advantage by more than a simple appointment to the donee. If the donee can use the property to pay off the donee's creditors, then the donee has taken for herself the economic benefit of the appointive property. The most influential list of ways in which the donee can take advantage of the appointive property for the donee's own benefit is found in the Internal Revenue Code (so influential that Restatement (Third) of Property § 17.3(a) uses the same list). In IRC §§ 2041 (estate tax) and 2514 (gift tax), a general power of appointment is defined as a power that allows the donee to appoint the appointive property to the donee, to the donee's creditors, to the donee's estate, or to the creditors of the donee's estate. If the donee can appoint to any one of those four objects, the power is general.

F A Q

Q: How can a donee "appoint to the donee's estate"?

A: Appointing to the estate means that the donee can exercise the power of appointment to make the appointive property part of her probate estate. The appointive property then is governed by the donee's will in the same way any other property in the probate estate is governed by the will.

If the permissible objects *do not* include the donee, then the power is **special** or **nongeneral**. Again, the IRC definition has come to dominate the law of powers of appointment. So long as the donee *cannot* appoint to the donee, the donee's creditors, the donee's estate, or the creditors of the donee's estate, the power is special (and Restatement (Third) of Property § 17.3(b) agrees). Of course, the donor of the power can define the permissible objects just about any way the donor wants. Many special powers have pretty narrowly defined permissible objects: the donee's issue, or the donee's surviving spouse and issue, or the donor's issue.

There are two other ways in which a power that would otherwise be general is classified as special. The first is illustrated by Example 10.2.

Example 10.2: T devises the residue of T's estate to Big Bank in trust, to pay income to T's child C for life, and on C's death to distribute the trust property as C and T's other child D shall together appoint, and in default of appointment T shall distribute the trust property to D.

C's ability to exercise this otherwise general power of appointment is limited because an appointment to anyone other than D takes the property away from D who will get it all if C does nothing, and D must join in any exercise of the power. In more general terms, the donee can exercise the power only with the **joinder** (agreement) of an **adverse party**, someone who will suffer economic loss if the power is exercised. Both the IRC (§ 2041(b)(1)(C)(ii)) and Restatement (Third) of Property (§ 17.3 cmt. e) classify such a power as nongeneral.

IRC § 2041(b)(1)(A) gives us the second way a power that allows the donee to appoint to herself can be nongeneral: the terms of the power limit the donee to using the appointive property only for the donee's health, education, maintenance, and support (often called a **HEMS standard**). This limitation creates an **ascertainable standard**, an objective limit on how much of the property the donee can use for the donee's own benefit. This is one instance, however, in which the property law of powers of appointment does not follow tax law. Restatement (Third) of Property says nothing about powers limited by ascertainable standards, although at least one state, New York, classifies such a power as special.

To sum up then, there are four basic types of powers of appointment:

1. Testamentary general powers of appointment
2. Inter vivos (lifetime) general powers of appointment (which may be presently exercisable or postponed)
3. Testamentary special powers of appointment
4. Inter vivos special powers of appointment (which may be presently exercisable or postponed)

F   A   Q

Q: Isn't a testamentary power a postponed power?

A: Yes, it is. The donee's ability to exercise it is postponed until the moment of death. However, the distinguishing feature of a testamentary power is that it can *only* be exercised in the donee's will. Since that's the case, the term "postponed power" is used to describe only powers that will become exercisable, if they ever do, during the donee's life.

Q: If the donor gives the donee authority to exercise the power during life, can the donee also exercise the power by will?

A: It depends on the words the donor uses. If the appointive property is to be distributed "as the donee shall appoint" without any mention of the method the donee must use, the power may be exercised during life or by will. However, if the donor specifies that the donee is to exercise the power "by deed," then the exercise must be by a document that would be effective during the donee's life to transfer the appointive property if the donee owned the appointive property outright.

B. Effects of Classification

Classification of a power of appointment is extremely important because it determines two significant questions: (1) What rights, if any, do the creditors of the donee have in the appointive property? (2) What are the estate and gift tax consequences of the power to the donee?

(1) Rights of Creditors

Let's say the donee of a power of appointment owes you money and hasn't paid, and you get a judgment for the amount of the debt. The donee appears to be judgment proof; at least, you can't find assets the donee holds outright sufficient to pay the debt. The donee, however, is the donee of a power of appointment over very valuable appointive property. Can you get at the appointive property to satisfy your judgment against the donee?

Traditionally the answer is a resounding no, no matter what sort of power the donee has. That answer makes sense if the power is any sort of special power; after all, the essence of the special power is the donee's inability to use the appointive property for the donee's own economic benefit. But the answer is the same for general powers of appointment, even though the essence of those powers is the donee's ability to use the appointive property for the donee's benefit. What gives?

What gives is one of those very old, very formal doctrinal distinctions. In this case, it's the long-standing doctrine that a power is not an interest. In other words, the donee of the power of appointment has no property interest in the appointive property. The only way the donee of a general power of appointment can acquire a property interest in the appointive property is to actually appoint the property to herself. The creditor can't force the donee to exercise the power, so that's that.

Another concept that has stood in the way of the creditor of the donee of a power of appointment is the **relation-back doctrine**, which says that the appointive property was and always is the property of the donor of the power until the donee exercises the power. The donee is only "filling in the blanks" in the donor's own disposition. That means the donor of the power is also the donor of whatever arrangements the donee makes by exercising the power. This is simply another way of saying that a power is not an interest. In the modern world, the relation-back doctrine is pretty much limited to special powers of appointment. Restatement

(Third) of Property § 17.4 comment f rejects the relation-back theory completely as a way of explaining power of appointment law and prefers to ask what sort of control over the appointive property the power gives to the donee.

If we do look at the situation of the donee of a presently exercisable general power from the point of view of control, it's clear that the only thing that stands between the donee of a general inter vivos power of appointment that's presently exercisable and the appointive property is what amounts to a direction to whoever has control of the appointive property (almost always a trustee) to deliver the appointive property to the donee. The donee's action has been compared to writing a check: the trustee (or whoever else has control of the appointive property) receives whatever document the donee has to deliver and must respond by delivering the appointive property requested by the donee to the donee. To put it more succinctly, being the donee of an inter vivos general power of appointment that's presently exercisable is almost exactly like being the owner of the appointive property subject to the power.

The force of that analogy has led some states to pass legislation that makes appointive property subject to a presently exercisable inter vivos general power subject to payment of the donee's debts. In addition, both Restatement (Third) of Property § 22.3 and Restatement (Third) of Trusts § 56 comments b and c take the position that appointive property subject to a presently exercisable general power is subject to satisfaction of the donee's debts.

On the other hand, the donee of a general testamentary power of appointment can indeed take the economic advantage of the appointive property for himself, but not during life. It's obvious then, and indeed it is the rule everywhere, that while the donee of a testamentary power is alive, the donee's creditors cannot reach the appointive property. But what about after the donee's death? After all, the donee could appoint the property in a way that makes it available to creditors, by appointing to the donee's estate (and thus making the appointive property part of the probate estate) or, if the power allows it, directly to creditors. Nevertheless, the traditional rule is that if the donee does not exercise the power, the donee's creditors cannot reach the appointive property. The converse is also true. If the donee *does* exercise a general testamentary power of appointment, then the donee's creditors can reach the appointive property. The appointment does not have to be to the donee's estate or creditors. Even if the donee appoints directly to named individuals, those appointees take the property subject to the right of the donee's executor to use the property to pay the donee's debts, at least if the probate estate is not sufficient to do so.

The Restatements (Third) of Property § 22.3 and of Trusts § 56 comments b and c, however, allow the donee's creditors to reach property subject to a testamentary general power of appointment whether the donee exercises the power or not, but only if the assets of the probate estate are insufficient to pay the decedent's debts and the expenses of administering the estate (in other words, the estate must be insolvent). At least one state, California, has a statute allowing the creditors of the donee's estate to reach property subject to a general testamentary power of appointment held by the donee, whether the donee exercises it or not — on the same terms as the Restatement. This California statute (Prob. Code § 682(b)) is unusual to say the least, and it seems that it will take some time before the position of the Restatements is widely adopted, if ever.

(2) Tax Effects

As we've already noted, the definition of a general power of appointment in the IRC estate and gift tax provisions has become the property law definition of a general power of appointment. Every other power of appointment is therefore special or nongeneral. The significance of this distinction is overwhelming. For transfer tax purposes, property subject to a general power of appointment, whether inter vivos or testamentary, and whether exercised or not, is the donee's property. Let's see some concrete examples.

Example 10.3: Mother's will devises her residuary estate to Big Bank in trust to pay the income to Daughter for life, and on Daughter's death the trust terminates and the trustee is to distribute the trust property as Daughter shall appoint in her will. On her death, Daughter's probate estate is valued at $2,500,000, and the trust property is valued at $3,000,000. Daughter's gross estate (i.e., her taxable estate before deductions) is $5,500,000. Why? Because Daughter is the donee of a general power of appointment.

Example 10.4: Mother's will devises her residuary estate to Big Bank in trust to pay the income to Daughter for life, and on Daughter's death the trust terminates and the trustee is to distribute the trust property as Daughter shall appoint in her will, except that Daughter may not appoint to herself, her estate, her creditors, or the creditors of her estate. On her death, Daughter's probate estate is valued at $2,500,000, and the trust property is valued at $3,000,000. Daughter's gross estate (i.e., her taxable estate before deductions) is $2,500,000. Why? Because Daughter is the donee of a special (nongeneral) power of appointment. The trust property is not subject to estate tax in her estate whether she exercises the power or not.

F   A   Q

Q: Does the donee have a general power of appointment if the only thing the donor says is that "the donee may appoint" and says nothing about permissible objects?

A: Yes, although there are a few court decisions that hold that the power must affirmatively allow the donee to appoint to at least one of the "general power quartet": donee, donee's creditor, donee's estate, creditors of donee's estate.

F   A   Q

Q: Is a power of appointment a special power if the donee can appoint to the donee's spouse or family?

A: Yes. It's easy to get confused about the meaning of "estate" in this context. Just because a permissible object of the power is someone who would take the donee's estate were the donee to die intestate, or is someone to whom the donee is likely to leave at least some of the donee's probate estate in the donee's will, the authority to appoint to such a person is *not* the same as appointing to the donee's estate.

The gift tax is relevant only if the power of appointment is a lifetime power of appointment. If the donee of a general power exercises it during life by appointing the appointive property to anyone other than the donee, the donee has made a gift that is potentially subject to gift tax. If the donee exercises an inter vivos special power of appointment by appointing the appointive property to anyone other than the donee, the donee *has not* made a taxable gift (unless the donee also had an interest in the property, for example, the donee was receiving the income from the appointive property, in which case the donee has made a gift of the value of the income interest).

There is a lot more to learn about powers of appointment and the transfer taxes, and we'll deal with some of that in Chapter 17. For now, it's enough to know that the property law dealing with the rights of a donee's creditors and the tax law agree on the treatment of special powers: the appointive property is not the property of the donee. Tax law and property law do not agree, however, when it comes to general powers. Although the property law is not uniform, on the whole, property subject to a general power of appointment is not the property of the donee when it comes to satisfying the donee's debts, but it is always treated as property of the donee when the question involves the donee's estate tax and gift taxes levied on transfers of property by the donee.

You may ask, what about income taxes and powers of appointment? IRC § 678(a) says that a person is the owner of any portion of a trust with respect to which the person "has a power exercisable solely by himself to vest the corpus or the income therefore in himself." That means for income tax purposes any trust property over which I have a presently exercisable general power of appointment really is my property. Any income or capital gain it generates is reported on my income tax return, and I get to use any deductions or capital losses generated by the property.

Sidebar

SPECIAL OR NONGENERAL?

The enormous influence that tax law has had on the property law of powers of appointment is most clearly seen in the terminology used for a power that is not a general power. When the first Restatement of Property was written, property subject to a general power of appointment was taxable only if the donee exercised the power. All others powers of appointment had no tax consequences. At the time, a "special power" was a power to appoint to a definable group, which did not include the donee. A power to appoint to everyone in the world who was not the donee was called a "hybrid" power and was seldom encountered and pretty much ignored.

In the 1940s, Congress created the modern law of taxation of powers of appointment, and all of a sudden, all general powers had tax consequences, but any power that was not general did not. What made a power not general was the lack of ability to appoint to the "quartet." The term "special" was still used for these powers, but now they were "special" because they were not general. What was once a "hybrid" power was now common, and although the term "special power" is often applied to it, "nongeneral," used in the Second and Third Restatements of Property, is really more accurate.

C. Creation of Powers of Appointment

Even though many powers of appointment are created in wills as part of a testamentary trust, creating powers of appointment is not at all like creating a valid will. It's more like creating a trust: all that's needed is manifestation of the intent to create a power of appointment. Granted, given the importance of powers of appointment in creating estate plans and the striking differences in the tax treatment of general powers as opposed to special powers, lawyers drafting powers of appointment are always careful to spell out the terms of the power as clearly as possible. As we'll see, there's a lot more that goes into drafting a power of appointment than clearly stating that a certain donee has a power to appoint and making it equally clear whether the power is special or general. However, that's a good place to start.

F   A   Q

Q: Is a power created if the donee appointed in the donor's will dies before the donor?

A: No. A power created in the donor's will is created at the moment the donor dies, and a power cannot be created in a donee who is dead when the power is created. Restatement (Third) of Property § 19.11 comment c, however, says that a power given to a donee by the donor's lifetime trust is created in the donee at the time the trust is created, even if the trust is revocable. Of course, any exercise of the power by the donee before the donor's death can be made meaningless by revoking the trust.

Just remember, all that's needed is a manifestation of intent. Let's say that the testator's will (not drafted by a lawyer) devises Blackacre with these words: "I direct that Blackacre shall be distributed in the discretion of my sister, X, to whomsoever she deems fit to distribute it to." That's a power of appointment, and it's also a general power because there's no limit on the permissible appointees, so the testator's sister can appoint Blackacre to herself.

D. Exercise of Powers of Appointment

(1) Intent to Exercise and Residuary Clauses

In the best of all possible worlds, it would be easy to decide if a donee had exercised a power of appointment. The donee would write *something* that said, more or less, "I hereby exercise the power of appointment given to me by Donor." As you have no doubt figured out, we do not live in the best of all possible worlds. The problems that usually arise involve testamentary powers of appointment. The exercise of inter vivos powers pretty much requires the donee to tell whoever has title to the appointive property (almost always a trustee) what the donee wants done by executing an instrument or performing an act sufficient to transfer the property if the donee had owned the property outright.

Exercising a power of appointment in a will (whether it's a power that can be exercised only by will or a power that can be exercised either during life or testamentarily) is another matter. That's because it has long been the law that the residuary clause of a will can manifest the intent to exercise a power of appointment of which the testator is donee, *even if the residuary clause makes no mention of the power of appointment.* This general rule of law is almost always held to apply only to general powers of appointment. If you think about it, that limitation makes sense. Being the donee of a general power of appointment pretty much makes you the owner of the appointive property. The residuary clause of your will, which disposes of *everything* in your probate estate that isn't disposed of by another provision of the will, can easily be understood to also act as an appointment of the appointive property to the devises of the residuary estate.

Different jurisdictions apply this rule in different ways. In some, courts implement the rule by having a very low threshold for finding the necessary intent to exercise the general power. In others, statutes state that the intent to exercise is presumed unless a contrary intent can be shown, and that threshold is usually pretty high. All in all, it has always been relatively easy for the donee of a general power of appointment to exercise the power without expressly mentioning it.

Restatement (Third) of Property § 19.4 modifies this traditional rule. Under the Restatement, the residuary clause of the will of a donee of a general power of appointment exercises the power only if the donor of the power did not name takers in default of exercise of the power. This rule is also the rule in UPC § 2-608. The rationale is that if the donor did indeed name takers in default, the donor would prefer that the appointive property pass to the takers in default rather than to the residuary beneficiaries of the donee's will through a residuary clause that is only presumed to exercise the power.

F   A   Q

Q: Does a will have to be admitted to probate to exercise a testamentary power of appointment?

A: You may be surprised to learn that the answer is no. If the language of the power simply requires the donee to exercise the power "by will," the power can be exercised by any document that meets the formal requirements for admission to probate as the donee's will. However, many documents creating testamentary powers of appointment (and many forms for creating such powers) include language requiring the donee to exercise the power in the donee's will "duly admitted to probate." Requiring the donee's will to be admitted makes it much easier for whoever has title to the appointive property (usually a trustee) to be certain whether the power has been exercised.

Given the very nature of a special power of appointment — the donee cannot take for herself any of the economic benefit of the appointive property — it makes sense that a residuary clause that says nothing about powers of appointment of which the testator is donee should not exercise a special power. And for once, law follows sense. Almost nowhere in the United States can a general residuary clause exercise a special power of appointment without making some reference at least to powers of appointment held by the testator. Almost. At least one state (New York) applies the same rule to general and special testamentary powers of appointment. A general residuary clause exercises the power unless the will shows the contrary intent. Of course, at least some of the residuary devisees must be permissible appointees of the special power (N.Y. Est. Powers & Trusts Law § 10-6.1(a)(4)).

(2) Blanket Exercise and Blending Clauses

So now we understand that a residuary clause can exercise a testamentary general power of appointment even if the will doesn't mention powers of appointment. Different questions arise if the will *does* mention powers of appointment but doesn't specifically identify the powers. A clause in a will exercising powers of appointment by a general reference to powers of appointment the testator may have is called a **blanket exercise clause**. Such a clause might read something like this: "I hereby exercise any power of appointment I may have as follows"; next is the actual appointment, the words describing the appointees of the appointive property. Of course, any special power of appointment the testator has will be exercised only if the appointees include permissible objects of the special power.

We'll consider the blanket exercise aspect first. Surely, you ask, there isn't anything problematic about a blanket exercise clause? It *says* the donee is exercising powers of appointment the donee has. Okay, maybe there's a special power in there and the appointees named in the blanket exercise clause are not permissible appointees of the special power, but that's easy to see and deal with; the power is simply not exercised. There's no need to infer intent to exercise, no need to construe language or figure the applicable law governing exercise by residuary clause. If only it were that simple. The complication comes from another very well-established bit of the law of exercise of powers. The donor of a power of appointment can place conditions on the donee's exercise of the power, and the most common is a requirement that the donee exercise the power by "specific reference" to the power.

Now a specific reference should mean just that. The donee can exercise the power only by identifying it in the will. For example: "I have a power of appointment given to me under the will of my late wife, [fill in name], [some forms then include the court in which the donor's will was admitted to probate and the date], and I hereby exercise the power by appointing the property subject to the power to" and then the actual disposition follows. But what about a blanket exercise clause? Can it be a specific reference? The traditional answer is yes. Or rather, there are many cases in which equity has come to the aid of the donee who didn't make a required "specific reference" but used a blanket exercise clause that will give the appointive property to persons, like family members, to whom the donee would likely make an appointment. (Restatement (Third) of Trusts § 19.10 and UPC § 2-704, one of the few UPC provisions dealing with powers of appointment, agree.)

F   A   Q

Q: Can a will exercise a power of appointment that was given to the donee after the will was executed?

A: Yes. A blanket exercise clause in the donee's will can apply to any power of appointment the donee has at death, whether the power was created before or after the execution of the will. The same rule applies to residuary clauses that exercise powers of appointment even without blanket exercise language. This rule is related to the rule that a will disposes of all the probate property the testator owns at death, no matter when acquired. The donor may prevent this result by requiring the donee to exercise the power in a will executed after the power is created. Many forms contain such a requirement.

EXERCISE BY THE DEAD

Recall that the will of a donee cannot exercise a power of appointment created after the donee's death. However, there are two ways in which language in the donee's will (most likely a blanket exercise clause) can exercise a power of appointment created in the will of a donor who dies after the donee. The first is incorporation by reference. If the donor's will refers to the donee's will, which is in existence when the donor's will is executed, it is possible for the donee's will to be incorporated into the donor's, and any part of the donee's will that could dispose of the appointive property can be given effect as part of the donor's will.

Another way is through the application of acts of independent significance. If the donor's will provides that certain property is to be disposed of to the persons named in the donee's will, then when the donee dies before the donor, the donee's will is a disposition of the donee's own probate estate and does not claim to dispose of the appointive property. From the point of view of the donor's estate, however, the donee's disposition of the donee's own property is an act that has significance apart from disposing of the donor's property, and the donor's will can "piggyback" on the donee's disposition of the donee's own property.

Just remember that some states take a very strict approach when it comes to enforcing an exercise by specific reference requirement. In some states (most notably New York (Est. Powers & Trusts Law § 10-6.1(b)) and California (Prob. Code § 632)), the only way to exercise a power to which the donor has attached a specific reference requirement is to include a specific reference to the power in the document purporting to exercise the power (and remember, that's almost always the donee's will).

(3) Blending Clauses, Capture, and Allocation

There's more to the question of whether a power of appointment has been exercised in the donee's will, and this additional aspect has to do with whether the residuary clause includes a **blending clause**. A blending clause is a blanket exercise clause or an exercise of a particular power that appears in the residuary clause of the will. A blending clause that includes a blanket exercise clause would read something like this: "I give the rest, residue, and remainder of my estate, both real and personal, including any property over which I have a power of appointment to," and then, of course, the words of disposition follow. A residuary clause that includes a reference to a specific power of appointment is also a blending clause: "I give the rest, residue, and remainder of my estate both real and person, including the property over which I have a power of appointment given to me under the will of my father," followed as before by the words of disposition.

Traditionally, the existence of a blending clause was the necessary prerequisite for the application of two doctrines related to powers of appointment: **capture**, which when it applies makes property subject to a general power of appointment exercised by the donee in the donee's will part of the donee's probate estate; and **allocation**, under which appointive property and the donee's probate property are used to satisfy the gifts made by the donee to maximize the fulfillment of the donee's intent.

Let's start with capture. Traditionally, the prerequisite for the application of the capture doctrine is an exercise of a general power of appointment through a blending clause that for some reason fails completely or in part. When that happens, the appointive property is treated as part of the donee's probate estate and passes with the rest of the property that passes under the residuary clause. The rationale is that the blending clause, the exercise of the power in the residuary clause that disposes of the donee's probate property, shows that the donee intended to take control of the appointive property for all purposes, not just for making the appointment. Here's an example.

Example 10.5: Testator is the donee of a general power of appointment that donee exercises through a blending clause (whether by including a blanket exercise clause in the residuary clause or by a specific reference to the power in the residuary clause). The residue is devised equally to the testator's sister-in-law and to a charity. However, the sister-in-law dies before the testator. Who should get the appointive property?

Under the usual rules for administering estates, one-half of the probate property passing under the residuary clause and one-half of the appointive property goes to each devisee. In other words, all the property disposed of by the residuary clause goes pro rata to each residuary devisee. Because the gift to the sister-in-law has lapsed (and remember that anti-lapse statutes almost never apply to someone who is not a relative by birth or adoption), the half of the probate property that is the subject of the lapsed gift either goes to the charity (if the no-residue-of-a-residue rule has been abolished) or passes in intestacy (if no-residue-of-a-residue is the law). One-half of the appointive property goes to the charity, but the appointment of the other half to the sister-in-law has failed. Under traditional law, that half of the appointive property is unappointed and goes back to the estate of the donor. But here the blending clause makes the doctrine of capture apply to the appointment, and the half of the appointive property that would otherwise be unappointed passes to the charity because it has been "captured" and made part of the donee's probate estate.

　　Allocation can apply to both special and general powers of appointment exercised by a blending clause in the donee's will. The doctrine says that the appointive property and the donee's probate property are used in a way that maximizes accomplishing the donee's intent. Here's an example of allocation applied to a special power of appointment.

Example 10.6: Child is the donee of a power of appointment over a trust created in the will of Child's parent. The power authorizes Child to appoint among Child's descendants. Child's will devises the residue of Child's estate by using a blending clause that devises the "rest, residue, and remainder" of Child's estate, "including any property over which I have a power of appointment" in equal shares to Child's son, S, and to the widower of Child's daughter, W. Child's probate estate passing under the residuary clause is valued at $500,000, and the appointive property is also valued at $500,000.

Let's assume that the residuary clause did indeed exercise the special power (that is, either the donor did not impose a specific reference requirement or, if the donor did, it was satisfied by the blending clause). Once again, the usual estate administration rule applies. One-half of every kind of property disposed of by the residuary clause goes to each devisee. Of course, W is *not* a permissible appointee of the special power because he's not a descendant of Child. If there's no way to fix this, the appointment of one-half of the appointive property has failed, and it will go back to the estate of the donor. (See Figure 10-1.) Enter the allocation doctrine. The appointive property is given to S, who is a permissible object of the power, and the property Child owned at death is given to W. Both S and W received one-half of the total $1,000,000 disposed of by the residuary clause. (See Figure 10.2.)

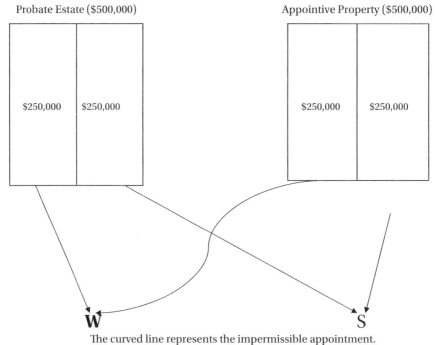

The curved line represents the impermissible appointment.

FIGURE 10.1   BEFORE ALLOCATION

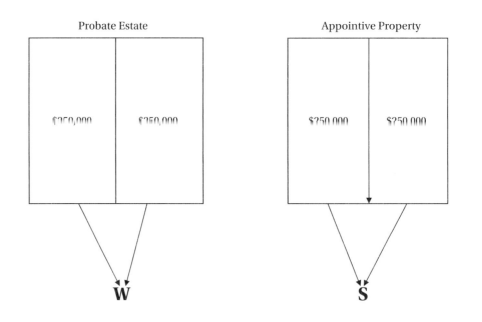

FIGURE 10.2   AFTER ALLOCATION

Other situations in which the allocation doctrine can maximize accomplishing the donee's intent are beyond what we need to know here. Just keep in mind that allocation is a possibility where (1) the donee has exercised a special or general power of appointment in a blending clause and (2) something other than a pro rata distribution of the appointive property and the property in the donee's probate estate comes closer to fulfilling the donee's intent.

We're not quite done. Restatement (Third) of Property makes a couple of changes in the way the doctrines of capture and allocation are applied. The first applies to both. As we've seen, traditionally the use of a blending clause is a necessary prerequisite to the application of either capture or allocation. Restatement (Third) of Property rejects that requirement of traditional law (§§ 19.2 cmt. e, 19.19 cmt. b (allocation), 19.21 cmt. b (capture)). Both doctrines are to be used whenever they produce a result closer to the donee's intent in exercising the power. The second change applies only to capture. Under § 19.21, capture will apply to make property subject to a general power of appointment part of the donee's residuary estate only where the appointment or part of it is ineffective *and* the donor of the power did not name takers in default of exercise of the power.

E. Miscellaneous Questions

There are just a few more aspects of the law of powers of appointment that we have to discuss.

(1) Failure to Appoint and Takers in Default

Recall from the material on capture and allocation what happens to the appointive property if the donee either does not exercise the power of appointment or does exercise it, but all or part of the appointment fails. The appointive property goes back to the estate of donor. That means that if the appointive property was part of a pre-residuary devise, the property would go to the residuary devisees; if they're already dead, it passes to their successors in interest. If the appointive property was part of the residuary devise, it probably goes to other residuary devisees; if there were none, it goes to the donor's heirs. In any event, it might require the services of a genealogist to figure out who is entitled to the property.

That's why every well-drafted power will include takers in default. The takers in default in turn will be described as persons alive when the donee's exercise fails or it is certain that the donee will not exercise the power. Here's a typical example of appropriate drafting.

Example 10.7: Testator devises property to X in trust to pay the income to Testator's Child for life and on Child's death to distribute the trust property "as Child shall appoint in Child's last will and testament duly admitted to probate which shall specifically refer to this power. The Trustee shall distribute any trust property not effectively appointed by Child to Child's issue living at Child's death, by representation, and if none to the then living issue of my [testator's] parents living at Child's death, by representation."

The takers in default under this power are always persons who are alive at the donee's (Child's) death. There's no need to trace property through the estates of persons long dead. Frankly, there's no excuse for not asking your clients where they want appointive property to go if the power is not exercised and then making sure that the power of appointment includes the appropriate takers in default.

(2) Choice of Law

One of the conundrums of the law of powers of appointment is choice of law. Specifically, is the question of the validity and effect of a donee's exercise of a power of appointment governed by the law that governs the appointive property or by the law that governs the instrument that the donee is using to exercise the power? Once again, that's a very abstract statement, so let's use the classic example of the problem.

Example 10.8: Mother's will devises property to Big Bank in trust to pay the income to Child for life, and on Child's death Big Bank as trustee is to distribute the property as "Child shall appoint in her last will duly admitted to probate." This is a testamentary general power. Child's will is indeed admitted to probate, and it makes no mention of the power of appointment, but the residuary clause reads, "I give, devise and bequeath all property I can dispose of by will of whatever kind and wherever located to my beloved alma mater, Whatsamatta University."

The governing law of Mother's trust is the law of State X where she was domiciled at death. The law governing Child's will is the law of State Y where she was domiciled at death. Under the law of State X, the residuary clause of a will cannot exercise any power of appointment unless it contains a least a blanket exercise clause. Under the law of State Y, the residuary clause of the donee's will can exercise a general power of appointment if the testator intends the clause to dispose of all of the property the testator can dispose of by will. Assume that the residuary clause in Child's will does indeed exercise the power under the law of State Y. Is the power exercised or not?

The traditional answer is no. The rationale is that the appointive property is trust property, and questions involving the trust and the trust property must be governed by law that governs the trust. Recently, a few courts have taken the opposite position. Their rationale is that the testator knows that the law of the testator's domicile governs the testator's will. Now that may be a legal fiction, but it is one that lawyers and courts have worked with for centuries. These newer decisions argue that it makes sense to apply the same rule to everything in the will including the question of whether the will exercises a power of appointment over trust property in a trust governed by the law of another state. Restatement (Third) of Property § 19.1 comment e agrees with the newer rule, citing in support the Restatement (Second) of Conflict of Laws § 275 comment c. Under the newer rule, therefore, the answer to the question posed by Example 10.8 is yes, the power was indeed exercised by the donee's will.

(3) Anti-Lapse Statutes and Powers of Appointment

We know that a gift in a will to devisee who does not survive the testator lapses and that anti-lapse statutes apply to some lapsed gifts. If the anti-lapse statute does apply, the statute designates a substitute taker of the lapsed gift, usually the issue of the devisee who survive the testator, by some system of representation. Do anti-lapse statutes apply to appointees of the exercise of a testamentary power of appointment who do not survive the donee whose will makes the appointment? There are few cases and almost no statutory law. Only two states have anti-lapse statutes (Cal. Prob. Code § 674; Wis. Stat. § 854.06) that apply to appointees under a testamentary power of appointment. Restatement (Third) of Property § 19.12 says an anti-lapse statute should be applied to an appointment to a deceased appointee as if the appointive property were owned either by the donee or the donor. That means that if the anti-lapse statute applies only to relatives of the testator, the statute will apply to an appointment to an appointee who dies before the appointment becomes effective (and that almost always means when the donee dies and the donee's will takes effect) if the appointee is related to either the donor of the power or to the donee.

Example 10.9: Donor's will devises the residue to T in trust to pay the income from the trust property to the donor's spouse for life, and on spouse's death T is to distribute the trust property as spouse appoints by will to the issue of donor's siblings and the issue of the spouse-donee's siblings. The donee's will appoints one-half of the trust property to one of the donor's nephews who predeceased the donee and one-half to a niece of the donee who also predeceases the donee. Who gets what?

Under the Restatement, if the anti-lapse statute that applies to the donee-spouse's will applies to devises to descendants of the grandparents of the testator whose will makes the lapsed gift, the statute applies to the entire appointment. One deceased appointee, the nephew, is a descendant of the donor's grandparents, and the other, the niece, is a descendant of the donee's grandparents. Under the most common anti-lapse statutes, one-half of the appointive property passes to the issue of the nephew who survive the donee-spouse, by representation, and the other half to the issue of the niece who survive the donee-spouse, by representation.

The UPC anti-lapse statute, § 2-603, conforms to the Restatement approach. It applies to deceased appointees if they are descendants of the grandparents of the donor or of the donee, even if the issue of the deceased appointee are not permissible objects of the power of appointment (UPC § 2-603(b)(5)). Figure 10.3 shows the analysis in visual form.

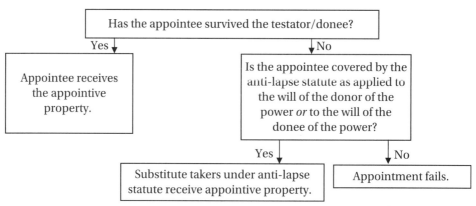

FIGURE 10.3 APPOINTEES OF TESTAMENTARY POWERS OF APPOINTMENT UNDER RESTATEMENT (THIRD) AND THE UPC

(4) Contracts to Appoint

Contracts and powers of appointment don't get along any better than contracts and wills do. It has long been the law that the donee of a power that is not presently exercisable — and that of course is the donee of every testamentary power — cannot make a contract to exercise the power in a specified way. Two reasons are given for this rule. First, the donee cannot exercise the power at the time the contract is made. The contract is equivalent to an appointment, so the donee has no authority to make the contract either. Second, the donor expected the donee to make the decision about whether and how to exercise the power when the power does indeed become exercisable. For the donee of a testamentary power, the time of exercise is the donee's death. Of course the exercise must be made in a will, but the idea is that the donor expects the donee to be able to decide on how to exercise the power in the last will the donee executes.

If the donee does exercise the power in accordance with the contract, the exercise is valid so long as the appointment is proper under the terms of the power. If the donee does not exercise the power in accordance with the contract, the damages the promise can get for breach are limited to the return of the consideration given to the donee.

Even though a donee of a power that is not presently exercisable cannot make a contract to exercise the power, the donee can **release** the power by doing whatever is necessary to show that the donee will not exercise the power. The donee literally "lets go" of the power. That means that the power is treated as if the donee kept it but didn't exercise it. If there are takers in default, the appointive property passes to them at the time the power could have been exercised; if there are no takers in default, the appointive property will pass through the estate of the donor. All powers can be released unless the donor manifests the intention that the power not be releasable.

(5) Complications in Understanding Special Powers

Special powers are subject to some rules that are related directly to the way these powers work. Although the donee of a general power of appointment has what amounts in many ways to ownership of the appointive property because the donee can take the economic benefit of the property for himself, the donee of the special power can decide only who is to enjoy the economic benefit of the property and may choose only among the permissible appointees designated by the donor (although that group may be very large indeed if the language of the power prevents the donee only from appointing to the general power quartet of the donee, the donee's creditors, the donee's estate, and the creditors of the donee's estate).

(a) Can the Donee Create a New Trust or a New Power of Appointment?

First, can the donee of a special power of appointment create a trust of the appointive property? The modern answer is yes. In addition, the donee may appoint to a trustee who is not the trustee of the trust that holds the appointive property. Restatement (Third) of Property agrees: §§ 19.13 and 19.14 in essence simply repeat the provisions of Restatement (Second). Traditionally, however, this was an unsettled question on which one could find conflicting authority. As a result, many forms for creating special powers of appointment still make it clear that a donee may appoint "in further trust" with any trustee of the donee's choosing.

Second, can the donee of a special power create a new power of appointment in an appointee? This is never a question for the donee of a general power. Almost all donees of general powers could first appoint the property to themselves and then dispose of it in any way they like. (Except, of course, donees restricted to appointing to their creditors or to the creditors of their estates. The power is a general power, but the donee can appoint the appointive property in outright ownership only to the creditors.)

While there does not seem to be a great deal of authority on the question, Restatement (Third) of Property § 19.14 says that the donee of a nongeneral (the Restatement term for special) power may create a power of appointment in an appointee so long as the permissible appointees of the new power are permissible appointees of the power the donee is exercising. The Restatement even allows the donee to create the new power in someone who is not a permissible appointee of the power the donee is exercising, so long as the permissible appointees of the new power are also permissible appointees of the power the donee is exercising to create the new power (§ 19.14 cmt. g).

(b) Is the Power Exclusive or Nonexclusive?

Third, there can be questions about how a donee is to exercise a special power when the permissible appointees are relatively small in number or a distinct class, like "the donee's children" or "the donor's descendants." If the donee does exercise the power, must the donee appoint something to each permissible appointee, or can the donee appoint all the appointive property to one appointee? In traditional terms, the question is whether the special power is **exclusive** or **nonexclusive**. An exclusive power allows the donee to appoint to only one of several permissible appointees. A nonexclusive power requires to donee to appoint some portion of the appointive property to each permissible appointee. (Restatement (Third) of Property § 17.5 uses the more accurately descriptive terms **exclusionary** and **nonexclusionary**.)

You should not be surprised to learn that what makes a special power exclusionary or nonexclusionary is the intent of the donor, which is by construing the language creating the power. When that language is ambiguous about intent and is in a will (which almost always means that the appointive property is the property of a testamentary trust), all the usual rules of construction apply, and the meaning of the words is determined by examining the words themselves in the context of the will. There are many cases construing the words of powers of appointment to decide whether the powers are exclusionary or nonexclusionary. Older cases found that the use of the word "among" (e.g., the donee may appoint "among the donee's children") indicated that the power was nonexclusionary. On the other hand, giving the donee the authority to appoint to "such" a group of permissible appointees meant that donor intended to create an exclusionary power. (For an extensive discussion of lots of cases, see Restatement (Third) of Property § 17.5 repr.'s note 3.) It is fair to say that more recent cases tend to construe ambiguous language to find that the power is exclusionary.

There's another reason to avoid construing language to create a nonexclusionary power: the doctrine of **illusory appointment**. This doctrine states that the donor of a nonexclusionary power intends the donee to appoint a reasonable amount to each appointee. Any appointment of less than that reasonable amount is "illusory"; it's really not an appointment at all. What is reasonable depends on the value of the appointive property and the number of permissible appointees. If the appointive property is worth $1,000,000 and there are five permissible appointees, we can be pretty sure that an appointment of $1,000 to four of the permissible appointees and the remaining $1,996,000 to the fifth is not acceptable. The $1,000 is such a small amount compared to the value of the appointive property that four of the appointments are illusory. It is much more difficult to figure out how much is enough. In our example, is the minimum appointment that's not illusory $100,000 (half of an equal division of the appointive property)? $50,000? Less? The only way to get a definitive answer if an appointee is unhappy is litigation (or perhaps a settlement of threatened litigation). You can see why a rule of construction that tries to avoid such questions could be considered a good thing.

F   A   Q

Q: Can a general power ever be nonexclusive (nonexclusionary)?

A: Yes, if the power is general because it authorizes the donee to appoint *only* to the donee's creditors or to the creditors of the donee's estate. (If the donee can appoint to the donee or to the donee's estate, the donee in effect can appoint to anyone by taking control of the property and then handing it out to anyone.) If the language of the power is construed to create a nonexclusionary power, the question is how little can the donee appoint to a creditor and still avoid the illusory appointment doctrine.

Q: Okay, then, is it at least possible for every special (nongeneral) power to be nonexclusive (nonexclusionary)?

A: No. Remember that before a power of appointment can be nonexclusionary, the class of potential appointees must be certain enough that an appointment could be made to each one. If the power is special because the donee is authorized to appoint to *anyone except* the donee, the donee's creditors, the donee's estate, or the creditors of the donee's estate, the number of potential appointees is unlimited, and it's simply impossible to require an appointment to each of them. Such a special power is *always* exclusive (exclusionary).

(c) Will a Gift in Default Be Implied if the Donor Does Not Name Takers in Default?

We know by now that every well-drafted power has takers in default. If there aren't any takers in default and the donee either does not exercise the power or does exercise it, but all or part of the appointment fails, the appointive property goes back to the estate of the donor. Here comes the exception. If the power is a special power with a limited number of permissible appointees (a power that could be a nonexclusionary power), the donee doesn't exercise the power, and there are no takers in default, then a court might very well find that the donor intended to create a gift in default of the exercise of the power to the permissible appointees. Some jurisdictions reach this result by classifying the power as an **imperative power**, which means that the power has to be exercised. If the donee does not exercise it, then the appropriate court will give the appointive property equally to the permissible appointees. Restatement (Third) of Property § 19.23 uses the implied gift-in-default characterization.

(d) Is the Appointment an Attempted Fraud on the Power?

In the modern world, there's little reason to create a general power of appointment unless there is some tax advantage to be gained by doing so, and occasionally there is, as we'll see in Chapter 17. A special power of appointment generally has no adverse tax effects for the donee, so most powers of appointment these days probably are special powers. The problem with the special power is that the limited list of permissible appointees is sometimes too limited. Think about the income beneficiary of a trust who has a special testamentary power of appointment to appoint among the donor's issue (the donor being the donee's parent); the takers in default are the donee's issue living at the donee's death, by representation; and if there are none, the issue of the donor, also by representation. This is all well and good except that the donee, who is married, has no issue. The donee and the donee's spouse have been using the income from the trust to pay for many of their basic expenses. If the donee dies first, the donee's spouse is not a beneficiary of the trust or a permissible appointee and will no longer be able to benefit from the trust property.

Worried that the spouse will be left short of money, the donee tries to work around the special power of appointment. The donee approaches a cousin who of course is a permissible appointee. The donee and the cousin agree that the donee will appoint to the cousin trust property worth a stated amount and that cousin will give two-thirds of the appointed property to the donee's surviving spouse. That's exactly what happens. The takers in default learn of the agreement between the donee and the donee's cousin, and they bring an action in the appropriate court to invalidate the appointment to the cousin. They will be successful. The donee has attempted what's known as a **fraud on the power**, a term that applies to any attempt to appoint for the benefit of an impermissible appointee, no matter how the donee tries to structure the deal. Any appointment that attempts to confer a benefit on an impermissible appointee is simply ineffective. The comments to § 19.16 of Restatement (Third) of Property inventory the usual devices donees use to try to get appointive property to impermissible appointees and also points out, not surprisingly, that *any* appointment motivated by the donee's desire to benefit someone who is not a permissible appointee is void.

SUMMARY

■ A power of appointment gives a person the power to dispose of property belonging to another person who has given the first person the power. The person giving the power is the donor; the person to whom it is given is the donee.

■ The donor creates a power of appointment by manifesting the intent to do so; no particular words are necessary.

■ Powers of appointment are classified by when they can be exercised — as soon as they are created (a presently exercisable power), after the occurrence of some event (a postponed power), or only in the will of the donee (a testamentary power). Presently exercisable powers and postponed powers once they become exercisable are classified as lifetime or inter vivos powers because the donee can exercise them during the donee's lifetime.

■ Powers of appointment are also classified based on the persons to whom the donee can appoint the property subject to the power. If the donee can take economic advantage of the property subject to the power for the donee, the power is a general power of appointment. If the donee cannot take advantage of the economic benefit of the property for the donee, the power is a nongeneral or special power of appointment.

■ Special powers of appointment are further classified as exclusive (or exclusionary) if the donee can appoint all of the property subject to the power to one of the permissible appointees to the exclusion of the others and as nonexclusive (nonexclusionary) if the donee cannot.

■ How a power of appointment is classified tells us two things: (1) what are the rights of the creditors of the donee in the property subject to the power, and (2) whether the donee will face estate, gift, or income tax consequences because of being a donee. Because of widespread use of powers of appointment in estate planning, the estate and gift tax consequences have long been considered the most important and the estate and gift tax definition of a general power of appointment — a power that allows the donee to appoint to the donee, the donee's creditors, the donee's estate, or the creditors of the donee's estate — has become the definition for property law purposes of what it means for the donee to take economic advantage of the property subject to the power for the donee's own benefit.

- Lifetime (inter vivos) powers of appointment are exercised by the donee's execution of a document sufficient to transfer the property if the donee had owned it outright.

- Testamentary powers of appointment can be exercised by the residuary clause of the donee's will, even though the clause makes no mention of powers of appointment. It is very unusual for the same rule to apply to a special power of appointment. These rules are default rules, and the donor can require the donee to exercise the power by specific reference to the power, although sometimes a reference to all or any powers held by the testator/donee is considered a specific reference.

- Uncertainties that frequently accompany the use of powers of appointment can almost all be avoided by careful drafting.

CONNECTIONS

Powers of Appointment and Wealth Transfer Taxes

The estate, gift, and generation-skipping transfer tax effects of powers of appointment are extremely important and are dealt with in Chapter 17.

Powers of Appointment and Revocable Trusts

Because the settlor of a revocable trust (Chapter 11) can end the trust and take outright ownership of the trust property, the settlor has a presently exercisable general power of appointment over the trust property which is one reason why the revocable trust property can be reached by the settlor's creditors.

Powers of Appointment and Protection of the Surviving Spouse

Statutes and decisions that expand the pool of property subject to the elective share beyond the probate property of the deceased spouse sometimes make property subject to a general power of appointment held by the deceased spouse subject to the elective share rights (Chapter 13) of the surviving spouse.

Powers of Appointment and Future Interests

Future interests that are transmissible at the death of the person who holds the interest give that person control over the identity of the person or persons who may eventually come into possession of the property at the distribution date (Chapter 7). While that may be a good thing, one of the arguments against transmissible future interests is that they are often transmitted unthinkingly. Giving the holder of a future interest a properly drafted power of appointment (including takers in default) exercisable if the holder dies before the distribution date is a more straightforward way of giving control over ultimate distribution to the person who first holds the future interest.

Powers of Appointment and the Rule Against Perpetuities

If the donee of a power of appointment validly appoints in further trust it is likely, indeed all but certain, that the donee has also created future interests. Like every other future interest, the future interests the donee creates are subject to the Rule Against Perpetuities (where it still is the law) (Chapter 12). How the Rule applies to these future interests, however, is dictated by the fact that they were indeed created by exercise of a power of appointment.

The Revocable Trust: The Ultimate Will Substitute

11

OVERVIEW

The revocable lifetime trust comes close to being the perfect will substitute: it makes all property nonprobate property, allows its creator to remains in complete control until death or incapacity, and disposes of property after death in much the same ways a will does. But don't be fooled. The revocable trust is still a trust, and the critical differences between the law of wills and the law of trusts are reflected in how the revocable trust functions, both during the lifetime and at the death of the person who creates it. Revocable trusts are a popular choice of estate planners, even more so now that modern statutes have made it easier to use them for making gifts at death.

A. WHY IT WORKS AND WHY IT'S NOT AN INVALID WILL SUBSTITUTE

B. CREATION OF REVOCABLE LIFETIME TRUSTS

  1. Creating the Trust
  2. Funding the Trust

C. HOW THEY WORK DURING THE SETTLOR'S LIFETIME

  1. The Relationship of the Settlor to the Trust Property
  2. Revoking the Trust
  3. Rights and Interests of the Beneficiaries Other than the Settlor

D. HOW THEY WORK AFTER THE SETTLOR'S DEATH

E. THE ROLE OF REVOCABLE TRUSTS IN ESTATE PLANNING

    1. To Fund or Not to Fund During the Settlor's Life
    2. Funding at Death — the Pour-Over Will

A. Why It Works and Why It's Not an Invalid Will Substitute

As we learned in Chapter 1, the revocable lifetime trust can be used to make any kind of property nonprobate property. Because the trustee has legal title to the trust property and because the office of trustee never dies, someone always has the legal authority to deal with the trust property. Unlike probate property that is orphaned by the death of its title holder, property in a revocable trust is never left helpless in this cold, cruel world. The trustee is always there to manage the trust property and always has the authority to sell, to acquire new property, and to distribute the property in accordance with the terms of the trust.

    Of course, any trust creates nonprobate property — title is held by the trustee and the office of trustee never dies. What makes the revocable lifetime trust different is the power to revoke retained by the person who creates the trust. So long as the settlor of the trust has the necessary capacity, she can change the trust at any time. In particular, the settlor of the trust can change the terms of the trust that are to take effect on the settlor's death.

F   A   Q

Q: If the settlor of the trust retains the power to revoke the trust, can he change the trust without revoking it?

A: For once a simple answer: yes. The power to revoke includes the power to change (more formally, "amend") the trust. The careful draftsperson will make sure, however, that the trust states that the settlor has the power to "revoke or amend."

This power to change the trust terms makes the revocable trust as flexible as a will. Don't worry if that sentence does not quite make sense. One of the problems with understanding the revocable lifetime trust is that you've probably never seen one and are therefore unsure about what such a document actually provides. What you need to realize is that a revocable trust can do anything a will can do when it comes to making a gift at death.

    Let's say that I want to make the following gifts at death:

> A general devise of $10,000 to my sister, the residue to my spouse, and, if my spouse does not survive, to my descendants, by representation.

You know that I can write my will to do exactly that by using language that gives these gifts: "I give $10,000 to my sister, Sally, if she shall survive me, and if she does not this gift shall be added to the residuary devise"; "I give the rest, residue and remainder of my estate to my spouse, and if my spouse does not survive me to my descendants who survive me, by representation." These gifts will be made by my executor once the will is admitted to probate and the executor has received letters testamentary.

I can do exactly the same thing by directing the trustee of my revocable trust to make these gifts after my death. The language will be a little different—trusts are usually written in the third person. The language will be something like this:

After the death of the settlor of the trust, the Trustee

1. Shall distribute $10,000 to the settlor's sister, Sally, if she shall survive the settlor, and if she does not this gift shall be added to the gift under clause 2.
2. Shall distribute the remainder of the trust property to the settlor's spouse, and if the settlor's spouse does not survive the settlor to the settlor's descendants who survive the settlor, by representation.

This language does the same thing as the language in the will. The trustee, however, does not have to wait for the probate process to be completed before having authority to make the gifts. The trustee's authority is always there once the trust is created. So it's accurate to say that the will makes gifts from the testator's probate property and the revocable lifetime trust makes gifts from the property that the settlor of the trust has made trust property. And because the settlor of the trust can change its terms or completely revoke it, it is as flexible and adaptable to changed circumstances as a will.

Now you should be having some doubts. Doesn't the revocable lifetime trust exactly fit the definition of an invalid will substitute? It's a document that's not a will that makes gifts at death. You know that the traditional way to decide whether a device is an invalid will substitute is to ask whether some interest passes to the beneficiaries during the life of the settlor of the device so that the gift really isn't being made at death. You also know that the persons who are going to receive gifts at the death of the settlor of the trust have future interests. Future interests are property, we know that. So doesn't the revocable lifetime trust pass the classic test?

It certainly should, and there is no doubt today that it does. While how the courts got to that conclusion is an interesting story, we don't have to tell it here. It's enough to know the revocable trust is a legally sufficient way to make gifts at death and is the functional equivalent of a will.

F   A   Q

Q: What kind of future interests do the beneficiaries of a revocable trust have while the settlor of the trust can exercise the power to revoke?

A: If the beneficiaries are not subject to any express conditions, they have vested remainders subject to divestment. The gifts in the trust are given when the trust is made, but they can be taken away by the power to revoke. That makes the exercise of the power to revoke a classic condition subsequent. Of course, if there are express conditions precedent like survival to the distribution date (usually the death of the settlor), the interests are contingent remainders. However, while the settlor is alive and has capacity, the beneficiaries' interests may be completely under the control of the settlor.

B. Creation of Revocable Lifetime Trusts

(1) Creating the Trust

Generally, a revocable trust must be created like any other trust. A trust of personal property may be oral while a trust holding real property must be in writing. We'll see at the end of this chapter, however, that if the trust is going to receive a gift from a will (usually the will of the settlor of the trust), the trust must be in writing. Some states have statutes that require additional formalities for all lifetime trusts or only for revocable trusts. These additional formalities usually reflect the legislature's decision that a trust that is a substitute for a will should be created with at least some formality.

(2) Funding the Trust

As we saw in Chapter 8, under the common law all that is necessary to make property trust property is for the owner to manifest the intention that the legal title to the property be transferred to the trustee. We also saw in Chapter 8 that Restatement (Third) of Trusts suggests that "good practice" dictates that property with formal, written title be transferred to the trustee by doing whatever is necessary to change that written title (§ 16 cmt. b). A handful of states have statutes that make that "good practice" mandatory for revocable trusts or all lifetime trusts. Once again, requiring a change of written, formal title to make property the property of a lifetime revocable trust at least shows that the legislature believes that a degree of formality is needed when a trust is a substitute for a will.

C. How They Work During the Settlor's Lifetime

Unlike wills, of course, the revocable trust intended as a will substitute does give an interest in the trust to the beneficiaries other than the settlor of the trust, but usually the settlor is the only beneficiary during the settlor's lifetime and is often the sole trustee.

(1) The Relationship of the Settlor to the Trust Property

(a) As Beneficiary

A testator retains complete control of the testator's probate property and enjoys all of the economic benefit from the property, giving it away only at death. The settlor of a revocable lifetime trust that is meant to function as a will substitute also wants to keep control of any property used to fund the trust and to keep all of the economic benefit of that property. Therefore the settlor is almost always the sole beneficiary of the trust while the settlor is alive. The trustee, who, remember is almost always the settlor, is given discretion to distribute trust income and principal to or for the benefit of the settlor. How does a typical funded revocable trust really work, then?

Q: Do revocable trusts have beneficiaries during the settlor's lifetime other than the settlor?

A: The settlor can pretty much create any trust terms regarding beneficiaries that he likes. One typical provision allows the trustee who is acting after the settlor becomes incapacitated to make discretionary distributions to members of the settlor's family. Such a provision can be especially useful if the settlor was supporting those family members because the trustee can now make distributions to those persons or pay their bills directly.

Example 11.1: Catherine Settlor is the trustee and sole beneficiary during her life of her revocable trust. (The trust terms include a provision under which a person named as successor trustee will take over when Catherine dies or if she becomes incapacitated.) She retitles her brokerage account in the name of the trustee, deeds her residence to the trustee of the revocable trust, and retitles her checking account (into which her pay is automatically deposited) in the name of the trustee. Every time Catherine writes a check to a pay a bill, she is the trustee making a distribution for her benefit as beneficiary. When she gives directions to her broker, she is investing and reinvesting the trust property as trustee. While she is carrying on her financial life as she did before she created the trust, she is now acting as trustee, managing trust property and making discretionary distributions.

Given the sort of control the settlor has, you can understand why the settlor of the trust is often said to have a presently exercisable general power of appointment (Chapter 10) over the trust property.

(b) As a Debtor

The power to revoke makes the trust property completely available to the settlor's creditors while the settlor is alive. For this purpose the settlor is treated like the owner of the trust property. Does that change if the settlor's interest is characterized as a presently exercisable general power of appointment in those jurisdictions that have the traditional rule that creditors of the donee of a presently exercisable general power of appointment cannot reach the property subject to the power to satisfy the donee's debts? Not at all. There is always an exception that applies when the donor and the donee of the power are the same person.

(c) As a Taxpayer

As far as the tax system is concerned, the revocable trust doesn't exist. For income tax purposes (federal and state) the income of the trust and any deductions related to the trust property belong to the settlor. For income tax purposes the revocable trust is one sort of **grantor trust**, a trust over which the settlor ("grantor" in Internal Revenue Code terms) has so much control that the settlor is treated as the owner of all of the trust property for income tax purposes.

The federal and state estate taxes also treat the revocable trust as totally transparent. All of the property in the trust at the settlor's death is part of the settlor's gross estate. Specific provisions of the IRC subject to estate tax property in a trust that the decedent created and in which the decedent retained an income interest and property in a trust created by the decedent and which the decedent can revoke (Chapter 17).

As far as the federal gift tax is concerned, if a distribution is made from the trust to a person other than the settlor, the settlor is making a gift that is subject to gift tax unless it qualified for one of several exemptions, which we'll discuss in Chapter 17.

Remember: *creating and funding a revocable trust will not diminish the settlor's taxes in any way.*

(2) Revoking the Trust

A well-drafted revocable trust will spell out how to exercise the power to revoke or amend, usually by requiring a writing delivered to a trustee. If the settlor is the sole trustee, then the delivery requirement is easily met. Restatement (Third) of Trusts § 63 and the UTC § 602(c) both say that clear and convincing evidence of the settlor's intent to revoke is enough to revoke the trust unless the terms of the trust make the method stated in the trust the exclusive way to revoke. Even in that case, substantial compliance with the prescribed method is sufficient. Both the Restatement and the UTC recognize revocation of a revocable trust by a provision in the settlor's will that expressly refers to the trust. The Restatement and the UTC also protect a trustee who is not the settlor who does not know about a revocation or amendment.

F   A   Q

Q: Will physically destroying a revocable trust revoke it?

A: It might, depending on the circumstances. But we can be pretty sure that the wills law presumption that a will last in the testator's possession and not found after death was destroyed by the testator with the intent to revoke it does not apply to a revocable trust. Other evidence of the settlor's intent to revoke would have to be found.

(3) Rights and Interests of the Beneficiaries Other than the Settlor

The rights of beneficiaries other than the settlor of the trust are not completely clear. Why? It's really the result of the dual nature of the revocable trust as will substitute and as a trust. We all know that the devisees named in the will of a living person have no interest in the testator's probate property. They have absolutely nothing to say about what the testator does or doesn't do with the property. If a revocable trust is going to be an effective will substitute, the settlor should be able to deal with the trust property without being answerable to the other beneficiaries. The revocable trust, however, is a trust, and the beneficiaries do have rights as beneficiaries. How can these two contradictory policies be reconciled?

In one situation, at least, there is an answer. The authorities agree that so long as the settlor of the trust has capacity to revoke the trust, the other beneficiaries of the trust have nothing to say about how the trustee (whether that's the settlor or someone else) is running the trust. (See Restatement Third of Trusts § 74(1) & repr.'s note). That's the position of UTC § 603(a), which says that while a trust is revocable by the settlor the rights of the beneficiaries are subject to the control of the settlor and the trustee's duties are owed only to the settlor. Both the UTC and the Restatement provisions go on to say that once the settlor lacks capacity to revoke the trust, the trustee is responsible to the beneficiaries other than the settlor. It is not certain, however, that the position of the UTC and the Restatement is accepted everywhere as the law.

If the settlor of the trust lacks capacity to revoke and the beneficiaries do not have any say in how the trustee is administering the trust, who can enforce the trust? There are two possibilities. First, if a court has determined that the settlor lacks capacity and appointed a conservator or guardian for the settlor, then the settlor's rights in the trust can be enforced by the conservator or guardian. Another possibility is that the settlor's agent acting under a power of attorney given by the settlor may be able to enforce the settlor's rights in the trust. All of which means that the trustee who is acting while the testator lacks capacity can be called to account by the settlor's legal representative but not by any other beneficiary of the trust.

The interests of the beneficiaries other than the settlor are almost always future interests that will vest in possession, if ever, at the settlor's death. In most states, these interests are governed by the law of future interests. That means they are not subject to lapse the way an equivalent gift in a will is, and what happens if the beneficiary dies before the settlor depends on whether the interest is transmissible. Of course, where UPC § 2-707 or a similar statute is the law, every interest in a trust is contingent on survival to the distribution and a beneficiary's future interest in a revocable trust is then much more like an interest under a will, especially if the statute, like UPC § 2-707, creates a substitute taker for the interest like an anti-lapse statute does. These examples illustrate what we're talking about.

Example 11.2: The residuary clause of Sandra's will reads: "I give the rest, residue, and remainder of my estate to my children, Anthony, Bettina, and Charles."

Example 11.3: The catchall term of Sandra's brother, Sam's, revocable trust reads: "After the settlor's death, the trustee shall deliver the remaining trust property to the settlor's niece and nephews, Anthony, Bettina, and Charles."

Sandra and Sam died in an airplane crash. Anthony had predeceased them both, survived by three children, Xavier, Yasmine, and Zina, who also survived Sandra and Sam. Anthony died testate, and his will was admitted to probate. Anthony devised his residuary estate to his wife Doreen.

It is overwhelmingly likely that the anti-lapse statute of the jurisdiction whose law governs Sandra's will in Example 11.2 applies to a devise to a child and that the lapsed devise is distributed to the child's issue who survive the testator, by representation. There is no indication that Sandra's will overrides the anti-lapse statute. That means that Xavier, Yasmine, and Zina will each receive 1/9 of their grandmother's residuary devise.

In the great majority of jurisdictions in the United States, the interests Sam's trust in Example 11.3 creates in his niece and nephews are future interests subject to the traditional rule that no requirement of survival to the distribution date is implied. Since Sam's revocable trust does not expressly require his niece and nephews to be living at his death to vest in possession, their interests are transmissible. Anthony's interest passed through his will to Doreen, and the trustee of Sam's trust will distribute 1/3 of the trust property that remains after all other distributions to Doreen.

If UPC § 2-707 governed Sam's trust, the trustee would distribute 1/9 of the trust residue to each of Anthony's three children.

Is this what Sam intended to happen if his niece or nephew predeceased him? We can't know, of course, but most commentators assume that Sam would be surprised to discover that his nephew's widow ends up with some of the property in Sam's trust. If that was not Sam's intent, he could have made his niece and nephews' interests contingent on surviving him and provided a gift to someone else should they not survive. Alternatively, Sam could allow his niece and nephews to decide how their shares of the trust are distributed if they die before him by giving them powers of appointment (Chapter 10). All of this simply shows that while a revocable trust can do everything a will can do, the legal contexts in which planning for accomplishing the testator's or settlor's ends differ.

F   A   Q

Q: The settlor is dead, and the beneficiaries of the trust want to question what the trustee did while the testator was alive. Can they?

A: Not for any period during which the settlor was in complete control, meaning while the settlor had capacity to revoke and while the settlor did not have capacity to revoke if the governing law wouldn't allow them to assert their rights as beneficiaries when the settlor lacked capacity. If someone other than the settlor was the trustee, the only person who could question the trustee's action would be the settlor's personal representative.

D. How They Work after the Settlor's Death

Once the settlor is dead, the big question is whether the trust is to continue or is going to terminate at that time. If the trust is going to terminate and the trust property is to be distributed outright to the beneficiaries, then that's what happens. The trust becomes equivalent to a will that makes only outright devises to the devisees. If the trust is to continue—it's the equivalent of a will that creates a testamentary trust—then the beneficiaries have the rights of any other trust beneficiaries. The trust property may be increased by a devise to the trustee in the settlor's will or by the death benefit under a life insurance policy of which the trustee was the beneficiary or by the addition of other property subject to a contractual will substitute that named the trustee as beneficiary, but all of the trust property is subject to whatever trust terms apply after the settlor's death. We can modify Figure 11.1 showing how property passes to beneficiaries of the gifts at death to look like this when a revocable trust is used as the principal vehicle for making those gifts.

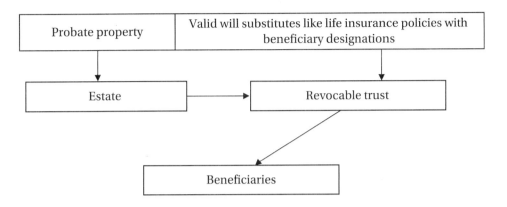

FIGURE 11.1   ROUTES FROM THE DECEDENT TO THE BENEFICIARIES OF THE GIFTS AT DEATH

One question, however, remains. We know that a decedent's probate property is subject to the payment of the decedent's debts. One of the purposes of the probate process is to provide a mechanism for getting those debts paid and a statute of limitations after which the decedent's creditors are barred. Is the property in a revocable trust subject to the payment of the settlor's debts after the settlor's death?

The answer is yes, although there are several different rationales for reaching that result. Statutes might make the trust liable. UPC § 6-102 makes all sorts of nonprobate property, including property held in a revocable trust, liable to pay the decedent's debts to the extent the probate estate is insufficient to do so. (The nonprobate property is also liable to pay the family allowances discussed in Chapter 13.) The UPC even extends the rules of abatement to the trust as if it were a will. Where there is no statute, courts have found ways to make property in a revocable trust available to pay the deceased settlor's debts. Some have simply decided that since the settlor had unlimited access to the property while alive, it must be available to pay the settlor's debts. Others have decided that if the probate estate is insolvent at the settlor's death, then the transfer to the beneficiaries of the trust at the settlor's death is a fraudulent transfer and can be undone by creditors. The abatement issue, however, often is not addressed in these opinions.

F   A   Q

Q: Assuming the settlor's revocable trust is subject to the settlor's debts, is all property added to the trust at the settlor's death subject to paying debts?

A: Property that is not otherwise liable for paying the decedent's debts will not become liable simply because it's added to a revocable trust at the settlor's death. For example, the death benefit under a life insurance policy is not subject to the insured's debts (unless the beneficiary is the probate estate). Making the trustee of the insured's revocable trust the beneficiary of a life insurance policy will not make the death benefit liable for paying the deceased insured's debts. The same rule applies to a retirement account otherwise immune from creditors' claims that is payable to the trustee of the account owner's revocable trust.

E. The Role of Revocable Trusts in Estate Planning

The revocable trust has many uses in modern estate planning in addition to avoiding probate. Some of these uses can be accomplished without funding the trust while the settlor is alive; others require funding. In addition, whether or not the trust is funded during the settlor's life, it is likely that the settlor will want to add whatever probate property the settlor has at death to the trust. Doing that properly requires understanding a specialized bit of wills and trusts law.

(1) To Fund or Not to Fund During the Settlor's Life

It's probably easiest to understand why a revocable trust would be funded during the settlor's life. If the settlor really wants to avoid the probate system, all of what would otherwise be probate property must be made trust property while the settlor is alive. But the settlor of a trust can have other reasons for funding the trust during life.

The settlor of the trust might want someone to manage the settlor's property. Perhaps the settlor is ill or believes that he will eventually lack capacity to make decisions about spending and investments. Of course, the settlor of the trust may be perfectly capable of managing his own property but would prefer that someone else do it. If the settlor is wealthy, a revocable trust with a bank as trustee can provide a vehicle for managing anything from a small to a large fortune. The bank as trustee can provide investment advice or hire others to do so, or the settlor can make the decisions and have the bank trustee deal mainly with record keeping and managing expenditures. In any event, should the settlor eventually lose capacity, the trust is already funded and settlor's property can be managed and the bills paid without anything more being done.

It is possible, however, to create a revocable trust that is not to have any property in it at all until the settlor dies. I can create a lifetime trust and designate the trust as the beneficiary of a life insurance policy or of a retirement savings account like an IRA or a pension plan like a 401(k) or a 403(b) plan. These plans often provide for a lump-sum payment if the account owner dies before retirement. Rather than have that lump sum pass outright to a beneficiary, the owner of the account might prefer that it pass to a trust to be managed by the trustee over the lifetime of the beneficiaries (or perhaps only until

Sidebar

TRUSTS AND RETIREMENT SAVINGS

While it is possible to make a trust the beneficiary of a retirement savings plan, it might not be wise to do so for income tax reasons. Retirement plans do not pay income tax, so what would be taxable income generated by the investments — dividends, interest, and capital gain realized when assets are sold — is not taxed in the hands of the plan. Only when the assets are withdrawn does the person receiving them pay income tax. The longer the assets can be kept in the plan the longer they can grow income tax free. Generally, when the owner of the plan dies, especially before retirement, and the beneficiary of the plan is a trust, the income tax rules may require a relatively rapid payout of the assets in the plan which means that whoever receives them will have to take most of the payout into taxable income and the distributed assets will no longer grow tax free. However, if the beneficiary is an individual, the beneficiary might be able to draw out the property over her own lifetime.

they attain a certain age). All of these arrangements are unremarkable and, in many states, blessed by statutes. Far more problematic is a devise in the testator's will to an existing trust, usually a lifetime trust created by the testator. Whether the trust has been funded before the testator's death or not, there are difficulties with the law of wills.

(2) Funding at Death — the Pour-Over Will

A devise from a will to an existing trust is usually called a **pour over**, and a **pour-over will** is a will that makes such a devise. The devise is usually the residuary devise, and the terms of the trust thus become the language that disposes of the bulk of the testator's probate estate. It may be hard to accept, but such an arrangement violates the Statute of Wills because by using it the testator is disposing of the probate estate, making a gift at death, in a document that is not a will.

```
F     A     Q
```

Q: Isn't a pour-over will simply a way of making a gift to an existing trust? What's the problem then with the Statute of Wills?

A: The problem comes in part from the law of trusts. Remember that a trust is not an entity; it's a relationship between the trustee and the beneficiaries in reference to the trust property. Thus a pour-over will isn't making a gift to the trust. Instead, it's making a gift of the legal title to the testator's probate estate to the trustee and a gift of the beneficial or equitable title to that property to the beneficiaries of the trust. And for once the law of wills behaves in an unformalistic way and recognizes that the gift in the pour-over will is to the beneficiaries of the trust. The trust terms are disposing of the probate estate, and since the trust is not executed like a will, the Statute of Wills is violated.

Courts worked around this problem using two well-established doctrines of the law of wills that we discussed in Chapter 5: incorporation by reference and acts of independent significance. Both doctrines allow a testator to dispose of property using the terms of a document that is not a will. If the document is in existence at the time the will is executed and the will refers to the document, the document becomes part of the will. Under acts of independent significance, an act that has significance apart from disposing of probate property can indeed dispose of a testator's probate property. The "act" that's involved here can be an existing trust. Both doctrines can be used to validate a pour-over will. Here's a traditionally worded residuary clause that makes a pour over.

Example 11.4: I give the rest, residue, and remainder of my estate, both real and personal and wheresoever situated, to the trustee of the trust created by me on July 7, 2011, to be held pursuant to the terms of that trust.

It's pretty clear that this residuary clause will incorporate the lifetime trust into the will. It clearly identifies the trust, and of course we assume that the trust is actually in existence at the time the will is executed. If the trust is funded before the testator's death so that it is "up and running," then the trust itself can be an act of independent significance and can dispose of the poured-over probate property. Perfect solution, right? Not quite.

Both doctrines have weaknesses when used to validate a pour-over will. Remember that incorporation by reference requires that the incorporated writing be in existence when the will is executed. It's not difficult to ensure that, but what if the settlor of the trust wants to amend it? If the amendment is to apply to the property poured over from the will, the will has to be executed again (or a codicil to the will must be executed; remember that the doctrine of republication by codicil says that a will is considered to be reexecuted when a codicil to it is executed). Perhaps even more troublesome is the effect of incorporation that makes the trust part of the will. That, in turn, means that the trust is treated as if it were created by the will; it's now a testamentary trust, which can have some disadvantages.

F   A   Q

Q: What are the disadvantages of a testamentary trust?

A: Perhaps the most common is that it is difficult to move the place of administration of the trust from the state in which the will was admitted to probate. Such a move might be desirable for several reasons. Think of a testator whose children are orphaned by the testator's death. The children are going to live with the guardians named in the testator's will, who live in a different state and are also the trustees of the testamentary trust created for the children. A court proceeding may be needed to allow the trustees to administer the trust in their home state. Without a change of the trust's situs (legal location), they'll have to have a brokerage account and a bank account in the state where the will was admitted to probate. Another difficulty is that in some states trustees of testamentary trusts are required to file formal accounts with the appropriate court at relatively frequent intervals. That's an expensive undertaking paid for by the trust.

Sidebar

WHAT IF THE STATE HAS NO POUR-OVER STATUTE?

If the testator's desire to have a pour-over will must conform to the traditional doctrines because the testator's will is governed by the law of a state that does not have a pour-over statute, the situation may not be as grim as our main discussion suggests. Restatement (Third) of Trusts § 19 goes some way to reducing and even eliminating the disadvantages inherent in the traditional doctrines, especially by stating in comment h that a lifetime trust that is not funded during life but that is the beneficiary of "one or more other dispositions or contracts," such as a life insurance policy or a pension plan, is "up and running" for purposes of using acts of independent significance to validate a pour over from the testator's will.

Using acts of independent significance to validate a pour over will does not have the disadvantages of using incorporation by reference, but it brings its own complications. Amendments to the trust will govern the poured-over property, so reexecuting the will whenever the trust is amended is not necessary. In the negative column, in order for the lifetime trust to be an act of independent significance, it must be up and running. In other words, it must be more than nominally funded; it is not possible to validate a pour over to an unfunded trust using the doctrine of acts of independent significance. That means that the testator cannot use an unfunded trust as part of the estate plan.

These problems with using the traditional doctrines to validate pour-over wills are not as important as they once were. Today, most states have statutes that validate pour-over wills. These statutes are usually very closely based on the

TABLE 11.1	Validating a Pour-Over Will		
Characteristic	Incorporation by reference	Acts of independent significance	UTATA
Trust must be in existence when will is executed	Yes	No	No
Will must be reexecuted if trust amended	Yes	No	No
Trust must be funded before settlor's death	No	Yes	No
Trust becomes a testamentary trust	Yes	No	No

Uniform Testamentary Addition to Trusts Act (UTATA), the latest version of which, promulgated in 1990, is incorporated into the UPC as § 2-511. These statutes simply get rid of the disadvantages of the traditional doctrines. For example, UPC § 2-511 validates a pour over to the trustee of a trust that has been established by the testator or by any other person during the testator's lifetime or at the testator's death by the devise to the trustee, so long as the trust is identified in the will and the trust is set forth in a writing. The trust can be executed "before, concurrently with, or after" the execution of the testator's will or it can be contained in the will of an individual who died before the testator. And it doesn't matter whether the trust is funded or not at the time of the pour over; the pour over is valid "regardless of the existence, size, or character of the corpus of the trust." Nor does it matter that the trust is amendable or revocable or that the trust was amended before or after the testator's death. Unless the testator's will provides otherwise, the property poured over is not held in a testamentary trust and is administered according to the terms of the trust, including any amendments made before or after the testator's death.

In short, UPC § 2-511 and other statutes like it give the testator the best of both worlds, as summarized in Table 11.1.

SUMMARY

■ A revocable trust can do anything a will can do when it comes to making a gift at death: all of the trust property is nonprobate probate; the settlor remains in complete control of the terms of trust and the trust property until death or incapacity, just as the testator can change her will at any time and remains in control of her probate property; and the trust terms can dispose of the trust property after the settlor's death in the same ways a will disposes of probate property after the testator's death.

■ The settlor of the revocable trust is treated as the owner of the trust property for purposes of both the income and the estate and gift taxes. Creditors of the settlor can reach the trust property during the settlor's life and often after the settlor's death.

■ The beneficiaries of a revocable trust other than the settlor have future interests that usually are governed by the law of future interests, which in turn means that what appear to be similar gifts in a will and in a revocable trust can turn out differently, especially if a named beneficiary dies before the settlor.

■ The rights of the beneficiaries of a revocable trust other than the settlor are subordinate to the rights of the settlor while the settlor is competent and often even after the settlor loses capacity.

■ One of the most important uses of the revocable trust is as the ultimate receptacle for all of the settlor's property. A pour-over will adds the testator's probate property to an existing trust, and although its workings were once awkward, jurisdictions now have statutes validating pour overs.

CONNECTIONS

Revocable Trusts and Wills

The revocable trust is the great engine for creating nonprobate property and is the closest thing to a true will substitute, much closer to a will than the methods of creating nonprobate property discussed in Chapter 6.

Revocable Trusts and Future Interests

Unlike wills, which do not create property interests in beneficiaries until the testator dies, revocable trusts usually create future interests in beneficiaries as soon as the trust is created. Giving the beneficiaries what the settlor wants them to have requires a thorough knowledge of the workings of conditions and the constructional laws discussed in Chapter 7.

Revocable Trusts and Trustee's Duties

A trustee's duties require the trustee to be totally unself-regarding. Chapter 16 makes it clear that the trustee, even a trustee who is a beneficiary, must put the interests of the beneficiaries of the trust ahead of the trustee's individual interests. The trustee of a revocable trust, whether or not the settlor acts as trustee, owes all of the trustee's duties to the settlor so long as the trust is revocable (although in some jurisdictions the settlor's loss of capacity will give life to the duties owed to other beneficiaries). Perhaps more than anything else, the nature of the trustee's duties makes the revocable trust an exceptional type of trust.

Revocable Trusts and Disability Planning

A funded revocable trust is an excellent device for managing the property of an incapacitated person and avoids some of the problems with other methods of doing so discussed in Chapter 14.

Revocable Trusts and Taxation

A funded revocable trust is not a device for reducing either income or estate taxes. The discussion in Chapter 17 explains how the estate tax law reaches any property in a trust created by a decedent during life and why during life the creator of the trust is treated as the owner of the trust property for federal income tax purposes.

Revocable Trusts and Protection of the Surviving Spouse

In some jurisdictions that follow the common law title theory of marital property, the revocable trust can be an effective means of frustrating the elective share rights of a surviving spouse. That is not the case under the UPC, where a revocable trust is part of the augmented estate in which a surviving spouse has certain rights (Chapter 13).

Trust Duration: The Rule Against Perpetuities

12

OVERVIEW

How long is too long? For holding your breath, you might say 90 seconds. For sitting in a dentist's chair, surely 90 minutes. And for eating the exact same dinner, 90 days probably qualifies. What about testators' control over the living? How long is too long for the dead to govern from beyond the grave? To answer that question, the common law has developed the Rule Against Perpetuities. But the Rule is anything but simple. In fact, sometimes it's downright silly. Modern law is chipping away at the Rule, sometimes substituting concrete answers like "90 years" for the "how long" question, and other times abolishing the Rule altogether. But the Rule still lives on, and so you must still read on.

A. INTRODUCTION

B. VESTING IN INTEREST

C. WHEN DOES THE PERIOD BEGIN?

D. WHO'S A "LIFE IN BEING"?

E. EXAMPLES OF REMOTE CONTINGENCIES

F. CONTINGENCIES RELATED TO PERSONS

G. REMORSELESS APPLICATION OF THE RULE

    1. Fertile Octogenarians and Precocious Toddlers
    2. Unborn Widows
    3. Administrative Contingencies

A. Introduction

The Rule Against Perpetuities has a fearsome reputation as the bane of all law students and, for that matter, of practicing lawyers. To a great degree, that reputation is deserved. The Rule in its common law, traditional formulation is simply weird. While many attempts have been made to simplify and modernize the Rule and make it easier to understand and apply, the changes cannot be understood without understanding the common law rule. To understand the workings of the Rule today, we first have to deal with it in its strictest form.

No doubt many of you know (or have some inkling) that a growing number of states have repealed the Rule. Even if you intend to take the bar exam or to practice in one of these jurisdictions, you should persevere in reading this chapter. First, you may have dealings with a jurisdiction in which some version of the Rule is the law. Second, the Rule addresses a very important question: how much control should the dead have over the living? More precisely, how much influence should the dead be able to exert by creating trusts for beneficiaries who have the economic benefit of the trust property, within the limits set by the trust's settlor, but who have no control over the trust property itself? To put it bluntly, for how long can the dead keep the living on an allowance?

One of the things you have to understand right at the beginning is that the Rule does not directly limit how long a trust can last. What it does do is limit the length of time that conditions precedent and subsequent can exist before they are resolved one way or the other. Why is that what the Rule does? The simple answer is because the Normans conquered England. One of the many oddities of the law of real property that comes from the feudal system created by William the Conqueror has to do with the inability of the owners of certain kinds of interests to transfer them during life. During the period when the Rule was developing, contingent interests and executory interests could not be transferred during the lifetime of their owners. So long as those interests existed in our old friend Blackacre, it was not possible to transfer fee simple ownership of Blackacre. That meant that Blackacre was not part of the market for land, and that meant that economic life was sort of frozen.

When the rules regarding alienability of land were developing into *the* Rule, land was the most important source of wealth in England. Now, that last statement may or may not be strictly true. It's very difficult to know whether the economic value of all of the land in England was greater or lesser than the value of tangible and intangible personal property, but it really doesn't matter. Land was the most socially significant form of wealth. The English aristocracy was a landed aristocracy. To have high social status required ownership of land.

That meant that if you were a high-ranking aristocrat who wanted your family to retain your exalted social position, you tried as hard as you (and your lawyers) could to make sure that your descendants could never lose ownership of the family lands. How you did that generally involved creating legal structures involving interests in the land that could not be transferred. After the Statute of Uses and the birth of the trust, keeping land from wandering out of the family involved contingent remainders and executory interests.

Conversely, if you were an aspiring aristocrat hoping to get your hands on sufficient real estate to support your hoped-for high status, you were not at all happy with the devices the existing aristocracy used to keep land from wandering away from their descendants, who may or may not have had the ability to hang on to the land had they had the authority to alienate it. These younger generation family members might be perfectly capable of staying at the top of the socioeconomic heap. They might also be completely incapable: prone to running up debts, lacking in the judgment necessary to hire competent managers of the family estates, simply bored with the whole thing. There could be any number of reasons someone sitting on some branch of the family tree in the future might want to sell the land to someone like you who had wealth but lacked social position.

The Rule developed as a judicially created compromise between the notion of free alienability — the idea that owners should be able to sell and buyers buy based on their own assessment of what was good for them, even if that meant that the social status of individuals and families could change — and the desire of those with wealth to ensure that their descendants would never suffer downward mobility.

The compromise allowed those with wealth to "lock it up" for the lifetime of someone alive when the arrangement was created, plus 21 years and any period of gestation. That meant that our hypothetical aristocratic (or perhaps merely very wealthy) landowner arranging what would happen on death could keep the land in the family for the lifetimes of the landowner's children plus the minorities of the children's children. That's the *what* of the Rule. It's the *how* of the Rule that has caused all of the misery.

B. Vesting in Interest

The *how* begins with understanding what the Rule requires when it requires that an interest "vest" within the perpetuity period of lives in being plus 21 years and a period of gestation. The "vesting" the Rule is concerned with is not vesting is possession, but

TABLE 12.1	How to Not Violate the Rule		
Interest	What prevents vesting in interest	What must happen before the perpetuities period runs out if interest is to be valid
Contingent remainder	Condition precedent to vesting in possession	Condition must be resolved one way or the other
Contingent remainder	Remainder persons are unascertained	Remainder persons must be born or it must be certain that they will never be born
Class gift	Class members being subject to partial divestment	Class must close
Executory interest	Vesting in possession subject to a condition subsequent	Condition subsequent must be resolved one way or the other

rather **vesting in interest.** To put it as simply and clearly as possible, a future interest is vested in interest *when its vesting in possession is not subject (1) to a condition precedent or (2) subsequent and (3) there are persons who would vest in possession were the distribution date to occur at any given time.* Elements 1 and 3 describe a contingent remainder: a remainder is contingent if its vesting is subject to a condition precedent or it is created in unascertained persons. Element 2 describes an executory interest: an executory interest will vest in possession only if the condition subsequent occurs. In addition, *a class gift is not vested in interest while it is subject to open.* Even if we can identify persons who would vest in possession were the distribution date to occur at any given time, the fact that the number of persons might increase or decrease and therefore change the amount of property each person vesting in possession would receive is enough to prevent the class gift from being vested in interest. To put this in more descriptive terms, *a future interest is vested in interest when we can identify the persons who will vest in possession, who will actually get possession of the property involved and how much of the property will be theirs.*

So here's the big payoff: only contingent remainders, executory interests, and vested remainders subject to open can be invalidated by the Rule. Invalidation happens only if we cannot be 100 percent certain that the condition precedent related to the contingent remainder or the condition subsequent related to the executory interest will be resolved and that the class will close before the expiration of the perpetuities period. Table 12.1 shows this same conclusion.

C. When Does the Period Begin?

So now we know what has to happen before the magic period runs. But when does the period start? The answer is pretty simple: when the future interest we're dealing with is irrevocable, that is, it cannot be taken back by the person who created it. This rule works in an especially odd way when applied to interests created by the exercise of a power of appointment, and we'll deal with those complications later in the chapter.

Putting powers of appointment aside, then, this is one aspect of the Rule that is mercifully simple to understand. If future interests are created in a will, usually by the creation of a testamentary trust, then the perpetuities period of "lives in being plus 21 years and a period of gestation" begins when the testator dies. The trust is created at that moment, even if it takes some time to probate the will and takes even more time to fund the trust by transferring probate assets to the trustee. Future interests in a lifetime irrevocable trust are created for perpetuities purposes when the trust is created. The trust is created by the transfer of property to the trustee or when the settlor declares a trust of property the settlor owns. Subsequent additions of property to the trust (by opening the lid of the trust box and putting more property inside) are usually said to relate back to the original creation of the trust so that a new perpetuities period does not begin. (Note that Restatement (Third) of Trusts § 29 comment g(1) takes the opposite position; the perpetuities period for future interests in property added to the trust after its creation begins at the time of the addition.)

The perpetuities period for future interests created by a revocable trust begins when the trust becomes irrevocable. That usually happens at the death of the settlor. The settlor can release the power to revoke while alive, however, and when the release becomes effective the trust becomes irrevocable and the perpetuities period begins then.

F A Q

Q: Does the perpetuities begin for future interests in a revocable trust if the settlor loses capacity to revoke?

A: No. The difficulties involved in establishing a loss of capacity are too great to make perpetuities issues turn on the determination. In addition, remember that if a testator loses capacity to make a new will, the will still has no effect on the testator's property until the testator dies.

These various rules can be summed up in one rule: the period begins to run when there is no living person who can become the fee simple absolute owner of the property in which the future interests subject to the Rule exist. Table 12.2 summarizes this rule.

TABLE 12.2	When the Perpetuities Period Begins
Interest created by	**Perpetuities period begins to run**
Testamentary trust	Date of testator's death
Lifetime irrevocable trust	Date trust is created (even for property subsequently added to trust)
Revocable trust	Date trust becomes irrevocable: death of settlor or date of settlor's lifetime release of power to revoke
Legal life estate/ remainder	If created by will, date of testator's death; if lifetime, date of delivery that makes the gift

And one last thing to remember: interests that remain in the transferor — reversions, rights of entry, and possibilities of reverter — are *not* subject to the Rule. They are considered to be vested in interest the moment they are created for historical reasons that we're not going to worry about.

D. Who's a "Life in Being"?

Now we come to perhaps the most puzzling element of the traditional Rule. Who is the "life in being" whose lifetime is the variable measuring stick of the Rule? What makes the answer difficult to understand is the very nature of the Rule and the way is it traditionally applied. Remember that a future interest is **void ab initio** (void from its creation) if we cannot be 100 percent certain that it will or will not vest within the period. What is usually called a **measuring life** is a person whose lifetime ensures that the future interest is valid. This is the life that proves the Rule has been obeyed. If there is no measuring life, the future interest is invalid.

The other thing you have to understand about the measuring life is that it must be a person who can be identified. Sure, there may be someone among the billions alive on earth when the future interest is created whose lifetime will make the future interest we're dealing with valid, but we cannot use that lifetime unless we can point to that person. Let's illustrate this using Examples 12.1 and 12.2.

Example 12.1: S devises property to T in trust to pay the income from the trust property to S's children for their lives, remainder to S's grandchildren.

First, note the word "devise." We recognize this means that the trust is created by a gift in a will and is a testamentary trust.

Second, if there are no grandchildren of S living at S's death, the remainder in the grandchildren is contingent because it is created in unascertained persons. If that is the case, there is reversion in S's successors in interest.

Third, if there are grandchildren living at S's death, then the remainder is a class gift and it is open — the living grandchildren have vested remainders subject to partial divestment. (This would also be true if a grandchild of S predeceased S, issue of that grandchild survived S, and an anti-lapse statute gave the dead grandchild's interest to the issue living at S's death.) There is no reversion in this case, of course, because the remainder is not contingent.

Fourth, the income interest in S's children is a present interest and is unquestionably valid because it vests the moment it is created. All of S's children alive when S dies take a share of the income. The class of S's children is closed when S dies. In other words, there is no condition precedent and the class is closed.

Fifth, the class gift to the grandchildren is perfectly valid under the Rule. If the remainder is contingent because there are no grandchildren, we know whether there will be grandchildren no later than the death of the last to die of S's children. We will be 100 percent certain whether the remainder will vest no later than the death of the last to die of S's children. If there are living grandchildren at S's death, then we know that the class will close physiologically when the last of S's children die. In both cases, *all of S's children are alive when the interests are created at S's death.* We will know whether the remainder will satisfy the Rule no later than the death of the last to die of these people, who are all lives in being. Thus, any one of S's children can be the measuring life. We don't have to know which one; all that is necessary is that we can be certain that the lifetime of one of these persons, all of whom are certainly alive at S's death, will be the lifetime that validates the remainder.

Example 12.2: S creates an irrevocable trust by trust agreement between S and T as trustee in which T agrees to pay the income from the trust property to S's children for their lives, remainder to S's grandchildren.

First, the future interests created by S are exactly the same as those in the previous example. If there are no living grandchildren of S at the time the trust is created, the remainder is contingent and there is a reversion in S. If there are living grandchildren, the remainder is vested subject to open (partial divestment) and there is no reversion.

Second, the interest of S's children is a class gift, but the class of S's children will close when S dies, and S clearly is alive when the trust is created.

Third, the remainder in the grandchildren is unquestionably invalid. Why? *Because S can have another child after the creation of the trust.* The lives in being at the creation of the interest who can be the lives that validate the remainder and whom we can identify are S and S's children living at the time the future interest is created. However, if S has another child, that child is not a life in being; and if it is that child whose death *more than 21 years after the deaths of S and all of S's children living at the time of the creation of the future interest* makes it certain that no grandchildren will ever be born or that closes the class of grandchildren, the remainder is invalid.

Fourth, because the birth of this **afterborn**, someone born after the future interest is created, *can happen*, we assume it *will happen* (more about this in a bit). The mere possibility that the occurrence of the event that must happen within the perpetuities period can be governed by the lifetime of someone born after the future interest is created, someone who is not a life in being, is enough to make the interest invalid from the moment of its attempted creation. That means that by creating this trust S has only created the life income interests in his children, and on the death of the last to die of his children, the reversion will take possession of the trust property through the operation of a resulting trust.

Here's the big point: sure, it's possible that the day S creates this lifetime irrevocable trust somewhere on earth a child is born who will outlive any afterborn child of S and therefore is a life in being who validates the remainder in S's grandchildren. The problem is, *we can't identify that person.* To prove that a future interest is not invalidated by the Rule, you *must* be able to point to a person whose lifetime ensures validity. In Example 12.1, we can point to any one of S's children living at his death. In the second example, we can point to no one. Is there someone who might validate the interest? Perfectly possible. Do we know who that is? No.

We can illustrate Example 12.2 with a time line.

June 1, 2009. S creates irrevocable trust. Living at that time are S and three children of S: A, B, and C. There are two possibilities: (1) The remainder is contingent because there are no living grandchildren of S, and (2) *the remainder is vested subject to open because there are living grandchildren of S.* Now we have to assume that S will have another child. How the birth of that child affects possibility (1) is in roman type and how it affects possibility (2) *is in italics.*

June 1, 2009. S's fourth child, Spoiler, is born.

June 1, 2069. The last of the lives in being (S, A, B, and C) dies.

June 1, 2090. The perpetuities period runs out. Spoiler is still alive. That means (1) if no grandchildren have been born up to now, they still can be, and therefore it is still possible for the remainder to vest because there will then no longer be unascertained persons; and (2) *the class of grandchildren is still open and won't close until Spoiler dies.* We simply cannot be certain that Spoiler will be dead before June 1, 2090, when the perpetuities period runs. The remainder is void from its attempted creation.

June 1, 2099. Spoiler dies, either ensuring that no grandchildren will ever be born or *closing the class.* Is it possible that this date is within 21 years of the death of someone who was alive on June 1, 2009? Absolutely. Can we identify that person? No way. Result: whoever has the reversionary interest takes the trust property through the operation of a resulting trust.

F   A   Q

Q: Doesn't the possibility of posthumously conceived children make the Rule unworkable?

A: Yes. If a person can have children who are conceived after that person's death, then classes will never close. This possibility is one reason, some say, for ending the Rule. If the Rule is going to continue to exist, the best solution is legislative. For example, UPC § 2-705(g) says that if the distribution date of a class gift is the death of the posthumously conceived child's parent, the child is considered to be alive at the parent's death if the child lives 120 hours after birth and was conceived within 36 months of the parent's death or born with 45 months of the parent's death.

If you take a good look at this time line, you'll notice something really strange: the trust has lasted *longer than the perpetuities period.* The trust ends when Spoiler dies, and that is after the end of the perpetuities period on June 1, 2090. Remember what we said at the beginning of the chapter: the Rule does not limit how long a trust can last. Spoiler vested in the income interest at birth, which happened during S's lifetime. Even if S is male and Spoiler were born after S's death, Spoiler is a trust beneficiary only if Spoiler is S's child; and that means Spoiler was *en ventre sa mere* during S's life and that Spoiler's legal existence for property law purposes relates back to the time of conception.

The Rule doesn't prevent the trust from enduring for Spoiler's entire lifetime, even though Spoiler is the dreaded afterborn. The Rule invalidates only the remainder whose vesting in interest depends on when Spoiler dies. Believe me, I'm not making this up.

E. Examples of Remote Contingencies

We've now dealt with the basics of the Rule. There's a lot more to learn, however, and we're going to approach this additional material by discussing examples based on remote contingencies, events not related to the births and deaths of persons that govern the resolution of conditions. We're going to make an arbitrary selection of a remote contingency, to wit, "when the Rock of Gibraltar crumbles." We start with Example 12.3.

Example 12.3: S transfers property to T in trust to pay the income from the trust property to A for life, remainder to B when the Rock of Gibraltar crumbles.

First, we know that the present interest in A vests when the trust is created and the remainder is contingent. Making vesting in possession contingent on being alive if something happens in the future is a classic condition precedent. S therefore has a reversion.

Second, we have no idea if and when the Rock of Gibraltar will eventually succumb to the ineluctable forces of erosion and turn into a great big pile of gravel. Clearly we can't say that we'll be certain whether the Rock will fall apart within 21 years of the death of S, A, and B, the only lives we can identify. Now, here's where you'll be tempted to make a mistake. But, you ask, B will certainly die and won't that end the possibility of B vesting in possession? No! Remember, under the traditional law, survival to the time of possession is never implied. If when B dies, Gibraltar is still looming over the strait that connects the Mediterranean with the Atlantic, the contingent remainder simply passes through B's estate ready to vest whenever the conditional precedent occurs.

Third, because we cannot be 100 percent certain that the condition precedent will occur or be certain not to occur within the perpetuities period, the remainder is invalid from its creation; and when A dies, the reversionary interest will take possession of the trust property through the operation of a resulting trust.

> **F   A   Q**
>
> **Q: If UPC § 2-707 is the law, wouldn't B's contingent remainder in Example 12.3 be valid?**
>
> A: Yes, it would. Because UPC § 2-707 is a default rule that makes every future interest in a trust contingent on the beneficiary's surviving to the distribution date, B's remainder is now contingent on being alive at the distribution date, which is when the Rock of Gibraltar crumbles. If when B dies the Rock is still standing, we know that B's remainder will never vest in possession. It's all over at B's death, and B of course is a life in being.

Here's the next example.

Example 12.4: S transfers property T in trust to pay the income from the trust property to A for life, remainder to B if B is living when the Rock of Gibraltar crumbles.

First, just as in the previous example, A vests in the present income interest for life when the trust is created. B has a contingent remainder; requiring the remainder person to be alive at some time in the future is a classic condition precedent.

Second, the condition precedent will be resolved no later than B's death. If when B dies the Rock is still standing, we know that the condition will never happen. B's interest is valid. Cold comfort to B, of course. The chances of B vesting in possession are as close to zero as you can get. Another way to put it is that on B's death it's all over, and the situation has been resolved by the end of a life in being. Of course, B's interest is worthless and the reversion is certain to take possession of the trust property, but at least the Rule was satisfied.

Here's our final example.

Example 12.5: S transfers property T in trust to pay the income from the trust property to A for life, remainder to B for life when the Rock of Gibraltar crumbles.

First, we've got the present interest vested in A at creation, and we have a remainder in a life income interest in B. There is a reversion in S, but not because B's remainder is contingent. S has given away only the income from the trust property. S never gave away the remainder in fee simple, so S indeed has a reversion. (Remember that under the traditional law of future interests, you can never create a remainder in yourself or a reversion in a third person. If you don't give away everything you have, you have a reversion.) B's interest by its very nature can vest in possession only if B is alive at the time of distribution. You might remember that a legal life estate or an equitable life income interest in a trust is vested subject to limitational defeasance, which is not the same as being contingent. A remainder in a life estate or life income held by a living person is usually referred to as vested, and it is certainly vested in interest for purposes of the Rule.

The preceding discussion should seem pretty ridiculous. Who would ever create a condition precedent that depends on some crazy remote contingency like the Rock of Gibraltar crumbling (or the Rockies tumbling, or who knows what else)? No one. However, when the Rule was being formulated, such remote contingencies were not at all odd. Remember that all of that development occurred in a world in which the fee tail was perfectly valid. The eventual dying out of someone's family line is indeed a remote contingency. Also, remember that accepted construction of "die without issue" was once "indefinite failure of issue," which meant a person died without issue when she had no living descendants. That event could happen many, many years in the future and was clearly a remote contingency.

There's another way in which you can see the relevance of the remote contingency examples. Remember that in our example involving Spoiler we described the little tyke as an "afterborn" and noted that when a condition might be resolved on the death of someone who was not alive when the perpetuities period began to run, an afterborn, the interest whose vesting depends on the resolution of that condition is invalid. The death of the afterborn is simply another kind of remote contingency. It's as impossible to be certain that someone born after the perpetuities period begins to run will die within 21 years of the death of someone who was alive when the period began to run as it is to be certain that the Rock of Gibraltar will crumble within 21 years of the death of someone alive when the perpetuities period began to run.

F. Contingencies Related to Persons

Most contingencies have to do with the birth and death of natural persons. Understanding how the Rule in its traditional formulation applies to those sorts of contingencies is greatly complicated by what is usually called the "remorseless application" of the Rule — or, to put it more colloquially, if it can happen we must assume it will happen.

The justification for this approach to applying the Rule to real life is actually quite sound, as crazy as it sometimes seems (and I assure you, after you read the next section you will find "crazy" is barely adequate to describe how the Rule traditionally works). The traditional view is that the Rule is designed to *frustrate* intent. The settlor of a trust may want to postpone vesting beyond the period allowed by the Rule, but that's simply not possible. To make sure that the bad intent is frustrated, the traditional approach of courts confronted with questions involving the Rule is to never give a future interest a break. If there is *any* way in which an arrangement can violate the Rule, then the Rule is violated. Traditionally, courts will not construe language creating future interests to avoid violations of the Rule, and the most unlikely things are treated as if they are going to come to pass. The lawyer most responsible for creating the traditional approach to the rule, the Boston practitioner and Harvard Law School professor John Chipman Gray, likened the Rule to an axiom of mathematics. There is no room to quibble or equivocate. If there is no measuring life that validates the interest, it's invalid. But oh what a bizarre world this approach has created.

G. Remorseless Application of the Rule

The "remorseless application" of the Rule can be summarized by examining three classic corollaries of that approach.

(1) Fertile Octogenarians and Precocious Toddlers

You no doubt understand by now that when trying to figure out whether a future interest is valid under the Rule, the critical question is whether a person can be born after the perpetuities period begins to run. Going back to Example 12.2 and Spoiler, obviously, if there was no possibility of Spoiler being born, there's no problem. That's why if the trust were a testamentary trust, the remainder in S's grandchildren would be valid. The trust would be created at S's death, and the possibility of S having children is over so there can never be an afterborn child (remember that we are ignoring the possibility of posthumous conception using stored gametes). If that's the case, then the class will close on the death of the last to die of S's children who are all lives in being when the interest is created and the perpetuities period begins to run; and that's perfectly valid. And if no grandchildren have been born by the time of S's death, the possibility of grandchildren will end with the death of the last child to die; if none have been born by that time, the contingent remainder will fail to vest on the death of a life in being.

Imagine, however, that when S creates the irrevocable trust in Example 12.2, S is a female aged 70. Even modern medical technology is unlikely to allow S to conceive a child before her death. Surely, then, we can be certain that Spoiler will not be born, that there can be no afterborn and the remainder is valid. Right? Wrong. Why? *Because under the traditional Rule, every person is presumed to be able to have children from the moment of birth until the moment of death.* When applied to a very old person, this is the rule of the **fertile octogenarian**; when applied to a prepubescent person, this is the rule of the **precocious toddler**.

At least in the modern world, you can imagine a grain of sense in the fertile octogenarian rule. Medical technology has made it possible for women to bear their genetic children (or to have their genetic children borne by another woman) beyond the traditional child-bearing years. And of course a child might be adopted at any time. Remember, however, that the fertile octogenarian rule was formulated *200 years ago* when human ingenuity could do nothing to extend a woman's reproductive capacity and when adoption was more or less unknown to the common law. The rule in fact can be traced to a specific case decided in the late eighteenth century, and modern scholarship tells us that given prevalent beliefs about human reproduction at that time, we cannot say that the judges who decided that case and the lawyers and later judges who followed it were being irrational by their own standards. (There's nothing to be said for the precocious toddler rule.)

(2) Unborn Widows

Another classic (mis)use of the remorseless quality of the common law rule is illustrated by Example 12.6.

Example 12.6: T devises property in trust to pay the income to T's son S for his life, then to pay the income to S's surviving spouse, if any, and then to distribute the trust property to S's issue then living by representation.

To apply the Rule to this example, we must first identify the interests created and the conditions that exist, if any. Here T has created a present interest in S, an equitable life estate, a remainder in a life estate in S's surviving spouse, and a contingent remainder in S's issue. The requirement that issue be living on the death of S's widow (if any) is a condition precedent.

Sidebar

COMMERICAL APPLICATIONS OF THE RULE

All of the examples we've been talking about involve applying the Rule to future interests created when a property owner makes a gift by creating a trust (or a legal life estate and remainder). In a few states, however, the Rule applies to commercial transactions, specifically, options on real estate. Most states, however, have repudiated this application of the Rule.

Second, when will the condition precedent be resolved? At S's widow's death, *and S's widow might be someone who was not yet born when the trust was created and the perpetuities period began to run*. Even if S is married at the time T creates the trust, it is possible that S's then spouse might die or they might divorce and that sometime later S might marry someone who was not a life in being when the trust was created, and that person might be S's surviving spouse. Unlikely? Perhaps, but for purposes of the common law Rule Against Perpetuities, the only response is "well, it *might* happen." And that's enough to make the contingent remainder void. We have yet another example of the possibility of an afterborn invalidating an interest that depends on a condition precedent that might be resolved on the death of the afterborn person.

This lunatic application of the common law rule is known as the **unborn widow** rule; an interest ends up being void because the resolution of a condition that must be resolved if the interest is to vest is tied to the lifespan of someone described as another person's surviving spouse and there is no guarantee that this hypothetical surviving spouse will turn out to be a life in being at the time the interest was created. Realize that if the reference were to a person who is currently S's spouse, the requirements of the Rule would be satisfied. In our example, if the remainder in a life estate had been created in "S's wife Makayla, if she shall survive him," the condition precedent would be resolved on the death of someone who was alive when the interest was created. The unborn widow problem arises because of the reference to a "generic" surviving spouse.

Realize also that the reminder in a life estate in S's widow is not void. That interest will vest in interest and possession (if it ever does) simultaneously at S's death, and S is clearly a life in being at the creation of the interest at T's death. This point often leads to confusion. After all, it does seem that the unborn widow rule should have something to do with the interest that is created in the surviving spouse who may not be a life in being when the perpetuities period begins to run. As we've seen, of course, it doesn't. The problem caused by this lovely example of the "remorseless application" of the Rule involves interests the vesting of which are linked to the death of the surviving spouse. Because the generic surviving spouse is not necessarily a life in being when the perpetuities period begins to run, the surviving spouse's death, like the death of any afterborn person, is a remote contingency.

(3) Administrative Contingencies

The third classic example of how the remorseless application of the Rule leads to crazy results involves what are usually called **administrative contingencies**, events that are precedent to vesting which involve not the birth and death of persons but rather the accomplishment of an administrative task involved with administering a testator's estate. Examples 12.7 and 12.8 give two typical examples.

Example 12.7: The residuary clause of T's will reads as follows: "I give the residue of my estate to my descendants who are alive when the administration of my estate is complete."

Example 12.8: The residuary clause of T's will reads as follows: "I give the residue of my estate to my descendants who are alive when my will is admitted to probate."

To understand the application of the Rule to these examples, we have to decide whether the conditions created by the language are conditions precedent. The answer is pretty clear: the only persons who are to receive a share of the testator's probate estate are the testator's descendants who are living when a specified event occurs in the future. That event, in turn, has nothing to do with the birth and death of persons, so the perpetuities period is 21 years, the "21-year period in gross." Okay, so you ask yourself, how in the world could it take more than 21 years to administer an estate or get a will admitted to probate? Remember we're dealing with the traditional Rule whose remorseless application requires us to test any nonvested interest against what might happen. Just as a 70-year-old woman *might* conceive a child and give birth, so it *might* take more than 21 years to administer an estate or to get a will admitted to probate. The possibility is enough to make the interests in the residuary estate invalid and result in a partial intestacy.

Realize that if the beneficiaries of the residuary estate were "my children living" when the condition precedent occurs, the interests *would* be valid because the testator's children are all lives in being at the testator's death and the condition precedent will be resolved in their lifetimes. What to a layperson might seem to be a small variation in words has a very big effect on the application of the Rule.

H. Class Gifts and the Rule Against Perpetuities

(1) The "All or Nothing" Rule

We already have seen some examples of the application of the Rule to class gifts, but we have yet to thoroughly examine the subject. What makes the interaction of the Rule and class gifts different from run of the mill perpetuities problems is first, the rule that a class gift which is subject to open is not vested in interest. Therefore, for a class gift to be valid, the class must close before the perpetuities period runs. In addition, a class gift can be subject to a condition precedent. The Rule as applied to class gifts, then, really has two prongs. A class gift is valid under the traditional Rule (1) if the class must close before the perpetuities period runs, and (2) if there is a condition precedent applicable to the class gift, it must be resolved as to all class members before the perpetuities period runs. If these two requirements are not met, then the gift is invalid as to all of the class members, a result that is often called the **all or nothing rule**.

We saw an illustration of the working of the first prong of the test in Example 12.2. Remember that the remainder in S's grandchildren in that example was invalid because of the possibility of the birth of an afterborn child of S whom we named Spoiler. Because the class of S's grandchildren would close on the death of the afterborn, the Rule is violated.

What makes this application of the Rule to class gifts especially complicated is the remorseless application, the what-might-happen approach. For example, we've seen how the fertile octogenarian rule works in the Spoiler example. Once a person can have a child right up to death, the possibilities for the birth of an afterborn who can influence the closing of a class always has to be taken into account. Add a condition precedent on top of that, and things get really complicated. Let's try a simple example.

Example 12.9: S devises property to T in trust to pay the income to S's daughter D for life, remainder to those of D's children who reach the age of 25.

Here we have a class gift to D's children. So first, will the class close in time? Absolutely — the class of D's children closes physiologically on D's death. It can't close any earlier under the rule of convenience because D is entitled to the income from the trust until her death. Now, we have to consider the condition. It is indeed a condition precedent because of the way it's worded. Only those children who reach the age of 25 are entitled to share in the distribution of the trust property. Now we have a problem. Remember that we must assume that D can have children until her death. If D does indeed die and close the class within four years of giving birth to a child, the condition precedent will not be resolved as to that child within the perpetuities period, and the entire remainder in D's children is void. On D's death, the trust property will pass to whoever has the reversion that passed through S.

How's that again? Here's our time line.

June 1, 2009. S dies and the trust is created. Living at that time are D and one child of D: X. There are two possibilities: (1) X is under the age of 25, and the remainder is therefore contingent because there is no remainder person who has satisfied the condition precedent; and (2) *X is 25 or older, and the remainder is vested subject to open or partial divestment because X has indeed satisfied the condition precedent.* Now we have to assume that D has another child. How the birth of that child affects possibility (1) is in roman type and how it affects possibility (2) *is in italics.*

June 1, 2010. D gives birth to Spoiler. That means (1) Spoiler now has a contingent remainder along with X, and (2) *Spoiler has an executory interest and will partially divest X if Spoiler reaches age 25.*

June 1, 2011. D dies. Under both (1) and (2), the class of D's children is closed. Because D is a life in being, the event closing the class, D's death, will always occur within the perpetuities period.

June 1, 2012. X dies before reaching age 25. The perpetuities period now has begun to run because both of the lives in being we could identify at the creation of the interest are dead. Under (1), assuming X is not 25 by June 1, 2012, X's interest would vanish because X did not fulfill the condition precedent. Under (2), *X's interest would be transmitted through X's estate because X had fulfilled the condition precedent.*

June 1, 2032. The perpetuities period has run, and Spoiler is 22 years old. Clearly, we cannot know whether Spoiler will reach age 25 or not. The condition precedent is unresolved, and the Rule Against Perpetuities is violated. The result is that the remainder in D's children is void from its creation, and on D's death whoever has the reversionary interest takes the trust property through the operation of a resulting trust. Once again, is it possible that Spoiler's 25th birthday, June 1, 2035, will occur within 21 years from the death of someone who was alive on June 1, 2009, when the perpetuities period began to run? Absolutely. Can we identify that person? No way. In fact, X certainly might be alive on Spoiler's 21st birthday, and if X dies on that very day, we will know whether Spoiler will turn 25 or not, within the perpetuities period because X of course is a life in being. But we can't be sure of that sequence of events.

Of course, if the condition precedent was a requirement of reaching age 21, then the remainder in D's children would be valid. No matter when D died, D's child would reach age 21 not later than 21 years after the death of D, who is a life in being at the time the perpetuities period begins to run. If the life income beneficiary were S's son and S died while the mother of his child was pregnant, the child would reach 21 within 21 years after the father's death, plus a period of gestation, and the remainder in the son's children would be valid. Remember that validity *does not* mean that the life income beneficiary's children will actually receive distribution of the trust property. They could all die before reaching age 21, and thus none of them would fulfill the condition precedent. But that's fine from a perpetuities point of view. So long as we are absolutely certain that the condition precedent will be resolved as to each class member within the perpetuities period, the remainder is valid.

There's another aspect of this example that sometimes can lead you astray. Remember alternative (2) where D's child X has already reached the age of 25 at the time the trust is created and the perpetuities period begins to run. Yes, X has fulfilled the condition precedent and would be entitled to a distribution from the trust property on D's death, were the remainder not invalid, of course. That does not mean that the class of D's children is closed by the rule of convenience when the trust is created. If it did, then the afterborn child of D could never enter the class and create all the difficulty. Think for a minute. The rule of convenience says that a class will close when a class member can demand distribution of his share of the property involved in the class gift. Can X demand distribution of X's share of the trust property? Of course not; the trust has to pay all the income from the trust property to D for D's life. While the trust has to pay income to the income beneficiary, the trustee can't distribute any trust property to a remainder person, even if that person has fulfilled the relevant condition precedent. Here's a good rule of thumb: while the trustee has the power to pay out income, a remainder beneficiary cannot close the class of remainder persons by the rule of convenience.

There are situations, however, in which the possibility of closing a class by the rule of convenience will prevent a future interest from violating the Rule. Let's try a deceptively simple example.

Example 12.10: T devises property to X in trust to pay the income to A for life, remainder to A's grandchildren.

There is no condition precedent involved with this remainder. All that is necessary for the remainder to be valid is absolute certainty that the class will close within the perpetuities period. When will the class of A's grandchildren close physiologically? When the last of A's children die. The possibility of A having children after T's death with the result that the class of A's grandchildren would remain open until the death of that afterborn child of A means that the Rule could be violated, and the remainder is then void.

However, there are several scenarios in which the class of A's grandchildren will close by the rule of convenience at A's death. Remember that there is no condition precedent here. Once A dies and the income interest is over, any grandchild is entitled to be paid, so if we know at the time T creates the interest at T's death that a grandchild of A will be able to demand her share of the remainder at A's death, we will know that the class will close on the death of a life in being, and the remainder is valid.

What circumstances could exist at T's death that would lead to that conclusion?

First, if there are grandchildren of A living at T's death, we know that the class of A's grandchildren will close at A's death because that grandchild will demand payment and close the class. Even if that grandchild dies immediately after T, there is no express condition of survival, the grandchild's interest in the remainder is transmissible, and the grandchild's successors in interest will demand payment and close the class at A's death.

Second, a grandchild of A was alive when T executed the will but died before T. If the anti-lapse statute applied and if the persons designated to take the predeceased beneficiary's interest by the anti-lapse statute exist (e.g., issue of the grandchild of A were living at T's death), then those persons (or their successors in interest) would close the class by the rule of convenience at A's death.

Third, and this possibility has nothing to do with the rule of convenience, none of A's children were living at T's death and therefore the class of A's grandchildren was closed physiologically at T's death.

We could multiply examples of the operation of the Rule on class gifts, but the analysis would always be the same. Are we 100 percent certain that the class will close 21 years after the death of a life in being when the perpetuities period began to run? If there is a condition precedent attached to the class gift, are we 100 percent certain that the condition will be resolved as to all of the class members; that is, are we 100 percent certain that we will know who among the class members has fulfilled the condition precedent and who has not within 21 years of the death of a life in being when the perpetuities period began to run? If the answer to either question is no, the class gift is completely invalid.

OK, I can't resist one more example. Analyze this.

Example 12.11: T devises property to X in trust to pay the income to A for life, remainder to A's grandchildren living at A's death.

Here we have a class gift to A's grandchildren and a condition precedent of survival to the distribution date of the trust property, which is A's death. The class of A's grandchildren could close physiologically beyond the perpetuities period. A could have an afterborn child, whose death need not necessarily occur within 21 years from the death of the people we can identify as being alive when the perpetuities period begin to run at T's death. This is exactly the same as our first example in which the possibility of the birth of the afterborn, Spoiler, meant that the class of grandchildren could close beyond the running of the perpetuities period.

But in this example the remainder *is* valid. Yes, it is, even though we have a condition precedent of surviving to the time of distribution of the trust property, which is A's death, and even though the class of A's grandchildren can close physiologically beyond the perpetuities period, as we've just said. The key is the rule of convenience. There are only two possibilities. First, there are no grandchildren of A living at A's death. The class is empty, the remainder fails, and the reversion takes possession of the trust property. Second, there is at least one grandchild of A living at A's death. That grandchild is entitled to payment. The right to receive distribution of the trust property at A's death will close the class of grandchildren by the rule of convenience. The class is closed, and the condition precedent is resolved at A's death. A is a life in being at T's death when the perpetuities period began to run, and therefore the condition precedent is resolved and the class is closed within the perpetuities period — in fact, with 21 years to spare.

(2) Exceptions to the "All or Nothing" Rule

(a) Gifts of a Specific Sum

There are two important exceptions to the all or nothing rule for class gifts. The first is directly related to a rule for closing a certain kind of class gift that we've already discussed. Remember the rule about closing the class when the gift is of a specific sum to each class member in Chapter 7? In that situation, the class closed at the death of the testator whose will made the gift, even if no class members were entitled to take at that time. If there are no class members, that's that. If there's a condition precedent to vesting in possession — "I give $5,000 to each of the children of my friend, X, who reach the age of 25" — and there are class members alive at the testator's death who have not yet fulfilled the condition precedent, the class still closes, and the executor will set sufficient funds to pay all of the class members if they all fulfill the condition precedent. If any of them don't, the beneficiaries of the residuary devise will take those funds. There is no perpetuities problem because all of the class members are living at the testator's death, and they are certainly lives in being at the time the perpetuities period begins to run.

What if the testator makes it clear that the class is to include the friend's children whether they are born before or after the testator's death? Under the usual rules, the class of X's children would close physiologically at X's death, but not all of the class members would necessarily fulfill the condition precedent within 21 years of X's death. X could have a child less than 4 years before death, and sure enough the condition precedent of reaching age 25 would not necessarily be resolved within 21 years. That means that the class gift is void as to all class members, right?

Wrong, not because your understanding of the way the Rule is applied to class gifts is deficient but because there is an exception that applies to gifts of a specific sum. Ever since the decision of the English Court of Chancery in the mid-nineteenth century, the rule has been that a gift of a specific sum to each member of a class that is invalid under the Rule as to some class members is good as to those class members whose gifts do not violate the Rule. In our example of the devise of $5,000 to children of X who reach age 25, the two children who are alive at the testator's death will get their $5,000 each if they live to age 25 because they themselves are lives in being and the condition precedent will be resolved as to them in their own lifetimes. The gift is invalid as to children of X born after the testator's death. The reason for this exception is that the executor knows how much money to set aside to pay the class members who have a chance of fulfilling the condition precedent.

That doesn't mean, however, that the number of class members has to be fixed at the time the perpetuities period begins to run. Try this example.

Example 12.12: Testator devises "$5,000 to each of the grandchildren of my friend, X, whether living at my death or born thereafter." Two children of X and one grandchild of X are living at Testator's death.

We can analyze this gift as follows:

- There is no condition precedent attached to the gift, so to satisfy the Rule the class needs only to close before the perpetuities period runs.
- Under the general rule for class gifts, this gift is invalid. The class of X's grandchildren living at Testator's death and born thereafter will close physiologically when the last of X's children die.
- X can have a child after Testator's death, the time when the perpetuities period began to run. Here's the dreaded afterborn.
- Because the class of X's grandchildren could close on the death of the afterborn and that death certainly could occur more than 21 years after the death of a life in being at Testator's death (the lives we can identify are X, X's two children, and the one grandchild), the class could close beyond the running of the perpetuities period, and the gift is invalid.
- The exception for gifts of a specific sum to each class member does apply, however, and the gift is therefore valid for the grandchild of X who is living at Testator's death and for all grandchildren born to the two children of X who

are lives in being at Testator's death. Those gifts will vest within the perpetuities period because these class members are born to lives in being. Any
grandchild born to an afterborn child of X is not part of the class.

(b) Gifts to Subclasses

The second exception is the **doctrine of subclasses**, which applies when it's
possible to divide a class gift into separate gifts to distinct subclasses. Again, we
can illustrate this doctrine with an example.

Example 12.13: Testator devises property to Big Bank in trust to pay the income to
Testator's son, S, for life, then to pay the income in equal shares to S's children for
their lives, and as each child of S dies, the trustee shall distribute to that child's issue,
then living, by representation, the fraction of the trust property equal to the number
1 divided by the number of S's children living immediately before the death of the
child to whose issue distribution is to be made. In other words, if at S's death S has six
children, at the death of the first of them to die, the trustee will distribute 1/6 of the
trust property to the child's descendants. At Testator's death, S and three children of
S are living. No grandchildren of S have even been born.

We can analyze this gift as follows:

- There is no condition precedent attached to the gift, so to satisfy the Rule the
  class of S's grandchildren needs only to close before the perpetuities period
  runs.
- Under the general rule for class gifts, this gift is invalid. The class of S's
  grandchildren closes physiologically when the last of S's children dies.
- S could have a child after Testator's death, the time when the perpetuities
  period begins to run. Once again, here's the afterborn.
- Because the class of S's grandchildren could close on the death of the afterborn and because that death certainly could occur more than 21 years after
  the death of a life in being at Testator's death (the lives we can identify are S
  and S's three children), the class could close beyond the running of the perpetuities period, and the gift is invalid.
- The trust in this example, however, does not create one single condition
  precedent; rather it creates several, one tied to the death of each of S's children. Every time a child dies, a condition precedent is resolved. There are as
  many class gifts as there are children of S, one gift to the surviving issue of each
  child. For purposes of satisfying the Rule, each class gift can be judged sep-
  arately. That means that the remainders contingent on surviving a child of S
  who was living at T's death are valid; the remainders contingent on surviving
  any child of S born after T's death are invalid.

Here's how it works in more detail. Assume that after T's death three more
children are born to S. When S dies, all six children survive. When one of the children
living at T's death dies, the share of the trust property resulting from the application
of the formula in the trust instrument is distributed to that child's issue then living, by
representation. On the death of a child of S born after T's death, the share of the trust
property resulting from the application of the formula passes by resulting trust to

whoever took the reversion from T's estate. That person or persons are the residuary beneficiaries or, if the trust was itself the residuary devise, then the reversion passed in intestacy. If we assume that T died unmarried, then the sole heir was S, and we have to determine who took the reversion through S's estate.

This useful escape from the draconian consequences of the all or nothing rule for class gifts is possible only when the settlor of the gift (Testator in Example 12.13) has created the subclasses by the terms of the gift. The remorseless application of the traditional Rule prevents a court from construing a class gift to be a gift to subclasses. If, in our example, the trust terms required the trustee to pay the trust income to the children of S until all the children are dead and then gave the remainder to S's grandchildren, the remainder would be invalid, even if at Testator's death there were living children of S. In applying the traditional Rule, no court would construe the language to create subclasses by separating the remainder to the children of S's children who are lives in being from the remainder to children of afterborn children of S.

I. Powers of Appointment and the Rule against Perpetuities

As we saw in Chapter 10, powers of appointment are powerful tools for bringing flexibility to the use of trusts. By designating someone to make the decision about how trust property will be distributed in the future, the settlor can hope that the decision will be made by wisely taking account of the facts that exist at the time the decision is made. The Rule is relevant here, too, and in ways that are easy to overlook. The Rule interacts with powers of appointment in two ways. First, it has something to say about the validity of the power itself, and second it also has something to say about the validity of future interests created by the exercise of the power.

(1) Is the Power Itself Valid?

The first question to ask about a power of appointment in relation to the Rule is whether the power itself is valid. The answer is yes, if it is certain that the power cannot be exercised beyond the perpetuities period. The rules for when the perpetuities period begins to run for the power are the same as for future interests: the period begins to run when the power is irrevocable. Therefore Table 12.2 also applies to power of appointment. If the appointive property is trust property, then the rules for future interests in trusts apply; if the appointive property is in a legal life estate/ remainder, then those rules apply. If you go back to Table 12.2, all you have to do at the top of the left-hand column is substitute "Power of appointment created in" for "Interest created by."

It is very unusual to create a power of appointment in an unborn person. Because the donor of the power is looking to the donee to make a good decision about how to distribute the trust property, the donee is overwhelmingly likely to be a person the donor knows. In fact, that person is often the life income beneficiary of the trust. That means that the overwhelming majority of powers of appointment are created in donees who are alive when the perpetuities period begins to run. Since they must exercise the power no later than their own deaths, the power itself does not violate the Rule.

There is one situation in which it can be easy to create a power of appointment that is invalid under the Rule. Even though powers of appointment are not held in a fiduciary capacity—that is, donees do not have fiduciary duties in exercising the powers they are given—in one situation a power held in a fiduciary capacity can run into trouble with the Rule. Here's an example.

Example 12.14: C transfers property to Big Bank in trust to pay the income to C's spouse for life, then to pay income and principal to C's children in such amounts and at such times as the trustee shall determine in its discretion, without considering other resources that may be available to the beneficiaries, until the death of the last to die of C's children, at which time the trust shall terminate and the trustee is to distribute the trust property to the American Cancer Society.

The remainder in the charity is valid because it is vested in interest from the moment of its creation; there is no condition attached to it at all. Were the remainder contingent, for example, if at the death of the last to die of C's children the trust was to terminate and the property distributed to C's descendants by representation and consequently there would be an implied condition of survival to the time of distribution, the remainder would be invalid. The condition could be resolved on the death of a child of C born after the perpetuities period began to run when C created the trust, and the resolution of a condition precedent on the death of an afterborn means that the Rule has been violated and the contingent remainder associated with the condition precedent is invalid.

That's not the case here, however, but we're not good with the Rule because of the trustee's power to make discretionary distributions. Because of the possibility of C having a child born after the creation of the trust (the afterborn), which possibility we have to take as a certainty under the traditional Rule, the trustee's power could last longer than lives in being plus 21 years. There are two views of what that means for the trustee's power. One view, which is probably the majority view of the few cases that have dealt with the problem, is that the power is void from its creation, just as is any future interest that violates the Rule. That result means that the power doesn't exist, and without the power the interest of C's children doesn't exist, so that at the death of C's spouse the remainder in the charity vests in possession.

There is a minority view that was strongly advocated by John Chipman Gray in his great treatise on the Rule. It was his view that the power in the trustee should be treated as a series of annual powers that would be good for 21 years after the death of a life in being. If that's the way a court sees it, then the trustee or trustees may exercise the power for 21 years after the death of C's spouse, at which time the power ends and the next interest in the trust, in our example, the remainder in the charity, vests in possession. The cases are practically nonexistent, and the question cannot be said to be definitively settled one way or the other.

F A Q

Q: If a discretionary power in a trustee is good for only a maximum of 21 years after the death of a life in being and, in the majority view, are void, why are discretionary trusts so popular even where the Rule still exists?

A: Where the Rule is still the law, it is possible to create a discretionary trust that will last for the maximum period allowed by the Rule, and the trustee's power will be valid for the entire duration of the trust. How is that done? Perhaps the most common way is to give the trustee the discretionary power for a period that ends 21 years after death of all of the descendants of the settlor living at the time the perpetuities period begins to run, which is when the trust is created if it's an irrevocable lifetime trust and the settlor's death if it's a testamentary trust. At that time, the trust terminates and the remainder vests in possession

If we imagine that a person has a child at age 25, and that the child has a child at age 25, and the grandchild has a child at age 25, by the time the person who is now a great-grandparent dies at 80, a not unusual life span, a trust ending 21 years after the death of the last to die of the testator's descendants living at the testator's death could last about 100 years if the great-grandchild has a life span of 80. Of course, the more young descendants the settlor has, the greater the chances for creating a long-term trust that does not involve a violation of the Rule.

(2) Future Interests Created by Exercise of the Power

There's more to powers of appointment and the Rule than the validity of the power itself. As we saw in Chapter 10, it is very common for donees to be given the power to appoint the appointive property in further trust, thus creating future interests. If the donee does that, it is very easy to violate the Rule. Why? Because of the special rules that govern when the perpetuities period begins to run with regard to future interests created by exercise of a power of appointment. To understand these special rules, we have to divide powers of appointment into two groups: (1) presently exercisable general powers of appointment, and (2) all other powers of appointment: all special powers and general testamentary powers.

The rule for future interests created by the exercise of a Group 1 power is simple. The perpetuities period begins to run when the power is exercised to create irrevocable future interests, just as it does when the settlor creates a trust of the settlor's own property. This rule makes a lot of sense. If I have a presently exercisable general power, I can take the appointive property for myself whenever I want. There should be no difference between telling the trustee of the trust whose property is the appointive property "transfer the property to me," and after the transfer is accomplished and I own the appointive property in my own name, I create a trust of the appointive property and telling the trustee, "continue to hold the property in a trust the terms of which I will set forth." (Or, telling the trustee to "transfer the property to a new trustee who will hold it on the following terms.") Look at the next example.

Example 12.15: Donee has a presently exercisable general power of appointment over the property in a testamentary trust created by Donee's grandparent. Donee instructs the trustee that Donee is creating a new trust with the same trustee, and under this new trust the trustee is to distribute all of the trust income to Donee's children until the death of the last child to die, at which time the trust terminates and the trustee is to distribute the trust property to the Donee's descendants then living by representation.

The new trust has no problems with the Rule. The condition precedent of survival will be resolved at the end of a life in being.

The rule for future interests created by the exercise of a Group 2 power is not so simple. If the donee of a Group 2 power exercises the power to create future interests subject to conditions that have to be resolved before the perpetuities period runs out, the perpetuities period begins *when the power was created.* This is the relation-back doctrine introduced in Chapter 10. I'll bet you can already see the delightful possibilities. Here's an example that is just like the previous example, except that the trust is created by the exercise of a Group 2 power.

Example 12.16: Donee has a special testamentary power of appointment over the property in a testamentary trust created by Donee's grandparent that allows Donee to appoint to the donee's issue outright or in further trust. Donee properly exercises the power in the Donee's will by creating a new trust with the same trustee. Under the terms of this new trust, the trustee is to distribute all of the trust income to Donee's children until the death of the last child to die, at which time the trust terminates and the trustee is to distribute the trust property to the Donee's descendants then living by representation.

The only difference in applying the Rule to this trust and to the trust in Example 12.15 comes from the application of the relation-back doctrine. In Example 12.16, the perpetuities period begins to run at grandparent's death when the power of appointment was created. The power of appointment is part of the grandparent's testamentary trust, so it was created when the trust was created. Once we know that the perpetuities period began to run at that time, we know that the trust is in big trouble.

It is possible, and in fact in this case it might actually be likely, that Donee's children living at Donee's death when the power is exercised include at least one person who was not alive (or in gestation) when grandparent died. There's the afterborn whose death is like any other remote contingency. Under the usual what-might-happen way the traditional Rule works, we have to assume that the afterborn will be the last of Donee's children to die and that death will happen more than 21 years after the death of any of Donee's children living at grandparent's death when the power was created. The result: the remainder is invalid because the condition precedent of being alive when the trust terminates could be resolved 21 years after the death of an afterborn. Rats.

But maybe things are not quite that bad. Did you notice that analysis of Example 12.16 started with the assumption that at least one of Donee's children was born after the creation of the power, which is when the perpetuities period began to run? Not only did you notice that, but you asked yourself, what if that's not true? What if when Donee dies, all of the Donee's children living at that time were also alive when grandparent died? If that's the case, is the Rule not violated? In that case, the trust will end on the death of a life in being at the time the perpetuities period began to run, which means the condition precedent will be resolved well within the perpetuities period and the contingent remainder is valid. You're right.

The application of the relation-back doctrine is the one aspect of the traditional Rule where we get a break; it's called the **second-look doctrine**. In determining the validity of interests created by the exercise of a Group 2 power of appointment, we get to take into account the facts at the time of exercise. This is the only time we don't look forward from the time the perpetuities period begins to run and ask "what might happen?" Instead, if the facts at the time the power is exercised mean that the Rule will not be violated, it's not violated, even though looking forward from the time the power was created it could have been. In Example 12.16, therefore, if at Donee's death, the time when the power is exercised, all of Donee's living children were also alive at grandparent's death when the power was created, the Rule is not violated. The afterborn isn't there, so all is well.

F A Q

Q: Does the application of the second-look doctrine require that the afterborn never be born?

A: No. The second-look doctrine says that whether the Rule is violated is determined by the facts at the time the Group 2 power is exercised. In Example 12.16, it doesn't matter if a child of Donee were born after the power was created. What matters is whether that person is alive *when the power is exercised.* If all of Donee's children living when the power is exercised were alive when the power was created, the Rule is not violated, no matter what happened in the time between the creation of the power and its exercise.

J. Prohibition on the Undue Suspension of the Power of Alienation

The traditional Rule is not the only legal device that has been devised to exert some control over the ability of property owners to control how that property is used in the future. Remember that the traditional Rule accomplishes its goal by limiting how long the resolution of conditions can be postponed into the future. As we've seen, the prohibition of remote vesting only indirectly limits how long a trust can last. There is another approach to regulating the control long-dead property owners can exercise over the living. This approach is purely statutory, and it limits the time during which the power of alienation can be suspended.

The **power of alienation** is the power to reassemble full fee simple ownership of property in the hands of one person. For example, think of the classic legal life estate created when G conveys Blackacre to A for life, then to B. So long as A can convey the life estate to C, and B can convey the life estate to C, the power to alienate is not suspended because all of the sticks in the bundle of fee simple ownership are in C's hands. If, however, the remainder were created in "the children of A who survive A," then the power of alienation is suspended until A's death because until A's death we can't identify the persons who will be able to convey the remainder interest. Say A has two children, X and Y, at the time the legal life estate and remainder are created. The conveyance by them of their interests to C won't give C fee simple ownership of Blackacre because all they convey to C is a contingent remainder. Ah, you say, but what if G conveys the reversion to C as well? (Remember that when G created a life estate and contingent remainders, G was left with a reversion.) Ah, you think on second thought, that won't do it. After all, X and Y may predecease A, and A's third child, Z, could survive A and end up vesting in possession, and the reversion, of course, vanishes. No matter how you look at it, the power to alienate is suspended during A's lifetime.

The first statute to set a limit to how long the power of alienation can be suspended was part of the Revised Statutes of the State of New York, which became law in 1830. At that time, the traditional Rule Against Perpetuities had not evolved into the Rule we know today (John Chipman Gray would not publish the first edition of his treatise, which was the first definitive statement of the traditional Rule as we know it, until 1886). Several states copied the New York rule in the nineteenth century, but today a prohibition on the undue suspension of the power of alienation is an important rule only in New York. And that's because only New York, it seems, maintains as part of its common law a rule that says if the beneficiaries of a trust cannot transfer their interests in the trust the power to alienate the trust property is suspended, even though the trustee can sell the trust property and reinvest the proceeds in different property. (New York also has enacted the traditional Rule against too remote vesting with some modifications to undo the ridiculous applications of the remorseless application rule. For both rules, the time period is the traditional life in being plus 21 years and a period of gestation.)

At this point, a light bulb should go off. What might prevent a trust beneficiary from transferring his interest in the trust? A spendthrift restriction, that's what. And just to make this more interesting, a New York statutory rule, also descended from the 1830 Revised Statutes, gives every income interest in a trust spendthrift protection unless the settlor of the trust provides otherwise (although the rule almost certainly applies only to mandatory interests). Take this all together, and in New York every trust suspends the power of alienation so long as a mandatory income interest lasts (unless, of course, the settlor has overridden the statutory spendthrift default rule). Here's the classic example of how the New York–style prohibition on the undue suspension of the power of alienation is more restrictive that the traditional Rule prohibiting remote vesting.

Example 12.17: Testator's will devises property to Big Bank in trust to pay the income to Testator's son, S, for life, then to pay the income to S's children for their lives, remainder to Doctors Without Borders.

We'll assume that the income beneficiaries cannot transfer their interests either because this trust is a New York trust and Testator did not override the default spendthrift rule or Testator expressly included a spendthrift restriction. Here's what we get if we apply the traditional Rule to this example:

- The perpetuities period begins to run at the creation of the trust, the date of Testator's death.
- The remainder in the charity is vested in interest from the creation of the trust. There is no condition of any kind attached to the remainder, so we've got no problems with the traditional Rule.
- The life income interest in S vests the moment the trust is created.
- The life income interest in S's children are a class gift. The class of S's children closes physiologically at S's death. There are no conditions attached to this remainder in income for life, so all that is necessary for validity under the traditional Rule is that the class close before the perpetuities period runs. It closes on the death of a life in being, S, so all is well.
- All interests are valid under the traditional Rule.

Now the analysis under the rule prohibiting undue suspension of the power of alienation (using the modern New York rule that limits the allowed period of suspension to the same lives in being plus 21 years and a period of gestation that applies to the traditional Rule):

- The power to alienate is suspended throughout the lifetimes of S and S's children.
- S can have a child after the trust is created. This child is an afterborn.
- Because the afterborn child might die more than 21 years after the death of S and any other lives in being (S's children living at Testator's death), the power to alienate could be suspended for longer than lives in being plus 21 years.
- Just as under the traditional Rule, if it might happen it will happen.
- Just as under the traditional Rule, the all or nothing rule applies to class gifts; if there is a violation as to one member of the class, the entire class gift is invalid.
- The income interest in S's children is invalid, and on S's death the trust property is distributed to the charity.

This example shows you that the rule against the New York version of undue suspension of the power of alienation can actually limit the length of time a trust lasts. This is a more direct limit on the power the dead have over the living than that exerted by the traditional Rule.

F   A   Q

Q: How important is it to understand the New York rule?

A: The New York rule against the undue suspension of the power of alienation is an important and interesting alternative to the traditional Rule as a method of limiting dead-hand control and certainly belongs in any policy discussion of the matter. And of course, if you intend to take the New York bar and practice in New York, understanding the New York rule certainly is important. (So go back and reread this section all you New Yorkers and aspiring New Yorkers!)

K. Results of Invalidity

What happens if an interest is invalid under the traditional Rule or under the anti-suspension of the power of alienation rule? As you've no doubt surmised from the examples we've discussed, the offending interest is treated as if it never existed. Perhaps the most common example is the contingent remainder being invalid under the Rule because the associated condition precedent could still be unresolved when the perpetuities period runs. The remainder just doesn't exist, and when the preceding, valid interests (which are usually income interests) come to an end, the reversion will become possessory. We saw that result in our examples involving our old friend Spoiler, the afterborn. Conditions that can be resolved on the death of an afterborn are resolved too late, and the interests whose vesting is controlled by such conditions are simply crossed out.

There's one application of the rule of invalidity that's not immediately obvious. It's possible for an executory interest to be invalid because resolution of the condition subsequent that must be resolved to determine whether the executory interest will vest by divesting the otherwise vested interest can happen after the perpetuities period has run. Here's an example.

Example 12.18: Testator devises property to Big Bank in trust to pay the income to Testator's son, S, for life, then to pay the income to S's widow for her life, then to terminate the trust and distribute the trust property to S's children, but if no children of S survive the widow, the trust property is distributed to Testator's niece, N.

Let's analyze the interests and apply the traditional Rule:

- S's income interest vests in possession when the trust is created, and that means that S is a life in being when the perpetuities period begins to run.
- The income interest in S's widow will vest in possession, if it ever does, at S's death; S is a life in being; the interest is valid.
- The remainder in S's children is vested subject to divestment. The condition is a classic condition subsequent. The remainder is given to the children and then taken away should the condition come to pass. The remainder in the children is valid under the traditional Rule — vested subject to divestment is vested in interest; it's vested enough. And, of course, the class of S's children closed physiologically at S's death, and S, you remember, is a life in being.
- Since the condition is a condition subsequent, the interest in N is an executory interest; it is invalid because the condition subsequent is resolved on the death of the widow who, of course, is the unborn widow.

Here's the point: not only is the executory interest invalid and simply eliminated from the trust, but *the condition subsequent is also invalid and treated as if it never existed.* That means that the children's remainder is indefeasibly vested. There is no possibility of its being divested even if none of them survive S's widow. If any of the children do die before the widow, that child's remainder interest is transmissible through the child's estate. So remember: if an executory interest is invalid because the condition subsequent that governs its vesting can be resolved beyond the running of the perpetuities period, the condition subsequent is simply crossed out and what was a vested remainder subject to divestment is an indefeasibly vested remainder.

There's another common law doctrine applied to interests that violate the Rule. The wonderfully named **doctrine of infectious invalidity** is used by courts to invalidate otherwise valid interests when the court believes that invalidating those interests better serves the intent of the settlor of the interests. The cases that apply the doctrine often involve quite complex situations. A simple example, however, will do for our purposes.

Example 12.19: Testator devises half of his residuary estate outright to his daughter and devises the other half to X as trustee to pay the income to Testator's son for his life, remainder to son's children who reach the age of 25.

By now you should be able to confidently declare the remainder in the son's children is void. It's a class gift, and although the class will close physiologically on the son's death, the possibility of an afterborn child of the son who might be less than

4 years of age on the death of the last life in being means that the condition precedent of reaching age 25 could be resolved too late. The result is that the entire class gift of the remainder is void. That means that after the son's death, the reversion will become possessory. Who got the reversion? If Testator's only heirs are the son and the daughter, then they each received one-half of the reversion at Testator's death. That, in turn, means that when the son dies, whoever got his share of the reversion will get possession of one-half of the trust property and the daughter or, her successors in interest take possession of the other half of the trust property. If you think about that result, it means that the daughter and her successors eventually get the benefit of three-quarters of the residue of the testator's estate, and the son's successors get the benefit of the remaining quarter.

Faced with this situation, a court could decide that the testator's intent was to benefit his two children and their successors (who are most likely their descendants) equally. The only way to get that result is to invalidate not only the remainder in the son's trust but the income interest in the son *and the gift of the other half of the residue to the daughter.* If the court does that, Testator dies intestate as to the residue of the probate estate, which then goes outright to the son and the daughter, one-half each. Striking down the entire residuary devise in the will is a pretty drastic step, and courts use the infectious invalidity doctrine only when they are truly convinced that the settlor of the invalid interest would rather have the entire arrangement fail than have the overall estate plan distorted by invalidating only those interests that run afoul of the Rule.

L. Limitations on Accumulations

There is another limitation on what sort of interests the settlor of a trust can create that is related to the Rule Against Perpetuities. This rule limits the length of time a trustee can be authorized to accumulate income. To make sure we understand what's going on here, we have to remember what trust income is — it's what the trust property produces as opposed to an increase in value of the property. The income produced by common stock is dividends; the income from bonds is interest; the income from real property is rent. Usually the trustee pays the income out to the current beneficiaries of the trust, and we've talked about how today it is very common to give the trustee discretion to decide how much income to pay to a beneficiary (with or without the settlor of the trust including in the trust terms directions to guide the trustee in making the decision).

The trustee's discretionary power to distribute income can include the option not to distribute all of the trust income for a certain period (usually a year). The income not distributed is **accumulated**. It can be accumulated for later distribution to the income beneficiaries or it could be added to the principal of the trust and produce more income for eventual distribution. In the extreme case, the settlor of the trust could instruct the trustee to accumulate all of the income for the entire term of the trust, presumably creating a really big payoff for the remainder beneficiaries.

The history of rules governing accumulations begins with the will of a wealthy Englishman, Peter Thellusson, who died in 1797. Thellusson's will directed that most of his estate, with the addition of all of the income the property earned during the lifetimes of his nine male descendants living at his death, would be distributed only after all nine were dead to his eldest male descendant living at that time. Peter's unhappy family challenged the will. The highest legal authority in England, the

House of Lords, held in 1805 that the will was valid.[1] The remainder was indeed contingent, but it would vest at the end of a life in being — the death of the last to die of the nine male descendants living at Thellusson's death — so the Rule Against Perpetuities was not violated. The Lords also held that under the common law, the direction to accumulate was valid because it did not extend beyond the perpetuities period. It would end at the same time the remainder vested.

The terms of Peter Thellusson's will, however, caused something of a popular outcry against the possibility of huge fortunes being accumulated for decades before finally coming into the hands of a single, now very rich, person. Parliament duly passed legislation severely limiting the ability to accumulate income. Both the Lords' decision in the will case and the Parliamentary act came after American independence, so for decades there was uncertainty about whether American common law included a rule allowing accumulations for the period of the Rule Against Perpetuities or some other rule. In the meantime, many states passed legislation dealing with accumulations, usually limiting accumulations to the period of the Rule Against Perpetuities.

In the rush to repeal or at least make ineffective the Rule Against Perpetuities by lengthening the perpetuities period to centuries, accumulations have been overlooked. Statutes dealing with accumulations have not been amended or repealed in coordination with changes in the perpetuities law, and where the "accumulations for no longer than lives in being plus 21 years" is common law, legislative alteration of the Rule Against Perpetuities leaves the law regarding accumulations unchanged.

You might ask, how can a trust that complies with the Rule Against Perpetuities violate a rule that limits accumulations to the classic perpetuities period? The same way the trust can violate the rule against undue suspension of the power of alienation. Remember Example 12.17 we used to illustrate the suspension rule? All we have to do is change the terms of the trust from mandatory payout of income to discretion in the trustee to distribute income and to accumulate what is not distributed.

Example 12.20: Testator's will devises property to Big Bank in trust to pay annually to Testator's son, S, for life so much or all of the income for the current year as the trustee shall determine in its sole discretion, at the end of every year adding to principal income not distributed, and after S's death to pay annually to S's children so much or all of the income for the current year as the trustee shall determine in its sole discretion, at the end of every year adding to principal income not distributed, and at the death of the last to die of S's children, the trust shall terminate and the trustee shall distribute the trust property, including accumulated income, to Doctors Without Borders.

As we've already seen, the Rule Against Perpetuities is perfectly happy with this trust. S's interest vests at Testator's death, the class of S's children closes at S's death, and S is a life in being. There is no condition precedent to the gift to S's children, so their gift is okay too. The charity is vested at the moment of Testator's death, so it's safe as well. However, the power to accumulate will last throughout the lifetimes of S's children (just like the power to alienate was suspended during the children's lifetimes so long as their interests were inalienable in Example 12.17). S could have a child after Testator's death, and now the power to accumulate will endure throughout the lifetime of the afterborn. Disaster. The result depends on governing

---

[1]Thellusson v. Woodford, 32 Eng. Rep. 1030 (Ch. 1805).

law. In some states, the power to accumulate is completely void; in others, it's void only for the period after the period runs out (that's the position of Restatement (Second) of Property § 2.2).

M. Curative Doctrines

Clearly, the Rule Against Perpetuities can destroy an estate plan because the consequences of a violation are overwhelming. Invalidating remainders and especially class gifts can completely rearrange the distribution of significant amounts of property. So in spite of the classic position that the Rule is to be remorselessly applied, courts and legislatures have departed from that position and taken various approaches to moderating the severity of the Rule.

Some courts have ignored the classic prohibitions and construed or even modified language to prevent a violation. For example, consider a class gift that violates the Rule only because of a condition precedent of reaching age 25.

Example 12.21: A devises property to T in trust to pay the income to B for life, remainder to B's children who reach the age of 25.

Remember that the only problem is that the age contingency is greater than 21. A court not tied to the strictest view of the Rule might be willing to reduce the age contingency to 21 on the theory that the testator would greatly prefer that to the destruction of the entire remainder. Or consider an unborn widow situation in which the surviving spouse is the same person the decedent was married to at the time of the creation of the future interest contingent on surviving the widow.

Example 12.22: A devises property to T in trust to pay the income to A's daughter, D, for life, then to her surviving spouse for life, remainder to D's descendants living at the surviving spouse's death by representation.

From the time A executed A's will to the time of A's death, D has been married to the same person. A court could construe "surviving spouse" to refer to D's current spouse, solving the problem.

(1) Statutory Limited Fixes

Unfortunately, perhaps, judicial intervention to prevent violations of the Rule through construing a fix to particular problems has been relatively rare. Some states have not waited for the courts and have passed legislation dealing with the more bizarre applications of the traditional what-might-happen approach. For instance, there are statutes reducing age contingencies to 21 if doing so will avoid a violation (which would solve the problem with the class gift in Example 12.21); defining all surviving spouses to be lives in being at the time the perpetuities period begins to run (ending unborn widow problems); creating a conclusive presumption that all administrative contingencies will be resolved within 21 years of the time the perpetuities period begins to run; creating conclusive presumptions about when persons can and cannot have children (ending fertile octogenarian problems, at least for females, and precocious toddler problems for both men and women); and even directing courts to construe language to avoid perpetuities problems.

Note that these statutory approaches leave the Rule essentially intact by addressing only the more absurd applications of its requirements. Only after determining the validity of a future interest under the traditional Rule can we ask if a specific statutory provision solves the problem. There have been attempts to address the difficulties with the Rule more comprehensively.

(2) Wait-and-See

The first attempt to remake perpetuities law, at least in the United States, was the "wait-and-see" approach, adopted by statute in Pennsylvania in 1947. This fundamental change in the Rule replaced the what-might-happen approach of the traditional Rule with a what-does-happen approach. Wait-and-see became the leading approach to reforming the Rule when it was adopted by the Restatement (Second) of Property § 1.3. Under the Restatement version of wait-and-see, if an interest is invalid under the Rule as traditionally applied, it is *not* void from the time of creation; we do not pretend it was never created. Instead, we identify persons who can be measuring lives and then wait to see if the nonvested interest does indeed vest within 21 years of the death of one of those persons.

Clearly, identifying those potential measuring lives is the whole game when it comes to wait-and-see. As we learned when we examined the traditional Rule, there may be *someone* alive when the potentially invalid interest is created within 21 years of whose death we can be sure that the interest will have vested or failed, but if we cannot identify that person, she cannot be the life that validates the interest. So to make wait-and-see work, we have to define the group in which the validating life must be found. Restatement (Second) § 1.3(2) identifies those lives as

- the settlor of the interest if the perpetuities period begins to run in his or her lifetime (this would almost have to involve the creation of an irrevocable lifetime trust or a legal life estate and remainder in real property by deed);
- everyone who is a beneficiary of the property in which the nonvested interest exists (if the number of beneficiaries is not "unreasonable") and the parents and grandparents of the beneficiaries living when the perpetuities period begins to run;
- the donee of a power of appointment alive when the period begins to run if the nonvested interest we're concerned with could be affected by the exercise of the power of appointment.

To illustrate the workings of wait-and-see, let's use the classic class gift example.

Example 12.23: A devises property to T in trust to pay the income to B for life, remainder to B's children who reach the age of 25.

Under the traditional what-might-happen approach, we know that the remainder in B's children is invalid because at B's death an afterborn child of B could be less than 4 years of age, and we cannot be certain that the child will or will not reach 25, fulfilling the condition precedent within 21 years of the death of any person we can identify. Under wait-and-see, however, B, all of B's children alive at A's death — the persons having beneficial interests in the trust property — and their living parents and grandparents are all measuring lives. So long as all of B's children reach 25 or die before that age within 21 years of the death of the last to die of the measuring lives, the remainder is valid. The odds of that happening, of course, are pretty good. First, B may not have a child within 4 years of B's death, and all of B's children will turn 25 or die trying within 21 years of B's death, and B is the measuring life. If B does have a child within 4 years of B's death, we wait to see if that child turns 21 or dies before that age within 21 years of the death of the last to die of all of the measuring lives. Again, if B has other children who were living when A died, the odds are that the afterborn will reach 25 or die before that age, within 21 years of the death of the last to die of B's children living when the interest was created at A's death.

As you can see, it is likely that everything will be resolved at B's death. If there really is an afterborn child of B under 4 at B's death, everyone will indeed have to wait and see whether or not the afterborn reaches 25 or dies before that age within 21 years of the death of one of the identified measuring lives. There will be a period of uncertainty, but presumably that's a small price to pay to prevent invalidation of interests that turn out to meet the requirements of the rule.

(3) Uniform Statutory Rule against Perpetuities (USRAP)

The Uniform Law Commission's trust and estates experts tried their hands at perpetuities reform in the 1980s, and in 1986 the Commission approved a uniform act creating a statutory rule against perpetuities. The USRAP occasioned a good deal of controversy but nevertheless had a fair number of enactments (although some of those were later repealed when the states involved further "reformed" their perpetuities law by simply abolishing the Rule).

Under USRAP, any nonvested interest has 90 years to vest. If after that time the interest is still not yet vested, a court may reform the interest to best carry out the intent of the person who created it. We can describe this as "90 years of wait-and-see and a judicial fix." More precisely, an interest is valid if at the time it is created it is certain to vest or fail with 21 years of the end of a life in being (in other words, the interest is valid under the traditional Rule) or if it vests or terminates within 90 years of its creation (UPC § 2-901(a); USRAP has been incorporated into the UPC, and we'll cite to those sections). Let's use our all-purpose example.

Example 12.24: A devises property to T in trust to pay the income to B for life, remainder to B's children who reach the age of 25.

We know that the remainder is invalid under the traditional Rule because of the possibility that B will be survived by an afterborn child under the age of 4. So under the first prong of USRAP, the remainder is invalid. That means that it falls under the second prong, and the remainder *is* valid if within 90 years of A's death (the time of the creation of the nonvested remainder) all of B's children have reached 25 or failed to do so. The odds of that happening are pretty good. If we assume that B has no children living at A's death and dies immediately after the birth of B's last child, B's death must come more than 65 years after A's death if there is to be any chance of violating the 90-year rule. Even if B is 1 year old when A dies, if the question of the remainder's vesting is still going to be open 90 years after A's death B must have a child when B is at least 66 years old. Possible, but not likely. All in all, few interests that do not satisfy the traditional test of the Rule when created will fail the 90-year test. Those that do are subject to reformation by a court "in the manner that most closely approximates the . . . manifested plan of distribution [of the settlor of the interest]" (UPC § 2-903(1)).

F   A   Q

Q: Why 90 years?

A: The drafters of USRAP explain the choice of the 90-year period in the general comment that precedes UPC § 2-901. They analyzed four hypothetical families "deemed to be representative of actual families" and determined that the youngest descendant of the settlor of a nonvested future interest at the settlor's death is about 6 years of age. The average remaining life expectancy of that 6-year old is 69 years, which when added to the 21 years of the traditional Rule equals 90 years.

(4) Restatement (Third) of Property

The very last part of the Restatement (Third) of Property includes a new rule against perpetuities. Section 27.1 states that a trust is subject to modification by a court if it does not terminate on or before the expiration of the perpetuity period. The period expires when the last measuring life dies, and the measuring lives are the settlor and the beneficiaries related to the settlor who are not more than two generations younger than the settlor and any beneficiaries who are not related to the settlor who are not more than two generations younger than the settlor. The measuring lives do not have to be alive when the trust is created. The idea is to limit the duration of trusts to two generations, the lives of the children and grandchildren of the settlor.

Example 12.25: Testator devises property to trustees named in the will to distribute income and principal among Testator's descendants living from time to time in the trustees' discretion. The trust shall terminate at the death of the last to die of Testator's children and grandchildren, and the trustees then shall distribute the trust property to the descendants of Testator then living by representation.

Under the traditional Rule Against Perpetuities, the contingent remainder in Testator's descendants is invalid because it could vest on the death of an afterborn grandchild. It would be valid only if none of Testator's children survived the testator. Then all of the grandchildren would be lives in being. In addition, the trustees' discretionary power violates the Rule because it can last longer than lives in being plus

21 years. Under the new scheme of Restatement (Third), the trust is completely valid because it ends when all of the beneficiaries who are one or two generations younger than the testator are dead. It doesn't matter when the beneficiaries are born. All that matters is their degree of relationship to the settlor.

BENEFICIARIES NOT RELATED TO THE SETTLOR

It's very easy to identify the measuring lives when the beneficiaries are related to the grantor: the settlor's children and grandchildren, nieces and nephews, great-nieces and -nephews, first cousins once and twice removed are all measuring lives. If the beneficiaries include persons who are not related to the grantor (or to the grantor's spouse or domestic partner, who is always in the same generation as the grantor), those beneficiaries are assigned to a generation based on the number of years between their births and the birth of the settlor. The scheme is the same as that used for generation assignment for purposes of the generation-skipping transfer tax (IRC § 2651(d)) (discussed in Chapter 17). A person born no later than 12.5 years after the settlor is in the settlor's generation, and a person born 12.5 years after the settlor but not more than 37.5 years after the settlor is one generation younger than the settlor (equivalent to the settlor's children). After that, every 25 years marks a new generation, so the second generation younger than the settlor includes persons born up to 62.5 years after the settlor.

If the trust does not end when the measuring lives are all dead, under § 27.2 the trust is subject to judicial modification. The result of the modification must be as close as possible to the settlor's original plan and must be within the perpetuities period. In the example above, let's say that under the terms of the trust the trust will terminate when the settlor has no living descendant, at which time the trustee is to distribute the trust property to a named charity. (This example is closely based on § 27.2 cmt. c, illus. 1.) When the last of the settlor's grandchildren die, any living descendant of the settlor and the trustee have standing to ask a court to modify the trust. Because the trust has lasted for the maximum period (the lives of the beneficiaries who are no more than two generations younger than the settlor, whenever born), the modification must result in the termination of the trust and the distribution of the trust property outright. The only real task for the court is to determine who is to receive the trust property. Given the terms of the trust, it is pretty clear that the property should be distributed by representation to the settlor's descendants living at the time of termination (the death of the settlor's last living grandchild). Of course, if that last grandchild to die were the last living descendant of the settlor, the trustee would distribute the trust property to the charity named in the trust.

Q: What happens under the Restatement scheme if after the perpetuities period runs no one who has standing asks a court to modify a trust that, by its terms, violates the Rule?

A: It's not clear. It seems that the drafters of the Restatement believe that the certainty of getting outright ownership of at least some part of the trust property will be incentive enough for a beneficiary to bring a modification proceeding. In addition, because the trustee has standing, it may be that the trustee would violate a fiduciary duty by failing to bring a proceeding to modify a trust that the trustee should know violates the Rule Against Perpetuities.

Of course, these provisions of Restatement (Third) of Property do not have the force of law. Whether this new rule against perpetuities does become law depends on whether a legislature enacts statutes that implement these provisions. Given the radical change from traditional perpetuities law embodied in these provisions, a court is unlikely to adopt them as a matter of case law.

(5) Saving Clauses

We can't leave the topic of perpetuities reform without mentioning what is probably the most common type of reform, which is really self-help — the inclusion of a **saving clause** in the document creating interests subject to the Rule. A saving clause will require any nonvested interests to vest when the perpetuities period runs out. If the interests are interests in a trust, the clause will require that the trust terminate and the trust property be distributed to the current beneficiaries. There are two ways to define the time when the perpetuities period runs out. The saving clause can refer to "21 years after death of the last to die of the descendants" of the person who created the interests living when the interest was created. The other is to define the period as running out 21 years after the death of the last to die of a group of persons living when the interest is created. These persons need not have any relationship to the property in which the nonvested interest is created, but must not be so great in number that they cannot be reasonably ascertained — "21 years after the death of the last to die of everyone listed in the Manhattan phone book on the day the interest is created" isn't going to work. While this alternative is probably more written about than actually used, it might work if you used the descendants of a famous person (who hasn't been dead too long) living at the time the perpetuities period begins to run.

It is also possible to write a saving clause into a trust designed to last for the maximum period allowed under the Rule. Here's the classic example that can be used by the settlor of such a trust who has living descendants.

Example 12.26: "I give my residuary estate to my trustee named in my will and my trustee shall distribute income and principal among my descendants living from time to time as my trustee shall determine in my trustee's sole discretion until 21 years after the death of the last to die of my descendants living at my death. At that time the trust shall terminate and my trustee shall distribute the trust property to my descendants then living, by representation."

This trust not only satisfies the Rule Against Perpetuities, but also satisfies the rule against the undue suspension of the power of alienation and a rule that limits accumulations to the perpetuities period. The contingent remainder in the testator's issue (remember, it's contingent because there is a condition precedent of survival to the

Sidebar

THE "ROYAL LIVES CLAUSE"

A saving clause that relies on a designated group of persons living when the interest is created is sometimes called a "royal lives clause." In a case decided by the English Court of Chancery, *In re Villar*, [1929] 1 Ch. 243, the testator created what amounted to a contingent remainder in the testator's descendants living 21 years after the death of all of the descendants of Queen Victoria living at the testator's death. There were some 120 descendants of the queen living at that time, and the court held that the remainder was valid. That's a lot of lives, but at least there are persons whose jobs involve keeping track of all of the members of the British aristocracy. Probably most commentators believe that the court in *Villar* should have found that the designated lives were too numerous, but the holding illustrates two important points: (1) designating a group of measuring lives is fine so long as (2) they are not so numerous that it's impractical to keep track of them.

distribution date) vests at the very moment the perpetuities period runs out, which is also when the trustee's discretionary power — also subject to the rule — ends. Because the trust ends when the period runs out, the power to alienate ceases to be suspended just as the perpetuities period runs out, and of course accumulation of trust income ends then as well.

N. The Future of the Rule against Perpetuities

The cynic might say, "What future?" The Rule, at least the classic Rule against too remote vesting, has been repealed in more than 15 states. The argument for repeal often goes something like this: the Rule is about making sure that property is not kept out of the market; in other words, the Rule is really about restraints on alienation. Although the law of trusts once severely limited the kinds of property in which a trustee could invest the trust property, today the law pretty much allows a trustee to invest in anything an individual could invest in so long as the trustee gets good results for the trust. Therefore, there is no need to limit the duration of trusts because the market for investments will operate just fine whether or not property is held in trust. Sometimes this argument is coupled with an argument disparaging the Rule as a device to prevent the evasion of feudal taxes, which is completely irrelevant in the modern world (and of course links the Rule in some vague way with taxes (always disliked) and feudalism (also disliked, although probably no one is quite certain why).

Repeal can mean a straightforward repeal of the Rule or a big increase in the period of time that can pass before an interest must vest — 360 years in one case and 1,000 in another. Usually the repeal does not apply to interests created in real property. The difficulty of conveying good title to land in which there are contingent interests — basically, all of the potential takers must be represented, and that requires appointing a guardian to represent their interests and a court to approve a sale as fair to everyone involved — means that unvested interests in real property really do act as restraints on alienation.

Several theories explain why repeal of the Rule, whatever the articulated reasons for it, has become such a popular legislative activity. Because it is possible to create a trust that is forever exempt from the generation-skipping transfer tax (discussed in Chapter 17), there has been pressure from estate planners and banks that hope to act as trustees for perpetual trusts to allow trusts to last "forever" so that the tax savings can be maximized. In addition, changing societal attitudes toward the accumulation of wealth may simply be making it more acceptable to create a pot of money that will support a person's descendants "forever." This second reason is related to the appearance of the self-settled spendthrift or asset protection trust. If you can create a trust that will be safe from the demands of the creditors of the beneficiaries including yourself, why not make the trust last forever?

The arguments for repeal of the Rule, however, never really deal with another rationale for the Rule: limiting the control of the dead hand. Although expressed at different times in different ways, one of the arguments in favor of the Rule has always been that it puts a necessary limit on how long a dead owner of property can dictate how that property is used — or, as we've mentioned before, on how long the dead can keep the living on an allowance. While there has been pushback against repeal, usually based on the argument that the control of the dead hand must be limited, it hasn't made much of an impression. Time will tell.

SUMMARY

■ The classic common law Rule Against Perpetuities requires that vesting in interest of a future interest occur within a set period of time measured from the creation of the interest. Vested in interest means that conditions precedent and subsequent are resolved and that open classes are closed.

■ The interest is valid only if it is possible to show that vesting in interest will occur no later than 21 years after the death of a life in being at the time of the creation of the interest, plus a period of gestation. In deciding whether the Rule is satisfied, the decision must be made looking forward from the creation of the interest, and no account is taken of actual events.

■ If an interest is void, it is void ab initio, from the moment of its creation, and is simply excised from the instrument that created it.

■ The classic common law Rule has been the victim of extremely doctrinaire application. The classic law of perpetuities is full of remarkable creatures like the precocious toddler, the fertile octogenarian, the unborn widow, and other oddities, all of which draw their vitality from the principle that in dealing with perpetuities, what *might* happen must be assumed to be *certain* to happen.

■ The common law includes limits on accumulation of trust income. Statutes exist that limit the suspension of the power of alienation. This alternative perpetuities regime directly limits the duration of trusts by requiring that someone have fee simple absolute ownership of the trust property at the end of the classic lives in being plus 21 years period.

■ Many attempts have been made to simplify the application of the classic common law Rule. Statutes have eliminated many bizarre assumptions that make the application of the Rule inane, provided that validity is judged on facts not assumptions, and replaced the classic period with a fixed number of years. Restatement (Third) of Property creates a new perpetuities regime that demands that trusts terminate after they have lasted for two generations.

■ Inclusion of a saving clause in a document creating interests subject to the Rule will prevent any violations.

■ All of the above is becoming ever more obsolete as more and more states abolish the Rule Against Perpetuities, at least as it applies to trusts. This movement is gaining ground, and it remains to be seen if the Rule has a future.

CONNECTIONS

Rule Against Perpetuities and Trusts (Beneficiaries Interests)

The Rule Against Perpetuities to some degree dictates the interests that can be given to beneficiaries of trusts. To the extent that the Rule is a consideration, the creation of contingent remainders and executory interests is disfavored (Chapter 9).

Rule Against Perpetuities and Trusts (Creation)

While the Rule does not directly limit the duration of a trust, the vesting requirement indirectly requires trusts to come to an end (Chapter 8). Both the prohibition on undue suspension of the power of alienation and the new rule against perpetuities in Restatement (Third) of Property directly limit the duration of trusts.

Rule Against Perpetuities and Powers of Appointment

Exercises of special powers of appointment and general testamentary powers of appointment that create future interests (Chapter 10) are constrained by the relation-back rule, which governs the application of the Rule Against Perpetuities to those future interests and starts the perpetuities running when the power was created.

Rule Against Perpetuities and Future Interests

The Rule Against Perpetuities exercises a good deal of influence on the law of future interests. Perhaps the most important example is the constructional rule that a condition precedent of survival to the time of distribution is never presumed but must be expressly stated (unless the future interest is created in a multigenerational class), thus limiting the creation of contingent remainders that are subject to the Rule (Chapter 7).

Rule Against Perpetuities and Wealth Transfer Taxes

As explained in Chapter 17, the workings of the generation-skipping transfer tax exemption amount has encouraged the creation of perpetual trusts and is a major contributor to state legislation abolishing or severely limiting the effect of the Rule Against Perpetuities.

Protection of the Family 13

These days we don't need family around to fend off woolly mammoths or blow on sparks while we rub two sticks together. But that doesn't mean

OVERVIEW

we don't still have strong bonds with our families. The protective instincts we feel for our kin are written into the law of wills and trusts too, in its treatment of surviving spouses, children, and a few other close relatives. You've learned already how much freedom our legal system gives property owners to dispose of their property as they wish at death. In this chapter, you'll see, on the other hand, that the law stops short of turning a completely blind eye to a decedent's spouse and descendants who, for one reason or another, were not provided for at decedent's death.

A. **PROTECTIONS DURING THE PROBATE PROCESS**

   1. Allowances
   2. Homestead
   3. Exempt Property

B. **PROTECTION FROM UNINTENTIONAL DISINHERITANCE**

   1. Children Omitted from a Parent's Will
   2. One Spouse Omitted from the Other's Will

C. **PROTECTION FOR THE SPOUSE FROM INTENTIONAL DISINHERITANCE: THE ELECTIVE SHARE**

   1. A Bit of History
   2. Modern Elective Share

A. Protections During the Probate Process

Whether a decedent is testate or intestate, administration of the estate takes some time. Two things relevant to the protection of the decedent's family can happen during the probate process. The first is designed to support the family until administration of the estate is complete, and the second is designed to ensure that certain property always goes to family members no matter what. In other words, the decedent's family receives these entitlements regardless of the extent of the decedent's debts.

(1) Allowances

Many state statutes allow the probate court to order the personal representative to pay an allowance out of the probate estate to the decedent's immediate family. The UPC version, § 2-404, states that the decedent's surviving spouse and minor children "whom the decedent was obligated to support" are entitled to "a reasonable allowance in money out of the estate for their maintenance during the period of administration." The only time limit on the payments applies when the probate estate is insolvent. In that case, the allowance may be paid for only one year.

(2) Homestead

Some states have a **homestead allowance** that makes the decedent's residence immune from creditor's claims. Florida's is particularly generous, keeping out of the hands of creditors a homestead of unlimited value so long as it passes to a relative of the decedent (and the list of eligible relatives is long). Other states model their homestead allowances on UPC § 2-402, which provides a very modest allowance that has nothing to do with the decedent owning a residence (the amount in brackets is $22,500). It belongs to the decedent's surviving spouse and, if none, to the decedent's minor children and adult children who were dependent on the decedent (usually because of a disability). This is an entitlement and therefore requires no exercise of discretion by the personal representative or the probate court.

The purpose of the UPC's homestead allowance is to facilitate the administration of estates so small that claims of a surviving spouse and dependent children should prevail over the decedent's creditors (UPC § 2-402 cmt.). States with much more generous homestead exemptions, especially where the exemption is a provision in the state constitution, seem to have a different policy reason for the exemption. In those situations, the policy seems to be one of strong protection against creditors no matter what amounts are involved. On the other hand, some states have no homestead exemption at all.

Q: Are these family protection exemptions later deducted in some way from the spouse's or children's share of the estate?

A: Generally, and certainly under the UPC, the answer is no. These special exemptions come "off the top" of the decedent's probate property, and what's left passes under the intestacy statute or will after debts and expenses are paid.

(3) Exempt Property

The third type of family protection available during probate exempts certain types of property from creditors' claims, at least up to some maximum value. The UPC provision, § 2-403, limits the exemption to $15,000 "in household furnishing, automobiles, furnishings, appliances, and personal effects." The decedent's surviving spouse is entitled to the exemption; if there is no surviving spouse, the decedent's children are entitled (and they do not have to be minors or dependents of the decedent).

States have different lists of exempt property and different maximum values. Behind all of the statutes, however, is a policy decision that certain types of property are so important to the decedent's surviving immediate family that creditors cannot reach them.

Sidebar

EXEMPT PROPERTY STATUTES AND HISTORY

Exempt property statutes have a long history, and often the list of exempt property has a distinctly antique ring to it. Here's some of the list in N.Y. Est., Powers & Trust Law § 5-3.1, amended in 2010: housekeeping utensils, musical instruments, a sewing machine, household furniture and appliances, "electronic and photographic devices," "the family bible or other religious books, family pictures, books, computer tapes, discs, and software, DVDs, CDs, audio tapes, record albums, and other electronic storage devices," "domestic and farm animals with their necessary food for sixty days, farm machinery, one tractor and one lawn tractor," a motor vehicle, and money and other personal property, to a maximum value of $92,500. The list is a wonderful combination of the nineteenth and the twenty-first centuries: note the *farm* tractor, the ultimate symbol of rural life, and the *lawn* tractor, the symbol of suburban life.

B. Protection from Unintentional Disinheritance

(1) Children Omitted from a Parent's Will

Nothing prevents a parent from disinheriting a child (or, for that matter, an adult child from disinheriting a parent). However, the law—or more precisely, legal systems descended from the English common law—usually have **pretermitted child statutes** that protect a child against what is regarded as unintentional disinheritance. The most limited form of statute applies to children born after the execution of the parent's will. Other statutes apply to any child of the decedent whenever born, and a small number of statutes apply not only to children but to all of the decedent's descendants.

Usually the omitted child receives her intestate share of the decedent's estate. That's an easy-to-apply remedy, but it can badly distort the decedent's estate plan.

Example 13.1: Husband and Wife have two children. They have reciprocal wills that leave everything to the survivor and, if the spouse does not survive, to the trustee of a testamentary trust, income to "my children, Ann and Bernard, until the youngest is 30 years of age." The trust then terminates, and the trust property is distributed to Ann and Bernard, to the issue of a child who has died before 30, and, if none, to the other sibling or his or her issue. The trustee is also named as guardian of the children's persons. After Wife gives birth to the couple's third child, Charles, Husband and Wife are involved in a car accident. Wife dies at the scene. Husband survives Wife by 120 hours and then dies.

Wife's probate estate thus passes to Husband and becomes part of his probate estate that passes to the trust. Because Charles is not mentioned in Husband's will, he is "pretermitted" and is entitled to his intestate share of his father's estate (1/3) while the other 2/3 is held in trust for his siblings. It is highly likely that the named guardian of the person will indeed be confirmed by the appropriate court as the guardian of the person for all three children, but while the guardian is also the trustee of the trust of which the two older children are beneficiaries, Charles's intestate share will be managed by a guardian of the property, with all the difficulties that involves. Whatever is left will be distributed to Charles when he's 18, even though the trust for his siblings lasts until the youngest is 30. In addition, the trustee (who, remember, is guardian of the person of all three children but not likely to be the guardian of Charles's property) has no say in how the guardianship property is used for Charles and may face difficult problems in making sure that the trust is used solely for the benefit of the two children who are beneficiaries.

As you can see, the operation of a pretermitted child statute can derange carefully made plans to care for surviving children. The UPC statute, § 2-302, tries to preserve the testator's estate plan by giving the omitted child (who must be born or adopted after the execution of the testator's will) a share in what the will gives the testator's other children. In Example 13.1, Charles would become a beneficiary of the trust. If the testator has children when the will is executed and the will gives them nothing, an afterborn child will receive nothing under the statute. An afterborn omitted child receives his intestate share only if the testator has no children when the will is executed. Even in that case, the omitted afterborn child will receive nothing if the will "devised all or substantially all of the estate to the other parent of the omitted child" and that parent survives the testator and is entitled to take under the will.

F   A   Q

Q: Can a child *en ventre sa mere* when its parent executes his will be an omitted child?

A: Yes. This is one of the few instances where the usual rule that once the child is born alive the child's legal existence goes back to the time of conception is not applied. Why? Because the child is better off, that is, the child will get the benefit of the pretermitted child statute if his legal existence *does not* start at the time of conception but rather at the time of birth.

No matter what the will provides, under the UPC the omitted afterborn child receives nothing from the probate estate if (1) it appears from the will that the omission was intentional (§ 2-302(b)(1), or (2)) the testator provided for the child by a transfer outside the will, which the testator intended to be in lieu of a devise under the will (§ 2-302(b)(2)). That intent can be shown by the testator's statements or it can be "reasonably inferred from the amount of the transfer or other evidence." The provisions UPC § 2-302 makes for pretermitted children really are default provisions.

F A Q

Q: What sort of transfer outside of the parent's will would satisfy UPC § 2-302(b)(2)?

A: Any number of options are available: making the child a beneficiary of a life insurance policy on the parent's life, a Totten trust, or another payable on death arrangement; making the child a beneficiary of a lifetime trust created and funded by the parent; or making an outright transfer to a custodial account under the Uniform Transfers to Minors Act.

F A Q

Q: Does a pretermitted child statute apply to a will substitute like a revocable lifetime trust?

A: No statute refers to anything other than the testator's will, and the few cases there are have refused to extend the pretermitted child concept to will substitutes. Interestingly, even Restatement (Third) of Property, which generally takes the position that wills rules should apply to revocable trusts that are will substitutes, discusses only wills in § 9.6 dealing with omitted children and simply describes cases refusing to extend the statutory provisions to will substitutes in item 17 of the reporter's note.

When it comes to determining whether the pretermitted child has been intentionally omitted from the will and thus cannot take advantage of the statute, existing statutes can be divided into two groups, named for the states where the type of statute was first enacted. Missouri-style statutes look only to the words of the will to decide whether the omission was intentional. Massachusetts-style statutes allow the use of extrinsic evidence to answer the question. UPC § 2-305(b)(1) says that the statute does not apply "if it appears from the will" that the omission was intentional, thus barring the use of extrinsic evidence. However, § 2-305(b)(2) expressly allows the use of extrinsic evidence to decide if a nontestamentary transfer to the child was intended by the testator to be "in lieu of" a testamentary provision. Restatement (Third) of Property § 9.6 comment i says that unless a statute provides otherwise, extrinsic evidence may be used to determine if an omission was intentional. (The reporter's note to § 9.6 contains an extensive discussion of the various state statutes and some important cases. According to the note, only the District of Columbia and Wyoming do not have pretermitted child statutes.)

FORCED HEIRSHIP

Giving parents free reign to disinherit their children is one way in which legal systems descended from English common law differ from the civil law–based systems of continental Europe, which are descended from Roman law. Statutes in civil law countries give children a "forced share" of the estate of their deceased parent. In the United States, only Louisiana, with its strong historical connection to the civil law, forbids the *intentional* disinheritance of a testator's children. The provision is constitutional and was last amended in 1995 to give forced heirship rights only to the testator's children 23 years or younger or who cannot care for their own persons or manage their own property because of lack of mental capacity or physical infirmity. The forced share is one-fourth of the testator's estate if there is one forced heir; if there is more than one, they share one-half of the estate equally (La. Const. art. XII, § 5.)

There is one provision that is very common and is included in UPC § 2-302(c). If the testator failed to provide for a child in the will because the testator incorrectly believed the child to be dead, the child is treated as an afterborn omitted child.

(2) One Spouse Omitted from the Other's Will

Omitted spouse statutes vary a good deal. Some simply revoke any existing will when the testator marries unless the will provides for the possibility of marriage. The results under statutes like these can be bizarre.

Example 13.2: Testator executes a will three days before she marries that gives her residuary estate to the person she is going to marry. If the will says nothing about the forthcoming marriage — suppose the residuary clause simply says "I give my residuary estate to X" — the marriage will revoke the will, and if the testator does not reexecute it before she dies, she will die intestate and her surviving spouse may not be her sole heir.

Modern statutes still protect the omitted spouse but do not revoke the will. Instead they award the omitted spouse the intestate share to which the spouse is entitled and leave the will intact. What's owed the spouse is like a debt, and it is satisfied first by whatever the will gives the surviving spouse, and then the devises in the will abate as they would whenever debts have to be paid. This is the approach of UPC § 2-301, which is similar to the omitted child provisions of § 2-302. Whenever the testator dies with a will executed before the marriage, the surviving spouse is entitled to his intestate share. There are three exceptions: (1) it appears "from the will or other evidence that the will was made in contemplation of the marriage"; (2) the will "expresses the intention" that it continue to be effective in spite of the testator's subsequent marriage; or (3) the testator provided for the spouse by a transfer outside of the will. Just as in the omitted child statute, that intent can be shown by the testator's statements, be "reasonably inferred" from the value of the transfer, or shown by "other evidence." In other words, extrinsic evidence is admissible on the question of whether the will was made "in contemplation of marriage" and on the effect of the nontestamentary transfer.

Another very important feature of UPC § 2-301 resembles the provisions in the omitted child statute that are designed to minimize disruption of the testator's estate plan. Even though the surviving spouse is entitled to the benefit of the statute, the spouse's entitlement is limited to the intestate share in that portion of the probate estate that is not devised to a child of the testator born before the marriage to the surviving spouse and who is not a child of the surviving spouse or to a descendant of such a child or which passes to a descendant of such a child through the operation of the anti-lapse statute (UPC § 2-603) or the operation of the statute abolishing the no-residue-of-a-residue rule (UPC § 2-604).

So how does Example 13.2 come out under UPC § 2-301 or a statute like it? It is pretty clear that the surviving spouse will be able to show that the will executed three days before marriage was "made in contemplation of the testator's marriage to the surviving spouse." The surviving spouse would indeed take the entire residuary estate.

No matter what the surviving spouse might take under an omitted spouse statute, in a non-community property state, she is entitled to the elective share that may be much more valuable than the interest that passes under the omitted spouse statute. In fact, a few states with elective share statutes do not even have an omitted spouse statute (New York being the most prominent; the omitted spouse statute applies only if the will was executed before 1930).

C. Protection for the Spouse from Intentional Disinheritance: The Elective Share

The one limit on testamentary freedom that is all but universal (in the United States, at least) is a prohibition on disinheriting the testator's surviving spouse. Before we begin exploring the mechanisms that are designed to frustrate a spouse's desire to disinherit the other spouse, we need some very basic knowledge. First, in the community property states, a married couple's community property divides at the death of one of the spouses. One-half is the probate property of the decedent, and the other half belongs to the surviving spouse. Because in these states there is no need to protect a spouse from intentional disinheritance, the statutes generally address only the spouse omitted from the will. Second, the intentional disinheritance statutes in the other states, usually called common law or title theory states, vary greatly in their effectiveness. Some are toothless; others create a robust regime of protection that is all but impossible to defeat. Even so, among the common law states, only Georgia does not have some sort of statute protecting the surviving spouse from intentional disinheritance.

F   A   Q

Q: How do the elective share statutes differ from the omitted spouse statutes?

A: First, they often apply to much more than the deceased spouse's probate property. Second, they are meant to prevent a testator from doing whatever he wants to do. The omitted spouse statutes are designed to prevent *unintentional* disinheritance and can be seen as remedying an oversight rather than frustrating intent.

(1) A Bit of History

The notion that one cannot intentionally disinherit one's spouse goes way back in the history of the common law. Under the classic common law, husbands and wives were treated differently. (This should come as no surprise since different treatment was the norm for centuries.) Suffice it to say here that neither of the historical devices, dower for widows and curtesy for widowers, make much sense in the modern world, where different treatment of spouses based on their gender would almost certainly

ECONOMIC PARTNERSHIP THEORY AND DIVORCE

The economic partnership theory of marriage has also had important consequences for divorce laws. Just about every, if not all, of the common law property states have statutes that provide for **equitable distribution** of a married couple's property on divorce. Under equitable distribution, the court hearing the divorce can divide up all of the couple's property, no matter how it is titled, on an equitable basis. That means, for example, that a spouse who worked, inside or outside of the home, and thus enabled the other spouse to qualify for a profession such as law or medicine, is often entitled to part of that spouse's future earnings. In addition, the need to equitably divide all property has led divorce courts to deal with all sorts of future interests, often deciding that a contingent remainder held by one of the spouses can be divided; if the interest does vest in possession in the future, the ex-spouses must share the property that comes into possession.

violate constitutional guarantees of equal protection. Starting in the last quarter of the twentieth century, a different view of the economic relationship between spouses began to emerge. The **economic partnership theory** describes marriage as an equal economic partnership in which both partners are equally responsible for the increase in the partnership's wealth. Its influence is clearly evident in the way modern elective share statutes answer a variety of common questions and is the policy rationale for the UPC elective share provisions.

(2) Modern Elective Share

(a) What Is the Size of the Elective Share?

There are different answers to this question, but the elective share is usually described as a fraction of the deceased spouse's property, and it's often one-half or one-third. What you should note is that it is not necessarily the same as the spouse's intestate share. Why? The intestacy statute is a default rule designed (at least in theory) to give those who do not write wills what they would want if they had thought about it. The elective share is the *minimum* a surviving spouse is entitled to receive from the deceased spouse. Another way to think about it is to realize that when the legislature enacts the intestacy provisions for a surviving spouse, it's writing into law its best judgment about how much of the probate estate the decedent wants the surviving spouse to have. When the legislature enacts the elective statute, on the other hand, it's writing into law what *society* has decided is the minimum share of the deceased spouse's property the survivor should have. The intestacy statute is supposed to further the deceased spouse's desires; the elective share statute frustrates the desire to disinherit the surviving spouse. In some states, however, there is a closer link between the elective share and the intestacy law. The elective share amount depends on whether the deceased spouse is survived by descendants. If he is, the elective share is less than if there were no surviving descendants.

What does the UPC do? The UPC elective share statute is very different from other elective share regimes. Under UPC §§ 2-202(a) and 2-203, the size of the elective share depends on the length of the marriage between the decedent and the surviving spouse. If the couple was married for 15 or more years, the survivor is entitled to 100 percent of the "marital property portion" of the property subject to the survivor's elective share rights (more on that in a minute). The marital property portion is 50 percent of that property, so the survivor of what in UPC terms is a long-term marriage gets an elective share equal to one-half of the property subject to the elective share. Survivors of shorter term marriages are entitled to smaller elective share percentages. The surviving spouse of a marriage that lasted less than one year is entitled to 3 percent of the 50 percent marital property, or 1.5 percent of the total property subject to the elective share right (you can see the entire schedule in UPC § 2-203). This "sliding scale" is one of the reflections of the economic partnership theory: the longer the partnership lasts, the more property it acquires.

There is another aspect of the UPC system that has to do with the size of the elective share. UPC § 2-202(b) guarantees the surviving spouse a minimum amount called the "supplemental elective share amount." If the elective share produced by the provisions already described is less than this supplemental amount, the surviving spouse is entitled to property sufficient to make up the difference. The current version of § 2-202(b) suggests a supplemental elective share amount of $75,000 by putting that amount in brackets.

(b) What Property Is Subject to the Elective Share?

This is obviously the big question. Think about a statute that gives the surviving spouse a percentage of the decedent's "estate." Without more, "estate" means "probate estate." A statute like this, and there are some, really provides the surviving spouse with very little protection. It's so easy to create valid will substitutes, including revocable trusts, that disinheriting the surviving spouse is almost laughably easy if the only property subject to the elective share right is the deceased spouse's probate estate.

States with what we'll call "probate estate elective share statutes" sometimes have judicially developed doctrines designed to give the surviving spouse additional protection. The cases usually deal with revocable trusts, but the reasoning seems to be the same no matter what will substitute is involved. That reasoning involves one or both of two tests: (1) is the nonprobate property arrangement "illusory" because the deceased spouse had control over the property, or (2) was the nonprobate arrangement created to defraud the surviving spouse of his rights? It is often not easy to apply these tests consistently, which makes it difficult to predict what a court will do. Very occasionally, a state high court will hold that a nonprobate property arrangement is always part of the probate estate for elective share purposes no matter what the circumstances of its creation. The most likely candidate for such treatment is a revocable trust created by the deceased spouse and funded before death. The complete control the settlor of a revocable trust has over the trust property is a pretty good justification for making that property subject to the elective share rights of the surviving spouse, even under a statute that limits those rights to the deceased spouse's probate estate.

Judicial decisions holding that nonprobate property is subject to the elective under probate estate statutes have been rare, and many decisions apply the illusory transfer and intent to defraud tests rather stringently. In some states, legislatures have dealt with the problem by creating a statutory list of nonprobate arrangements and transfers that are automatically included in the pool of property subject to the elective share rights of the surviving spouse. Usually the list includes revocable trusts created and funded by the deceased spouse, payable on death accounts (to the extent they hold the deceased spouse's property), property jointly held by the decedent and another with right of survivorship (again, to the extent that the decedent was the source of the property), and some outright transfers to others especially if they are made close to death. Of course, if the surviving spouse is the beneficiary of these nonprobate arrangements or the donee of near-death transfers, what the spouse receives usually counts toward satisfying the elective share.

What does the UPC do? The UPC goes very far in the direction of creating a statutorily defined pool of property subject to the elective share. The UPC term for this pool of property is the **augmented estate**. It is truly comprehensive. It includes, of course, the deceased spouse's probate estate net of funeral and administration expenses, enforceable debts, the homestead and family allowances, and exempt property (UPC § 2-204). It includes all sorts of nonprobate property arrangements in which the decedent has an interest (including property subject to a presently exercisable general power of appointment, which includes a revocable trust), and irrevocable transfers made by the decedent during the marriage over which the decedent retained certain forms of control or an interest in the property. All of these are included in the decedent's augmented estate to the extent they pass to someone other than the surviving spouse (UPC § 2-205). The augmented estate also includes all nonprobate transfers passing to the surviving spouse (UPC § 2-206). So far, this is not very surprising, but the UPC goes much further. The augmented estate includes *the surviving spouse's property* as well as the surviving spouse's nonprobate transfers to others that would be included in the augmented estate were the surviving spouse the decedent (UPC § 2-207).

These four elements — the deceased spouse's probate estate, nonprobate transfer to others and to the surviving spouse, and the surviving spouse's property and nonprobate transfers to others — make up the augmented estate (UPC § 2-203(a)), and the elective share is 50 percent of the marital property portion of the augmented estate, which is defined by the sliding scale of UPC § 2-203(b) that we've already mentioned.

Why does the UPC define the elective share by taking into consideration the property of both the deceased spouse and the surviving spouse? The policy behind this innovative provision is the economic partnership theory. Since both spouses have contributed to acquiring their accumulated wealth, the survivor's elective share should be measured taking into account all of the partnership property. One consequence of this approach is that a surviving spouse who is wealthier than the deceased spouse may be entitled to receive nothing more than what the survivor already has. Here's an example.

Example 13.3: Husband and Wife have been married for 25 years when Husband dies testate. Husband's net probate estate is $200,000, none of which passes to Wife under his will; his nonprobate transfers to others are $300,000; his nonprobate transfers to Wife are $100,000; and Wife's property and nonprobate transfers to others total $1,000,000. The total augmented estate is $1,600,000, the marital property portion is 50 percent, or $800,000; and of that, Wife is entitled to 100 percent after a marriage of 15 years or longer. That's $800,000, but Wife's share of the augmented estate is $1,000,000. Result: Wife's elective share right is satisfied without any further transfers of property.

Without this combining of the property of the deceased spouse and the surviving spouse, which is unique to the UPC, Wife would be entitled to the elective share percentage of 50 percent of Husband's augmented estate of $600,000, or $300,000. The $600,000 includes $100,000 of nonprobate transfers to Wife, but she is entitled to an additional $200,000. It's worth asking whether the wealthier spouse should have a claim on the poorer spouse's property. The UPC at least decides that the answer is no.

F   A   Q

Q: What does the term "marital property" mean?

A: Generally, this is a concept that does not really apply in the world of wills and trusts (although remember that in the UPC elective share scheme, the concept of the "marital property portion" of the "augmented estate" is very important). Usually the concept of "marital property" is important in the law of divorce where it describes the property the court can divide between the divorcing spouses.

(c) Must the Spouse Accept an Income Interest?

Another way elective share statutes differ is whether the surviving spouse must accept an income interest in a trust rather than outright ownership of property in satisfaction of the elective share. Probate estate elective share statutes almost always simply give the surviving spouse some share of the deceased spouse's "estate." That means that the surviving spouse is entitled to outright ownership of the share. The result of successfully exercising the right of election is money (or more likely property) in the surviving spouse's pocket.

Some elective share statutes that expand the pool of property subject to the elective share right beyond the probate estate allow the surviving spouse's entitlement to be satisfied at least in part by the right to all of the income from a trust. The most extreme form of such a statute allows the deceased spouse to satisfy the entire elective share right by giving the surviving spouse all of the income for life from a trust funded with the elective share amount.

Example 13.4: State X's elective share statute says that a surviving spouse is entitled to the income for life from a trust funded with one-half of the deceased spouse's "property" and defines property to include the net probate estate (after debts and expenses are paid), various nonprobate property arrangements, and transfers to others than the spouse. Wife dies with a net probate estate of $300,000 and $300,000 of nonprobate transfers other than to Husband. Under a 50 percent elective share statute that allows the elective to be satisfied by giving the survivor an income interest in a trust funded in an amount equal to the elective share amount, Wife can satisfy Husband's elective share right by creating a testamentary trust with the $300,000 of probate property and giving Husband all of the income from the trust for life. Husband is entitled to nothing more, and Wife can give the remainder in the trust to whomever she wishes — the couple's children, her children by a prior marriage, her collateral relatives, or a charity.

Allowing satisfaction of the elective share entitlement by giving the surviving spouse an income interest in a trust clearly expresses the idea that the purpose of the elective share is to require the deceased spouse to continue to fulfill the spousal support obligation. If the economic partnership theory is the policy behind the elective share, however, it is easy to conclude that the proper elective share amount is one-half of the partnership property and that the surviving spouse should own that one-half outright because under that theory the surviving spouse is receiving through the elective share property what he has earned.

Some non-UPC statutes that expand the pool beyond the probate estate require outright ownership of the elective share by the surviving spouse. Under others, the surviving spouse may have to accept an income interest, but the extent to which the income interest satisfies the elective share right may not be linked to the value of the trust property that is producing the income. Instead the commuted value of the income interest, calculated actuarially, counts toward satisfying the elective share right. If the spouse has additional interests in the trust (e.g., the trustee may invade principal for the spouse's support), more of the value of the trust property might count toward satisfying the elective share.

What does the UPC do? The foregoing discussion could certainly lead you to believe that the UPC elective share scheme requires that the surviving spouse receive outright ownership of the elective share. That's not the case, but it is not at all obvious from the text of the UPC provisions. Section 2-208(b)(2) states that the "value of property" includes the commuted value of any present or future interest. That provision means that the value of the property received by the surviving spouse from the deceased spouse would include the actuarially calculated value of income interests and even future interests (think of an irrevocable lifetime trust created by the deceased spouse to pay the income to the settlor's daughter by a previous marriage, with an indefeasibly vested remainder to the surviving spouse).

The analysis, however, can't stop there. Before the 1993 revision of the UPC elective share provisions, § 2-207(a)(3) counted as a transfer to the surviving spouse, and therefore as counting toward the satisfaction of the elective share, any part of the augmented estate that passed to the surviving spouse but was disclaimed by the surviving spouse. The revision removed that provision. The conclusion must be that the surviving spouse can disclaim a property interest in the augmented estate, and it will not count toward satisfying the elective share right. That, in turn, means that the surviving spouse can disclaim an income interest and take the elective share amount outright, a conclusion confirmed by the comment to UPC § 2-209.

Example 13.5: Husband and Wife have been married for 25 years when Husband dies testate. Husband's net probate estate is $1,000,000, all of which passes to the trustee named in the will to pay the income to Wife for life, remainder to Husband's descendants by representation (Husband's descendants are offspring of a prior marriage; Husband and Wife never had children). No nonprobate transfers to others by Husband are part of the augmented estate. His nonprobate transfers to Wife are $100,000. Wife's property and nonprobate transfers to others total $100,000. The total augment estate is $1,200,000; the marital property portion is 50 percent, or $600,000; and of that, Wife is entitled to 100 percent after a marriage of 15 years or longer. Her own part of the augmented estate totals $100,000, so she is entitled to an additional $500,000.

Assume that the commuted value (present value) of the income interest, taking into account Wife's actuarial life expectancy and whatever discount rate is applicable (the interest rate that is assumed to prevail for Wife's life expectancy), is $500,000. Wife has two choices. She can accept the income interest, and her elective share right will be satisfied. In the alternative, she can disclaim her interest in the trust, causing the remainder to accelerate. The trust property will then belong to Husband's descendants who survive Husband by representation. They must then pay $500,000 to Wife in satisfaction of her elective share.

Why might Wife disclaim her interest in the trust? Perhaps she feels she will get more economic benefit from property she can manage herself than from an income interest in the trust, which must be impartially managed by the trustee to balance her interest in current income and the remainder owners' interest in maximizing growth. Another factor could be her desire to increase her own estate so that she can make a larger gift at death. Whatever Wife's reasons, under the UPC she can require that the elective share amount pass to her outright.

(d) Election by an Incapacitated Spouse

There is one thing that is certain in the law of the elective share: no election can be made on behalf of a deceased spouse. The elective share is a personal right that can only be exercised personally by the surviving spouse. Modern statutes almost always provide that an election can be made on behalf of an incapacitated spouse by the spouse's fiduciary, a guardian, or a conservator. There is more diversity on the question of whether an agent for the surviving spouse acting under a power of attorney can make the election, even if the power of attorney expressly authorizes the agent to do so. In answering the question, it may make a difference whether the spouse is incapacitated.

Several questions must be faced when making an election for an incapacitated spouse. First, is the election the right thing to do? Think of the surviving spouse who is receiving Medicaid. The deceased spouse's will gives the surviving spouse nothing, and the surviving spouse receives no nonprobate property. Clearly, if the spouse does not claim the elective share right, he will continue to be without assets and will continue to qualify for Medicaid (or for any other government assistance program that is means tested). In some states, failure to claim the elective share is treated as a transfer of the property the surviving spouse would have received, and that transfer will disqualify the surviving spouse from receiving further assistance for some period of time (during which, of course, the surviving spouse has no assets to use to pay for care). In short, the surviving spouse must take the elective share, or a guardian must make the election on the spouse's behalf, and the property must be used to pay for the surviving spouse's care. A similar question arises under statutes that require the surviving spouse to have outright ownership of the elective share. Assume the surviving spouse is incapacitated and the deceased spouse created a trust for the survivor with relatively generous provisions for the surviving spouse: a mandatory interest in income and a discretionary power in the trustee to invade principal for the surviving spouse's health and maintenance. Should the surviving spouse's fiduciary assert the elective share right, even though that means that management of the property will be in the hands of a guardian of the property and that the terms of the guardianship are probably much less flexible than the trust terms?

Usually the fiduciary is required to act in the best interests of the surviving spouse. Some courts have taken a very inflexible view of "best interests" and decided that outright ownership is better than being the beneficiary of a trust, even if the surviving spouse is incapacitated and the property will be managed by a guardian of the property. Other courts have taken a more realistic view. Noting that the surviving spouse is economically better off as a beneficiary of the trust created by the deceased spouse, these courts have decided that asserting the elective share right and thus destroying the trust is not in the surviving spouse's best interests.

What does the UPC do? If the election is made by a properly authorized fiduciary for the surviving but incapacitated spouse (like a guardian or an agent under a power of attorney), the property obtained for the surviving spouse must be placed in a trust that conforms to the provisions of the Uniform Custodial Trust Act (UPC § 2-212(b)). The Act creates a discretionary trust as to income and principal, for a single beneficiary, in this case the incapacitated surviving spouse. Distributions are to be made "with regard to" the beneficiary's other property.

F   A   Q

Q: Doesn't the custodial trust go against the economic partnership theory since any remaining trust property returns to the estate of the first spouse to die?

A: You certainly can look at it that way. It can be argued that following the economic partnership theory to its logical conclusion means the surviving spouse should have outright ownership of the elective share amount, and any of the property that remains at the surviving spouse's death should be part of her probate estate. Why that result should change if the surviving spouse is incapacitated at the time of the first spouse's death is worth thinking about.

Interestingly enough, the remainder of the custodial trust passes under the residuary clause of the deceased spouse's will as if the deceased spouse had died immediately after the surviving spouse or to the deceased spouse's heirs determined under UPC § 2-711 (heirs determined as if the ancestor died at the distribution date). Property in a custodial trust at the surviving spouse's death will therefore return to the estate of the first spouse to die (although all of the trust property could be consumed for the needs of the surviving spouse).

D. Community Property

We've already mentioned community property. Something we haven't done is list the community property states:

- Arizona
- California
- Idaho
- Louisiana
- Nevada
- New Mexico
- Texas
- Washington State

In addition, Wisconsin is the only state to have adopted the Uniform Marital Property Act, which in essence creates a community property regime without giving it the name. Finally, Alaska statutes allow a married couple to create a trust the terms of which make the property used to fund it community property.

As we've already learned, when the marriage ends the community property divides in half. When the end comes through divorce, the result certainly can be the equivalent of equitable distribution. When the end comes at the death of one of the spouses, the result can be like the 50/50 division of the augmented estate under the UPC elective share scheme. The survivor automatically owns one-half of the community property and the other half is the probate estate of the deceased spouse (some of which may go to the survivor in intestacy, under the decedent's will, or as an omitted spouse under a premarital will). The key to gauging the similarity is determining what property is community property.

(1) What Property Is Community Property?

The broadest definition of community property is all property gained by the spouses through their efforts. The simplest example is earnings from employment outside of the home. All wages are community property. Anything bought with community property is also community property. If one spouse invests his earnings in stocks and bonds, those stocks and bonds are community property.

Property brought to the marriage by the spouses or received through inheritance or gift is **separate property**. In some states, the earnings on separate property are separate; in others, they are community.

Example 13.6: Husband inherits 1,000 shares of ExxonMobil from his mother. The shares are separate property. Anything bought with the proceeds of sales of the stock is separate property. Dividends paid on the stock are community property in Idaho, Texas, and Louisiana, and separate property elsewhere.

Sidebar

COMMUNITY PROPERTY AND THE FEDERAL INCOME TAX

Under a community property system, both spouses' earnings are community property, meaning for income tax purposes that each spouse pays federal income tax on one-half of the total income. At one time, if one spouse had much more taxable income than the other, the resulting "income split" would result in a much lower overall tax bill compared to a similarly situated couple in a common law state. But by creating the joint return and taxing married couples as a unit, Congress removed the community property advantage (and put an end to the movement to adopt community property in some common law states to obtain the income tax benefits for married couples).

One common question that comes up involves improvements to separate property paid for with community property or made by the efforts of one of the spouses.

Example 13.7: Wife brings a mortgaged residence to the marriage. The house is separate property, but $100,000 of community property is used to pay the mortgage, which is equivalent to 50 percent of the total cost of acquiring the house. In some states, the community is entitled only to reimbursement of the $100,000 amount paid. In others, half of the value of the house is community property because that's the proportion of the acquisition costs paid by the community.

Example 13.8: Husband is the sole proprietor of a business at the time of marriage. He continues to work in the business during the marriage, taking very little salary and other compensation and investing most of the enterprise's earnings in the business. In some states, the community is entitled only to the value of Husband's services that were not fully compensated. In others, the community would have some interest in the business itself.

Example 13.9: Wife owns a life insurance policy on her own life. After marriage she continues to pay the premiums out of her earnings, which are now community property. At her death the policy proceeds are likely to be community property in proportion to the total amount of premiums paid with community property. But even this rule is not uniform. In Texas, at least, the policy is separate property, and the community is entitled only to the value of the premiums paid with community property.

F   A   Q

Q: Is it possible to hold property as joint tenants with right of survivorship in a community property state?

A: The answer has always been yes for joint tenants who are not married to each other. A married couple could always create a joint tenancy by first turning community property into separate property and then creating the joint tenancy with right of survivorship. Today, eight of the nine community property states (all except Louisiana) recognize community property with a right of survivorship. A couple who uses this device can make community property nonprobate property.

Sidebar

COMMUNITY PROPERTY AND THE ESTATE TAX

When a community property spouse dies, the probate estate includes one-half of the community property, and the gross estate for federal estate tax purpose also includes one-half of the community property. This creates a disparity between common law and community property married couples analogous to that under the income tax. At the very least, when a community property spouse dies, one-half of the community property will not be taxed until the death of the surviving spouse. Congress responded by creating the estate tax marital deduction, which allowed a deduction from the taxable estate of gifts to a surviving spouse in an amount not to exceed one-half of the taxable estate. The marital deduction is more generous today, but its beginning was this attempt to equalize the estate tax treatment of common law and community property.

Usually a sale of community property by one spouse for consideration is upheld as a proper exercise of the spouse's right to manage the community property. (Once only the husband was the manager of the community, but that rule has fallen to equal protection.) In some states, however, selling real property held by the community requires the consent of both spouses.

The community property system is not a straightjacket, and couples can usually change separate property to community property and vice versa by an express agreement. In California, this process is known as **transmutation**, which probably makes you think of turning lead into gold.

The community property system can raise many fact questions that do not need to be addressed in common law title states (e.g., whether a spouse consented to a gratuitous transfer of community property). In addition, transfers by one spouse that require the consent of the other can be reached by the other spouse no matter when they were made so long as it was during the marriage. Elective share statutes that go beyond the probate estate usually limit the outright gratuitous transfers by the decedent that are subject to the elective share to those made within a year or two of death (two years under UPC § 2-205(3)).

(2) The "Widow's Election"

Remember that the survivor of a community property marriage is the automatic owner of one-half of the community property. There is no need to make an election of any sort. Sometimes, however, the deceased spouse will offer the surviving spouse a choice. The will creates a trust for the surviving spouse of *all* of the couple's community property. If the surviving spouse does not accept the trust, she must be content with outright ownership of half of the community property. This device is known as the **widow's election**, although, of course, it applies to widowers as well. The income, estate, and gift tax effects of the widow's election are quite complex and depend in part on how the election is structured.

F   A   Q

Q: Why would a surviving spouse accept the "widow's election"?

A: There are many reasons. The survivor might feel more secure as the beneficiary of a trust holding all of the community property than as the outright owner of one-half. The survivor might also prefer that all of the property be managed by the trustee, especially if the survivor believes that he lacks the skills necessary to manage the property. In addition, if the survivor is incapacitated or has capacity but is ill, the decedent probably hoped to avoid problems of guardianship for the survivor. Of course, accepting the election means that the spouse creating the trust has control over who receives the remainder (unless the survivor is given a power of appointment). Another reason involves uncertainty over what is community property. The surviving spouse might decide accepting the interest in the trust is better than litigating over how much of the property included in the trust really is community property.

E. Moving from One Marital Property Regime to the Other

When a married couple changes domicile from a community property jurisdiction to a common law jurisdiction or vice versa, they should be sure to consider the ways the move affects their estate planning.

(1) From Common Law to Community Property

The most important effect on a couple from a common law state is the loss of the elective share. The couple will begin to accumulate community property once they have established domicile in the community property state, but the property brought with them remains separate property. Especially if the couple retires to the community property state and neither is working for compensation, the amount of community property created between the move and the death of the first spouse may be negligible.

California, Idaho, Louisiana, and Washington State try to help the surviving spouse when the decedent's property is separate property brought into the state. These four states have defined a category of property as **quasi-community property**, which is property acquired while the spouses were domiciled in a common law property state that would have been community property had the couple been domiciled in the community property state at the time of acquisition. When the spouse who acquired the property dies, the surviving spouse owns one-half of the quasi-community property. However, if the nonacquiring spouse dies first, the decedent has no interest in the quasi-community property.

Example 13.10: While H and W are domiciled in New York, W invests some of her earnings in stock and bonds held in a brokerage account. The couple moves to California. On W's death, H owns one-half of the investments in the brokerage account. If H dies first, he *does not* have any rights in the brokerage account.

Of course, enforcing the surviving spouse's rights to quasi-community property may require resolving some difficult questions of fact, especially if the property of the deceased spouse was acquired many years ago. If the couple wants to address the question before one of them dies, they could transmute separate property into community property and give the survivor the usual rights of a community property spouse.

Arizona, New Mexico, and Texas also recognize the quasi-community property concept but apply it only when the couple divorces, not on the death of a spouse.

(2) From Community Property to Common Law

The community property couple who move to a common law state often want to make sure that the community property they bring to the common law state retains its character as community property. The general principles of conflicts of law do say that the character of community property is not changed by the married couple moving their domicile to a common law state. That general principle is codified in the Uniform Disposition of Community Property Rights at Death Act, which has been adopted in fourteen common law states.

Example 13.11: H and W move from California to New York where they take the proceeds of the sale of their Malibu home, which was community property, and buy a condominium in New York City. Because New York has adopted the Uniform Disposition of Community Property Rights at Death Act, H and W easily can hold title to the condominium as community property.

F. Pensions Public and Private

One important source of protection for the family is not really part of the law of wills and trusts. Retired workers are all entitled to an income stream from the federal Social Security system, and many are also entitled to private work-related pensions.

(1) Social Security

The Social Security system provides what amounts to a publically funded pension for workers. Employees and employers both pay into the system under the provision of the Federal Insurance Contribution Act (FICA). In 2012, the rate of tax for employees was 4.2 percent on the first $110,100 of wages (this is a reduction from the otherwise applicable rate of 6.2 percent which will continue through at least February 2012).

The employer pays an amount equal to 6.2 percent on the same amount of wages. In addition, a rate of 2.9 percent is levied on all wages to fund the Medicare system and is also split between the employer and the employee. Self-employed persons pay the entire amount of both taxes (15.3 percent) on their earnings. When a person who has paid into the system retires, he is entitled to a monthly payment, the amount of which is based on the amount of wages taxed, the length of time worked for which taxes were paid, and age at retirement.

Family members of a worker who is entitled to benefits may themselves be entitled to payments from the Social Security system. A spouse is entitled to benefits if she is over 62 years of age (which is the minimum retirement age). A spouse is also entitled to benefits no matter what her age if the spouse is caring for the worker's child who is younger than 16 or who is disabled and entitled to benefits based on the worker's earnings record.

F A Q

Q: What's the difference between Medicaid and Medicare?

A: Medicaid is a means-tested joint federal and state program that provides healthcare for indigent persons. Medicare is a federal program that provides healthcare for persons older than 65 (and for some younger disabled persons). The former is financed out of general revenues, both state and federal, and the latter is financed by a federal payroll tax (under FICA).

A surviving spouse is also entitled to benefits based on the deceased spouse's earning record if he is at least 60 years old (50 years old if also disabled) or if he is caring for a child of the worker who is under 16 or disabled and entitled to benefits. Finally, and this may surprise you, an ex-spouse of a worker may also be entitled to benefits based on the worker's earnings record. Once again, the claimant must be 60 years old (50 if disabled) or caring for a child of the worker who is eligible for benefits based on the worker's earnings. In addition, the ex-spouse must not be eligible for an equal or higher benefit based on his own earnings record and must not be married (unless remarriage occurred after age 60, 50 if disabled).

As you can see, children are also entitled to benefits based on a parent's earnings record.

Sidebar

SOCIAL SECURITY AND POSTHUMOUS CONCEPTION

The provision of the Social Security system that provides benefits for children of a covered worker and for a spouse caring for those children is the reason for much litigation over the status of posthumously conceived children. Almost all of the reported cases have been brought by widows seeking the benefits to which their children would be entitled as the children of their deceased husbands. The litigation aims to receive judicial recognition of the children's paternity, which will result in eligibility for benefits.

They must be unmarried and under 18 years of age. If the child is in elementary or secondary school as a full-time student, benefits continue to age 19. If the child became disabled before the age of 22, she is eligible for benefits at any age.

The Social Security system is an important source of support for workers and their families. However, it is a source of support only. Although the law that funds the system has the word "insurance" in its title, Social Security is not an insurance system. While the benefits a worker receives are tied to some degree to the amount the worker has paid into the system, it is abundantly clear that a participant in the system does not have an account with her name on it that holds the participant's contributions. Money contributed by current workers fund current benefits, and those workers' benefits will be funded by future contributions (and by accumulated surpluses). In any event, however, Social Security is an important source of income for retirees as well as disabled persons.

(2) Private Employment-Related Pensions

In Chapter 6 we talked about the effect of the Employee Retirement Income Security Act (ERISA), specifically its federal preemption provision, on state laws revoking beneficiary designations of an ex-spouse. Another provision of ERISA is very important for surviving spouses. A married person who participates in a plan covered by ERISA (and that's any pension or benefit plan sponsored by an employer) must take any annuity benefit under the plan as a **joint and survivor annuity** with the person's spouse. That means that the annuity amount is paid over the joint lifetimes of the employee and the spouse, and the spouse will continue to receive the annuity even if the employee dies first. The spouse can waive this right in a notarized waiver executed during the marriage. That means that a prenuptial agreement cannot waive the right (nor can it be waived if the worker is under age 35).

F   A   Q

Q: What are the Social Security and pension rights of the survivor of a marriage between two persons of the same sex?

A: Under the Defense of Marriage Act, the federal government is required to recognize as a marriage only that between a man and a woman. Therefore, the survivor of a same-sex marriage is not entitled to Social Security benefits as a surviving spouse (even if caring for the decedent's children) nor does the spouse have a right under ERISA to a joint and survivor annuity in the other spouse's pension plan.

Now is the time to note that pension plans come in two varieties. Under a **defined benefit plan**, the amount of the pension benefit is guaranteed and is set by a formula that is usually tied to the employee's level of compensation just before retirement. Such plans are becoming rarer and exist today primarily in the public sector. The other type is a **defined contribution plan** in which the employee (and often the employer) makes contributions to the employee's account that are not included in the employee's taxable income. The contributions are invested, and when it's time to retire the employee either takes the account in a lump sum (and almost always turns it into an IRA from which periodic distributions are made) or uses it to buy an annuity (a joint and survivor annuity if the employee is married and the spouse has not waived her rights in the retirement plan). The amount available depends on how the investments the employee has made have performed. Thus the benefit is anything but "defined."

SUMMARY

■ A decedent's family may have several different types of interests in the decedent's property: an allowance out of the probate estate, a homestead exemption, and an entitlement to a certain amount of personal property free from the claims of the decedent's creditors.

■ Pretermitted child statutes and omitted spouse statutes protect the decedent's children and spouse from unintentional disinheritance. These statutes are not at all uniform, and some of them can lead to substantial distortion of the decedent's estate plan.

■ All the common law property states except Georgia have statutes that purport to prevent the intentional disinheritance of a surviving spouse by giving the surviving spouse an elective share in the deceased spouse's property. These elective share statutes vary principally in what property is subject to the elective share right and whether the surviving spouse can demand outright ownership of the share.

■ The community property system is a completely different approach to protecting a surviving spouse. During the marriage, all the property that comes into the marriage belongs equally to the two spouses. On death, the community splits in half: half the property belongs to the surviving spouse and the other half is the probate property of the deceased spouse.

■ The Social Security system provides public pensions for retired workers as well as disability benefits for workers and their families. Private work-related pensions are subject to federal law that requires certain benefits for a surviving spouse.

CONNECTIONS

Family Protection and Wills

The law of family protection is one of the very few formal limitations on testamentary freedom, but much of the law discussed in this chapter is supposedly designed to implement the decedent's intent by remedying a mistaken omission of a spouse or child. Only the elective share laws are truly intent defeating.

Family Protection and the Definition of Family

Just as answering the questions "who is a spouse?" and "who is a child?" are critical to the workings of the intestacy statute (Chapter 2) as well as to the interpretation of wills, they are equally critical to the law discussed in this chapter. The question of the status of children of assisted conception, in fact, has been raised judicially most often in connection with Social Security survivor benefits.

Family Protection and Nonprobate Property

The proliferation of forms of nonprobate property (Chapters 6 and 11) has made the law preventing disinheritance of a surviving spouse much more complicated. Where at one time giving the surviving spouse some part of the deceased spouse's probate estate was likely to give the surviving spouse real protection against disinheritance, today the ease with which almost any sort of property can be turned into nonprobate property means that probate-estate-only elective share statutes are not effective.

Family Protection and Wealth Transfer Taxation

Neither estate taxes nor gift taxes apply to outright transfers between opposite-sex spouses, or to certain transfers to trusts of which the spouse of the transferor is the beneficiary (Chapter 17). If the transfer occurs at the death of the first spouse to die and is made to a trust that qualifies for exemption from estate tax, the surviving spouse's interest in the trust may not satisfy the spouse's elective share rights.

Dealing with Illness, Disability, and Last Things

14

Life spans in the United States continue to increase, helped by ever-advancing medical technology. But living longer than previous genera-

OVERVIEW

tions doesn't necessarily mean living well, and some of us will reach a time when we cannot make reasoned decisions about our property, financial matters, healthcare, or even the day-to-day tasks of living. Our legal system provides mechanisms that authorize surrogate decision makers to make choices for incapacitated persons. These arrangements include durable powers of attorney, revocable trusts, and guardianship for property; statutory devices that guide healthcare surrogate decisions; and, in some jurisdictions, laws regulating third-party decisions about the disposition of decedents' remains. The longer we live, the more important it becomes to understand how these elements fit into the modern estate plan.

A. THE CONCEPT OF SURROGATE DECISION MAKING

B. DEALING WITH PROPERTY BELONGING TO AN INCAPACITATED PERSON

    1.   Powers of Attorney
    2.   Guardianship

C. HEALTHCARE DECISIONS

D. DISPOSITION OF REMAINS

A. The Concept of Surrogate Decision Making

We are all going to die. That's as certain as certain can be. That's humbling enough, but many of us, before we die, will become unable to care for ourselves or to make decisions about financial or healthcare issues. Loss of capacity has many causes, but the result is the same. Someone may have to make the decisions that we can no longer make for ourselves. Just as the law provides various ways for making gifts at death, it also provides a variety of devices for authorizing others to make certain decisions for us during our lifetimes when we cannot make those decisions for ourselves.

Two basic concepts are often used when decisions have to be made for an incapacitated person and the devices used to give others the authority to make decisions do not give clear guidance. One is the **substituted judgment standard**. Under that standard, the decision maker is to do what the incapacitated person would do in the situation. Deciding what that action would be usually requires an investigation of what the incapacitated person did in analogous situations and, frankly, some guesswork.

The other approach to these uncertainties is the **best interests standard**. Under this standard, the decision maker does what he thinks is in the best interests of the person for whom the decision is being made. Courts may use either standard in deciding what a decision maker should do.

Here's a simplified example. The **protected person** (the person whose affairs are being managed by a guardian) can no longer live alone. The person needs help to carry on the normal functions of daily life: preparing food, going to the bathroom, dressing, maintaining personal hygiene. On many occasions the protected person has made it clear to family members and friends that staying in her home is of the greatest importance. Because of the protected person's disabilities, she would need full-time qualified help to safely remain living at home. The alternative is to move the protected person to an institutional setting such as an assisted living facility. The person who has decision-making authority for the protected person must choose a course of action.

Under a substituted judgment standard, the decision should be to do what is necessary to allow the protected person to live at home. The protected person's wishes are known, and it is clear that in this situation the protected person would decide to remain at home. Using the best interests standard, however, could lead to a different result. If the protected person needs 24-hour care, an institutional setting makes sense. Staff will always be available. If caregiving depends on the regular arrival of healthcare aides at the protected person's home, then bad weather, illness, or staffing difficulties could leave the protected person without services for periods of time. In addition, although the protected person may have the financial resources to pay for 24-hour home care right now, those resources may be exhausted before the protected person's death or before her condition worsens and home care is simply impossible.

Government programs, principally Medicaid, may pay for the protected person's care once she is indigent. However, finding a place for a patient whose bills will be paid by the government might be difficult. It is certain that the decision maker will have a much wider choice of institutional placements if the protected person is going to pay for care with her own resources—a "private pay" patient.

As you can see, the standards can lead to very different decisions. As you can also see, there is nothing clear-cut about how to apply either standard. In our example, an institutional placement for the protected person might be possible using a substituted judgment standard. The rationale could be that if the protected person knew about the ins and outs of Medicaid and long-term care, she would have decided that it would be better to be a private pay patient than stay at home and wait to become indigent. Using the best interests standard could result in a decision to care for the protected person at home. If the decision maker concludes that the protected person's desire to stay at home is so strong that removal from the home would harm the protected person's health and that the protected person is unlikely to live long enough to exhaust the available financial resources, then staying at home may indeed be in the protected person's best interests.

B. Dealing with Property Belonging to an Incapacitated Person

If a person is incapacitated, some other person is going to have to deal with the incapacitated person's property. Sometimes there is no need to take any legal steps to empower a surrogate decision maker. If the incapacitated person's property is held jointly with a person who has capacity — a spouse, partner, relative, or friend — the other joint holder will be able to make decisions about the property. Checks can be written and investments bought and sold without the need to do anything more. Somewhat similarly, if the now incapacitated person's property is held in a revocable trust of which the person is the beneficiary, the trustee can manage the person's property. So long as there is a trustee who can act, the incapacitated person's bills will be paid, investments made, and funds made available to do whatever needs to be done for the beneficiary of the trust.

F   A   Q

Q: Does the existence of a way to manage an incapacitated person's property mean that legal proceedings to appoint a decision maker can be completely avoided?

A: Perhaps not. Even if there is someone with full authority to make decisions about the incapacitated person's property, that person may not have the authority to makes decisions about the incapacitated person's person — where to live, what sort of medical treatment should be given, how personal relationships are to be managed (who may visit the incapacitated person and when). In other words, even though all decisions related to the incapacitated person's property can be taken without bringing any legal proceeding, it may be necessary to have a proceeding to appoint a guardian of the person (rather than of the property) of the incapacitated person.

Even if the incapacitated person does not hold property jointly or is not the beneficiary of a revocable trust, a legal proceeding to appoint a surrogate decision maker is not a foregone conclusion. Another way to ensure that property management decisions are made for an incapacitated person can be put in place before such management is needed, through a power of attorney.

(1) Powers of Attorney

One of the most common ways to arrange for a decision maker to manage a person's property when the property owner cannot is to use a **durable power of attorney** in which a property owner (the **principal**) grants to another person (the **attorney-in-fact** or **agent**) authority to make decisions about the principal's property. The authority can be narrow — to carry out a specific real estate closing — or very broad — to do anything the principal could do. In essence, the principal gives the attorney-in-fact the authority to sign the principal's name to whatever documents are necessary to carry out a transaction. In fact, the traditional way an attorney-in-fact signs for the principal looks like this:

[Signature of principal]

By

[Signature of attorney-in-fact (or agent)]
Attorney-in-fact (or Agent)

F   A   Q

Q: What's the difference between an attorney-in-fact and an agent?

A: "Attorney-in-fact" is the traditional term in agency law. Several modern statutes, including the Uniform Power of Attorney Act, use the term "agent" instead. The idea is that someone who is not knowledgeable about the law of agency is much more likely to understand the term "agent" than a term that seems to have something to do with lawyers but really doesn't. Although lawyers sometime act as agents under a power of attorney for clients, there is absolutely no requirement that the agent be a lawyer.

The power of attorney is an aspect of the law of agency, which generally deals with legal questions that arise when one person has authority to act for another. The law of agency is an ancient part of the common law and is a huge topic in its own right. In fact, agency is the subject of a Restatement. The classic law of agency, however, has one feature that prevents using it as a way of coping with a principal's disability: *the agency relationship ends when the principal becomes incompetent.* Today, however, every state has statutes that permit the creation of a durable power of attorney under which the agent's authority *does not* terminate if the principal becomes incompetent. (Under some statutes, including the Uniform Power of Attorney Act (UPOAA) (incorporated into the UPC as article 5B, §§ 5B-101 through 5B-302), durability is the default rule; all powers of attorney are durable unless they state otherwise.) Today, so long as it makes a sufficiently broad grant of authority to the agent, a durable power of attorney can provide all that is needed to manage the property of an incapacitated person.

The challenge in drafting a durable power of attorney for the types of situations we're discussing is making the grant of authority sufficiently comprehensive so that third parties who are asked to accept the agent's authority will do so. Many lawyers have developed elaborate power of attorney forms aimed at answering questions about the scope of authority before they arise, but developing such a comprehensive form can be a complex task. Some states have enacted statutes that address the problem by creating a **statutory short form power of attorney**. The statute has separate sections whose language grants comprehensive authority to the agent to do everything related to, for example, real estate transactions. All the authority described in the real estate section is granted to the agent by simply indicating that the principal is granting authority related to "real estate transactions." Some statutes include forms that list the topics of the statutory sections granting authority, and the principal grants the authority given in those sections by initialing the topic. (This is how the form included in the UPOAA works.) The idea is that if the statute says that the statutory language is intended to be truly comprehensive, then third parties can be sure that the agent really has the necessary authority to carry out a particular transaction. To give you a better idea of how these statutory short forms work, here's the "initial grant of authority" section of the form in the UPOAA:

F   A   Q

Q: What's a "springing" durable power of attorney?

A: A **springing durable power of attorney** by its terms becomes effective only when the principal becomes incapacitated. One problem often identified with springing powers is the difficulty of creating a workable test for determining when the principal has lost capacity. Rather than create a springing power, some principals simply don't give the agent the power of attorney at the time it's executed and rely on their attorney or someone else to decide when to give the agent the document so that the agent can begin to act.

I grant my agent and any successor agent general authority to act for me with respect to the following subjects as defined in the [act]:

(INITIAL each power you want to include in the agent's general authority. If you wish to grant all of the powers you may initial "All Preceding Powers" instead of initialing each power.)

(_____) Real Property

(_____) Tangible Personal Property

(_____) Stocks and Bonds

(_____) Commodities and Options

(_____) Banks and Other Financial Institutions

(_____) Operation of an Entity or Business

(_____) Insurance and Annuities

(_____) Estates, Trusts, and Other Beneficial Interests

(_____) Claims and Litigation

(_____) Personal and Family Maintenance

(_____) Benefits from Governmental Programs or Civil or Military Service

(_____) Retirement Plans

Sidebar

FINANCIAL INSTITUTIONS AND POWERS OF ATTORNEY

Many lawyers complain about financial institutions, especially banks, refusing to honor a power of attorney because it was not executed on the bank's own form or because, in the bank's view, it does not give the agent the authority to do what he is trying to accomplish. The banks' fear is liability for doing something that exceeds the agent's authority or for honoring a fraudulent power of attorney. Many statutes try to encourage all third parties to accept powers of attorney by exonerating the third party from any liability for honoring a power of attorney that appears to be properly executed, especially if execution includes notarization of the principal's signature, and by providing ways for the third party to rely on the agent's assertion that the grant of authority is both comprehensive and valid. (The Uniform Power of Attorney Act exemplifies this approach.)

The law continues to develop, however, and this is yet another area in which state laws differ greatly.

(_____) Taxes

(_____) All Preceding Powers

There's another list of powers in the Uniform Act's form:

My agent MAY NOT do any of the following specific acts for me UNLESS I have also INITIALED the specific power:
    (CAUTION: Granting any of the following powers will give your agent the authority to take actions that could significantly reduce your property or change how your property is distributed at your death. INITIAL ONLY the specific powers you WANT to include in the agent's authority.)

(_____) Create, amend, or revoke an inter vivos trust

(_____) Make a gift, subject to the limitations of the [act] and any special instructions in this power of attorney

(_____) Create or change rights of survivorship

(_____) Create or change a beneficiary designation

(_____) Authorize another person to exercise the authority granted under this power of attorney

(_____) Waive the principal's right to be a beneficiary of a joint and survivor annuity, including a survivor benefit under a retirement plan

(_____) Exercise fiduciary powers that the principal has authority to delegate

[(_____) Disclaim or refuse an interest in property, including a power of appointment]

As you can see, the second list of things the agent can do almost all involve altering the principal's estate plan, either by giving gifts that change the amount and nature of the principal's probate property that will pass under the principal's will or in intestacy, or by altering nonprobate property arrangements. A good deal of litigation involves agents exercising authority under a power of attorney in ways that alter the principal's arrangements for making gifts at death. Often these cases involve the agent making gifts to herself or to members of the agent's family. Statutes have been paying more attention to this issue, and the UPOAA is an example of that heightened attention. The approach taken by the act is to make sure that the principal expressly authorizes the grant of such authority to the agent. The idea, of course, is that the principal will be especially careful in granting such authority and will select a truly trustworthy agent. In addition, requiring an express grant of authority makes it easier to hold the agent accountable when the agent does something that is not authorized.

F A Q

Q: Can the agent under a durable power of attorney make a will for the principal?

A: The answer is a resounding no. Executing the principal's will is one thing that simply cannot be done by an agent. Two others are exercising the principal's right to vote and contracting a marriage for the principal. However, some power of attorney statutes allow the principal to give the agent authority to amend existing revocable trusts and even to create a revocable trust. Creating a revocable trust is not very different from writing a will, of course, but this is one instance in which traditional law is being left behind by developments in the law of making gifts at death.

Authority to make gifts illustrates another important feature of the power of attorney: what duty does the agent have to the principal? There is no doubt that the agent is a fiduciary, which means that the agent must act solely in the principal's interest. We'll investigate the fiduciary duties of trustees at great length in Chapter 16, but the agent under a power of attorney is not quite like a trustee. Remember that the law of agency developed long before a durable power of attorney was even possible. Principals were always competent. They could give orders to their agents, and if they gave a degree of discretion to their agents, they could always supervise how it was used. A principal who lacks capacity to act, however, cannot supervise an agent. Nor can the incompetent principal give instructions to the agent.

F   A   Q

Q: What level of capacity is needed to validly create a power of attorney?

A: That's a surprisingly difficult question to answer. Even the Uniform Power of Attorney Act does not require the principal to have any particular level of capacity at the time the power of attorney is executed. About the best we can say is that a principal must know what it means to grant authority under a power of attorney and know to whom the authority is being granted. This is almost certainly a higher level of capacity than that needed to create a valid will and is probably akin to standard contractual capacity.

In addition, agents exercising authority granted by a durable power of attorney often are doing things with the principal's property that are necessary to carry on daily life. When choices have to be made, it is frequently unclear whether a best interests standard or a substituted judgment standard should be used to guide decision making. Sometimes, too, the agent is a family member who will benefit at least indirectly from the actions taken in the principal's interest. The traditional law of fiduciary relationships absolutely forbids a fiduciary from personally benefiting from the exercise of the fiduciary's powers. Such situations involve a conflict of interest that violates the duty of loyalty that a trustee, for example, owes to the beneficiaries of the trust. The law governing agents under durable powers, however, is developing in ways that recognize an agent who is a family member may legitimately benefit from some actions taken for the principal. For example, UPOAA § 114(d) provides that "[a]n agent that acts with care, competence, and diligence for the best interest of the principal is not liable solely because the agent also benefits from the act or has an individual or conflicting interest in relation to the property or affairs of the principal." This provision illustrates another trend in recent legislation: spelling out in some detail the nature of the agent's fiduciary duties in ways that distinguish them from the duties of other fiduciaries.

GIFTS AND POWERS OF ATTORNEY

The history of agents making gifts using the authority granted in a power of attorney is completely tied up with the creation of the durable power of attorney. For many reasons related to the federal estate tax (and many equivalent state taxes), it can be advantageous for a person who is very near death to make gifts to those who would benefit after death under the person's estate plan. Often the prospective donor is without capacity to make a lifetime gift. The agent under a durable power, however, can act. The IRS has challenged some of these gifts on the grounds that the agent did not have the authority to give away the principal's property. The resulting litigation generally has decided that an agent acting under a power of attorney could not make a gift of the principal's property unless the authority to make gifts was expressly granted. Lawyers began to add the authority to make gifts to their forms, and states with power of attorney statutes that include definitions of grants of authority added the authority to make gifts, often limiting the amount of the gifts and requiring the principal to add language to the power of attorney to grant broader authority. As the provisions of the Uniform Power of Attorney Act illustrate, legislatures are beginning to address the issue.

Finally, there is one more aspect of the use of durable powers of attorney that is driving changes in the law. It takes no great leap of the imagination to understand that the agent under a durable power of attorney that grants very broad authority has enormous control over the property of another person. An unscrupulous agent can steal a great deal, to be blunt. Statutory provisions that require an express grant of authority to make gifts and to alter nonprobate property arrangements, like those in the UPOAA's form, are one way to trying to prevent fraud by reminding principals how much authority they are giving the agent. On the other hand, however, the growing complexity of statutory forms and increasing formal oversight of agents have begun to make the durable power of attorney resemble more formal methods for dealing with a disabled principal.

(2) Guardianship

If the durable power of attorney is the least formal method of dealing with disability, and the next step on the road to formality is the revocable trust, guardianship is the end of the road. While procedures and even terminology vary from state to state, we'll use the term **guardianship** to refer to court proceedings that result in the appointment of a person to make decisions for an incapacitated person after the court has made a finding that the person is incapacitated.

In some ways, the sort of guardianship we are dealing with here is like a guardianship of the property of a minor we discussed in Chapter 2. The guardian manages the protected person's property, paying bills and sometimes dealing with making decisions about the protected person's personal life, combining guardianship of the property with guardianship of the person. The degree of court supervision over the guardian's actions varies from state to state. Often, like the guardian of a minor, the guardian of an incapacitated adult can spend the protected persons' income as a routine matter but needs court permission to use capital assets to pay current expenses. While a guardian of the property of a minor is often a lawyer, guardians of protected persons are often family members.

F   A   Q

Q: Does the appointment of a guardian or conservator of a person's property mean the person lacks capacity to make a will?

A: Not at all. A person can have the relatively low level of capacity necessary to make a will yet lack the capacity to manage financial affairs. On the other hand, a completely competent person might need a guardian or conservator to deal with the person's property because of purely physical infirmities.

The distinguishing feature of all guardianship proceedings is that they involve a court. The allegedly incompetent person is entitled to counsel, and most if not all states have mechanisms for making an independent assessment of the capacity of the person who is the subject of the proceeding. Many modern statutes allow the court to tailor the conservatorship to the needs of the protected person. In essence, the law of guardianship has begun to recognize degrees of incapacity. The policy is to give decision-making power to another person only to the degree it is necessary for the health and safety of the protected person.

That is not to say that the powers of a guardian are always limited. In some states, and under the UPC (§ 5-411(a)(7)), the guardian (called a conservator under the UPC) with court approval can make a will for a protected person, amend or revoke an existing will, or create a revocable trust. The terms of the estate plan created by a guardian or conservator are set by using the substituted judgment standard.

Although we've now spent some time on the differences between the durable power of attorney and guardianship as ways for dealing with disability, in some ways they are more alike than different when they are compared to the revocable lifetime trust, another legal mechanism for managing the property of a disabled person. Here are the important similarities and differences:

- Who selects the person who has authority to deal with the property?

  The *revocable trust* and the *power of attorney* are ALIKE because the *trustee* and the *agent* are selected by the person whose property they manage, the *settlor* and the *principal*.

  Guardianship is DIFFERENT because the person managing the property is selected by the court (although in some states a person can nominated a guardian before becoming incompetent; the court may but need not appoint the nominated person).

- To whom is the person managing the property responsible?

  The *power of attorney* and *guardianship* are ALIKE because the *agent* and the *guardian* are responsible and owe duties only to the *principal* or the *protected person.*

  The *revocable trust* is DIFFERENT because the *trustee* may owe fiduciary duties to all of the beneficiaries of the trust, not just the (now incapacitated) *settlor.* (The law in this area is not settled; in some states, even if the settlor/sole beneficiary for life is incapacitated, the other beneficiaries cannot question the actions of the trustee; only the settlor's guardian can do that.)

- Who makes the decision about the power granted to the person managing the property?

The *power of attorney* and the *revocable trust* are ALIKE because the *settlor* and the *principal* are in complete control, in the first instance, of the terms of the trust; and in the second, of the what authority to grant the agent.

Guardianship is DIFFERENT because the authority of the *guardian* is controlled by the relevant statute and the court creating the guardianship.

■ Can the arrangement be kept private?

The *revocable trust* and the *power of attorney* are ALIKE because neither really is a public document; they are created by purely private action.

Guardianship is DIFFERENT because it is created in a court proceeding.

C. Healthcare Decisions

Whatever the differences and similarities among the durable powers of attorney, revocable trust, and guardianship, when it comes to managing the affairs of a disabled or incapacitated person, there is one thing they have in common in almost all, if not all, jurisdictions: the decision maker cannot make decisions about the healthcare of the settlor, principal, or protected person. Appointing a decision maker for healthcare issues almost always requires executing another document. In addition, instructions regarding treatment decisions, known as **advance directives** (but often called, somewhat confusingly, a **living will**), may have to be included in another, separate document. In some states, the two documents can be combined, and that's the approach of the Uniform Health Care Decisions Act (UHCDA), which has been fairly widely adopted by the states, sometimes with modifications.

F   A   Q

Q: Must advance directives be in writing?

A: In many states, no. Wishes about life-sustaining treatment can be proved by testimony from others about the patient's statements while competent. Good practice, however, is to put the desires and instructions in writing in a form recognized by the relevant jurisdiction.

If a person has not appointed a healthcare decision maker, the task of making decisions for an incapacitated person falls to the spouse (under some statutes, a domestic partner) or next of kin, meaning children or parents if there are no children (this should remind you of the list of persons who can be administrator of an intestate estate). Of course, decision by committee is difficult, especially when the decision involves life and death. To try to mitigate the difficulties, many states have enacted statutes that create a hierarchy of decision makers, starting with the person's spouse. If there is more than one person entitled to make decisions, majority rules, and if there is a tie, no one can make decisions and it's off to court to have a decision maker appointed.

The way all of this is supposed to work, of course, is that a decision maker selected by the now incapacitated person is to make decisions in accordance with the clear written instructions given by the person who can no longer make decisions for herself. What if there are no written advance directives that cover the situation? The usual standard for surrogate decision making in this area is substituted judgment, based on what the surrogate decision maker knows of the individual's beliefs and desires. The UHCDA says that in the absence of knowledge of the individual's desires, the decision is to be made "in accordance with the surrogate's determination of the patient's best interests," taking into account the patient's "personal values" to the extent the surrogate decision maker knows about those values (§§ 2(e), 5(f)).

As you no doubt understand, appointing a surrogate decision maker for healthcare and formulating advance directives, along with the preparation of a durable power of attorney, have become standard parts of creating an estate plan.

D. Disposition of Remains

The very last thing to consider in this chapter is indeed the very last thing—the disposition of the decedent's remains. Funerary customs are an important part of any society, and they vary greatly among human cultures. In the United States, most human remains are buried, although entombment above ground in a mausoleum seems to be becoming more common as traditional cemeteries are pressed for space. Cremation is another option. The ashes (sometimes called cremains) can then be scattered, buried, or placed in the equivalent of a mausoleum called a columbarium. The important thing to recognize is that most people have very strong feelings about the disposition of their remains and often wish to make sure that their desires are carried out.

If the decedent has not made his wishes known before death, the surviving family makes decisions about the disposition of the decedent's remains. Long-settled common law gives priority for making those decisions to a surviving spouse; if no spouse, then to children; and if no children, then to close collateral relatives. There are many cases in which surviving family cannot agree on what to do, and courts have often been called on to settle the resulting disputes by determining what the decedent would have wanted (an example of a substituted judgment standard). For example, if it can be shown that the decedent regularly carried out religious observances, a court would most likely decide that the decedent would prefer to be buried in accordance with that particular religious tradition.

Some states have enacted statutes that allow a person to designate someone to make all the arrangements necessary for the disposition of the person's remains in accordance with binding instructions. The resulting document is analogous to and even looks a little like a designation of a surrogate healthcare decision maker coupled with what amounts to advance directives with regard to funerary rites and burial or cremation. In those states, the proper creation of binding directions for

INCREASING ORGAN DONATION

Human organs suitable for transplantation are in chronically short supply, making the discussion of how to increase organ donation an important one. While some have suggested that marketing human organs is an appropriate solution, Congress has forbidden the sale of human organs (National Organ Transplant Act of 1984, 42 U.S.C. § 274(e)). Other commentators have suggested tax deductions or credits for donation. One of the more promising ideas, which some European nations have implemented, is to make consent to donation the default rule; a person has to affirmatively opt out of the presumed consent regime. Where the presumed consent rule has become law, organ donation has often increased dramatically. For now, though, state laws concerning organ donation vary, but federal regulations require hospitals that participate in Medicare to make a "routine request" of all prospective donors' families.

disposition of the client's remains is yet another aspect of routine estate planning. The statutes often create a hierarchy of persons entitled to make decisions about funeral arrangements in disposition of remains in the absence of written instructions. While the hierarchy is usually the same as under the common law, these statutes often give a surviving domestic partner (defined in a variety of ways) the same priority as a surviving spouse.

There is another aspect of the disposition of human remains that is truly the opposite of death. The transplantation of human organs is almost routine and would be even more common were there a sufficient supply of donated organs. There are statutes in all states governing organ donation after death. Most of these statutes are based on some version of the Uniform Anatomical Gift Act, first promulgated by the Uniform Law Commission in 1968 and revised in 1987 and 2006. The statutes create procedures for giving consent for the donation of one's organs — which in many states can be done by signing a donation form incorporated into a driver's license — and for the giving of consent by surviving family members of a prospective donor.

SUMMARY

■ Making decisions for an incapacitated person usually involves using a substituted judgment or a best interests standard. The former involves attempting to make the decision the incapacitated person would make; the latter, the decision that is best for the incapacitated person under the circumstances.

■ Planning for incapacity is now a standard part of estate planning. The principal planning devices are durable powers of attorney and revocable trusts. These arrangements are relatively informal and private, and the grant of authority remains under the control of the person making the arrangements.

■ Guardianship is the formal, public means of managing incapacity. It requires a court proceeding; the authority of the guardian can be quite limited, but in any event is controlled by law.

■ Decisions about medical treatment usually require the execution of documents other than a power of attorney or revocable trust. These documents both appoint someone to make healthcare decisions and give guidance on how to make those decisions, especially when they concern withdrawal of life-sustaining treatment. In the absence of a grant of authority, statutes in many states give that authority to family members.

■ Decisions about the disposition of a decedent's body are also the province of family members. In some states, statutes provide a mechanism for authorizing a person to carry out instructions for disposition of one's remains.

CONNECTIONS

Disability Planning and Revocable Trusts

Although we usually think of the revocable trust as the premier device for avoiding probate (Chapter 11), it can also be an excellent way to manage the property of someone who lacks capacity to handle his own affairs.

Disability Planning and Fiduciary Obligation

While the fiduciary obligations of court-appointed guardians and most trustees are well understood (if not always observed) (Chapter 16), the obligations of the trustee of a revocable trust (Chapter 11) are not quite as well defined. Even less clear are the fiduciary obligations of agents under durable powers of attorney. In particular, the strict fiduciary duty of loyalty is modified in recent legislative enactments like the UPOAA.

Disability Planning and Protection of the Family

Giving someone the authority to make decisions regarding the property of an incapacitated person can have profound effects on the incapacitated person's family. The authority given to many agents under durable powers of attorney includes the ability to significantly alter the principal's arrangements for making gifts at death and may alter the amount of property subject to the elective share (Chapter 13).

Charitable Trusts

15

O V E R V I E W

Charitable trusts differ from other trusts because they do not have ascertainable beneficiaries and are exempt from the Rule Against Perpetuities (where it still exists). This special treatment is justified by the public benefits provided by charitable trusts. The desire to preserve these public benefits has led to more flexible rules about how courts can modify charitable trusts. Enforcing the duties of trustees of charitable trusts is also the subject of special doctrines and rules because of the absence of ascertainable beneficiaries. While for many decades public officials have enforced charitable trusts' terms, both case law and statutes have begun to give settlors of charitable trusts and donors of charitable gifts standing to enforce the terms of their gifts.

A. **RANGE OF CHARITABLE ENTITIES**

B. **PURPOSES FOR WHICH CHARITABLE TRUSTS CAN BE CREATED**

    1. Traditional Limits
    2. Purpose Trusts
    3. Discriminatory Provisions

C. **CY PRES**

D. **SUPERVISION OF CHARITABLE TRUSTS**

    1. Role of the State Attorneys General
    2. Persons Who Have a Special Interest
    3. Emerging Role of the Donor

A. Range of Charitable Entities

Charitable entities are organized in two main ways: as trusts and as corporations. In the twenty-first century, the corporation is the more common form by far. But the much older law of charitable trusts has greatly influenced the law applied to charitable corporations, so what we discuss in this chapter is important for understanding all ways of making charitable gifts.

B. Purposes for Which Charitable Trusts Can Be Created

(1) Traditional Limits

As we've seen in Chapter 8, trusts can be created for a truly breathtaking range of purposes. The only limit is set by public policy, which on the whole is a very generous limit setter when it comes to private trusts. Things are a little different when we're talking about charitable trusts because charitable trusts are free from some of the restrictive rules that apply to private express trusts. Most strikingly, a charitable trust is not subject to the Rule Against Perpetuities (where it still exists). A charitable trust can last forever. The other principal difference between charitable trusts and private trusts has to do with the requirement that a trust have identifiable beneficiaries. A charitable trust can have indefinite or unascertained beneficiaries. How, then, is a charitable trust enforced if there are no identifiable beneficiaries who can call the trustee to account? We'll deal with that question in a bit.

Given these exemptions from the law generally applicable to trusts, it's not surprising that the category of "charitable trust" has long been limited to trusts that are created to accomplish what courts describe as socially desirable purposes. The ancestors of the usual list of permissible charitable purposes, however, are not cases. The usually accepted list goes back to the English Statute of Charitable Uses of 1601. The latest form of the list is in Restatement (Third) of Trusts § 28, which states that charitable purposes include

(a) the relief of poverty,
(b) the advancement of knowledge or education,
(c) the advancement of religion,
(d) the promotion of health,
(e) governmental or municipal purposes, and
(f) other purposes that are beneficial to the community.

UTC § 405(a) reproduces the substance of this list with only minor stylistic variations.

The last category, of course, is not easily defined. As the Restatement puts it, when it comes to deciding whether a particular purpose is indeed charitable because

Sidebar

CHARITABLE, BENEVOLENT, OR PHILANTHROPIC?

A good deal of case law exists on whether a gift for "benevolent" purposes is also a gift for "charitable" purposes. English precedent going back to the early nineteenth century holds that the term "benevolent" is not the same as "charitable" but the term "philanthropic" is. Therefore, a gift in a will to the trustees named in the will who are to use the income from the property "for such benevolent or philanthropic purposes as the trustees select" is not a charitable trust. The law in the United States is not uniform. Many states have case law that maintains the distinction, but a few states have statutes that recognize gifts in trust for benevolent purposes as the equivalent of charitable trusts.

it is beneficial to the community, "much depends on the time and the place at which the questions arises" (§ 28 cmt. *l*). One example the Restatement does give involves trusts to relieve the suffering of animals, to prevent cruelty to animals, or to provide a home for stray or abandoned animals.

Don't confuse this very broad list of charitable purposes with the charitable tax exemption rules or the deductions allowed for charitable donations. Federal tax law plays a very important part in setting the rules for making charitable gifts and deducting charitable donations, as well as for administering charitable institutions, including charitable trusts. (Remember too that state law on charitable purposes applies to the question of whether an organization is exempt from real property taxation, state or local.) And although tax law and the traditional list of charitable trust purposes overlap, they also differ in important ways.[1]

Sidebar

WHAT'S IN A NAME?

Many charities have similar-sounding names. When your client wants to make a gift at death to a specific charity, you must identify the charitable organization properly. Usually this requires getting in contact with the organization or at least visiting its Web site. If your client expects a tax deduction for the gift, you must also make sure that gifts to the organization are deductible (unless it is a very well-known public charity like the American Red Cross). You might ask the organization for a copy of its exemption letter or consult the list of all tax-exempt organizations published by the IRS. If there is any doubt about what charitable organization the decedent meant, the result is likely to be a construction proceeding.

F A Q

Q: Can a trust have both charitable and noncharitable beneficiaries?

A: Yes, but. The "but" has to do with tax issues. In tax talk, such trusts are called **split interest trusts**, and if the settlor wants to get a tax deduction for the value of the charitable portion of the trust, the trust must conform to some fairly complex rules found in IRC §§ 664, 2055, and 2522 (discussed briefly in Chapter 17). Split interest trusts are valuable tools for accomplishing estate planning when estate and gift taxes are an issue and are also valuable in income tax planning. As far as the property law of trusts is concerned, however, split interest trusts have identifiable beneficiaries who have standing to enforce the trust, and the noncharitable beneficiaries have interests that must be valid under the Rule Against Perpetuities (where it still exists).

(2) Purpose Trusts

What if a person who intends to create a trust without definite beneficiaries fails to create a valid charitable trust? The property ends up wherever the circumstances require; for example, if the gift were made by the residuary clause of the testator's will, the property would pass in a partial intestacy.

One of the most striking trends in modern trust law, by far more developed in common law jurisdictions outside of the United States, is the validation of these failed trusts as **purpose trusts**, trusts without definite beneficiaries created for some purpose other than charitable, which we mentioned in Chapter 8's discussion

---

[1]If you're interested, you can find the list of types of organizations to which contributions are deductible for income tax purposes in IRC § 170(c) and the list of purposes for which a tax-exempt organization can be created in § 501(c)(3).

of the requirement that a trust have beneficiaries. As we learned there, one type of this sort of trust that is now widely valid in the United States (and under UTC § 408) is a trust for the care of a specific animal, often called a **pet trust**. The UTC does go further, however. Section 409 allows the creation of a noncharitable trust with "without definite or definitely ascertainable beneficiaries" for a valid purpose that can last no more than 21 years.

(3) Discriminatory Provisions

One of the best examples of how changing times can affect the law is how courts have treated charitable trusts with racial or religiously restrictive conditions since the civil rights revolution began in the 1960s. It is not unusual to find trusts created to give scholarships to persons of only one race or gender (usually white and male) or that limited benefits to persons of a certain religion or not of a certain religion.

When these trusts have been tangled up with public institutions—for example, where some public body serves as trustee—the courts have had little difficulty in removing the offending provision by finding state action and consequently a violation of the equal protection guarantee of the Fourteenth Amendment to the U.S. Constitution. A trust to provide college scholarships to white graduates of a particular public high school cannot stand if the trustee is the school board. The next question is whether the trust should continue without the discriminatory provision or instead come to an end. Courts have usually allowed a trust to continue without the impermissible restriction by using doctrines that allow courts to alter charitable trusts to carry out the donor's intent as closely as possible. We'll discuss the principal doctrine, cy pres, in a minute.

What happens if the charitable trust is not connected to state action in any way? The provisions may still violate state or federal anti-discrimination laws. If that's the case, the courts face the same question of whether to strike the discriminatory provision and allow the trust to continue or to allow the trust to fail because it can no longer be carried out. The more common result is to allow the trust to continue on a nondiscriminatory basis by removing the impermissible restriction.

F   A   Q

Q: Can I create a charitable trust to provide college scholarships to the descendants of my grandparents?

A: No. This really isn't a question of invidious discrimination, but rather one of charitable purpose. Limiting beneficiaries to the relatives of the settlor is an attempt to turn a private trust into one that receives certain privileges because it benefits the public in some way. Similarly, the tax law has rigorous provisions designed to ensure that trusts receiving favorable tax treatment are not masks for providing benefits to the family or friends of the settlor rather than to the public.

There are no hard and fast rules here. What is certain is that answering the question of what is and isn't acceptable involves questions of constitutional requirements, statutory and administrative provisions, and public policy, all of which interact in complex ways.

C. Cy Pres

Courts are usually quite adamant in their refusals to rewrite wills and trusts to better accomplish what the persons who created them intended. The approach to charitable trusts is quite different, a difference embodied in the doctrine of **cy pres** (from *cy pres comme possible*, "as near as possible"). Cy pres allows courts, under certain conditions, to apply a charitable trust's provisions to a purpose that *as closely as possible* matches the original settlor's purpose.

What is it about charitable trusts that led to the development of this exceptional doctrine? Surely it is related to the public nature of the charitable trust. Remember that a trust is charitable only if the trust property is devoted to a purpose that in some way benefits the public, even if that benefit comes by helping individuals. If the exact purposes for which the trust was created cannot be carried out, the courts have been willing to make changes in the trust terms to ensure that the trust continues to benefit the public. This willingness is especially evident where the descendants of the settlor have a reversionary interest that would come into possession of the trust property were the trust to fail.

Before the question of whether to use the cy pres doctrine is ever reached, the charitable trust in question has to fail in some way. The traditional view is that a charitable trust fails when its purpose is or has become unlawful, impossible, or impractical to carry out. We've already seen examples of the first: a trust may have provisions that with the passage of time and the change of context turn out to violate constitutional, statutory, or regulatory provisions or are contrary to public policy. "Impossible" could include provisions for the support of an institution or a cause that no longer exists because of societal or technological change. A trust to provide scholarships to attend a college that no longer exists is impossible to carry out. A trust to provide a park for a city becomes impossible to carry out when the park land is taken by eminent domain to build a highway. "Impracticality" often involves insufficient funds. A gift in trust to erect a hospital may be impractical to carry out because the amount is insufficient to build and operate a modern hospital.

Both Restatement (Third) of Trusts § 67 and UTC § 413 take an important step beyond the traditional rules by allowing a court to use cy pres doctrine when a particular charitable purpose becomes "wasteful." The Restatement makes it clear that "wasteful" means that the amount of funds available so far exceeds what is necessary to carry out the charitable purpose of the trust "that continued expenditure of all of the funds for that purpose, although possible to do so, would be wasteful" (§ 67 cmt. c(1)). Another way to explain this concept of "wasteful" is to apply it when the trust generates surplus funds. Sometimes the cure for the "wasteful" gift is straightforward. A trust created to provide a limited number of scholarships to a particular school produces much more income than is necessary to fund the stipulated number of scholarships. A court would likely use cy pres to authorize the awarding of a greater number of scholarships than provided by the terms of the trust. That's easy. Far more complicated are cases in which the available funds seem to some observers as far exceeding what can usefully be spent on the specified charitable purposes. Consider a trust whose income is to be expended on the relief of the poor and needy in a county where the median and average family incomes far exceed that of other counties in the relevant metropolitan area.

Is it "wasteful" to spend large sums on a very small number of needy persons when in the same community, broadly defined, there are far more people in need of aid? Should a court use the cy pres doctrine to expand the geographical scope of the trust's charitable activities because there is so much money available that it can be "spread around"? That's not an easy question to answer. The settlor's intent is clear, and the charitable purpose is clearly not illegal, impossible (there will always be at least some needy persons in the richest community), nor impractical (something can always be done for those persons). How much deference must be given to the settlor's freedom to dispose of wealth as the settlor decides? How much weight can a court give to the needs of the broader community? And what is the "community," anyway? Is the rich suburban county part of a community that includes a relatively poor city? These are not easy questions, and it remains to be seen how courts will address them where UTC § 413(a) is the law or where courts accept the formulation of Restatement (Third) of Trusts § 67.

F   A   Q

Q: Does cy pres apply only to charitable trusts?

A: No. Courts have applied the doctrine also to gifts to charitable corporations. One classic case, *Matter of Neher*, 18 N.E.2d 625 (N.Y. 1939), involves a gift to a unit of local government. The testator placed her property in trust for the Village of Red Hook to use as a hospital named for the testator's husband. The highest court of New York agreed with the village that it did not have the resources to operate a hospital, that the stated purpose was therefore impractical, and that the doctrine of cy pres allowed the village to memorialize the testator's husband by building on the property an administration building named for the testator's husband.

Traditionally, the first step in applying cy pres to a charitable trust whose purpose can no longer be carried out is to determine whether the settlor had a **general charitable intent** or an intent to make the charitable gift only for the original purposes of the trust. That inquiry is where all the "art" of applying the doctrine takes over. Finding the intent of the donor of the charitable gift is an exercise shaped by formal rules of construction as well as by a court's insights into what the donor had in mind. As always with construction questions, it is sometimes difficult to escape the conclusion that the court's reasoning comes after a decision about what the donor meant. In the context of deciding whether cy pres is applicable to a failed charitable gift, a court's search for the donor's intent is often shaped by a predisposition to find a way to preserve benefits for society, especially if the alternative is to allow the property to pass to the donor's heirs or residuary beneficiaries.

The "traditionally" beginning the preceding paragraph is necessary because this is another area in which Restatement (Third) of Trusts and the UTC have made a change that can be characterized as radical. The blackletter of Restatement § 67 begins with the phrase "unless the terms of the trust provide otherwise." Under the Restatement, therefore, the application of cy pres is the default position. UTC § 413 codifies that position. Under the UTC, as under the Restatement, the donor's general charitable intent is assumed. The comment to UTC § 413 is completely candid about the reason for abandoning the need to find that general charitable intent: "Courts are usually able to find a general charitable purpose to which to apply the property, no matter how vaguely such purpose may have been expressed by the settlor."

The UTC also deals expressly with another aspect of the application of the cy pres doctrine in a way that expands the ability of the court to use cy pres. Comment b to

Restatement § 67 says that terms of the trust providing for disposition of the trust property should the charitable purpose fail are to be given effect and preclude the application of cy pres. UTC § 413(b), on the other hand, says that a trust provision that results in distribution to a noncharitable beneficiary prevails over the court's power to use cy pres *only* if under the provision the trust property reverts to the settlor and the settlor is still alive or if the trust were created not more than 21 years ago. The UTC goes very far to preserve charitable trusts.

Figure 15.1 sums up the current state of the cy pres doctrine.

FIGURE 15.1   Cy pres doctrine

A court may apply cy pres to a charitable gift if the gift is, when made, or becomes

> ### Unlawful
> (e.g., involves discrimination forbidden by constitutional provisions, statute, or regulation or is contrary to public policy);

Or

> ### Impossible
> (e.g., a beneficiary (usually an institution) no longer exists);

Or

> ### Impractical
> (e.g., the amount of the gift is insufficient to carry out the charitable purpose);

*Or, **under Restatement (Third) of Trusts § 67 and UTC § 413(a),***

> ### Wasteful
> (e.g., a trust to provide a small number of scholarships generates several times the income necessary to fund those scholarships).

*And, **under traditional law,***

> The donor of the gift had a general charitable intent as opposed to the intent to carry out only the stated charitable purpose.

*And, **under Restatement (Third) of Trusts § 67,***

> ### The terms of the trust do not provide otherwise
> (e.g., the terms provide otherwise if on the failure of the charitable gift the trust property reverts to the settlor or passes to the settlor's descendants).

And, under UTC § 413,

> **The terms of the trust do not provide for distribution of the trust property to a noncharitable beneficiary should the trust end; but if they do, the terms do not prevent the application of cy pres**
>
> *unless*
>
> beneficiary is the settlor and the settlor is alive
>
> *or*
>
> fewer than 21 years have passed since the creation of the trust.

D. Supervision of Charitable Trusts

As we've seen, one of the major differences between charitable trusts and private trusts is that charitable trusts do not have definite beneficiaries. Indeed, the primary distinguishing characteristic of charitable trusts is that the beneficiaries are indefinite, or, to put it more precisely, the beneficiaries of a charitable trust are the public at large. Or to put it another and more modern way, the charitable trust is a purpose trust without ascertainable beneficiaries. However you conceptualize the matter, a charitable trust does not have identified beneficiaries who can make sure that the trustees, or for that matter the donees of charitable gifts not in trust, are doing what they are supposed to be doing. In formal legal terms, who has standing to sue to enforce the terms of the gift?

(1) Role of the State Attorneys General

The answer is the state attorneys general, whose offices also supervise charitable corporations and other charitable entities. The attorney general's authority extends to bringing a cy pres proceeding, either on its own or in collaboration with the trust's trustees or the gift's donees. In supervising charities, the attorney general's authority includes investigating compensation paid to officers, the appropriateness of investments, and how the charitable purpose is being carried out.

A good deal of scholarly commentary maintains that state attorneys general do not provide that much real supervision of charities, including charitable trusts, for lack of resources or for politics reasons, among others. Making generalizations about all 50 state attorneys general is difficult, but these sorts of concerns are reflected in the developing law of the supervision of charities.

(2) Persons Who Have a Special Interest

One category of private individuals does have standing in most U.S. jurisdictions to enforce the terms of a charitable gift: persons with a "special interest" in carrying out the trust's charitable purpose. The courts often have not been very generous in finding this type of standing, however, because they fear that numerous lawsuits against charities might result. Although baseless, these suits would be expensive to fend off, draining assets that should be devoted to the charitable purpose. However, in some circumstances, granting standing to those with a special interest may be the only way to enforce a charitable gift, especially given the limitations of the attorney general's ability (or perhaps willingness) to deal with every possible violation.

F   A   Q

Q: What's a relator got to do with the attorney general enforcing a charitable trust?

A: Public officials like the attorney general sometimes bring suit "on the relation" of a third person, who pays the costs of the litigation. In a way, the third person asks the attorney general to allow her to carry on the suit based on the attorney general's standing. The attorney general may control the conduct of the suit and may later withdraw the authorization given the relator.

What amounts to a special interest is decided on a case-by-case basis and involves some complexities. All we need to say for now is that courts continue to create common law by balancing the concerns about preventing harassment of charitable trustees while ensuring that the terms of charitable gifts are enforced.

(3) Emerging Role of the Donor

Perhaps the hottest topic in the law of enforcing charitable trusts is the growing number of cases in which the donor has been recognized as having standing to enforce the gift. Not so long ago (indeed just before the beginning of the twenty-first century), it was blackletter that the settlor of a charitable trust (or the donor of any charitable gift) lacked standing to enforce the terms of the trust (or of the gift) unless the settlor (or donor) had reserved the right to do so in the trust terms (or in the terms of the gift). That rule was not unique to charitable trusts; the settlor of a private trust cannot sue to enforce the trust unless the settlor has retained an interest in the trust or has retained the power to enforce the trust. This general rule really is a rule. The reporter's notes to Restatement (Third) of Trusts § 94 comment d(2) read, "The basic rule . . . has been consistently recognized in treatise statements of

> **Sidebar**
>
> **PRINCIPLES OF THE LAW OF NONPROFIT ORGANIZATIONS**
>
> The law of charitable trusts is important for the law of all charitable gifts, not just those made in trust. And although that means much of what the Restatement (Third) of Trusts says about charitable trusts is relevant to all charitable gifts, many aspects of the administration of charities are not part of the law of trusts. The ALI has an ongoing project to create not a Restatement of the law but a statement of the Principles of the Law of Nonprofit Organizations. When the project is completed, it will be an important tool for understanding the law of charities beyond what we've dealt with here.

common law" and in the prior Restatements, including in § 391 of Restatement (Second) of Trusts. The notes also observe that the general rule has not been subjected to the sort of criticism that has arisen in the charitable trust context, "perhaps reflecting a general satisfaction with traditional doctrine."

No one would say today that there is satisfaction with the traditional doctrine as applied to charitable gifts, whether in trust or not. The change in the law has been driven by several forces, including some very high-profile cases; greater suspicion of large, wealthy charitable institutions; and perhaps a greater assertiveness on the part of donors, who feel that they have obligations to ensure that their gifts are being put to proper uses, especially when their names are associated with them. In addition, courts seem to be more open to arguments resting on the asserted inability of the attorney general to deal with every instance of possible wrongdoing by trustees of charitable trusts and managers of charitable corporations.

For whatever reasons, the rule with regard to charitable trusts is indeed changing. And the change has come not only from decided cases. Legislation allowing settlors to enforce charitable trusts has begun to appear on the statute books, often because a state has adopted UTC § 405(c), which reads, "The settlor of a charitable trust, among others, may maintain a proceeding to enforce the trust." It is not surprising, then, to find that Restatement (Third) of Trusts § 94(2) has joined in, jettisoning the rule of prior Restatements as applied to charitable trusts by listing the settlor as one of the persons who can sue for enforcement of a charitable trust, at least under some conditions. Clearly, the law of settlor standing will continue to develop.

SUMMARY

■ Charitable trusts differ from private express trusts in that they do not have ascertainable beneficiaries and are not subject to the Rule Against Perpetuities (where it still exists).

■ Charitable trusts can be created only for purposes that benefit the public.

■ Courts have long used the doctrine of cy pres to carry out a donor's general charitable intent if his or her specific charitable trust or charitable gift cannot be carried out exactly according to its terms. Both Restatement (Third) of Trusts and the UTC liberalize the use of cy pres.

■ While the task of enforcing charitable trusts and gifts traditionally has belonged to the state attorneys general, one of the most dramatic changes in the law of charitable trusts and gifts has been the increasing willingness of courts and statutes (including the UTC) to give donors in general, including the settlors of charitable trusts, standing to enforce their gifts.

CONNECTIONS

Charitable Trusts and Trusts (Modification and Termination)

The traditional law of modification and termination of private express trusts focuses on enforcing the intent of the settlor (Chapter 8). Private benefits are controlled by the person who created them, even from the grave. When it comes to charitable trusts and charitable gifts in general, courts have long used the doctrine of cy pres to alter the terms of trust and charitable gifts not in trust to preserve the donor's intent to benefit the public.

Charitable Trusts and Trusts (Requirements for a Valid Trust)

While charitable trusts require a trustee and trust property as do other express trusts, there is no need for a charitable trust to have ascertainable beneficiaries, which a private express trust must have (Chapter 8). The general public is the beneficiary of the trust, which means that enforcement is traditionally also in the hands of the representative of the public, the state attorney general.

Charitable Trusts and Fiduciary Duties (Enforcement)

The lack of ascertainable beneficiaries means that the state attorney general is charged with enforcing the fiduciary duties (Chapter 16) of trustees of charitable trusts.

Fiduciary Obligation and Trusts and Estates

16

If you own a pet or ever babysit your little brother, congratulations! You are a fiduciary. Well, at least *unofficially* you're a fiduciary. In the legal sense, a fiduciary is someone who is obliged to act solely for another party's benefit, which in our context means trustees and personal representatives. (Fiduciaries are found in many other areas of the law too; in fact, the lawyer-client relationship is one important example.) The law that governs trustees and personal representatives divides roughly into three parts: prohibitions, commands, and rules governing third-party relationships. Breaches of fiduciary duties are serious concerns for beneficiaries, of course, but also for society in general, given the level of trust involved.

O V E R V I E W

D. DUTIES OWED DIRECTLY TO BENEFICIARIES

1. To Inform
2. To Account
3. To Inquire

E. DAMAGES FOR BREACH

1. Violations of the Duty of Loyalty
2. Violations of the Duty of Prudence

F. EXCULPATORY CLAUSES

G. LIABILITY OF THIRD PARTIES

H. TRUSTEE LIABILITY TO THIRD PARTIES

A. What Fiduciaries Cannot Do: The Duty of Loyalty

The essence of being a **fiduciary** is acting solely for the benefit of whoever is owed the fiduciary obligation. While fiduciary obligations are found in many areas of law, for our purposes we're talking about the duties trustees and personal representatives owe to the beneficiaries of trusts and estates. One of the most important elements of the fiduciary obligation is the **duty of loyalty**, which is often summarized by the rule that the trustee or personal representative is to administer the trust or estate solely in the interests of the beneficiaries. The duty of loyalty from the perspective of the trustee or personal representative is "all for you, beneficiaries, and none for me."

(1) Self-Dealing

The most striking doctrinal manifestation of the duty of loyalty is the prohibition on **self-dealing**, which is what happens when a fiduciary is on both sides of a transaction involving the property of the trust or estate, usually selling as fiduciary and buying as an individual. Traditionally, the law has allowed the fiduciary no defense (with the few exceptions that we discuss in a minute). Self-dealing is a breach of the duty of loyalty, period. This unforgiving approach is known as the **no further inquiry rule**.

Classically, the only defenses to the no further inquiry rule are that the settlor (or testator) authorized self-dealing in the trust terms (or the will), or that the beneficiaries consented. Consent can come only after full disclosure; and even then, the fiduciary must act in good faith and the entire transaction must be fair to the beneficiaries. A court may authorize the self-dealing as well, but that almost always requires the beneficiaries' consent.

Realize that transactions that involve self-dealing are *voidable*, not void. That is, if the beneficiaries do not complain, nothing happens. Even if the beneficiaries are unhappy, if they wait too long to ask a court to set aside the transaction, the statute of limitations will bar any action.

The UTC codifies the duty of loyalty in § 802. Subsection (b) makes any transaction involving trust property that the trustee enters into for the trustee's personal benefit voidable by a beneficiary. In addition to the exceptions we've already mentioned, § 802(b) adds approval of the court, the beneficiary's failure to object before the running of the statute of limitations provided in § 1005, and a relevant contract that was entered into before the trustee "became or contemplated becoming trustee." The UTC codification generally agrees with the treatment of self-dealing in Restatement (Third) of Trusts § 78. The blackletter of § 78(c) states that the trustee is "strictly prohibited "from engaging in self-dealing" except in "discrete circumstances," which generally are those enumerated in UTC § 802.

Keep in mind that although the exceptions have expanded over the years, the basic rule is still that self-dealing is a breach of the duty of loyalty, no further inquiry necessary. The reference in Restatement (Third) of Trusts § 78(c) to "discreet circumstances" emphasizes the strength of the basic rule. There are no general exceptions, only a limited number of special situations in which it is clear that the benefit to the trust and the beneficiaries outweighs the inherent evil of self-dealing.

Since the last decade of the twentieth century, commentators have become more critical of the no further inquiry rule, arguing that it should be replaced by the requirement that the trustee act in the best interests of the beneficiaries. If exceptions to the no further inquiry rule continue to multiply, a best interest standard may finally supplant it.

Sidebar

RULES AND STANDARDS

The discussion of whether the (relatively) bright line of the no further inquiry rule is better than a best interests of the beneficiaries standard is one more example of the conflict between rules and standards that appears in many areas of law. The conflict is always between an inflexible rule and a court-applied standard. The first presumably is efficient because actors know ahead of time what is and is not allowed. On the other hand, maybe a court should decide whether a fiduciary's self-dealing furthers beneficiaries' interests enough to outweigh any harm. The disadvantage, of course, of involving a court is more time and money. So what's better, a rule or a standard? That's something lawmakers, judges, and lawyers will be discussing probably forever.

(2) Conflicts

Another category of transactions that is forbidden to fiduciaries is **conflicts of interest** between the fiduciary's duty of loyalty to the beneficiaries and the fiduciary's loyalty to or affection for other persons. The classic example is a sale of trust property to the fiduciary's child. The child-parent relationship means that the fiduciary is interested in both sides of the transaction. To put it less abstractly, what's stronger, the fiduciary's duty to obtain the highest possible selling price for the trust beneficiaries' benefit or the parent's interest in selling at the lowest possible price for her child's benefit? The law acknowledges that some temptations are too strong to resist. Rather than expect the fiduciary to deal at arm's length with any person to whom the fiduciary feels personal loyalty, the law says "don't even try." (See the long and broad list of parties that create such a conflict of interest in UTC § 802(c) and the more or less identical list in UPC § 3-713 applicable to personal representatives.)

The duty of loyalty, to use an *au current* term, is robust. Exceptions are few and closely circumscribed, and violations that do not fall under an exception cannot be excused no matter how appealing the circumstances.

(3) Co-Fiduciaries

It is not uncommon for an estate to have **co-fiduciaries**, that is, more than one executor or trustee. While all fiduciaries of estate and trusts have the same fiduciary duties to the beneficiaries, co-fiduciaries have special duties related to monitoring one another.

Even before we can ask what happens when one of several co-fiduciaries breaches fiduciary duties, we have to know how co-fiduciaries resolve disagreements among themselves. The traditional rule is that if there is more than one executor of an estate, each one can exercise many powers without the concurrence of the others. UPC § 3-717, however, provides that co-executors must act concurrently, unless the will provides otherwise. The section also provides that co-executors can delegate one of their number to act for all and allows less than unanimous action if an emergency must be addressed. Just to make things a little confusing, the traditional rule for co-trustees is that they must act unanimously, but UTC § 703(a) allows co-trustees who cannot agree to act by majority decision, and Restatement (Third) of Trusts § 39 agrees. What happens when an even number of co-fiduciaries divide evenly on a question? The only solution is to go to court. (Memo to self: advise clients who insist on multiple fiduciaries to designate an odd number.)

F   A   Q

Q: Why appoint more than one executor or trustee?

A: Sometimes a parent wants to treat children equally right down to making them all executors or trustees. A settlor might want to supplement the expertise of a corporate trustee with the insights of an individual who knows the beneficiaries. In some situations, tax considerations make it wise to appoint more than one trustee. But unless you have a very good reason to appoint co-fiduciaries, it's probably best avoided, if only not to burden the trust or estate with the payment of more than one commission.

Once we have multiple fiduciaries who do not need to act unanimously, we have to think about what happens when the majority agrees on something that the dissenters believe is a breach of duty. Generally, a trustee or personal representative who does not join in a prohibited action is not liable, although equally generally a co-fiduciary cannot sit back and do nothing if he knows that co-fiduciaries are up to no good. Reasonable care must be used to prevent a breach of duty and to remedy one once it's occurred. Whatever "reasonable care" might be in any given situation, it surely cannot mean indulging in willful ignorance. (UTC § 703 codifies these rules and embodies the generally accepted principles.)

B. Managing the Property: The Duty of Prudence

The second major branch of fiduciary duty, at least as it applies to trustees, is the **duty of prudence**, which governs the trustee's management of the trust property. If we use our "trust as a box" metaphor from Chapter 8, what we're dealing with here is the duty that governs the trustee's actions when she puts on the magic gloves that allow her to reach through the side of the box, take property out to sell it, and put back in property purchased with the proceeds of sale.

Personal representatives are also subject to the duty of prudence. Estate administration, however, usually does not involve investing and reinvesting for the long haul. Personal representatives often have to decide on which investments to sell to raise cash to pay taxes and other expenses of estate administration as well as general devises of cash, but that's not the same as making decisions about investing trust property of a trust that may last for decades. As we'll see, the Uniform Prudent Investor Act applies only to trustees.

(1) From Prudent Person to Prudent Investor

Until the 1990s, the **prudent man rule** (now often called the **prudent person rule**) was *the* rule that governed how trustees are supposed to invest trust property. By far the most commonly cited formulation of the rule comes from the 1830 Massachusetts case that first stated it, *Harvard College v. Amory*.[1] The court told trustees to invest by observing "how men of prudence, discretion and intelligence manage their own affairs, *not in regard to speculation, but in regard to the permanent disposition of their funds, considering the probable income, as well as the probable safety of the capital to be invested*" (emphasis added).[2] This formulation was adopted by most jurisdictions in the United States.

If you just look at those words with completely fresh eyes, they seem to state a flexible standard that can be applied in different ways to different situations. What happened as the case law developed, however, was quite different. The requirement to avoid speculation became a flat prohibition on taking almost any risk at all, and the need to consider "probable income" became a flat prohibition on investing in anything that does not produce income. Some investments came to be regarded as per se imprudent because they were "speculative." This category included equity investments (shares of stock) in companies that did not pay regular dividends, in other words, that did not produce a regular return that is traditionally regarded as income.

Now imagine the dilemma of the trustee who has responsibility for a sprinkle trust enduring for the maximum period allowed by the Rule Against Perpetuities. The settlor created the trust in 1980 to benefit all of the settlor's descendants, of which there are many. Because the trust is likely to last 80 or 90 years, the trustee must make at least some investments that will grow in value to keep pace with inflation. The trustee is conscientious and, in the 1980s, is very aware of the possibilities for making money in the new world of high tech. When Microsoft goes public in 1986, the trustee decides that investing in the company by buying the newly available shares is an excellent way to invest for growth. Yes, the investment is somewhat risky, but the company has an established track record, and the potential for growth is very great. If the trustee had bought 1,000 shares on the day the company went public and never sold any, today, after several stock splits, the trust would own 288,000 shares. The cost of each of those shares is $0.097. The growth has been very impressive indeed.

Sidebar

THE LEGAL LIST

An even more restrictive approach to proper investing of trust property is the "legal list" of investments. These lists, formulated by courts or set forth in statutes, usually authorize trustees to invest only in government bonds, first mortgages on real property, sometimes corporate bonds, and even more rarely some common stocks. Without trust terms that expand the authority of the trustee to invest beyond the list, the legal list (or the prudent man rule in the absence of a legal list) sets the limits.

---

[1] 26 Mass. (9 Pick.) 446 (1830).
[2] *Id.* at 461.

But Microsoft did not pay a dividend until 2003. Under the more stringent applications of the prudent man rule, an investment in Microsoft was per se imprudent from 1986 until 2003. That's a lot of growth forgone. What makes that result even more maddening is that the trustee cannot justify the investment in this stock that does not pay dividends by pointing to the other investments in the trust fund that do pay dividends or interest. In fact, let's say that the trustee decided back in the 1980s that it was impossible to identify which new high-tech companies would be the most successful. After identifying how much of the trust property should be invested in this emerging technology, the trustee bought shares in a number of companies that seemed to be the best bets. You might think this was sensible or even "prudent." No such luck. Let's say that the trustee bought shares in five companies. Three were failures that ended up in bankruptcy, and the trust lost money on those investments. One was moderately successful, and the trust's investment did grow in value. The fifth was Microsoft, which increased in value greatly. If a beneficiary takes the trustee to court and accuses him of violating the duty of prudence by making investments that became worthless (or resulted in large losses), the trustee cannot defend by pointing out that the gains in Microsoft alone far exceeded the losses and the total investment in high tech turned out to be very profitable.

This sort of application of the prudent man rule became more and more problematic in the second half of the twentieth century. Economists studying the behavior of financial markets became certain that (1) any sensible investment program requires taking some risks, (2) the possibility of higher return is the compensation for higher risk, and (3) the exact mix of levels of risk that is appropriate depends on the goal of the investor. To put it bluntly, if an investor never suffers a loss or has an investment go completely bust, she probably is not taking sufficient risks and is forgoing the possibility of extraordinary returns. In short, it makes no sense to prohibit a trustee from doing what our hypothetical investor in Microsoft did just because a stock does not pay a dividend. It makes even less sense to punish a trustee for pursing an investment strategy that is successful because on the way to that success some investments didn't pan out.

F   A   Q

Q: Is a trustee always liable if an investment declines in value?

A: Not at all. Values go up and down all the time, and no trustee could always know the best time to buy or sell an investment. Liability usually comes from not paying attention at all (e.g., a trustee who never seriously reviews a trust's investments or who, with only a reasonable amount of investigation, could have foreseen a dramatic loss of value). Here's something to think about. Is a trustee who invested trust funds with Bernard Madoff liable for the losses from what turned out to be a gigantic fraud? If so many were taken in, is it reasonable to expect better from a trustee? No doubt the courts will have a chance to decide.

The newer point of view is known as the **modern portfolio theory**. It recognizes that different levels of risk are appropriate depending on the purpose for which the portfolio was created. For example, it makes sense to take greater risks in exchange for the greater possibility of high returns in the form of growth in value if you're investing a 401(k) account that belongs to a 30-year-old. With more than three decades to go before retirement, growth is necessary just to keep up with inflation, and there is plenty of time to make up any losses. Once the owner of the account is 60, however, growth becomes less important than conserving value. There is little time before retirement to make up for any losses, and therefore the level of investment risk should be relatively low. This emphasis on the overall performance of the portfolio leads to another important tenet of modern portfolio theory: no one investment is per se imprudent. What's important is how all of the investments work together to best accomplish the purposes for the which the investments are being made.

Modern portfolio theory has powered the most important development in the law of fiduciary duty and the law of trusts in many decades. The prudent man rule has been driven from the scene by the **prudent investor rule**, which embodies the insights of modern portfolio theory. The triumph of the new rule was facilitated by the ALI and Uniform Law Commissioners. In the late 1980s, the ALI began to work on a revision of the Restatement (Second) of Trusts' provisions dealing with the duty of prudence. The law professors and practitioners working on the revision were convinced that the soundness of modern portfolio theory was well demonstrated by empirical research. They rewrote the trust investment provisions of Restatement (Second) of Trusts (§§ 227-229) to state the prudent investor rule. These sections are now §§ 90-92 of Restatement (Third) of Trusts. The Uniform Law Commissioners then drafted and promulgated in 1994 the Uniform Prudent Investor Act (UPIA), which has been adopted in at least 46 states and the District of Columbia.

The heart of the Restatement provisions and the UPIA is the requirement that the trustee manage and invest the trust assets as a prudent investor would, keeping in mind the "purposes, terms, distribution requirements, and other circumstances of the trust" (UPIA § 2(a); Restatement (Third) of Trusts § 90). Both formulations require that the trustee's decisions be evaluated as part of an overall strategy with levels of risk and return reasonably suited to the trust. How to decide on that strategy depends on the circumstances. Some examples of the circumstances that might be relevant to the trust and its beneficiaries are found in UPIA § 2(c): general economic conditions; the possible effect of inflation or deflation; the expected tax consequences of investment decisions or strategies; the role each investment plays in the overall portfolio, which may include financial assets, interests in closely held enterprises, tangible and intangible personal property, and real property; the expected total return from income and the appreciation of capital; and other resources of the beneficiaries.

Clearly, the prudent investor standard is very different from what the prudent man rule had become. To drive that home, the UPIA in § 2(e) expressly states that "a trustee may invest in any kind of property or type of investment consistent with the standards of this [act]." Investments that are per se imprudent no longer exist. In their place are investments that only are or are not appropriate to the trust.

(2) Diversification

Another aspect of the prudent investor standard deserves separate consideration because it has become the most litigated feature of the new rules. Both Restatement (Third) of Trusts (§ 90(b)) and UPIA (§ 3) state that the trustee has a duty to diversify the trust's investments unless it is "prudent not to do so" (Restatement) or "because of special circumstances, the purposes of the trust are better served without diversifying" (UPIA). The reason for this emphasis on diversification is directly related to the way modern portfolio theory deals with risk. Remember that a certain degree of risk is necessary to obtain reward, and the degree of risk the trustee undertakes is directly related to the purposes and circumstances of the trust and its beneficiaries. One of the best ways to deal with risk is to diversify investments so that all sorts of levels of risk are represented in the trust's portfolio.

Remember that the high-tech example started with a long-term sprinkle trust. Because the trust will run for generations and the number of beneficiaries will most likely increase, looking for growth in the overall value of the trust portfolio by seeking out greater risk for greater reward is perfectly appropriate. This is exactly the sort of circumstance in which the prudent investor standard is meant to accommodate, a level of risk that the prudent man standard (at least as it developed) could not abide. On the other hand, think about a testamentary trust created by the testator to take care of the living expenses of the testator's surviving spouse or domestic partner. The trust terminates at the survivor's death and passes outright to the testator's descendants by representation. The trustee of that trust would be prudent to take on a much lesser degree of risk than the trustee of the long-term trust. The primary purpose of the trust is to provide for the survivor, so the conservation of the value of the trust portfolio is important. In addition, if the trust will last for a relatively short period, it might not be possible to recoup losses. Diversification is still important. Risk can always be reduced by selecting an array of investments, which it is hoped will not all decrease (or increase for that matter) in value in unison. It's just that our hypothetical support trust will diversify by investing in relatively low-risk investments.

The best-known litigation about diversification involves trusts heavily invested in a single common stock that formed the original funding of the trust. Usually at one time the stock was a "blue chip" investment, seemingly never losing value and indeed always becoming more valuable. Often the settlor or testator (many of these trusts are testamentary) was very attached to the particular investment. Either the settlor worked for the corporation, or the settlor's parent had, or the settlor had simply made a good investment long ago and was determined never to let it go. Sometimes the trust permits the trustee to retain ownership of the investment or even requires the trustee to do so. The security then declines in value, and the beneficiaries want to make the trustee pay for failing to diversify the trust's portfolio.

Where the trust is silent about retaining the original assets, trustees who fail to diversify investments usually do not fare well in court. Even though a stock is an acceptable investment in the trust's portfolio and even though the trustee is not liable for the decrease in value because the decision to retain the investment in stock was not imprudent, failing to diversify is often judged to violate the duty of prudence. Had the trust portfolio been property diversified, the decrease in value of this one investment would not have so greatly diminished the value of the entire portfolio.

Both Restatement (Third) of Trusts § 91 and UPIA § 1(b) make it clear that the prudent investor standard is a default rule and that the trustee has a duty to conform to the trust requirements regarding investments. However, the statutory language says that the trustee's reliance on the trust provisions regarding investments must be "reasonable," and the Restatement makes that reliance subject to the rules allowing modification of and deviation from the terms of the trust that require the trustee to seek modification when adhering to the trust terms would substantially harm the trust or the beneficiaries. Even a flat prohibition on selling a particular asset or the inclusion in the terms of the trust of a mandatory investment strategy can be overridden by a court when adhering to the trust terms would cause substantial harm. Exactly what the balance should be between the interests of the beneficiaries as protected by the default rules governing prudence and the settlor's view of prudence expressed in the trust terms is the subject of ongoing debate. As cases are decided, the shape of the law may become clearer; but for now, this question in particular is in play.

(3) Delegation

Conforming to the prudent investor standard can be a daunting task. Under the prudent man standard, it could be argued that the trustee of a relatively short-term trust, say a testamentary trust for the support of the testator's surviving spouse, was doing the right thing by investing heavily in bonds and in some "blue chip" stocks that paid a steady stream of dividends. Today, under the prudent investor standard, the same investment plan might be acceptable, but determining whether that's the case requires considering the factors listed in the UPIA. Some of these factors, which form the core of the prudent investor standard, involve the general economic climate and outlook. In short, properly making decisions under this new standard may be beyond the competence of the trustee.

This need for expertise in making investment decisions is the principal driver of another important change in traditional law. For a very long time, trust law was quite clear about a trustee's delegation of the exercise of the trustee's powers to others: couldn't do it. Delegating purely ministerial acts such as keeping certain records or even completing tax returns was more or less acceptable, but as Restatement (Second) of Trusts § 171 comment h stated in no uncertain terms: "A trustee cannot property delegate to another power to select investments." Full stop. That flat prohibition does not work very well in the world of the prudent investor standard and the need for investment expertise.

Even before the adoption of UPIA took off, the no delegation rule had been changing around the margins. The revision of Restatement (Second) of Trusts that produced the prudent investor rule accelerated the process by completely revising § 171 (now § 80 of Restatement (Third)) to permit delegation where it is prudent to do so; comment f(1) and § 90 comment j make it clear that it may indeed be prudent to delegate some aspects of making decisions about investments. For example, while the trustee must set the trust's investment objective (e.g., sustaining a long-term trust for an entire family) and at least approve the investment strategies designed to accomplish that objective, formulating those strategies can be delegated to others who have the appropriate expertise. The delegation must be prudently done, of course, and the trustee is responsible both for selecting the agent and supervising his performance. These rules are codified in UPIA § 9 and in almost exactly the same words in UTC § 807. Both statutes require the trustee to use "reasonable care, skill, and caution" in selecting the agent, establishing the terms of the delegation, and monitoring the agent's performance.

There is a flip side of this as well. The trustee who has special expertise is required to use it. UPIA § 2(f) and UTC § 806 say exactly that, and apply both to trustees who have special expertise and to those who represent themselves as having special expertise, which is why they were named trustees. That means that a trustee who is a professional investor or a bank can be held to a higher standard than a family member who is acting as trustee but who has no knowledge of financial markets or even of the basics of investing. That person, of course, should consider delegating investment making authority.

(4) Subsidiary Duties Related to the Property

When it comes to trust property, the trustee's primary duty is to manage it prudently, and today that means in accord with the prudent investor standard. Other duties too relate to the trust property and are usually regarded as secondary or subsidiary to the duty of prudence.

(a) Secure

The trustee must secure the trust property, or as UTC § 809 puts it, take "reasonable steps to take control of and protect" the trust property. The same duty in Restatement (Third) of Trusts § 76(2)(b) is expressed in terms of collecting and protecting. The trustee has a duty to see that the property given to the trust becomes trust property. How that is done depends on the nature of the property and sometimes on the terms of the trust. Taking control of financial investments probably means opening a brokerage account titled in the name of the trustee as trustee of the trust and transferring the assets to that account. If the trust property includes physical securities like stock certificates (which are becoming less and less common), the trustee must take possession of them; if it has registered title, the trustee must register the property in her name as trustee of the trust.

If the trust is a testamentary trust, the trustee must make sure that the executor transfers the probate property that is trust property to the trustee. How long before that happens depends on the complexity of the estate administration. If the executor commits a breach of duty that damages the value of the trust property, the trustee must seek redress. UTC § 812 deals with collecting trust property and requires the trustee to make sure that trust property in the hands of someone other than the trustee, including a former trustee, is delivered to the trustee and requires the trustee to seek redress for a breach of trust by a former trustee.

Sometimes the trustee is not expected to take possession of trust property. For example, if the trust includes tangible personal property — think of artwork or jewelry — the terms of the trust may say that the beneficiary gets to use the property, in which case the beneficiary will have possession. The same applies to a residence owned by the trust. A beneficiary may be entitled to live there, giving him possession.

(b) Care For

This one is pretty obvious. The trustee has to take care of the trust property. That's the "protecting" part of Restatement (Third) of Trusts § 76(2)(b) and UTC § 809. This duty includes properly insuring trust property from whatever hazards threaten it (e.g., fire insurance, theft insurance). Protection also includes pursuing claims the trust may have and defending claims against the trust.

(c) Earmark

Trust property has to be identified as trust property. UTC § 810(c) requires the trustee to "cause the trust property to be designated so that the interest of the trust, to the extent feasible, appears in records maintained by a party other than the trustee or beneficiary." Restatement (Third) of Trusts § 84 comment d requires the same thing. This is a requirement that you probably don't think much about, but what it means is that securities must be registered in the name of the trustee as trustee of the trust, the appropriate deeds or other instruments filed in the land records, and other assets with registered titled (motor vehicles, boats, airplanes) be registered in the name of the trustee as trustee (all of which will have been done if the trustee has properly secured the trust property).

If assets do not have registered title, for example, tangible personal property, the trustee has to maintain appropriate records. For example, jewelry belonging to the trust but in the possession of a beneficiary should be listed and described in a writing kept with the records of the trust. While they are not very common any more, financial instruments like bearer bonds (bonds payable to whoever has possession of them) without registered title should also be properly listed and described and kept safe, most likely in a safe deposit box rented by the trustee as trustee. The whole idea is to make sure that the trustee does not claim that profitable investments actually belong to the trustee individually and not to the trust.

F   A   Q

Q: What do ears have to do with it?

A: "Earmark" refers to making a notch or other mark on the ear of domestic animals, like cattle or sheep or goats, to indicate ownership. Over time, the term has come to refer to any way to indicate ownership of specific property, especially when it is not easy to differentiate the property owned from similar property.

There is one way in which the modern world has changed the law of earmarks. As we've noted before, once upon a time financial investments were represented by pieces of paper. If you owned stock in a company, you had a stock certificate; if you owned a bond, you had a piece of paper that represented the debt. Today most financial investments don't exist in tangible form. Many bonds are "book entry" bonds; they exist only in the records of one of the parties to the complicated legal arrangements creating the debt. Investments in stock are usually held in nominee name. A brokerage firm owns stock certificates representing many millions of shares and buys and sells as required to service their customers. The customer has a brokerage account that keeps a record of what the customer owns. In essence, the account is just a record in a computer's memory. It took some doing for trustees to own stock in nominee name, that is, to open a brokerage account in the name of the trustee as trustee of the trust and hold financial investments in that account. Today, statutes in all jurisdictions allow trustees to hold financial investments in this way. An example is UTC § 816(7)(B) and (D).

(d) No Comingling

The last of these subsidiary duties is probably the one most violated by inexperienced individual trustees. Trustees must not comingle trust property with their own. The reasons are pretty obvious: the trustee by commingling, for example, could mistakenly use trust property for her own benefit or put trust funds within the reach of her personal creditors. Unfortunately, inexperienced trustees often do exactly that, keeping the trust's cash and their own in a single checking account or buying a certificate of deposit with their personal funds and trust funds and taking title solely as an individual and not as trustee.

There are always exceptions, of course. Restatement (Third) of Trusts § 84 comment b states the no commingling rule, but notes that the rule is not absolute. There is always an exception implied when the settlor of the trust implicitly authorizes the commingling by, for example, transferring into trust an interest in real property in which the trustee is a tenant in common. The trustee still must properly earmark the trust's interest.

The prohibition on commingling also applies to property of separate trusts with the same trustee. There is an exception here as well. So long as the trustee keeps adequate records, the trustee may invest property of different trusts as a whole. For example, the trustee could invest property of more than one trust in Blackacre, so long as the trustee's records adequately show the trusts' separate interests as tenants in common. In the same vein, UTC § 810(d) allows the trustee to "invest as a whole the property of two or more separate trusts" so long as the trustee keeps adequate records.

C. The Duty of Impartiality

The **duty of impartiality** is far easier to state than it is to properly carry out. UTC § 803 states it succinctly: if a trust has two or more beneficiaries, "the trustee shall act impartially in investing, managing, and distributing the trust property, giving due regard to the beneficiaries' respective interests." Restatement (Third) of Trusts § 79 is more elaborate. It includes a requirement that the trustee act "impartially and with due regard for the diverse beneficial interests created by the terms of the trust" when communicating with the beneficiaries. Section 70(d) also expressly requires the trustee to make sure that the trust produces income "reasonably appropriate to the purposes of the trust and to the diverse present and future interests of its beneficiaries."

The Restatement's reference to sufficient production of income gets to the heart of the impartiality dilemma. Remember Chapter 9's example of the trustee of a trust giving mandatory income to A, remainder on A's death to A's issue? The trustee invests only in municipal bonds. The income beneficiary is most pleased to receive lots of tax exempt income, but the remainder beneficiaries are not so happy when they get a sum equal to the original funding of the trust, which now is worth far less because of intervening inflation.

The unitrust (introduced in Chapter 9) can provide a good solution to the impartiality problem, under certain circumstances. (After reading the first half of this chapter, you should also see how the unitrust could be a solution to problems posed by the prudent investor standard.) The trustee must invest to accomplish the purposes of the trust. If the trust is a long-term trust with several generations of beneficiaries, fulfilling that duty means investing for growth. That in turn means that it likely will be difficult to produce sufficient income, traditionally defined, to satisfy the income ben-eficiaries. Do you see that the trustee of such a trust has a much easier time when the interest of the current beneficiaries is expressed as a unitrust percentage? So long as the value of the trust property increases, the amount paid to the current beneficiaries will increase; and the remainder beneficiaries have a better chance of receiving property that has increased in value, at least enough to keep up with inflation.

That is the theory at least, and the theory is so appealing that many jurisdictions have adopted some form of a statutory unitrust. Some of these statutes make the unitrust the default rule. After the effective date of the statute, any trust that creates an income interest, mandatory or discretionary, gives the beneficiaries entitled to that interest a unitrust interest of whatever percentage is stated in the statute. The stated unitrust percentage is also a default rule, and the settlor can choose a different per-centage. The settlor can also opt for the traditional definition of income. Some statutes create a unitrust option that settlors can select by reference to the statute, leaving the traditional definition of income as the default. Most statutes allow trustees to convert an existing trust into a unitrust with court approval and also to convert a unitrust to a trust governed by the traditional law of income and principal with court approval.

F   A   Q

Q: If the trust doesn't produce enough income, why not just give trustees the power to invade principal for the benefit of income beneficiaries?

A: Many older trusts were created when producing reasonable amounts of income was easier, so settlors (and lawyers) didn't think it necessary to give trustees the power to invade principal. Some states allow income beneficiaries, especially surviving spouses, to ask a court to authorize an invasion of principal if the income produced by the trust is insufficient to accomplish the purposes of the trust. Under the modern unitrust statutes, these trusts could be converted into unitrusts. Even when trustees have the power to invade principal, however, they are sometimes reluctant to use it. Some commentators conclude that trustees resist invading principal to avoid facing unhappy remainder beneficiaries when the trust ends.

Whether the trust is a unitrust or is governed by traditional principal and income law, the trustee's choices affect the balance between the interests of current and future beneficiaries. Those choices often have to do with investment decisions, but we saw in Chapter 9 that they also involve allocating receipts between income and principal. In making those allocations, the trustee must treat the beneficiaries impartially. As we also saw in Chapter 9, every jurisdiction has statutes that provide default rules for allocating between principal and income, and following those default rules satisfies the duty of impartiality.

In every case, however, it is the settlor's purpose in creating the trust that must be carried out. If the trust terms express the settlor's intention to favor one beneficiary or group of beneficiaries over another, the trustee must honor that intention. Being "impartial" does not mean treating the beneficiaries equally. It means impartially carrying out the purposes for which the trust was created.

Consider yet again a trust created by testator's will with a mandatory income interest for the testator's surviving spouse or domestic partner. The trust terminates at the death of the survivor, and the trust property goes outright to the testator's issue. The duty of impartiality requires that the trustee act with due regard to the respective interests. The duty of prudence, as stated in the UPIA, requires the trustee to invest to fulfill the purposes for which the settlor created the trust, and now things get interesting.

If the trust is not a unitrust, the trustee is required to invest to produce a level of income for the income beneficiary that fulfills the settlor's purpose. The more certain we can be that the settlor wanted the trust managed to principally benefit the surviving spouse or partner, the less likely the trustee will be found liable to the remainder beneficiaries for investing to produce income at the expense of appreciation. That conclusion certainty will be easier to get to if the trust terms include language that tells the trustee that the interest of the surviving spouse or partner is more important than the interests of the remainder beneficiaries. Often trusts for surviving spouses or domestic partners include just that sort of language. If that's the case, the trustee's decision to invest to favor income production over growth will not result in liability to the remainder beneficiaries, but the failure to do so would open the trustee to liability to the income beneficiary.

What happens if the trustee has one of the varieties of discretion we discussed in Chapter 9? As we noted there, no matter how "absolute" the discretion may be, its exercise is always ultimately under the control of the courts; and the courts will enforce the trustee's duty to treat the beneficiaries impartially by exercising the discretion in conformity with the settlor's purpose in creating the trust. Let's go back yet again to the trust created for a surviving spouse or partner, only this time, in addition to the mandatory income interest, the trustee has discretion to invade principal for the income beneficiary in the trustee's "sole and absolute discretion" (what Restatement (Third) of Trusts calls "extended discretion"). Even though the trustee has a good deal of leeway in deciding how to exercise the power to invade principal (to open the lid of the trust box, reach in, take out some property, and give it to the beneficiary), the trustee must act "in good faith and in accordance with the terms and purposes of the trust and the interests of the beneficiaries" (UTC § 814(a)). Once again, the clearer the settlor's instructions, the easier it is for the trustee to do what's supposed to be done. Of course, if the discretion is governed by a standard like "support," it also can be easier for the trustee to decide on a proper course of action.

Do you see why being a trustee is often not exactly a piece of cake?

D. Duties Owed Directly to Beneficiaries

The final group of duties we're going to examine contains those a trustee owes directly to beneficiaries. Fulfilling these duties requires the trustee to communicate directly with beneficiaries.

(1) To Inform

As we've seen, a trust (other than a charitable trust) must have ascertainable beneficiaries. Someone must be able to enforce the trustee's fiduciary duties. The settlor cannot unless she is a beneficiary or somehow has reserved rights in the trust instrument (and, of course, many settlors die long before their trusts end). It makes perfect sense that the beneficiaries must know about the trust and about the nature of their interests to be able to make sure the trustee does what he is supposed to do. The duty to inform has two aspects: (1) what the trustee must tell beneficiaries without their asking, and (2) what response the trustee must make to beneficiaries' inquiries.

Restatement (Third) of Trusts § 82 deals with the duty to furnish information to beneficiaries. The blackletter says a trustee has duty to inform "fairly representative beneficiaries" of the existence of the trust, of the fact that they are beneficiaries, of the right to obtain further information, and of "basic information concerning the trusteeship." The "fairly representative beneficiaries" also must be kept "reasonably informed" of changes involving the trusteeship and "other significant developments concerning the trust and its administration," especially when the information is needed by the beneficiaries to be able to properly protect their interests. The trustee has a duty to inform all beneficiaries of "significant changes" to their status and to respond to a request from any beneficiary for information about the trust or its administration. All beneficiaries are entitled to reasonable access to trust documents, including a copy of the trust, and the trust records and to inspect the trust's property holdings.

As you can see, we can classify the duty to inform not only by whether the trustee is required to tell the beneficiaries something or is required to answer requests, but by which beneficiaries get what. The key term in this second classification is "fairly representative beneficiaries." That term is defined in comment a(1) to § 82. In most cases, according to the comment, the beneficiaries who represent all are those currently entitled or eligible to receive distributions of income or principal ("entitled" or "eligible" will depend on whether interests are discretionary or mandatory), and those who would be entitled or eligible were the current interests to cease or the trust terminate. Here's a simple example.

Example 16.1: Testator's will devises property to Big Bank in trust to pay the income to testator's child D for life, trust terminating on D's death, at which time the trust property is distributed to D's descendants then living by representation, and, if none, to the descendants of testator's parents then living by representation.

We can analyze Example 16.1 this way:

- ■ **D** as income beneficiary is always a fairly representative beneficiary because only **D** is interested in the trust income.

The persons who are fairly representative beneficiaries of the remainder interest are

- ■ If **D** has no living descendants, then **D's Siblings** are fairly representative beneficiaries because they are the presumptive remainder beneficiaries; they would vest in possession of the trust property were **D** to die today.
- ■ If **D** has **Adult Children**, then they are fairly representative beneficiaries of the remainder interest because they would vest in possession of the trust property were **D** to die today.

- If **D** has only **Minor Children**, they are fairly representative beneficiaries because they would vest in possession were **D** to die today, but the trustee can discharge its duty to inform by informing the **Minor Children's** other parent as representative of the children or the **Siblings** because they, like the **Minor Children**, have a contingent remainder in the trust.

To state all this in more general terms:

- *Fairly representative beneficiaries of the income interest:* Current permissible recipients of income, whether the income interest is mandatory or discretionary. Adult, competent beneficiaries can represent minor or incapacitated beneficiaries.
- *Fairly representative beneficiaries of the remainder interest*: Those beneficiaries who would come into possession of the trust property were the trust to terminate now. Adult, competent beneficiaries can represent minor or incapacitated beneficiaries. (Yes, this is all very much like the concept of virtual representation we discussed in Chapter 9.)

Note, however, that the trustee has a duty to provide some basic information to *all* beneficiaries, not just those who are "fairly representative." The reason is pretty simple: without knowledge of their interests, beneficiaries cannot enforce their rights as trust beneficiaries. Of course, some beneficiaries have more remote interests than others. Take another look at our example above. Let's say that D has living children and grandchildren. The odds of any other descendants of the testator's parents coming into possession of the trust property at D's death are pretty slim. Nonetheless, they are beneficiaries and are entitled to information. But comment e to § 82 takes a very practical approach and states that a court may limit how often beneficiaries may request information and how much information beneficiaries can get, "weighing the remotest substantiality of their interests in the trust against the burdens, intrusiveness, and privacy considerations that may be involved." In other words, if beneficiaries who have little chance of ever getting any trust property make unreasonable demands, a court can impose limits (although realize that going to court is not costless).

F A Q

Q: Must the trustee satisfy a beneficiary's demand for a complete copy of the trust instrument?

A: What authority there is seems to say yes, although once again, the court might allow the trustee to hand over a redacted version if there's a good reason like preserving the privacy of other beneficiaries or concerns about the behavior of the beneficiary making the request. Where litigation may be involved, however, nothing but a complete copy will do. This is another area in which revocable trusts used as will substitutes may be treated somewhat differently from other trusts. Wills are more or less public documents once admitted to probate. To keep the complete terms of a revocable trust from the beneficiaries after the settlor's death would make the trust a secret will, which is unheard of in our system of law.

It's not the just the court that can impose limits. Traditionally, the settlor can put at least some limits on the trustee's duty to inform and the beneficiaries' rights to request and receive information. Restatement (Third) of Trusts continues this recognition of the settlor's power in comment a(2) to § 82, which states that "the terms of the trust" may change the amount of information a trustee is required to give as well as how often and to whom it is given. Comment e also recognizes that the settlor may have very good reasons for limiting the trustee's duty to disclose "in order, for example, to lessen the risk of unnecessary or unwarranted loss of privacy" or because of the possibility of bad effects on immature beneficiaries or on those whose lives are particularly troubled. The settlor or trustee may also simply believe that the beneficiary who knows too much will lose all incentive to earn her own living. The Restatement, however, insists that the beneficiary (and, in the case of a minor beneficiary, a proper representative) must receive enough information to allow the beneficiary to properly protect his interest in the trust. And that really is the rock bottom principle.

There is one very big exception to all of this: while the settlor of a revocable lifetime trust has the power and capacity to revoke the trust, the rights of the beneficiaries other than the settlor are completely under the settlor's control; the trustee must follow the settlor's instructions (Restatement (Third) of Trusts § 74). So the trustee, even if she is not the settlor, has no duty to tell the beneficiaries other than the settlor anything, whether those beneficiaries ask or not. This extreme modification of the usual rules really makes the revocable trust very much like a will. Wills don't create any interests in their beneficiaries until the testator dies. Revocable trusts are so often created as will substitutes, as we saw in Chapter 11, that the Restatement, and just about everyone else, agrees that the beneficiaries of a revocable trust should have no more rights that the beneficiaries of the will of a living person, at least while the settlor still has capacity to revoke the trust and undo the entire arrangement. Once the settlor lacks capacity, however, the Restatement generally takes the position that the other trust beneficiaries have all the rights of trust beneficiaries generally, although there is some authority that makes the trustee answerable only to the incapacitated settlor's court-appointed fiduciary (a conservator or guardian).

The UTC's codification of the trustee's duty to inform generally follows the Restatement (Third) of Trusts and in fact agrees completely on the revocable trust. UTC § 603(a) says that while a trust is revocable and the settlor has capacity to exercise the power to revoke, the settlor controls the rights of the beneficiaries and the trustee's duties are owed only to the settlor. As we saw in Chapter 11 the phrase "and the settlor has capacity to revoke the trust" is in brackets, however, which means that it is optional.

When we get to irrevocable trusts, UTC § 813(a) requires the trustee to keep the "qualified beneficiaries" reasonably informed about the administration of the trust and about "material facts," knowledge of which the qualified beneficiaries need to protect their interests. In addition, a trustee must "promptly respond" to a beneficiary's request for information unless it is unreasonable "under the circumstances." All of this is very similar to Restatement (Third) of Trusts § 82 with which we started this discussion. Some beneficiaries must be kept informed, and all beneficiaries are entitled to have reasonable requests for information answered. "Qualified beneficiary" is defined in UTC § 103(13), and it turns out to be the same as the "fairly representative beneficiary" of Restatement § 82.

UTC § 105 AND TRUST TRANSPARENCY

It's clear that the UTC was not enthusiastic about the 2004 amendments to § 105(b). The comment to § 105 says: "The placing of these provisions in brackets does not mean that the Drafting Committee [for the UTC which proposed the amendments] recommends that an enacting jurisdiction delete §§ 105(b)(8) and (b)(9). The Committee continues to believe that § 105(b)(8) and (9), enacted as it is, represent the best balance of competing policy considerations. Rather, the provisions were placed in brackets out of a recognition that there is a lack of consensus on the extent to which a settlor ought to be able to waive reporting to the beneficiaries, and that there is little chance that the states will enact §§ 105(b)(8) and (b)(9) with any uniformity." A triumph of pragmatism over conviction about proper policy.

The UTC goes on, however, and in § 813(b) requires a trustee to "promptly" provide a copy of the trust to any beneficiary who requests it and to give the qualified beneficiaries certain basic information about the trust, including informing them of their right to request a copy of the trust instrument. If you read only UTC § 813, it seems that the Code has left out a very important part of the law set forth in the Restatement: the ability of the settlor to alter these duties of the trustee. You must remember, however, that the UTC is pretty much one big default rule except for those provisions that § 105(b) makes "mandatory." Section 813(b) is one of those mandatory provisions, and no provision of the UTC has caused as much discussion, much of it critical, than this transparency requirement. Some states adopting the UTC modified this requirement, often drastically. Recognizing the degree of disagreement over these provisions, in 2004 the Uniform Law Commission amended § 105(b) to put in brackets clauses (8) and (9), which reference the requirements of § 813(b).

This is yet another area in which figuring out the law in a particular jurisdiction requires careful research. For now, however, the rules we've discussed in this section as set out in Restatement (Third) of Trusts and the UTC are summarized in Table 16-1. (The information in Table 16-1 does not apply to revocable trusts, at least when the settlor is competent to exercise the power to revoke.)

| TABLE 16.1 | The Duty to Inform under Restatement (Third) and the UTC |

Information or action by beneficiary	Restatement (Third)	UTC	
		without 2004 amendments	with 2004 amendments
Existence of trust	T'ee must promptly inform frb (§ 82(1))	T'ee must inform qb 25-years-old w/in 60 days (§ 813(b)(3))	Settlor may override
Copy of trust	"ordinarily" all beneficiaries entitled (§ 82 cmt. e)	T'ee must give to all beneficiaries upon request (§ 813(b)(1))	Not altered; still a mandatory term
Information about T'ee (name, address, phone)	T'ee must promptly inform frb (§ 82(1)(a))	T'ee must inform qb 25-years-old w/in 60 days (§ 813(b)(2))	Settlor may override

TABLE 16.1	*(Continued)*		
Information or action by beneficiary	**Restatement (Third)**	**UTC**	
		without 2004 amendments	**with 2004 amendments**
Facts about administration	T'ee must keep frb "reasonably informed" especially of information needed to protect beneficiaries' interests (§ 82(1)(c))	T'ee must keep qb "reasonably informed" about administration and of "material facts" needed to protect interests (§ 813(a))	Not altered; still a mandatory term
Requests for information about administration	T'ee has duty to respond; but trust terms may modify	T'ee must promptly respond unless "unreasonable under the circumstances" (§ 813(a))	Settlor may override

Note: T'ee = trustee; frb = fairly representative beneficiaries; qb = qualified beneficiaries.

(2) To Account

The trustee's next duty to beneficiaries is to account. As discussed in earlier chapters, an accounting is a formal statement of everything the trustee has done with the trust property. First, it shows what the trustee did when the trustee put on those magic gloves and reached into the trust box to deal with the property. It shows all sales of trust property, all reinvestments of the proceeds, and all the income from the property collected by the trustee. It also shows all the distributions the trustee made, whether they were made to the beneficiaries by sending income through the income spout, by opening up the trust box to make a distribution of principal to the beneficiaries, or to pay administration expenses like the trustee's commission, investment advisor fees, and accounting and legal fees. Many states have formal rules for how the accounting should be put together, detailing what appears on which of many schedules. How often a trustee must account is also jurisdiction specific and varies from once a year to no set schedule. But no matter what the rules about form or frequency, the goal is the same: to present a complete picture of how the trustee has carried out the trustee's duties.

No matter what the accounting looks like, the ultimate reason for preparing it is always the same. The trustee creates an elaborate statement of his actions to present for approval. In essence, the trustee wants to be told that the beneficiaries have no grounds to complain about how he has administered the trust and carried out his fiduciary duties. Clearly the next question is who gives that approval. The beneficiaries certainly can, but there's always the problem of minor beneficiaries or even unborn beneficiaries if the account is not the final accounting on the termination of the trust. A court can give the approval and issue a formal decree approving the account and releasing the trustee from any further responsibility. Formal court approval happens only on notice to all the beneficiaries, who will then have the opportunity to examine the accounting and make objections. If there are minor or incapacitated beneficiaries who cannot be virtually represented, a guardian ad litem will be appointed to represent their interests. Often the court can examine the accounting on its own initiative and raise questions about the trustee's actions. Of course, even a court decree settling the account is only as good as the information contained in the account. There are cases in which a decree has been revoked because the trustee negligently presented false information in the account.

F A Q

Q: Do executors and administrators have a duty to account?

A: Yes, and they usually have all the options for seeking approval of the account that a trustee has. Formal approval by a court is most likely where there have been disputes about the administration of the estate, where assets are particularly difficult to value, where the estate assets declined greatly during the course of administration, and where minors or charities are among the beneficiaries.

A court decree settling the account and discharging the trustee from further liability is the only thing on which the trustee (or personal representative) can fully rely to put an end to the responsibilities and duties of the fiduciary relationship. Formal court accountings can be expensive and time consuming, however, and in some instances may not be necessary. When all the beneficiaries are adults and the administration of the trust has been straightforward, approval of the accounts by the beneficiaries may be enough to allow the most scrupulous trustee (or the trustee's most anxious successor in interest) to sleep peacefully. Here's an example.

Example 16.2: Testator's will devises property to surviving spouse to pay the income to surviving spouse for life, at which time a child of Testator and surviving spouse becomes successor trustee, the trust terminates, and the trust property is distributed to the issue of Testator and surviving spouse by representation. At surviving spouse's death, all of the remainder beneficiaries who vest in possession are adults with full capacity.

The surviving spouse's personal representative will produce the account for the surviving spouse's trusteeship. Because all of the persons who have an interest in the trust property are competent adults, if they are content with the way their parent or grandparent managed the trust, it's almost certainly unnecessary to have a formal accounting. The trustee's personal representative will present the account to the remainder beneficiaries and ask them to execute what's usually called a **receipt and release** that acknowledges receipt of the trust property to which they are entitled and releases the trustee (here, the trustee's estate) from any liability.

What separates the duty to account from the duty to inform in general? The principal difference is the formality of the accounting and its association with a court proceeding, especially in the jurisdictions that require trustees of testamentary trusts to account at fixed intervals. A formal procedure for informing beneficiaries about what the trustee is doing with the trust property is quite different from giving beneficiaries the sort of information we discussed under the heading of "duty to inform."

That distinction, however, is not made by Restatement (Third) of Trusts or the UTC, which both include the duty to account as part of the duty to inform. Restatement (Third) of Trusts § 83 deals with the duty "to keep records and provide reports." Comment b states that a beneficiary's right to request information includes "a right to request and receive accountings or comparable reports." The same comment states that this duty can be fulfilled by providing beneficiaries with informal reports so long as they "reveal trust assets and liabilities, receipts and disbursements, and other transactions involving trust property," and also tell the beneficiaries how much compensation the trustee has received and how it was calculated. These are all of the things an accounting traditionally includes. The comment also quite rightly notes that both the form and frequency of accountings are governed by statute in many states.

UTC § 813 (which in fact is captioned "Duty to Inform and Report") pretty much codifies in subsection (c) the Restatement provisions. The comment to § 813 makes it clear that the drafters of the UTC agree with the Restatement about the lack of importance to be given to the form of the report: "The Uniform Trust Code employs the term 'report' instead of 'accounting' in order to negate any inference that the report must be prepared in any particular format or with a high degree or formality." UTC § 813(c), by the way, is not a mandatory provision under UTC § 105 and therefore could be modified by the settlor. However, any attempt to include in the trust terms a provision that purported to allow the trustee to refuse to account would be contrary to public policy and might also contradict other statutes.

It's quite correct to conclude that both the UTC and the Restatement want to increase the likelihood and frequency of reports to the beneficiaries by encouraging the use of reports that are less formal, perhaps easier to understand, and certainly less expensive to produce than traditional accountings. Remember, though, that state statutes, even in states that have enacted UTC § 813, may require the trustee to formally account at fixed intervals, and even more likely when the trust terminates or when the trusteeship ends. In addition, a beneficiary, or at least a beneficiary with an interest that is not too remote or contingent, may ask a court to require the trustee to account.

(3) To Inquire

To inquire about what from whom? About the beneficiaries' circumstances and needs from the beneficiaries themselves. To fulfill her core duty to administer the trust in the interest of the beneficiaries, a trustee must make whatever effort is reasonably necessary to obtain information essential to this duty.

What efforts are reasonably necessary depends, of course, on the circumstances. As we saw in Chapter 9, trustees often have discretion in making distributions of income and principal to the beneficiaries, and that discretion is often guided by some sort of standard relating to the support or maintenance of the beneficiaries. If the trustee is going to make distributions that fulfill the trust purpose to provide support and maintenance, the trustee has to know what the beneficiaries need.

It's clear that the trustee cannot just sit there and wait for the beneficiaries to ask. It's also clear that the trustee's duty isn't fulfilled by asking the beneficiaries to "tell me what you think you need" and letting it go at that. If there is no answer, the circumstances may be such that the trustee will have to ask more detailed and precise questions. Even if the trustee gets an answer, the answer may be clearly incomplete or show that a beneficiary really doesn't understand what's being asked. Once again, the trustee will have to follow up and make the effort to get useful information. If the terms of the trust tell the trustee to take into account a beneficiary's other resources in deciding how to exercise discretion to distribute to that beneficiary, the trustee will have to find out the extent of those resources (Restatement (Third) of Trusts § 50 cmt. e(1) & repr.'s note).

Failure to make the kind of inquiries necessary to properly administer the trust can lead to liability for breach of trust, although that is not always the case. As we will see in a minute when we discuss exculpatory clauses, the settlor can reduce the standard of care the trustee must use so as to make liability unlikely. It is still possible, however, for a court to fashion an equitable remedy such as ordering an additional distribution to the beneficiaries or imposing a constructive trust on trust property distributed to other beneficiaries.

E. Damages for Breach

The general rule governing damages for breach of trust is pretty clear. As UTC § 1002(a) and Restatement (Third) of Trusts § 100 put it, the trustee who commits a breach of trust is liable to the beneficiaries for the greater of the amount necessary to restore the value of the beneficiaries' interests had the breach not occurred or the profit the trustee made by committing the breach. The amount necessary to make the trust whole is known as a **surcharge**. Applying that general rule to all the different ways in which a trustee's duties can be violated, however, is where matters start to get complicated.

(1) Violations of the Duty of Loyalty

Violations of the duty of loyalty usually involve the trustee's using trust property for his personal benefit. The beneficiaries' equitable interest in the trust property allows them to pursue any property the trustee has acquired through a breach of his duties. This principle is called **tracing** or the **trust pursuit rule** and gives the trust beneficiaries an advantage over the other unsecured creditors of the trustee should the trustee be insolvent when the beneficiaries get around to enforcing their rights (Restatement (Third) of Trusts § 100(b)). Before we get to some examples, there is one situation in which tracing won't help.

If the trustee's breach involves dissipating the trust property, which means that after the trustee commits the breach the property is simply gone, tracing is useless. An example is the trustee who uses trust property to buy services for herself, say, by writing a check on the trust account to pay for an elaborate meal in an expensive restaurant. Granted, the trustee and the trustee's guests have been well fed, but there's nothing the beneficiaries can point to and say "that was bought with trust property." In a case like this, the beneficiaries are no better off than any other creditor of the trustee. They can obtain a judgment for the amount of the restaurant bill. If the trustee is bankrupt when they try to collect the judgment, however, they have to stand in line with all the other unsecured creditors of the trustee.

To illustrate how tracing does work, let's say the trustee used $5,000 of trust funds to buy for her personal account 500 shares of X Corporation stock at $10 per share.

Example 16.3: At the time the beneficiaries obtain a court decree establishing the trustee's liability, the 500 shares of X Corporation are worth $10,000. The beneficiaries would almost certainly choose the option of recovering the profit the trustee made and elect to recover the shares.

Example 16.4: At the time the beneficiaries obtain a court decree establishing the trustee's liability, the 500 shares of X Corporation are worth $2,500. The beneficiaries can recover the $2,500 plus surcharge the trustee what amounts are necessary to make the trust whole.

All these examples involve what amounts to the trustee stealing from the trust. Given the no further inquiry rule that traditionally governs self-dealing, the same rules apply when the trustee has done nothing wrong other than engaging in self-dealing.

Example 16.5: Trustee purchases 500 shares of X Corporation from the trust at $10 per share for a total of $5,000, which is the full fair market price, to provide the trust with cash needed to pay accounting and legal fees. At the time the beneficiaries obtain a decree determining the trustee's liability, the 500 shares of X Corporation are worth $10,000. The beneficiaries will almost certainly elect to recover the profit made by the trustee and elect to recover the shares.

What should the trustee in our example have done? Sell the 500 shares on the open market. What if there is no market for X Corporation stock because the company is a closely held family corporation? If there's no other way to raise the necessary cash, the trustee should have taken out a loan with a commercial lender or, as a last resort, loaned the trustee's own funds to the trust at the current market rate of interest.

F   A   Q

Q: Do the rules dealing with damages apply to personal representatives?

A: Yes. Executors and administrators can breach the duty of loyalty and engage in self-dealing in the same ways trustees can. They can also breach the duty of prudence in the same ways, although personal representatives usually do not make long-term investments. The prudent investor standard might require the sale of assets even though the proceeds of sale are not required to meet the cash requirements of the estate, however, and failure to do so could certainly lead to liability. (Remember that although the UPIA applies only to trustees, its principles will no doubt be influential in judging the investment performance of those non-trustee fiduciaries.)

(2) Violations of the Duty of Prudence

Damages for failing to fulfill the duty of prudence are the same as those for breaching the duty of loyalty: the greater of what is required to restore the value of the trust property or the trustee's profit (Restatement (Third) of Trusts § 100). The latter remedy, however, is less likely to be relevant than it is when self-dealing is involved, if only because the trustee is likely making investments by buying and selling in the relevant markets. The trustee has not taken trust property for his personal use, so tracing really isn't an option, as we will see in more detail in a bit. So the question almost always comes down to how to restore the trust's value to what it would have been had the breach not occurred. Before the widespread adoption of the prudent investor standard, figuring out the trustee's liability for making an imprudent investment started with the amount of the trust's **lost capital**. Here's an example.

Example 16.6: Trustee buys 500 shares of Dodgy Corporation at $10 a share for a total of $5,000. An investor who did the minimum investigation before investing in Dodgy Corporation would have concluded that any investment in the corporation was so speculative as to be imprudent no matter what the surrounding circumstances. A year later, the soundness of that conclusion is evident when Dodgy files for bankruptcy protection and the stock becomes worthless.

The beneficiaries of the trust bring a proceeding that results in a decree holding the trustee liable for violating the duty of prudence. What are the damages? The lost capital is $5,000, the amount invested in the now worthless stock. The beneficiaries recover that amount from the trustee plus a surcharge in the amount necessary to make the trust whole. Conceptually that amount should be what the $5,000 would be worth had it been properly invested. In reality, however, the surcharge, at least traditionally, was calculated by using the statutory interest rate applied to unpaid judgments for the period from purchase of the stock until the date of the decree. The amount of interest would be reduced by any income produced by the investment (here, dividends).

Now that the prudent investor standard is the law just about everywhere, thinking about how to calculate the amount of surcharge, the damages assessed to make the trust whole, has changed. The same revision of Restatement (Second) of Trusts that produced the prudent investor standard also rewrote the sections dealing with remedies for breach of trust. The aim of the revision is to bring the total return concept that is at the core of the prudent investor standard to the measurement of damages. In Example 16.6, the starting point for measuring damages is the same, the $5,000 that was "lost" by making an imprudent investment. Instead of simply applying the statutory rate of interest, however, the next step is to "adjust" the $5,000 for the total return, positive or negative, that would have been earned had the $5,000 been prudently invested. That means taking into account not only income (interest and dividends) from proper investments, but also any appreciation or depreciation in their value. According to the Restatement, the measure of total return should be "based on a total return experience for suitable investments of comparable trusts" (Restatement (Third) of Trusts § 100).

Sidebar

APPRECIATION DAMAGES

You might see discussion in the cases of something called "appreciation damages." These damages are traditionally awarded when the trustee or personal representative committed a breach by selling property the fiduciary was required to retain. If the property had increased in value by the time the beneficiaries obtained a court decree establishing the fiduciary's liability, the damages were the value of the property *at the time of the decree*, even if the fiduciary did not own the property and the tracing (trust pursuit) remedy was not available. Modern trusts and wills seldom require the trustee or personal representative to retain specific property, but the concept is not obsolete. It has been held to apply to fiduciaries who engaged in self-dealing.

The appropriate rate of return might be difficult to establish or it might be as straightforward as using the rate of return of the other, prudent, investments in the trust. This might be a particularly good measure when this particular investment is the trustee's only violation of the duty of prudence. When the trustee's breach is more extensive, for example, when almost all of the trust property was not prudently invested, it might be necessary to use a broad-based index of publicly traded securities like the Standard & Poor's 500, an index based on the values of the stock of 500 widely traded public corporations.

F   A   Q

Q: Are fiduciaries ever liable for punitive damages?

A: Conventional wisdom is that fiduciaries are seldom, if ever, liable for punitive damages. The accuracy of that view is not what it once was. While many cases have refused to consider the imposition of punitive damages absent fraud or actual malice, some more recent case decisions have imposed punitive damages when the fiduciary's bad behavior is not fraudulent or malicious but simply really bad.

Remember that the total return approach to damages for breaches of the duty of prudence is simply a variation on the basic theme that damages are designed to make the trust whole. Once the duty of prudence is governed by the total return ideas behind the prudent investor standard, the measure of damages should indeed be set by referring to what prudent investing would have accomplished for the trust. That means, of course, that the same measure of damages can apply to some situations involving breach of the duty of loyalty. Consider the situation in which the breach involves the trustee taking money or property from the trust and using it to acquire property in the trustee's own name. As we saw, if the acquired property has increased in value by the time the beneficiaries obtain a court decree establishing the trustee's liability, they will likely elect to take the property for the trust. If the acquired property has decreased in value, the beneficiaries can get back the amount paid plus whatever is needed to make the trust whole. Under the prudent investor approach, that amount might be measured not by a rate of interest but by the total return concept (Restatement (Third) of Trusts § 100 cmt. b(1)).

F. Exculpatory Clauses

Trusts are private arrangements, and as we've seen, even the most ambitious codification of trust law in American history, the UTC, is basically a default statute that is subordinate to the terms of the trust (except for the mandatory provisions of § 105(b)). Does the primacy of the settlor's arrangements extend to the rules governing the duties of trustees? To a great degree, the answer is yes. Many trusts include **exculpatory clauses** that purport to limit the trustee's liability. These clauses are valid, at least to the extent that they are substantively and procedurally sound.

As far as substance goes, no clause can completely exonerate a trustee from all liability. Otherwise there would be no trust. If there is no trust when there are no beneficiaries who can enforce the trustee's duties, then there is equally no trust when the beneficiaries cannot enforce the trustee's duties because of a provision of the trust's terms. Provisions purporting to prevent any court from reviewing the trustee's decisions are unquestionably unenforceable. Where to draw the line is the question. UTC § 1008(a)(1) invalidates any exculpatory clause that purports to exempt a trustee from liability for breach of trust "committed in bad faith or with reckless indifference to the purposes of the trust or the interest of the beneficiaries." This is a generally accepted formula, although some of the cases draw the line at "gross negligence," which is probably a lot like reckless indifference. An exculpatory clause that excused the trustee from errors made in good faith and without willful neglect would therefore pass muster.

The procedural limitation has to do with how the exculpatory clause got into the trust in the first place. In the best of all possible worlds, any exculpatory clause would be the result of the settlor's considered decision to include it. The decision might be made in response to the request of the prospective trustee, but it would be the settlor's decision to raise the threshold for liability in order, for example, to induce a trustee to serve. If the settlor's decision to include the clause is not freely made, however, a court will not enforce it. Once again, the UTC codifies the generally accepted common law. Section 1008(a)(2) invalidates any exculpatory clause that made it into the trust as a result of the trustee's abuse of a fiduciary or confidential relationship with the settlor.

How we answer the question of whether an exculpatory clause was included in a trust as a result of abuse depends a good deal on who bears the burden of proof: the beneficiary who is trying to invalidate the clause or the trustee who is trying to use it as a shield. Some cases put that burden on the beneficiary. Most commentators, many other cases, and UTC § 1008(b) put the burden on the trustee to prove that the clause was *not* included in the trust as the result of abuse. The UTC provision, for example, requires the trustee to prove that the existence of the clause and its contents "were adequately communicated to the settlor" and that the clause is "fair under the circumstances." The drafters of the UTC considered § 1008 so important that they made it one of the provisions that trust terms cannot override (§ 105(b)(10)).

CERTIFICATION OF TRUST UNDER THE UTC

Third persons who wish to make sure that a proposed transaction is within a trustee's authority often demand to see the complete trust instrument. This is not a big deal for testamentary trusts since wills are part of the public record, but lifetime trusts are quintessentially private documents. UTC § 1013 attempts to preserve the privacy of lifetime trusts (and make things easier for the trustees of testamentary trusts) by authorizing a trustee to make a certification of the existence of the trust and the extent of the trustee's authority. The person receiving the certification may rely on the facts it states and act without fear of liability. The section even provides for the award of damages against a person who, having received a certification, still demands a copy of the entire trust if the demand was not in good faith.

G. Liability of Third Parties

Let's say you buy a classic 1936 Rolls Royce from a trustee who has breached her fiduciary duties by selling the car to you. Will you be liable? Or will you simply drive away from the transaction in higher style than when you arrived?

It used to be the rule that, as a third party, you dealt with a fiduciary at your peril. Simply knowing that you were buying property that was part of an estate or trust (in other words, that the person you were dealing with had legal but not beneficial title to the property involved) was enough to require you to make sure that the trustee or personal representative was not acting beyond the powers given in the will or trust or exercising improperly the powers that were granted. Needless to say, that made dealing with fiduciaries somewhat difficult. In fact, Restatement (Second) of Trusts § 297 comment f requires a transferee "who knows or should know" that the person making the transfer holds the transferred property in trust to inquire into the terms of the trust to make sure that the transfer is proper. The second trust Restatement was completed in 1959, and the law has developed quite a bit since.

That development has been away from requiring a person dealing with a trustee or a personal representative to inquire about the scope of the fiduciary's powers and their proper exercise. UPC § 3-714 states flat out that "the fact that a person knowingly deals with a personal representative does not alone require the person to inquire into the existence of a power or the propriety of its exercise." UTC § 1012(b) sets forth the same rule in almost the same words for those dealing with trustees: a person who deals in good faith with a trustee "is not required to inquire into the extent of the trustee's powers or the propriety of their exercise." Restatement (Third) of Trusts § 108 agrees with the UTC. These changes responded to criticisms that the older position did not provide trust beneficiaries with real protection and that trust beneficiaries are better off when no useless obstacles hinder the purchase and sale of trust property in the market.

Under modern law, a third party who qualifies as a **bona fide purchaser**, someone who gives value in exchange for the purchased property and who is without notice of competing claims, is not liable for any breach of trust caused by the transaction. You probably recall the term "bona fide purchaser" from your contracts and property classes, and the concept is the same in our context. Both UTC § 1012 and Restatement (Third) of Trusts § 108 refer to the commercial law and other Restatements(e.g., Restatement (Third) of Restitution and Unjust Enrichment §§ 66-69). The aim is to put all commercial transactions on the same footing.

Sidebar

NEGOTIABLE INSTRUMENTS, SECURITIES, THIRD PARTIES, AND DAMAGES FOR BREACH

The law governing the relationship between fiduciaries and third-party transferees of trust property when the property is negotiable instruments or securities is found in the law governing those commercial transactions. The Uniform Commercial Code is what's relevant when the property is a negotiable instrument. The laws applicable to securities govern transactions in that type of property. UTC § 1012(e) expressly states that the other laws relating to commercial transactions or the transfer of securities by fiduciaries prevail over the UTC provisions.

F A Q

Q: Since every liable third party is one side of a transaction that has a breaching fiduciary on the other, can the beneficiaries recover from both?

A: Generally no (unless the recovery from the third party still leaves the trustee liable for punitive damages). Usually the beneficiaries will pursue their remedies against the party able to pay.

However, even a bona fide purchaser will not be protected if he knew of the breach of trust. The difficult part of that rule is the "knowing" about the breach of trust. But if knowledge of the breach can be proved, the third party certainly will be liable to the beneficiaries. A third party who has notice of a trustee's breach is an involuntary trustee of the property acquired. It is not surprising, therefore, that beneficiaries have the same remedies against the third party that they have against the trustee. They can trace the cash the third party received in a sale to the trustee. If the third party bought property from the trustee, the beneficiaries can get it back, along with whatever more is necessary to make the trust whole.

H. Trustee Liability to Third Parties

In carrying out their duties, trustees often have to contract or interact with third parties in ways that could lead to liability if things go wrong. Until the second half of the last century, trustees were personally liable in these situations. If they were not at fault personally, they could seek reimbursement from the trust and might even be able to pay a judgment directly from the trust, but they personally were liable for the amount of the judgment. In addition, the plaintiff could sue only the trustee as an individual. If the plaintiff obtained a judgment but the trustee was insolvent, the plaintiff was out of luck, no matter how much property was in the trust. Here's an example involving a trustee and, in parentheses, a personal representative.

Example 16.7: The trust (probate estate) includes an apartment building. A guest of a tenant is injured on the premises and sues in tort. The injured party must sue the trustee (personal representative) individually. If the injured party recovers, the resulting judgment can be collected only from the trustee (personal representative), who will then be entitled to reimbursement from the trust (probate estate). If the trustee (personal representative) is insolvent, the injured party is out of luck. And if the trust property (probate estate) is insufficient to reimburse the trustee (personal representative), there is authority that says the trustee (personal representative) is out of luck—she is liable for the entire judgment.

The same rule applied to contracts entered into by the trustee or personal representative in course of the administration of the estate or trust. Unless the contract made it clear that the trustee or personal representative would not be personally liable should things go wrong, the fiduciary was personally liable for any judgment but could seek reimbursement from the trust or probate estate.

F   A   Q

Q: Why did traditional law require contract and tort claimants to sue fiduciaries as individuals?

A: Because neither trusts nor estates are legal entities but are relationships between the fiduciary, the beneficiaries, and the property, the law doesn't consider them really "there." Also, both types of relationships are creatures of equity rather than common law, making it impossible to sue the trust or estate or even the fiduciary as fiduciary. Only after these contract and tort cases proceeded against the fiduciary as an individual did equity deal with reimbursing the fiduciary from the property of the trust or estate.

All this began to change about the middle of the twentieth century as legislatures, often following the lead of uniform acts, changed the law. UPC §§ 3-808 (personal representatives) and 7-306 (trustees), UTC § 1010, and Restatement (Third) of Trusts §§ 105 and 106 (trustees) end personal liability for the fiduciary (unless the fiduciary is personally at fault) and allow the plaintiff to sue the fiduciary in his fiduciary capacity.

Sidebar

ENVIRONMENTAL LIABILITY

Federal statute imposes liability for remedying certain environmental problems on the owner of contaminated land, whether or not the owner played any part in creating the problem (42 U.S.C. § 9607). When the statute became law in 1980, it created a good deal of concern that fiduciaries might be personally liable for costs of assessment and cleanup that exceeded the value of the property in the trust or estate. In 1996, the statute was amended to make it clear that fiduciaries were liable for costs of environmental remediation only to the extent of the property of the trust or estate. In the meantime, many states amended their statutes to the same effect and also to make clear that fiduciaries had the power to conduct environmental assessments and to refuse to accept contaminated property. The UTC's provision is § 816(13).

SUMMARY

- The principal duties of the fiduciary are loyalty, prudence, and impartiality.

- The duty of loyalty includes a strict ban on self-dealing and engaging in transactions that involve conflicts of interest.

- The duty of prudence involves the investment of trust or estate property. The UPIA has radically changed the law governing the duty of prudence by introducing the prudent investor standard, which judges the propriety of a trustee's investments by judging how well they are designed to carry out the settlor's purpose in creating the trust.

- The duty of impartiality requires the fiduciary to treat the beneficiaries in accordance with the purposes of the trust. The prudent investor standard has affected the law of impartiality by making the unitrust interest an attractive alternative to a traditional income interest.

- The fiduciary also has a duty to inform the beneficiaries of the details of their interests in the trust or estate so that they can properly protect their interests. The UTC's formulation of the trustee's duty to inform has been controversial, and the law in this area is developing.

- Subsidiary duties involve making sure the trust property can be recognized as trust property.

- Damages for breach of fiduciary duties always involve making the trust or estate whole, whether by awarding interest on the judgment against the trustee, or applying the total return concept to the value lost through the trustee's wrongdoing.

- Exculpatory clauses can lessen the degree of care required of a trustee or personal representative but cannot prevent all court supervision of a fiduciary. An exculpatory clause is invalid if it results from the abuse of a fiduciary relationship between the settlor or testator and the drafter of the trust or will. The UTC puts the burden of showing a lack of abuse on the party attempting to take advantage of the exculpatory clause.

- Because neither a trust nor an estate is a legal entity, the law once required a person injured in the course of the administration of the trust or estate to sue the trustee or personal representative individually. The fiduciary could then recover from the trust or estate if the trustee were not personally at fault. Modern law, including the UPC, the UTC, and the Restatement (Third) of Trusts, allows the injured person to sue the trustee or personal representative in the fiduciary capacity and to recover directly from the trust or estate.

CONNECTIONS

Fiduciary Obligations and Beneficiaries' Interests (In General)
Fulfilling the duty of impartiality requires understanding the interests of the various beneficiaries. The discussion in Chapter 9 is highly relevant, therefore, to any discussion of the duty of impartiality.

Fiduciary Obligations and Beneficiaries' Interests (Principal and Income)
The duty of impartiality is closely tied to balancing the interests in income with interests in principal. The principles discussed in Chapter 9 and the rules of the Uniform Principal and Income Act play a crucial role in deciding how the duty of impartiality should be fulfilled.

Fiduciary Obligations and Representation
Proceedings for fiduciary accounting often require the use of the doctrines of representation discussed in Chapter 8. The principles of representation also inform the concepts of "fairly representative beneficiaries," which is critical to the Restatement (Third) of Trusts' view of the duty to inform, and "qualified beneficiaries," which is the UTC equivalent.

Fiduciary Obligations and Future Interests
The enforcement of fiduciary duties is often complicated by their being owed to persons with future interests, some of whom may be unascertained (Chapter 7) and must be somehow represented in court proceedings involving the trustee (Chapter 8).

Fiduciary Obligations and Revocable Trusts
The duties of the trustee of a revocable trust are different from those of most trustees because of the revocable trust's resemblance in so many ways to a will, which in turn means that while the settlor of the trust is alive and has the power to revoke, the trustee's duties are owed only to the settlor.

Wealth Transfer Taxation and Income Taxation of Estates and Trusts

17

The estate, gift, and generation-skipping transfer taxes are known collectively as the wealth transfer taxes. Since the law of wills and trusts is

OVERVIEW

really all about transferring property, whether at death or during life, these taxes play an important role in how estate plans are structured. Particularly important is how these taxes apply to trusts. Whatever the property law that governs making a valid will, creating a valid will substitute, or creating a valid trust, the tax consequences of doing so are dictated by a separate body of law. Estates and trusts are also income taxpayers, so those rules too play an important role in estate planning, especially when using trusts.

A. Introduction

Estate planning is sometimes described as being **tax driven** because minimizing taxes is usually an important goal. Which taxes are estate planners trying to avoid?

The gift tax, the estate tax, the generation-skipping transfer tax (GST tax), and the income tax, all four of which are federal taxes. Some states have estate taxes of their own, less than a handful have gift taxes of their own, a large handful levy a GST tax, and most subject estates and trusts to state income taxes.

Now we have to qualify the previous paragraph in some maddeningly complex ways. The complications involve the first three taxes, which are known collectively as **wealth transfer taxes**. The estate tax was enacted in 1916. The gift tax was enacted in 1924, repealed in 1924, and reenacted in 1932. The GST tax was enacted in 1976 but repealed *ab initio* (as if it never had been enacted) in 1986, at which time a new GST tax was enacted.

The system in place in 1986 simply went rolling along until the 1990s when two components of the system, the GST tax and the estate tax, became embroiled in political controversy. The estate tax in particular was the focus. Excoriated as the "death tax," it was portrayed as the destroyer of family farms and small businesses. Whatever the empirical evidence about the effects of the tax, these attacks proved popular, and in 2001 Congress passed and then President George W. Bush signed the Economic Growth and Tax Relief Reconciliation Act of 2001 (EGTRRA). The new law included some of the most extensive reductions in federal income taxes ever enacted (including a reduction in the maximum tax rate on long-term capital gains and certain dividends to 15 percent). The new law also phased out both the estate and GST taxes. Both taxes expired at midnight on December 31, 2009. However, both taxes were scheduled to come back to life exactly one year later. In fact, the law would have returned just as it was before the enactment of EGTRRA. In the meantime, the gift tax remained in place throughout 2010 (although at a reduced rate).

Also for 2010, another long existing aspect of the taxation of inherited property changed. For decades, one of the fundamentals of income taxation was the rule that property received from a decedent received a new **basis** at the decedent's death. Basis is an income tax concept. It is the value that is subtracted from the value received on a disposition of the property to determine whether there is capital gain or loss. Usually the basis of property is what taxpayer paid for the property, although basis can be adjusted for many reasons. The new basis acquired at the death of the owner of the property is equal to the value for estate tax purposes, generally the value on the date of death, and could be higher or lower than the original basis. If it is higher, of course, all the appreciation in value that occurred from the time the decedent acquired the property until death will never be subject to income tax, although it is part of the value of the estate subject to estate tax.

EGTRRA repealed the new basis rule for 2010. Instead of a new basis, property received from the decedent dying in 2010 retained the basis it had in the hands of the decedent. This is known as **carryover basis**. There is more to carryover basis, however. The decedent's personal representative could increase the basis of property passing from the decedent by $1,300,000 and property passing to, or in a qualified trust for, the surviving spouse could have its basis increased by an additional $3,000,000.

Throughout 2009 and 2010, estate planners were in a quandary. Planners did not believe that the estate tax would be repealed for 2010, and most believed Congress would do something to prevent the resurrection of the pre-EGTRRA estate and GST taxes in 2011. Fingernails were bitten to the quick by the time Congress did act in December. On December 17, 2011, President Barack Obama signed tax legislation that extended the estate and GST taxes pretty much as changed by EGTTRA (with some new features that we'll note) for two more years.[1] Now the changes will expire at midnight December 31, 2012, and things will go back to the way they were before EGTRRA unless Congress acts. Estates of decedents dying in 2010 are given the option of paying estate tax (as modified by the 2010 legislation) or not paying tax but using carryover basis. We're not going to spend more time on carryover basis because it will probably affect only a small number of estates.

We do have to discuss the gift tax as well as the estate and GST taxes. Why? First, the taxes are with us for now at least. Second, several states have their own estate taxes and GST taxes that are almost all based on the federal taxes. Finally, some of the law of making gifts at death has been strongly influenced by the provisions of the wealth transfer taxes. Understanding how those taxes operate will help to complete your understanding of the property law we've been discussing.

B. Wealth Transfer Taxes — Gift and Estate Tax Integration

We're going to discuss the gift, estate, and GST taxes as they operate in 2010 through 2012 (what we'll call the "extension period"). This isn't going to be a very detailed discussion, but it should give you a general understanding of how the system works with an emphasis on provisions that influence the property law of making gifts at death.

Ever since 1976, the gift and estate taxes have been more or less integrated. The basic idea is that taxable transfers during life (taxable gifts) and the final taxable transfer at death are all part of one long series of gifts culminating in the final gift at death. The system allows every person to make aggregate taxable transfers of up to $5,000,000 in 2010 and 2011 and because the amount is adjusted for inflation, $5,120,000 in 2012 without paying tax. That's because we each have a **unified credit** against the transfer taxes that offsets the tax that would be levied on $5,000,000 (plus inflation adjustments) of taxable transfers. Once the unified credit is used up, the tax on taxable transfers is 35 percent. (Tax on lesser amounts is less than 35 percent and is completely offset by the credit.) The first thing to note is that part or all of the value of transfers sheltered by the credit can be used up by making taxable gifts during life. Here's an illustration using the $5,000,000 exemption amount:

Assume that our generic Taxpayer has $7,000,000 of wealth. To keep things simple, we'll assume that the assets never appreciate in value, that the extension period rules govern, and that Taxpayer dies one year after making the taxable gift.

Lifetime taxable gift:	$1,000,000
Tax on $1,000,000:	330,800
Gift tax unified credit:	330,800
Tax due:	0
Taxable estate:	6,000,000 (7,000,000 − 1,000,000)
Tax on $7,000,000:	2,430,800 (6,000,000 + 1,000,000 of lifetime taxable gifts)
Unified credit:	1,730,800
Tax due:	700,000

---

[1]Tax Relief, Unemployment Insurance Reauthorization, and Job Creation Act of 2010, Pub. L. No. 111-312, 124 Stat. 3296.

Now you no doubt have several questions. We'll deal with what I guarantee are the most important.

Q: Why is the estate tax calculated on $7,000,000? After giving away $1,000,000 during life, Taxpayer has $6,000,000 left to be taxed, right?

A: Remember that the gift and estate taxes are integrated. That means that the taxable estate is treated as a gift at death. The tax due at death is calculated by adding the taxable gifts made during life (the **adjusted taxable gifts**) to the taxable estate, the taxable amount of the gift at death. The system is cumulative. If Taxpayer had not made any lifetime taxable gifts and died with a $7,000,000 taxable estate, the tax due would be exactly the same: $700,000.

Q: How come the full unified credit of $1,730,800 is subtracted when calculating the estate tax? Didn't Taxpayer use up $330,800 of the credit during life?

A: Yes, but remember the $1,000,000 of taxable gifts was added to the taxable estate and the estate tax calculated on the total amount. If we bring already taxed gifts back into the calculation, then we have to subtract the entire unified credit in calculating the tax due, including that part of the credit used to offset the tax on the lifetime taxable gifts.

Now there's another aspect of the system that we have to consider. Obviously, it is unlikely that values will stay constant the way we've assumed they will for this example. With luck, asset values will increase over time. That means that Taxpayer will have more than $6,000,000 at death, so the tax will be more than the $700,000 we calculated. However, the $1,000,000 Taxpayer gave away will also be worth more by the time Taxpayer dies. That increase in value will never be taxed in Taxpayer's estate. To illustrate that point, let's assume everything appreciates 10 percent between the time of the $1,000,000 gift and Taxpayer's death. The situation at death:

Taxable estate:	$6,600,000 (7,000,000 − 1,000,000 plus 10% appreciation)
Tax on $7,600,000:	2,640,800 (6,600,000 + 1,000,000 of lifetime taxable gifts)
Unified credit:	1,730,800
Tax due:	910,000

If the gift had not been made when it was, Taxpayer's taxable estate would be $7,700,000:

Taxable estate:	$7,700,000 (7,000,000 + 10% appreciation)
Tax on $7,700,000:	2,675,800
Unified credit:	1,730,800
Tax due:	945,000

The difference between the $910,000 of tax due when Taxpayer makes the lifetime gift and the $945,000 tax due when the gift is not made is $35,000, which is the amount of the estate tax on the $100,000 of appreciation in the value of the $1,000,000 that Taxpayer did not give away. The point is that *making lifetime gifts can reduce the donor's total transfer taxes by removing the appreciation on the property given away from eventual taxation in the donor's estate.* Now you may think that more is better, so why not give away more than $1,000,000 and get much more appreciation out of the estate? Indeed, why not? The answer is uncertainty. It's impossible to know what estate tax rates will be in the future, or if there will be a tax at all, so calculations showing substantial estate tax savings by making large gifts today may end up being meaningless. It's equally impossible to know what the future may bring in the way of unexpected emergencies of every sort: illness, natural disasters, economic downturns. Give too much away and what might have been a manageable problem could become a disaster.

There is another tax advantage to making lifetime gifts that's worth illustrating, and it involves deliberately making a taxable gift. We need some bigger numbers to make this illustration work, so we'll give our Taxpayer a taxable estate of $60,000,000. Taxpayer makes a taxable gift of $10,000,000 in 2011.

Lifetime taxable gift:	$10,000,000
Tax on $10,000,000:	3,480,800
Gift tax unified credit:	1,730,800
Gift tax due:	1,750,000
Taxpayer has left:	48,250,000 (60,000,000 − 10,000,000 gift − 1,750,000 tax paid)

Let's assume that Taxpayer dies more than three years later (why three years? we'll see in a minute) and that values have not increased. We'll also assume that the 2011-2012 rates are in effect.

Taxable estate:	$48,250,000
Tax on $58,250,000:	20,367,500 (48,250,000 + 10,000,000 of lifetime taxable gift)
Unified credit:	1,730,800
Gift tax paid:	1,750,000
Tax due:	16,887,500
Total tax on the transfer of 60,000,000:	18,637,500 (1,750,000 gift tax + 16,887,500 estate tax)

Now compare this with what happens *without* the lifetime gift:

Taxable estate:	$60,000,000
Tax on $60,000,000:	20,980,800
Unified credit:	1,730,800
Tax due:	19,250,000

The total tax paid is $612,500 *less* when Taxpayer makes a lifetime gift of $10,000,000. Why? *Because the $1,750,000 used to pay the gift tax is not itself taxed.* The difference is equal to the estate tax on that $1,750,000 (calculated in this example at the 35 percent in effect during 2011 and 2012). The gift tax is **tax exclusive**; the money used to pay the tax is not itself subject to tax. The estate tax is **tax inclusive**; the money used to pay the tax is itself subject to the tax. (The income tax is tax inclusive as well.)

Now you might wonder whether everyone who has the necessary wealth makes large taxable gifts right before death (usually called **deathbed gifts**) and gets the money used to pay the gift tax out from under the estate tax. They don't because under IRC § 2035(b) the gross estate includes any gift tax paid on any gift by the decedent or the decedent's spouse within three years of the decedent's death. In the example, if Taxpayer died within three years of making the $10,000,000 gift, the $1,750,000 would be part of the gross estate, the estate tax would be calculated on $60,000,000, and the total of the estate and gift taxes paid would be $19,250,000.

(1) Gift Tax

Now that we have an idea of how the gift and estate taxes work together, we have to step back and consider the basics of how the taxes work on their own. We'll start with the gift tax and the most basic question of all: what is a gift? A **donor** makes a gift when the donor transfers property to the **donee** to the extent the donor does not receive consideration in money or money's worth, that is, the transfer is **gratuitous**. Not every gratuitous transfer is a taxable gift, however. To make a taxable gift, the donor must relinquish *dominion and control* over the property. Of course, if the donor writes a check to the donee, the donor has clearly relinquished dominion and control when the donee cashes the check. The interesting questions usually arise when the donor makes a transfer to a trust.

Example 17.1: Donor transfers $1,000,000 to Trustee, in trust, to pay the income to Donor for life, and at Donor's death the trust terminates and the Trustee is to pay the trust property free of trust to the issue of Donor's domestic partner then living by representation.

What's the gift? The value of the remainder interest. The donor has kept the income from the property and has relinquished dominion and control only over the remainder.

Example 17.2: Donor transfers $1,000,000 to Trustee, in trust, to pay the income to Donor for life, and at Donor's death the trust terminates and the Trustee is to pay the trust property free of trust to the issue of Donor's domestic partner then living by representation. Donor retains the right to revoke the trust at any time by a signed writing delivered to Trustee.

What's the gift? There isn't one. By keeping the power to revoke, Donor has retained dominion and control over all of the property transferred to Trustee.

Example 17.3: Donor transfers $1,000,000 to Trustee, in trust, to pay the income to Donor for life, and at Donor's death the trust terminates and the Trustee is to distribute the trust property as Donor shall appoint among her domestic partner's issue in her last will and testament admitted to probate. Donor may appoint in such amounts as she sees fit, and may appoint outright or in further trust with her trustee or with another trustee, and if Donor does not exercise the power of appointment, the Trustee is to distribute the trust property free of trust to the issue of Donor's domestic partner then living by representation.

What's the gift? There isn't one. Donor has retained the income from the trust property. The special power of appointment allows Donor to decide who will enjoy the property at Donor's death, which means that Donor has retained control sufficient to prevent a gift of the remainder interest.

How is the gift of the remainder in Example 17.1 valued? It must be valued using **actuarial principles**. The value of the gift is the value *today* of the right to receive the $1,000,000 transferred to the trust at the end of Donor's life. Calculating that value requires that we know how long Donor is expected to live and what the **discount rate** is, the rate at which money is expected to increase in value over Donor's remaining life expectancy. The basic idea is that the right to receive $1 a year from now is worth the amount you have to invest today to have a dollar one year from now. So the value of the right to receive $1,000,000 at Donor's death (the future interest over which the donor relinquished dominion and control) is the amount we'd have to invest today to have $1,000,000 at the end of Donor's life expectancy. This is how it's done, even if the $1,000,000 is not $1,000,000 in cash but rather property: stocks (whether publicly traded or not), bonds, real estate, or anything else.

Of course, we don't know when Donor is going to die. But that's not a problem. We know what Donor's likely life expectancy is based on our experience with the lifespans of large numbers of people. This knowledge is summarized in **actuarial life expectancy tables**, which were first created for insurance companies so they could figure out how to set the premiums on life insurance policies. Today the IRS publishes life expectancy tables that must be used in actuarial calculations involved in taxation. These tables are revised periodically based on census data. The discount rate that must be used is calculated monthly and published by the IRS. It's based on the interest rate on government bonds. If Donor makes a taxable gift of the remainder in a trust funded with property worth $1,000,000 and Donor is 60 years of age and the discount rate is 4.2 percent, the value of the remainder is $447,680. That means if we invest $447,680 today and it grows 4.2 percent a year, by the end of the Donor's actuarial life expectancy we'll have $1,000,000. The higher the discount rate, the smaller the value of the remainder because the higher the rate of growth, the less we need to start with. If the discount rate is 5.2 percent, the value of the remainder is $380,330.

What happened to the rest of the $1,000,000? That's the value of the income interest, the value today of receiving the income on the $1,000,000, calculated at the discount rate, for the remaining years of Donor's life expectancy. Once again, we use the discount rate to calculate the value. The value of the right to receive a dollar in income one year from now is the value that if invested at the discount rate will grow into one dollar during that year. The value of the income interest is the sum of all of those values for the number of years the income interest will last. In this case, the number of years is Donor's actuarial life expectancy. Of course, if the Donor does not retain dominion or control of the transferred property, then the entire value of the property transferred is the value of the gift.

F	A	Q

Q: What happens if the donor's actual lifespan is different from the actuarial assumption or the trust property increases in value at more or less than the discount rate used in valuation?

A: Nothing. Actuarial valuation is based on averages. While individual taxpayers may do better or worse than the actuarial predictions, the U.S. Treasury deals with a very large number of actuarial valuations, and over time the wins and losses balance out. In *Ithaca Trust Co. v. United States*, 279 U.S. 151 (1929), the U.S. Supreme Court approved of using actuarial valuation in taxation based on the idea that, on average, the government came out even.

If a gratuitous transfer is subject to the gift tax, then it is called a **completed gift for gift tax purposes**. Otherwise, the transfer is **incomplete**. In Example 17.1, the gift of the income interest is incomplete, and the gift of the remainder interest is complete. In Examples 17.2 and 17.3, the entire transfer is an incomplete gift. Remember that the donor need not transfer the donor's property. As we saw in Chapter 10, the exercise of a lifetime general power of appointment is a transfer of the appointive property, which can certainly be a taxable gift if the terms of the exercise mean that the donee of the power is giving up dominion and control of the appointive property.

You might wonder why Examples 17.1, 17.2, and 17.3 involve remainders given to the descendants of Donor's domestic partner. That's because if in Example 17.1 the remainder had been given to Donor's descendants or the descendants of Donor's spouse, the life income interest retained by Donor would be valued at zero for gift tax purposes.

That result comes from Chapter 14 of the IRC (§§ 2701-2704), which contains special valuation rules that apply to certain transfers between family members. For our purposes, § 2702 is the most important. It provides that an interest retained by the settlor of a trust, the creation of which transfers an interest to a "member of the family" (for this purpose, the settlor's spouse, any ancestor, or any lineal descendant of either the settlor or the settlor's spouse, the settlor's siblings, and a spouse of any ancestor, descendant, or sibling), will be valued at zero for gift tax purposes unless the retained interest is an annuity interest (a fixed dollar amount) paid at least annually or a unitrust amount, a payment at least annually of a fixed percentage of the value of the trust property determined annually. Congress enacted these provisions because it concluded that the temptation to manipulate trust investment strategy to benefit remainder beneficiaries was simply too great. Remember that the gift tax is paid on the actuarial value of the remainder when the settlor of the trust retains the income interest. Having done that, the settlor could suggest that the trustee invest to sacrifice the production of income to growth of the value of the trust property. The settlor could even be trustee and carry out this program directly. The idea is to make the actual value of the remainder at the distribution date exceed as much as possible the actuarially determined value used for gift tax purposes. Requiring that the settlor retain an annuity or unitrust interest limits the ability to manipulate the ultimate value of the remainder by requiring either a minimum value for the income payments to the settlor or a tying of those payments to the total value of the trust.

Some of the most important provisions of the gift tax sections of the IRC deal with exclusions from taxable gifts. These provisions identify transfers that even though they are completed gifts are not treated as taxable gifts. The most significant is the **present interest exclusion**. Any person can make completed gifts with a total value of up to $13,000 a year to any individual and not pay any gift tax. The only requirement is that the gift be a present interest. While the case law fleshing out the definition of a present interest is quite voluminous, all we need to know for now is that transfer involves a present interest if the donee can enjoy the property at the moment the transfer is complete.

Example 17.4: Donor directs her broker to transfer 200 shares of X Corporation worth $100 per share at the time of transfer to the brokerage account of Donor's Older Son. The first $13,000 of value is excluded, and the taxable gift is $7,000. Donor also directs her broker to transfer 200 shares of Y Corporation worth $100 per share to Donor's Younger Son. The first $13,000 of value is excluded, and the taxable gift is $7,000. Total taxable gifts: $14,000.

Example 17.5: Donor transfers $1,000,000 to Trustee, in trust, to pay the income to Donor's Daughter for life, and at Daughter's death the trust terminates and the Trustee is to pay the trust property free of trust to Daughter's issue then living by representation.

The first $13,000 of the actuarial value of the income interest qualifies for the present interest exclusion. None of the value of the remainder qualifies because it is a future interest. The taxable gift is $987,000 (1,000,000 − 13,000).

Why does the law include the present interest exclusion? The legislative history indicates that Congress was trying to keep small, everyday sort of gifts like birthday, holiday, or anniversary gifts out of the gift tax system. Over time, the present interest exclusion has taken on a life of its own as an important planning tool. Careful estate planners, however, will often caution their clients to make a present interest exclusion gift of something less than the full $13,000 to leave room for those routine gifts.

There are two other exclusions that are of great importance, especially because both are unlimited in amount. The first is for transfers to pay another person's medical bills. Any medical expense that can be deducted for income tax purposes qualifies for this exclusion, including doctor and hospital bills and insurance premiums. The second exclusion is for tuition expenses. A grandparent can pay her grandchild's tuition in any amount for any level of education and not worry about making a taxable gift. The exclusion is for *tuition* only; it does not include room, board, books, or other fees. Furthermore, to qualify for the exclusion, the payment must be made directly to the provider (e.g., the doctor or school). Both these exclusions are in addition to the basic present interest exclusion.

> ## Sidebar
>
> ### SPLIT GIFTS
>
> Let's say that Grandparents would each like to make a present interest exclusion gift to Grandchild. Only Grandmother, however, has enough cash in her brokerage account to make the $26,000 gift. No problem. The IRC allows married couples to split gifts, that is, to treat a taxable gift as if it were made one-half by each spouse no matter which spouse has title to the property given. Electing split gift treatment requires the filing of a gift tax return on which the spouse whose property is not being used for the gift consents to be treated as the donor of one-half of the property.

Example 17.6: During 2010, Grandparent pays Grandchild's private secondary school tuition in the amount of $25,000, pays an orthodontist's bill of $7,000, transfers $12,000 in cash to a custodial account for Grandchild established under the Uniform Transfer to Minors Act, and gives Grandchild birthday and holiday gifts worth $900. Total completed gifts: $44,900; total taxable gifts: $0.

F   A   Q

Q: How does one make a present interest exclusion gift to a minor, other than by having a guardian of the property appointed?

A: One way is by making the gift to a custodial account under the Uniform Transfer to Minors Act. IRC § 2503(c) also allows gifts to a trust for a minor to qualify for the present interest exclusion, so long as the minor is the only beneficiary, the income from the property is expended for the minor or accumulated for eventual distribution to the minor, and the trust terminates and is distributed to the minor (or the minor can demand distribution) at age 21. If the minor dies before that age, the property must be payable to the minor's estate or the minor must have a general power of appointment over the trust property. Without this special provision, the value of the remainder interest would not qualify for the exclusion.

Two other important exclusions from taxable gifts are structured as deductions, not exclusions. The first is the **marital deduction**. Outright transfers between spouses do not incur gift tax. There are special rules for obtaining the marital deduction when one spouse creates a trust of which the other spouse is a beneficiary and another set of special rules when the recipient spouse is not a U.S. citizen. We'll talk about the marital trust rules when we talk about the estate tax because the rules are the same. The second is the **charitable deduction**. The charitable deduction is unlimited in amount. Generally, any charitable gift that can be deducted for income tax purposes also qualifies for the gift tax charitable deduction. There are special rules that govern obtaining the deduction when a trust that has both noncharitable and charitable beneficiaries, and we'll talk about those too when we get to the estate tax.

(2) Estate Tax

And now we indeed have gotten to the estate tax. The most fundamental question we have to answer in dealing with the estate tax is "What is the decedent's **gross estate**, the property subject to estate tax before deductions and credits?" It *is not* limited to the probate estate. If it were, the estate tax would be as toothless as an elective share limited to probate property. Although as we've seen, some states have never really grappled with expanding the pool of property subject to the elective share beyond the deceased spouse's probate estate, Congress realized from the very beginning of the estate tax that limiting the taxable estate to the probate estate would be foolish. The statutory language Congress used to expand the probate estate was the subject of frequent litigation. Today, fortunately, the meaning of these IRC sections is pretty well understood, at least as they apply to straightforward situations. The statutory language that defines the gross estate is found in IRC §§ 2033 through 2044. Section 2033 includes in the gross estate interests in property owned by the decedent—in other words, the decedent's probate property. Several of these sections address specific kinds of property.

F   A   Q

Q: What's the difference between an inheritance tax and an estate tax?

A: An estate tax is levied on the estate as a whole. The amount of tax depends on the value of the taxable estate. An inheritance tax is levied on the recipients of the property subject to the tax (although the estate usually pays the tax). The amount of tax depends on the identity of the recipient of the property. Property passing to close family members is taxed at a low rate, if at all; property passing to nonrelatives is usually taxed at the highest rate.

---

§ 2042 Proceeds of Life Insurance. Life insurance is one of the oldest forms of non-probate property. The death benefit paid because of an insured's death is included in the insured's gross estate if the deceased insured held **incidents of ownership** in the policy. An incident of ownership is any power over the policy that allows the decedent to get an economic benefit from the policy. Common examples are the ability to borrow against the accumulated cash value of the policy, the ability to cash the policy in, and the power to name a beneficiary. The person who owns the policy always has

incidents of ownership. Usually the insured procured the policy and is the owner. That means that the death benefit is part of the insured's gross estate when the insured dies unless the insured has disposed of the incidents of ownership by giving away ownership of the policy (which will have gift tax consequences).

F   A   Q

Q: Is the death benefit paid from a life insurance policy tax-free?

A: The death benefit paid to the beneficiary of a life insurance policy is generally not taxable income in the hands of the beneficiary; in other words, it is *income tax* free. However, the death benefit may be subject to estate tax in the insured's estate.

§ 2040 Joint Interests. This section applies to all joint arrangements with right of survivorship (including tenancy by the entirety) where the decedent was one of the joint holders of the property involved. The decedent's gross estate includes all of the jointly held property unless the decedent's estate can show that some or all of the property originally belonged to the other joint holder or holders. There is a special rule applicable when the other joint holder is the decedent's spouse (assuming the spouse is a U.S. citizen). In that case, one-half of the property is included in the decedent's gross estate no matter who contributed what to acquiring the property. Here are some examples.

Example 17.7: Decedent and her brother, B, are joint holders with right of survivorship of a brokerage account. On Decedent's death, her gross estate will include all of the property in the account unless her personal representative can show what part of the property in the account came from B. If the personal representative can show that B contributed 40 percent of the funds that went into the account, Decedent's gross estate will include 60 percent of the value of the account.

Example 17.8: Decedent and her husband, H, both U.S. citizens, are joint holders with right of survivorship of a brokerage account. On Decedent's death, her gross estate will include one-half the value of the account, no matter who contributed what. There is no need to trace contributions.

§ 2039 Annuities. The gross estate includes the value received because of the decedent's death by a beneficiary of an annuity the decedent was receiving or had the right to receive. If the beneficiary receives an annuity rather than a lump sum, the value included is calculated actuarially.

Example 17.9: At time of his death, Decedent was retired and receiving a pension in the form of an annuity. Decedent's sister, S, is the beneficiary of the payments remaining at Decedent's death. Decedent's gross estate includes the present value of those payments calculated actuarially.

§ 2041 Powers of Appointment. All appointive property subject to a general power of appointment held by the decedent as donee is included in the gross estate. As we

discussed at some length in Chapter 10, a power of appointment is general if it allows the donee to appoint to the donee, the donee's estate, the donee's creditors, or the creditors of the donee's estate. This list of potential appointees that makes a power general for tax purposes, as we noted, has also become the standard definition of a general power of appointment for property law purposes. As we saw also in Chapter 10, under § 2041 a power that would otherwise be general is not if its exercise is subject to an "ascertainable standard" such as "health, education, maintenance, or support" (HEMS).

The statute creates an interesting and important wrinkle in the rules that apply to powers of appointment. A lapse of a general power is a release, and a release is an exercise (subject to the important exception known as the five-and-five rule discussed below). So if I have a general power of appointment and let it go by releasing it, I've transferred the appointive property and almost certainly made a gift to whoever takes the appointive property if the power is not exercised (the takers in default, if there are any.) Also, if I have a general power that I can exercise until a certain time, at which time the power expires, and I don't exercise it and the power does expire, I am treated as if I had released the power. An example should make that clearer.

Example 17.10: Donor transfers property to Trustee, in trust, to pay the income to Donor's Daughter for her life, and at Daughter's death the trust terminates and the Trustee is to pay the trust property free of trust to the issue of Daughter's domestic partner then living by representation. Daughter may withdraw $10,000 of trust property between November 15 and December 15 of every year by sending a signed notice to the trustee stating that she is exercising the withdrawal power. The power is a general power of appointment because Daughter can appoint to herself. If Daughter does not exercise the power, under the general rule of § 2041 she would be treated as taking the $10,000 out of the trust and putting it back in. That means that Daughter has made a taxable gift of the actuarial value of the remainder interest in the $10,000 ($10,000 minus the value of her income interest in the $10,000). There are also unpleasant estate tax consequences, as we'll see shortly.

These sorts of withdrawal powers, however, are very useful when the settlor of a trust wants to give a beneficiary the peace of mind of knowing that he can have a distribution of trust property without waiting for the trustee to exercise discretion to invade the trust principal. So popular and useful are such powers of withdrawal that Congress created an exception from the lapse-release-exercise rule. The lapse is treated as a release only to the extent the property subject to the power of withdrawal exceeds the greater of $5,000 or 5 percent of the value of the property from which the withdrawal would come (the **five-and-five rule**). In Example 17.10, Daughter would suffer no adverse tax consequences from the lapse of her power if the value of the trust property when the power lapsed on December 15 was at least $200,000 because 5 percent of $200,000 is $10,000. A power that fits this exception is often referred to as a **five-and-five power** and is a popular device for giving beneficiaries access to trust principal.

The other gross estate provisions in the IRC are not limited to specific kinds of property. These provisions are generally applicable to transfers made by the decedent where the decedent retained certain interests in or powers over the transferred property. We need to take a minute to understand the policy behind these provisions. The transfer taxes are excise taxes on the privilege of transmitting property. That is how they have always been understood, and indeed that is why they are constitutional. Because they are excise taxes, they do not have to be apportioned among the states by population in accordance with Article I, § 2, clause 3 of the U.S. Constitution. And because they are excise taxes, it is constitutional to include in the gross estate property that the decedent transferred during life in such a way that economic enjoyment of the property passes to others only at the decedent's death.

That's very abstract, so here's the classic example.

Example 17.11: Decedent transfers $1,000,000 to Trustee, in trust, to pay the income to Decedent for life, and at Decedent's death the trust terminates and the Trustee is to pay the trust property free of trust to Decedent's issue then living by representation.

At Decedent's death, the life income interest is over. It simply vanishes, and with it vanishes Decedent's enjoyment of the economic benefits of the trust property. Decedent's death is the distribution date for the remainder interest. At that moment, the remainder vests in possession and the economic benefit of the trust property passes to the remainder beneficiaries. The statute includes in Decedent's gross estate all of the property in which Decedent had the income interest. Even though Decedent no longer had legal title to the property — that's in Trustee — and even though Decedent had beneficial or equitable title only to the income produced by the property, the tax falls on the entire value of the property enjoyment of which passes at Decedent's death. Three sections of the IRC deal with interest and powers retained by the decedent in a lifetime transfer of property.

§ 2036 Transfers in Which the Decedent Retained the Income from the Transferred Property or the Power to Designate Who Enjoys the Income from the Property. This section applies when the decedent had transferred property but retained the income from the property that is an *interest* (§ 2036(a)(1)) or *the power* to designate the persons who will enjoy the property or the income from the property (§ 2036(a)(2)) for the decedent's life or for a period that does not actually end before the decedent's death. (Example 17.11 falls under § 2036(a)(1).)

Now you can understand why the lapse of a power of appointment that is not sheltered by the five-and-five rule has adverse estate tax consequences. In Example 17.10, if the trust property was worth $100,000 when the power of withdraw lapsed, Daughter made a $5,000 transfer to the trust (5 percent of $100,000 equals $5,000, which means $5,000 of the $10,000 lapse is treated as a lapse). Not only has Daughter made a taxable gift equal to $5,000 minus the value of her income interest in the $5,000, but she has also transferred $5,000 to the trust because of the lapse of her general power of appointment. Under the terms of the trust, she is entitled to the income from that $5,000. Were she to die immediately after the lapse, $5,000 of the trust property would be included in her gross estate under § 2036(a)(1). Going forward, she is the transferor of 1/20 of the trust property, and even if there are no more lapses (either because she exercises the power or the trust property is always worth at least $200,000 at the time of the lapse), when she dies 1/20 of the trust property is included in her gross estate. If there are more lapses not sheltered by the five-and-five, more and more of the trust property will be included in her gross estate at her death.

§ 2037 Transfers Taking Effect at Death. In spite of its broad title, this section applies to an interest in property transferred by the decedent to the extent that (a) the interest can be enjoyed only by surviving the decedent; *and* (b) the decedent

had retained a reversionary *interest* in the property, the value of which immediately before the decedent's death exceeds 5 percent of the value of the property. Here's an example.

Example 17.12: Decedent transfers property to Trustee in trust to pay the income to B for life, and at B's death the trust terminates and Trustee is to distribute the property free of trust to Decedent if Decedent is then living and, if not, to Decedent's issue then living by representation. Decedent's issue will receive possession of the trust property only if they survive Decedent because, of course, they must be alive at B's death and Decedent must have died before B if the issue's contingent remainder is going to vest in possession. If at Decedent's death during B's lifetime the actuarial value of Decedent's remainder (calculated as if Decedent were going to live out her actuarial life expectancy) exceeds 5 percent of the value of the property, then the value of the trust property minus the value of B's remaining income interest is included in Decedent's gross estate.

§ 2038 Revocable Transfers. This section includes in the gross estate any property transferred by the decedent where the enjoyment of the property was subject to change at the time of the decedent's death by reason of a *power* held by the decedent to alter, amend, revoke, or terminate the terms of the transfer or where that power was relinquished during the three years prior to the decedent's death.

Sections 2036 and 2038 will include in the gross estate just about every valid will substitute that is not included by the more specific sections, and often both sections will apply. Table 17.1 shows how one would analyze the most powerful will substitute trust, the lifetime revocable trust.

Any sort of payable on death (POD) account or transfer on death (TOD) account will also be included because the creator of the account or other arrangement almost always enjoys the income from the property involved for life and, in any event, has the power to revoke the arrangement. That power to revoke also means that the creation of the arrangement did not involve a taxable gift because the power to revoke makes the transfer incomplete for gift tax purposes. As we've seen, however, a transfer can be complete for gift tax purposes but still be included in the gross estate for estate tax purposes. Think about Example 17.1 for a moment. We used that example of a trust in which the settlor retained the income to illustrate the concept that only part of a transfer can be a completed gift. Now you also know that when the settlor dies *the entire value of the trust property will be included in the settlor's gross estate under § 2036(a)(1).* Completed gift for gift tax, but included in the gross estate.

TABLE 17.1	Revocable Trusts Included in the Gross Estate	
Trust term	Interest or Power	Applicable Provision
Settlor receives all of the income from the property settlor transferred for life.	Interest	§ 2036(a)(1)
Settlor can revoke the trust.	Power	§ 2038(a)(1)

Because it's pretty obvious when a transferor retains an interest, it's safe to say that *retained interests* don't cause many surprises when it comes time to figure out the decedent's gross estate. Most of the unwelcome surprises are probably caused by *retained powers*. Often the power has tax consequences for the decedent because the decedent ends up being trustee and as trustee has powers that lead to inclusion in the gross estate under § 2036(a)(2) or 2038(a)(1).

Under § 2036(a)(2), transferred property is included in the gross estate when the transferor retains the power to "designate the persons who shall possess or enjoy the property or the income therefrom." Think of all the ways a trustee can make such "designations." Clearly, if the trustee has discretion in distributing income or principal or both, the trustee does indeed have the power to designate who enjoys the trust property and the income from it. In addition, depending on the terms of the trust, these distribution powers may also be powers to "alter, amend, revoke, or terminate" under § 2038(a)(1). The only way the creator of a trust can safely hold discretionary distribution powers as trustee is if the powers are limited by an ascertainable standard. This is not the HEMS standard in § 2041 that applies to powers of appointment but is a product of case law. While any language that the court concludes creates a standard that a court can enforce is sufficient, careful drafters stick to the HEMS language when limiting trustee powers that are or might be held by the settlor.

There is one group of powers that the transferor can hold as trustee without any danger of causing inclusion of the trust property in the gross estate. As we saw in Chapter 16, the exercise of administrative powers such as allocating receipts between income and principal and making investments can indeed determine which beneficiaries will benefit from the trust property. The trustee can invest for growth and "starve" the income interests or vice versa. We know, of course, that the trustee has fiduciary duties that require her to treat the beneficiaries impartially and that can be enforced by a court. It has been clear for a generation that such powers do not implicate § 2036 or § 2038 because of the constraints placed on the trustee by enforceable fiduciary duties.

Nevertheless, the decision to make the settlor of a trust a trustee must be made with great care. In fact, inclusion in the gross estate can result even if the settlor is not trustee when the trust is created. Section 2038 applies to powers that the decedent can exercise at death whether or not the power was retained at the time of the transfer of the property. In addition, if the settlor can remove a trustee and appoint a "subordinate party," in general terms a family member, the powers of the trustee will be imputed to the settlor and that will mean inclusion of the trust property in the gross estate if the powers are not limited by an ascertainable standard. Even more striking, it is clear that the powers of the trustee will be imputed to the settlor if the settlor can appoint herself trustee should a vacancy occur in the trusteeship, even if the settlor cannot cause the vacancy. If you study estate planning in any detail, you will spend a good deal of time and energy learning the ins and outs of drafting to make sure that the trustee appointment and selection terms of the trust don't cause estate tax complications.

Now that we've got the basics of the gross estate, we have to talk a little about the deductions from the gross estate that are subtracted to arrive at the **taxable estate**, the value on which the tax is calculated. The IRC allows deductions for the estate's expenses such as the cost of the decedent's funeral, executor's commissions and lawyer's fees, and the decedent's debts paid by the estate out of property that is subject to creditors' claims. These deductions are important, but even more important are two others: the charitable deduction and the marital deduction.

(a) Charitable Deduction

As under the gift tax, there is an unlimited estate tax deduction for gifts to charity. That means that it is possible to eliminate the estate tax in any estate, no matter how large, by giving the exclusion amount ($5,000,000 in 2010 and 2011 and $5,120,000 in 2012) to the decedent's family or to anyone else and giving the rest of the estate to charity. Charitable gifts are a part of many estate plans. Sometimes these are outright gifts to charity. Sometimes the decedent creates a private foundation that is itself a charity. Private foundations are heavily regulated by the IRC, but nevertheless are often an important part of estate planning for the wealthy. Sometimes the decedent wants to create a trust to benefit both private individuals (usually family members) and charity. These split interest trusts, which can also be created during life and result in a gift tax charitable deduction, are subject to a complex set of rules. The basic idea, however, should be familiar to you. The purpose of the rules is to prevent manipulation of the administration of the trust to starve the charitable interest.

Split interest trusts come in two basic varieties: **charitable remainder trusts**, in which noncharitable beneficiaries are given the initial interest and the remainder is given to charity; and **charitable lead trusts**, in which the charity is given the initial interest and the remainder is given to noncharitable beneficiaries. The provision designed to prevent **manipulation requires** that the income interest in either sort of trust be either an annuity interest or a unitrust interest. Thus split interest trust come in four varieties:

1. Charitable remainder annuity trusts (**CRATs**)
2. Charitable remainder unitrusts (**CRUTs**)
3. Charitable lead annuity trusts (**CLATs**), and
4. Charitable lead unitrusts (**CLUTs**)

As we've seen, the potential for manipulating the trust to the disadvantage of the charitable beneficiaries is simply one example of how trustees' powers to allocate receipts between principal and income and to select investments can shift benefits from one set of beneficiaries to another. As we've also seen, one aspect of the trustee's fiduciary duty is the requirement that the trustee treat the beneficiaries impartially, and that duty is powerful enough to negate the application of §§ 2036(a)(2) and 2038(a)(1) to these administrative powers. Congress was not willing to trust in the enforcement of fiduciary duty to ensure that trustees of split interest trusts would not attempt to shift benefits to the private beneficiaries at the expense of the charitable beneficiary. Instead, Congress decided to require that the initial interest in the trust be an annuity interest, that is, a fixed sum payable at least annually, or a unitrust interest, which, as we saw in our discussion of principal and income and the prudent investor standard, ensures that both income and remainder interests will share in appreciation or depreciation of the trust property.

Properly drafting a split interest trust requires close attention to some complex requirements. Fortunately, the IRS has produced model forms for several varieties of split interest trusts, and many practitioners begin their drafting with those forms.

(b) Marital Deduction

The second and perhaps even more important deduction is the marital deduction. Like the charitable deduction, it is unlimited in amount and can be used in conjunction with the exclusion amount to eliminate estate tax on the estate of any decedent who has a surviving opposite-sex spouse. There are several requirements for obtaining the marital deduction for property that passes to a surviving spouse and additional requirements if the surviving spouse is not a U.S. citizen. (The rules governing the marital deduction for transfers to noncitizen spouses are quite complex and beyond the scope of this discussion, for which we'll assume both spouses are U.S. citizens.) The most important is that a **terminable interest** will not qualify. The surviving spouse has a terminable interest in property if interests in the property pass from the decedent to both the surviving spouse and to others and if at the end of the surviving spouse's interest those others will enjoy the property. That means that unless one of the exceptions discussed below is not met, merely giving the spouse a life income interest in a trust will not create a marital deduction.

Nothing prevents the decedent from simply making an outright devise to the surviving spouse or from making the surviving spouse the beneficiary of a POD or TOD arrangement. If the decedent has used a revocable lifetime trust, the trust can always terminate at death and distribute the trust property outright to the surviving spouse. That might not be what the decedent wants, however. The surviving spouse may be ill or lack capacity so that placing management of the property in the hands of a trustee may be the wisest thing to do. The decedent might not want the surviving spouse to be able to give away the property during life or at death, especially if the decedent has descendants by other marriages or relationships. In short, there are many reasons for the decedent's preferring to give the surviving spouse only equitable ownership of the property involved in the marital deduction.

F   A   Q

Q: Will a unitrust interest satisfy the requirement that the surviving spouse receive all of the income of a gpa or QTIP marital deduction trust?

A: Yes, generally a unitrust interest will satisfy the "all the income" requirement, although there are some complexities related to how state law defines a unitrust interest and does or does not allow trustees of existing trusts to convert a traditional income interest to a unitrust interest.

IRC § 2056 provides three different sorts of trusts that will qualify for the marital deduction. Once the right sort of trust is created, any trust property that would qualify for the marital deduction were it given to the surviving spouse qualifies for the marital deduction, even if the surviving spouse is entitled to only the trust income. An **estate trust** need only provide that at the surviving spouse's death the trust property is paid to the surviving spouse's estate. The surviving spouse doesn't even have to have any interest in the trust during his lifetime, but no one else may have an interest in trust property during the surviving spouse's lifetime. The second is a **general power of appointment (gpa) trust** (also known as a § 2056(b)(5) trust after the relevant Code provision). The surviving spouse must (1) be entitled to all of the income from the trust property for life, and (2) have a general power of appointment over the trust. The third is a **QTIP (qualified terminable interest property) trust**. Qualified terminable interest property is property in which the spouse has a "qualified income interest" for life, which simply means that the surviving spouse is the only income beneficiary of the trust during her life and that no one else can have any interest in the trust property while the surviving spouse is alive. For example, the trustee cannot have authority to invade principal for anyone other than the spouse. If the trust created for the surviving spouse includes a qualified income interest, the decedent's executor can elect to make the trust property QTIP, and the marital deduction will be obtained in the decedent's estate for all of the QTIP.

F   A   Q

Q: Does the Code define what it means to give the spouse all of the income from a gpa or QTIP marital deduction trust? Why doesn't the Code require an annuity or unitrust interest like it does for split interest trusts?

A: Since the beginning of the marital deduction, the "all of the income" requirement has been satisfied by giving the spouse the rights of an income beneficiary under the state law that governs the trust. In this case, the Code relies on a trustee's fiduciary duty to treat the beneficiaries impartially and the surviving spouse's ability to enforce that duty should the trustee try to favor the remainder interest. Marital deduction trusts sometimes include language stating that the surviving spouse's needs are paramount and permitting or even requiring the trustee to favor the surviving spouse's present interest in the trust over the future interest of the remainder beneficiaries. It is also common to include a provision giving the surviving spouse the power to direct the trustee to sell trust property that does not produce income and reinvest the proceeds in income-producing property.

Whatever property is in an estate trust, a general power of appointment trust, or a QTIP trust at the surviving spouse's death will be included in the surviving spouse's gross estate. Taking the deduction in the estate of the first spouse to die, therefore, results in a postponement of estate tax from the time of the first spouse's death to the death of the survivor. The requirements for each type of marital deduction trust and how the trust property is taxed in the surviving spouse's estate is shown in Table 17.2.

There is also a marital deduction for gift tax purposes (IRC § 2523). The terminable interest requirement is the same as it is under the estate tax. That means that if one spouse wants to make a lifetime gift to the other in trust, one of the three acceptable trusts—estate trust, gpa trust, or QTIP trust—must be used. Any outright gift from one spouse to the other qualifies for the deduction, so a married couple never has to worry about making taxable gifts to each other. Remember, however, that under the federal Defense of Marriage Act, only a marriage between a man and a woman is recognized as a marriage, so the marital deduction applies only to opposite-sex married couples. Same-sex couples, even if they are married, cannot take advantage of the marital deduction for federal estate and gift tax purposes.

It's pretty easy to understand the "no marital deduction on death" for same-sex couples upon death.

Sidebar

MARITAL DEDUCTION TRUSTS AND THE ELECTIVE SHARE

Using a marital deduction trust as the primary device for making a gift to a surviving spouse at death can cause complications with the elective share. No matter how much property funds an estate, a gpa, or a QTIP trust, not a penny of it will count toward satisfying the surviving spouse's elective share right in those states whose statutes entitle the surviving spouse to outright ownership of the elective share amount. That in turn means that using a QTIP trust will not necessarily guarantee that a decedent controls the disposition of all of the remaining marital deduction property at the surviving spouse's death. The surviving spouse could simply exercise the elective share right, thereby giving up the income interest in the QTIP and getting outright ownership of the elective share amount.

Example 17.13: Amanda and Javier are a married couple. When Amanda dies in 2011 with a taxable estate before the marital deduction of $7,000,000, her estate will owe no federal estate tax so long as she leaves the difference between the applicable exclusion amount,

TABLE 17.2	**Comparing the Three Types of Marital Deduction Trusts**		
	Estate Trust	gpa Trust	QTIP trust
Surviving spouse's minimum interest during life	None	All income	All income
Other interests during surviving spouse's life	None	Spouse may appoint principal to others	None
How included in surviving spouse's gross estate	Remainder payable to surviving spouse's estate (IRC § 2033)	Spouse has general power of appointment (IRC § 2041)	Express provision in IRC § 2044
Can spouse control recipient of trust property at death?	Yes, by devise in the will	Yes, by exercise of the power of appointment	No

$5,000,000, and $7,000,000 (= $2,000,000) to Javier in a form that will qualify for the estate tax marital deduction. If Amanda leaves the entire $7,000,000 to Javier, of course, there will be no estate tax. (Javier's gross estate will always include the property for which the marital deduction was obtained in his wife's estate to the extent he does not consume it.)

Example 17.14: Abigail (Amanda's sister) is married to her partner, Jacinda. When Abigail dies in 2011 with a taxable estate of $7,000,000, her estate will owe no federal estate tax only if she leaves the $2,000,000 that exceeds the applicable exclusion amount to charity (at least, that's the most straightforward way). If she leaves the entire $7,000,000 to Jacinda, her estate will owe $700,000 in federal estate tax. (Jacinda's gross estate will also include the property she receives from Abigail to the extent she does not consume it.)

The gift tax results are sometimes more subtle. However, when financial assets or real estate is involved, the results are also clear.

Example 17.15: Amanda and Javier buy a house. Amanda provides the entire purchase price, and the couple takes title to the home as joint tenants with right of survivorship. Because the joint tenancy is unilaterally severable from the moment it is created, Amanda has made a gift of one-half the value of the home to Javier. This gift is not taxable because of the unlimited marital deduction. In addition, no matter which spouse dies first, one-half of the value of the house is included in the decedent's gross estate under IRC § 2040.

Example 17.16: Abigail and Jacinda also buy a house. Abigail provides the entire purchase price, and the couple takes title as joint tenants with right of survivorship. Because the joint tenancy is unilaterally severable from the moment it is created, Abigail has made a gift of one-half the value of the home to Jacinda. There is no marital deduction, so Abigail has made a taxable gift of one-half of the value of the home to Jacinda (minus the present interest exclusion, if it has not already been used up in the year of the purchase of the house). In addition, under § 2040 the gross estate of the first spouse to die will include the entire value of the home unless the estate of the decedent can prove the extent of the other joint owner's contribution to acquiring the property.

Example 17.13 can also illustrate one of the few innovations in the 2010 extension of the estate tax: the introduction of **portability** of the applicable exclusion amount. Note in 17.13 that whether Amanda creates a trust to hold her applicable exclusion amount or gives everything to Javier, her estate pays no federal estate tax, but Javier's taxable estate will include everything he received from Amanda to extent he does not consume it or give it away. Until the enactment of the 2010 law, unless Amanda used her applicable exclusion amount, she lost it. If Amanda dies in 2011 or 2012, however, her executor can elect to give to Javier her unused applicable exclusion amount—the exclusion amount is now "portable." Together, Amanda and Javier can transmit $10,000,000 ($10,120,000 if the first spouse to die dies in 2012) on the death of the second to die, even if the entire amount is taxed in the estate of the second to die. (And no, you can't go through life accumulating unused exclusion amounts from a series of predeceased spouses; the amendment to IRC § 2010 that creates portability prevents that.)

(3) Generation-Skipping Transfer Tax

We have to consider one more wealth transfer tax, the generation-skipping transfer tax. The GST tax is applicable to the following situations (all defined in IRC § 2612).

Example 17.17: Decedent devises property to Big Bank in trust to pay the income to Child for life, and on Child's death the trust terminates and the trust property is distributed free of trust to Child's descendants by representation. The GST tax is levied on the trust property at Child's death, which is a **taxable termination**, the end of an interest (here the income interest) in a trust belonging to a person one generation younger than the person who transferred property to the trustee (the **transferor**) by reason of which the property passes to a person two or more generations younger than the transferor.

Example 17.18: Settlor (grandparent) creates an irrevocable lifetime trust by transferring property to Trustee. Trustee has extended discretion to distribute income and principal to Settlor's descendants until 21 years after the death of all of Settlor's descendants living at the time of the creation of the trust. While at least one of Settlor's children is alive, Trustee makes a distribution of income or principal to a beneficiary who is at least two generations younger (grandchild or younger) than Settlor/Transferor. The GST tax is levied at that time on the amount distributed. The event is a **taxable distribution**, a distribution from a trust to a person who is two or more generations younger than Transferor. There will also be a taxable termination when the last of the children dies and, if the trust is still in existence, when the last of the grandchildren dies (so long as all of the children have already died). These events are also taxable terminations: the end of the interest of an entire generation after which only a person two or more generations younger than the transferor has an interest in the trust.

Example 17.19: Grandparent's will includes a general or specific devise to Grandchild. Alternatively, Grandparent makes an outright gift to Grandchild. Both of these transfers are examples of a **direct skip**, a transfer subject to estate or gift tax made by a decedent or donor (again, who is a transferor) to a person two or more generations younger than the transferor.

Why does the tax apply to these particular situations? The policy behind the imposition of the tax is straightforward: a transfer of wealth should be taxed once in every generation. It's easiest to see how this policy is applied in Example 17.17. Decedent/Transferor's estate will pay an estate tax (if the taxable estate is large enough). Had the property placed in trust been given outright to Child, it would have been included in Child's gross estate (to the extent Child did not consume it) and might have given rise to an estate tax before the property passed on to Child's descendants; and if Child gave it away before death by making a taxable gift, there would be gift tax consequences. The end of Child's life income interest, however, is not a taxable event. The income interest simply vanishes at Child's death. The GST tax was created to ensure the payment of a tax at Child's death — that is, to ensure the payment of a tax in what would otherwise be a "skipped" generation.

Q: How are persons assigned to generations if they are not related to the transferor?

A: Generation assignment is made by comparing a nonrelative's birth date to the birth date of the transferor. A person born no more than 12 ½ years after the transferor is in the transferor's generation; someone born 12 ½ years after the transferor but not more than 37 ½ years after is in the first generation younger. Then each subsequent 25-year period is a new generation. This is the same scheme used in the Rule Against Perpetuities set out in Restatement (Third) of Property.

In Example 17.18, the tax is imposed to prevent the use of a multigenerational sprinkle trust to avoid the tax. The distribution to the younger generation beneficiary is treated as if it had been made to the older generation beneficiary and then given in a transfer subject to gift tax to the beneficiary who receives the distribution. (Note, however, that there is one GST tax levied on a taxable distribution or a direct skip to a great-grandchild or more remote descendant.) Example 17.18 is equivalent to 17.16 without the trust involved. The outright gift is treated as if Grandparent gave the property to Child in a taxable transfer; Child then gave it to Grandchild in a taxable transaction.

The tax is quite severe. It is equal to the highest estate and gift tax rate, which in 2011 and 2012 was 35 percent. So in Example 17.17, if at the time of the taxable termination the taxable amount (the value of the trust property minus certain allowable deductions, mainly for expenses involved in winding up the trust) were $1,000,000, the GST tax would be $350,000. It's not quite that simple, however, because everyone has a **GST exemption** amount, just like we all have an applicable exclusion amount for the estate and gift taxes. That amount is equal to the estate and gift tax applicable exclusion amount ($5,000,000 in 2010 and 2011 and $5,120,000 in 2012), but unlike the estate tax exemption it is not portable between spouses. As you might imagine, the exemption allows one to make direct skips up to the amount of the exclusion without paying GST tax (only the gift or estate tax would apply). But it can actually be a better deal than that. Let's say that when Decedent in Example 17.17 died in 2011, she had not used any of her GST exemption during life so that the entire $5,000,000 was available for her personal representative to allocate. If the property passing to the trust were exactly equal to the amount of exemption allocated to the trust, *the trust would never be subject to GST tax no matter how large its value at the time of the taxable termination.*

The mechanism for getting to that result is a bit complex. The amount of tax due is defined as the taxable amount multiplied by the **applicable rate**, which it turn is determined by multiplying the maximum estate and gift tax rate by the **inclusion ratio**, which is determined by subtracting the **applicable fraction** from the number 1 (IRC §§ 2641, 2642). All of that is not as complicated as it looks. The applicable fraction is a fraction, the denominator of which is the value of the property funding the generation-skipping trust or involved in the direct skip and the numerator is the amount of exemption allocated. Therefore, if the trust in Example 17.17 is funded with $5,000,000 and Decedent's personal representative allocates her entire GST tax exemption to the trust:

- The applicable fraction is 5,000,000/5,000,000 = 1.
- The inclusion ratio then is $1 - 1 = 0$.
- The applicable rate is (maximum estate and gift tax rate) $\times 0 = 0$.

No matter how much property is involved in the taxable termination, the GST tax will be zero. We get the same result with the trust in Example 17.18. If Settlor/Transferor allocates enough exemption to reduce the inclusion ratio to zero, then there will never be GST tax paid on an otherwise taxable distribution (nor on the taxable terminations that occur when the interests of an entire generation end). And Example 17.18 shows why one important reason for the slow death of the Rule Against Perpetuities is the GST tax. If a multigenerational sprinkle trust can be made forever exempt from GST tax, why shouldn't it last forever? What keeps it from lasting forever? The Rule? So . . . bye-bye Rule Against Perpetuities.

There is a good deal more to the GST tax, but we've discussed enough for you to understand when it applies, how the exemption can be used, and how that use has made the future of the Rule Against Perpetuities quite dim indeed.

(4) Income Taxation of Estates and Trusts

There is one other tax that we have to discuss. Estates and trusts are taxpayers just like natural persons are. We file a Form 1040 to pay our federal income tax; a personal representative or trustee files Form 1041 to pay the federal income tax of the estate or trust. The taxable income of an estate or a trust is calculated in much the same way as the taxable income of a natural person is calculated, with one very big exception: estates and trusts deduct from gross income the distributions they make out of income to beneficiaries. The deduction is limited by the estate or trust's **distributable net income (DNI).** DNI is roughly (and I do mean roughly) equal to the estate or trust's **accounting income** (dividends, interest, rents, and so forth). What that means is that capital gains realized by the estate or trust are generally taxed to the estate or trust. If taxed to the estate or trust, distributions of capital gains are not included in the beneficiaries' gross income.

There are many more rules that apply to the calculation of DNI, and yes, there are special rules that apply to distributions from unitrusts (which, remember, are not tied to the traditional accounting income of the estate or trust). As a broad generalization, and that's all we need here, trust income is taxed to the beneficiaries who receive it, and the trust pays the income tax on the capital gains realized by selling assets that are part of the trust principal. Of course, the trustee of a discretionary income trust may not distribute all of the trust's income in any one year, and that retained income is taxed to the trust. There is often an incentive, however, not to have ordinary income (i.e., income that is not capital gains or qualified dividends, both of which in 2011 and 2012 were subject to a maximum 15 percent rate) taxed to the trust. The income tax rate schedule for estates and trusts is very compressed; the highest rate is reached at an amount of taxable income that is less than one-tenth of the amount at which an unmarried individual reaches the maximum rate.

There are some trusts, however, whose income is taxed neither to the beneficiaries nor to the trust because some individual is treated under the IRC as the "owner" of the trust, which means that all of the trust's income and deductions are reported on that individual's Form 1040. The person most likely to be treated as the owner of a trust is the person who created it. The IRC uses the term "grantor" for the creator of a trust, and these trusts are knows as grantor trusts. For a trust to be a grantor trust, the grantor must retain certain interests in or powers over the property transferred to the trust. The rules are set out in IRC §§ 671 through 677 (§ 678 tells us when someone other than the grantor is treated as owner of the trust for income tax purposes). The powers and interests retained are the income tax analogues to the retained powers and interests that cause inclusion of transferred property in the gross estate for estate tax purposes.

We don't need to examine these rules in any detail, although a thorough understanding of them is absolutely essential to doing competent estate planning, especially because there are some significant differences between the income tax and the estate tax rules. What you need to know now is that these **grantor trust rules** are completely and utterly distinct and separate from the law of trusts. Every grantor trust is a proper trust with a trustee, beneficiaries, and property. As far as property law is concerned, a grantor trust is a properly recognized relationship between those three necessary elements of a valid trust. For income tax purposes, however, *the trust does not exist.* In *Helvering v. Clifford,*[2] the U.S. Supreme Court established the principle that the rules of property law do not necessarily dictate the result for purposes of taxation.

Grantor trusts play a very important role in modern estate planning. And that observation brings us full circle. We've investigated in some detail the property law rules that govern making gifts at death (and, to some degree, during life). The application of those rules in twenty-first-century American society is greatly influenced by the tax system. When it comes to what we broadly call estate planning, one truly cannot have one without the other.

SUMMARY

- The estate and GST taxes were repealed for one year at the beginning of 2010, but in December 2010 were retroactively restored and extended through 2012. It is widely hoped that Congress will act before the taxes are restored to their pre-2001 rules on January 1, 2013.

- The gift and estate taxes are integrated. To calculate the estate tax, the taxable estate and certain taxable gifts made during life are added together.

- A taxable gift is a transfer of property made without receiving consideration in money or money's worth in return.

- Gifts made during life have the advantages (1) of removing from the donor's estate and thus from the estate tax any appreciation on the property given that occurs from the date of gift to the date of the donor's death, and (2) removing from the donor's estate the funds used to pay the gift tax. The gift tax is tax exclusive.

- Gifts of income streams and of future interests are valued actuarially.

---

[2]309 U.S. 331 (1940).

- There are important exclusions from the gift tax for gifts of present interests as well as for gifts related to medical and educational expenses.

- The estate tax base includes the decedent's probate estate plus various transfers made during life in which the decedent retained specified powers or interests as well as certain kinds of property, which are governed by specific rules. It also includes the funds that will be used to pay the estate tax; the estate tax is tax inclusive.

- The two most significant deductions for both estate and gift tax purposes are the marital and charitable deductions.

- The GST tax is designed to ensure that transfers of wealth are taxed in each generation. The effects of the tax are mitigated by an exclusion that also applies to trusts and can make a trust completely exempt from the tax no matter how long it lasts.

- Estates and trusts pay income tax, although they are allowed a deduction for the income they distribute to beneficiaries.

- Some trusts are not taxpayers, however. The retention of certain powers or interests by the settlor, specified in the IRC, means that the trust property is treated for income tax purposes as if it was owned by the settlor. In much more limited instances, a beneficiary is treated as the owner of the trust property for income tax purposes.

CONNECTIONS

Wealth Transfer Taxes and Trusts

The terms of a trust will determine whether the creation of the trust (Chapter 8) is a completed gift for gift tax purposes and whether the trust will be part of the settlor's or a beneficiary's gross estate. Grants of discretion to trustees, the selection of who is to be trustee, as well as the creation of powers of appointment all have important transfer tax consequences.

Wealth Transfer Taxes and Powers of Appointment

The tax definition of a general power appointment has become the property law definition as well (Chapter 10). The estate and gift tax consequences facing the donee of a general power of appointment can be severe and must always be taken into account when creating powers of appointment.

Wealth Transfer Taxes and Fiduciary Duties

Although certain powers held by a settlor as trustee can indeed have gift and estate tax consequences, doing what trustees always do — selling trust property and reinvesting the proceeds, allocating receipts between income and principal—are not those sorts of powers because their exercise is controlled by general fiduciary duties, especially the duty to treat all beneficiaries impartially (Chapter 16). There are two situations where the tax law does not trust that duty to sufficiently constrain manipulation and requires present interests to be either unitrust interests or annuities: split interest charitable trusts and trusts in which the settlor retains the income and the remainder is given to family members.

Wealth Transfer Taxes and Protection of the Surviving Spouse I

The marital deduction is an overwhelmingly important aspect of estate planning for married opposite-sex couples. The ability to place property in trust and still obtain a marital deduction is in tension with those statutes that allow the surviving spouse to demand outright ownership of the elective share amount (Chapter 13).

Wealth Transfer Taxes and Protection of the Surviving Spouse II

The estate tax rules that expand the reach of the gross estate beyond the decedent's probate estate are analogous in both purpose and substance to the rules found in some elective share statutes that expand the pool of assets subject to the elective share beyond the deceased spouse's probate property (Chapter 13).

Index